Dictionary of Literary Biography

Documentary Series

1 *Sherwood Anderson, Willa Cather, John Dos Passos, Theodore Dreiser, F. Scott Fitzgerald, Ernest Hemingway, Sinclair Lewis,* edited by Margaret A. Van Antwerp (1982)

2 *James Gould Cozzens, James T. Farrell, William Faulkner, John O'Hara, John Steinbeck, Thomas Wolfe, Richard Wright,* edited by Margaret A. Van Antwerp (1982)

3 *Saul Bellow, Jack Kerouac, Norman Mailer, Vladimir Nabokov, John Updike, Kurt Vonnegut,* edited by Mary Bruccoli (1983)

4 *Tennessee Williams,* edited by Margaret A. Van Antwerp and Sally Johns (1984)

5 *American Transcendentalists,* edited by Joel Myerson (1988)

6 *Hardboiled Mystery Writers: Raymond Chandler, Dashiell Hammett, Ross Macdonald,* edited by Matthew J. Bruccoli and Richard Layman (1989)

7 *Modern American Poets: James Dickey, Robert Frost, Marianne Moore,* edited by Karen L. Rood (1989)

8 *The Black Aesthetic Movement,* edited by Jeffrey Louis Decker (1991)

9 *American Writers of the Vietnam War: W. D. Ehrhart, Larry Heinemann, Tim O'Brien, Walter McDonald, John M. Del Vecchio,* edited by Ronald Baughman (1991)

10 *The Bloomsbury Group,* edited by Edward L. Bishop (1992)

11 *American Proletarian Culture: The Twenties and The Thirties,* edited by Jon Christian Suggs (1993)

12 *Southern Women Writers: Flannery O'Connor, Katherine Anne Porter, Eudora Welty,* edited by Mary Ann Wimsatt and Karen L. Rood (1994)

13 *The House of Scribner, 1846–1904,* edited by John Delaney (1996)

14 *Four Women Writers for Children, 1868–1918,* edited by Caroline C. Hunt (1996)

Yearbooks

1980 edited by Karen L. Rood, Jean W. Ross, and Richard Ziegfeld (1981)

1981 edited by Karen L. Rood, Jean W. Ross, and Richard Ziegfeld (1982)

1982 edited by Richard Ziegfeld; associate editors: Jean W. Ross and Lynne C. Zeigler (1983)

1983 edited by Mary Bruccoli and Jean W. Ross; associate editor: Richard Ziegfeld (1984)

1984 edited by Jean W. Ross (1985)

1985 edited by Jean W. Ross (1986)

1986 edited by J. M. Brook (1987)

1987 edited by J. M. Brook (1988)

1988 edited by J. M. Brook (1989)

1989 edited by J. M. Brook (1990)

1990 edited by James W. Hipp (1991)

1991 edited by James W. Hipp (1992)

1992 edited by James W. Hipp (1993)

1993 edited by James W. Hipp, contributing editor George Garrett (1994)

1994 edited by James W. Hipp, contributing editor George Garrett (1995)

1995 edited by James W. Hipp, contributing editor George Garrett (1996)

Concise Series

Concise Dictionary of American Literary Biography, 6 volumes (1988-1989): *The New Consciousness, 1941-1968; Colonization to the American Renaissance, 1640-1865; Realism, Naturalism, and Local Color, 1865-1917; The Twenties, 1917-1929; The Age of Maturity, 1929-1941; Broadening Views, 1968-1988.*

Concise Dictionary of British Literary Biography, 8 volumes (1991-1992): *Writers of the Middle Ages and Renaissance Before 1660; Writers of the Restoration and Eighteenth Century, 1660-1789; Writers of the Romantic Period, 1789-1832; Victorian Writers, 1832-1890; Late Victorian and Edwardian Writers, 1890-1914; Modern Writers, 1914-1945; Writers After World War II, 1945-1960; Contemporary Writers, 1960 to Present.*

Sixteenth-Century British Nondramatic Writers

Sixteenth-Century British Nondramatic Writers

Edited by
David A. Richardson
Cleveland State University

A Bruccoli Clark Layman Book
Gale Research
Detroit, Washington, D.C., London

The paper used in this publication meets the minimum requirements
of American National Standard for Information Sciences–Permanence
Paper for Printed Library Materials, ANSI Z39.48-1984. ∞™

Library of Congress Cataloging-in-Publication Data

Sixteenth-century British nondramatic writers. Fourth series / edited by David A. Richardson.
    p. cm. – (Dictionary of literary biography; v. 172)
"A Bruccoli Clark Layman book."
Includes bibliographical references and index.
ISBN 0-8103-9935-0 (alk. paper)
1. Authors, English – Early modern, 1500–1700 – Biography – Dictionaries. 2. English literature – Early modern, 1500–1700 – Bio-bibliography – Dictionaries. 3. English literature – Early modern, 1500–1700 – Dictionaries. 4. Sixteenth century – Biography – Dictionaries. I. Richardson, David A. II. Series.
PR411.S584 1996
820.9'003'03 – dc20   96-43211
                                              CIP

[B]

10 9 8 7 6 5 4 3 2 1

For all students of English Renaissance literature

Contents

Plan of the Series

The advisory board, the editors, and the publisher of the *Dictionary of Literary Biography* are joined in endorsing Mark Twain's declaration. The literature of a nation provides an inexhaustible resource of permanent worth. We intend to make literature and its creators better understood and more accessible to students and the reading public, while satisfying the standards of teachers and scholars.

To meet these requirements, *literary biography* has been construed in terms of the author's achievement. The most important thing about a writer is his writing. Accordingly, the entries in *DLB* are career biographies, tracing the development of the author's canon and the evolution of his reputation.

The purpose of *DLB* is not only to provide reliable information in a convenient format but also to place the figures in the larger perspective of literary history and to offer appraisals of their accomplishments by qualified scholars.

The publication plan for *DLB* resulted from two years of preparation. The project was proposed to Bruccoli Clark by Frederick C. Ruffner, president of the Gale Research Company, in November 1975. After specimen entries were prepared and typeset, an advisory board was formed to refine the entry format and develop the series rationale. In meetings held during 1976, the publisher, series editors, and advisory board approved the scheme for a comprehensive biographical dictionary of persons who contributed to North American literature. Editorial work on the first volume began in January 1977, and it was published in 1978. In order to make *DLB* more than a reference tool and to compile volumes that individually have claim to status as literary history, it was decided to organize volumes by topic, period, or genre. Each of these free-standing volumes provides a biographical-bibliographical guide and overview for a particular area of literature. We are convinced that this organization – as opposed to a single alphabet method – constitutes a valuable innovation in the presentation of reference material. The volume plan necessarily requires many decisions for the placement and treatment of authors who might properly be included in two or three volumes. In some instances a major figure will be included in separate volumes, but with different entries emphasizing the aspect of his career appropriate to each volume. Ernest Hemingway, for example, is represented in *American Writers in Paris, 1920–1939* by an entry focusing on his expatriate apprenticeship; he is also in *American Novelists, 1910–1945* with an entry surveying his entire career. Each volume includes a cumulative index of the subject authors and articles. Comprehensive indexes to the entire series are planned.

With volume ten in 1982 it was decided to enlarge the scope of *DLB*. By the end of 1986 twenty-one volumes treating British literature had been published, and volumes for Commonwealth and Modern European literature were in progress. The series has been further augmented by the *DLB Yearbooks* (since 1981) which update published entries and add new entries to keep the *DLB* current with contemporary activity. There have also been *DLB Documentary Series* volumes which provide biographical and critical source materials for figures whose work is judged to have particular interest for students. One of these companion volumes is entirely devoted to Tennessee Williams.

We define literature as the *intellectual commerce of a nation:* not merely as belles lettres but as that ample and complex process by which ideas are generated, shaped, and transmitted. *DLB* entries are not limited to "creative writers" but extend to other figures who in their time and in their way influenced the mind of a people. Thus the series encompasses historians, journalists, publishers, and screenwriters. By this means readers of *DLB* may be aided to perceive literature not as cult scripture in the keeping of intellectual high priests but firmly positioned at the center of a nation's life.

DLB includes the major writers appropriate to each volume and those standing in the ranks immediately behind them. Scholarly and critical counsel has been sought in deciding which minor figures to include and how full their entries should be. Wherever possible, useful references are made to figures who do not warrant separate entries.

Each *DLB* volume has a volume editor responsible for planning the volume, selecting the figures for inclusion, and assigning the entries. Volume editors are also responsible for preparing, where appropriate, appendices surveying the major periodicals and literary and intellectual movements for their volumes, as well as lists of further readings. Work on the series as a whole is coordinated at the Bruccoli Clark Layman editorial center in Columbia, South Carolina, where the editorial staff is responsible for accuracy of the published volumes.

One feature that distinguishes *DLB* is the illustration policy – its concern with the iconography of literature. Just as an author is influenced by his surroundings, so is the reader's understanding of the author enhanced by a knowledge of his environment. Therefore *DLB* volumes include not only drawings, paintings, and photographs of authors, often depicting them at various stages in their careers, but also illustrations of their families and places where they lived. Title pages are regularly reproduced in facsimile along with dust jackets for modern authors. The dust jackets are a special feature of *DLB* because they often document better than anything else the way in which an author's work was perceived in its own time. Specimens of the writers' manuscripts are included when feasible.

Samuel Johnson rightly decreed that "The chief glory of every people arises from its authors." The purpose of the *Dictionary of Literary Biography* is to compile literary history in the surest way available to us – by accurate and comprehensive treatment of the lives and work of those who contributed to it.

The *DLB* Advisory Board

Introduction

The Early Modern period from 1485 to 1603 in England is commonly referred to as "the Renaissance" and as "the age of the Tudors," for it can be conveniently divided into the reigns of Henry VII, Henry VIII, Edward VI, Mary I, and Elizabeth I — an unbroken string of idiosyncratic Tudor monarchs. But there is no single theory, history, concept, or tag for sixteenth-century British nondramatic literature — none at least that inspires widespread and lasting conviction. In matters of literary history, each defining term and every generation of scholarship has been succeeded by new information, interpretations, and labels.

Scholarship about sixteenth-century English writing was dominated in the early twentieth century by historical, philological, and bibliographical work, with the New Criticism especially prominent at midcentury. The latter half of this century — and especially the final third — has seen an explosion of scholarship influenced by Freudian and other psychologies, Marxist theories of history and economics, feminist and gender issues, deconstruction, and a vast array of other French theory. Each has had or is having its day, as the New Historicism, for instance, is succeeded by "New New Historicism," and received studies of the British literary empire are reassessed in light of postcolonial anthropological and ethnographic criticism. The present state of sixteenth-century literary history is nothing less than effervescent, so that canonical features that dominated yesterday are challenged by others today and likely to be displaced tomorrow.

Two important background studies for sixteenth-century scholarship are Jacob Burckhardt's *The Civilization of the Renaissance in Italy* (1860) and E. M. W. Tillyard's *The Elizabethan World Picture* (1944). Some of the most influential works of the twentieth century include Douglas Bush's *The Renaissance and English Humanism* (1939), Hallett Smith's *Elizabethan Poetry: A Study in Conventions, Meaning, and Expression* (1952), C. S. Lewis's *English Literature in the Sixteenth Century, Excluding Drama* (1954), Mikhail Bakhtin's *Rabelais and His World* (1968), Michel Foucault's "What Is an Author?" (1979), and Stephen Greenblatt's *Renaissance Self-Fashioning from More to Shakespeare* (1980). For a quick overview of the scholarly status quo, see Michael J. Marcuse's listings of "Literature of the Re-

naissance and Earlier Seventeenth Century" (1990) and Leah S. Marcus's essay on "Renaissance / Early Modern Studies" (1992). An evolving history of sixteenth-century literature is implicit — often aggressively explicit — in "Recent Studies in the English Renaissance" (annually in *Studies in English Literature,* winter issue), and readers will quickly spot trends from articles in respected journals such as *English Literary Renaissance* and from reviews in *Renaissance Quarterly* and *The Sixteenth Century Journal.* Although now more than two decades old, *The New Cambridge Bibliography of English Literature* (1974–   ) is an invaluable guide to primary and secondary materials, including literary history. *The State of Renaissance Studies: A Special Twenty-fifth Anniversary Symposium in Honor of Dan S. Collins* (1995) is a more current critical and bibliographic starting point.

Most of the writers treated in this Fourth Series lived well into the seventeenth century. Some — such as Thomas Dekker, John Marston, Anthony Munday, and Henry Peacham — lived into the 1630s, and Elizabeth Melville and William Percy into the 1640s. Most of their works were conceived or published, however, before the death of Queen Elizabeth. For example, Charles Whitworth observes that while the life of Thomas Lodge exactly spans the reigns of Elizabeth Tudor (1558–1603) and James Stuart (1603–1625), his contributions to the Golden Age of English literature occur between 1589 and the end of 1596. Wyman H. Herendeen's account of William Camden applies to Lodge and every other author under consideration here: "His life and career were products of late Tudor educational, religious, political, and social structures."

Thus, all of the nondramatic writings discussed in this volume are rooted in the sixteenth century. Variously they are representative or culminating works of the Tudor era or transitional — even seminal — influences upon Stuart authors. In James VI of Scotland, I of England, may be seen a royal author spanning both ages, while in William Shakespeare is seen the supreme author in English for these and all times.

As in *DLB 132, DLB 136,* and *DLB 167,* this introduction does not pronounce on what is past or passing, nor does it predict what is to come in our understanding of sixteenth-century literary history. Instead, it highlights some recurrent motifs in the articles making up this volume – motifs and emphases that will inevitably change with the discovery of new documents, reinterpretations of standard texts, and the rise and fall of theoretical schools in the universities. The articles in this volume demonstrate several aspects of sixteenth-century British nondramatic literature: a continuing history of literary innovation, writing across many genres, complex interaction among patrons and authors, deep-seated commitment to education and didacticism, continuation of the Protestant Reformation, much nondramatic political writing, radically new treatments of law and history, various humanistic concerns, and substantial developments in professional writing as a career. This introduction can be complemented by similar treatments of other sixteenth-century British nondramatic writers in *DLB 132, DLB 136,* and *DLB 167.*

Innovation. The writers treated in this volume, like those in the earlier series, are conveniently labeled "Renaissance authors," but they were far more than literary discoverers and revivers, or adapters and imitators, of "reborn" classical texts. Their works were often strikingly new, even revolutionary. Collectively, their literary biographies document innovation on a scale perhaps unequaled in the history of English and in a heterogeneous diversity that almost defies classification. The fact that many of these innovations happened near the end of the century suggests that specific political, economic, religious, technical, and literary stimuli continued to be enormously fruitful across decades or even the entire century. It also suggests that change generally provoked further change among writers of many genres and every degree of excellence.

In this volume, pride of place for innovation must be given to King James VI of Scotland, whose first law upon emerging from his minority in 1584 was not political but poetic. His *Reulis and Cautelis [rules and regulations] to Be Observit and Eschewit in Scottish Poesie* (1584) is described by Jenny Wormald as "guidelines for the new culture of the Scottish court," the only work laying down "rules for the glory of *Scottish* poetry." It is contemporaneous with Sir Philip Sidney's *Apology for Poetry* (1595) in English. Together the two volumes introduced an age of unparalleled literary and dramatic creativity over which Elizabeth and James presided for four decades until her death in 1603 and his in 1625. While Elizabeth reigned in Westminster as Gloriana patronizing Shakespeare and Edmund Spenser, at the Scottish court James ruled as Apollo over his "Castalian band" of poets, including William

Fowler, who made the first translation into English (Scots) of Niccolò Machiavelli's *Il Principe (The Prince,* 1513). In experimenting with the sonnet, the king himself seems to have anticipated Spenser's variant rhyme scheme: *ababbcbccdcdee.*

The sonnet developed throughout the century in more than forty thousand surviving examples, from Sir Thomas Wyatt's and Henry Howard, Earl of Surrey's early adaptations of Petrarch to Sir Walter Ralegh's encomium of Elizabeth accompanying Spenser's *Faerie Queene* of 1590. As late as 1609 Shakespeare's 154 sonnets still invited innovation: they and Spenser's eighty-nine sonnets in *Amoretti* (1595) are virtually unique in advising marriage. Shakespeare's are also unusual for including sexual consummation, and while they are not the first, they are a model of the distinctive break from what Dennis Kay calls the "shackles of patronage" toward a "poetry of self-discovery."

At the same time, amorous motifs and encomiastic motives transcended the sonnet to inform other court lyrics by Shakespeare's older contemporary Edward de Vere, seventeenth Earl of Oxford. Kay remarks that Oxford and Sir Edward Dyer were "the first of Elizabeth's courtiers to woo her, to 'court' her in verse." As "a self-conscious setter of trends," Oxford challenged the older generation's moral suspicion of verse and set the precedent that a "flamboyant display of eloquence" confers luster upon the court.

Yet eloquence and morality meet in John Dowland's *First Book of Songs or Ayres* (1597). According to Elise Bickford Jorgens, this is "not only Dowland's first, but the first English publication in what was to be a favored genre for the next two decades, celebrated then and now for its careful attention to the union of music and poetry." In the same lyric mode, Dowland's younger contemporary Thomas Campion has been called by T. S. Eliot "except for Shakespeare . . . the most accomplished master of rhymed lyric of his time." Walter R. Davis calls Campion's preface to Philip Rosseter's *Book of Ayres* (1601) a "manifesto" advocating the relatively simple lute song or ayre over the fashionable and intricate madrigal. His lyrical innovation is the marriage or overt connection of music and poetry.

Another first at the end of the century is Richard Barnfield's "Tears of an Affectionate Shepherd Sick for Love" (1594), "the first deliberately concentrated defense [of homoeroticism] in English," according to Kenneth Borris. Barnfield's longest and most controversial poem, it is based on Virgil's second eclogue about a shepherd's wooing a younger male (a classical work that seems to have been especially fashionable in the 1590s). Barnfield's "Tears" has been called "the most explicitly homosexual [poem] of the entire English Renaissance"; but given its pastoral subject and Ovidian context of sexual ambiguity, pursuits, and rivalries in love, it need not be pederastic. Nor is it necessarily misogynistic, for it shows that same-sex love can be more advantageous and moral than heterosexual love, that it is not inferior per se. The same premises and values inform Barnfield's *Cynthia* (1595) and his pastoral ode and twenty homoerotic sonnets appended to it.

In a wholly different vein and language, Elizabeth Weston lived an expatriate's life on the Continent and was one of seven English authors – and the only woman – in Thomas Farnaby's *Index Poeticus* (1634) of distinguished Latin authors, past and present. Also a Neo-Latinist, Camden earned a reputation as the first modern English historian for his monumental *Britannia* (1586) with its "more thorough and accurate periodizing of British history than any previous writer had managed." It was the first major work in England to reproduce archaeological materials such as ancient coins, inscriptions, monuments, and ruins; they are a serious component of Camden's historical analysis, placing his "chorographia" in the "vanguard of early modern cultural histories," according to Wyman H. Herendeen.

Translators outnumbered Neo-Latin authors, however, and include Thomas Lodge, who in 1614 made the only English translation of Seneca's complete prose until modern times. Much other translation was from classical Latin and Greek, but John Florio worked from modern vernaculars, including the Italian versions of Jacques Cartier's first two voyages (1580); Konrad Eisenbichler identifies Florio's prefatory epistle as "one of the earliest documents to advocate colonization." Florio may also have been the anonymous translator of the first English version of Giovanni Boccaccio's *Decameron* (1620). His best-known work is his first complete translation of Michel de Montaigne's *Essais* (1580) from French into English (1603). An immediate success, it became a powerful impetus for popularizing the essay form in English and a resource for authors such as Shakespeare, Ben Jonson, Robert Burton, and Ralegh. Florio's preface to Montaigne is an apology for translations, arguing that they make learning accessible to all and that "learning cannot be too common, and the commoner the better."

The vernacular was simultaneously gaining ascendancy in the professions. William Fulbecke,

for example, is described by D. R. Woolf as one of the "earliest authors of works in English on the canon and civil laws," which had traditionally been composed in Latin or French. His *Parallel or Conference* of the civil, canon, and common laws (1601–1602) is "one of the earliest English texts in comparative jurisprudence." Although his concern was to defend a powerful monarchy that found itself hemmed in by laws, he was one of the first common lawyers to think about "general principles which English law shared with other legal systems."

Other innovations (in approximate chronological order) characterize British writing at the end of the sixteenth century. Edward de Vere, seventeenth Earl of Oxford, was the first Elizabethan courtier poet to make a name as a published writer. In his *School of Abuse* (1579) Stephen Gosson initiated one of the central critical debates of English literature that eventually closed the theaters in 1642. Anthony Munday published *Zelauto* in 1580, which makes him the first Elizabethan writer of prose fiction without university training. The distinction is notable, avers Richard L. Branyan, because the work has "more vigor and clarity" than its model (John Lyly's *Euphues*), "contains fewer superfluous allusions, and is more readable today than Lyly's books." In *Scilla's Metamorphosis* (1589) Thomas Lodge was the first English poet to use the iambic sixain (*ababcc*) in a long narrative poem. His long narrative poem is an important early example of the Elizabethan epyllion, or Ovidian minor epic, and his verse form is now popularly known as Shakespeare's "Venus and Adonis stanza." (For related experiments with quantitative prosody and with topomorphology or strategically placed patterns in poetry, see the articles on Campion, Ralegh, and Shakespeare.)

In the realm of satire, Thomas Lodge was the first to identify the genre with Satyrs (in 1589) and was immediately imitated by George Puttenham, who used the connection in his *Art of English Poesie* (1589). Lodge's *Fig for Momus* (1595) is the first English collection of verse satires and epistles on a classical model. Camden's *Remains of a Greater Work Concerning Britain* (1605) contains the first "collection" of medieval poetry.

Genres. A recurrent trait of these late-sixteenth-century writers is that they are remarkably diverse, producing both prose and verse on virtually every subject in a myriad of nondramatic genres. King James leads the list. Although he wrote much less often after assuming new responsibilities in 1603, he was active through the turn of the century in a variety of genres and subjects: as translator of the Psalms and as author of political polemic, theology, political theory, speeches and letters, poetry, and poetic theory. In the early 1580s his poems showed "a talent for sheer light-hearted enjoyment." A collection of his earlier work, *The Essays of a Prentice in the Divine Art of Poesie* (1584), includes sonnets, a translation in heroic couplets of Guillaume de Salluste, Seigneur du Bartas's *Uranie*, and probably the best of his poems, the allegorical *Phoenix*. This volume also includes *Reulis and Cautelis* (noted above), which is his literary criticism setting forth rules for specific literary forms with an emphasis on ear-pleasing rhythm. (Although the sonnet came late to Scotland, at least seven hundred were written by James's countrymen between the 1580s and 1630.) James's later collection, *Poeticall Exercises* (1591), includes the major poem *Lepanto* and his translation of du Bartas's *Les Furies*.

In 1588, adding theologian-king to his role as poet-king, James published his first biblical commentary, on Revelation – a vitriolic Protestant attack on the Antichrist and his minions in the persons of the Pope, Jesuits, and Turks. Later he wrote more in the same vein in *Triplici nodo* (1607), *A Premonition* (1609), and *A Remonstrance for the Right of Kings* (1615). At the end of the century, in entirely unoriginal, hurried, and turgid prose, he wrote *Daemonologie* (1597) to refute skeptical works on witchcraft by Johann Weyer and Reginald Scot. He turned to political theorizing in *Basilikon Doron* (1599) and *The Trve Lawe of Free Monarchies* (1598). The first, a spirited, practical manual of kingship for Prince Henry, became enormously popular upon James's accession in 1603; the second asserts the integration of church and state in a full-scale argument for the divine right of kings. In another genre altogether, many examples of James's table talk were collected and published posthumously.

Shakespeare attained his majority only two years before James and achieved his reputation primarily from his plays. Yet, as Kay observes, he was first celebrated for his nondramatic narrative poems, *Venus and Adonis* (1593) and *Lucrece* (1594), which illuminate his activities as a poet "emphatically of his own age, especially in the period of extraordinary literary ferment in the last ten or twelve years of the reign of Queen Elizabeth." His two long poems are closely related to the epyllion, or Ovidian minor epic, flourishing brilliantly during the 1590s and attracting other writers such as Christopher Marlowe, Michael Drayton, John Marston, John Heywood, George Chapman, Thomas Lodge, and Francis Beaumont.

This popular minor genre of "Ovid anglicized" is characterized by a strong medieval tone, a melancholic narrator, personified psychological abstractions, and an abundant measure of irony, humor, and eroticism. Lodge's contribution is *Scilla's Metamorphosis* (1589), while Marston in *Pygmalion's Image* (1598) "scrupulously redeems the pleasure principle," according to James P. Bednarz: the poem is part of a Renaissance move to free Ovid from encrustations of a "stultifying and often absurd layer of didactic theory." Alternative interpretations, however, are less forgiving, identifying the poem as a parody or mock-epyllion. Marston himself says in his *Scourge of Villainy* (1598) that he could not possibly have imitated Ovid's model in a state of "sad seriousness"; his intent was to "note the odious spot / And blemish" that deforms modern poetry. Richard Lynche's little-known *Love of Dom Diego and Ginevra* (1596) is also an Ovidian minor epic with the erotic subject matter, length, and rhetorical devices typical of the genre. Like Spenser's *Epithalamion* (1595) following the eighty-nine sonnets of his *Amoretti*, it is appended to Lynche's thirty-nine sonnets of *Diella*, thus making Lynche and Spenser unusual in providing separate, happy endings to English sonnet sequences.

Among sonnets at this time, none are more famous than Shakespeare's for their examination of both idealized and raw physical love, for literary memorializing and remorseless images of time and death. Kay remarks that they are also part of Protestant England's "secularization of introspection," functioning like the Penitential Psalms of David in the sixteenth-century scriptural tradition and translations by Sir Thomas Wyatt and Mary Sidney.

While Shakespeare's sonnets tower above those of his contemporaries in this volume, much can still be learned from the mediocre and conventional. For example, *Zepheria* (1594) is an anonymous sequence full of bad rhymes and startling neologisms. Little esteemed by modern editors and readers, it has traditionally been disparaged by scholars such as Sidney Lee, who says that it "limps clumsily along a most cacophonous path" and infers that the author was a law student who "mistook legal technicalities for poetic imagery." But as L. M. Storozynsky comments, the poems should probably be read in a spirit of parody, for they exaggerate all the hyperbolic conventions of description, comparison, excess apostrophe, and bombastic diction of Petrarchan love poetry – perhaps to mock Romeo and other love-struck gallants of the tradition.

Likewise, Bartholomew Griffin's *Fidessa: More Chaste than Kind* (1596) is little known but typical of sixteenth-century sonneteering and indicative of its popularity. Griffin has been accused of "achieving fine verbal and aural effects where there is little or no meaning," notes Storozynsky; but a variation of one of his sonnets was reprinted by Isaac Jaggard in *The Passionate Pilgrim* (1599), a collection published as if its contents were written entirely by Shakespeare. Another Shakespeare imitator was Richard Lynche, who joined Griffin and a handful of Elizabethan writers in publishing both sonnet sequences and long narrative poems (others included Samuel Daniel, Giles Fletcher the Elder, Lodge, and Spenser). Lynche's *Diella* (1596) almost certainly recalls Daniel's *Delia* (1592) by its name and by the device of linking the last sonnet to the following narrative. Other variations on the sonnet tradition include Robert Tofte's carefully arranged sequence of ten-, twenty-, and twenty-four-line love poems in *Laura* (1597) and John Davies of Hereford's ten *Sonnets to Philomel* (1591–1594), nine *Gulling Sonnets* (1594–1595), and an epithalamium (1595) composed of ten sonnets, including one as introduction followed by one for each of the nine Muses.

In addition to these sonnets and the ayres of Dowland and Campion, the short poem, or lyric, appears in a dazzling array from authors such as Edward de Vere, seventeenth Earl of Oxford, and in many contexts — most notably at the end of the century in several literary anthologies, the successors to Richard Tottel's *Songs and Sonnets* (1557). Lodge, for example, is the primary contributor to *The Phoenix Nest* (1593), with sixteen lyrics in a wide variety of forms and complex metrical patterns. His fourteen poems in *England's Helicon* (1600) are outnumbered only by Bartholomew Young's twenty-five and Sir Philip Sidney's fifteen. Similarly, several of Barnfield's lyrics appeared in successful anthologies, often attributed to Shakespeare.

If genre may be reduced even further to the scale of the word, then Florio deserves recognition beyond his translation of Montaigne's *Essais* for his Italian-English dictionary, *A World of Words*. First published in 1598 and expanded in 1611, this compilation became the standard of the seventeenth century and the basis for many successors. Its humanistic preface praises English for the "richness of its lexicon" — a richness that informs all levels of society including the lowest, which is reflected in Thomas Dekker's glossary of "canting" language in his *Lantern and Candlelight* (1608).

On a scale somewhat larger than single words, the pithy proverb or sententious saying engaged Florio to cull six thousand apothegms from Italian literature and publish them in *Giardino di ricreatione*

(1591); he compares his compilation to those of Desiderius Erasmus in Greek and Latin (published 1500 and following) and Thomas Heywood in English (1550 and following). Printed with *Giardino,* the twelve dialogues of his *Second Fruits* are in part exercises in the use of proverbs, which Florio marks in the text with asterisks. The first part of his earlier *First Fruits* (1578) comprises forty-four elementary dialogues of increasing difficulty — a genre that Fulbecke used for his *Parallel or Conference* of the civil, canon, and common laws. In Shakespeare's *Lucrece,* Tarquin and Lucrece debate in an extended dialogue; the poem also contains several sententiae (wise sayings) that are set off typographically.

Among the masters of small-scale genres, lyricist Thomas Campion published more than four hundred Latin epigrams (1595, 1619), stating in the preface to Rosseter's *Book of Ayres* that what epigrams are to poetry, ayres are to music. At about the same time, Davies also wrote forty-eight epigrams (1595?) that earned him the epithet "the English Martial" after the Roman poet, whose works were a standard text at Westminster School. The purpose of Davies's epigrams is to attack pretentious inadequacies in love, in honor, and at court; their principal object is the gull, one who seems but is not wise.

Closely related to the epigram is formal satire. While John Marston is remembered today chiefly as a dramatist for *The Malcontent* (1602–1603), in his own time he was noted as "a literary voice of violent disaffection" in verse satire of "stylistic and emotional excess," of "hysterical rage." The butt of his invective in *Certain Satires* (1598) is the gentry and abuses of language and literature. James P. Bednarz observes that "in an age when satirists were generally expected to cultivate an acerbic tone," *The Scourge of Villainy* distinguished itself as "the most truculent, hysterical, and some would say obscene, voice of late-Elizabethan invective." It attacks religious abuse by both Catholics and Protestants, sexual perversions (including bestiality and incest), and criticism of *Certain Satires*. Bednarz notes that "Satire 7" seems to abandon the ideal of discovering moral integrity or reforming modern society and loses its way in an "abyss of agonizing self-doubt." Ben Jonson called Marston a "Hercules in poetry," and his "language of unreconciled alienation" is apparent in such Shakespearean characters as Hamlet, Lear, Timon, Thersites, and Iago.

Satirists such as Marston had to change their writing careers after 1 June 1599, when John Whitgift, Archbishop of Canterbury, and Richard

Bancroft, Bishop of London, issued their Order of Conflagration, a generic ban on satires and epigrams that suppressed Marston's *Pygmalion's Image* and *The Scourge of Villainy* along with works by Everard Gilpin, Joseph Hall, Christopher Marlowe, John Davies, Thomas Middleton, Thomas Nashe, and Gabriel Harvey. Such official censorship made all aspects of authorship and publishing highly problematic.

Satire was later revived in Dekker's only known controversial writing, *The Double PP* (1606), an anti-Jesuit satire that includes a verse caricature "Picture of a Jesuit," a prose inventory of Jesuit terrorism in Europe, and a verse narrative about Protestant armies that encompass all the estates of England and defeat the Pope and his Romish armies. Dekker's *News from Hell* (1606) is an epistolary moral satire and one of many spinoffs from Nashe's *Pierce Penniless* (1592); its description of hell includes a burlesque scene of the ferryman Charon. *The Gull's Horn Book* (1609) is Dekker's satiric courtesy book that Frederick O. Waage describes as "drenched in irony, since the urban conduct it supposedly promotes is presented by the speaker as absurd and degenerate." His *Raven's Almanac* of the same year (1609) is "a mock-prognostication dedicated to gallants and gulls," with satiric predictions for each season interspersed with droll stories.

Dekker's descriptive forte is apparent in a collaborative enterprise, *Jests to Make You Merry* (1607). George Wilkins contributed jests and Dekker the unrelated tales of Cock Watt ("the spirit of Newgate"), including descriptions of activities by a variety of female criminals. *The Bellman of London* (1608) is probably Dekker's "most successful work as a prose writer," with the Bellman as a "guide to candlelight crime," including a diversity of rogue types from the aristocratic Upright-Men to the Kinchyn Company (little boys) and an anatomy of their different kinds of scams, fraud, and thievery. Closely related to this low-life rogue literature is Dekker's *Strange Horse Race* (1613), which includes a parodic text of the devil's will where all vices are given to urban criminals. Dekker supplemented the ninth edition of Sir Thomas Overbury's characters with six new prison-related figures, emphasizing their typically diabolic inner natures, as in his Creditor, Sergeant, Yeoman, and Jailer. *Dekker His Dream* (1620) is an autobiographical vision of Apocalypse and hell, where the torments are biblical and the sufferers are urban criminal types.

The prose romance emerging at the end of the sixteenth century was shaped by Sidney, Nashe, and Lyly (see *DLB 167*). It is exemplified later by Dekker's *Penny-wise, Pound-foolish* (1631), a novella of domestic romance about a wayfaring sailor eventually reconciled with his wife and rewarded with a fortune. Almost fifty years earlier, William Warner's *Pan His Syrinx* (1584) is a compendium of the conventions of Greek prose romances: lost parents and children, love stories, confused identities, shipwrecks, surprise denouements, and spectacular reunions, all in a complex and convoluted story line. Revised in 1597 to reduce the stylistic influence of Lyly's euphuism, Warner's book influenced Robert Greene and later the plays of Dekker and Robert Daborne.

The best-known romance by an author in this volume is Lodge's *Rosalynde* (1590), which had reached a fourth edition before Shakespeare transmuted it into *As You Like It*. Like Sidney's *Arcadia,* it synthesizes chivalric adventure narrative, pastoralism, and lyric poetry. Among Lodge's several lesser-known works, Charles Whitworth calls *Euphues' Shadow* "the nearest imitation of Lyly's *Euphues* that has survived." Throughout Lodge's prose there are elements of violence and villainy, but his last romance, *A Margarite of America* (1596), "outdoes almost anything in [Matteo] Bandello, Greene, or Nashe in decadent horror and sheer bloodiness." It is "extraordinarily bleak and bloody," a tale of "human depravity and motiveless malignity" with "no repentance and redemption, no reward for virtue." As Lodge himself says, it is "replenished with all vice and impoverished of all virtue."

At the opposite end of the moral spectrum stands Lancelot Andrewes and his sermons, for aside from his stature among advanced humanist scholars, one of his chief roles was preacher. He is generally regarded as "a Jacobean churchman," and his reputation "largely rests upon the great festival sermons he preached for over two decades to the Jacobean court," but his first sermon to Queen Elizabeth as court preacher was during Lent in 1590. In contrast to Calvinist moralism with its emphasis on guilt and personal experience, Andrewes's festival sermons are richly textured, traditional works of mystery and piety. Beginning in 1604 almost until his death, he preached at court on Christmas, Easter, Pentecost, and often on Good Friday or during Lent. A humbler devotional work and Dekker's sole example of the genre is his *Four Birds of Noah's Ark* (1609), in the tradition of Protestant primers and prayer books.

Possibly the best-known reflective work of this period is John Davies's *Nosce Teipsum* (1599). Composed of two elegies on human knowledge and the soul of man, it was continuously reprinted through the eighteenth century. Also well known is Davies's complexly symbolic *Orchestra* (1596), which Robert Wiltenburg describes as showing that "all of life is best comprehended under the figure of dance, representing ordered change through time." The poem may have originated in an entertainment as "a fanciful 'disputation' for a Middle Temple audience."

In recent decades Fulke Greville, first Lord Brooke, has been increasingly recognized for his reflective verse (all published posthumously), with some claims that he is a religious poet comparable to John Donne. He considered his *Treatise of Religion* as the most important of his shorter philosophical poems, in it (as in *An Inquisition upon Fame and Honor*) rejecting the stoic equanimity he advocates in *A Letter to an Honorable Lady* (1633; probably composed 1595-1601) and implicitly rejecting a Calvinist doctrine of predestination. John Gouws describes war in Greville's *Treatise of Wars* as "a divine scourge of human wickedness — a trial of the Elect . . . a purge for the excesses of peace — an instrument for sustaining the vicissitudes of the fallen condition." Several of his *Caelia* poems record his growing self-understanding during the reign of James I, while *A Treatise of Humane Learning* shows his commitment to the tradition of Renaissance skepticism and his rejection of both Montaigne's relativism and Francis Bacon's humanistic optimism.

Less philosophical and more empirical is a growing body of travel literature, for travel in the Early Modern period was increasingly replacing ancient books as a source of knowledge. Hence, travel writing became what Raymond-Jean Frontain calls "one of the most popular forms of Elizabethan and Stuart reading." Richard Hakluyt, for example, paid Florio to translate Jacques Cartier's *First Voyages* (1580) from Italian. In the early seventeenth century, Thomas Coryate in his travel writings is a serious empiricist, "as specific in his description of a desert mirage as of a Jewish circumcision rite." He traveled in Europe, to the lands of classical and biblical antiquity, to parts of the Ottoman Empire, and to the court of the Great Mogul. His account (published 1611) of a 1,975-mile trip made largely on foot in 1608 is "an extraordinary mixture of the most energetic personal experience, sharp social observation, religious polemic, architectural description, and humanist fascination with monuments and their inscriptions" — a sprightly synthesis of John Leland, Thomas Hoby, and Will Kemp.

Equally eclectic is William Warner's major work, his encyclopedic verse chronicle *Albion's England* (1586). This volume is a precursor of Michael Drayton's *Poly-Olbion* (1612), combining world and British history with the narrative and allegorical techniques of Spenser's *Faerie Queene* (1590, 1596). Ursula Appelt describes it as the most diverse collection of stories in sixteenth-century British literature, combining the genres of chronicle, epic, romance, burlesque, fabliau, beast fable, and love story. It reflects both the developing prose romance and the short-lived verse chronicles of the sixteenth century, both the historical methods of Raphael Holinshed and the moralizing of *A Mirror for Magistrates* (1559-1609) Warner was considered by many of his contemporaries to be an equal of Homer, Virgil, Horace, and Ovid — and of Spenser, Shakespeare, and Sidney. But *Albion's England* has not stood the test of time: Appelt observes, "Warner's poor literary judgment was equalled by the quality of his execution."

In addition to the variety of genres represented throughout the sixteenth century in this volume, many of the writers practiced a remarkable diversity in their own works. At the end of the century, for example, Charles Whitworth observes that the output of Thomas Lodge was "more varied and more copious than that of most of his contemporaries," for Lodge wrote almost every kind of literature: lyric poems by the dozens, prose romances, plays, sonnets and sonnet sequences, narrative poems, satires in verse and prose, satiric and admonitory pamphlets, fervent devotional tracts of Jesuit orthodoxy, medical treatises, large-scale translations, and moral complaints in dialogue. *A Fig for Momus* (1595), his last verse collection, comprises fifteen secular meditations categorized as satires, epistles, and four Horatian eclogues cast as dialogues. Yet writing was not Lodge's most important vocation, being confined largely to the few years between 1589 and 1596, when he left England for medical study at Avignon and a new career.

Variety, however, is no guarantee of quality, as can be seen from the prolific hack writing of Anthony Munday: plays, a pamphlet, city pageants, ballads, lyrics, an update of John Stowe's chronicle history of London, translations of prose romances, and possibly his most entertaining book, *The English Roman Life* (1583), about his travels on the Continent. He was also a precursor of modern journalists in his *View of Sundry Examples* (1580), a collection of sensational nonfiction news stories replete with murder, suicide, and didactic pronouncements about the consequence of sin and God's inescapable wrath.

More distinguished in their diversity are Ralegh and Greville. In addition to some trenchant lyrics, Ralegh wrote prose treatises on shipbuilding, agriculture, economics, warfare, and the nature of the soul. His *Discovery of Guiana* (1596) has been called one of the most fascinating adventure stories ever written; and while in the Tower of London he composed his monumental *History of the World* (1614).

Greville wrote short poems, closet dramas, sonnet sequences, and verse treatises on several topics. His *Caelica* sonnets, like those of Sidney, respond to Petrarchan love literature, but cynically deny the possibility of ideal mortal love. He also wrote "discursive poems" such as *A Treatise of Monarchy* (1670; composed 1599–1610) on that form of government as problematic but superior to aristocracy and democracy. John Gouws describes Greville's *Dedication to Sir Philip Sidney* (1652; composed 1610–1612) as "a laudatory biography of Sidney as an ideal subject" and observes that its "encomiastic history of Queen Elizabeth I's reign" is an indirect censure of her successor, James I. Greville's *Letter to an Honorable Lady* reflects the literary traditions of the *consolatio* and the Senecan epistle in trying to persuade an ill-used lady to lead a life of "stoic, Christian patience"; the attitude is rejected in his Calvinistic *Inquisition upon Fame and Honor* (1633; composed 1612–1614).

Patronage, networking. The confluence of Greville, Ralegh, Queen Elizabeth, and King James brings to the fore one of the most important principles underlying writing at the end of the sixteenth century and the beginning of the seventeenth: authors typically depended upon some form of patronage for social, economic, and artistic survival. At the same time, they often knew and were able to help each other within the relatively confined network of the literary community. Thus, a successful literary life in Renaissance England often depended not only on the marketplace but also on whom the author knew.

Greville, for instance, pursued an active literary life for almost fifty years (from the late 1570s to the 1620s), making him, according to Gouws, "the principal courtly writer of the Elizabethan and Jacobean eras (apart from his short-lived friend Sir Philip Sidney)." He derived his social position from the patronage of Elizabeth and James, and in turn actively patronized other writers. He was responsible for William Camden's appointment as Clarenceux King of Arms in the Herald's Office, and he supported the work of John Speed in history, Bishop Joseph Hall in religion, Samuel Daniel in literature, and John Coke in politics, the latter becoming secretary of state under Charles I.

Ralegh well understood the patronage system and accordingly wrote most of his works for self-advancement at court. As early as 1574 he attended Lyon's Inn and Middle Temple in London not only to study law but also to form contacts for furthering his ambitions in public life. He seems to have known the earl of Oxford around 1578–1579, and he may have met Spenser in 1580 in Ireland. A decade later he generously promoted Spenser's publication of *The Faerie Queene*. Ralegh's own career fared less well, for after Elizabeth's death in 1603, he found himself out of favor with James and was imprisoned for thirteen years. Even in prison, however, he worked on his monumental *History of the World* for Prince Henry as a hope for winning release, but he stopped work after Henry's death of typhoid fever in 1612.

The supreme patron treated in this volume is, of course, King James, who both presided over the literary culture of his age and contributed to it. His Scottish courtier poets called themselves "the Castalian band" and were recognized internationally. His wife, Anne of Denmark, was the first to patronize Ben Jonson, and the preeminent Protestant translation of Scripture for almost four hundred years is known as the Authorized or King James Version of the Bible in recognition of his leadership. Jenny Wormald summarizes his literary and artistic significance thus: "For some forty-five years, King James shaped and dominated the cultural scene, presiding over the flowering of poetry in Scotland and of the masque in England; and through his extensive political and theological writings, he had a political and intellectual influence which went far beyond the practical pursuits of kings."

Even writers who depended wholly on royal largesse had something to offer their patrons in return. Elizabeth Weston, for example, was much praised by European humanists and epitomizes the symbiotic relationship of writer and patron in her expatriate appeals to Emperor Rudolf II in Prague: in exchange for magnanimous help for an impoverished widow and her orphaned daughter, she would bear witness to the *humanitas* of the Rudolphine circle and a specifically English witness to its imperial scope.

Sometimes the reward system paid off handsomely even for lesser writers and sometimes despite impolitic behavior. For example, Robert Wiltenburg describes John Davies as perhaps the most representative of the minor poets of the 1590s, a role that depended on serving at once his own interests and those of some idea or person such as his sovereign or patron. His success is apparent in his being asked to write an epithalamium for the wedding in 1595 of Elizabeth Vere (daughter of the earl of Oxford and granddaughter of William Cecil, Lord Burghley) to William Stanley, sixth Earl of Derby and a patron of acting companies. Davies had attracted the favorable notice of the Cecil family and of Queen Elizabeth before 1598, but then he publicly attacked a friend and was disgraced and banished from the court. His attempt to regain Elizabeth's favor in *Hymns of Astraea* (1599) is a tour de force of ingenious acrostics and encomium. (Related works are Dekker's martial encomiums in his *Artillery Garden* of 1615 and *Wars, Wars, Wars* of 1628.) Davies restored his social and professional status with the help of his widely respected *Nosce Teipsum* and the intervention of powerful friends such as Charles Blount, the queen, Robert Cecil, and Sir Thomas Egerton. After the accession of James in 1603, Davies rapidly rose to knighthood and enjoyed many legal and political appointments in Ireland, including the offices of solicitor general and attorney general.

Patronage and networking made the Jacobean court fertile ground for other authors, too. After 1604 John Florio was an active participant in court life, serving as Groom of the Privy Chamber for Queen Anne and Italian tutor for some of the royal children. He enjoyed extensive political connections with Robert Cecil (Burghley's son) and the earls of Southampton, Leicester, Rutland, Bedford, and especially Essex, and he managed to survive Essex's fall unscathed. He seems to have had mixed relationships in a literary circle that included his brother-in-law Samuel Daniel, John Eliot, Nashe, Harvey, Hakluyt, and Shakespeare. His monumental translation of Montaigne's *Essais* was made possible by a network of other patrons and friends, including the countess of Bedford, Lady Anne Harington, Matthew Gwinne, Theodore Diodati, and Daniel. Similarly, Thomas Coryate was able to move to London with the patronage of two members of his godfather's family; then Prince Henry apparently gave him a pension and supported him, possibly as some kind of unofficial court jester. Coryate was regularly part of a circle at the Mermaid Tavern that included Jonson, Donne, Inigo Jones, and their associates.

Closely related to court patronage is support from the Established Church, which benefited many writers, including Lancelot Andrewes, as already noted. Arond 1586 Andrewes became chaplain for both Archbishop Whitgift and Queen Elizabeth. Despite Secretary of State Francis Walsingham's Puritan theology, he patronized Andrewes

with nominations to several ecclesiastical appointments. At the same time, Andrewes moved easily within the intellectual orbit of Camden, Hakluyt, Bacon, and other members of the Society of Antiquaries. Earlier, a "shrewd choice of patrons" led Henry Peacham the Elder to several appointments in his religious career. He dedicated the 1577 edition of his *Garden of Eloquence* to John Aylmer, Bishop of London, who ordained him priest in 1578. Peacham's *Sermon on Job* (1591), dedicated to Margaret Clifford, Countess of Cumberland, and her sister Anne Dudley, Countess of Warwick, may have been instrumental in his receiving a double benefice at North and South Leverton.

Sacred and secular patronage was gradually being eroded by entrepreneurial capitalism and professional writing in Elizabethan and Jacobean England, but it was far from moribund. Shakespeare's career, for example, was dramatically affected by microbes and politics when the Privy Council, fearing plague and civil unrest, closed London theaters from 23 June 1592 until June 1594. As Dennis Kay observes, this crisis became an opportunity for Shakespeare to turn from lowly scriptwriting for the public theater to the more conventional course of pursuing art and patronage. His first publication, *Venus and Adonis,* reveals his social and literary aspirations: his choice of Richard Field as printer shows his ambition to associate himself with "unambiguously high art productions," and his dedication to the earl of Southampton shows his desire for "direct aristocratic patronage." In his sonnets, however, an apparent pitch for patronage may be qualified, for some scholars have argued that the poems direct attention to the speaker's subjectivity rather than to the ostensible object of praise, thus identifying the so-called birth of the author in Early Modern literature.

In any event, and whether or not he is the mysterious "Mr. W. H." of the sonnet's dedication (written by their printer, Thomas Thorpe), Southampton figures prominently as a Renaissance patron, as does Edward de Vere, seventeenth Earl of Oxford, who was also a distinguished author. Oxford was intermittently prominent at Elizabeth's court from 1564 to 1582, leading what Kay describes as the "turbulent and unsettled life" of a courtier, although he fit the strict definition only off-and-on, when he actually received room and board (the *bouge,* or living allowance) at court. Kay observes that "no other prominent courtier was so well known as the author of published English verse" and that Oxford was praised both as a potential patron and as an accomplished writer himself.

He sponsored a dramatic troupe and influenced other authors, including Ralegh, Arthur Gorges, and Sidney. John Lyly was his most significant protégé. Oxford was himself tutored by his uncle Arthur Golding (half brother to his mother), who was associated with the earl of Leicester and the Sidney circle and whose translation of Ovid's *Metamorphoses* figures importantly in Shakespeare's works.

As patron, Oxford was the recipient of dedications to a wide range of works, including translations of classical texts, scientific and medical works, translations of John Calvin's sermons, antiquarian histories of Britain, defenses of the military profession, and Angel Day's *English Secretary* (1586). Lyly, Munday, and Greene all dedicated fiction to him. A great deal of poetry and music was also dedicated to Oxford, including Thomas Watson's *Hekatompathia* (1582), John Soowthern's *Pandora* (1584), and John Farmer's *Forty Several Ways* (1591). From 1586 until his death in 1604, by command of Queen Elizabeth and King James he received £1,000 annually from the unfilled bishopric of Ely as "relief to his financial problems." Kay sums up Oxford's importance as "a significant figure at a crucial time. Both his writing and his reputation played an important role in making skill in writing vernacular verse an accomplishment to be prized and admired."

Patronage and networking also appeared among the unskillful and outside the court or church. William Percy, for example, was a minor poet with an unenviable reputation, being classed by Sidney Lee among the "Poetae Minimi" and his works as "invariably grotesque" among the "debased developments" of the sonnet. Nonetheless, Percy is of interest at least for his connection to Barnabe Barnes, who dedicated his *Parthenophil and Parthenophe* (1593) to him. Percy reciprocated with a madrigal to Barnes at the end of his own sonnet sequence, *To the Fairest Coelia* (1594). At Gloucester Hall, Oxford, after 1589, he was apparently regarded as a patron of a small literary circle that included Charles Fitzgeoffrey and the three Mychelbourne brothers (Edward, Thomas, and Lawrence). Later in London, the group may have included the dramatists John Ford and John Webster.

Another instance shows how not every writer was happy with the system. William Warner was patronized by the Lords Hundson — Henry and George Carey — but without much reward or advancement. His bitterness toward "ingrateful and ungracious readers" may suggest the neglect of patrons or more generally disgust with the disregard

for poetry in his day. But a break between author and patrons can be inferred from Warner's changing the dedication of *Albion's England* from the Careys to Sir Edward Coke in its 1606 edition.

Among notable poet-musicians, however, the system seems to have been advantageous in material and other ways. Renaissance composers were typically dependent upon patronage of the rich and famous — more so than their literary counterparts, according to Elise Bickford Jorgens. Because Thomas Campion took up the practice of medicine at the age of nearly forty, he did not have to earn his livelihood as a poet-musician or rely on the favors of patronage, but he did seek recognition in print and remuneration from the court. His older contemporary William Byrd was particularly successful, for example, in his appointment to the Chapel Royal in 1570. Byrd's courtly and literary connections included the earl of Oxford, whose lyric "If Women Could Be Fair and Never Fond" he set to music. Byrd's longtime musical and literary patrons included the Petre family, who maintained an underground congregation of recusants. Others in his Catholic environment were Edward Paston of Norfolk Hall, who held a prodigious collection of musical manuscripts, including much by Byrd. Paston was head of Catholic Appleton Hall and also patron of Thomas Morley, a composer, student of Byrd, and fellow Catholic sympathizer.

Few writers benefited as much from an extensive literary circle and lifelong patronage as William Camden, who later become a patron in his own right. Beginning as early as his student days at Oxford, he was first supported by Dr. Thomas Cooper, later the bishop of Winchester and one of many episcopal ties in Camden's life. He spent part of his career in Christ Church College, where he valued his relationship with Sir Philip Sidney. He eventually become headmaster of Westminster School, which had close institutional ties with Christ Church. At Westminster from 1575 to 1597, Camden was patronized by the dean of its cathedral, Gabriel Goodman, befriended by its headmaster, Edward Grant, associated with its steward, William Cecil, Lord Burghley — and thus connected directly to the older courtly humanism of Roger Ascham and the court itself through Westminster's performances of plays at court annually or more often. Camden was active in the Society of Antiquaries from its founding. The publication history of his *Britannia* (1586–1607) is coextensive with his many reports at meetings of the society, and his collaborative and collegial research methods affected the practice of history and literature throughout England.

In a literary vein, Camden's life and works are interconnected with those of Sidney and Spenser, which together provide three quite different perspectives of the English Renaissance at its peak. Singularly beneficial to Camden was his close association with a former student, Robert Cotton, whom he helped to collect books, manuscripts, and antiques, in the process developing a large correspondence with scholars and friends in England and Europe. Their relationship seems to have been a creative symbiosis of building a collection for Cotton and allowing Camden free use of it for his own studies. In his maturity Camden became a benefactor as well as beneficiary of the system both as a contributor to Westminster School and Oxford University, where he established the first lectures in history in 1622, and as Clarenceux King of Arms, a strategic role in the competitive patronage system at court.

Other writers benefited simply from the stimulating give-and-take of literary association. Campion's circle at Peter House, Cambridge, apparently included Abraham Fraunce, Harvey, Percy, and Nashe; around 1586–1594 he would have known Francis Davison at Gray's Inn. Barnfield certainly knew contemporary writers such as Thomas Watson, Fraunce, Marlowe, Francis Meres, and Michael Drayton. Gosson's intellectual circle at Corpus Christi College, Oxford, was "vigorously religious," according to Arthur F. Kinney, including Richard Hooker and others who eventually held such appointments as Archdeacon of Lincoln, Canon of Exeter, and chaplain to Queen Elizabeth. Gosson's own prose style was much influenced by the lectures of John Rainoldes.

The richness and complexity of literary association is perhaps best seen in the heterogeneous career of Lodge. He is typically discussed in the context of other authors, especially the "University Wits," among whom he was almost always outshown and outclassed by writers such as Lyly, Marlowe, Nashe, and Greene. Yet he was influential even upon Shakespeare, who borrowed the substance of *As You Like It* from Lodge's *Rosalynde,* his model for *Venus and Adonis* from *Scilla's Metamorphosis,* and elements of his Roman plays from *The Wounds of Civil War* (written 1586 or 1587). Lodge wrote with Marlowe for the Chamberlain's Men in the late 1580s, and Marlowe borrowed from his *Wounds of Civil War* for *Tamburlaine* and *Edward II.* Lodge exchanged salvos with Gosson over Gosson's *School of Abuse,* and he seems to have been

on good terms with Sidney, to whom he later dedicated *A Looking Glass for London and England* (1594). With an active literary career concentrated in prose fiction and lyric poetry around 1589–1596, he seems to have kept good company: he addressed his *Fig for Momus,* eclogues in dialogue form, to Spenser, Daniel, and Drayton. And in *England's Helicon* he shared pages with George Peele, Drayton, Greville, Marlowe, Ralegh, Shakespeare, Sidney, and many others – perhaps thanks to its publisher Nicholas Ling, who had published *Rosalynde.*

Relationships among authors were not always harmonious, however. James P. Bednarz notes that Marston's satires were greeted with "considerable acrimony" by several of his contemporaries such as Joseph Hall and John Weever. Ben Jonson was his "most persistent critic" as they exchanged insults in the so-called Poets' War at the turn of the century – yet Marston's last published poem is a commendatory piece in the first edition of Jonson's *Sejanus* (1605).

Finally, the precarious relationship among authors and between authors and patrons is apparent in Gosson's dedicating his *Ephemerides of Plato* to Sidney. His unsolicited dedication is notable both as an urgent request from a fellow author for patronage and as an annoying impertinence from a stranger.

Education, didacticism. For most of the authors in these sixteenth-century volumes, teaching, studying, and rigorous education were natural extensions of reading and writing. King James himself was known as "the king of scholarship and wit." He reflected his upbringing when he exclaimed during a visit to the Bodleian Library in Oxford in 1605, "Were I not a King I would be a University-man; and if it were so that I must be a prisoner . . . I would have no other prison than this library, and be chained together with these good authors." In his youth his principal tutor was the European humanist, classicist, and poet George Buchanan, followed by Peter Young, who built up James's library with scholarly books in addition to medieval romances and poetry. The collection was the nucleus of the Royal Library that moved to the British Museum in 1759.

Several authors in this volume were professionally involved in formal education, none more fully than William Camden, for whom the role of educator complemented his other accomplishments as historian, poet, and herald. He was much influenced in his own upbringing by Protestant institutions and became an influence himself as recordkeeper and then headmaster of Westminster School. Lord Burghley had reestablished Westminster in part to recapture an emphasis on Greek, so it is understandable that Camden's *Institutio graecae grammatices compendiaria* (1595) became the school's authorized Greek grammar beside William Lily's Latin textbook.

Camden's classroom success and his subsequent effect on writers are reflected in the relatively large number of elegies in Greek in the memorial collection published at his death. His influence also extended to Westminster's dramatic tradition and beyond, as attested by Ben Jonson's warm acknowledgments. Camden's humanistic attention to classical languages was reinforced by Lancelot Andrewes, who served as dean of Westminster and was popular with his students for informal instruction as well as lessons in Hebrew and Greek. Similar influence and interaction can be noted in Lodge, who was educated at Merchant Taylors' School under Richard Mulcaster (Spenser's mentor) and tutored by Edward Hoby at Oxford, where he may have begun to write plays.

Outside of the universities and schools such as Westminster and Merchant Taylors', John Florio earned his living by teaching Italian language and conversation. His textbook *First Fruits* embodies humanistic concern for the beauty and utility of modern vernaculars. Dedicated to the earl of Leicester, it includes an Italian grammar and a series of forty-four dialogues that seem to reflect a European moral agenda (Florio was the son of a Reform minister) and a degree of condescension toward English insularity, dress, and morals. His *Second Fruits* is much less preachy and more enthusiastic about the intellectual ferment of the late sixteenth century. It does, however, defend Italy against Roger Ascham's charges of moral contamination, arguing reasonably that good and evil exist in every nation.

Teaching is both means and end in Stephen Gosson's first important book, *The School of Abuse*. Its central metaphor is the schoolroom, and moral instruction is the chief criterion by which all literature is to be judged. Gosson's basic premise is that good art instructs in virtue through models of virtuous action, with the proviso that art appeals to emotion and can thus subjugate reason. He is always careful, however, to emphasize that his attack is not on art itself but upon its abuses.

Gosson's subsequent *Apology for the School of Abuse* (1579) abandons his earlier moderate Christian humanism for a theologically conservative and antihumanistic attack on the theater. (His two works may be the immediate causes of Sidney's *Defense of Poetry* (1595), itself an exercise in judicial rhetoric.) A third work, *Plays Confuted in Five Actions*

(1582), is logical, relentlessly Aristotelian, and, according to Arthur F. Kinney, "the single most significant attack on plays in the entire Tudor period." Gosson's fundamental premise and metaphor here is that plays are "addle eggs," rotten in concept and actuality because they are the creation of the devil. Where his first attacks rely on humanist allusion to antiquity and classical rhetoric, this final one rests absolutely on inductive and deductive logic and the certainty of Scripture and the Church Fathers. In addition to this prose, Gosson's surviving poems are heavily didactic, commonplace, and unimaginative. (Apparently his plays were, too, although they have not survived.)

Other didactic authors are more subtle than Gosson but sometimes appear contradictory or confused in their use of literature for instruction. For example, John Marston's first publication, *The Metamorphosis of Pygmalion's Image and Certain Satires,* seems to be a self-contradictory volume. His epyllion "celebrates the absolute triumph of libido," according to Bednarz, who calls it "an erotic mythological narrative in which sexual fantasy is extravagantly rewarded." The five satires following, however, represent Marston's "notorious voice of moral indignation."

In William Warner's prose romance *Syrinx,* didactic idealism clashes with reality. In seven moralizing tales, Warner creates an irresolvable contradiction between providentialism and arbitrary Fortune, so he allows his main characters finally to escape the world to live "happily ever after" on a totally isolated island. Perhaps more successful is *Albion's England,* in which he treats historical subject matter with the techniques of verse romance. The result is history in a collection of heterogeneous stories that teach and delight, if taken in small doses — a happy achievement of the literary ideals of Horace and Sidney.

Reformation. Despite England's officially Protestant religion during most of the sixteenth century, a small but vital Catholic subculture included literary and artistic figures such as John Dowland, who converted to the Catholic Church, and recusant William Byrd. The Counter-Reformation itself provoked Protestant Anthony Munday to use his literary talents to help root out suspected recusants and pursue Martin Marprelate. In 1579 Munday feigned apostasy so that he could spy from the English College in Rome. (Gosson, too, was apparently engaged by Walsingham to spy on Jesuit activities in Rome on behalf of Elizabeth's government.) Munday's *Brief Discourse of the Taking of Edmund Campion* and a pamphlet on the arraignment and execution of E. Duckett (both 1581) are graphic anti-Catholic propaganda. He seems intent upon being recognized as patriot and Protestant, but there is an odor of opportunism in that his pamphlets are highly inaccurate and he published his account of Campion only a week after the arrest. Munday's book *The English Roman Life* (1582), however, is a detailed, interesting, and credible account of his observations in Rome.

At about the same time, Anne Dowriche's *French History* (1589) treats mid-sixteenth-century Catholic persecution of Huguenots in France. The work is a verse martyrology in three parts that expresses grassroots Puritan fears and expose political motivations of religious persecution. Dowriche's further purpose is to "restore again some credit if I can unto poetry, having been defaced of late so many ways by wanton vanities." For Dowriche's younger contemporary Elizabeth Melville, too, poetry existed to serve religious truths. *Ane Godlie Dreame* (1603) is an account of her intense personal experiences in the Scottish (Presbyterian) Reformation, including her religious melancholy and a prophetic dream-vision of Jesus as her companion. Like John Bunyan's Christian later in the century, her narrator serves roles as pilgrim, prophet, and preacher, but in the cause of Scottish Presbyterianism.

Other writers served the English Church in other ways. Thomas Coryate manifested a highly festive spirit in nearly all of his activities and writings, including an oration he wrote and delivered in 1606 for a local celebration: he defended the "old-time holiday pastimes" that had thrived under Queen Elizabeth but were coming under increasing attack from Puritans. Lancelot Andrewes was an eminent scholar as well as preacher, bishop, and educator. He admired Richard Hooker and is probably responsible for saving Hooker's manuscripts after his untimely death in 1600. He was appointed in 1604 as director of one of the committees charged with preparing the Authorized Version of the Bible (1611). Diligent at recruiting worthy priests, he was equally active at removing corrupt or negligent ones such as Richard Barwicke. Andrewes is usually regarded as an early leader of anti-Calvinist reaction and as spiritual and intellectual father of Anglo-Catholicism.

No religious writer was more visible, however, than King James himself. Like Andrewes, his formative years were in the sixteenth century, but his works and influence continued for twenty-five years of his life and for almost four hundred years worldwide among Protestants through the Author-ized or King James Version of the Bible. In the highly political context of the Reformation, several of his mature writings attacked the Catholic Church and asserted the controversial right of the king to rule the church, and not vice versa: *Basilikon Doron* and *The Trve Lawe of Free Monarchies; Triplici nodo; Triplex Cuneus, or An Apologie for the Oath of Allegiance* (1608); *A Premonition of All Most Mightie Monarches;* and *A Remonstrance for the Right of Kings.*

Politics. For King James and many others, religion was inseparable from politics, both on the international scene and domestically. Lancelot Andrewes, for example, was James's spokesman in his annual sermons on the Gunpowder Plot and the Gowrie Conspiracy, where he articulated royalist ideology with its cosmological and psychological consolations. He won an international reputation when at the king's bidding he wrote two long Latin treatises on the obedience of subjects to their princes. Yet despite Andrewes's access to considerable power — he was privy councillor, high commissioner, bishop, and a peer in the House of Lords — he chose not to exercise that power. As Debora Shuger says, he seems "too gentle to have been an effective politician."

A generation earlier, Elaine V. Beilin says that Dowriche's *French History* arose from political persecution of Protestants on the Continent. It reflects "fundamental Puritan fears and warnings": unless Scripture is the highest law for ruler and people alike, England might suffer the disastrous history of France.

Even the Elizabethan love lyric was not insulated from deep-seated political and religious faction. A tiff between Oxford and Sidney over the use of a tennis court informs "Whercas the Heart at Tennis Plays," but the poem's implications extend to Oxford's standing on his social rank with Sidney, who was a commoner, and his distancing himself and his Catholic leanings from the views of the earl of Leicester, his protégé Sidney, and the rest of their strongly Protestant faction. Thus, in an ostensibly private lyric, Oxford challenges Protestant ascendancy in public matters of national and international consequence. Likewise, Lyly's dramas written while he was in Oxford's employ are politically resonant; however, with what Kay describes as "a courtly obliquity and ambiguity," they are not directly allegorical of Queen Elizabeth but rather generally suggestive — a far safer tactic for a vulnerable author.

More explicit and potentially more dangerous to the author is Shakespeare's *Lucrece.* Its "Argument" puts Tarquin's private violence into the public context of Roman political history; his brutality finally drove Rome to root out his family and replace kings with consuls – not a happy prospect for a Tudor monarch such as Elizabeth. Later, during the reign of James, Fulke Greville's extant closet dramas depict the dangers of absolute and corrupt monarchy, both its public vices and its inescapable effect on individuals – a somberly pessimistic view of what Gouws calls "the irremediable fallibility and degeneracy of human nature since the Fall."

Even epideictic (ceremonial) rhetoric and the encomium had political resonance, as in Ralegh's praise of Elizabeth in *The Ocean to Scinthia* and "Like to a Hermit Poor in Place Obscure." As Jerry Leath Mills observes, "If Ralegh did not actually invent . . . 'political Petrarchism,' he certainly developed it to new levels of self-serving appropriateness."

Law and history. At the end of the sixteenth century, literature and politics spilled over into law and history in the works of William Fulbecke. His first legal book, *A Direction or Preparative to the Study of the Law* (1600), shows a marked preference for the clarity of written codes over ambiguous custom. Fulbecke repeatedly advocates the "convenient liberty" offered by strong laws as protection from exploitive magistrates and an unruly multitude. As an important historian as well, Fulbecke was contemptuous of popular rule and took the Roman civil wars of the first century as proof of its instability. His *Historical Collection* (1601) tries to link the end of Livy's history of the Roman republic to Tacitus's account of the early empire – but also demonstrates "the mischiefs of discord and civil dissension" he anticipated in a disputed succession to Elizabeth's throne. In his first publication, a late Tudor moral tract titled *A Book of Christian Ethics* (1587), Fulbecke makes interesting use of analogies from law; his style is markedly influenced by Lyly's distinctive euphuism.

Literary and rhetorical modes informed other legal writing and careers, too. Dekker's *Dead Term* (1608) anatomizes London life with emphasis on legal customs; it includes personifications of London and Westminster complaining and boasting to each other of their respective virtues and vices. While John Davies is included in this volume as a poet, his legal career was strikingly successful in Ireland, where he served as barrister, solicitor general, attorney general, King's Sergeant, and Speaker of the House of the Irish Parliament before 1619. Back in England, he pursued a similar career but died before assuming office as Lord Chief Justice.

Among historians, William Warner depended chiefly on previous chroniclers and traditional apodixes (premises) for *Albion's England,* his verse chronicle glorifying England as beneficiary of God's providence. It is compiled from well-known works by William Caxton, Ranulf Higden, Robert Fabyan, Thomas Cooper, Richard Grafton, Raphael Holinshed, William Camden, and John Stow, with other borrowings from Hooker, Calvin, Saint Augustine, Boccaccio, and near-verbatim extracts from Hakluyt's explorations.

Camden, by contrast, may fairly be considered the precursor of the modern cultural historian. Best known for his topographical *Britannia* and the Latin *History of England* (1615, 1625), he relied on an objective use of original documents and other kinds of cultural artifacts to read history. He traveled widely in England and studied vernacular languages, especially Anglo-Saxon and Welsh, to help his understanding. Camden's principles arose from a fundamental skepticism about man's ability to know the past and his readiness to challenge commonplace assumptions such as the legend of Brutus. His work is part of the development of empirical methods and the "new historiography" to be articulated thirty years later by Francis Bacon in his *Novum Organum* (1620). The *Britannia* deeply influenced future historiography with its attention to specialization, sharp periodization, diverse interpretation of events, and politically controversial work. The *History of England* is clearly a model for modern, secular political biography with its awareness of complex causes and refusal to rely on sententious and providential readings of human affairs.

Other historians used their discipline for a variety of other purposes. As noted above, the first part of Greville's *Dedication to Sir Philip Sidney* is a laudatory biography of his friend; the second part is an encomium of Queen Elizabeth and by indirection a censure of King James. Gouws suggests that its posthumous publication in 1652, long after Greville's death in 1628, was part of an effort to use the reputations of Sidney and Elizabeth to influence foreign policy in Commonwealth England.

In Ralegh's contemporaneous *History of the World,* the theme of mutability and impermanence figures large, as do two conflicting presumptions: that God is the first cause whose providential plan is revealed by history, and (with Jean Bodin, Niccolò Machiavelli, and Francis Bacon) that human beings are responsible for their own condition in a world of their own making – the premise of a secular "political science." Irrespective of his personal conviction, Ralegh thoroughly embarrassed King James for stressing what Mills sums up as "the vanity of human pomp, the transitory nature of earthly rule, and the proposition that no monarch stands above the law of God."

Humanism. Many of the authors discussed in this volume can be profitably considered under the broad and diverse rubric of humanism. With some notable exceptions after a century of Tudor rule, humanist concerns tended to focus nationally, even locally. For example, *Albion's England* by Warner is typical in glorifying British history, attacking Catholicism, and satirizing mythological characters. This popular and patriotic chronicle resembles Spenser's *Faerie Queene* in warning of the dangers of internal strife and foreign intervention, and depicting England as the special beneficiary of God's providence.

Language, too, was a matter of nationalism. Throughout the century, writers continued to study classical languages; but when Henry Peacham published his *Garden of Eloquence* (1577) in English, he implied that eloquence is as readily attainable in the vernacular as in Latin. His work followed distinguished models, including Richard Sherry's *Treatise of Schemes and Tropes* (1550, 1555), Johannes Susenbrotus's Latin *Epitome troporum ac schematum* (1540), and Erasmus's *De Copia* (1512). It led to distinguished successors such as Angel Day's *English Secretary,* Fraunce's *Arcadian Rhetoric* (1588), and Puttenham's *Art of English Poesie* (1589).

At the end of the century, Robert Tofte's translations of modern French and Italian literature reinforced the humanists' assumption that English was an artful language. So do the many translations by Florio, Lynche, and Munday; and the large number of translations dedicated to the earl of Oxford suggest that his famed eloquence gave him "something of the stature of a champion of the vernacular," according to Dennis Kay. The rise of scientific discourse in the seventeenth century, however, promoted a plain style of discourse, so the humanists' eloquence came to be regarded as unnecessary ornament, interfering with clear, economical expression. (More-extensive discussions of rhetoric and style may be found in the articles on Andrewes, King James, Gosson, Greville, Oxford, Peacham, Ralegh, and Shakespeare. For these authors, rhetorical language is profoundly integral to meaning and effect.)

An important humanist principle is commitment to the active life as complement or alternative to contemplative and voluptuous modes. Active service to his prince may be one reason for Greville's choosing a career at court, but he was frustrated there by the distrust of Burghley, Robert Cecil, and the queen herself for his radical Protestant attitudes. Ralegh was both more and less successful; despite an unhappy end, Mills describes him as "the most credible embodiment that Tudor-Stuart England has to offer of the ideal of the Renaissance man": soldier, privateer, explorer, projector of colonization, courtier, poet, scientist, historian — a résumé that challenges if not displaces the romantic image of Sidney as the all-round ideal of the age. If Ralegh accomplished nothing else, his projects for New World colonization offered to serve England's well-being through permanent settlement of families, development of a nautical academy, and learning aboriginal languages.

Two writers, Andrewes and Camden, stand out as exceptions to the commonplace that British humanism became increasingly insular. In his role as scholar-bishop, Andrewes is the most prominent English representative of the international late-Renaissance humanist community of scholars, jurists, and churchmen. Known affectionately as "a saintly scholar," he was actively engaged with leading members of the European intellectual community, himself interested in science and history, and a leader in oriental and patristic studies. Like all good scholars, he studied regularly and systematically.

From his early association with Westminster School, Camden enjoyed international scholarly respect from both Protestants and Catholics in Hungary, Italy, Flanders, and France. At the same time, in addition to his fluency in other European languages, he collected vernacular Anglo-Saxon and Welsh to augment his historical understanding. As Wyman H. Herendeen observes, his *Britannia* is part of a literature of "national self-consciousness in which serious literary genres — historical, poetic, and topographical — are appropriated to a Protestant poetic directed towards Britain's cultural identity." In this respect, Camden is much like Sidney, Spenser, and other Elizabethan Protestant humanists, but he was rigorously secular and undogmatic in pursuing principles of causation and tolerating multiple influences. His resulting attempts at objectivity were at odds with Sidney's reactionary literary attitudes, with Spenser's ignoring distinctions between poetry and history, and with the polemics of both humanist and emerging Counter-Reformation histories. After 1600 his life showed several changes in the place of the humanistic scholar since the mid sixteenth century, including his career outside a university and his working on an unorthodox range of national rather than classical texts.

Professional writing and popularity. One final observation may be drawn from the writers treated in this volume. Despite a historical and continuing reliance on patronage, authors increasingly found themselves able to earn a living from their craft. Lodge, for example, represents the new literary professionalism of the 1590s, surviving chiefly as an author until 1596, when he changed to a medical career. It is true that many sixteenth-century authors such as Richard Lynche were published anonymously or nearly anonymously, a fact from which L. M. Storozynsky infers a widely held disdain for the writing and printing trades. It is also true that satirists had to change their careers after the Order of Conflagration of 1 June 1599, when official censorship made all aspects of authorship and publishing highly problematic. Nonetheless, as Richard H. Branyan observes of hack writer Anthony Munday, a good living could be made even from mediocre writing.

Such growth of a writing profession may be explained in part by developments in printing technology, in part by expansion of the reading public. In any event, it depended upon an ample supply of works that people wanted to read and were willing to pay for. The authors in this volume provided an abundance of such works. Gosson, for example, influenced the stage and opponents of the drama for more than fifty years, his *School of Abuse* going through several editions of three thousand copies or more, each calling forth plays and pamphlets in response. John Davies's most famous work, *Nosce Teipsum,* was republished several times before his death in 1626 and was continuously in print through the eighteenth century. Elizabeth Melville's *Ane Godlie Dreame* was often republished in seventeenth- and eighteenth-century editions — "more than any other single volume by a British woman who lived before 1640," remarks Carolyn R. Swift. As Western thinkers ceased to believe that all important truths are available only from ancient books, travel literature became one of the most popular forms of reading during the sixteenth century, hence the popularity of Coryate's accounts of his peregrinations.

Other, more prolific writers were equally popular. During a period of fifty years Lodge's prose romance *Rosalynde* went through ten editions by 1642. His 1602 translation of the Jewish historian Josephus was his most popular work after *Rosalynde,* reaching seven editions by 1670. Dekker's *That Wonderful Year* (1603) was published in three editions during its first year, and his *Lantern and Candlelight* was popular enough to go through a complex sequence of eight editions. Ralegh was successful both in print and marketing: his *History of the World* and a medical invention, "Balsam of Guiana," sold vigorously for more than a hundred years.

Shakespeare's sonnets had a limited commercial success, with only the unauthorized edition of 1609 before 1640. His *Lucrece,* however, went through at least eight editions before 1640, appealing both to Southampton and to a large portion of the reading public who may have wanted to distinguish themselves from the vulgar crowd. By 1640 *Venus and Adonis* saw fifteen editions, apparently stimulating erotic fantasies and physical desire in a plague-ridden London. Shakespeare's "Venus and Adonis stanza" was extremely popular in courtier verse such as that of Ralegh, Arthur Gorges, and Edward Dyer, as well as Spenser, Sidney, Lodge, and the earls of Essex and Oxford. Dennis Kay observes that Shakespeare was a great popularizer, translating high art of the court into "palatable and sentimental commercial forms." Even these widely disseminated nondramatic works, however, did not begin to approach the financial profit of the plays.

This introduction has described nine large topics that are prominent in the articles in this volume: literary innovation, variety of genres, author/patron and author/author relationships, education and didacticism, the Protestant Reformation, nondramatic political writing, treatments of law and history, humanism, and developments in the profession of writing as a career. This account can be complemented by similar descriptions of other sixteenth-century British nondramatic writers in *DLB 132, DLB 136,* and *DLB 167.*

It is appropriate to conclude this introduction with Shakespeare, for he is a polestar among English nondramatic as well as dramatic writers. Yet, like Sidney and Spenser, his creativity could not have flourished without the writing environment created by his contemporaries. More than 150 of them are treated in the four series of *Sixteenth-Century British Nondramatic Writers* (a list of these authors and works is provided at the end of this volume). As Mark Eccles proposed in 1942 and 1982, hundreds of other Renaissance writers can be profitably studied for their works and biographies. A few of the more notable writers include Roger Ascham; William Cecil, Lord Burghley; Abraham Fraunce; Henry Howard, Earl of Surrey; Francis Meres; Robert Parsons; George Puttenham; John Rainoldes; Richard Staneyhurst; George Turbervile; and Thomas Whythorne. For a fuller understanding of the context of Shakespeare, Sidney, Spenser, and their contemporaries, much valuable work remains for present and future students of Renaissance literature.

Note: Titles in the front matter of articles have been checked against *A Short-Title Catalogue of Books*

Printed in England, Scotland, and Ireland and of English Books Printed Abroad 1475–1640, second edition (1976–1991) and other sources and are given, as far as possible, with original spelling and punctuation but modernized capitalization. With the exception of Scottish authors and Spenser, titles and quotations in the texts of the entries are modernized for capitalization, spelling, and punctuation to make them more readily accessible to modern readers. The introduction to each series is specific to that volume. The "Checklist of Further Readings," however, is cumulative and therefore most complete in *DLB 172.*

– David A. Richardson

Acknowledgments

This book was produced by Bruccoli Clark Layman, Inc. Karen L. Rood is senior editor for the *Dictionary of Literary Biography* series. Samuel W. Bruce was the in-house editor.

Production manager is Samuel W. Bruce. Photography editors are Julie E. Frick and Margaret Meriwether. Photographic copy work was performed by Joseph M. Bruccoli. Layout and graphics supervisor is Emily Ruth Sharpe. Copyediting supervisor is Laurel M. Gladden. Typesetting supervisor is Kathleen M. Flanagan. Systems manager is Chris Elmore. Laura Pleicones and L. Kay Webster are editorial associates. The production staff includes Phyllis A. Avant, Ann M. Cheschi, Melody W. Clegg, Patricia Coate, Joyce Fowler, Brenda A. Gillie, Stephanie C. Hatchell, Kathy Lawler Merlette, Pamela D. Norton, Delores Plastow, William L. Thomas Jr., and Allison Trussell.

Walter W. Ross, Steven Gross, and Mark McEwan did library research. They were assisted by the following librarians at the Thomas Cooper Library of the University of South Carolina: Linda Holderfield and the interlibrary-loan staff; reference-department head Virginia Weathers; reference librarians Marilee Birchfield, Stefanie Buck, Stefanie DuBose, Rebecca Feind, Karen Joseph, Donna Lehman, Charlene Loope, Anthony McKissick, Jean Rhyne, Kwamine Simpson, and Virginia Weathers; circulation-department head Caroline Taylor; and acquisitions-searching supervisor David Haggard.

In preparing these four volumes on *Sixteenth-Century British Nondramatic Writers,* the editor has been supported by a summer stipend from the National Endowment for the Humanities and a Research and Creative Activities Award from Cleveland State University. The editor is grateful for student and staff assistance at Cleveland State University from Hugh Kennedy, Hua Liu, and Claire Bean and for administrative support from Department of English Chairmen John Gerlach and Earl R. Anderson. For technical support in regularizing computer files, thanks to Scott Haver of Instructional Computing in the College of Arts and Sciences. The editor especially acknowledges the meticulous assistance of Michael D. Bohnert.

Dictionary of Literary Biography® • Volume One Hundred Seventy-Two

Sixteenth-Century British Nondramatic Writers

Dictionary of Literary Biography

Lancelot Andrewes

(1555 – 25 September 1626)

Debora K. Shuger
University of California, Los Angeles

See also the Andrewes entry in *DLB 151: British Prose Writers of the Early Seventeenth Century.*

BOOKS: *The Wonderfull Combate (for Gods Glorie and Mans Saluation) betweene Christ and Satan. In Seuen Sermons,* anonymous (London: Printed by John Charlwood for Richard Smith, 1592); republished as *Seven Sermons on the Wonderfull Combate between Christ and Sathan,* as Andrewes (London: Printed by Dorothy Jaggard for I. Jaggard & Michael Sparke, 1627);

Tortura Torti sive ad Matthaei Torti librum responsio (London: Robert Barker, 1609);

Responsio ad apologiam Cardinalis Bellarmini, contra praefationem monitoriam Jacobi regis (London: Robert Barker, 1610);

Scala Coeli: Nineteen Sermons Concerning Prayer, anonymous (London: Printed by N. O. for Francis Burton, 1611);

Articles to Be Inquired of by the Churchwardens and Sworn-Men in the Primary Visitation of the Right Reverend Father in God, Lancelot, Lord Bishop of Winton (London: B. Norton & J. Bill, 1619);

Reverendi in Christo patris, Lanceloti, episcopi Wintoniensis, opuscula quaedam posthuma, edited by William Laud and John Buckeridge (London: Richard Badger & Andrew Hebb, 1629) – includes the first printing of Andrewes's *Two Answers to Cardinall Perron* (circa 1618); *Two Speeches in the Starr-Chamber; Letters to Du Moulin* (circa 1618–1619); *Concio ad Clerum in Synodo Provinciali Cantuariensis Provinciae* (1593); *De decimis* (circa 1587); *De usuris* (1585); *Concio ad Clerum pro gradu doctoris* (circa 1587);

Lancelot Andrewes; portrait by an unknown artist (Jesus College, Oxford)

XCVI. Sermons, edited by William Laud and John Buckeridge (London: Printed by George Willer for Richard Badger, 1629);

Stricturae: Or, a Briefe Answer to Cardinall Perron's Reply (London: Printed by Felix Kyngston for Richard Badger & Andrew Hebb, 1629);

A Patterne of Catechisticall Doctrine, anonymous (London: Printed for W. Garrett, 1630; revised and enlarged, 1641); enlarged again as *The*

Morall Law Expovnded (London: Printed for Michael Sparke, 1642); revised as *The Pattern of Catechistical Doctrine at Large* (London: Printed by R. Norton for G. Badger, 1650);

Institutiones piae; or Directions to Pray, anonymous, edited by Henry Isaacson (London: H. Seile, 1630); republished as *Holy Devotions, with Directions to Pray* (London: Printed for H. Seile, 1655);

A Sermon of the Pestilence. Preached at Chiswick, 1603 (London: Richard Badger, 1636);

Of Episcopacy. Three Epistles of Peter Moulin Doctor and Professor of Divinity. Answered by . . . Lancelot Andrewes (London, 1647);

A Manuel of Directions for the Sick, edited by Drake (London: Printed for Humphrey Moseley, 1648);

A Manual of the Private Devotions and Meditations of . . . Lancelot Andrewes, translated and edited by Drake (London: Humphrey Moseley, 1648); published in the original Greek and Latin as *Preces privatae* (Oxford: E Theatro Sheldoniano, 1675);

A Learned Discourse of Ceremonies Retained and Used in Christian Churches, attributed to Andrewes (London: C. Adams, 1653);

Apospasmatia sacra; or a Collection of Posthumous and Orphan Lectures, Delivered at St. Paul's and St. Giles His Church, attributed to Andrewes (London: Printed by R. Hodgkinsonne for H. Moseley, 1657);

The Form of Consecration of a Church or Chappel (London: T. Garthwait, 1659).

Editions: *The Works of Lancelot Andrewes,* 11 volumes, edited by J. P. Wilson and James Bliss (Oxford: J. Parker, 1841–1872; reprinted, New York: AMS Press, 1967);

The Preces Privatae of Lancelot Andrewes, translated and edited by F. E. Brightman (London: Methuen, 1903);

The Manual for the Sick, edited by Brightman (London: Rivingtons, 1909);

Lancelot Andrewes: Sermons, edited by G. M. Story (Oxford: Clarendon Press, 1967).

OTHER: "Notes on the Book of Common Prayer," in *Commentary on the Book of Common Prayer,* by William Nicholls (London: R. Bonwicke, W. Freeman, 1710).

As his early biographers and eulogizers (including George Herbert and John Milton) attest, Lancelot Andrewes, the grave and erudite Jacobean churchman, came to exemplify the saintly scholar-bishop, still a potent cultural ideal in the first half of the seventeenth century. Usually treated as one of the early leaders of the anti-Calvinist reaction – the spiritual father, as it were, of Anglo-Catholicism – he was also an eminent scholar, one of the few English scholars of his day to achieve a European reputation. He is among the foremost English representatives of the late-Renaissance *respublica litterarum,* the international community of scholars, jurists, and churchmen engaged in advanced humanist scholarship. His subsequent reputation, however, largely rests upon the great festival sermons he preached for more than two decades to the Jacobean court, sermons characterized by a dense, compact prose and a deep reverence before the central mysteries of Christian devotion.

Lancelot Andrewes was born in 1555, the eldest child of a prosperous London merchant. He attended Cooper's Free School for a couple of years and then around 1565 went to study under Richard Mulcaster at the Merchant Taylors' School. Already a brilliant student, in 1571 Andrewes received one of the six newly endowed Greek scholarships at Pembroke Hall, and so, like his fellow student at Merchant Taylors', Edmund Spenser, Andrewes left Mulcaster for Cambridge – where John Whitgift was still master of Trinity – on the eve of the Admonitions Controversy. During his college years Andrewes acquired a prodigious knowledge of foreign languages (more than fifteen, according to his biographer John Buckeridge). Andrewes's early theological sympathies seem to have inclined toward Geneva, since he participated in a university version of the Puritan "prophesyings" along with Chaderton and Knewstubs, both later Puritan representatives to the Hampton Court Conference. In 1575 he received his B.A. and was elected to a fellowship at Pembroke; the M.A. came three years later, at which time Andrewes became the catechist for Pembroke, delivering a highly successful series of lectures, posthumously published as *A Pattern of Catechistical Doctrine* (1630). He was appointed junior treasurer at Pembroke in 1580 and senior treasurer in 1581 – unlike most Renaissance Englishmen, Andrewes managed other people's money conscientiously and competently. He received his B.Div. in 1585, writing a thesis on usury.

In 1586 Andrewes was appointed chaplain to the earl of Huntingdon, who invited him to northern England to confer with recusants. Around the same time, he also became the chaplain for both Whitgift (archbishop since 1583) and Queen Elizabeth I. He took his doctorate in divinity around 1588, but the degree seems to have been held up slightly because of Puritan opposition, evidence that Andrewes's theological views had altered. Some time before this, Walsingham, a Puritan supporter, offered to make Andrewes the reader of controversies at Cambridge; Andrewes refused on ideological grounds, and Walsingham apparently dismissed him but later (whether respecting his integrity or for some other reason) continued to act as his patron, nominating him in 1589 to the vicarage of St. Giles, Cripplegate, and to prebends at St. Paul's and Southwell. In the same year Andrewes was also elected the master of Pembroke Hall.

During the following decade Andrewes turned down two bishoprics, Salisbury in 1596 and Ely in 1599, since he refused to alienate their revenues — a condition of acceptance under Elizabeth. He did, however, accept honorary membership in Gray's Inn in 1590 and a prebendary at Westminster in 1597; in the latter office he participated in Edmund Spenser's funeral in 1599. At the same time, Andrewes also began his career as a court preacher, delivering his first sermon to the queen in Lent of 1590. His most interesting theological essay also dates from this period, the "Judgment of the Lambeth Articles" (1660), a hesitant but unequivocal critique of the central tenets of doctrinal Calvinism. This piece was not printed until the Restoration, but in 1600 Andrewes gave direct offense by preaching in defense of priestly absolution, a novelty that caused a minor commotion. The next year, however, he was made dean of Westminster. William Camden was headmaster at the time, and in 1602 Richard Hakluyt became prebendary. Andrewes was drawn into the intellectual orbit of these men, in 1604 becoming a member of the Society of Antiquaries (shortly thereafter dissolved by James I); their works are among the few secular texts listed in the inventory appended to Andrewes's will.

Like his friend and patron Fulke Greville, first Lord Brooke, Andrewes quickly rose to national prominence under King James. Beginning in 1604, for twenty years Andrewes preached at court on Christmas, Easter, Pentecost, the anniversaries of the Gunpowder Plot and Gowrie Conspiracy, and, less regularly, on Good Friday or during Lent. In the same year he also took part in the Hampton Court Conference and, at its conclusion, was appointed director of one of the committees entrusted with preparing a new translation of the Bible. The first twelve books of the Authorized Version are the work of Andrewes's group.

In 1605 Andrewes accepted the bishopric of Chichester and the office of the lord almoner; four

Title page for the enlarged edition of the lectures Andrewes delivered at Pembroke Hall in the 1570s

years later he received the far more valuable bishopric of Ely. Andrewes paid a price for these promotions. The Oath of Allegiance, imposed by James after the Gunpowder Plot, raised an international controversy; the king first wrote a defense of the oath — the *Triplici nodo, triplex cuneus* (1608) — but assigned Andrewes to respond to Bellarmine's confutation of the royal propagandist. The result was that Andrewes produced two long Latin treatises on obedience to princes: *Tortura Torti* (1609) and *Responsio ad apologiam Cardinalis Bellarmini* (1610). These works won Andrewes an international reputation and also made him the favored candidate for the next archbishop of Canterbury, succeeding Richard Bancroft, who died in 1610. On his deathbed, however, the earl of Dunbar ordered his servants to remove his heart after his death and present it to

James in a golden cup with the sole request that George Abbot, then bishop of London, be installed at Canterbury. Andrewes remained at Ely to enjoy the company of the great Protestant philologist Isaac Casaubon, who had left France for England in 1610 and quickly became Andrewes's intimate friend, accompanying him to Ely in 1611. Three years later, the dying Casaubon called for Andrewes to administer his final communion.

In 1613 Andrewes was appointed to the commission set up to look into the divorce of the earl of Essex, to which, under considerable royal pressure, he agreed — a capitulation that the wisdom of hindsight has often condemned. Three years later James made him a member of the Privy Council and then, in 1619, bishop of Winchester and dean of the Chapels Royal. As a member of the House of Lords, in 1621 he sat on the committee that heard evidence against Francis Bacon, a longtime friend. At the age of seventy Andrewes retired from public life, too ill even to attend James on his deathbed. He died on 25 September 1626 and was buried at the Church of St. Saviour's, Southwark; Bishop Buckeridge of Rochester preached his funeral sermon.

Andrewes was a fairly important Jacobean churchman, a revered scholar-bishop, and a preacher. Any adequate assessment of his life must take into account all three roles. As privy councillor, high commissioner, bishop, and member of the House of Lords, he had access to considerable political power, which he apparently chose not to exercise. Contemporary accounts note that he generally remained silent or absented himself when secular matters were being discussed, although he was a capable and unusually honest administrator — rare virtues for a Jacobean official. Modern scholars have censured his unwavering devotion to James — especially his coerced assent to the Essex divorce — but while submissive to the royal will, Andrewes in turn helped restrain the king's habitual vulgarity. He tended to avoid the pastoral duties annexed to his episcopal office, rarely preaching in his dioceses or conducting visitations. On the other hand, he was one of the few Jacobean bishops who actively attempted to recruit worthy priests (both anti-Calvinist and Calvinist) and conversely to remove the corrupt or negligent ones, as, for example, one Richard Barwicke, who was later deprived of his office for pouring communion wine from a bottle lodged in his breeches with its neck sticking out of the codpiece. Although a high churchman, Andrewes, unlike William Laud, did not impose his liturgical tastes on reluctant parishes. Both as bishop

and civil servant, he seems too gentle to have been an effective politician.

Part of Andrewes's renown, in fact, derived from his otherworldly detachment from ecclesiastical and secular politics. Contemporary memorials eulogize him not as an influential court prelate but as a saintly scholar, daily spending morning and evening in study and prayer — this last occupation preserved in his *Preces privatae* (1675), a deeply devout and moving set of private devotions he composed for his own use. The early biographies particularly stress his generosity to poor parishioners and struggling scholars, much of it given anonymously, as well as his openhanded hospitality. They also note his remarkably broad learning. A leading English orientalist and patristic scholar, Andrewes also displayed an unusual interest in scientific and historiographic scholarship, as his brief membership in the Society of Antiquaries would suggest. Bacon, who first met Andrewes in 1593, consulted him about the *Advancement of Learning* and *Cogita et visa* and, a year after his fall, dedicated the *Advertisement Touching an Holy War* to him. Andrewes also praised Selden's highly controversial *History of Tithes,* a work most clergymen wished banned. A few of Andrewes's later works, particularly the *Stricturae: Or, a Brief Answer to Cardinal Perron's Reply* (written circa 1618; published 1629) and *A Learned Discourse of Ceremonies* (1653), are good examples of humanist historical scholarship.

Andrewes's friends and correspondents included the principal members of the European *respublica litterarum:* Casaubon, Vossius, Heinsius, Erpinus, and Hugo Grotius (whom he apparently distrusted). He admired Richard Hooker and is probably responsible for preserving his manuscripts after Hooker's untimely death in 1600. He likewise befriended younger scholars, sending William Bedwell, one of the first English Arabists, to Leiden at his own expense to complete his studies. Probably in 1615 he first met George Herbert, then only twenty-two; they discussed predestination and sanctification, and afterward Herbert sent the aged bishop a long letter in Greek, which so impressed Andrewes that he "put it into his bosom, and did often show it to many scholars." Herbert later dedicated the *Musae responsoriae* to Andrewes.

Andrewes's closest episcopal colleagues — Neill, Overall, Laud, John Cosin — were the principal architects of what has variously been termed English Arminianism, high churchmanship, or Anglo-Catholicism. In many ways, Andrewes was the spiritual and intellectual leader of this movement away from the Calvinist consensus of the

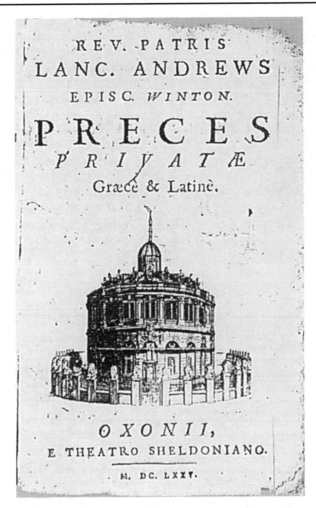

REV. PATRIS
LANC. ANDREWS
EPISC. *WINTON.*
P R E C E S
P R I V A T Æ
Græcè & Latinè.

O X O N I I,
E THEATRO SHELDONIANO.
M. DC. LXXV.

Title page for the original Greek and Latin version of the work published in English as A Manual of the Private Devotions and Meditations of . . . Lancelot Andrewes *(1648)*

Elizabethan church, a movement based rather on the revival of patristic studies than on Dutch Arminianism. In a Latin court sermon preached in 1613, Andrewes summarized this new interpretation of the dogmatic foundations of English Protestantism: the Church of England rests upon "one *canon* given by God in Scripture, *two Testaments, three Creeds, four general Councils, five centuries, and the succession of Fathers* during that period." Christian antiquity supplements *sola Scriptura;* Calvin is not mentioned. Although, at James's request, Andrewes kept silent his doubts concerning Calvinist theology (which his earlier critique of the Lambeth Articles nevertheless makes quite clear), he was allowed to reintroduce the elaborate and un-Calvinistic ceremonial of the ancient liturgies; his private chapel at Ely Palace became the model for subsequent Anglo-Catholic experiments with the beauty of holiness.

Andrewes's patristic scholarship and devotion to Christian antiquity suffuse his sermons. The great festival sermons in particular recall the rich, mysterious textures of ancient and medieval Christian preaching: the Latin Fathers' elaborate, schematic wordplay, the antithetic rhetoric of Christian paradox, the haunting personifications of late-antique *allegoresis,* the gravely tender Christological narratives of Franciscan piety. They seem strikingly different from the characteristic products of post-Reformation theology; they lack the moralism, the emphasis on guilt and punishment, the concentration on subjective experience – on the pilgrim's progress – typical of Protestant sermons (including those of John Donne). Although criticism has generally ignored Andrewes's series of political sermons on the Gunpowder Plot and Gowrie Conspiracy, they are of interest for their evocation of the emotional power of Jacobean absolutism, the deep resonance notions of divine right and sacred kingship still possessed (for some Englishmen) during this period. Like the court masques, these sermons articulate the cosmological and psychological consolations of royalist ideology.

Andrewes's sermons are best known for their distinctive style: a combination of homey, colloquial brevity and a highly formalized verbal patterning combining antithesis, schematic parallelism, and macaronic sound play. This drastically un-Ciceronian prose is the result of merging a native plain style with the intricate, aural rhetoric of patristic and medieval *kunstprosa*. A passage from Andrewes's 1618 Christmas sermon is characteristic:

> He, to come thus into *clouts,* himself! But yet, all is well; all children are so: but, *in praesepi,* that is it, there is the wonder: *Children* lie not there; He doth: There lieth He; the *Lord of glory,* without all *glorie.* Instead of a *Palace,* a *poor stable;* of a *cradle* of state, a beast's *cratch;* no pillow, but a lock of hay; no hangings, but dust and cobwebs; no attendants, but *in medio animalium* (as the Fathers read the third of *Abakuk*): For, if the *Inne* were full, the *stable* was not empty, we may be sure.

Noteworthy in this passage are the extremely simple Anglo-Saxon vocabulary punctuated by Latin polysyllables; the brief *membra* (averaging five syllables) that give Andrewes's style its abrupt, staccato rhythm; the persistent antithetic parallelism; the colloquial directness of "all is well" or "we may be sure"; and the iconographic detail – the rhetorical embodiment of the traditional paradoxes of the Incarnation. This use of verbal patterning to articulate the order of things characterizes Andrewes's sermons; they presuppose a prereferential view of language, in which the thing is implicit in the name, in which words – their sounds, etymology, sequence – disclose the hidden rhythms of sacred history. "Structuralism *with* a transcendental subject," as Stanley Fish wittily puts it.

Despite the syntactic stylization, Andrewes's prose has a colloquial immediacy, a capacity to register the tonalities of inner experience. In the Nativity sermon of 1618, Andrewes points out that, without angelic guidance, the shepherds were unlikely to have taken a child lying in a manger for the Messiah; had someone suggested it, "they would have shaken him off, and said, with as great scorn as they, *Nunquid poterit iste salvare nos,* what shall this be our *Saviour* trow?" Andrewes infuses a conversational pungency into

the colorless Latin, which vividly captures the shepherds' commonsensical incredulity. These little, flickering dramas of human response surface momentarily amid the stylized rhythms of Andrewes's prose – a baroque intertwining of specificity and abstract design, of moment and eternity, of energy and pattern. T. S. Eliot remarked of these sermons, "they rank with the finest English prose of their time, of any time" – an assessment that does not seem excessive.

Bibliography:

Elizabeth McCutcheon, "Recent Studies in Andrewes," *English Literary Renaissance,* 11 (Winter 1981): 96–108.

Biographies:

John Buckeridge, *A Sermon Preached at the Funeral of the Right Honorable and Reverend Father in God, Lancelot, Late Lord Bishop of Winchester,* in *The Works of Lancelot Andrewes,* volume 5, edited by J. P. Wilson and James Bliss (Oxford: J. Parker, 1841–1872), pp. 237–298;

Henry Isaacson, *An Exact Narration of the Life and Death of . . . Lancelot Andrewes* in *The Works of Lancelot Andrewes,* volume 11 (1872), pp. i–xxxiv;

Robert L. Ottley, *Lancelot Andrewes* (Boston: Houghton Mifflin, 1894);

Florence Higham, *Lancelot Andrewes* (London: Student Christian Movement Press, 1952);

Paul A. Welsby, *Lancelot Andrewes: 1555–1626* (London: S.P.C.K., 1958).

References:

J. W. Blench, *Preaching in England in the Late Fifteenth and Sixteenth Centuries: A Study of English Sermons 1450–c. 1600* (Oxford: Blackwell, 1964);

Horton Davies, *Like Angels from a Cloud: The English Metaphysical Preachers, 1588–1645* (San Marino, Cal.: Huntington Library, 1986);

T. S. Eliot, *For Lancelot Andrewes: Essays on Style and Order* (Garden City, N.Y.: Doubleday, 1929);

Kenneth Fincham, *Prelate as Pastor: The Episcopate of James I* (Oxford: Clarendon Press, 1990);

Stanley Fish, "Sequence and Meaning in Seventeenth-Century Narrative," in his *To Tell a Story: Narrative Theory and Practice* (Los Angeles: University of California Press, 1973), pp. 59–75;

Nicholas Lossky, *Lancelot Andrewes the Preacher (1555–1626): The Origins of the Mystical Theology of the Church of England,* translated by Andrew Louth (Oxford: Clarendon Press, 1991);

Douglas Macleane, *Lancelot Andrewes and the Reaction* (London: George Allen, 1910);

Elizabeth McCutcheon, "Lancelot Andrewes' *Preces Privatae:* A Journey through Time," *Studies in Philology,* 65 (April 1968): 223–241;

W. Fraser Mitchell, *English Pulpit Oratory from Andrewes to Tillotson: A Study of Its Literary Aspects* (London: S.P.C.K., 1932);

B. J. Opie, "The Devil, Science, and Subjectivity," *English Literary Renaissance,* 6 (Autumn 1976): 430–452;

H. C. Porter, *Reformation and Reaction in Tudor Cambridge* (Cambridge: Cambridge University Press, 1958);

Maurice F. Reidy, S.J., *Bishop Lancelot Andrewes: Jacobean Court Preacher* (Chicago: Loyola University Press, 1955);

Debora Kuller Shuger, *Habits of Thought in the English Renaissance: Religion, Politics, and the Dominant Culture* (Berkeley: University of California Press, 1990);

P. G. Stanwood, "Patristic and Contemporary Borrowing in the Caroline Divines," *Renaissance Quarterly,* 23 (Winter 1970): 421–429;

G. M. Story, "The Text of Lancelot Andrewes's Sermons," in *Editing Seventeenth-Century Prose,* edited by D. I. B. Smith (Toronto: A. M. Hakkert, 1972), pp. 11–24;

Joan Webber, "Celebration of Word and World in Lancelot Andrewes' Style," *Journal of English and Germanic Philology,* 64 (April 1965): 255–269.

Papers:
Paul Klemp of the University of Wisconsin at Oshkosh has identified several unpublished sermons attributed to Andrewes in manuscripts at Cambridge. In *Court Culture and the Origins of a Royalist Tradition in Early Stuart England* (Philadelphia: University of Pennsylvania Press, 1987), R. Malcolm Smuts quotes part of a poem satirizing the Spanish Match (from British Library, Harl. MSS 4955, fol. 70), which he attributes to Andrewes.

Richard Barnfield

(June 1574 – March 1627)

Kenneth Borris
McGill University

BOOKS: *Greenes Funeralls,* by "R. B. Gent.," possibly Barnfield (London: Printed and sold by John Danter, 1594);

The Affectionate Shepheard, anonymous (London: Printed by John Danter for T. Gubbin and E. Newman, 1594);

Cynthia. With Certaine Sonnets, and the Legend of Cassandra (London: Printed for Humfrey Lownes, 1595);

The Encomion of Lady Pecunia: or The Praise of Money (London: Printed by G. Shaw for John Jaggard, 1598); revised and enlarged as *Lady Pecunia, or The Praise of Money* (London: Printed by W. Jaggard and sold by John Hodgets, 1605).

Editions: *The Poems of Richard Barnfield,* edited by Montague Summers (London: Fortune Press, 1936);

The Complete Poems, edited by George Klawitter (Selinsgrove, Pa.: Susquehanna University Press, 1990).

Several of Richard Barnfield's lyrics seemed fine enough that they were long ascribed to William Shakespeare; yet Barnfield himself has rarely been read, studied, or anthologized. His obscurity results more from his homoerotic interests than from poetic limitations, for Barnfield is one of the most unusual, interesting, and technically accomplished minor Elizabethan poets.

Little is known of his life, aside from Alexander B. Grosart's findings (circa 1876) and the essential new research of Fred Clitheroe. Born in June 1574 at Norbury Manor in Staffordshire to Richard Barnfield and Mary Skrymsher Barnfield, the poet was the privileged scion of prosperous landowning families of the region and the eldest son, with three siblings: Robert, John, and Dorothea. In 1572 the estate of his uncle,

James Skrymsher, at whose manor Barnfield was born, included fifteen thousand acres; the poet's father had patrimonially inherited the manors of Edgmond, Wyndersley, Church Pulverbache, and Pykstock in 1568. In 1581, however, when the poet was nearly seven, the birth of his sister may have caused his mother's death, for she was buried only two months after Dorothea's baptism on 25 March. This association of circumstances could well have influenced the poet's sexual development. Or, as Clitheroe suggests, his mother might have been the Barnfield spouse who attempted to cut her sleeping husband's throat with a knife in bed at Newport in 1581 and then fatally slashed her own with a rusty arrow some days later.

Barnfield's early education was most likely undertaken by William Lee, the rector of Edgmond and a fellow of New Hall, Oxford. Admitted to Brasenose College at Oxford in 1589, Barnfield was sent down for some misdemeanor in 1591, but he was permitted to return after paying 6s. 8d. and agreeing to deliver a declamation in hall within six weeks. The poet obtained his B.A. in February 1592; that year he also performed exercises for the M.A., but no record of the outcome exists. His publications display classical learning, with Latin epigraphs and mottoes, and both Latin and Greek literary allusions and borrowings. In the early 1590s Barnfield moved to London and may have sought entrance to Gray's Inn to study law, although his name does not appear in the index of admittances. Meanwhile, he developed literary connections, probably including Thomas Watson, Abraham Fraunce, Christopher Marlowe, Francis Meres, and Michael Drayton.

Barnfield precociously published most of his poetry before he was twenty-two, and almost all of it appeared in print before 1599.

He may have written much of *Greene's Funerals*, by "R. B. Gent." (1594), a collection of so-called sonnets defending Robert Greene against posthumous attacks by Gabriel Harvey and others. Later that year Barnfield's far more poetically adept *The Affectionate Shepherd* appeared anonymously, dedicated to Lady Penelope Rich – Sir Philip Sidney's "Stella." The main grouping consists of two long pastorals, "The Tears of an Affectionate Shepherd Sick for Love" and "The Shepherd's Content," both on country life and amorous cares, followed by a love sonnet as coda. Barnfield then archly juxtaposes his lugubrious "Complaint of Chastity" with a parodic experiment in classical hexameters, "Helen's Rape; or, A Light Lantern for Light Ladies."

The first and title poem, Barnfield's longest and most controversial, is based on Virgil's second eclogue, in which a shepherd woos a younger male. Previously translated by both Fraunce and William Webbe and partially imitated in Edmund Spenser's *Shepheardes Calender* (1579), this eclogue seems to have been especially fashionable. Barnfield creatively expands Virgil's model to reflect a wider range of loves, perhaps recalling the sexual diversity of Longus's pastoral romance *Daphnis and Chloe*. Barnfield's Daphnis, the speaker throughout and to some extent the poet's pastoral persona, pursues a younger Ganymede; but so does Guendolena, whom a far older and unnamed man pursues in turn. Though Daphnis refers to Ganymede as a "boy," the poem need not be pederastic, despite the criticisms of C. S. Lewis and others. Barnfield was only twenty when he published the work. Moreover, Elizabethans could apply *boy* and its synonyms as endearments well beyond even late adolescence. Ganymede rejects Daphnis's courtship, and so Daphnis undergoes rapid metaphoric aging, like Spenser's Colin Clout. There may be some personal allegory, but the only such reading contradicts basic facts. Guendolena is supposedly Penelope Rich, while Daphnis-Barnfield pursues Charles Blount as Ganymede; but Daphnis castigates Guendolena in the poem while extolling Rich in the dedication, and Blount was eleven years older than Barnfield, whereas Ganymede is clearly younger than Daphnis.

Barnfield's self-designation has strategic significance that demonstrates his literary acuity. Named for the laurel, Daphnis is the legendary inventor of pastoral beloved by Hermes and favored by Apollo and a prototypical pastoralist in Theocritus's *Idylls*, lovelorn for offending Aphrodite. Besides elegiacally celebrating Daphnis as a handsome pastoral

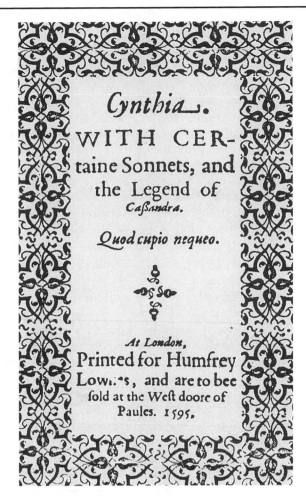

Title page for the poem Richard Barnfield called "the first imitation of the verse of that excellent Poet, Master Spenser, in his Faerie Queene*"*

leader of Bacchic rites who loves peace and whose praises are to endure, Virgil's *Eclogues* link him with ambiguities of sex and gender: in the eighth eclogue a shepherd assumes the persona of Daphnis's female lover, who summons him magically. An Ovidian context, also unnoticed by Barnfield's previous commentators, is even more telling:

> I won't tell you about the love affair of Daphnis, the shepherd of Ida, for everyone knows the story – how the nymph, angry at the thought of a rival, turned him into stone. So fierce is the indignation felt by lovers! Nor shall I tell how once the laws of nature were altered, and Sithon hovered between both sexes, now male, now female.

Thus Ovid's Alcithoe introduces the story of Hermaphroditus, "possessed of a dual nature, which could not be called male or female, but seemed to be at once both and neither" (*Metamorphoses*, 4.274–388, translation by Mary M. Innes). The whole context concerns sexual ambiguities, pursuits, and rivalries – Barnfield's pastoral subjects in this poem. His linkage of Ganymede with his chosen persona further evokes the Ovidian allusion, for the mythical Ganymede's earthly home was also Mount Ida. Clearly, then, Barnfield can deploy classical learning with subtle and pointed effect. The relationship between him and Daphnis is complex, for Barnfield virtually identifies himself with Daphnis in the dedication yet somewhat distances himself later (and in other poems), so that Daphnis's discourse ironically reveals some limitations in the character's conduct and personality. Barnfield's critics unfortunately tend to oversimplify this most elusive and ambiguous relationship.

Though more pastorally appealing than many Elizabethan treatments of the genre, *The Affectionate Shepherd* distinguishes itself most with its once-daring reappraisals of love and sexuality. Bruce R. Smith has called it "the most explicitly homosexual" poem of the English Renaissance. Daphnis first considers, "If it be sin to love a lovely Lad, / Oh then sin I, for whom my soul is sad." But as he reveals the qualities of his desire, any question of its possible sinfulness disappears. Guendolena and her suitor function as foils. Addressing Ganymede, Daphnis argues that Guendolena craves only Ganymede's body, whereas Daphnis appreciates his mind and virtues as well. This argument is not misogynist (contrary to Smith), for the poem does not identify Guendolena's attitude with women in general. Since Guendolena in turn is sexually harrassed by her repellent suitor, the poem implies that same-sex love can be clearly more moral and advantageous than some forms of love between persons of opposite sexes, not inferior or wrongful per se.

Previous commentators (including Smith) unfortunately miss this general theme and thus tend to find the poem disjointed or merely escapist. Though Gregory W. Bredbeck observes that "the passion of Daphnis . . . certainly makes more sense than the heteroerotic love in the poem, which is explained in terms of slapstick mishaps, deathly misfires, and divine mistakes," even he does not draw the appropriate thematic conclusions. Whereas some critics claim that Daphnis's concluding ethical counsel to Ganymede conflicts with the poem's subject, Barnfield structures the poem to challenge assumptions that homoerotic love is sinful or immoral, broaching those views at the outset only to discredit them. Following classical precedents, Renaissance defenses of such love commonly emphasize its edifying potential, and Barnfield's poem seems the first deliberately concentrated defense in English.

His astute evocation of literary and mythical precedents for ambiguous, alternate, or protean sexualities aptly reinforces his defense of same-sex love and shows too how readily the ancients were invoked for its justification. Pastoral provides the apt generic context for reassessing the vexed relations between this personal desire, its idyllic fulfillment, and social convention. Classical pastoralists treated homoerotic love naturally, and the genre enables a writer to posit a more humanly authentic world that critically departs from current cultural norms.

Barnfield's preface for his next volume, *Cynthia* (1595), claims encouragement from readers of *The Affectionate Shepherd* but disavows publically imputed authorship of two previous, unidentified books, one of which could be *Greene's Funerals*. Probably under considerable social pressure, the poet further claims that his former homoerotic poetry was "nothing else but an imitation of *Virgil*"; Sidney, for example, calls such love "abominable filthiness" in *The Defence of Poetry* (1595). Then Barnfield offers the delightful title poem as "the first imitation of the verse of that excellent Poet, Master Spenser, in his *Faerie Queene*." In this dream vision Jove reviews the judgment of Paris and awards the prize to "a maiden queen" who incorporates all graces and virtues, alluding to Elizabeth.

Somewhat cheekily, Barnfield immediately appends twenty finely wrought homoerotic English sonnets to Ganymede, which seem wholly independent of Shakespeare's sonnets to a young man, not published until 1609. By including them, Barnfield disclaims his prefatory Virgilian disclaimer. The Daphnis-Ganymede story then continues in a mysterious pastoral ode, "Nights Were Short, and Days Were Long," worthy of inclusion in any Elizabethan selection. Daphnis, the speaker relates, now loves Eliza instead, perhaps referring only to the queen. Barnfield does not, however, thus accept "traditional values" and, in effect, retract his positive treatments of same-sex love, as Smith and Bredbeck assert. Daphnis turns to Eliza only because she seems more beautiful and Ganymede rejects him – yet Daphnis still ambivalently perceives Ganymede as "beauty's bed." The poem conveys no sense that there is anything wrong with homoerotic desire itself or with acting on it.

Concluding with "Cassandra," which mixes complaint narrative with minor epic, or epyllion, Barnfield turns the Trojan story into a mythical etiology of supposed female inconstancy and deceptiveness. Sexism and misogyny were Elizabethan norms, however, and Barnfield evinces less than many writers of his time. Ironically, those putative feminine qualities originate from Cassandra's reactions to male sexual harassment, so that males seem ultimately to blame. A second edition of *Cynthia* appeared in 1598.

The poet's last collection, *The Encomion of Lady Pecunia* (1598), forsakes topics of love, gender, and sexuality for social satire of avarice and selfishness. This volume has four sections, each with a title page, and consists of three long poems and a final assortment including Barnfield's most acclaimed work, "As It Fell upon a Day." Following Desiderius Erasmus, the title poem ironically praises folly: Barnfield wittily mocks avarice through encomiums of "the fairest Fair Pecunia, / The famous queen of rich America." After rising to that prophetic strain, he offers "The Complaint of Poetry for the Death of Liberality," a pastoral elegy in which Poetry laments Bounty's demise; the resultant decline of literature, learning, and society; and the plight of the poor. The tone further darkens in the following "Combat, between Conscience and Covetousness, in the Mind of Man," an allegorical dream vision in which these two personifications verbally duel for mastery and Conscience loses. But the concluding section, "Poems in Divers Humors," reveals the positive standard animating the satire. This assortment celebrates joys of music and literature, faithful friendship, beauty, and, in elegies on Sidney and Barnfield's aunt, persons outstanding in learning, gallantry, kindness, and generosity. The section and volume close with a strategically deployed, epigrammatic memento mori, doubly conclusive in its terminal position and implying that the genuine pleasures are to be savored fully while life remains. Barnfield's published poems all gain strength and significance from their contextual position in his volumes. In 1605 a second, revised edition appeared, mainly adding praise of James I and omitting most short poems because of spatial constraints. However, the title poem of both editions subversively criticizes England for especial abuses.

Some lyrics from these volumes appear in Elizabethan anthologies. *The Passionate Pilgrim* (1599) includes "As It Fell" and "If Music and Sweet Poetry Agree," from *Lady Pecunia,* but attributes them to Shakespeare, whose editors long continued to follow suit. John Bodenham's *Belvedere; or, The Garden of the Muses* (1600), a compilation of extracts from diverse poems, draws from Barnfield and lists him among select modern English poets. *England's Helicon* (1600), which Bodenham helped compile, includes three of Barnfield's published poems and implies his authorship of another, "The Unknown Shepherd's Complaint," by appending one of his

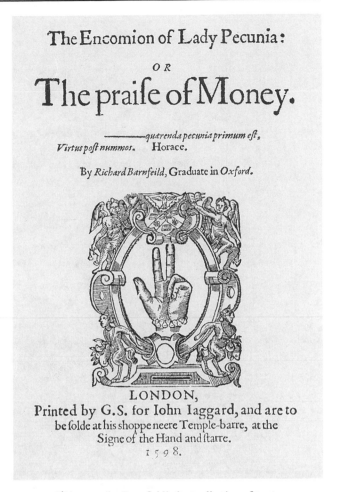

The Encomion of Lady Pecunia:

OR

The praiſe of Money.

——————*quærenda pecunia primum eſt,*
Virtus poſt nummos.   Horace.

By *Richard Barnfeild*, Graduate in *Oxford*.

LONDON,
Printed by G.S. for Iohn Iaggard, and are to be folde at his shoppe neere Temple-barre, at the Signe of the Hand and ſtarre.
1 5 9 8.

Title page for Barnfield's last collection of poetry

poems retitled "Another of the Same Shepherd's." "Shepherd's Complaint" is probably correctly attributed to Barnfield, for it depends much on anaphora, a rhetorical scheme he tends to overwork. This poem further appears in *The Passionate Pilgrim* as Shakespeare's.

Barnfield may have stopped publishing because he lacked sufficient confidence in his own primarily lyric talent. He most admired the vastly adventurous Spenser and gave *Cynthia* the epigraph *Quod cupio nequeo* (what I desire I cannot do). While that may be partly a lament of the frustrated lover, the poet was still only twenty-one; and the epigraph has clear literary reference, since Barnfield deprecates his poetic abilities several times within the volume. Nevertheless, his prefaces, inclusion in anthologies, the commendatory poem for *Cynthia,* and the second editions show his poetry was reasonably well received. Unlike many Elizabethan writers, he never complains of criticism, and Meres includes him with the "best" English pastoralists in *Palladis Tamia* (1598).

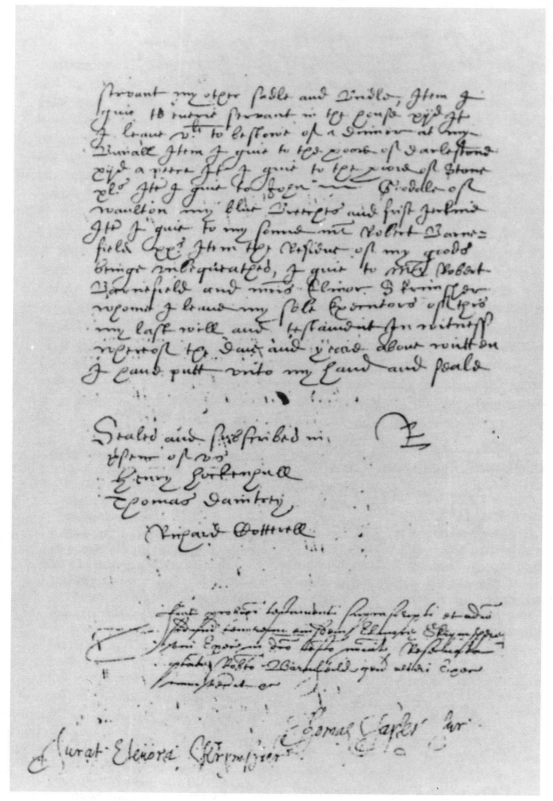

Second page of Barnfield's will, with his mark ("R") at right (Lichfield Joint Record Office, B/C/11)

By 1606 Barnfield had probably returned to country life in Staffordshire; sometime between 1605 and 1627 he took up residence in the village of Darlaston, where he died. In 1604 his father became armigerous and also, Clitheroe has discovered, disinherited the paternally eponymous poet, then aged thirty, by settling the estate on the second son, Robert, who had just married. The marriage contract, written in 1602, specifies "heirs begotten or to be gotten." That apparent concern may well have begun a main factor in the poet's deprivation, either because prospects of his marriage and continuation of the line currently seemed remote; or, if he had already married, because his father rejected the match. Ironically, Robert sold off the family estate of Edgmond in 1608, and not he but the poet eventually produced the male heir their father probably desired: the poet's will, written in 1627, includes a son and granddaughter, though no wife, who presumably died earlier. Her name and the duration of their marriage, which could have begun at any point between 1594 and 1612, are unknown; the most likely candidate, Elizabeth Barnfield, died in 1625. Though the poet's relations with his siblings and father's family seem to have been strained, he remained close to his maternal relatives; he was an executor for his uncle James's important estate in 1619. On account of his father's sanction, the poet left a modest, unlanded estate when he died in March 1627. The inventory values his books at ten shillings, his wardrobe at more than forty-three pounds.

In the *Theatrum Poetarum* (1675) Edward Phillips, the nephew and student of John Milton, still ranked Barnfield with Thomas Lodge, Robert Greene, and Nicholas Breton. That reputation quickly faded, however, for his texts became extremely rare, probably in part because of their homoerotic content. In the nineteenth century the poet's standing progressively rose as new editions of his work appeared. In *The History of English Poetry* (1871), editor W. Carew Hazlitt awarded Barnfield "the first place" among Elizabethan minor writers for his "undoubted genius," and in 1880 Algernon Swinburne dubbed him "our first-born Keats." Thus, in his entry on Barnfield for the *Dictionary of National Biography* Edmund Gosse declares that "only of late . . . something like justice has been done to the great poetical qualities of Barnfield."

Yet despite efforts to promote Barnfield, his reputation again plummeted in this century. Where Walter W. Greg remarks in his *Pastoral Poetry and Pastoral Drama* (1906) that Barnfield's poetry surpasses "the barren level" of Elizabethan pastoral

through "charm of poetic style and love of natural beauty," Lewis is scandalized by supposed pederasty, and so in his *English Literature in the Sixteenth Century, Excluding Drama* (1954) he polices the canon in a highly influential critique that presses unprecedented and trumped-up literary charges. Citing the line "Bath'd in a melting sugar-candy stream," he claims that Barnfield's *Affectionate Shepherd* exemplifies "very bad 'bad Golden'" style. Yet William Hazlitt observes that "surely no author . . . has fairer pretensions to be regarded as a writer of genuine, untainted vernacular English." Barnfield uses diverse styles as his purposes require, and Lewis's quotation misrepresents the first volume. Moreover, in context, such passages critically reflect Daphnis's overeager excesses in blandishment with authorial verbal irony. Lewis's further attacks are also misleading. Daphnis digresses absurdly, he claims, in a "lecture on the flavours of fish"; but that passage is actually just a six-line stanza and advances the argument in an aptly countrified way. In the only book on Barnfield to date, Harry Morris explicitly follows Lewis, condemning "perverted love" while multiplying spurious literary indictments. For instance, when the speaker of "The Complaint of Poetry" claims to transcend mortality, Morris attributes the voice to Barnfield and finds him "unthinking" and "ridiculous." But as the title and poem make clear, the speaker throughout is Poetry. Lewis and his disciple are so comprehensively reductive that few have since been able to take Barnfield's poetry seriously. Smith surpasses even these critiques by dismissing Barnfield's work as pornographic "poems of masturbation," a characterization that simply is not warranted by the material.

Barnfield's vicissitudes largely result from the interactions of literary canonicity with politics and prejudice. When credited to Shakespeare, his poems were not patronized but found worthily Shakespearean. Since his texts have no established canonical sanctity, he readily serves some critics as a scapegoat for the sexual challenges posed by some more prominent Elizabethan writers. Yet, beginning with Thomas Warton, even Barnfield's admirers tend to warn against "perversion" or claim that his amorous poetry is merely classically imitative or rejects physical love, despite its sensuous, impassioned language and imagery. A notable exception is Frank Kermode, who in his *English Pastoral Poetry from the Beginnings to Marvell* (1952) ignores sexual issues to emphasize rather that Barnfield's "success can hardly be denied. The blend of native and classical elements, and the richness with which his fancy invests the pastoral properties, combine to make his poems uniquely attractive at first glance."

Whatever the modern reader makes of the homoerotic poems, Barnfield's wit, clever wordplay, tactful self-presentation, concern for friendship, generosity toward other poets, ethical commitment, polished technique, and critical revaluation of social conditions are attractive. Besides Spenser, he judiciously applauds Sidney, Drayton, Samuel Daniel, and Shakespeare. No poetaster himself, Barnfield strives for variety and innovation both technically and thematically. Often he opts for smooth Spenserian musicality, sometimes producing passages of remarkable lyric beauty, such as in the opening of "Nights Were Short," his pastoral ode in *Cynthia*. He also achieves far different effects, as the chiseled toughness of his "Life of Man" shows. Displaying much percipience in his stylistic appropriations from Spenser, Barnfield even anticipates recent trends in Spenser studies by repeatedly identifying Spenser's ingenious profundity as his most surpassing literary attribute: "whose deep conceit is such, / As passing all conceit, needs no defense" ("If Music and Sweet Poetry Agree").

In any case, because of current interest in the literary implications of gender and sexuality and in expressions of dissent from dominant ideologies, Barnfield's work will undoubtedly attract increasing attention. His treatments of sexuality are still too novel and challenging for many critics, and he deserves much credit for his outspokenness, precocious not only for his own years but for his epoch. Having also been sent down at Oxford and disinherited, he was clearly an independent-minded man who contested the prescriptions of contemporary authority, not unlike Marlowe, and thus suffered heavy social sanctions. Study of this intriguing personality and his texts offers many opportunities, for his critical repertoire is still virtually embryonic.

References:

Alan Bray, *Homosexuality in Renaissance England* (London: Gay Men's Press, 1982), pp. 60–61;

Gregory W. Bredbeck, *Sodomy and Interpretation: Marlowe to Milton* (Ithaca, N.Y. & London: Cornell University Press, 1991), pp. 148–167;

Fred Clitheroe, *The Life and Selected Writings of Richard Barnfield, 1574–1627* (Newcastle: Lymes Press, 1992);

Scott Giantvalley, "Barnfield, Drayton, and Marlowe: Homoeroticism and Homosexuality in Elizabethan Literature," *Pacific Coast Philology*, 16 (1981): 9–24;

Jonathan Goldberg, *Sodometries: Renaissance Texts, Modern Sexualities* (Stanford, Cal.: Stanford University Press, 1992), pp. 68–69;

Harry Morris, *Richard Barnfield, Colin's Child* (Tallahassee: Florida State University Press, 1963);

James M. Saslow, *Ganymede in the Renaissance: Homosexuality in Art and Society* (New Haven: Yale University Press, 1986);

Bruce R. Smith, *Homosexual Desire in Shakespeare's England: A Cultural Poetics* (Chicago: University of Chicago Press, 1991), pp. 99–115.

Papers:

Some claim Barnfield authored most of a brief commonplace book containing various short poems, one published by Ben Jonson and another by Barnfield, and a heterosexually bawdy parodic eclogue in prose (Folger Shakespeare Library, MS V.a.161). Contrary to Bray and Goldberg, then, any argument about Barnfield based on this manuscript is purely fanciful. No other papers are known to be extant, except the poet's will (Lichfield Joint Record Office, B/C/11).

William Byrd

(circa 1543 – 4 July 1623)

Elise Bickford Jorgens
Western Michigan University

BOOKS: *Cantiones, quae ab argumento sacrae vocantur,* by Byrd and Thomas Tallis (London: Thomas Vautrollier, 1575);

Psalmes, Sonets and Songs of Sadnes and Pietie (London: Thomas East, 1588);

Liber primus sacrarum cantionum (London: Thomas East, 1589);

Songs of Sundrie Natures (London: Thomas East, 1589);

Liber secundus sacrarum cantionum (London: Thomas East, 1591);

Mass for Four Voices [published without title page] (N.p., circa 1592–1593);

Mass for Three Voices [published without title page] (N.p., circa 1593–1594);

Mass for Five Voices [published without title page] (N.p., circa 1595);

Gradualia ac cantiones sacrae (London: Thomas East, 1605);

Gradualia seu cantionum sacrarum, liber secundus (London: Thomas East, 1607);

Psalmes, Songs and Sonnets . . . Fit for Voyces or Viols (London: Thomas Snodham, 1611).

Editions: *English Church Music, Part 1,* edited by P. C. Buck and others, Tudor Church Music 2 (London: Oxford University Press, 1927);

Gradualia, Books 1 and 2, edited by Buck and others, Tudor Church Music 7 (London: Oxford University Press, 1927);

Masses, Cantiones and Motets, edited by Buck and others, Tudor Church Music 9 (London: Oxford University Press, 1928);

The Collected Works of William Byrd, edited by E. H. Fellowes, revised by Thurston Dart and others (London: Stainer & Bell, 1937–1950);

Songs of Sundry Natures, edited by Fellowes, revised by Philip Brett, The English Madrigalists 15 (London: Stainer & Bell, 1962);

Psalms, Sonnets and Songs of Sadness and Piety, edited by Fellowes, revised by Brett, The English Madrigalists 14 (London: Stainer & Bell, 1963);

Psalms, Songs and Sonnets, edited by Fellowes, revised by Dart, The English Madrigalists 16 (London: Stainer & Bell, 1964);

Keyboard Music I, edited by Alan M. Brown, Musica Britannica 27 (London: Stainer & Bell, 1969; revised, 1976);

The Byrd Edition, edited by Brett and others (London: Stainer & Bell, 1970–);

Keyboard Music II, edited by Brown, Musica Britannica 28 (London: Stainer & Bell, 1971; revised, 1976).

The life and activities of Elizabethan composer William Byrd exhibit many connections with the literary world of his time. As a composer of secular vocal music, Byrd knew and used contemporary poetry as texts for his songs, and he likely knew many prominent poets personally. For many years he held the patent for music printing, in effect controlling broad dissemination of poetry in the medium of song (in both his own songbooks and those of other composers of the day) and affording a rare view into the complex world of publishing and patronage. The prefaces to his many printed volumes of vocal music show him to have been a thoughtful and articulate author, seriously concerned with the nature of the musico-poetic relationship: Byrd originated the expression "framed to the life of the words," often used to characterize the special association of music and poetry in the English Renaissance. His private life also involved members of literary circles. Byrd was a practicing Catholic, and an account of his life brings into focus a small but important subculture of recusant Catholics who held prominent positions in Elizabethan society, a group that included literary figures as well.

William Byrd was born around 1543, and Anthony Wood's comment in *Athenae Oxonienses* (1691–1692) that he was "bred up under Tallis" has led to the supposition that he was one of the Children of the Chapel; if he was a choirboy in the Chapel Royal under Mary Tudor, he would have been in-

William Byrd

troduced to the Catholic liturgy and its music at a young age. Nothing certain is known of Byrd's parentage and almost nothing of his first twenty years. The first documented record of his career is dated 1563, when he accepted a position as organist at Lincoln Cathedral and apparently began composing English liturgical music. He was appointed to the Chapel Royal in February 1570, but he seems not to have relinquished the Lincoln position until 1572, at which time he is presumed to have begun sharing the responsibilities of organist of the Chapel Royal with the aging Thomas Tallis.

In September 1568, while he was still at Lincoln, Byrd married Juliana Birley; their two eldest children, Christopher and Elizabeth, were baptized at St. Margaret's-in-the-Close, Lincoln, in 1569 and 1572. A third child, Thomas, born in 1576, was named after his godfather, Thomas Tallis, and is the only one of the Byrd children who became a musician. Juliana Byrd must have died sometime around 1586, and Byrd married a second wife, Ellen. Two more children, Rachel and Mary, are mentioned in later documents, but their birth dates are not recorded and it is not known whether they were the children of Juliana or Ellen Byrd.

Composers in late-Renaissance England were even more dependent than their literary counter-parts upon the patronage of the rich and famous, and Byrd seems to have excelled at negotiating these avenues of support. He achieved the pinnacle of success in Elizabeth's Chapel while remaining faithful to the desire expressed in his will to "live and die a true and perfect member of God's holy Catholic Church." The roster of notable Elizabethans who offered him their aid, and the times and places at which it was offered, suggests that his devout adherence to his religious beliefs and practices was not a hindrance and may even have been an asset in providing the contacts he needed.

In 1573 or 1574 Byrd secured from the earl of Oxford the lease of the manor of Battails Hall in Essex, generating the first of six litigations over property rights that occupied Byrd throughout his life – in this instance, an attempt by a third party to establish that he had a prior claim to the lease. Battails Hall may never have been home to the Byrds, but it is the first indication of the composer's association with the poet Edward de Vere, the seventeenth Earl of Oxford and the author of "If Women Could Be Fair and Never Fond," which Byrd set as a song text in his 1588 collection *Psalms, Sonnets and Songs.* Oxford, like many others of the nobility in the early decades of Elizabeth's reign, probably had Catholic sympathies – at least until about 1580 when he denounced his former friends Henry Howard, Charles Arundel, and Francis Southwell as Catholics. Given what is known of Byrd's later contacts, it is tempting to assume a Catholic connection in addition to the artistic kinship, but there is nothing more than coincidence to suggest that Byrd's association with Oxford extended to religious matters.

From 1575 to 1596 Byrd and Thomas Tallis held the royal patent for printing music and music paper in England. Together they published *Cantiones . . . sacrae* in 1575. The volume was dedicated to Elizabeth I, probably as a gesture of thanks for her granting of the patent; it contained Latin motets – fourteen each by Tallis and Byrd – some of them related to the Roman Catholic liturgy and advertised in the prefaces as the heralds of renown for English music on the Continent. Publication of this collection was recognized in literary circles, for the noted Elizabethan educator and grammarian Richard Mulcaster provided a set of commendatory verses to grace its opening. As a business venture, however, the volume was not successful. Byrd and Tallis ceased publication, and while Elizabeth came to Byrd's aid with the lease of income property when the publishing business proved not to be lucrative, all music printing in England languished for the next thirteen years. The partnership ended with Tallis's death in 1585, though Byrd retained the monopoly.

In about 1577 Byrd moved his family to Harlington in West Middlesex, where they lived until 1592. This residence and Stondon Place, the next and last of Byrd's homes, assume significance from their apparent role in his religious life: from this time on his open involvement with the Catholic community increased. The first documented indications of Byrd's recusancy come with the move to Harlington in 1577, when his first wife, Juliana, was cited for failure to attend Reformed church services. The citations continued regularly, Juliana's name often accompanied by the name of John Reason, a servant in the Byrd home, and by 1580 Byrd's name had begun to appear in lists of those suspected of providing meeting places for recusants. In 1583 John Reason was caught delivering a letter from the composer, along with some of his music, to a Catholic household. During that year Byrd was among a group of Catholics who met with several well-known Jesuits, including the poet Robert Southwell (who was known as a Jesuit missionary), Father William Weston (a Jesuit priest), and another Jesuit missionary, Father Henry Garnet, in an eight-day assembly that included a sung mass, with chorus

and instrumentalists. By 1585 Byrd himself began to be included in citations for absence from services.

Byrd's escalating recusant activities do not appear to have affected his professional life. A substantial amount of his music composed for the English liturgy exists, including two complete services (the "Short" and the "Great") and two more partial services, a litany, three preces with psalms or responses (antiphonal petitions, or prayers), and more than sixty English anthems, or similar devotional pieces, many of them for liturgical use. On stylistic grounds, Joseph Kerman has placed the composition of the Great Service, Byrd's most significant work for the Anglican liturgy, in the 1580s. It seems likely that much of the remaining English liturgical music also dates from this middle period, although none of the English church music except the anthems and devotional songs was published during the composer's lifetime, making precise dating impossible.

In 1588, despite the restrictions said to make printing music unlucrative, Byrd resumed the publication of music he and Tallis had discontinued, this time turning the venture into a small but flourishing business with more import for the appreciation and dissemination of literature. He added two more volumes to the *Cantiones* (1589 and 1591, dedicated respectively to Catholic patrons Charles Somerset, Earl of Worcester, and John Lumley, Baron Lumley) and entered the secular trade with *Psalms, Sonnets and Songs of Sadness and Piety* in 1588 and *Songs of Sundry Natures* in 1589, the latter dedicated to Henry Carey, Baron Hunsdon, who was lord chamberlain and a first cousin of the queen.

All four of these volumes include works that had been circulating in manuscript during the previous decade, and many of them have texts attributable to well-known poets. Like the Latin motets of the *Cantiones,* many of the songs in Byrd's two secular volumes are pious and devotional. In addition to the psalm settings in the 1588 collection, several of the secular songs are moralistic in character (such as the two poems attributed to Sir Edward Dyer, "I Joy Not in No Earthly Bliss" and "My Mind to Me a Kingdom Is"), appearing alongside more worldly offerings such as Sir Philip Sidney's "O you that hear this voice" (the sixth song from *Astrophil and Stella,* 1591), Thomas Deloney's "Farewell, false love, the oracle of lies," and Oxford's "If women could be fair and never fond." This volume also contains a setting of stanzas from Henry Walpole's "Why do I use my paper, ink, and pen," written as an epitaph on the Jesuit father Edmund Campion, who was executed in 1581. The 1589 collection contains a set-

Title page for Byrd's first book of secular music

ting of one of Geoffrey Whitney's moralistic poems from *A Choice of Emblems* (1586), five more of which appeared in the final secular volume in 1611. It is clear, then, that Byrd's songs themselves were common vehicles for poetry of the period to become more widely circulated.

Byrd was also responsible for the publication of about ten volumes of songs by other composers, his role as publisher allowing him to play an even more prominent part in making both literary and musical composition much more broadly available to a public audience. Most of the songs in these collections — like Byrd's own compositions — are musically conservative in style. Two of the books, however, are collections of Italian madrigals with English lyrics, Nicholas Yonge's *Musica Transalpina* (1588) and Thomas Watson's *Italian Madrigals Englished* (1590), giving impetus to the coming vogue for madrigals in England. Watson was a well-known poet in his own right, and Yonge, though a musician, had regular contact with a literary circle.

Each of their volumes included two of the earliest original English madrigals, with music by Byrd himself, prominently announced along with Byrd's permission to publish on the title pages. In *Musica Transalpina* Byrd's contributions were set to translations of two portions of Ludovico Ariosto's *Orlando Furioso* (1532), while in *Italian Madrigals Englished* he turned to English verse as well, providing two different settings of Watson's "This Sweet and Merry Month of May," reputedly at Watson's request. The composer-publisher thus clearly established his name in the vanguard of the celebrated confluence of literature and music in the English Renaissance.

When Byrd reinstituted the printing of music in 1588, the market must have been essentially dead. The prefaces and dedicatory epistles attached to the printed collections of songs of 1588–1591 point to the need to *develop* an audience for printed music, which Byrd was apparently successful at doing. In many ways these prefaces and dedications are conventional for their time, reflecting the conditions of patronage, but in subtle ways they also show an urgency that is not characteristic of, for instance, literary dedications of the period, which commonly have at least a posture of nonchalance.

Byrd seems at pains to please everyone and by almost any means. In "The Epistle to the Reader" at the start of *Psalms, Sonnets and Songs,* he announces his intent to provide songs to suit all moods and humors, declaring, "If thou delight in music of great compass, here are diverse songs, which being originally made for instruments to express the harmony and one voice to pronounce the ditty, are now framed in all parts for voices to sing the same." The emphasis is on broad appeal, not artistic effect. The notion is confirmed a few sentences later when he says, "Whatsoever pains I have taken herein, I shall think to be well employed if the same be well accepted, music thereby the better loved and the more exercised." In the prefatory note to *Songs of Sundry Natures* in the following year, Byrd declares that "my last impression of music . . . hath had good passage and utterance" and "since the publishing thereof, the exercise and love of that art [has] exceedingly increased." The composer is therefore "encouraged thereby, to take further pains therein, and to make thee [Baron Hunsdon, the dedicatee] partaker thereof, because I would show myself grateful to thee for thy love and desirous to delight thee with variety, whereof (in my opinion) no science is more plentifully adorned than music."

In 1592 or 1593 Byrd moved to Stondon Massey in Essex, where he lived until the end of his life. The house, Stondon Place, belonged to William

Shelley, a Jesuit sympathizer who forfeited his properties to the Crown for his part in a plot to establish Mary, Queen of Scots, on the English throne. Byrd, by an odd twist of fate, leased it from the Crown, securing from Elizabeth in 1595 a lease extending the family's right to occupancy through the lives of his son Christopher and his daughters Elizabeth and Rachel. After Shelley's death in 1597, his widow tried to evict Byrd, instituting a long and difficult legal battle, but Byrd held fast and, after Mrs. Shelley's death in 1610, bought Stondon Place from John Shelley, the heir to the property.

Despite his having leased Stondon Place after its forfeiture from a Catholic family, this move seems to have been congenial to – if not motivated by – Byrd's desire to maintain an active religious life as a Catholic. The area was one of several in Elizabethan England in which recusant families were clustered, and the Petre family, who lived near Stondon Massey at Ingatestone, maintained an underground congregation of recusants. The Petres were Byrd's patrons, the recipients of dedications of some of Byrd's published compositions, and during the 1590s he probably composed most if not all of his music for the Catholic liturgy for use in masses celebrated in their home. Book 2 of the *Gradualia* is dedicated to Lord Petre of Writtle in terms that strongly suggest that this music was composed for use in services in the Petre household. (Book 1 of the *Gradualia* was dedicated to the Catholic Henry Howard, Earl of Northampton and the second son of the poet Surrey.)

Throughout this period and to the end of his life, Byrd and other members of his family continued to be cited for recusancy, as in a passage from the Chelmsford Diocesan Registry, Essex Archidiaconal Records, 11 May 1605, which also names his second wife, Ellen:

William Byrd [and] Elena [his wife presented] for Popish recusants. He is a gentleman of the King's Majesty's Chapel and as the minister and churchwardens do hear, the said William Byrd with the assistance of one Gabriel Colford who is now at Antwerp, hath been the chief and principal seducer of John Wright. . . . And the said Ellen Byrd, as it is reported and as her servants have confessed, have appointed business on the Sabbath day for her servants of purpose to keep them from Church . . . and the said Ellen refuseth conference, and the minister and Churchwardens have not as yet spoke with the said William Byrd because he is from home – and they have been excommunicate these seven years.

After 1590 Byrd wrote more for the Roman Catholic liturgy, using his printing monopoly to publish three masses during the mid 1590s (circa 1593 to 1595); although none has a title page, Byrd's authorship is clear. His motets of this period, after the publication of the 1589 and 1591 *Cantiones,* use liturgical texts, in contrast to the laudatory or devotional texts of the earlier motets, suggesting that they were intended for use in the rite rather than for personal devotions. These liturgical motets were published in 1605 and 1607 in the two sets of *Gradualia* – daring publications even for Byrd as they coincide with the resurgence of anti-Catholicism in England rising out of the Gunpowder Plot; both sets seem to have been withdrawn and republished in 1610. Musicologists James Jackman and Kerman have demonstrated that these motets comprise interchangeable segments that can be arranged in varying configurations to produce complete mass settings. They are considerably shorter and less elaborate than the nonliturgical motets of the *Cantiones* in keeping with their apparent use in celebrations of the mass in recusant households.

After 1596 Byrd no longer held the monopoly for music printing. He published nothing more until 1605 and no new secular music until *Psalms, Songs and Sonnets* (1611). This volume sums up the public persona of this brilliant and ambitious man. Dedicated to Francis Clifford, Earl of Cumberland – who was not a Catholic – the volume includes some songs from earlier books but is made up mostly of works composed in the intervening twenty years. Byrd's prefatory matter is dramatically different from what had appeared in earlier books, adopting a new, less fawning tone, urging that care and practice go into the performance of his songs, and replacing the early collections' exhortation to potential buyers with a touching statement from the almost seventy-year-old man: "The natural inclination and love to the art of music, wherein I have spent the better part of mine age, have been so powerful in me, that even in my old years which are desirous of rest, I cannot contain myself from taking some pains therein." The concern in the address "To all true lovers of music" is with performance rather than purchase, with discrimination and taste rather than breadth of audience, and the urge to create rather than to sell seems to have determined the decision to publish.

Psalms, Songs and Sonnets begins with "The Eagle's Force Subdues Each Bird that Flies," set to a poem by Thomas Churchyard concerning the futility of tangling with princes. The volume also includes settings of five moral emblems from Geoffrey Whitney's *A Choice of Emblems* (1586) and settings of several psalms but only three songs in the amorous

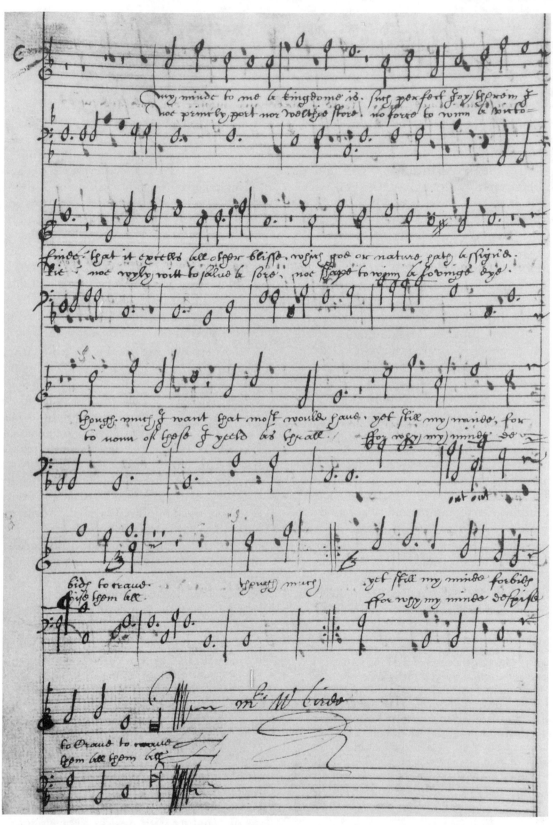

Manuscript of Byrd's score for "My Mind to Me a Kingdom Is," a poem attributed to Sir Edward Dyer (Christ Church, Oxford, Ms. 439)

vein of the earlier songs for popular appeal; one is a reprint of one of the settings of Watson's "This Sweet and Merry Month of May." While the pious tone of Byrd's earlier song texts is unchanged in this last volume, it is joined by a bitterness that might easily be read politically: number 2 (by Whitney) begins "Of flatt'ring speech with sugared words beware: / Suspect the heart whose face doth fawn and smile, / With trusting these the world is clogged with care"; the anonymous number 23 contains the lines "To govern he is fitless / That deals not by election / But by his fond affection. / O that it might be treason, / For men to rule by will, and not by reason."

The 1611 volume also contains a song to a text ("Crowned with Flowers") apparently written by Edward Paston, a Norfolk landowner and collector of music who was responsible for at least the preservation, if not the composition, of a dozen consort songs by Byrd that have survived only in Paston's prodigious manuscript collections. Byrd, in fact, seems to have been a household favorite, as almost all the manuscripts extant from Paston's collections contain some of his music and some are devoted exclusively to his works. Paston was the head of Appleton Hall, another of the Catholic houses of the period, and although he led a retired country life in his later years, he cultivated both music and literature. He appears to have offered his support to Thomas Morley, another composer with Catholic sympathies who was Byrd's student and the recipient of the publishing patent after Byrd. Paston was also a sometime poet and accomplished translator of poetry who knew Whitney (one of the *Emblems* set to music by Byrd is dedicated to Paston) and may have had associations with Dyer and Sidney. The musicologist Philip Brett speculates that Paston became interested in the young William Byrd in London in the 1570s and that both were known to members of Elizabethan literary circles; it is certainly tempting to think that Byrd met Dyer and Whitney, and perhaps Sidney and other literary figures, in Paston's company. Paston's taste, like Byrd's, was conservative and moral: the songs from his manuscripts include Byrd's setting of Thomas Churchyard's "What Steps of Strife" (one of three songs by Byrd based on Churchyard's "Shore's Wife" from *Mirror for Magistrates,* 1559) and some moralizing elegies that Paston apparently contributed to the collections.

Byrd died, presumably at Stondon Place as he wished, on 4 July 1623, and it is assumed that he was buried there. In 1923, at the time of the tercentenary of his death, a commemorative tablet was placed in the wall of the church at Stondon. The only known portrait of William Byrd is by G. Van der Gucht and is not reliably authentic, as it was engraved around 1729 for use in an unpublished history of music by Niccolo Francesco Haym.

Byrd's vocal music has sometimes been called unliterary because it was not responsive to the nuances of a poetic text in the ways that the madrigal and later lute song of the English Renaissance made famous. The 1611 collection of songs is the source of the well-known declaration that its music is "framed to the life of the words," but what Byrd meant by this was somewhat different from the aesthetic of text setting favored by his contemporaries. Byrd's work can best be seen as focused on the listener as reader, making poetry more accessible by reinforcing its formal contours and strengthening its rhetorical force, so that the words themselves are clearly and accurately perceived. For Byrd, music used in this fashion had a moral purpose: to facilitate the understanding of worthy texts.

Although Byrd's profession and commitment were focused in the sacred music for both Catholic and Anglican practices and almost none of the approximately thirty manuscripts each of music for viol consort and for keyboard was published during his lifetime, Oliver Neighbour notes that pavanes and galliards for keyboard occupied the composer for over forty years. Byrd wrote these keyboard pieces the way a poet of his day wrote sonnets, and they became for him a medium for compositional experimentation. Present-day admiration for Byrd falls as much on the keen musical intelligence revealed in these pieces of abstract music as on the persistent spirituality that informs the greatest of the sacred compositions.

In his study of Byrd's masses and motets, Kerman comments that Byrd was more interested in offering a service to his church than in courting the favor of posterity. History, however, has conferred on Byrd a reverence not accorded to many. During his lifetime he enjoyed the highest esteem afforded to a musician by his society: a gentleman of the Chapel Royal from 1570 to his death, he was praised by his well-known pupil Thomas Morley as a great master; John Baldwin, who copied out *My Lady Nevell's Book,* asserts in a lengthy manuscript poem about contemporary musicians that Byrd "doth excel all at this time"; and he was extolled in the Cheque Book of the Chapel Royal at the time of his death as "the Father of Music." Henry Peacham, in *The Complete Gentleman* (1634), offers extravagant praise for a musician whose compositions must by that time have seemed old-fashioned:

For motets and music of piety and devotion as well for the honor of our nation as the merit of the man, I prefer above all other our phoenix, Mr. William Byrd, whom in that kind I know not whether any may equal. I am sure none excel, even by the judgment of France and Italy, who are very sparing in the commendation of strangers in regard of that conceit they have of themselves.

Byrd continues to draw both scholarly and aesthetic admiration from musicologists, performers, and audiences. Although most of his output in secular song is not truly of the madrigal genre, Edmund H. Fellowes felt compelled to include the songs in his monumental and pioneering series, The English Madrigalists, and he wrote the only real biography of the composer. Recent musical scholarship has focused on the sources of Byrd's musical styles and techniques. Literary interest in Byrd could well center on the dedications and prefaces that show him to have increasing rhetorical command. Beyond these, Byrd holds a rarefied, almost ascetic reputation as a master craftsman of peculiarly British sensibilities. He even appears as a character in the novel *English Music* (1992) by the English author and critic Peter Ackroyd: the main character, who has learned from his father the "English music" comprising centuries of British literature, painting, architecture, and music, enters the lives of several literary characters, the milieu of some British landscape paintings – and the studio of William Byrd – where he learns both discipline and art from the celebrated composer.

Bibliography:

Richard Turbet, *William Byrd: A Guide to Research* (New York: Garland, 1987).

Biography:

Edmund H. Fellowes, *William Byrd* (London: Oxford University Press, 1936; second edition, 1948).

References:

H. K. Andrews, *The Technique of Byrd's Vocal Polyphony* (London: Oxford University Press, 1966);

Philip Brett, "Edward Paston (1550–1630): A Norfolk Gentleman and His Musical Collection," *Transactions of the Cambridge Bibliographical Society,* 4, part 1 (1964): 51–69;

Brett, "Word-Setting in the Songs of Byrd," *Proceedings of the Royal Musical Association,* 98 (1972): 47–64;

Alan Brown and Richard Turbet, eds., *Byrd Studies* (Cambridge: Cambridge University Press, 1992);

Peter le Huray, *Music and the Reformation in England, 1549–1660* (New York: Oxford University Press, 1967);

James Jackman, "Liturgical Aspects of Byrd's *Gradualia,*" *Musical Quarterly,* 49 (January 1963): 17–37;

Joseph Kerman, *The Elizabethan Madrigal: A Comparative Study* (New York: American Musicological Society, 1962);

Kerman, *The Masses and Motets of William Byrd* (Berkeley: University of California Press, 1981);

Adrian Morey, *The Catholic Subjects of Elizabeth I* (Totowa, N.J.: Rowman & Littlefield, 1978);

Oliver Neighbour, *The Consort and Keyboard Music of William Byrd* (Berkeley: University of California Press, 1978);

David C. Price, *Patrons and Musicians of the English Renaissance* (Cambridge: Cambridge University Press, 1981).

Papers:

The principal holdings of William Byrd's manuscript compositions, letters, and personal records are at the British Library; the Bodleian Library, Oxford; the Christ Church Library, Oxford; and the Cambridge University Libraries.

William Camden

(2 May 1551 – 9 November 1623)

Wyman H. Herendeen
University of Windsor

BOOKS: *Britannia sive florentissimorum regnorum, Angliae, Scotiae, Hiberniae, chorographica descriptio* (London: R. Newbery, 1586; revised and enlarged, 1587; revised and enlarged again, London: G. Bishop, 1590; revised and enlarged, London: G. Bishop & J. Norton, 1607); translated by Philemon Holland as *Britain, or a Chorographicall Description of England, Scotland, and Ireland* (London: G. Bishop & J. Norton, 1610);

Institutio graecae grammatices compendiaria in usum regiae scholae Westmonasteriensis (London: E. Bollifant, 1595);

Reges, reginae, nobiles et alii in ecclesia collegiata B. Petri Westmonasterii sepulti, usque ad annum 1600 (London: E. Bollifant, 1600); revised as *Reges, reginae, nobiles et alii in ecclesia collegiata B. Petri Westmonasterii sepulti, usque ad annum 1603* (London: E. Bollifant, 1603); revised again as *Reges, reginae, nobiles et alii in ecclesia collegiata B. Petri Westmonasterii sepulti, usque ad annum 1606* (London: E. Bollifant, 1606);

Anglica, Normannica, Hibernica, Cambrica, a veteribus scripta (Frankfurt: Marne, 1603);

Remaines of a Greater Worke Concerning Britaine (London: Waterson, 1605; revised and enlarged, 1614);

Actio in Henricum Garnetum, Societatis Jesuiticae in Anglia Superiorem (London, 1607);

Annales rerum Anglicarum, et Hibernicarum, regnante Elizabetha, ad annum M.D.LXXXIX (London: Waterson, 1615); translated [from the French translation by P. De Bellegent] by Abraham Darcie as *Annales. The True and Royal History of Elizabeth, Queene of England* (London: B. Fisher, 1625); enlarged as *Tomus alter annalium rerum Anglicarum, et Hibernicarum, sive pars quarta* (Leyden, 1625; London: T. Harper, 1627); translated by T. Browne, as *Annales. Tomus alter & idem* (London: T. Harper, 1629).

Editions: *A Discoverie of Certaine Errours . . . in the "Britannia," 1594 . . . By Ralph Brooke . . . To*

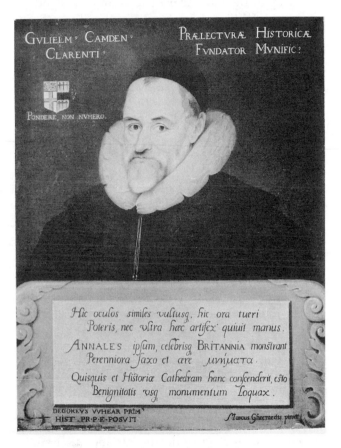

William Camden; portrait by Marcus Gheeraerts the Younger (Bodleian Library, Oxford)

which are added . . . *Mr. Camden's Answer*, edited by John Anstis (London: Printed for J. Woodman & D. Lyon, 1724);

William Camden: Remains Concerning Britain, edited by R. D. Dunn (Toronto: University of Toronto Press, 1984).

OTHER: *A Collection of Curious Discourses Written by Eminent Antiquarians*, 2 volumes, edited by Thomas Hearne (London: W. & J. Richardson, 1771) – includes Camden's "Of the Antiquity, Office, and Privilege of Heralds in England"; "Of the Diversity of Names in This Is-

land"; "Of the Etymology and Original of Barons"; "Of Epitaphes"; "Of the Antiquity, Variety, and Reason of Motts with Arms of Noblemen and Gentlemen in England"; "Of the Antiquity, Power, Order, State, Manner, Persons, and Proceedings of the High Court of Parliament in England"; "The Antiquity, Authority, and Succession of the High Steward of England"; "The Antiquity and Office of the Earl Marshal of England"; and "Of the Antiquity of the Christian Religion in this Island";
"Poems by William Camden," edited and translated by George B. Johnson, special issue of *Studies in Philology,* 72 (December 1975).

William Camden – educator, historian, poet, and herald – was a major influence in each of the four areas of his personal and professional life. Best known for his topographical work, the *Britannia* (1586), and for the *Annales rerum Anglicarum . . . regnante Elizabetha* (1615; translated as the *History of Elizabeth,* 1625), his place in the intellectual currents of his own and later generations is not confined to individual works, but extends to the fertile and changing relationship between poets and historians from the late sixteenth century to the Restoration. His view of the past and the scholarly methodologies he used to represent and interpret it were recognized by contemporaries for their originality in England. The characteristics associated with modern historiography were emerging in Italy and France in the sixteenth century and found full and mature expression in Camden's work. Widely known and esteemed throughout the European intellectual community, Camden exerted a shaping force on the individuals, social institutions, literary genres, and political currents of his time. Relying heavily on the objective use of original documents and other kinds of cultural artifacts to read history, recognizing that many secular factors contribute to the shaping of history, and ready to acknowledge the historian's fallibility and frequent recourse to myth, Camden is a precursor of the modern cultural historian.

William Camden was born on 2 May 1551 in the Old Bailey, an area caught between medieval London and Renaissance Westminster. His life and career were products of late-Tudor educational, religious, political, and social structures. His father, Sampson Camden, was a member of the Painter-Stainers, a company whose fortunes declined with those of the aristocracy, although Camden retained close ties with them up to the time of his death. Through his connection with the guild, Camden forged an early association with heraldry that was renewed in middle age, when he became Clarenceux, King of Arms. His maternal family were the Curwens, an old and well-connected Lancashire family reputed to have connections with Catherine Parr; from them may have come some of the opportunities and connections that enabled Camden to rise from an otherwise inauspicious childhood.

From his early youth Camden was dependent on Protestant institutions, particularly the heavily doctrinal educational system that influenced his intellectual and political development. He was first educated in London at Christ's Hospital, the former monastic premises of the Grey Friars, converted by Edward VI in 1552 into a hospital and school for the city's poor and orphaned. Camden's bout with the plague in 1563 is the first episode in a life frequently troubled with ill health. After his recovery he went to the more prestigious St. Paul's School, itself deeply imbued with traditions of religious reform and humanism instilled by its founder, John Colet, and first master, William Lily, only a generation previously. There, in the community presided over by Alexander Nowell, dean of St. Paul's, and John Cook, headmaster, both lifelong friends of William Cecil, Lord Burghley, Camden was assimilated into the intellectual and political currents that would direct his career and would, in turn, be influenced by him. Later in life Camden spoke of his interest in antiquarian matters even as a youth, and it is likely that these tastes were fostered at the chapter and school of St. Paul's, much as they were for like-minded Londoners who benefited from Nowell's influence, including William Harrison and Edmund Spenser.

In 1566 Camden began his career at Oxford – when Robert Dudley, Earl of Leicester, became chancellor and encouraged the Puritan factions in the religious controversies of the university. Although Camden emerged from Oxford with a clearly focused idea of new historiographical methodology and many personal connections that would continue to serve him, it appears to have been a more deeply frustrating period than is usually suggested, possibly because of his early identification with parties unsympathetic to Leicester, including his first patron at the university, Dr. Thomas Cooper. Camden began as a chorister and servitor at Magdalen College, where he was under Cooper, later Bishop of Winchester – one of many episcopal ties in his life. Camden's position as chorister seems not to have been merely a financial exigency, for he had a lifelong interest in music. A series of disappointments plagued the financially dependent student at Oxford. Talented though he was, he failed

Title page and illustrations of Stonehenge and ancient coins from the 1600 edition of Camden's topographical history of Britain

to get a fellowship and moved to Broadgates Hall, where Richard and George Carew were fellow students, and then to Christ Church, taking up residence with Thomas Thornton, where Philip Sidney also resided. Camden valued highly his connection with Sidney and recalls it later when writing the *Britannia.*

Camden's peripatetic existence at Oxford suggests the vulnerability of a person in his position, needing to find support as well as intellectual compatibility. In 1569 he was a fellowship candidate at All Souls College and was again blocked by university politics and religious controversy. Tradition has been that his candidacy was resisted by the Catholic faction, but this oversimplifies Oxford politics at the time and overlooks Camden's discomfort with the Puritans and the pattern of his compatability with conservative religious parties. His own account, in a letter to Archbishop James Ussher dated 10 July 1618, is that he was passed over for "defending the Religion established," which would locate him with Elizabeth and Burghley's compromise and could refer equally to Puritan or Catholic opposition.

In spite of these frustrations, throughout his life Camden maintained close connections with the university, Christ Church, and the many individuals he met there. Further, Westminster School had close institutional ties with Christ Church, and the professional path leading to his post at Westminster no doubt began at Oxford. The college's curriculum accommodated noncanonical subjects congenial to Camden such as geography, astronomy, geometry, and history, and like Westminster, it had a deeply rooted dramatic tradition.

Camden's training at Oxford, like his major work, has its origins in Erasmian humanism but also diverges from it because of contemporary pressures. In 1570, after four years studying logic at Oxford, he left without taking the B.A., which a gentleman could easily afford to forgo, but not a man of Camden's background. His relationship with the university continued to be checkered, and he petitioned unsuccessfully for his degree in 1570 and again, successfully, in 1574. His struggle with the authorities continued when, fifteen years later, after the success of the *Britannia,* he supplicated the university for the degree of master of arts, having spent the equivalent of sixteen years of study after the bachelor's. This petition also seems to have been thwarted.

For four years after he left Oxford in 1571, Camden's activities are unknown. He may have traveled the country indulging his antiquarian appe-

tites; but for a man without visible means of support, this seems an unlikely luxury. Tradition has it that he enjoyed the patronage of Gabriel Goodman, Dean of Westminster, but the beginning of their friendship is also unknown. The thread of his history reappears with the formal commencement of his duties at Westminster School in 1575. His life at Westminster, as second master from 1575 to 1593, then as headmaster until 1597, was one of stability and productivity.

With the friendship of Goodman and the headmaster, Edward Grant, Camden joined an intellectual and political community closely associated with William Cecil, Baron Burghley, who was steward of Westminster and maintained a residence there. With his former secretary Goodman as dean, Burghley presided over the chapter, with its twelve prebends forming, according to Stow, something akin to a school of theology within the city. Men such as Burghley, Grant, Goodman, and Richard Bancroft made Westminster a place of learning having direct ties with an older courtly humanist tradition characterized by Roger Ascham, whose letters were edited in 1576 by his close friend Grant. Camden made his literary debut with the contribution of an elegy to this collection. It was a fitting debut for a young scholar trained in the humanist traditions and milieu that Ascham exemplified and that, if they did not exactly perish with Elizabeth's former tutor, were radically transformed in the early modern London inhabited by Camden.

The Westminster School that Camden entered in 1575 had been reestablished at Burghley's instigation during the early years of Elizabeth's reign. Its curriculum was designed to recapture some of the original objectives of St. Paul's, particularly its emphasis on Greek; its organization and administration were tailored to its unique place as part of the complex that included the abbey, Westminster Palace and the major government offices, Parliament, and the chapter library (which also served the school). Although officially a secular body administered by the headmaster, it was run by the dean and prebends and closely overseen by Burghley. It also had a longstanding tradition of school drama that was richer than that of most schools because each of the three different kinds of student — the queen's scholars, the choir boys, and the town boys (oppidans) — put on at least one annual performance. The choristers (known as "the children of Westminster") had particularly close connections to the court. Although the choir boys were officially separate from the school, Camden sang with them, and the separation seems to have been largely a formality.

Camden stepped naturally into his duties at Westminster, helping place the school foremost among the many institutions reformed during the Tudor period. His contribution to Greek education is a good example of his place in the continuum of the humanist tradition. His *Institutio graecae grammatices compendiaria in usum regiae scholae Westmonasteriensis* (1595) was modeled after William Lily's *Short Introduction of Grammar* (1509?), prepared for St. Paul's; it assumed the status of authorized Greek grammar alongside Lily's Latin text. Camden's real classroom success is evident from the comparatively large number of contributions in Greek in the collection of elegies published at his death, *Camdeni Insignia* (1623).

He also served the school's dramatic traditions, as is evident in Ben Jonson's warm acknowledgments of his teacher's influence, particularly in Epigram 14 and in his dedication to Camden of the 1616 Folio of *Every Man in His Humor* and (originally) *Cynthia's Revels* (1600). Jonson's neoclassicism, unique among his contemporary dramatists, bears the stamp of the Westminster curriculum, as does his epigrammatic verse and his relative comfort with Greek.

Camden served the school's implicit commitment to Elizabethan church policy, as well, particularly Burghley's view of it, through his self-professed success in using the school to bring Catholics within the Protestant fold, and in training many young men who later became bishops. Camden had a major hand in the changes in the use, administration, and physical arrangements of the library, which served both chapter and school; he was made its custodian and then librarian in addition to his other duties, thus securing control over an important research tool. The terms of Jonson's praise of his teacher and friend in Epigram 14 provide a compact anatomy of the Christian-humanist virtues that contemporaries found in Camden:

> Camden, most reverend head, to whom I owe
>   All that I am in arts, all that I know,
> (How nothing's that?) to whom my country owes
>   The great renown and name wherewith she goes;
> Than thee, the age sees not that thing more grave,
>   More high, more holy, that she more would crave.
> What name, what skill, what faith hast thou in things!
>   What sight in searching the most antique springs!
> What weight, and what authority in thy speech!
> Man scarce can make that doubt, but thou canst teach.
> Pardon free truth, and let thy modesty,

> Which conquers all, be once overcome by thee.
> Many of thine this better could than I;
> But for their powers, accept my piety.

From an early date in his association with the school, Camden enjoyed the respect of members of the international scholarly community. Many Protestant scholars traveling to England sought him out, including the itinerant Hungarian scholar Parmenius, the Italian lawyer Alberico Gentili, and the Flemish geographers Gerardus Mercator and Abraham Ortelius, whose encouragement in 1576 provided the impetus for the *Britannia*. Catholics also figured among Camden's expanding range of correspondents as his yet-unpublished work became better known. He dates his friendship with Barnabe Brisson, chief justice of France, to 1581, when he was in England. Thomas Smith's posthumous collection and publication of many of Camden's letters in 1691 records the network of European scholars that continued to widen throughout Camden's life. In addition, he traveled extensively in England, gathering antiquarian and topographical information, and (as he relates in the section on languages in *Remains* [1605]) he followed the example of men such as Laurence Nowell, William Lambarde, John Jocelyn, and Francis Tate, and studied the vernacular languages, particularly Anglo-Saxon and Welsh, to assist his historical understanding.

The appearance in 1586 of the *Britannia,* a thick, unassuming octavo in Latin that was dedicated to Burghley, hardly took the scholarly community by surprise, but it did present them with something previously unseen. In its original state it was still rather rude, and between 1586 and 1607 Camden spent much of his career perfecting it in form and content. During this time it underwent six major revisions and brought into the research process numerous individuals, so that its impact was amplified considerably. Coextensive with its publication history were the founding and active years of the Society of Antiquaries. The topics of the reports for their meetings often drew on or ultimately contributed to editions of the *Britannia* or Camden's related work. In addition, many individuals around the country assisted Camden by providing information about such matters as local lore, antiquities, inscriptions, and coins. Thus the *Britannia* embodies a historiography; and through his collaborative and collegial research methods, Camden further affected the way that history and related literary forms were being practiced and experimented within England.

Frontispiece and title page for the English translation of Camden's Annales rerum Anglicarum, et Hibernicarum, regnante Elizabetha *(1615)*

Notwithstanding its originality, the *Britannia* is a humanist text having close links with the classical models that it converts to national ends. As Camden stresses, it is not a history, although its chorographic form, in which the description is organized around the regional geography, accommodates historical material. Following the model of Pausanias's *Description of Greece* (circa 150), it foregrounds national landscape, community, and manners, rather than narrated events. Thus it shows Camden's rejection of the tradition of rhetorical history, with its emphasis on providential patterns reinforcing dynastic political structures. Camden's historiography intentionally suppresses the political dogma of history in order to present a version of social change that is accommodating rather than prescriptive or confrontational in nature.

The *Britannia* participates in the revival of topographical forms that was taking place across Europe in the aftermath of the Reformation, when nations were in the process of political, religious, and social redefinition. A major impetus for this in England came from one of Camden's major sources, John Leland, whose unpublished *Itinerary* (written 1535–1543, published 1710–1712) was begun in direct response to the dissolution of the monasteries by Henry VIII. Others as well were working in topographical forms resembling the overall design of the *Britannia,* including William Harrison, whose *Description of Britain* forms part of Raphael Holinshed's *Chronicle* (1577), and William Lambarde, who confined his planned description of the counties to a one-volume *Perambulation of Kent* (1576) out of deference to Camden. The interest in topographic forms in Britain was spearheaded in its early years by the Protestant publisher Reginald Wolf, and, if it avoided explicit political controversy, it was nevertheless a by-product of political change. Thus, they share the general form and focus of classical and medieval *topographia,* describing actual physical landscapes, noting their distinctive natural physical qualities, their antiquities, the people, their manners, customs, local legends, and laws. However, in Camden and his contemporaries, the chorographic form is brought into the context of early modern Europe.

Thus, the *Britannia* is part of a literature of national self-consciousness in which various literary genres — historical, poetic, and topographical — are appropriated to a Protestant poetic directed toward

Britain's cultural identity. In this, it is an expression of Camden's generation and his affinity with others educated in an Elizabethan Protestant humanism, particularly Sidney and Spenser. The lives and major work of these three writers are closely interconnected and provide three quite different versions of the English Renaissance at its peak. Camden's relationship to these two contemporaries and their work, and his influence on succeeding generations, locate him in the mainstream of the changes occurring in early modern England.

Biographically and literarily, the *Britannia* looks back to Camden's time at Oxford with Sidney, and it suggests contrasts as well as affinities that are important for understanding the historian and his work. The most important and perhaps also the most influential of his university peers, Sir Philip Sidney, Leicester's nephew, was Camden's social superior. They were intellectually, socially, and temperamentally different. Sidney was a would-be man of action for whom letters were part of a humanist training and poetry a leisurely activity to which he never entirely reconciled his gentlemanly self; he "encouraged" Camden as only a nobleman could. In successive editions of the *Britannia,* Camden expressed his respect for Sidney and gratitude for this support, making full use of that connection as only a commoner could. Sidney's support was not that of patron but that of a schoolfellow whose life would no doubt follow a path quite different from Camden's. Academically they had similar interests, but they cannot have agreed on much other than the general merit of liberal learning and disputation. Aside from their strong patriotism, their political, social, and religious views must have been more often at odds than harmonious, Sidney's petulance and his bellicose Protestantism tending to Puritan extremes quite alien to Camden.

Oxford nurtured their literary interests and raised in both men similar intellectual questions; the literary fruit of these years proved to be similar in kind but different in character. Both men wrote major works responding to the same questions about the nature and status of the imagination and of history, and they stand in distinct opposition to one another. Sidney's *Apology for Poetry* (1595) places poetry above its rival disciplines: theology, philosophy, and history. History was imaginative literature's major competition after the second half of the century. Up to the death of King James I, writers continued to experiment creatively and freely with different combinations of the two disciplines. Sidney's view, however, is that of a purist. Intolerant of any impurities in the crystalline air the poet

breathes, he devalues the particular kind of truth of history in favor of poetry's transcendent truth and insists on the incompatibility of the two. Important as it is, the *Apology for Poetry* is derivative and theoretically reactionary, attempting to deny what is happening in various literary and intellectual modes. Its inflexibility and intolerance suit the man and his favorite literary genre: heroical poetry.

The *Britannia* also contends with the relation between historical fact and poetic fiction. The historiography that Camden was the first in England to articulate and practice has its roots in humanistic historical philology; it calls for the use of original documents, objective and accurate reporting of facts, and the clear distinction between what was and what might or should have been. Separating history and rhetoric, Camden's work, like its Italian and French counterparts, is part of the growth of empirical methods occurring in other disciplines as well. While it has its classical models in Tacitus and Polybius, Camden's historical method is markedly different from the prevailing rhetorical humanist treatment of history, such as that described in Spenser's letter to Sir Walter Ralegh. Embracing such palpable fictions as Geoffrey of Monmouth's Brutus myth and the imperfectly historical Arthurian lore, such writers harness the political and moral potential of their form; among the finest achievements in this tradition is Edmund Spenser's *Faerie Queene* (1590, 1596). While Sidney tries to invalidate the claims of the other modes and to give sole authority to the poet, Spenser the peacemaker sees them all as the offspring of Dame Rhetoric and ignores the different ontologies distinguishing poetry and history. In contrast, Camden builds on the distinctive strengths of both, using poetry in the *Britannia* to comment on history without blurring the differences between the two modes as Spenser does. Camden's methodology would prove to be that of the future.

It is this reworking of traditional forms and content through new methodologies that emerged from Italian and French historical writers, including Giovanni Biondo, Francesco Guicciardini, and Jean Bodin, that earned Camden the reputation as the first modern English historian. In light of the traditional elements and humanist origins of his work, the modern historian can appreciate his originality among his contemporaries without exaggerating his work's revolutionary nature. His treatment of the historical past stands out as rigorously secular, undogmatic in the pursuit of causation in human affairs, and tolerant of multiple influences acting on events. This attempt at objectivity is alien to the polemical dimension of both humanist and emergent Counter-Reformation histories. Camden's prose tends to a low or middle style, using irony, understatement, and occasional metaphoric expressions. Camden attempts to re-create the past of Roman Britain accurately, through extensive quotation of original texts and the use of nonliterary evidence and without relying on hearsay, as Sidney accuses historians of doing. However, underlying these methods is a fundamental skepticism about the ability to know the past and a readiness to question previously held assumptions such as the legend of Brutus. This new historiography, which has consistently been identified with Camden, is firmly in the Baconian tradition – thirty years before its characteristics are articulated in the *Novum Organum* (1620).

During the many years of its refinement the *Britannia* evolved into a well-designed folio of historical archaeology with the resources of the print medium adapted to its needs. Hoping to see as far as possible into the past of the ancient Britons, Camden had to work from the window provided by literary documents and other data surviving from the Roman occupation. He thus achieves two complementary goals – the recovery of the British past and its assimilation in the Roman world. Sifting through the strata of the past necessitated a more thorough and accurate periodizing of British history than any previous writer had managed. The opening sections thus provide brief histories of the country's inhabitants – British, Roman, Saxon, Norman, Pict. Camden's emphases on the tribe and on topography further depoliticizes his approach to history – or more precisely, changes the configurations of political history.

In successive editions Camden also added to and organized the types of nonliterary material brought to bear on historical analysis. Engravings of ancient British, Roman, and Saxon coins, inscriptions, monuments, and ruins provide visual data comparable to the extensive quotations that Camden cites from his sources. The *Britannia* is the first major work in England to use and reproduce such archaeological material as a serious component of its historical analysis, placing Camden in the vanguard of early modern cultural historians. The antiquarian movement that flourished in the next century drew directly on his example, learning from his methods, and editing and amplifying the *Britannia*. Thus, the *Britannia* not only broadened Camden's already-established reputation, but it also carried its influence into the future, acting as an agent of change in a way that Sidney's *Apology for Poetry,* for example, did not.

Along with its nearly exact contemporary, Spenser's *Faerie Queene,* the *Britannia* raises questions about the relation between myth and history. Camden and Spenser were aware of each other's work and were probably personally acquainted. Spenser admired Camden and in *The Ruines of Time* (1591) praised him as the "nourice of antiquitie," making him the model historian and Sidney the model poet. Moved mainly by the patriotic spirit that he felt infused Camden's historical knowledge, Spenser either failed to notice that the historiography undermined his own use of legendary material, or was content to ignore these fundamental differences. He drew on the *Britannia* for the chronicle material embodied in *Faerie Queene* II.x and III.iii, and for the topographical detail and design of the marriage of Thames and Medway in IV.xi–xii.

Their shared interest in historical topography suggests a long and close understanding between the two going back to the late 1570s, when Spenser was writing his "Epithalamion Thamesis," which is described in his 1580 correspondence with Gabriel Harvey. Never published and probably incorporated into *Faerie Queene* IV.xi–xii, the "Epithalamion Thamesis" closely resembles its exact contemporary, Camden's Latin fragment, the "De Connubio Tamae et Isis," which is interwoven through the *Britannia*. The correspondences in date, form, and content are so close that the precise relation between the two works is unclear. William Vallans's *Tale of Two Swans* (1590) also makes the association between the two river poets and the antiquarian John Leland and his river poem, the *Cygnea Cantio* (1545), making clear that the connection between history, poetry, and topography was a recognized area of literary experimentation. Furthermore, the literary and biographical links among Camden, Spenser, and Sidney are many and were recognized by contemporaries, as in Joseph Hall's "To Camden" (1600?), and strongly suggest that the three were working to resolve similar generic and intellectual problems of how to reconcile the dross of history with the gold of the imagination.

In spite of these affinities, Spenser, as well as Sidney, presents a treatment of history and myth that would soon be untenable. Spenser's *Faerie Queene* was the last national epic able to blend unquestioningly the poetic, legendary, and historical materials that in the *Britannia* were segregated. Camden's work and his influence set the course for the future. National epics such as Michael Drayton's *Poly-Olbion* (1612, 1622) and Samuel Daniel's

Part of a letter from Camden to Robert Cotton, dated 15 March 1596, concerning the queen's recovery from an illness (British Library, Ms. Cott. Jul. c. III, fol. 64ª)

Civil Wars (1595, 1609), with their self-conscious use of historical fact, reflect the impact of Camden's example.

Similarly, the direction of historical writing in prose was heavily influenced by Camden, with the result being increased specialization, sharper periodization, greater divergence in writers' interpretations of history, and more politically controversial work – as seen in Daniel's *History of England* (1612), the reports presented at the Society of Antiquaries, and in the scholarship of men such as Robert Cotton and John Selden. The history and development of the Society of Antiquaries is closely linked to the publication and revision of the *Britannia*. Camden was a founding member, and the refinement of his own historiography carries directly into the methods used and subjects examined in the regular meetings of the society, held in the College of Arms at Derby House. Although motivated in part by a patriotic concern for the national past, their inquiries were often of inherently political significance, addressing topics dealing with social structures (such as the antiquity of parliaments, laws, shires, and cities) and with titles and offices (such as the offices of the earl marshal and the heralds). At least eleven of Camden's essays for the Society of Antiquaries appear among those gathered in *A Collection of Curious Discourses* (1771); they deal with questions of arms,

titles, language, epitaphs, and names. In method and subject matter the work of the Society of Antiquaries questions the nature of the social structure by scrutinizing it closely, which may have contributed to the society's failure to secure a royal patron and its eventual discouragement under King Charles.

Important for all aspects of Camden's antiquarian and literary activities was his close association with his former student Cotton, a member of Parliament best known for his library, itself an adjunct to his political life. Precocious bibliophile that he was, Cotton began collecting while young and was involved with the Society of Antiquaries even in its early years. He and Camden worked closely together throughout their lives, traveling in England to collect books, manuscripts, and antiquities, and corresponding with scholars and friends in England and Europe. Cotton's London residence was adjacent to the Westminster Abbey complex, and it is clear that the doors of his library were always open to Camden; in his will Camden states that his friend should have first access to his collection in order to reclaim unreturned material. For many contemporaries, the names Cotton and Camden were interchangeable. Cotton had financial resources that Camden did not, and the latter seems to have been content helping build Cotton's collection and using it for his own studies.

Following the publication of the *Britannia,* Camden's lot improved. He was put in charge of the library at Westminster in 1587, adding twenty shillings to his salary of ten pounds. In 1589 he was made a prebend at Ilfracomb by Bishop John Piers, a stall he held for the rest of his life. In March 1593 he replaced Edward Grant as headmaster, a post he retained four years. In the meantime, he continued his travels, although from 1594 his health, never robust, began to deteriorate.

By 1597 Camden was tiring of his onerous duties as educator, and there is evidence that he desired a change, although he reputedly refused the position of mastership of requests. At the recommendation of Fulke Greville, Lord Brooke, his name was presented to the queen for the newly vacant post of Clarenceux, King of Arms. On 23 October 1597, after serving one day as Richmond Herald to satisfy prerequisites of office, Camden was created Clarenceux, one of the three kings of arms, the others being Garter (principal herald) and Norroy. The kings of arms were the senior heralds in the College of Arms and were answerable to the earl marshal. They were responsible for matters of arms throughout the kingdom, and their duties included court attendance and representation of the monarch; the granting and confirming of arms, for which they were expected to make visitations to designated regions; the marshaling of tournaments and royal and noble processions; and the enforcement of all privileges, rights, and restrictions pertaining to matters of degree and title. The heralds held a strategic place within the competitive patronage system at court, and so enjoyed considerable influence and had ample opportunity for profit and abuse of power. Camden's appointment was irregular. It situated a firm ally of Burghley in the center of the College of Arms precisely at the time when the increasingly erratic Essex became earl marshal. While his appointment must have angered many observers, only Ralph Brooke's complaints survive in his diatribe titled *A Discovery of Certain Errors . . . in the "Britannia"* (1599). It would seem that Camden was too well respected or too well connected to challenge.

From the date of Camden's appointment, and no doubt directly linked to it, the College of Arms began a period of much-needed reorganization and reform. His influence, intellectually and administratively, resembles that at Westminster School and among the Society of Antiquaries, with which the College was closely associated. The society met at Derby House, in Garter's offices, and many of the essays presented deal with issues related to the College of Arms. The two organizations, under Camden's presiding genius, were part of the cultural redefinition of the relationship between the nobility and the Crown in England. During Camden's tenure, the interests and methods of heralds and antiquarians came closer together. A work such as his *Reges, reginae, nobiles et alii in ecclesia . . . Westmonasterii* (1600), a descriptive guide to the royal and noble monuments in the abbey, is a good example of how the two offices converged to make a significant statement in support of episcopacy.

During the Jacobean period, Camden's travels became less frequent, and he used the extraordinary powers that James granted him to delegate his visitations to deputies. As the last revised editions of the *Britannia* were completed, he also finished several related projects, including the edition of English chronicle material, *Anglica, Normannica, Hibernica, Cambrica, a veteribus scripta* (1603), and an interesting miscellany of material left over from the *Britannia* titled the *Remains,* dedicated to Robert Cotton.

Both of these works show how the place of humanist scholar had changed since the mid sixteenth century, reshaped by the political, religious, and material conditions of Camden's generation. A classical scholar trained in Greek, he was cut off from a university career, studying instead national history, a topic having grown in interest since the Reformation. Rather than editing classical or scriptural texts, he dedicated himself to placing Britain in the classical tradition and editing works of national importance, such as the *Anglica, Normannica, Hibernica, Cambrica, a veteribus scripta,* edited from work by Sir Thomas More, William Gemeticensis, Giraldus Cambrensis, and others. Not a courtier-scholar or professor, he lived on the urban edge of the court, or in particular, its political and legislative sphere.

The *Remains* illustrates how Camden's scholarship responds to the intellectual currents of his generation. This richly varied collection reveals the unorthodox range of subjects that Camden felt to be of historical interest. In it he attempts a comparative and historical study of English, prints the first collection of medieval poetry, and shows a wide-ranging curiosity about social customs and habits. The work, idiosyncratic as it is, reflects how vernacular material once regarded as marginal had assumed a place of interest for a broad range of readers.

Camden studiously maintained his place at the periphery of literary and social London. After a

Camden's monument in Westminster Abbey

riding accident in 1607 that immobilized him for nearly a year, he traveled little, and in 1609 he settled into a house in Chislehurst, Kent, near London but outside the reach of the plague. He then turned his attention to one last major literary achievement, the *Annales rerum Anglicarum, et Hibernicarum, regnante Elizabetha,* or the *History of Elizabeth,* a work that reflects Camden's eminence as a historian and a man close to but disengaged from the court.

Written in chronicle form, the *History of Elizabeth* is, nevertheless, methodologically consistent with the historiography of the *Britannia.* It also marks quite a different literary role for Camden. In 1606 he began his correspondence with Jacques De Thou, who was writing his massive *History of His Own Time* (1604–1608), and the *History of Elizabeth* draws on De Thou's method of close documentation of contemporary history.

Camden was originally encouraged to undertake this commemorative work by Lord Burghley, who supplied him with private documents for the purpose. Around 1608, when it became apparent

that such a record was needed and that no one else was willing to perform it, the project was renewed, with the assistance of Cotton and his library. Camden was encouraged further by James, who was interested in countering the negative view of his mother, Mary, Queen of Scots, that De Thou presents. The history drew Camden and Cotton into a politically sensitive situation in which the king's interference threatened Camden's intellectual integrity. He hastened the first part of the work (up to 1589) to completion, fearing its premature publication. Dedicating the work to Cotton and apostrophizing Truth, Camden acknowledges the sensitivity of its subject. He sent a copy of the completed manuscript to Pierre Dupuy with instructions that it not be translated until after his death.

The work is recognized as a model of the modern, secular political biography, with its awareness of the complex causes of events and its refusal to resort to sententious and providential readings of human affairs. The 1625 English translation, from a French edition by Abraham Darcie, shows how in later years Camden's work fueled the fires of conservatism and the cult of Elizabeth.

In spite of his growing preference for retirement, Camden assumed a place of considerable eminence among the intellectual community of London. After James consented to Matthew Sutcliff's proposal for the establishment of Chelsea College, dedicated to issues of religious policy, Camden was appointed its historian in 1610. However, the last five years of his life were fraught with poor health, and, as Camden wrote to Bishop James Ussher in 1618, he "purposed to sequester" himself "from worldly business and cogitations." His presence gave rigor to the College of Arms and led to the demise of the old school of heralds exemplified by Brooke, and the emergence of the antiquarian scholar-herald such as Dugdale. Apparently there was a move in Camden's last years to buy him out of office, probably because of his reliance on deputies, but this attempt was thwarted, partly through the influence of Cotton and partly through the clearly stated powers of deputation granted to him.

The beneficiary of distinctively Tudor foundations and institutions, Camden repaid his debts to society as a benefactor, in particular to Westminster School, to which he regularly made gifts, and Oxford University. In 1622 he completed the arrangements for establishing the first lectureship in history at Oxford, thus taking his place among patrons helping to reshape the curriculum through endowments of new areas of study. Degory Wheare was the first occupant of the Camden Chair of History. Camden died on 9 November 1623, bequeathing a gift of silver plate to the Painter-Stainers in his father's name. Attended by the members of the College of Arms (except Brooke) and an impressive procession of mourners from all estates, Camden's funeral was an apt reflection of the man who in his prime refused titles and honors and served in letter and deed the principles of meritocracy in the public sphere.

With remarkable consistency Camden has retained a firm and respected place in the wide margins of Elizabethan and Stuart intellectual history. This situation is largely a result of his protective covering as an antiquarian and that discipline's underestimated place in the history of ideas and the political currents of early modern Britain. His originality among British historical writers has rarely been questioned, although specific details of individual works are occasionally challenged — topographical details in the *Britannia* or specifics of his heraldry, for example. Similarly, Camden's influence on poets and historians

has been well established but not thoroughly analyzed. However, as the antiquarian's place in intellectual and political history is reassessed, Camden's understated role in the cultural history of the period also calls for reassessment. In *Of Reformation in England* (1641) John Milton anticipated the direction of modern cultural studies when he recognized that Camden's antiquarianism concealed a profound political commitment — as he saw it, an idolatry of the past that came close to Catholic sympathies. Camden's historiography and influence are clearly well entrenched, but they are also incompletely appreciated. As scholars better understand how antiquarians and literary-historical writers participated in the political dynamic of their culture, Camden's commentators will undoubtedly find that he had a more active role in shaping Elizabethan and Stuart culture than he is currently accorded.

Letters:

V. cl. Gulielmi Camdeni et illustrium Virorum ad G. Camdenum Epistolae, edited by Thomas Smith (London, 1691).

References:

Richard L. DeMolen, "The Library of William Camden," *Proceedings of the American Philosophical Society,* 128 (December 1984): 326–409;

William Huse Dunham, "William Camden's Commonplace Book," *Yale University Library Gazette,* 43 (1969): 139–156;

F. S. Fussner, *The Historical Revolution: English Historical Writing and Thought, 1580–1640* (London: Routledge & Kegan Paul, 1962);

Wyman H. Herendeen, *From Landscape to Literature: The River and the Myth of Geography* (Pittsburgh: Duquesne University Press, 1986);

Herendeen, "'Like a circle bounded in itself ': Jonson, Camden, and the Strategies of Praise," *Journal of Medieval and Renaissance Studies,* 11 (Fall 1981): 137–167;

Herendeen, "Spenserian Specifics: Spenser's Appropriation of a Renaissance Topos," *Medievalia et Humanistica,* new series 10 (1981): 159–188;

Herendeen, "'Wanton discourse and the engines of Time': William Camden — Historian among Poets-Historical," in *Renaissance Rereadings: Intertext & Context,* edited by Maryanne Cline Horowitz, Anne J. Cruz, and Wendy A. Furman (Urbana: University of Illinois Press, 1989), pp. 142–156;

Herendeen, "William Camden: Historian, Herald, and Antiquary," *Studies in Philology,* 85 (Spring 1988): 192–210;

Thomas D. Kendrick, *British Antiquity* (London: Methuen, 1950): 143–165;

F. J. Levy, "The Making of Camden's *Britannia,*" *Bibliothèque d'Humanisme et Renaissance,* 26 (1964): 76–97;

Levy, *Tudor Historical Thought* (San Marino, Cal.: Huntington Library, 1967);

Linda van Norden, "The Elizabethan College of Antiquaries," dissertation, University of California, Los Angeles, 1946;

Stuart Piggott, "William Camden and the *Britannia,*" *Proceedings of the British Academy,* 37 (1951): 199–217;

Maurice Powicke, "William Camden," *Essays and Studies,* new series 1 (1948): 67–84;

Kevin Sharpe, *Sir Robert Cotton, 1586–1631: History and Politics in Early Modern England* (Oxford: Oxford University Press, 1979);

Hugh Trevor-Roper, *Queen Elizabeth's First Historian: William Camden and the Beginnings of English "Civil History"* (London: British Library, 1971);

C. E. Wright, "The Elizabethan Society of Antiquaries and the Formation of the Cottonian Library," in *The English Library before 1700,* edited by Francis Wormald and C. E. Wright (London: Athlone Press, 1958), pp. 177–197.

Papers:

There are many surviving collections of papers by and relating to Camden, some of the most important of which are at the Beinecke Library, Yale University (Ms. 370), the Bodleian Library, University of Oxford (Mss. C.7.2. Art; Ashmolean 846; Douce 68; Rawlinson B.70; Smith 1, 2, 18, 19, and 74), and the British Library (Mss. Add. 5408; 36,294; Cotton Cleo. E.i.; Jul. F.vi.; Faust. E.i.; Titus F. VII–VIII).

Thomas Campion

(12 February 1567 – 1 March 1620)

Elise Bickford Jorgens
Western Michigan University

See also the Campion entry in *DLB 58: Jacobean and Caroline Dramatists.*

BOOKS: *Thomae Campiani Poemata. Ad Thamesin. Fragmentum Umbra. Liber Elegiarum. Liber Epigrammatum* (London: R. Field, 1595);

Observations in the Art of English Poesie (London: Printed by R. Field for A. Wise, 1602);

The Discription of a Maske, Presented before the Kinges Majestie at White-Hall, on Twelfth Night Last, in Honour of the Lord Hayes (London: Printed by J. Windet for J. Brown, 1607);

A New Way of Making Fowre Parts in Counter-point, by a Most familiar, and Infallible Rule. Secondly, a Necessary Discourse of Keyes, and Their Proper Closes. Thirdly, the Allowed Passages of All Concords Perfect, or Imperfect, Are Declared. Also by Way of Preface, the Nature of the Scale Is Expressed, with a Briefe Method Teaching to Sing (London: Printed by T. Snodham for J. Browne, circa 1610); reprinted in *A Brief Introduction To the Skill of Musick. In Two Books. . . . The Third Edition Enlarged. To Which Is Added a Third Book Entituled, The Art of Descant, or Composing Musick in Parts, By Dr. Tho. Campion. With Annotations thereon by Mr. Chr. Simpson,* by John Playford (London, 1660);

A Relation of the Late Royall Entertainment Given by the Right Honorable the Lord Knowles. . . . Whereunto Is Annexed the Description, Speeches and Songs of the Lords Maske (London: Printed by W. Stansby for J. Budge, 1613);

Two Bookes of Ayres. The First Contayning Divine and Morall Songs: The Second, Light Conceits of Lovers (London: Printed by T. Snodham for M. Lownes & J. Browne, circa 1613);

Songs of Mourning: Bewailing the Untimely Death of Prince Henry. Worded by Tho. Campion. And Set Forth to Bee Sung with One Voyce to the Lute, or Violl: by John Coprario (London: Printed by T. Snodham for J. Browne, 1613);

The Description of a Maske: Presented in the Banqueting Roome at Whitehall, on Saint Stephens Night Last, At the Mariage of the Right Honourable the Earle of Somerset (London: Printed by E. Allde & T. Snodham for L. Lisle, 1614);

The Third and Fourth Booke of Ayres (London: T. Snodham, circa 1617);

Tho. Campiani Epigrammatum Libri II. Umbra. Elegiarum liber unus (London: E. Griffin, 1619).

Editions: *Campion's Works,* edited by Percival Vivian (Oxford: Clarendon Press, 1909; reprinted 1966);

Songs from Rosseter's Book of Airs, edited by E. H. Fellowes, English School of Lutenist Song Writers, second series, nos. 4 & 13 (London: Stainer & Bell, 1922);

First Book of Airs, edited by Fellowes, English School of Lutenist Song Writers, second series 1 (London: Stainer & Bell, 1925);

Second Book of Airs, edited by Fellowes, English School of Lutenist Song Writers, second series 2 (London: Stainer & Bell, 1925);

Third Book of Ayres, edited by Fellowes, English School of Lutenist Song Writers, second series 10 (London: Stainer & Bell, 1926);

Fourth Booke of Ayres, edited by Fellowes, English School of Lutenist Song Writers, second series 11 (London: Stainer & Bell, 1926);

The Works of Thomas Campion, edited by Walter R. Davis (New York: Doubleday 1967; London: Faber & Faber, 1969);

Four Hundred Songs and Dances from the Stuart Masque: With a Supplement of Sixteen Additional Pieces, edited by Andrew J. Sabol (Providence, R.I.: Brown University Press, 1978; London: University Press of New England, 1982).

OTHER: "Poems and Sonets of Sundrie Other Noblemen and Gentlemen," in *Astrophil and Stella,* by Sir Philip Sidney (London: Thomas Newman, 1591) – includes Campion's "Harke, All You Ladies that Doo Sleepe";

"What Faire Pompe Have I Spide of Glittering Ladies"; "My Love Bound Me with a Kisse"; "Love Whets the Dullest Wittes, His Plagues Be Such"; and "A Daie, a Night, an Houre of Sweete Content";

A Booke of Ayres. Set Forth to Be Song to the Lute, Orpherian, and Base Violl, by Philip Rosseter Lutenist (London: P. Short, 1601) – includes 21 poems and a preface by Campion.

Thomas Campion's importance for non-dramatic literature of the English Renaissance lies in the exceptional intimacy of the musical-poetic connection in his work. While other poets and musicians talked about the union of the two arts, only Campion produced complete songs wholly of his own composition, and only he wrote lyric poetry of enduring literary value whose very construction is deeply etched with the poet's care for its ultimate fusion with music. The development of this composite art was Campion's lifelong project, which made a modest but lasting impression on the modern assessment of the nature of lyric poetry in England in the last decade of the sixteenth century and the first two decades of the seventeenth. A practicing physician in his later years, Campion occupied a curious place somewhere between the well-trained courtly amateur and the professional craftsman in poetry, music, and drama – particularly the masque. Although he did not earn his livelihood as a musician nor rely on favor garnered through the system of literary patronage, he did seek the recognition of print and the remuneration of the professional craftsman at court. He produced an accomplished oeuvre in both poetry and music (mostly in the form of songs for which he provided both lyrics and musical settings), and he wrote treatises on both arts. His *Observations in the Art of English Poesie* (1602) and *A New Way of Making Four Parts in Counterpoint* (circa 1610) are conservative works, drawing extensively on earlier authors, yet both treatises and the songs they support offer startling innovations as well, and the musical treatise continued to appear – incorporated without acknowledgment into John Playford's *Brief Introduction to the Skill of Music* (1660) – throughout the seventeenth century.

Born on 12 February 1567, Thomas Campion was the second child of John and Lucy Campion; a sister, Rose, preceded him by two years. His early family life was complicated by the vicissitudes of living in a time of shorter life expectancy than that of the present day: Lucy Campion was a widow with a young daughter, Mary, at the time of her

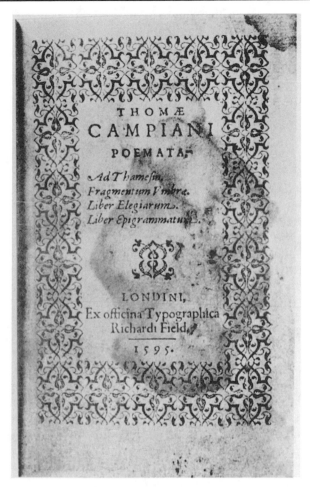

Title page for Thomas Campion's first book, a collection of Neo-Latin poetry

marriage to Thomas's father, John, making Thomas the third child in the household. When John died in October 1576, Lucy married a third time in August 1577, and then died in March 1580, leaving at least Rose and Thomas in the guardianship of their stepfather, Augustine Steward. When Steward also remarried in 1581, Thomas, then fourteen, and his new stepbrother were sent away to Cambridge, apparently not even returning home for vacations.

Campion left Peterhouse, Cambridge, in 1584. Although he did not take a degree, the three years he spent at Cambridge must have been significant for the acquaintances he would have made: Abraham Fraunce, Gabriel Harvey, and Thomas Nashe were all at Cambridge during Campion's years in residence. In 1586 he made an even more decisive move for the direction he was to take, enrolling at Gray's Inn, a law school more celebrated for its development of the artistic tastes and talents of the young men who entered than for its rigorous legal training. At Gray's Inn, Campion made many friends, including the poet Francis Davison, and performed in plays and masques.

From that point on, as Campion's adult life was taking shape, the known facts are few and details are vague. He left Gray's Inn probably sometime around 1594, and eventually his references to people from other parts of the city make clear that he had moved to St. Dunstan's-in-the-West, where other musicians lived. He may have been with Essex in the siege on Rouen in 1591; he described the actions of the cowardly Barnabe Barnes during this siege in his Latin poem *In Barnum* (1619). He went to the University of Caen in 1602, studied medicine, and took up a medical practice in London at the age of nearly forty; Walter R. Davis, in *Thomas Campion* (1987), suggests that this was a practical course, since the £260 his mother had left in trust for him had run out, forcing him to find a way to earn a living.

Evidence is more plentiful of the lifelong enterprise for which Campion is known today: his published literary and musical works and the two treatises devoted to these arts. These begin, appropriately, with five songs probably written for incorporation into a masque. They appeared in 1591 in a pirated edition of Sir Philip Sidney's sonnet sequence *Astrophil and Stella* published by Thomas Newman. Attributed to "Content," the five lyrics can be ascribed to Campion with good assurance, as the first reappeared in the *Book of Ayres* (1601) and the third and fourth were translated to Latin epigrams in his *Liber Epigrammatum* (1595). Sidney's influence is evident, particularly in the second poem, which is written in rhymed Asclepiadics following Sidney's "O Sweet Woods the Delight of Solitariness," and in the fifth, which mimics several devices found in Sidney's experimental lyrics in *Arcadia* (1590, 1593). While these are youthful and derivative poems, they point decisively toward the hallmarks of Campion's later style, with careful attention to the pacing of words and syllables, the disposition of a few polysyllabic words in the context of a line made up of the monosyllables he noted as frequent in the English tongue, and the fine-tuning of the succession of vowel sounds within the line. Clearly his interest in these musical details was present from his earliest attempts.

Campion's next published work was in Latin, *Thomae Campiani Poemata* (1595), and included the incomplete epic "Ad Thamesin," celebrating the defeat of the Spanish Armada; part of a long Ovidian poem, "Fragmentum Umbra"; sixteen elegies; and 129 epigrams. While Latin titles begin and end the list of Campion's oeuvre, and the Latin poems

make up nearly a third of his published work, much of the later collection is revision or completion of the poems begun in this 1595 collection. Thus, *Tho. Campiani Epigrammatum Libri II* (1619) includes the completed *Umbra* and revised versions of eleven of the elegies plus two additional elegies; "Ad Thamesin" is dropped.

The one portion of the earlier Latin collection that is significantly continued up to the printing of the later volume is the epigrams; their number reaches 453 by the time of the final publication. Like the other Latin poems, the epigrams are fashionable, the sorts of things all young poets wrote. They are clearly derived from Roman models as well as earlier Renaissance poets. They are important in Campion's development, however, for the sharp attention they focus on character and subject. It seems likely that the epigrams engaged the poet's thinking throughout his career, honing his ability to distill portraits of people and descriptions of things and events into a few short but precise lines and sharpening his skill with the aphoristic turn that characterizes much of his work. These traits take on significance in the more graceful English lyrics he set as songs; indeed, Campion himself drew the connection, announcing in the preface to *A Book of Ayres*, "What epigrams are in poetry, the same are ayres in music, then in their chief perfection when they are short and well seasoned."

The point at which Campion turned from being what Davis calls "a coterie poet in Latin" to a writer of English lyrics for music is hard to determine. By 1597, however, he had apparently begun to be associated with the chief players in the development of the English lute song, for he contributed a dedicatory poem to John Dowland's *First Book of Songs or Ayres* in that year. This collection was not only Dowland's first, but the first English publication in what was to be a favored genre for the next two decades, celebrated then and now for its careful attention to the union of music and poetry.

Campion's entry into the field came in 1601 with the publication of Philip Rosseter's *Book of Ayres*. By 1604 Rosseter was the king's lutenist and remained active in court entertainment throughout most of King James's reign. He was Campion's best friend and the sole inheritor named in Campion's will. It is fair to say, however, that little would be known of Rosseter today had he not collaborated with Campion in this collection. The book was presented for publication by Rosseter, and it was he who wrote the dedication to Campion's friend and supporter Sir Thomas Monson, but Campion contributed the first twenty-one songs and is almost certainly the author of the brief but groundbreaking treatise on song presented as an address "To the Reader."

As already noted, Campion's prefatory remarks to *A Book of Ayres* introduce the comparison of the ayre, or solo song, to the epigram, suggesting both brevity and simple, straightforward delivery as the desirable characteristics. He objects to "many rests in music," proclaiming, "in ayres I find no use they have, unless it be to make a vulgar and trivial modulation seem to the ignorant strange, and to the judicial tedious." He argues against the fashionable madrigal, which he describes as "long, intricate, bated with fugue, chained with syncopation, and where the nature of every word is precisely expressed in the note." His own songs, by contrast, he describes as "ear-pleasing rhymes without art," and he declares that "we ought to maintain as well in notes, as in action, a manly carriage, gracing no word but that which is eminent and emphatical." Davis, in the introduction to *A Book of Ayres* in his 1967 edition of Campion's works, refers to this document as a manifesto — an apt word, for the songs in this book are presented simply, with a single treble vocal part and a relatively unadorned lute accompaniment with a bass line for viola da gamba, thus looking forward to the continuo song that would gain favor in England by the 1630s.

Campion's poems in *A Book of Ayres* include some of his best-known compositions and present the essence of his contribution to the lyric genre: the aphoristic "Though You Are Young and I Am Old"; "I Care Not for These Ladies," with its artfully simple portrait of "kind Amarillis / The wanton country maid"; the celebration of intellectual beauty in "Mistress, since you so much desire / To know the place of Cupid's fire" (to be parodied in his earthier version, "Beauty, Since You So Much Desire," published later in *The Fourth Book,* 1617); "Come, Let Us Sound with Melody," the only instance of classical quantitative meter (Sapphic) that Campion rendered musically in the manner of the French *musique mesurée*. While the later books would present some wonderful new songs and some refinements of the features exhibited in this first collection, they would introduce no radical new techniques or striking developments. In 1601 Campion was nearly thirty-five years old, and despite the paucity of earlier publication he seems to have arrived at his own mature understanding of the kind of art he would produce. Its most significant hallmarks are the formal properties associated with music noted above. But in substance, too, the mature Campion is already present. He is a keen ob-

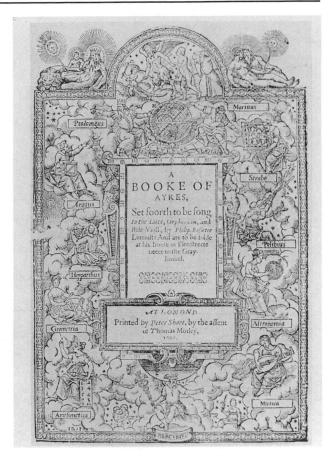

Title page for Campion's collaboration with composer Philip Rosseter, the poet's first effort as a musical lyricist

server of human frailty, particularly that brought on by the conflicts of love and sexuality. He is also a moralist. Although it would be difficult to abstract a single, consistent moral code from these lyrics, Campion does not hesitate to offer his vision of what is proper. While religious lyrics do not form a prominent part of this collection, the piety of "The Man of Life Upright" or "Come, Let Us Sound" is conventional, and in both sacred and secular veins Campion's epigrammatic turn to the timeless aphorism is notable.

What is new in the 1601 *Book of Ayres* is the overt connection with music, both in performance and in its impact on the nature of poetry. The analyst who seeks examples of how Campion's music represents text in these songs is oddly stymied. There are occasional instances of word painting, and the rhythmic and metrical interaction of music and poetry bears close observation, but it is the fusion of the two elements in the best songs that is striking, affecting the reader-listener with the sense that a musical declamation was in the poet's ear from the start. In this and in Campion's espousal of

OBSERVATIONS
in the Art of English
Poesie.

By *Thomas Campion*.

Wherein it is demonstra-
tively prooued, and by example
confirmed, that the English toong
will receiue eight seuerall kinds of num-
bers, proper to it selfe, which are all
in this booke set forth, and were
neuer before this time by any
man attempted.

Printed at London by RICHARD FIELD
for *Andrew Wise.* 1602.

Title page for Campion's treatise on poetic meter

the principle of quantitative meters for an English poetry, there is a relation to the experiments called musique mesurée practiced in France by the group known as the Pléiade. Yet in Campion's best poetry the stiffness and artificiality of the French experiments yield to a supple, musical handling of the sounds of words that bespeaks much more than theory alone.

One of the tantalizing gaps in Campion's biography occurs around the question of his musical training. Some have speculated that Campion learned music from his new friends Dowland and Rosseter in the late 1590s, and it is sometimes suggested that Rosseter helped him with the musical settings for his contributions to *A Book of Ayres* (as it has also sometimes been assumed that Campion provided the texts for Rosseter's half, although Davis rejects this hypothesis). On the other hand, the musical settings of all of Campion's songs merge so well with their texts as to create a medium that does not readily admit of division into separable components. In the absence of clear knowledge that,

for instance, Campion did not play the lute, it seems reasonable to take him at his word and acknowledge the settings as his representations of his theories about the new medium of the ayre.

In the year after *A Book of Ayres* Campion published his manifesto on poetry, *Observations in the Art of English Poesie*. His intent is stated on the title page of the book: "Wherein it is demonstratively proved and by example confirmed that the English tongue will receive eight several kinds of numbers, proper to itself, which are all in this book set forth and were never before this time by any man attempted." Following in the direction indicated by Sidney and taken up in the famous correspondence between Edmund Spenser and Gabriel Harvey, Campion embarks on a defense of quantitative meters in English, illustrating each with an example of his own composing. His singular contribution to this short-lived movement lay in his eschewing the notion that a classical ideal could be recaptured by imposing classical rules of scansion on English poetry. Instead, Campion set out to align the quantity of the classical meters with the natural stress patterns of English. In the final chapter of the treatise – "The Tenth Chapter, of the Quantity of English Syllables" – he begins the "rules of position" with the observation that "above all the accent of our words is diligently to be observed, for chiefly by the accent in any language the true value of the syllables is to be measured. . . . Wherefore the first rule that is to be observed is the nature of the accent, which we must ever follow."

There can be no doubt that Campion's writing of this treatise grew out of his interest in the associations of music and poetry as much as from his admiration and emulation of Sidney. On the first page he refers to the organization of syllables in terms of "the length and shortness of their sound" and continues by comparing poetry with music. "The Eighth Chapter, of Ditties and Odes" brings the connection full circle; here the author notes that "it is now time to handle such verses as are fit for *ditties* or *odes,* which we may call *lyrical,* because they are apt to be sung to an instrument, if they were adorned with convenient notes."

The most controversial feature of the *Observations* was the second chapter "declaring the unaptness of rhyme in poesie." Rhyme, Campion noted, is a rhetorical figure of the category *figura verbi,* having only a surface appeal, and ought "sparingly to be used, lest it should offend the ear with tedious affection." He refers later to "the childish titillation of rhyming" and comments that "there is yet another fault in rhyme altogether intolerable, which is that it enforceth a man oftentimes to abjure his matter and extend a short conceit beyond all bounds of art." As the lyric poets of the day were regular users of rhyme, it is not surprising that Campion offended many in declaring that "the facility and popularity of rhyme creates as many poets as a hot summer flies." The *Observations* did not go unremarked, prompting Samuel Daniel's 1603 rejoinder, *A Defense of Rhyme,* in which Daniel points out that Campion's quantitative meters are not new. But the treatise does offer theoretical insight into the particular kind of care about words that drove this poet-composer.

Sometime during the year of the publication of the *Observations,* Campion went to France, embarking at the age of thirty-eight on a course of medical studies at the University of Caen in Normandy, a reputable but not distinguished medical school in a university better known for its poetry contests. Three years later, with medical degree in hand, he returned to London to set up practice. Again little is known about this aspect of the poet's life. His ear-

lier friend and supporter Sir Thomas Monson became his patient, as is recorded in accounts of their implication in the Sir Thomas Overbury murder in 1613, but otherwise the record is silent on his medical practice, noting instead his continued involvement in the world of literature and music.

Edward Lowbury, Timothy Salter, and Alison Young, the authors of *Thomas Campion: Poet, Composer, Physician* (1970), have attempted to see an influence from Campion's medical practice on his poetry, but the evidence is sparse. In the final chapter of the book, they note that images of wounds and healing are relatively frequent and that while pain and death are common subjects for poets, in Campion's poetry they are presented in an almost clinical manner. They conclude, however, that while images of disease, healing and death or, more profoundly, those of human frailty and suffering could result from Campion's study and practice of medicine, it would be difficult to deduce from the poems alone that the poet was also a physician.

In any event, Campion's medical practice does not seem to have interfered with his artistic career as he moved into the world of courtly entertainment with *Lord Hay's Masque* (1607). This work, commissioned by James's court for the marriage of James Hay, one of the king's favorites, to Honora Denny, the daughter of one of James's early supporters, was the first of three masques for which Campion provided the libretti; the other two, both performed in 1613, were for even more important weddings, those of the Princess Elizabeth to Frederick Count Palatine (*The Lord's Masque,* 1613), and of Robert Carr, the Earl of Somerset and James's new favorite, to Lady Frances Howard, whose earlier marriage to the earl of Essex had been annulled (*The Squire's Masque* or *The Somerset Masque,* 1614).

With these masques Campion moved into the center of the country's artistic elite; he was composing for the royal court and enjoyed the advantages of increased prestige and visibility and of the lavish expenditures with which James indulged his taste for luxury. The masque had become a highly politicized form of entertainment used by the king to reinforce his role and status. It was also the occasion for spending large sums of money for the best and the latest that money could buy in costume, in sets and stage design and machinery, and in music and dance, putting Campion in direct contact with the leading designers, dancers, and musicians and, significantly, with other composers who would set his libretti. Thus, while Campion's masques have an important place in the dramatic literature of the period, they are also significant for their impact on his continued nondramatic output in the form of additional volumes of songs, many of which bear the traces of composers associated with the masque such as Nicholas Lanier and the Italianized Englishman Giovanni Coperario, as well as some working in the more native English traditions.

In November 1612 England was shocked by the death of Prince Henry. With the *Songs of Mourning: Bewailing the Untimely Death of Prince Henry* (1613), Campion contributed to the outpouring of elegies occasioned by the death of the young heir. The musical settings for these songs were composed not by Campion but by Coperario. Little documentary information exists about the nature of this collaboration, but as these poems are different in significant ways from Campion's other work, it seems likely that the musical connection with Coperario effected some changes in Campion's creative process. The poems are addressed to members of the royal family, to "the Most Disconsolate Great Britain," and finally to the world, and they seek to confront the particular states of anguish that these various constituencies might be expected to feel in the face of the young prince's death. They have neither the aphoristic certainty nor the witty perspicacity of the best of Campion's lyrics, but seem instead heavy and contrived. More tellingly, the formal properties of these poems lack the grace and classical balance of his better lyrics. In the third song, "Fortune and Glory May Be Lost and Won," for instance, the eleven lines of varying lengths that make up the stanza suggest the Italian madrigal form rather than Campion's more characteristic rhymed, balladlike stanzas. The rhythm of the lines is also less finely honed, and one does not hear the delicate movement of vowels and space for consonants that he perfected in other works. His collaboration with Nicholas Lanier in "Bring Away This Sacred Tree" for *The Squire's Masque* in 1614 may have involved Campion's writing a parody or *contrafactum* to Lanier's already-existing music. Perhaps these songs are also *contrafacta,* assembled quickly for the immediate purpose of lamenting the country's tragic loss.

Campion's remaining songbooks were published in pairs and were clearly ascribed to him, without the mediating presence of a Rosseter. *Two Books of Ayres* (circa 1613) presents, according to the author, a retrospective collection, containing "a few" songs out of many "which, partly at the request of friends, partly for my own recreation, were by me long since composed." This characteristic amateur posture of the age is probably also an accurate representation of Campion's activity as a poet

and composer. The book was published without date, but internal evidence suggests that it was sometime around 1612 or 1613, more than a decade after the previous collection in collaboration with Rosseter. One of its lyrics, "Though Your Strangeness Frets My Heart," had obviously been in circulation prior to this date, for another composer, Robert Jones, used it as a text for his own song, published in his collection *A Musical Dream* (1609).

The best-known songs in the 1613 books are notable for precisely the features that characterize all of Campion's work. "Never Weather-Beaten Sail," for example, illustrates the intricate and careful creation of musical and verbal rhythm out of the accentual pattern of the words and the sensitive distribution of the vowel sounds. This song also epitomizes the sense one frequently has with Campion that the sacred and the secular are not far apart — a sense reinforced by the almost erotic urgency of both music and words in the last line: "O come quickly, sweetest Lord, and take my soul to rest."

The musical treatise, *A New Way of Making Four Parts in Counterpoint,* was also published around this time, most likely around 1610. It is primarily a summary of the rules of counterpoint as set down by the sixteenth-century German musical theorist Sethus Calvisius. For musical historians the most important feature of Campion's document is its insistence on the importance of the bass line rather than the tenor as the foundation of harmony, an essential development in the advent of the new baroque styles in music.

The final song book, *The Third and Fourth Book of Ayres,* published sometime after February 1617, is again at least in part a retrospective collection. The two books are dedicated respectively to Sir Thomas Monson, referring to his recent release from prison, and his son, John Monson. Several songs in the third book especially have a world-weariness about them, as if their author had experienced disillusion and disaffection ("Why Presumes Thy Pride" or "O Grief, O Spite"). The best, however, are expansive lyrics celebrating the better times ("Now Winter Nights Enlarge") and the perpetual joys and frustrations of love ("Kind Are Her Answers," "Shall I Come, Sweet Love, to Thee?," or, in the fourth book, "I Must Complain").

Campion's implication in the sordid events surrounding the murder of Sir Thomas Overbury rate discussion, as they span the years from 1613 to 1617 and must have had a profound impact on Campion during that time. The confusing series of events was prompted by Overbury's overt opposition to the marriage of Robert Carr and Frances

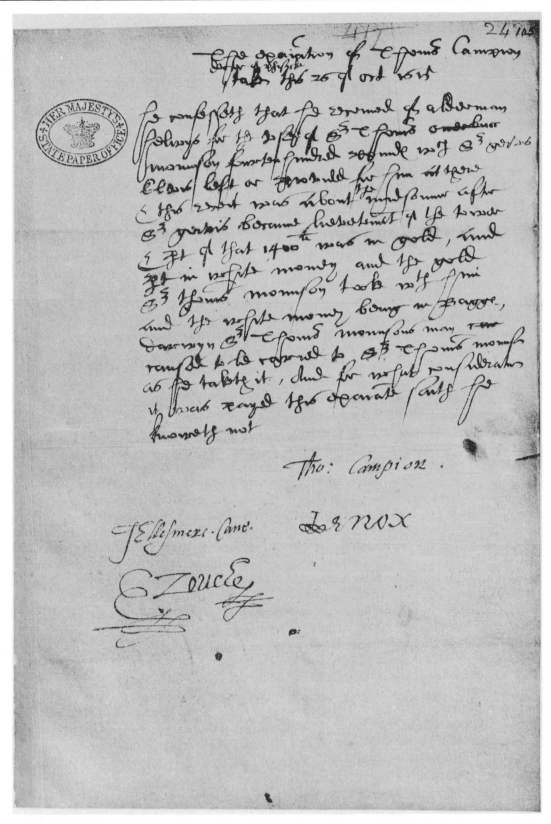

*Minutes of the 26 October 1615 examination of Campion in the case of Sir Thomas Overbury's murder, signed
by Campion and the examiners (Her Majesty's State Paper Office, S. P. Dom. James I. lxxxii)*

Howard (for which Campion wrote *The Squire's Masque*). Carr and Lady Frances had sufficient influence that they were able to get Overbury imprisoned and eventually poisoned. Campion's friend Sir Thomas Monson was implicated because of his association with the Howards and his involvement in selling the office of Lieutenant of the Tower of London to Sir Jervis Elwes, who assisted Carr and Lady Frances in accomplishing the murder. Campion was implicated because, as Monson's friend and physician, he unwittingly transported the money for the sale of the office from Elwes to Monson. Carr and Frances were eventually convicted of the crime and imprisoned in the Tower of London until 1622; Elwes and two other accomplices were hanged. Monson and Campion were both acquitted, having persuaded the justices that neither of them knew of the plot to poison Overbury, although Monson was confined to the Tower from October 1615 until February 1617 while the case was being investigated. Campion, as Monson's physician, was allowed to visit him under the supervision of the new lieutenant. The dedication for *The Third and Fourth Book of Ayres,* addressed to Monson, refers to Monson's having finally gained his freedom, and the tone of the poem is celebratory. Nevertheless, the protracted episode almost certainly had a permanent impact on Campion.

Thomas Campion died on 1 March 1620, at age fifty-two. He was buried on the day of his death at St. Dunstan's-in-the-West, Fleet Street. He had never married, and although he had carved an important place for himself in the musical and literary world of James's court, he cannot be said to have been a success, at least not by late-twentieth-century standards. With six collections of songs in print, three masques presented at court and their descriptions published, and an apparently adequate midlife career as a physician, Campion was able to leave only twenty-three pounds to his longtime friend and collaborator, Philip Rosseter. There is no record of any more musical or English literary work after 1617, and as noted above, the 1619 collection of Latin verse contains considerable reprinting of the 1595 collection. Even though the outcome of the Monson-Overbury scandal was positive for Campion and his friend Monson, it seems likely that these events prompted his withdrawal from the glittering world of courtly flattery and intrigue.

Throughout his career and for some years after his death, Campion's poetry appeared regularly in manuscript commonplace books, both literary and musical. These books document another kind of fame than the poet's movement in the court's entertainment world, showing instead a broad appeal in those literary circles where poetry was read and admired. Campion's poems appear in these household collections beginning in the early 1590s and continuing sporadically throughout the seventeenth century. In assessing Campion's unique contribution to the musical lyric of his day, it is also useful to recognize that his poems were frequently chosen by other composers as texts for their songs.

In the nondramatic literature of the late Renaissance, Campion's contribution holds an ambiguous position. He was neglected for almost two hundred years, but in the late 1800s he was rediscovered by A. H. Bullen, who published the first collected edition and started a resurgence of interest and admiration that would include T. S. Eliot and Ezra Pound. In *The Use of Poetry and the Use of Criticism* (1933) Eliot calls Campion, "except for Shakespeare . . . the most accomplished master of rhymed lyric of his time." His lyrics and the songs in which he presented them strongly reflect his period's style, and Davis finds Campion's influence in the works of such poets as Pound, W. H. Auden, and Robert Creeley. Campion has been called a poet of the ear, and his careful respect for the nature of the language and its capacities for pleasing intonation was a significant development. Yet although his poems continue to be anthologized, they represent a refinement of the sixteenth-century lyric rather than a departure and did not offer as much to a new generation as, say, John Donne's bold innovations did. For the literary historian, then, his poems remain beautiful miniatures, revered for their intrinsic worth more than for their significance.

In current critical debates, Campion's art is on the fringes. The gentle sarcasm of the more epigrammatic lyrics offers some pictures of the age, and some (such as "Though You Are Young and I Am Old") present themselves as timeless aphorisms. Critics interested in gender studies will find a full range of the period's gender clichés, from the heartless and fickle women to the dismissive or broken-hearted lovers. But the important formal properties of his style are of little interest to cultural criticism.

References:

Walter R. Davis, *Thomas Campion* (Boston: Twayne, 1987);

Edward Doughtie, *English Renaissance Song* (Boston: Twayne, 1986);

Doughtie, "Sibling Rivalry: Music *vs.* Poetry in Campion and Others," *Criticism,* 20 (1978): 1–16;

Martha Feldman, "In Defense of Campion: A New Look at His *Ayres* and *Observations," Journal of Musicology,* 5 (Spring 1987): 226–256;

Elise Bickford Jorgens, *The Well-Tun'd Word: Musical Interpretations of English Poetry, 1597–1651* (Minneapolis: University of Minnesota Press, 1982);

David Lindley, *Thomas Campion* (Leiden: E. J. Brill, 1986);

Edward Lowbury, Timothy Salter, and Alison Young, *Thomas Campion: Poet, Composer, Physician* (New York: Barnes & Noble, 1970);

Winifred Maynard, *Elizabethan Lyric Poetry and Its Music* (Oxford: Clarendon Press, 1986);

Stephen Ratcliffe, *Campion: On Song* (Boston & London: Routledge & Kegan Paul, 1981);

David A. Richardson, "The Golden Mean in Campion's Airs," *Comparative Literature,* 30 (Spring 1978): 108–132;

Louise Schleiner, *The Living Lyre in English Verse from Elizabeth through the Restoration* (Columbia: University of Missouri Press, 1984), pp. 4–45;

Ian Spink, *English Song: Dowland to Purcell* (London: B. T. Batsford, 1974), pp. 15–37.

Papers:

The principal sources of manuscript copies of the poems and songs are the British Library; the Bodleian Library, Oxford; Christ Church College Library, Oxford; the Fitzwilliam Museum, Cambridge; the Edinburgh University Library; the National Library of Scotland, Edinburgh; Trinity College Library, Dublin; and the New York Public Library.

Thomas Coryate
(1577 or 1579 – December 1617)

Raymond-Jean Frontain
University of Central Arkansas

See also the Coryate entry in *DLB 151: British Prose Writers of the Early Seventeenth Century.*

BOOKS: *Coryats Crudities. Hastily Gobled up in Five Moneths Travells in France, Savoy, [etc. With 2 Orations] (by H. Kirchnerus, in Praise of Travell. [And] the Posthume [Latin] Poems of the Authors Father. – G. Coryate.)* (London: Printed by William Stansby for the author, 1611);

Coryats Crambe, or His Colwort Twise Sodden, and Now Served as the Second Course to His Crudities (London: William Stansby, 1611);

Thomas Coriate Traveller for the English Wits: Greeting. From the Court of the Great Mogul (London: W. Jaggard & Henry Fetherston, 1616); republished as *Thomas Coryate, Traveller for the English Wits, and the Good of This Kingdom* (London: W. Jaggard & Henry Fetherston, 1616);

Mr. Thomas Coriat to His Friends in England Sendeth Greeting: from Agra in the Easterne India, the Last of October, 1616 (London: John Beale, 1617).

Editions: *Coryate's Crudities; Reprinted from the Edition of 1611. To Which Are Now Added, His Letters from India, &c. and Extracts Relating to Him, from Various Authors: Being a More Particular Account of His Travels (Mostly on Foot) in Different Parts of the Globe, Than Any Hitherto Published. Together with His Orations, Character, Death, &c.,* 3 volumes (London: Printed for W. Cater, Samuel Hayes & J. Wilkie, 1776);

Coryate's Crudities Hastily Gobbled Up in Five Months Travels etc., 2 volumes (Glasgow: James MacLehose, 1905);

Coryate's Crudities (1611) (London: Scolar, 1978).

OTHER: "Master Thomas Coryate's Travels to and Observations in Constantinople and Other Places in the Way Thither, and His Journey Thence to Aleppo, Damascus and Jerusalem," in *Purchas His Pilgrimage. Or Relations of the World and the Religions Observed in All Ages,* fourth edition, by Samuel Purchas (London:

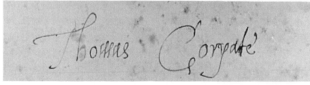

Printed by W. Stansby for Henry Fetherston, 1626), pp. 1811–1831.

Thomas Coryate, the self-proclaimed "Peregrine of Odcombe" or "Odcombian Leg-stretcher," was renowned in his day first for having toured Europe largely on foot and, afterward, for traveling through the lands of classical and biblical antiquity and portions of the Ottoman Empire and visiting the court of the Great Mogul before dying in India at around age forty. Through his books, letters, and orations he was a tireless self-promoter, so laboriously fashioning for himself the image of the learned wit that he was as often the butt of jokes as the author of them. Coryate is best understood, however, as a comic or bourgeois Faustus: a tireless inquisitor whose pride in his investigations is tempered by his own self-mocking humor or undercut by the oftentimes pedestrian nature of his interests.

Despite contradictory evidence, Coryate was probably born in Odcombe, Somerset, sometime between 25 June and 29 September in either 1577 or 1579. He was the only son of the Reverend George Coryate, the village rector, and his wife, Gertrude. In 1594 he entered Winchester College, Oxford, where his father had studied as a youth. Later, as a commoner in Gloucester Hall (now Exeter College), he studied logic and rhetoric as well as the Greek and Latin authors he quoted liberally and with evident pride in the orations he delighted in making throughout his adult life.

Coryate seems to have been at Oxford for about three years. His leaving without taking a degree may signify nothing more than his deciding not to take holy orders. He was at home at Odcombe in 1606, when, as he reports in *Coryate's Crambe* (1611), the local churchwardens and other "friends of the parish . . . solicited me to set abroad my wits and invent some conceited and plausible matter" that might help replenish the church's exhausted funds. He organized a mock battle between a muster of one hundred of his parish's men and "two cohorts" of "Oppidanes" from the neighboring town of Yeovil, which concluded with a skirmish in the town square before an audience of about two thousand locals. To round off the day's festivities, Coryate justified the fantastic revelry in the first of many orations. Confessing that "drunkenness, gluttony, swearing, lasciviousness," and other sins "seem to be the inseparable accidents and individual adjuncts of Church-ales," he argued that when conducted soberly — as clearly he assumed theirs had been — such festivals are valuable, "first for the breeding of love betwixt neighbors, and secondly, for the raising of a stock for the supporting and maintenance of our Church, and the Church affairs." His apologia is not only an early defense of the holiday pastimes that thrived under Elizabeth and were coming increasingly under attack by Puritan factions during Coryate's day, but it is also an excellent example of the festive spirit that characterizes nearly all of Coryate's activities and writings.

George Coryate's death on 4 March 1607 necessitated the family's removal from the parsonage. Presumably at this time Thomas Coryate left Odcombe for London, where he seems to have enjoyed the patronage of two members of his godfather's family: Sir Edward Phelips, the builder of Montacute House, which Coryate would, with obvious affection, compare favorably with the best examples of continental architecture; and Sir Robert Phelips, Edward's son and one of the gentlemen of the Privy Chamber extraordinary to Prince Henry. Thomas Fuller reports that Henry gave Coryate a pension and employed him as a servant. This role may have been that of a sort of unofficial court jester.

Between 1606 and 1612 Coryate was regularly in the company of a group of witty intellectuals who gathered at the Mermaid Tavern: Ben Jonson, John Donne, Inigo Jones, Richard Martin, Hugh Holland, Lionel Cranfield, and Laurence Whitaker. Not only would they supply mock-commendatory verses for *Coryate's Crudities* (1611) when it was published, but Coryate's open letters to the group "from the Court of the Great Mogul" and "from Agra" supply two of the surviving records of his activities during the last years of his life, as well as the only conclusive evidence of the Mermaid Tavern gatherings.

On 14 May 1608 Coryate began the journey that would make him famous. After embarking from Dover, he traveled through France and northern Italy to Venice, where he remained just over six weeks, then back again through Switzerland, the Rhine Valley, and the Low Countries, returning to London on 3 October. He estimated that he traveled a total of 1,975 miles, mostly on foot. The resulting narrative, which he published in 1611, is an extraordinary mixture of energetic personal experience, sharp social observation, religious polemic, architectural description, and humanist fascination with monuments and their inscriptions. Recalling its Tudor precedents, it is a striking cross between John Leland's narrative of his journeys as King's Antiquary in *The Laborious Journey and Search* (1549), Thomas Hoby's description of European cities and of his travels from one to another in *A Book of the Travels and Life of Me* (1547–1564), and Will Kemp's madcap *Nine Days Wonder* (1600). A "second course" to *Coryate's Crudities* appeared later the same year, in which Coryate published the text of the orations he had delivered while on his travels, as well as additional commendations from English literati.

Coryate's trip to Venice was but a dry run for a more ambitious tour. On 20 October 1612 he set out to visit the lands of Greek and biblical antiquity, traveling by merchant ship through the Bay of Biscay and across the Mediterranean, arriving at the

Title page for Coryate's account of his European travels

wealth in the Elizabethan imagination, and the initial implementation of trade agreements that would lead to British colonial domination of India in succeeding centuries. Coryate arrived in Ajmer, on the Indian coast, ten months later, boasting that he had spent only fifty shillings during the entire trip.

What little information that has survived of Coryate's last two years comes from English ambassador Sir Thomas Roe (who supplied Samuel Purchase with Coryate's "observations," printed in *Purchase His Pilgrims,* 1626) and Roe's chaplain, Edward Terry. Roe describes being met upon his arrival in India by "the most famous unwearied Thomas Coryate (who on foot passed most of Europe and Asia and was now arrived in India, being but the beginning of his purposed travels)," and indeed Coryate's curiosity seemed inexhaustible. In his last surviving letter, sent from Agra in October 1616, he expresses his intention to take to the road again, resolving to see "ancient Babylon and Nimrod's Tower, some few miles from Nineva, and . . . Cairo in Egypt, heretofore Memphis, upon the famous river Nilus," tarrying in each place only long enough "to observe every principal matter there, and so be gone." Coryate died in December 1617, however, near the mouth of the Tapti River on the West Indian coast, and he was buried somewhere between Swally and Surat, although local legend identifies as his a tomb on the Gulf of Cambay used as an admiralty marker.

As Anthony Grafton demonstrates in his *New Worlds, Ancient Texts: The Power of Tradition and the Shock of Discovery* (1992), a major shift in epistemological models took place between 1550 and 1650, as Western thinkers were forced to substitute for the authority of ancient texts the evidence of discoveries made through travel. Travel writing quickly became one of the most popular forms of Elizabethan and Stuart reading, demanding an almost scientific detachment of the writer, who weighed popular prejudices regarding the world outside Britain's island fortress against the evidence of his own experience, even while paradoxically continuing to satisfy the reader's taste for novelty.

Few Elizabethans were as determined as Coryate to weigh against the evidence of his own senses the reports of the miraculous Middle East and of the even more fabulous Indies circulated by medieval pilgrims, by merchants such as Marco Polo, and by the highly imaginative Sir John Mandeville. "Master Coryate," notes Purchase, "was indeed a curious viewer of so much as his bodily eyes could comprehend." He climbed Mount Tabor by grabbing hold of scrub that grew

Venetian island of Zante on 13 January 1613 and proceeding from there to the Turkish-ruled island of Chios. By 22 February Coryate's ship had anchored off the coast of the Troad, where he visited what were thought to be the ruins of ancient Troy. He spent ten months in Constantinople as the guest of the English ambassador Paul Pindar before setting sail on 21 January 1614 for the Holy Land. Landing at Iskanderum at the port of Aleppo (which he called "the principal emporium of the Orient world"), he journeyed in a caravan of Armenian pilgrims south to Damascus and Jerusalem, where he toured the biblical sites.

Coryate was originally to have returned home at this point; but after returning to Aleppo in May 1614, he set out instead to explore the caravan routes that led through the Persian Empire to the lands of the Great Mogul. The honorable East India Company received its charter from the queen at the close of the century on 31 December 1600; thus, Coryate's life spanned both the exploratory travels of John Newberry through India in the 1580s, which established the Indies as a place of fabulous

The tomb north of Suvali, India, popularly identified as that of Coryate

on the steep mountainside, visited a Venetian brothel so as to be able to describe its appointments and the charms of its world-famous courtesans, and raised a ruckus when denied entrance to a Catholic cloister where he was determined to observe the nuns at their devotions.

Coryate's Crudities also includes the first published English description of such conveniences as the umbrella and the table fork. He was as interested in the smallest domestic detail of other nations – such as the Italian custom of allowing children to run about in their shirts both as relief from the heat and to allow them to relieve themselves without a mother or nurse stopping to undo their clothing – as he was in such public ones as the Ottoman legal code, which prescribed hanging for anyone careless enough to allow a fire to start or the pouring of molten lead into the mouth and ears of anyone found drinking during the holy days. Coryate was likewise as specific in his description of a desert mirage as of a Jewish circumcision rite. His extraordinary willingness to partake of local customs did not extend to matters of religion, however: a vociferous Protestant who had the Jerusalem cross tattooed on his wrist, Coryate never tired of debating religion

and caused a near riot when he attempted to convert a Venetian rabbi in his own synagogue. In addition, Coryate was a tireless examiner of ruins, a scrupulous transcriber of their inscriptions, and he was rigorous in his consideration of their significance; he saw himself as a scholar whose collections of antiquities would eventually surpass those of Sir Robert Cotton.

But Coryate continues to deserve attention as much for his writing as for his traveling. He loved languages and took a humanist's delight in their acquisition: "I learn the Persian, Turkish, and Arabian tongues, having already gotten the Italian (I thank God)," he wrote from abroad. Language allowed him to transcend social as well as national boundaries, as when he delivered a carefully prepared oration before the Great Mogul in Persian. Language was also a means of fashioning and displaying an ambitiously erudite self – one that, however, seemed to tire Coryate's contemporaries quickly. In editing Coryate's surviving notes for posthumous publication, Purchase promised not to "obtrude Master Coryate's prolixity on the patientest reader," and poets as diverse as John Donne and John Taylor were driven to express in print their exasperation at

Coryate's excesses. At his worst he could be as tedious as William Shakespeare's Holofernes but at his best as animated and zestful as Ben Jonson. As Jonson himself wryly comments in "A Character of the Author," which prefaces the *Crudities,* Coryate "is a great and bold carpenter of words, or (to express him in one of his own) a Logo-daedale."

Geographers have paid more attention to Coryate than have literary historians. The first Englishman to have traveled as far as India to see for himself what foreign parts were like, Coryate has provided invaluable evidence for the reconstruction of Middle Eastern and central Asian cultural and social systems in the late Renaissance. Yet the same detail so highly valued by the modern geographer often proves tedious to other readers, and the absence of a modern edition of Coryate's works ensures his inaccessibility. His canon offers opportunity for serious research, however. In the persona he constructs for himself in his narrative and letters, and particularly in his orations, Coryate provides an excellent middle-class example of Renaissance self-fashioning. What is more, his extraordinary tone of self-mocking goodwill merits consideration in any study of Renaissance festivity and play, for his is essentially a ludic self. One of the great incarnations of the Elizabethan spirit of transgression and exploration, Coryate is also one of the period's great literary fools.

Biography:

Michael Strachan, *The Life and Adventures of Thomas Coryate* (London: Oxford University Press, 1962).

References:

Douglas Bush, "The Literature of Travel," in his *English Literature in the Earlier Seventeenth Century,* second edition (New York: Oxford University Press, 1962), pp. 180–191;

Mary B. Campbell, *The Witness and the Other World: Exotic European Travel Writing, 400–1600* (Ithaca, N.Y.: Cornell University Press, 1988);

Authur Freeman, "Improbable Journeys," in his *Elizabeth's Misfits: Brief Lives of English Eccentrics, Exploiters, Rogues, and Failures 1580–1660* (New York: Garland, 1978), pp. 167–187;

Edgar Hinchcliffe, "Thomas Coriati Testimonium," *Notes and Queries,* 15 (October 1968): 370–375;

Anthony Parr, "Thomas Coryate and the Discovery of Europe," *Huntington Library Quarterly,* 55 (1992): 579–602;

Boies Penrose, "Tourists in the East," in his *Travel and Discovery in the Renaissance* (Cambridge, Mass.: Harvard University Press, 1952), pp. 213–228;

Louis B. Wright, "The Wonders of Travel," in his *Middle-Class Culture in Elizabethan England* (Chapel Hill: University of North Carolina Press, 1935), pp. 508–548.

Sir John Davies

(April? 1569 – 8 December 1626)

Robert Wiltenburg
Washington University

BOOKS: *Epigrammes and Elegies,* by Davies and Christopher Marlowe (Middleburg?: Nimmo, 1595?);

Orchestra, or a Poeme of Dauncing (London: Printed by J. Roberts for N. Ling, 1596);

Nosce Teipsum. This Oracle Expounded in Two Elegies (London: Printed by R. Field for J. Standish, 1599);

Hymnes of Astraea, in Acrosticke Verse (London: Printed for J. Standish, 1599);

A Discoverie of the True Causes Why Ireland Was Never Entirely Subdued, untill His Majesties Raigne (London: Printed by W. Jaggard for J. Jaggard, 1612);

Le Primer Report des Cases et Matters Resolves en les Courts del Roy en Ireland (Dublin: J. Franckton, 1615);

Nosce teipsum. . . . Hymnes of Astraea. Orchestra. Not Finished (London: Printed by A. Mathews for R. Hawkins, 1622);

The Question Concerning Impositions (London: Printed by S. G. for H. Twyford & R. Marriot, 1656).

Editions: *The Works in Verse and Prose of Sir John Davies,* 3 volumes, edited by Alexander B. Grosart (Blackburn: Printed for private circulation, 1869–1876);

The Complete Poems of Sir John Davies, 2 volumes, edited by Grosart (London: Chatto & Windus, 1876);

The Poems of Sir John Davies, edited by Clare Howard (New York: Columbia University Press, 1941);

The Poems of Sir John Davies, edited by Robert Krueger (Oxford: Clarendon Press, 1975).

OTHER: Francis Davison, *A Poetical Rhapsody Containing Diverse Sonnets, Odes* (London: Printed by N. Okes for R. Jackson, 1608) – includes five poems by Davies.

Sir John Davies is perhaps the most interesting and the most representative of the minor poets of the 1590s. While studying law at the Middle Temple, he took a leading role in the quick-shifting literary fashions of the time, and he produced in *Orchestra* (1596) and *Nosce Teipsum* (1599) two works of enduring and general interest. Though often more "verser" than poet, he is nonetheless a verse maker of rare energy, inventiveness, skill, lucidity, and charm — and his poems at their best possess the sharpness, grace, and memorability of an impulse or a moment perfectly realized. He aimed always to be "speaking well . . . / Hoping thereby honor and wealth to gain" (Epigram 34) — hoping, that is, to persuade his hearers of the merits both of his case and of himself. His frequent successes in poetry and affairs depended upon serving at once his own interests and those of some person or some idea greater than himself: sovereigns or patrons, ideas of true wit and sophistication, of love and sociability, of the possibility and dimensions of self-knowledge, and, finally, of the centrality of law as the guarantor of civility and prosperity in human affairs. Throughout his works the reader finds little of doubt or anguish but much vivacity, together with the lawyer's calm faith that the most authoritative tradition, properly known and sifted, discerningly applied and extended, will be adequate to emergent occasions, and with the faith of the practical rhetorician in verse and prose that much may be gained, and many may be profited, by reading, thinking, writing, and speaking well.

Davies was born at Chicksgrove in Tisbury, Wiltshire, and was christened in the parish church on 16 April 1569. His father, also named John, was a wealthy tanner whose own father, also John, had come into Wiltshire from South Wales with Sir William Herbert, first Earl of Pembroke. His mother, Mary, née Bennett, was a daughter of the most prominent local family. In 1580, the year of his father's death, Davies began his formal studies, first at Winchester School from 1580 to 1585 and later at Queen's College, Oxford, which he entered on 15 October 1585. He left Oxford after about a year

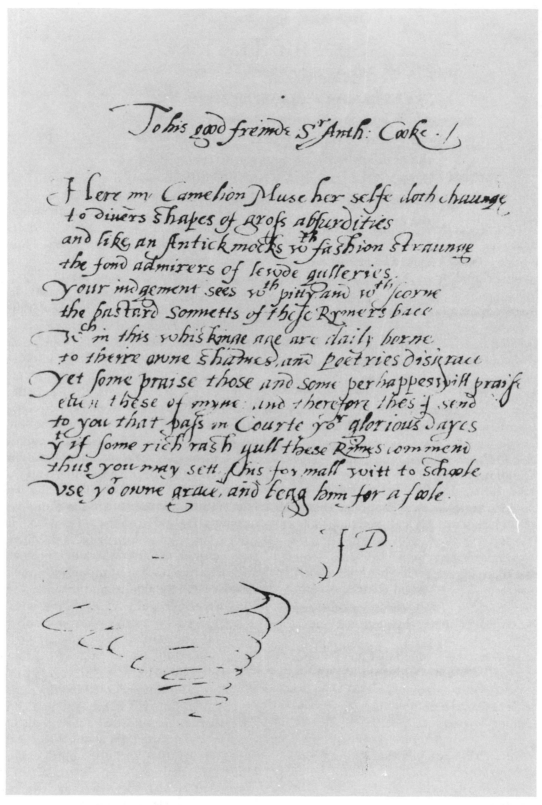

John Davies's dedicatory sonnet to Sir Anthony Cooke in the manuscript for the "Gulling Sonnets" (Chetham's
Hospital and Library, Manchester, Ms. A.4.15 [8012])

and a half, evidently without taking a degree, and went to London to follow the law, initially spending a year at New Inn, one of the Inns of Chancery, before being admitted to its affiliated Inn of Court, the Middle Temple, which he entered on 10 February 1588.

The Inns of Court, those "noblest nurseries of humanity and liberty," as Ben Jonson called them in his dedication for the 1616 Folio edition of *Every Man Out of His Humour,* were just the place for a talented, ambitious young man from the country. Davies thrived at the Middle Temple, excelling in the legal curriculum of presentation, disputation, and conversation offered there, and was called to the bar on 4 July 1595, after the minimum period of seven years. Meanwhile, he had been making friends (notably Richard Martin, a handsome, charismatic contemporary, and William Fleetwood, with both of whom he traveled to Holland in 1592 to meet the jurist Paul Merula), making trouble (the three were among those cited or punished for provoking Candlemas riots at the Temple in 1591 and 1593), and, finally, making a reputation as a witty and graceful poet, with sonnets and antisonnets, epigrams, an epithalamium, *Orchestra,* and other pieces.

Davies's earliest poems leave an impression, as G. A. Wilkes observes in "The Poetry of Sir John Davies" (1962), "of eager versatility, of readiness to spill his energies into any form that beckoned." If sonnets were wanted, he could produce the "Ten Sonnets, to Philomel" (circa 1591–1594), a conventional exercise but clean, facile, pleasing, and pointed. Yet early on Davies shows himself more than a clever imitator of the mode with nine "Gulling Sonnets" (1594–1595), in which his "chameleon muse" was among the first to satirize the affected Petrarchism, strained conceits, and labored techniques of "gulls" whose wits are merely "formal" — that is, who mistake or misvalue form over matter. The joke throughout, as Davies notes in the dedicatory sonnet to Sir Anthony Cooke, is that his parodies, sailing as close as possible to the prevailing wind, may actually be taken seriously. The best is the fifth, a wonderful parody of "correlative verse":

Mine eye, mine ear, my will, my wit, my heart,
Did see, did hear, did like, discern, did love,
Her face, her speech, her fashion, judgement, art,
Which did charm, please, delight, confound, and move.

Here the obsessive, artificial multiplication of parallels crowds out not only passion but sense and wit as well. Davies's challenge to the artful abuses of the sonneteers remains at the level of style rather than, as John Donne was beginning to do, challenging the adequacy of their conception of love.

The same limitations apply to Davies's roughly contemporaneous first publication, the *Epigrams and Elegies* (1595?), printed together with some elegies by Chistopher Marlowe. This collection of forty-eight epigrams, ranging in length from four to thirty-six lines, caused Davies to be hailed as the English Martial. As Martial's work was a standard text at Winchester, and the making of epigrams a favorite exercise, it is not surprising that Davies has caught something of Martial's tone and tactics. Yet his persona and purposes remain narrower than those of the Roman poet. Davies undertakes in the name of "all good wits and spirits" to attack the "general vice that merits public blame."

The recurrent object of Davies's satire is a new figure of his own discerning, the gull. The second epigram is devoted to defining the "true and perfect gull" and, after quatrains sketching his pretentious inadequacies in love, honor, and at court, concludes, "But to define a gull in terms precise, / A gull is he which seems, and is not wise." This definition implies something more than simple folly, more even than mistaking form for substance — though the gull's life, whether he be old or young, Puritan or libertine, lawyer or soldier, male or female, is a catalogue of just such mistakes. At bottom, his condition involves a disabling obliqueness, a want of self-awareness and self-possession, a want of the discerning wit that sees one's self, one's needs, one's true situation. Priscus, a typical example, has risen "from low to high estate" and excuses his forgetting of his old friends with the plea, "For at this time my self I do not know" (Epigram 31).

In other hands such material might provoke searching social, moral, or psychological analyses; in still others, high tragedy. For Davies, however, even the meditations of his melancholy gull reach no higher than the social effects of "long cloaks" versus those of "great black feathers" (Epigram 47). In this lightly amusing social comedy, the line between wits and gulls, between those who always get the point and those who never do, remains clear and is never crossed. This may well seem an opportunity lost for an ambitious young provincial who had begun to know the satisfactions of being part of the in-crowd and had yet to discover the pain of being out of it.

Just how "in" Davies had become is indicated by his being asked to provide an epithalamium for an important public wedding, that of Elizabeth Vere, daughter of the earl of Oxford and granddaughter of William Cecil, Lord Burghley, to William Stanley, Earl of Derby, on 16 January 1595. Although the epithalamium may have formed part of a larger masque of the Muses, it stands on its own as a series of ten sonnets — one introductory, the others in the persons of each of the nine Muses, who comment upon and bless the marriage. The sequence is elegantly wrought: as a literary conceit; as a careful, knowledgeable compliment to the couple and their families; and as gentle advice to "Love not that Love that is a child and blind, / But that heroic, honorable Love . . . Which links true friends" in order "That with your days your joys may multiply."

This commission had probably resulted from the success of Davies's *Orchestra, or A Poem of Dancing,* entered in the Stationers' Register 25 June 1594 and finally published in 1596. The expanded title describing it as "Judicially proving the true observation of time and measure, in the authentical and laudable use of dancing" suggests its likely origin as an entertainment, a fanciful disputation for a Middle Temple audience — a supposition strengthened by the effusive dedication of "This sudden, rash, half-capriole of my wit" to his friend Richard Martin, who may well have taken a part in its presentation.

Davies says that the poem was written in fifteen days, and indeed the earliest version — preserved in the Leweston Fitzjames manuscript and including stanzas 1–108 and 127–131 — is notable for swift, playful, dazzling variations upon its unifying theme. Eleven introductory stanzas efficiently establish the mock-Homeric framework (that the poem will tell the "one thing he forgot" in the story of Ulysses), invoke a "light Muse," and set the shimmering, seductive scene in which Antinous, chief of Penelope's wooers, will exercise his "cunning courtesy" in an effort to persuade her to dance. She modestly resists this "new rage," this innovative "misrule" and "misgovernment," but is willing to hear more. Antinous then begins a lengthy persuasion in which he not only proves the antiquity of dancing but argues that all of life is best comprehended under the figure of the dance, representing ordered change through time. This figure is applied throughout time and space: from the beginning when Love persuaded the warring elements "To leave their first disordered combating" to the present dancing of the natural elements — stars, sun, earth, moon, planets, sea, and rivers; then to the social dance of the offices and ceremonies of human life — love, poetry, religion, government, and speech; and finally to the most intimate actions and passions of the human body and soul.

The recurrent theme is that "Kind Nature first doth cause all things to love, / Love makes them dance and in just order move." All is in motion, and to the extent that this motion exhibits order (dances) it contributes to the cosmic harmony, the universal dance of nature and of time. What better can people do than to participate in this quintessential art, the "child of music and of love," "The fair character of the world's consent, / The heav'n's true figure, and th'earth's ornament"?

Penelope, however, is unswayed by this "tedious praise of that she did despise," turning upon its head Antinous's conceit of dancing as the child of personified Love, who is, in her chaste view, "the hateful father vile / That doth the world with sorceries beguile." Antinous replies with a distinction between "true Love" and "mischievous Lust," but the persuasion is incomplete and ends with Antinous's plea for renewed inspiration.

The additional verses (109–126) that appear in the published version were probably added for a court performance and introduce new elements and emphases. The praise of concord in marriage (109–112) sorts rather oddly with Antinous's purpose but leads to a clear moral statement (doubly emphasized by its italicization in the 1622 edition) explicitly asserting the harmony of the potentially disruptive dance of natural Love with the needs of human social order: "For of Love's maze it [dancing] is the curious plot, / And of man's fellowship the true-love knot." The revised poem ends with a magic mirror vision of perfected dancing in Elizabeth's court (119–126), a final image that should convince Penelope if anything can.

Of the delights afforded by *Orchestra,* there is no dispute. Modern opinion has been less sure how far, beyond appreciating the tour de force, to attribute to the poem philosophic seriousness, as E. M. W. Tillyard did, expressive of Davies's own thinking or, more plausibly, that of his time. Recently it has been suggested by J. R. Brink that there may be implicit comment on the succession crisis, or (at the behest of the Cecils) subtle criticism of the earl of Essex, but the poem's aesthetic and rhetorical exuberance — its own evident delight in the dance of words, lines, and figures and in its often-tested and triumphantly confirmed powers of invention — remains the dominant impression and effect.

Having achieved the professional advancement to utter barrister and published the widely praised *Orchestra,* and having attracted the favorable notice of the Cecils and of the queen, Davies, the

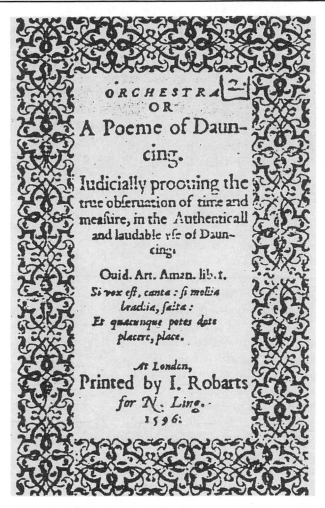

*Title page for Davies's mock-Homeric poem on the history and
importance of dance*

tanner's son from Wiltshire, had come far socially, and his professional and social future seemed assured. More surprising, then, is the incident that provides the defining crisis of his early career, the public attack on 9 February 1598 on his sometime friend Richard Martin. According to the minutes of the Middle Temple:

> While the Masters of the Bench and other fellows were quietly dining publicly in the hall, John Davies, one of the Masters of the Bar, in cap and gown, and girt with a dagger, his servant and another with him being armed with swords, came into the hall. The servant and the other person stayed at the bottom of the hall, while he walked up to the fireplace and then to the lower part of the second table for Masters of the Bar, where Richard Martin was quietly dining. Taking from under his gown a stick, which is commonly called "a Bastinado," he struck Martin on the head with it till it broke, and then running to the bottom of the Hall he took his servant's sword out of his hand, shook it over his own head, and ran down to the water steps and jumped into a boat. He is expelled, never to return.

Clearly, this event was theatrically staged, a public revenge calculated to punish and humiliate Martin. The causes of the breach are not fully known but can be inferred. The two men were of different types: Martin is described in Benjamin Rudyerd's *Prince D'amour* (1660) as being "of a cheerful and gracious countenance . . . tall bodied, and well-proportioned; of a sweet and fair conversation . . . of a noble and high spirit . . . so eloquent in ordinary speech . . . that . . . study could not mend it"; Davies, in John Manningham's diary (written 1602–1603) as one who "goes waddling with his arse out behind as though he were about to make every one that he meets, a wall to piss against." Other satiric jabs make fun of Davies's pock-marked face and awkward gait. His affection for Martin was at its height in the 1596 dedication to *Orchestra,* where he calls him "mine-own-self's better half," but Martin's election as the prince of love presiding over the Candlemas revels of 1597–1598 brought whatever latent stresses there may have been to a head. Rudyerd's account of the progress of the festivities lampoons Davies under the name of Stradilax, an ambitious, garish maladroit, who, despite his increasingly desperate efforts to gain acceptance, is finally rejected and excluded by the prince and his circle. Davies took a wounded lover's self-destructive revenge.

The result was disgrace and banishment. Davies spent the next two and a half years conducting a campaign to regain his place and to restore his prospects. One part of that campaign was the publication of *Nosce Teipsum* and the *Hymns of Astraea* (1599) – the fruits of his involuntary retirement, probably at Oxford. The *Hymns of Astraea* present an astonishing tour de force, twenty-six acrostics keyed to ELISA BETHA REGINA (because the constellation Virgo contains twenty-six stars) in which the queen, her body, mind, virtues, and effects are exhaustively praised under the figure of Astraea, virgin goddess of the spring, remnant of the Golden Age, and agent of its restoration. The mythological resources are deftly manipulated, and Davies achieves a surprising degree of sense, grace, and ease, given the constrictions of the form and the limitations of purpose.

Nosce Teipsum, comprising two elegies – "Of Human Knowledge" and "Of the Soul of Man, and the Immortality Thereof" – is Davies's best-known work, being several times republished in his lifetime and continuously reprinted during the next two centuries. There has long been some mild uncertainty about its date of composition, and some part of it may have been in existence as early as 1592, but the balance of probabilities supports the traditional account that places it in 1598–1599 and discerns in it signs of Davies's recent experiences. As James L. Sanderson observes, the effectiveness of the poem lies not simply in the confident urbanity with which two millennia worth of arguments about the soul, its nature, and its powers are organized and presented in lucid, effortless-seeming quatrains – even the clearest of expositions tires at length – but in an underlying rhythm of falling and rising, of loss and recovery, that supports the whole. This rhythm is made explicit in the advice given in the final stanzas:

> Study the best and highest things that are,
> But of thy self an humble thought retain.

> Cast down thyself, and only strive to raise
> The glory of thy Maker's sacred name.

The two elegies enact both the casting down and the raising up. The first begins in the confusion and corruption of man's fallen condition, in which the reasoning soul is darkened and obscured, questioning whether knowledge is even possible "When *Reason's* lamp . . . is now become a sparkle." The aroused consciousness of the gap between what man has been and what he has become leads the speaker close to despair:

> *I know* my Body's of so frail a kind,
>   As force without, fevers within can kill;
>   *I know* the heavenly nature of my mind,
>   But 'tis corrupted both in *wit* and *will:*
> *I know* my *Soul* hath power to know all things,
>   Yet is she blind and ignorant in all;
>   *I know* I'm one of *Nature's* little kings,
>   Yet to the least and vilest things am thrall,
> *I know* my life's a pain, and but a span,
>   *I know* my *Sense* is mocked with every thing;
>   And to conclude, *I know* my self a *Man,*
>   Which is a *proud* and yet a *wretched* thing.

The second elegy immediately begins the rebuilding. Direct apprehension having been lost in the Fall, God yet reserves to man "an *inward light,"* a power of reflection sufficient to begin and to carry through the inquiry into the soul's nature. All the traditional questions are raised: what is it, where is it, how does it operate, what is its relation to the body, to the senses, to God? These questions receive the traditional, mostly Thomist, answers: the soul is both substance and spirit, participating in both earth and heaven; it uses and rules the senses; its operations are represented as the twin powers of the "judging *Wit,* and choosing *Will* "; it is, of its nature, dissatisfied with even the best of earthly "wealth, pleasure, praise" and finds rest and assurance only in the eternal. This analysis of the soul's nature and powers is completed by adducing reasons for and answering objections against its immortality, appealing finally to the consensus of all religions and cultures: "For how can that be false which every tongue, / Of every mortal man affirms for true[?]" By the final "acclamation" this exhaustive anatomy of the question of the soul has so much restored the speaker's own soul and informed his own reason that he is prepared to receive the wisdom needed to govern his condition: to "take heed of *overweening,"* to "study the best and highest things," to embrace humility, and to "Use all thy powers that blessed power to praise, / Which gives thee power to *be,* and *use the same."*

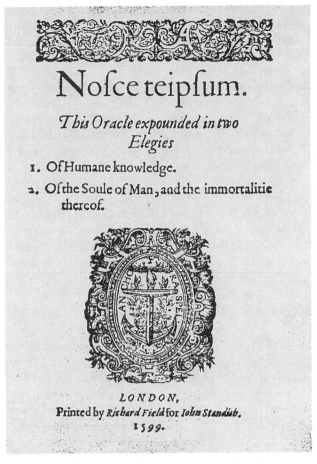

Nosce teipsum.

This Oracle expounded in two Elegies

1. Of Humane knowledge.

2. Of the Soule of Man, and the immortalitie thereof.

LONDON,
Printed by *Richard Field* for *Iohn Standish*.
1599.

*Title page for Davies's best-known work, a philosophical poem
about the soul and human reason*

The restoration of Davies's social and professional status required in addition the intervention of powerful patrons and friends – Charles Blount, Lord Mountjoy, who had encouraged him to publish *Nosce Teipsum* and dedicate it to the queen; Sir Robert Cecil; and Sir Thomas Egerton, the Lord Keeper – who finally effected his reinstatement at the Middle Temple on 30 October 1601. The temporary disgrace had the paradoxical benefit of stimulating Davies to cultivate his contacts with these courtiers, who continued to help him. In 1601 he sat as the member of Parliament for Corfe Castle. In 1602 he supplied a typically resourceful, cleverly constructed "Contention between a Wife, a Widow, and a Maid" for Cecil's entertainment of the queen at Hatfield – the occasion for which the "Rainbow Portrait" of Elizabeth was evidently produced as a memorial.

Davies's fortunes soared with the accession of James I in 1603. The writer was among those who traveled to Scotland to congratulate the new king and, upon being recognized as the author of *Nosce Teipsum,* was embraced by him. Soon Davies was in Ireland serving under Mountjoy, the Lord Deputy. He was knighted in Dublin on 18 October 1603; he was appointed solicitor-general for Ireland on 25 November; and on 19 April 1606 he was advanced to attorney general. Early in 1609 he married Eleanor, the daughter of George Touchet, Lord Audley and Earl of Castlehaven. He was made the king's sergeant in 1612, and he became speaker of the house of the Irish Parliament in 1613 – he had to be seated, by force, in the lap of a rival claimant. He acquired wealth and lands in Ireland, where he remained until 1619.

Davies's Irish career was notable in several respects. His vivid reports and trenchant analyses of Irish conditions, regularly communicated to Cecil, formed the basis for much of English policy in Ireland, policy that Davies then executed. His *Discovery of the True Causes Why Ireland Was Never Entirely Subdued* (1612) was a work of original and thoroughgoing scholarship that diagnosed the errors of English policy over several centuries; it was frequently republished during the following two centuries. His analysis in that book, and in the eloquent "Discourse of the Common Law" (addressed to Egerton) that introduces *Le Primer Report des Cases et Matters Resolves* (1615), depends upon the fundamental recognition that "to give laws unto a people," not conquest or command, is first among "the true marks of sovereignty." In failing to exert itself in this respect, the English government has left the Irish in a pitiable state, prey to English adventurers who "might oppress, spoil, and kill them without controlment," and to the uncertainties and inequities of the indigenous "brehon" law, with its loose and variable handling of such crucial matters as rights of property and inheritance and regular penalties for crimes. He pleads for the extension of the benefits of the English common law – "the most perfect, and the most excellent, and without comparison the best . . . as coming nearest to the Law of Nature" – throughout Ireland. For, he continues, in a world without justice,

> we should not know what were our own, what another man's, what we should have from our ancestors, what we should to our children . . . there would be nothing certain, nothing sure; no contracts, no commerce, no conversation among men, but all kingdoms and states would be brought to confusion, and all human society would be dissolved.

By an irony of history, the chief accomplishment of this idealistic lawgiver was the plantation of Ulster, meant as a model to the rest of Ireland, in which Irish and English were to live together under common (English) law. Davies's analysis and practice remained of consequence to English imperial legal thinking for centuries.

Davies's life after his return to England in 1619 was mostly a postscript to his earlier history. He versified a portion of the Psalms and published a collection of his poetry that included *Nosce Teipsum, Hymns of Astraea,* and *Orchestra.* Only *Orchestra* was altered, a dedication to Prince Charles – who was fond of masking and dancing – replacing that to Martin, and the title page no longer offering to "judicially prove" but merely to "express" the "Antiquity and Excellency of Dancing." The dialogue and the persuasion had, of course, never been finished, even in 1596; and Davies now makes the signs of incompleteness unmistakable, canceling the somewhat dated appeals to the muses of Spenser, acknowledging a lacuna, substituting five stanzas in further praise of Elizabeth's court, and deliberately marking the final irresolution with "So &c. &c."

Davies's marriage was a mixed blessing: two sons died young, and his wife was given to acrostics and to prophecies, including that of her husband's death. When she put on mourning three days before the fatal day, Davies is said to have commented: "I pray weep not while I am alive, and I will give you leave to laugh when I am dead." He lived, however, to see his daughter, Lucy, married to Ferdinando Hastings, later Earl of Huntingdon. Davies also pursued his legal career, serving the king's interests and being named lord chief justice but dying of an apoplexy on 8 December 1626, before he could assume the office. John Donne preached his funeral sermon.

Davies's poetry, with its wit and inventiveness, its clarity and ease, has continued to please readers for nearly four centuries and to provide material – particularly in its form, technique, and contemporary influence – of enduring scholarly interest to historians of literature and culture. Davies's dual career in literature and law presents a clear case study in some of the social contexts and purposes of Elizabethan poetry. Yet one must also consider what it is that makes his work, in Robert Krueger's phrase, "excellent in its kind, but irretrievably minor." Perhaps it lies in his attitude toward boundaries, the imaginary lines separating and linking realms of experience and regions of the soul. Davies resolutely draws, strengthens, and patrols such borders wherever he can in the service of reason and of reason's dominion in psychic, social, and political life. In this he achieved some successes both in life and in art, but his confident, benevolent, remorseless imposition of English law in Ireland also sowed the seeds of lasting strife; and one must recognize that the author of *Orchestra* was also the author of the outrage against Martin. More-adventurous poets recognize that the heart, too, has its reasons, subtler and less regular perhaps but no less urgent than those of the mind, and they continually explore, cross, and recross those boundaries. Davies's self-exploration never extends so far.

Bibliographies:

James L. Sanderson, "Recent Studies in Sir John Davies," *English Literary Renaissance,* 4 (Autumn 1974): 411–417;

P. J. Klemp, *Fulke Greville and Sir John Davies: A Reference Guide* (Boston: G. K. Hall, 1985).

References:

J. R. Brink, "The Composition Date of Sir John Davies' *Nosce Teipsum,*" *Huntington Library Quarterly,* 37 (November 1973): 19–32;

Brink, "The 1622 Edition of Sir John Davies's *Orchestra*," *Library,* 30 (March 1975): 25–33;

Mary Carpenter Erler, "Sir John Davies and the Rainbow Portrait of Queen Elizabeth," *Modern Philology,* 84 (May 1987): 359–371;

P. J. Finkelpearl, *John Marston of the Middle Temple* (Cambridge, Mass.: Harvard University Press, 1969);

Robert Krueger, "Sir John Davies: *Orchestra* Complete, *Epigrams,* Unpublished Poems," *Review of English Studies,* 13 (February 1962): 17–29; (May 1962): 113–124;

Hans S. Pawlisch, *Sir John Davies and the Conquest of Ireland* (Cambridge: Cambridge University Press, 1985);

James L. Sanderson, *Sir John Davies* (Boston: G. K. Hall, 1975);

Theodore Spencer, "Two Classic Elizabethans: Samuel Daniel and Sir John Davies," in *Theodore Spencer: Selected Essays,* edited by Alan C. Purves (New Brunswick, N.J.: Rutgers University Press, 1966), pp. 100–122;

E. M. W. Tillyard, *Five Poems, 1470–1870* (London: Chatto & Windus, 1948), pp. 30–48;

G. A. Wilkes, "The Poetry of Sir John Davies," *Huntington Library Quarterly,* 25 (August 1962): 283–298.

Papers:

The more significant extant manuscripts of Sir John Davies include one at Edinburgh University Library (Laing Ms. III. 44, a collection of Davies's poems originally belonging to his daughter, Lucy); one at the Bodleian Library, Oxford (Ms. Add. B. 97, compiled by Leweston Fitzjames, a younger contemporary at the Middle Temple); one at All Souls, Oxford (Ms. 155, copied from the papers of Sir Christopher Yelverton); and one at Alnwick Castle, Northumberland (Ms. 474, a presentation copy of *Nosce Teipsum* with corrections and dedicatory verse in Davies's own hand).

Thomas Dekker

(circa 1572 – August 1632)

Frederick O. Waage
East Tennessee State University

See also the Dekker entry in *DLB 62: Elizabethan Dramatists.*

BOOKS: *The Pleasant Comedie of Old Fortunatus* (London: Printed by S. Stafford for W. Apley, 1600);

The Shoemakers Holiday. Or The Gentle Craft. With the Life of Simon Eyre, Shoomaker, and Lord Maior of London (London: Printed by V. Sims, 1600);

Blurt Master-Constable. Or The Spaniard's NightWalke, by Dekker and perhaps Thomas Middleton (London: Printed by E. Allde for H. Rockytt, 1602);

Satiro-Mastix. Or The Untrussing of the Humorous Poet (London: Printed by E. Allde for E. White, 1602);

The Pleasant Comodie of Patient Grissell, by Dekker, Henry Chettle, and William Haughton (London: Printed by E. Allde for H. Rocket, 1603);

1603. The Wonderfull Yeare. Wherein Is Shewed the Picture of London, Lying Sicke of the Plague (London: Printed by T. Creede, sold by N. Ling, J. Smethwick & J. Browne, 1603);

The Batchelars Banquet: Or a Banquet for Batchelars: Wherein Is Prepared Sundry Dainties Dishes, sometimes attributed to Dekker (London: Printed by T. Creede, sold by T. Pavier, 1603);

Newes from Graves-End: Sent to Nobody, attributed to Dekker (London: Printed by T. Creede for T. Archer, 1604);

The Meeting of Gallants at an Ordinarie: or The Walkes in Powles, attributed to Dekker and perhaps Middleton (London: Printed by T. Creede, sold by M. Lawe, 1604);

The Honest Whore, with, the Humours of the Patient Man, and the Longing Wife [part 1], by Dekker and Middleton (London: Printed by V. Simmes & others for J. Hodgets, 1604); republished as *The Converted Curtezan* (London: Printed by V. Simmes, sold by J. Hodgets, 1604);

The Magnificent Entertainment: Given to King James upon His Passage through London (London: Printed by T. Creede, H. Lownes, E. Allde & others for T. Man the Younger, 1604);

The Double PP. A Papist in Armes. Encountred by the Protestant. A Jesuite Marching before Them (London: Printed by T. Creede, sold by J. Hodgets, 1606);

Newes from Hell; Brought by the Divells Carrier (London: Printed by R. Blower, S. Stafford & V. Simmes for W. Ferebrand, 1606); enlarged as *A Knights Conjuring. Done in Earnest: Discovered in Jest* (London: Printed by T. Creede for W. Barley, 1607);

The Seven Deadly Sinnes of London: Drawne in Seven Severall Coaches, Through the Citie Bringing the Plague with Them (London: Printed by E. Allde & S. Stafford for N. Butter, 1606);

Jests to Make You Merie: With the Conjuring Up of Cock Watt, by Dekker and George Wilkins (London: Printed by N. Okes for N. Butter, 1607);

North-ward Hoe, by Dekker and John Webster (London: Printed by G. Eld, 1607);

The Famous History of Sir T. Wyat. With the Coronation of Queen Mary (presumably the same play as *Lady Jane*), by Dekker, Webster, Thomas Heywood, Chettle, and Wentworth Smith (London: Printed by E. Allde for T. Archer, 1607);

West-ward Hoe, by Dekker and Webster (London: Printed by W. Jaggard, sold by J. Hodgets, 1607);

The Whore of Babylon (London: Printed at Eliot's Court Press [?] for N. Butter, 1607);

The Dead Tearme. Or Westminsters Complaint for Long Vacations and Short Termes (London: Printed by W. Jaggard, sold by J. Hodgets, 1608);

The Belman of London: Bringing to Light the Most Notorious Villanies Now Practised in the Kingdome (London: Printed by N. Okes for N. Butter, 1608);

Lanthorne and Candle-light. Or the Bell-mans Second Nights Walke (London: Printed by G. Eld for J. Busbie, 1608; corrected and amended edition, London: Printed by E. Allde for J. Busby,

1609); enlarged as *O per se O, or a New Crier of Lanthorne and Candle-Light* (London: Printed by T. Snodham for J. Busbie, 1612); enlarged again as *Villanies Discovered by Lanthorne and Candle-Light* (London: Printed by W. Stansby for J. Busby, 1616; enlarged again, London: Printed by A. Mathewes, 1620); enlarged again as *English Villanies* (London: Printed by A. Mathewes, sold by J. Grismond, 1632);

Foure Birds of Noahs Arke (London: Printed by H. Ballard for N. Butter, 1609);

The Guls Horne-Booke (London: Printed by N. Okes for R. S., 1609);

The Ravens Almanacke Foretelling of a Plague, Famine, and Civill Warre (London: Printed by E. Allde for T. Archer, 1609);

Worke for Armorours: or, The Peace Is Broken (London: Printed by N. Okes for N. Butter, 1609);

The Roaring Girle. Or Moll Cut-purse, by Dekker and Middleton (London: Printed by N. Okes for T. Archer, 1611);

If It Be Not Good, the Divel Is in It. A New Play (London: Printed by T. Creede for J. Trundle, sold by E. Marchant, 1612);

Troia-Nova Triumphans. London Triumphing, or, The Solemne Receiving of Sir J. Swinerton after Taking the Oath of Maioralty (London: Printed by N. Okes, sold by J. Wright, 1612);

A Strange Horse-Race, at the End of Which, Comes in the Catch-Pols Masque (London: Printed by N. Okes for J. Hunt, 1613);

The Artillery Garden (London: Printed by G. Eld, 1616);

Dekker His Dreame. In Which, the Great Volumes of Heaven and Hell to Him Were Opened (London: Printed by N. Okes, 1620);

The Virgin Martir, A Tragedie, by Dekker and Philip Massinger (London: Printed by B. Alsop for T. Jones, 1622);

A Rod for Run-Awayes. Gods Tokens, of His Feareful Judgements, upon This City (London: Printed by G. Purslowe for J. Trundle, 1625);

Brittannia's Honor: Brightly Shining in Severall Magnificent Shewes or Pageants, to Celebrate R. Deane, at His Inauguration into the Majoralty of London, October the 29th. 1628 (London: Printed by N. Okes & J. Norton, 1628);

Warres, Warres, Warres (London: Printed by N. Okes for J. G., 1628);

Londons Tempe, or The Feild of Happines. To Celebrate J. Campebell, at His Inauguration into the Maioralty of London, the 29 of October, 1629 (London: Printed by N. Okes, 1629);

London Looke Backe, at That Yeare of Yeares 1625 (London: Printed by A. Mathewes, sold by E. Blackmoore, 1630);

The Blacke Rod: and the White Rod. (Justice and Mercie.) Striking, and Sparing, London (London: Printed by B. Alsop & T. Fawcet for J. Cowper, 1630);

The Second Part of the Honest Whore (London: Printed by Eliz. Allde for N. Butter, 1630);

A Tragi-Comedy: Called, Match Mee in London (London: Printed by B. Alsop & T. Fawcet for H. Seile, 1631);

Penny-Wise Pound Foolish or, a Bristow Diamond, Set in Two Rings, and Both Crack'd (London: Printed by A. Mathewes for E. Blackmoore, 1631);

The Noble Souldier. Or, A Contract Broken, Justly Reveng'd. A Tragedy (London: Printed by J. Beale for N. Vavasour, 1634);

The Wonder of a Kingdome (London: Printed by R. Raworth for N. Vavasour, 1636);

The Sun's-Darling: A Moral Masque, by Dekker and John Ford (London: Printed by J. Bell for Andrew Penneycuicke, 1656);

Lust's Dominion, or The Lascivious Queen (presumably the same play as *The Spanish Moor's Tragedy*), by Dekker, Haughton, John Day, and John Marston (London: Printed by F. K., sold by Robert Pollard, 1657);

The Witch of Edmonton, by Dekker, Ford, and William Rowley (London: Printed by J. Cottrel for Edward Blackmoore, 1658).

Editions: *The Non-Dramatic Works of Thomas Dekker,* 5 volumes, edited by A. B. Grosart (London, 1884–1886);

The Plague Pamphlets of Thomas Dekker, edited by F. P. Wilson (Oxford: Clarendon Press, 1925);

The Overburian Characters, edited by W. J. Paylor (Oxford: Basil Blackwell, 1936);

The Dramatic Works of Thomas Dekker, 4 volumes, edited by Fredson Bowers (Cambridge: Cambridge University Press, 1953–1961);

Thomas Dekker . . . Selected Writings, edited by E. D. Pendry (Cambridge, Mass.: Harvard University Press, 1968);

Thomas Dekker's A Knight's Conjuring (1607), edited by Larry M. Robbins (The Hague: Mouton, 1974);

Cyrus Hoy, *Introductions, Notes, and Commentaries to texts in "The Dramatic Works of Thomas Dekker,"* 4 volumes (Cambridge: Cambridge University Press, 1980–1981).

PLAY PRODUCTIONS: *Sir Thomas More,* probably by Anthony Munday, with revisions by Dek-

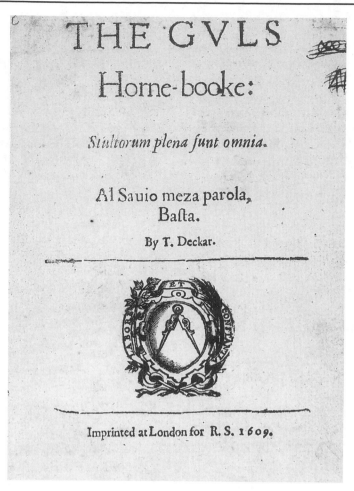

THE GVLS

Horne-booke:

Stultorum plena funt omnia.

Al Sauio meza parola,
Bafta.

By T. Deckar.

Imprinted at London for R. S. 1609.

Title page for Thomas Dekker's satiric courtesy book

ker, Henry Chettle, probably William Shakespeare, and perhaps Thomas Heywood, probably not produced, circa 1598;

Paeton, London, Rose theater, January 1598;

The Famous Wars of Henry I and the Prince of Wales (also known as *The Welshman's Prize*), by Dekker, Chettle, and Michael Drayton, London, Rose theater, March 1598;

Earl Godwin and his Three Sons, parts 1 and 2, by Dekker, Drayton, Chettle, and Robert Wilson, London, Rose theater, spring 1598;

Black Bateman of the North, part 1, by Dekker, Drayton, Chettle, and Wilson, London, Rose theater, May 1598;

The Mad Man's Morris, by Dekker, Drayton, and Wilson, London, Rose theater, July 1598;

Hannibal and Hermes, part 1 (also known as *Worse Afeard than Hurt*), by Dekker, Drayton, and Wilson, London, Rose theater, July 1598;

Pierce of Winchester, by Dekker, Drayton, and Wilson, London, Rose theater, July–August 1598);

Worse Afeard than Hurt (presumably part 2 of *Hannibal and Hermes*), by Dekker and Drayton, London, Rose theater, September 1598;

Conan, Prince of Cornwall, by Dekker and Drayton, London, Rose theater, October 1598;

The Civil Wars of France, parts 1, 2, and 3, by Dekker and Drayton, London, Rose theater, autumn 1598;

The First Introduction of the Civil Wars of France, London, Rose theater, January 1599;

Troilus and Cressida, by Dekker and Chettle, London, Rose theater, April 1599;

Agamemnon (apparently the same play as *Orestes' Furies*), by Dekker and Chettle, London, Rose theater, summer 1599;

The Shoemakers' Holiday, London, Rose theater, summer 1599;

Page of Plymouth, by Dekker and Ben Jonson, London, Rose theater, September 1599;

The Tragedy of Robert II, King of Scots, by Dekker, Chettle, Jonson, and perhaps John Marston, London, Rose theater, autumn 1599;

The Stepmother's Tragedy, by Dekker and Chettle, London, Rose theater, October 1599;

Old Fortunatus, London, Rose theater, autumn 1599;

Patient Grissell, by Dekker, Chettle, and William Haughton, London, Rose theater, January 1600;

Lust's Dominion (possibly a revision of an earlier play and presumably the same play as *The Spanish Moor's Tragedy*), by Dekker, John Day, Haughton, and Marston, London, Rose theater, spring 1600;

The Seven Wise Masters, by Dekker, Chettle Haughton, and Day, London, Rose theater, March 1600;

The Golden Ass, or Cupid and Psyche, by Dekker, Chettle, and Day, London, Rose theater, May 1600;

Fair Constance of Rome, part 1, by Dekker, Drayton, Munday, Wilson, and Richard Hathway, London, Rose theater, June 1600;

Fortune's Tennis, London, Rose or Fortune theater, September 1600;

Sebastian, King of Portugal, by Dekker and Chettle, London, Fortune theater, May 1601;

Satiromastix, London, Globe theater and Paul's theater, autumn 1601;

Blurt, Master Constable, by Dekker and perhaps Thomas Middleton, London, Paul's theater, circa 1601–1602;

Pontius Pilate (anonymous play of circa 1597), prologue and epilogue added by Dekker, London, Fortune theater, January 1602;

Tasso's Melancholy (anonymous play of circa 1594), revised by Dekker, London, Fortune theater, January 1602;

Jephthah, by Dekker and Munday, London, Fortune theater, May 1602;

Caesar's Fall (also known as *Two Shapes*), by Dekker, Drayton, Munday, Middleton, and John Webster, London, Fortune theater, May 1602;

Sir John Oldcastle, part 2, by Drayton, Hathway, Munday, and Wilson (1600), revised by Dekker, London, Boar's Head or Rose theater, September 1602;

A Medicine for a Curst Wife, London, Boar's Head or Rose theater, September 1602;

Sir Thomas Wyatt (presumably the same play as *Lady Jane*), by Dekker, Webster, Chettle, Heywood, and Wentworth Smith, London, Boar's Head or Rose theater, autumn 1602;

Christmas Comes but Once a Year, by Dekker, Chettle, Heywood, and Webster, London, Boar's Head or Rose theater, November 1602;

The Magnificent Entertainment, by Dekker (with Zeal's speech by Middleton), streets of London, 15 March 1604;

The Honest Whore, part 1, by Dekker and Middleton, London, Fortune theater, spring 1604;

Westward Ho, by Dekker and Webster, London, Paul's theater, late 1604;

The Honest Whore, part 2, London, Fortune theater, circa 1604–1605;

Northward Ho, by Dekker and Webster, London, Paul's theater, 1605;

The Whore of Babylon, London, Fortune theater, winter 1605–1606;

The Roaring Girl, by Dekker and Middleton, London, Fortune theater, April–May 1611;

If This Be Not a Good Play, the Devil Is in It, London, Red Bull theater, May–June 1611;

Troia-Nova Triumphans, streets of London, 29 October 1612;

Guy of Warwick, by Dekker and Day (Stationers' Register, 15 January 1620), unknown theater;

The Virgin Martyr, by Dekker and Philip Massinger, London, Red Bull theater, October 1620;

Match Me in London, London, Red Bull theater, circa 1621;

The Witch of Edmonton, by Dekker, John Ford, and William Rowley, London, Cockpit theater, 1621;

The Noble Spanish Soldier (perhaps a revision of an earlier, circa 1600, collaboration with Day), unknown theater, circa 1622;

The Wonder of a Kingdom (apparently a revision and abridgment of a collaboration with Day), unknown theater, circa 1623;

The Bellman of Paris, by Dekker and Day, London, Curtain or Red Bull theater, licensed 30 July 1623;

The Welsh Ambassador (in part a revision of *The Noble Spanish Soldier* and perhaps a collaboration with Ford), unknown theater, circa 1623;

The Sun's Darling, by Dekker and Ford, London, Cockpit theater, licensed 3 March 1624;

The Fairy Knight, by Dekker and Ford, London, Red Bull theater, licensed 11 June 1624;

The Late Murder of the Son upon the Mother, by Dekker, Ford, Rowley, and Webster, London, Red Bull theater, September 1624;

The Bristow Merchant, by Dekker and Ford, London, Fortune theater, licensed 22 October 1624;

Lord Mayor's pageant, streets of London, 29 October 1627;

Britannia's Honor, streets of London, 29 October 1628;

London's Tempe, streets of London, 29 October 1629.

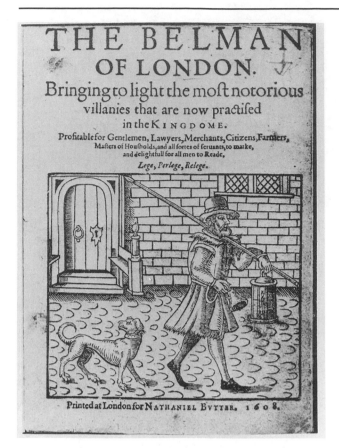

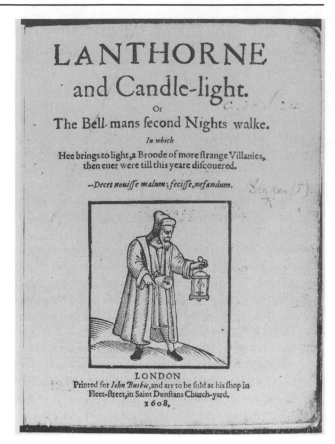

Title pages for Dekker's two pamphlets featuring the Bellman of London

Thomas Dekker is best known as a major Elizabethan and Jacobean dramatist, author of *The Shoemakers' Holiday* (1599), *The Honest Whore* (1604–1605), and many other plays. Although some of his nondramatic works – such as *The Wonderful Year* (1603) and *The Gull's Hornbook* (1609) – are well known, the richness and extent of his nondramatic work are often obscured. *The Wonderful Year,* Dekker's first known prose work, achieved three editions in 1603, after he had been for at least five years a prolific playwright. Dekker's inspiration for the book may have been economic, since the plague closed the theaters from 1603 to spring 1604; but it was obviously inspired also by the "wonderful" coincidence of the plague, Queen Elizabeth I's death on 19 March 1603, and the accession of James I, for whose London entry in spring 1604 Dekker devised *The Magnificent Entertainment.*

The Wonderful Year follows two patterns: temporal and spatial. Temporally, it moves from an idealized pastoral springtime to the royal death and accession to the plague's dark season. Spatially, it moves from the cosmic order of nature, to the spheres of royalty (where succession affirms social order), to the *urbs* of the common people, disordered and distempered by plague. These sequences express the author's moral vision. Spring bacchanals are forms of misrule, for which God through the plague takes retribution. The prose spring scene is followed by alternating verse and prose on the death and succession: James has been greeted as spring was, by arrogant, materialistic celebration. The final, longest section details in prose the consequences of sin. Allegorical evocations of implacable death and scenes of collective disaster alternate with anecdotes describing the plague's capture of those who presumptuously believed they had escaped it, as well as the cruelty of the uninfected to the afflicted.

Three anonymous books of 1603–1604 – *The Bachelor's Banquet, News from Gravesend,* and *The Meeting of Gallants at an Ordinary* – have been attributed to Dekker, but with insufficient evidence. The years 1604–1605 were a period of intense dramatic activity for the author, and it is no wonder that his next nondramatic pamphlet did not appear until 1606, inspired, as was his allegorical play *The Whore of Babylon* (1605–1606), by the Gunpowder Plot, revealed in November 1605.

The pamphlet, Dekker's only known entry into the realm of controversial writing, was *The Double PP,* an anti-Jesuit satire. It begins with a caricatural "Picture of a Jesuit" in verse, followed by a prose inventory of Jesuit terrorism in Europe. A second section characterizes in verse the heraldically named soldiers in the "Romish Army," encountering the Protestant Army led by the "second Brute" (or Brutus, that is, James I), and consisting of all estates of England, from nobility to artificers. In the book's final poem, the Protestants defeat the Pope.

The year 1606 began a five-year hiatus in Dekker's dramatic production and publication, and a proliferation of nondramatic writing. The first of these works, *News from Hell,* expanded in 1607 as *A Knight's Conjuring,* is among several spinoffs from Thomas Nashe's *Pierce-Penniless, His Supplication to the Devil* (1592), featuring the motif of diabolical and earthly communication. Nashe's book is an epistolary moral satire, written by the narrator to the Devil. Dekker's is the reply, as dictated to the speaker by the illiterate Devil, in the form of a Lucianic hell description. Dekker's speaker, complimenting Nashe, describes the arrival in Hell of Nashe's Knight of the Post with Nashe's *Pierce Penniless,* what he sees there, and the Devil's answer to each of the book's articles. *News from Hell* trails off with a burlesque scene involving the ferryman Charon.

Returning to his favorite terrain, Dekker wrote *The Seven Deadly Sins of London* (1606), presented as an interlude of iniquity with seven players (eight, if the Devil is included). First, as a warning to London, it evokes the wages of sin paid by other great world cities, and London's own suffering in the 1603 plague. After this induction are described the triumphal entries into London of the seven sins, which include Politic Bankruptcy, Lying Candlelight (nocturnal crime), Sloth, Apishness (extravagant apparel), Shaving (financial fraud), and Cruelty, whose chariot leads the procession.

In 1607 Dekker collaborated with journeyman writer George Wilkins on a jestbook, *Jests to Make You Merry,* to which Wilkins probably contributed the jests and Dekker the unrelated tales of Cock Watt, the spirit of Newgate, as well as other material on prisons and prisoners. Cock Watt describes his appearances to various criminals, besides the activities of "morts" (thieves' female consorts) and of other female criminals: "glimmerers," "reachers," and "foists." Finally Cock Watt visits a tavern, gets arrested, and starts reciting a paradoxical encomium of sergeants.

Dekker also expanded and disguised *News from Hell,* retitling it *A Knight's Conjuring,* with a new title page and dedication, the removal of references to Nashe, and two substantial additions at the beginning and end. In the first, a pastoral idyll is broken by a storm conjured by some men trying to raise Nashe's emissary Knight from Hell with the Devil's letter. A new conclusion fulfills the speaker's offer in *News from Hell* to lift the reader up to the paradisal Insulae Fortunatae, where he can visit the Grove of Bay Trees inhabited only by poets and musicians, among whom are named Geoffrey Chaucer, Edmund Spenser, Christopher Marlowe, Robert Greene, George Peele, and Nashe himself.

The success of nocturnal Cock Watt may have brought Dekker down to the earth and, in 1608, to his most successful work as a prose writer. As successor to Cock Watt as a guide to candlelight crime, he invented the Bellman of London, who in an eponymously titled pamphlet gives the reader a guided tour of the London underworld — some of it original, some cribbed or adapted from earlier chroniclers of urban and rural villainy such as Thomas Harman and John Audeley. The Bellman protests to his readers that his goal is to "conquer these savages." In so doing, he describes escaping city corruption to the pastoral countryside, where he ironically discovers and witnesses the ceremonial meeting of a villains' parliament. After describing this ritual, the Bellman provides a directory of rogue types, from the aristocratic Upright-Men to the Kinchyn Company (little boys). Then he expands his coverage to anatomizing the different kinds of scam, fraud, and thievery they practice, categorized as "laws": Cheating Law, Vincent's Law, and so on.

The Bellman of London (1608) inspired at least one imitation (not extant), which Dekker mentions in his sequel, *Lantern and Candlelight* (1608). There is an extant response to the latter, the anonymous *Martin Markall, Beadle of Bridewell* (1610), which accuses Dekker of plagiarism. *Lantern and Candlelight,* which became more popular than *The Bellman of London,* going through a complex sequence of eight varying editions, additions, and deletions, includes a glossary of canting language and the narrative framework of a devil's mission from Hell to get rid of the Bellman. This devil encounters and describes all kinds of London villainies, and ends by meeting the Bellman and giving him the account, a "map of vices." The text was subsequently revised in 1612, 1616, and 1632.

Dekker's *The Dead Term* (1608), a medley of prose and verse, discusses varied aspects of London

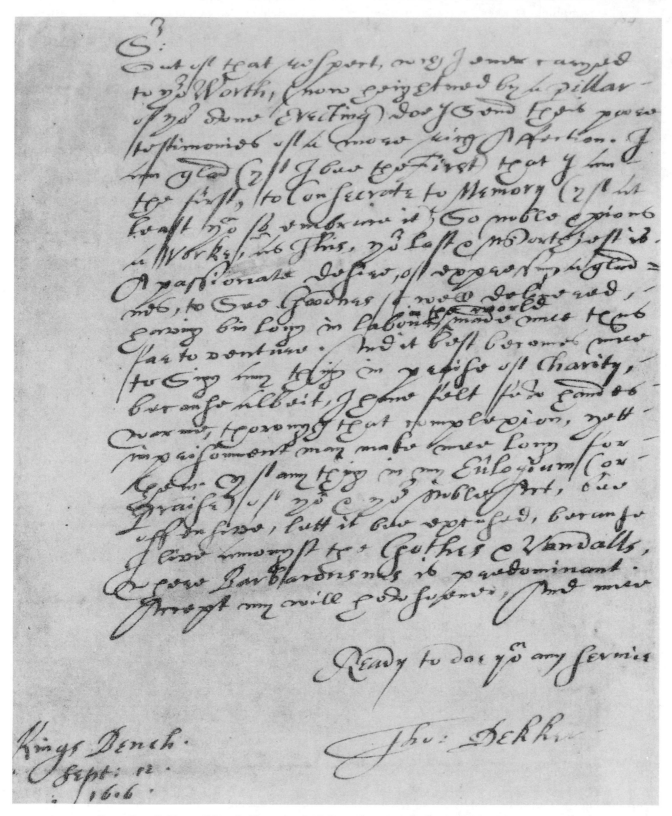

Letter from Dekker to Edward Alleyn, dated 12 September 1616 (Dulwich College, Ms. I, art. 108)

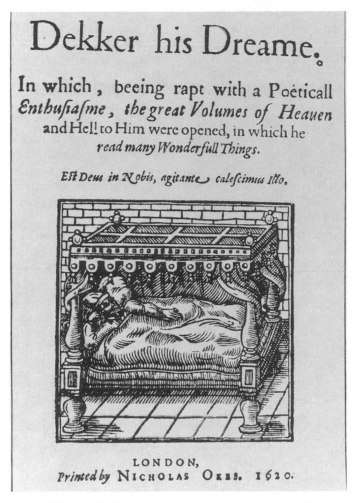

Title page for Dekker's vision of the Apocalypse and Hell

life, with emphasis, as the title suggests, on legal customs and practices. Westminster and London, personified, complain and boast to each other: Westminster complains of London's vices and her own emptiness during the summer dead term when courts are not held; London complains about and describes her vices, and expresses jealousy that Westminster has so few.

The year 1609 marks the pinnacle of Dekker's productivity and virtuosity in prose and verse. *Four Birds of Noah's Ark* is his only devotional work. It partakes of the Protestant primer and prayer-book tradition and is really four books – named for the Dove, Eagle, Pelican, and Phoenix – each with its own title page. As the birds ascend in majesty, so do the prayers: those of the Dove are for normal mortals, of the Eagle for high estates, of the Pelican against deadly sins, and of the Phoenix on the benefits gained by Christ's life and death.

The Gull's Hornbook is a satiric courtesy book, inspired by Friedrich Dedekind's popular *Grobianus*

(1549; English translation, 1605). Dekker's gulls are rurals from "the old world of simplicity" trying to succeed in the city's "new world of sophistication." The author takes the gull through a typical day, going from advice on sleeping late in the morning to walking the streets at night; there are chapters on important locales such as St. Paul's Cathedral, playhouses, and taverns. *The Gull's Hornbook* is drenched in irony, since the urban conduct it supposedly promotes is presented by the speaker as absurd and degenerate.

The Raven's Almanac (1609) is another generic satire, a mock-prognostication dedicated to gallants and gulls, young lawyers and sons of citizens, with a quarter of the year for each. As well as telling droll stories, the Raven predicts winter plagues (of vice, not disease), summer famine, and autumn civil war between rich and poor. *Work for Armorers*, an economic allegory similar to the martial *Double PP*, takes this civil war seriously. The narrator has retreated from the plague to his history library, when he is interrupted by the ragged army of Poverty, marching against Money. Poverty, advised by Discontent, Hunger, and others, gains many poor adherents. Money, advised by Parsimony, enters the city, which is then besieged by Poverty. After several maneuvers exposing in different ways the exploitation of the poor by the rich, plague and famine attack both armies, so they declare a truce. At the end, "the rich men feast one another (as they were wont) and the poor were kept poor still in policy, because they should do no more hurt."

Dekker's playwriting resumed briefly in 1611, with *The Roaring Girl*. But when his next new pamphlet, *A Strange Horse Race*, appeared in 1613, he had already been committed for debt in 1612 to the King's Bench Prison, where he remained for more than six years. *A Strange Horse Race* first erratically chronicles different kinds of races — horse races, races of the body's elements, and of the moral vices and virtues. A Hell scene is then described, followed by the text of the Devil's parodic will (attributing vices to the usual urban criminals) and a masque celebrating the birth of new vices. The whole work has an air of desperate and disordered improvisation.

The Artillery Garden (1616) was published during Dekker's third year of imprisonment, and he presents himself in its dedication as a victim of warfare the poem will celebrate. It is a history of a personified London, with the end of glorifying the Artillery Company, the City Trainband (home guard), and their exercise yard. Dekker asserts that "the scope of this poem, is to consecrate to memory the worth both of men and military exercise, now practiced in the artillery garden." It concludes with an encomium of Prince Henry, who had died in 1613, suggesting Dekker's sympathy for Henry's Protestant militancy.

In 1616 an expanded edition of *Lantern and Candlelight* was published, and in the same year the ninth edition of Sir Thomas Overbury's poem "A Wife" appeared, which included new "characters," of which six prison-related examples are probably by Dekker. The notoriety of Overbury's poisoning in the Tower in 1613 and the trials of the perpetrators made the poem and the characters — expanded in each new edition — best-sellers. Dekker's characters are both realistic and metaphorically rich. Their inner natures are emphasized. Creditor, Sergeant, Yeoman, and Jailer are diabolical; for each, "the misery of poor men . . . are the offals on which he feeds." The prisoner is at most "one who has lost his way."

After he had been released and refound his way as a playwright, Dekker capitalized on his imprisonment with *Dekker His Dream* (1620) — his personal, biblically glossed vision of the Apocalypse and of Hell as they appeared to him during his imprisonment. Written in eccentric, passionate couplets, it evokes the preliminary social chaos, Christ's coming in glory, and the Last Judgment. Then it turns to a classical underworld (for which Dekker apologizes), where the torments are biblical and their sufferers again urban criminal types. At the end, an angelic exposition of the eternality of punishment causes an uproar that wakens the dreamer.

After his playwriting career ended (apparently around 1624), Dekker wrote only a few more nondramatic works. One is *Wars, Wars, Wars* (1628), a short verse pamphlet praising English martial art in the manner of *The Artillery Garden*. He concludes, however, that his pamphlet is really a paradoxical encomium, since war is really "gloomy night," and peace "bright day."

Two other late works are plague pamphlets. *A Rod for Runaways* (1625) bears a grim allegorical woodcut of Death conquering London. It chastises the runaways who flee the plague-stricken city rather than standing their ground, leaving it — "thou mother of my life, nurse of my being" — desolate. Dekker provides reasons for staying and anecdotes of the folly and danger of fleeing, and, always the storyteller, ends with a long section of tales about bizarre plague deaths. *The Black Rod and the White Rod* (1630) begins by figuring the world as a theater's stage from which, the play over, actors exit in common clothes to go to their common home, the grave. Dekker then reviews the 1603 and 1625 plagues, the statistics and circumstances of the then-current one, and adds words of consolation, exhortations to prayer, and visions of the afterlife. The tone is that of an elderly speaker preoccupied with his own end, concerned more with heavenly than with earthly things.

Dekker's final substantial work, *Penny-wise, Pound-Foolish* (1631), is a novella of domestic romance, perhaps derived from his last produced play (written with John Ford), *The Bristow Merchant* (1624). Its conceit involves the "wonderful worth of a penny"; Ferdinand and Annabella of Bristol wed, but Ferdinand is drawn to London and adultery. He returns, is reconciled, and goes to sea with only a penny from Annabella, "to purchase a pennyworth of wit." After his return he falls again. The plot twists to his final permanent reconciliation with Annabella, his fortune restored by the beggar to whom he gave her penny and who managed to turn it into great riches.

Dekker probably died in August 1632, after managing to complete a final revision of *Lantern and Candlelight.* In his essay "Thomas Dekker, the Restoration of St. Paul's, and J. P. Collier, the Forger" (1963), F. David Hoeniger published two manuscript poems, "A New Ballad of the Dancing on the Ropes" and "Paul His Temple Triumphant," along with a pathetic letter of presentation to "Mr. Simon English, Counselor at Law," signed "Tho: Dekker." The latter, in which Dekker allows himself "threescore years," celebrates the restoration of St. Paul's in true Dekkerian style, including allusions to works of John Donne, its dean, who died in March 1631.

The "antique" and "sick" Dekker of these last words had an impressive achievement to look back on, and not just as a playwright. Unfortunately, despite their subtlety and diversity of genre, style, and topical reference, Dekker's nondramatic works have received scant critical attention, most of which has been incidental to discussions of his dramatic works. Nevertheless, despite their often occasional origin, Dekker's work was among the best and (in the case of the Bellman books) best-selling prose of the Jacobean period.

Bibliographies:

Samuel A. Tannenbaum, *Dekker: A Concise Bibliography* (New York: Privately printed, 1939);

Tannenbaum and Dorothy R. Tannenbaum, *Supplement to a Bibliography of Thomas Dekker* (New York: Privately printed, 1945);

Dennis Donovan, *Thomas Dekker, 1945–1965: Elizabethan Bibliographies, Supplements, No. 2* (London: Nether Press, 1967);

Doris Adler, *Thomas Dekker: A Reference Guide* (Boston: G. K. Hall, 1983).

References:

Julia Gasper, *The Dragon and the Dove: The Plays of Thomas Dekker* (Oxford: Oxford University Press, 1990);

F. David Hoeniger, "Thomas Dekker, the Restoration of St. Paul's, and J. P. Collier, the Forger," *Renaissance News,* 16 (Spring 1963): 181–200;

A. V. Judges, *The Elizabethan Underworld* (London: Routledge, 1930);

Frederick O. Waage, *Thomas Dekker's Pamphlets, 1603–1609, and Jacobean Popular Literature,* 2 volumes (Salzburg: Salzburg Studies in English Literature, 1977).

Papers:

Two letters in Thomas Dekker's hand, written while he was a prisoner in the King's Bench Prison, are preserved among the papers of Edward Alleyn in the library of Dulwich College, London. Dekker's deposition (dated 3 February 1625) in the legal suit over his play *The Late Murther of the Son upon the Mother* (now lost) is preserved in the Public Records Office, London. The manuscript for the play *Sir Thomas More* is located in the British Library, London (Harleian Ms. 7368); that for *The Welsh Ambassador* is in the Public Library of Cardiff, Wales.

John Dowland

(1563 – February 1626)

Edward Doughtie
Rice University

BOOKS: *The First Booke of Songes or Ayres of Fowre Partes with Tableture* (London: Printed by Peter Short, 1597);

The Second Booke of Songs or Ayres, of 2. 4. and 5. Parts: With Tableture (London: Printed by Thomas East for George Eastland, 1600);

The Third and Last Booke of Songs or Aires. Newly Composed to Sing to the Lute (London: Printed by Peter Short for Thomas Adams, 1603);

Lachrimae, or Seaven Teares Figured in Seaven Passionate Pavans, with Divers other Pavans . . . Set forth for the Lute, Viols, or Violons, in Five Parts (London: Printed by John Windet, 1604);

A Pilgrimes Solace. Wherein Is Contained Musicall Harmonie of 3. 4. and 5. Parts, to Be Sung and Plaid with the Lute (London: Printed by Thomas Snodham for Matthew Lownes & John Browne, 1612).

Editions: *The English Lute-Songs,* edited by Edmund H. Fellowes, revised by Thurston Dart and others, first series 1-2, 5-6, 10-12, and 14 (London: Stainer & Bell, 1920-1971);

Seven Hymn-Tunes: Lamentatio Henrici Noel, 2 volumes, edited by Fellowes, Tudor Church Music, second series 79-80 (London: Oxford University Press, 1934);

Ayres for Four Voices, edited by Dart and Nigel Fortune, Musica Britannica, 6 (London: Stainer & Bell for the Royal Musical Association, 1953);

The Collected Lute Music, edited by Diana Poulton and Basil Lam (London: Faber & Faber, 1974);

Complete Consort Music, edited by Edgar Hunt (London: Schott, 1985).

OTHER: *The Whole Booke of Psalmes: With Their Wonted Tunes* (London: Printed by Thomas Est, 1592) – includes six harmonizations by Dowland;

A New Booke of Tabliture (London: Printed by William Barley, 1596) – includes seven lute pieces by Dowland;

Andreas Ornithoparcus His Micrologus, translated by Dowland (London: Printed by Thomas Adams, 1609);

Robert Dowland, *Varietie of Lute-Lessons: Viz. Fantasies, Pavins, Galliards . . . Selected out of the Best Approved Authors. . . . Whereunto Is Annexed Certaine Observations Belonging to Lute-Playing: By John Baptisto Besardo. . . . Also a Short Treatise . . . by J. Douland* (London: Printed by Thomas Snodham for Thomas Adams, 1610) – includes several contributions by John Dowland;

Dowland, *A Musicall Banquet. Furnished with Varietie of Delicious Ayres, Collected out of the Best Authors in English, French, Spanish and Italian* (London: Printed by Thomas Snodham for Thomas Adams, 1610) – includes three songs by John Dowland;

William Leighton, *The Teares or Lamentacions of a Sorrowfull Soule* (London: Printed by William Stansby, 1614) – includes two settings of Leighton's verses by Dowland;

Thomas Ravenscroft, *The Whole Booke of Psalmes* (London, 1621) – includes a harmonization of Psalm 100 by Dowland.

Known in his own time as a virtuoso performer on the lute, John Dowland is today remembered mainly as a composer of vocal and instrumental music. Except for a few pieces of minor verse — four commendatory rhymes for others' books, a Latin quatrain, and a translation — he is not known to have written poetry. It is possible that he could have written some of the lyrics to his songs, but there is no evidence that he did. Dowland owes his place in literary history to his role as a collector and preserver of poems and as a kind of musical interpreter of them.

John Dowland was born in 1563. His birthplace is not known, but it was probably in England, and not, as some earlier scholars thought, in Ireland. He did spend a fair amount of his life outside

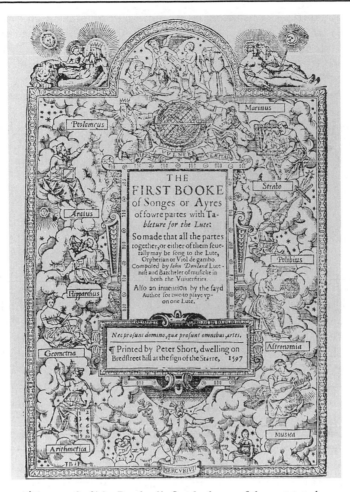

*Title page for John Dowland's first book, one of the most popular
musical publications of the English Renaissance*

of England, however. He was in the service of Sir Henry Cobham in the early 1580s in Paris, where he converted to Catholicism. Back in England, despite his growing reputation as a lutenist and the bachelor of music he received from Oxford in 1588, and despite his connections with courtiers such as George Carey, Henry Noel, and possibly Fulke Greville, first Lord Brooke, and the earl of Essex, Dowland was unable to get a place among the royal musicians. He thought, rightly or wrongly, that his religion stood in his way. This frustration may have contributed to the melancholy persona that he was to cultivate in coming years.

In 1594 he returned to the Continent at the invitation of Heinrich Julius, Duke of Braunschweig; after a time he proceeded to the court of Moritz, Landgrave of Hessen, at Cassel. Both rulers apparently offered him positions, but he had conceived the idea of going to Rome to study with the well-known composer of madrigals Luca Marenzio. Dowland visited Venice, Padua, Genoa, Ferrara, and Florence but seems to have been frightened out of continuing to Rome. He retreated to Nuremberg, where on 10 December 1595 he wrote a letter to Sir Robert Cecil about English Catholics in Italy who spoke of secret missions into and out of England and of words against the queen. He returned to Cassel and served the landgrave until Henry Noel, his "old master and friend," wrote in December 1596 that "her Majesty hath wished divers times your return." Dowland returned only to find that Noel had died on 26 February 1597. As a memorial to his friend Dowland wrote a set of seven four-voice "funeral psalms" called "Lamentatio Henrici Noel." The manuscript is inscribed "Gio. Dolande infelice Inglese" (John Dowland, unhappy Englishman).

The "unhappy Englishman" seems to have found that his hopes for royal preferment died with his friend. He nevertheless took advantage of his presence in England to publish his *First Book of Songs or Airs* (1597), which proved to be one of the most popular musical publications of the English Renaissance. It established the format for the ayre, which consists of a dominant melody with accompaniment: performance options include not only a single voice with lute and/or bass viol but also four voices, or whatever voices and instruments happen to be available.

Dowland invests the publication with a learned, humanistic tone: he cites Plato in the dedication and brags in his address to the reader that he has degrees from both Oxford and Cambridge. Thomas Campion provides a Latin epigram comparing Dowland to Orpheus. Dowland goes on in his address to describe his continental travels and to drop the names of foreign princes and musicians with whom he has associated. In pleading for a favorable reception he says, "The courtly judgment I hope will not be severe against [the songs], being it self a party," which suggests that courtiers are among the anonymous poets represented. Many of the texts have no independent sources, but two (numbers 2 and 21) are by Greville and one (number 18) is probably by Sir Henry Lee – it was sung at the ceremony marking his retirement as the queen's champion in 1590. Sir Henry Wotton provides a glimpse of how the courtly coterie used songs when he writes in *A Parallel between Robert, Late Earl of Essex, and George, Late Duke of Buckingham* (1641) that once, when the earl of Essex feared loss of favor with the queen, he "chose to evaporate his thoughts in a sonnet (being his common way) to be sung before the queen" by Robert Hales. At least one of the lyrics – number 5 – may be by Essex, and it is possible that numbers 3, 4, 6, and 19 were used by courtiers to lobby the queen.

Dowland dedicates the book to Sir George Carey, second Baron Hunsdon and the queen's Lord Chamberlain (distributor of posts for the royal household), whom he thanks for "honorable favors" that upheld his "poor fortunes." Dowland's characteristic note of melancholy complaint is heard in several of the songs, as in "Burst forth My Tears" (number 8), "Go, Crystal Tears" (number 9), and "All Ye Whom Love or Fortune Hath Betrayed" (number 14), in which he sings his "sorrows like the dying swan."

Dowland's fortunes, if not his temperament, began to improve. On 15 November 1598 he was appointed lutenist to Christian IV, King of Denmark and brother-in-law to the duke of Braunschweig and to King James VI of Scotland. From Denmark, Dowland sent the copy for his *Second Book of Songs or Airs* (1600) to his wife in England; she sold it to George Eastland for twenty pounds and half of what might be got from Lucy, Countess of Bedford, for dedicating the book to her. This dedication is less personal than others Dowland wrote: he probably knew that the countess had patronized poets, for several – including John Donne and Ben Jonson – had written poems to her.

The *Second Book of Songs or Airs* includes the song version of Dowland's best-known work, "Flow, My Tears," or as it was known in instrumental versions, "Lachrymae." This study in melancholy became Dowland's signature: he signed a Nuremberg gentleman's album "Jo: dolandi de Lachrimae." The song is alluded to in several contemporary sources, notably plays by Francis Beaumont and John Fletcher, Ben Jonson, John Webster, Philip Massinger, and Thomas Middleton; "to sing Lachrymae" even became a proverb. If any song text is a candidate for speculatively assigning to Dowland, it is this one. Not only are the personal associations strong, but the verse is also in an irregular form, suggesting that it was written as a contrafactum to fit Dowland's previously composed pavane. Other songs from the *Second Book of Songs or Airs,* like those in the first, use texts by Fulke Greville (number 18) and (probably) Sir Henry Lee (numbers 6–8). Several songs have the appearance of being part of a larger context, such as a masque, play, or other court entertainment (numbers 3–8, 14, and 22). Most of the songs seem to derive from the pre-Denmark period, when Dowland was operating on the fringes of the English court.

Dowland sent the copy for his *Third and Last Book of Songs or Airs* (1603) from Denmark sometime before 21 February 1603. It bears a grateful dedication to John Souch, soon afterward to be knighted by James I, and an epistle that rises above the usual defensiveness of many Elizabethan prefaces: "As in a hive of bees all labor alike to lay up honey, opposing themselves against none but fruitless drones; so in the house of learning and fame, all good endeavorers should strive to add somewhat that is good, not malicing one another, but altogether bandying against the idle and malicious ignorant."

Some of the texts in this collection are of a newer fashion: one poem is by Thomas Campion (number 17), and one with a risqué cavalier joke (number 6) was popular in manuscripts throughout the seventeenth century. Old themes recur, however, such as melancholy and tears (numbers 5, 8, 10, 11, and 15). Many of these songs also seem to have courtly connections: two (numbers 3 and 18) have texts probably by the earl of Essex, who had been executed in 1601. Several have flattering allusions to Queen Elizabeth (numbers 2, 3, 6, and 7)

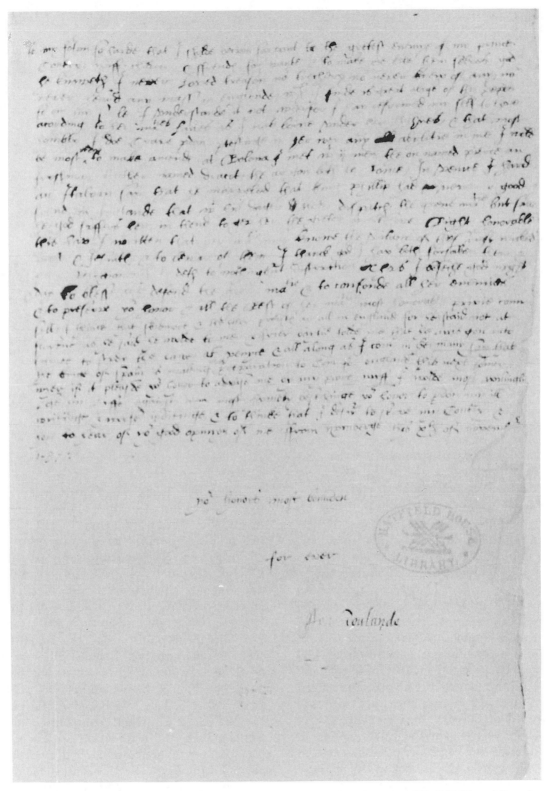

Last page of a letter from Dowland to Sir Robert Cecil, dated 10 November 1595 (Hatfield House Library)

Music for Dowland's "Sweet, Stay a While," in A Pilgrim's Solace *(1612)*

and may have been part of some Accession Day show. But the queen died on 24 March 1603, probably just as the book came from the printer.

Later that summer Dowland followed his book to England in order to seek a post at the new court. He was faced with a problem of some delicacy: how could he ask King James to steal his brother-in-law's servant? Dowland's strategy was to dedicate *Lachrimae, or Seven Tears Figured in Seven Passionate Pavans* (1604), a collection of instrumental consort music that opens with a series of variations on his best-known tune, to Queen Anne of Denmark. The dedication offers excuses for tardiness in returning to Denmark and includes this eloquent sentence: "And though the title doth promise tears, unfit guests in these joyful times, yet no doubt pleasant are the tears which music weeps, neither are tears shed always in sorrow, but sometime in joy and gladness." The work was published around April 1604; but Dowland was back in Denmark by July, his attempt having failed. He seems to have offended Christian IV by staying away longer than the period allocated by royal permission. Other problems may have arisen, but whatever the immediate cause may have been, Dowland was dis-

missed on 24 February 1606. He then returned to England for good.

Dowland's next publication was a vigorous prose translation of a rather old-fashioned treatise on music by Andreas Vogelsang, or Ornithoparcus, which had originally been published in Leipzig in 1517. It has a fulsome dedication to Robert Cecil, Earl of Salisbury, acknowledging "special favors and graces," which suggests that Cecil may have helped Dowland on his return. The epistle is dated 10 April 1609, from his "house in Fetter-lane."

The next publications involving Dowland seem designed to give his son, Robert, then about nineteen, a professional boost. Robert was nominally the editor of the two anthologies published in 1610, *Variety of Lute Lessons* and *A Musical Banquet,* but the elder Dowland contributed significant works to each, and many of the other works are by composers of his generation. He provided nine lute pieces for the first collection, and the landgrave of Hessen, his old patron, and older lutenists such as Anthony Holborne, Gregory Howet, and Daniel Batchelar also contributed. John Dowland also included his translation of J. B. Besard's "Necessary Observations Belonging to the Lute" and his own

"Other Necessary Observations." These works are brief and technical but clear; it is worth noting that Dowland invokes Pythagorean science in describing how to set frets on the lute. Two pieces are credited to Robert, but one seems to be a set of variations on one of his father's tunes.

A Musical Banquet collects airs by English and foreign composers, including three songs by John Dowland, one with a text by Sir Henry Lee, and another, "In Darkness Let Me Dwell," one of the most powerful and dramatic expressions of Dowland's melancholy. The words first appeared with John Coprario's music in *Funeral Tears* (1606), a collection of songs mourning the death of Charles Blount, Earl of Devonshire and eighth Lord Mountjoy. Dowland's setting transfigures a mediocre poem through music that combines native and "advanced" Italian elements, poignant dissonances, and passionate declamation. In other songs Holborne set a poem by George Clifford, Earl of Cumberland and Lee's successor as the queen's champion; Richard Martin and Batchelar set texts by the earl of Essex; and Robert Hales, the queen's favorite singer, set an anonymous poem. Three songs have texts by Sir Philip Sidney. Robert dedicated *Variety of Lute Lessons* to Sir Thomas Monson, thanking him for educating him while his father was abroad. The dedicatee of *A Musical Banquet* was Sir Robert Sidney, Robert's godfather.

Sometime before 1612 the elder Dowland became lutenist to Theophilus Howard, Lord Walden, for he identifies himself as such on the title page of his last collection of airs, *A Pilgrim's Solace* (1612). The book, which is dedicated to Walden, includes two songs that were probably composed for Walden's wedding (numbers 20 and 21). In his epistle to the reader Dowland reminds his countrymen of the honors and employment he received abroad and complains about his recent reception by younger musicians, especially singers who are ignorant of the elements of music and blindly ornament vocal lines and who consider Dowland old-fashioned. Dowland did, in fact, reach back for some of his texts to one first set by William Byrd in 1588 (number 13), one from a pageant performed in 1592 (number 18), one by Nicholas Breton published in 1602 (numbers 14–16), and part of a long poem the earl of Essex wrote shortly before his execution in 1601 (number 10). But two texts have since crept into the Donne *dubia* (numbers 2, 3), and one is attributed to William Herbert, Earl of Pembroke (number 1). The melancholy note is still much in evidence in several songs (numbers 7, 9, and 10), but in some it takes on a religious cast (numbers

12–17). The music is inventive and adventurously expressive, showing no signs of stagnation.

To reflect more generally on Dowland's treatment of verse beyond the formal parallels of verse unit and musical period: his musical settings interpret their texts mainly by giving them a physical sound – a voice. This voice usually reinforces the general mood suggested by the text through fairly common musical means: serious matter evokes slow tempos; melancholy subjects, minor modes and dissonances; humor, major tonality and lively rhythms. Dowland's songs often go further in that they give a sense of emotional genuineness to verse that seems to be no more than Petrarchan cliché, as in "In Darkness Let Me Dwell." "Go, Crystal Tears" is another example that treats a conventional love lament with gently melancholy yet persuasive music. Another poem in the same vein, "Me, Me, and None But Me," is so exaggerated in sentiment that it is hard to take seriously; the music subtly mocks the poem by naively illustrating "I draw too long this idle breath" with long notes and "fly to heaven above" with an ascending scale, all in a rather cheerful major mode. A better poem such as the aubade "Sweet, Stay Awhile" evokes a rich musical treatment that begins by suggesting the languor of the waking lovers with long and longing notes and then continues with the urgency of "O stay, or else my joys must die," with dramatic exclamation and rapidly repeated sequences on "my joys." Less impressionistic analysis can be accomplished with more precise reference to the music, but there is a certain amount of irreducible subjectivity in such interpretation, just as there is in determining the tone of voice in a conversation.

Shortly after the publication of *A Pilgrim's Solace,* perhaps because of Walden's friendship with the musical Prince Henry (who died later in the year), or perhaps because Walden's father, Lord Thomas Howard, Earl of Suffolk, was lord chamberlain, Dowland was at last appointed to be one of the royal lutenists. Having finally attained his goal, he contributed to a few collections but wrote little more original music. Henry Peacham referred to him in *Thalia's Banquet* (1620) as "Doctor" Dowland, a title he is given in subsequent references. When King James died in 1625, Dowland played in the ensemble at his funeral. In February 1626 Dowland himself died; he was buried at St. Ann, Blackfriars, on 20 February and was succeeded in the King's Music by his son, Robert.

Dowland's reputation as the archetypal musician, the *Anglorum Orphei,* held firm for years after his death. He was celebrated in poems by Campion,

Richard Barnfield, Peacham, and Josuah Sylvester; his songs were alluded to in plays and poems. Although some of his songs and psalm settings continued to be printed and sung, his popularity declined with that of the lute, until the early music revival of this century made the full range of his work available and critically esteemed.

References:

Edward Doughtie, *English Renaissance Song* (Boston: Twayne, 1986);

Doughtie, ed., *Lyrics from English Airs, 1596–1622* (Cambridge, Mass.: Harvard University Press, 1970);

Elise Bickford Jorgens, *The Well-Tun'd Word: Musical Interpretations of English Poetry 1597–1651* (Minneapolis: University of Minnesota Press, 1982);

Wilfrid Mellers, *Harmonious Meeting: A Study of the Relationship between English Music, Poetry and Theatre c. 1600–1900* (London: Dobson, 1965), pp. 81–103;

Diana Poulton, *John Dowland* (London: Faber & Faber, 1972; revised edition, Berkeley: University of California Press, 1982);

Ian Spink, *English Song: Dowland to Purcell* (London: Batsford, 1974), pp. 15–43;

Robert Toft, " 'Musicke a Sister to Poetrie': Rhetorical Artifice in the Passionate Airs of John Dowland," *Early Music,* 12 (1984): 173–199;

John M. Ward, *A Dowland Miscellany,* special issue of the *Journal of the Lute Society of America,* 10 (1977);

Robin Headlam Wells, "John Dowland and Elizabethan Melancholy," *Early Music,* 19 (November 1985): 514–528.

Anne Dowriche

(before July 1560 – after 1613)

Elaine V. Beilin
Framingham State College

BOOK: *The French Historie. That Is; a Lamentable Discourse of Three Bloodie Broiles in France for the Gospell of Jesus Christ* (London: Thomas Orwin for Thomas Man, 1589).

Motivated to write a historical poem by intense religious conviction and a mission to reform poetry, Anne Dowriche was one of a small number of women who published poetry in the sixteenth century. In her preface she states that she wrote *The French History* (1589) to edify, comfort, and stir up her Protestant readers to "care, watchfulness, zeal, and ferventness in the cause of God's truth," choosing poetry in order to restore its "credit" and to move her audience. Her twenty-four-hundred-line poem, an ardently Protestant account of the French civil wars, is framed as a narrative history, a providential justification of the Reformed church, and a political diatribe against tyranny. Through her poem Dowriche participated vigorously in contemporary religious and political controversies, and although some of her verses lumber along, she created vivid and memorable scenes and characters.

Anne Edgcumbe Dowriche was the daughter of Sir Richard Edgcumbe and Elizabeth Tregian Edgcumbe of Mount Edgcumbe, Cornwall. The Edgcumbe arms, three boars' heads, appear on the verso of the title page of *The French History*. Although no birth record appears to be extant, Dowriche was born before 1 July 1560, when she is mentioned in Sir Richard's will. In *Records of the Edgcumbe Family* (1888), W. H. Edgcumbe suggests that Anne and her sister, Honour, were still children when the will was written, since Sir Richard provides for their education in the document. On 29 November 1580 an Exeter marriage license was issued for "Mr. Dowrishe, Rector of Lapford, and Anna Edgecombe, gentlewoman." Hugh Dowriche matriculated at Hart Hall, Oxford, in 1572, when he was nineteen, became bachelor of divinity in 1581, and was licensed to preach in 1583. He also served as rector of Honiton, Devon, from 1587 to 1598. Transcriptions of baptismal records exist for his and Anne's three children: Mary (born 1587), Anne (born 1589), and Hugh (born 1594); another son, Elkana, apparently the eldest, is remembered in the 1590 will of his grandfather, Thomas Dowriche. G. E. Trease lists the children's names as Elkana, Walter, Mary, and Elizabeth, so there may have been other births.

Sources on Dowriche's biography include a few local records and family papers, bibliographical notices, and an inaccurate entry in the *Dictionary of National Biography,* which surmises incorrectly that she was the daughter of Peter Edgcumbe, who died in 1607. This Peter (Piers or Pearse) Edgcumbe was actually the "loving brother" to whom she dedicated her poem – the dictionary incorrectly identifies the dedicatee as the Pearse Edgcumbe who died in 1628; he was actually Dowriche's nephew. Although Dowriche was married only once, the *Dictionary of National Biography* identifies a second husband as Richard Trefusis. In fact, it was another Anne Edgcumbe, Dowriche's niece and Piers Edgcumbe's daughter, whose first husband was Richard Trefusis. Family genealogies clarify their separate identities, as does a document of 1613 that names both the aunt, Anne Dowriche, and the niece, Anne Trefusis.

The Edgcumbes were a prominent family of Cornwall and Devon. Dowriche's father, Sir Richard, served in various county offices, and her brothers were both members of Parliament. In 1553 Sir Richard completed Mount Edgcumbe, his great house overlooking Plymouth Sound. Presumably Dowriche lived there. In the manuscript "A Friendly Remembrance of Sir Richard Edgcomb," her nephew, the historian and poet Richard Carew of Antony, describes her father as a "fine old English gentleman" who possessed "very good grace in making English verses." He was also a generous, charitable man whose house was famous for hospitality. In his *Survey of Cornwall* (1602), Carew describes Sir Richard's deer park, round turrets, and his great hall, ranking the house "for health, pleasure, and commodities, with any subject's house of his degree in England." The house was burned out during World War II and has since been rebuilt.

Anne Edgcumbe married into the well-to-do Dowriche family of Dowriche House near Sandford, Devon. In his will, her father-in-law, Thomas Dowriche, leaves to his "well-beloved daughter-in-law" four pounds, "to make her a ring," and to his grandson Elkana "the gilt silver goblet weighing nineteen ounces" as well as five pounds toward Elkana's preferment. It is worth noting that Elkana's name clearly indicates the dominant interest of Anne and Hugh Dowriche in biblical studies: breaking with a long tradition of family names on both sides, they gave their first-born a biblical name meaning "provided by God."

Following the publication of his wife's learned poem, Hugh Dowriche also wrote a work steeped in exegesis, *The Jailor's Conversion* (1596). Both Dowriches inscribe the prefaces to their books from Honiton, Devon – Anne on 25 July 1589 and Hugh on 30 June 1596. There was apparently some local interest in Anne's poem, since a variant copy was printed for the Exeter bookseller William Russell. From their specifically godly language and from Hugh Dowriche's dedication to his "first friend," Valentine Knightley, a member of a prominent Puritan family, it appears that the Dowriches were members of an active Puritan circle. Commendatory verses by "A. D." prefacing Hugh Dowriche's book echo lines in *The French History,* "that all things done to God's elect are always for the best." In *The Jailor's Conversion,* she repeats the doctrine: "And all that haps to His elect, / Is always for the best." Indeed, this belief is fundamental to Dowriche's providential reading of history.

In the dedication to "the right worshipful her loving brother, Master Pearse Edgecombe," Dowriche distinguishes between the simple form of her poem, which is "base and scarce worth the seeing," and the excellence of her subject matter. Even the conventional self-deprecation of dedications is outdone by her warning, "If you find any thing that fits not your liking, remember I pray, that it is a woman's doing." But while Dowriche appears to be treading cautiously on ground rarely covered by a woman, she also emphasizes her pleasure in "collecting and disposing" her history, and in her pref-

ace titled "To the Reader" she announces her arrival as a new poet with a mission.

Dowriche introduces her religious goals in this preface, explaining that she chose to write about the French religious wars as a warning against Satan's strength and as an example of the patient suffering of the godly, in this case the Huguenots persecuted by the Catholic regime. Since everyone already knew about English "noble martyrs," Dowriche took as her source Thomas Tymme's *The Three Parts of Commentaries, Containing the Whole and Perfect Discourse of the Civil Wars of France* (1574) – a translation of Jean de Serres's *Commentariorum de statu religionis & reipublicae in regno Galliae libri* (1572–1575) transforming its events into verse and amplifying speeches to make a more stirring poem; yet, she stresses, "here is no more set down than there is signified."

While she zealously recounts a one-sided Huguenot version of the wars, Dowriche was apparently justifying her invented speeches in the light of contemporary discussions about historical truth. Thus, she closely follows her chronicle source, yet also elaborates certain dramatic moments with orations by Anne du Bourg and other martyrs, as well as by her Catholic villains and even by Satan himself. In her choice of scenes – the affair of the Rue St. Jacques in 1557, the death of Anne du Bourg in 1559, and the massacre of St. Bartholomew in 1572 – Dowriche makes a case for the political motivation of religious persecution, highlighting crucial moments in the conflict between the Catholic monarchy and the Huguenot nobles and bourgeoisie. Her religious and political agenda is also served by her integration of scriptural parallels, introduced to give a providential framework to her history of the godly martyrs. Not at all meekly, she wishes "to restore again some credit if I can unto poetry, having been defaced of late so many ways by wanton vanities."

Dowriche's understanding of poetic convention is reflected in the narrative framework she creates for her history. Two narrators speak, an English man and a French exile, the latter occupying most of the poem. The opening lines depict a first-person narrator walking in the woods where he overhears a fearful "shrilling voice" lamenting the miseries of war-torn France. Developing an *ubi sunt* theme, this "godly French exile" mourns the loss of "mutual love that Prince and people had" and the ensuing tyranny that has brought France to disastrous civil war. The sympathetic Englishman offers his hospitality in return for

Title page and verso, with the Edgcumbe family coat of arms, for Anne Dowriche's historical poem

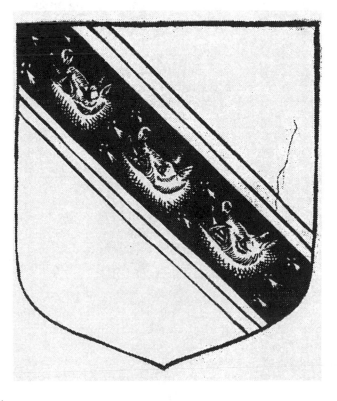

the exile's story. It may be that Dowriche's two male narrators reflect her source, a French work translated by an Englishman; or she may have perceived that her subject matter would be more acceptably clothed in male discourse.

The first of the poem's three parts is set in 1557 during the reign of Henry II. The new religion takes hold among "God's elect," but Satan arrives to urge his forces to destroy them. Closely following her prose source, Dowriche constructs an archetypal battle between good and evil: the chief heroes are the godly men and women who secretly participate in the Reformed church and bravely suffer the consequences of discovery; the chief villains are the Catholic Queen Catherine de Medici and the powerful Guise family, all of whom Satan constantly urges to eradicate the followers of Luther. During his first oration, Satan tells his followers that "when in fields they join their joyful Psalms to sing, / We must give out that they conspire which way to kill the King." When the Reformers are attacked after their secret prayer meetings on the Rue St. Jacques, Dowriche creates both a political lesson and a parable of demonic persecution. While some of the "godly troop" escape, "The greater sort were taken then, and straight to prison led." Among the prisoners are "women of great parentage which were with shame reviled" by the mob on the streets. Here Dowriche closely follows Tymme, using much of his phrasing, including the "women of great parentage . . . [who] were shamefully entreated and unhonestly handled of the people."

Throughout her poem, Dowriche follows Tymme's Protestant linking of religious persecution with French politics and foreign affairs, citing particularly the common Catholic fears of Protestant sedition, strongly denied by both authors. Most historians concur with her in seeing the events of 1557 as seminal. Indeed, Barbara Diefendorf suggests in *Beneath the Cross: Catholics and Huguenots in Sixteenth-Century Paris* (1991) that the affair of the Rue St. Jacques defined the beginning of popular violence against the new religion and, further, that there were "complex interrelations between popular violence and monarchical politics."

In the second and third parts of her poem, Dowriche's principal interest is in dramatizing and interpreting the course of religious persecution, popular violence, and monarchical politics. She creates a providential scheme in which the Huguenots are scripturally justified Christian martyrs, but she also dramatizes political resistance to tyranny. Her martyrology probably owes as much to Foxe's *Actes and Monuments* (1563) for manner as it does to Tymme's translation for matter. She may also have been influenced by the resistance theory of François Hotman, whose *De Furoribus Gallicis* (1573) was included as "A True and Plain Report of the Furious Outrages of France," in the tenth book of Tymme's *The Three Parts of Commentaries*.

Dowriche's hero in the second part is Anne du Bourg (Annas Burgeus), a counsellor in the Senate of Paris who publicly confronted Henry II and, in Tymme's version, "very boldly and freely uttered his mind" about ending the punishment of Protestants. The king immediately ordered du Bourg's arrest and sentenced him to death. *The Three Parts of Commentaries* – and other contemporary histories – record at length du Bourg's final oration to the Senate. Dowriche created her own versified version of this speech and apparently invented another, his address to the king. In the impassioned language of the martyr, the poem gains considerable strength as Dowriche exploits both the dramatic setting and the potential for rhetorical fireworks. When du Bourg faces Henry II, his speech is bold and stirring:

> And if the hidden truth the Lord will now reveal,
> To daunt the same (o noble King) your force shall not prevail.
> What giant can withstand of truth the piercing might?
> What earthly force of shining sun at noon can quench the light?
> If truth do conquer kings, if truth do conquer all,
> Then leave to love these popish lies; let whorish Babel fall.

This excerpt demonstrates Dowriche's fervent language, well suited to the speaker; at the same time, its meter is unremittingly regular, the beat simply punctuating the propaganda in rhyming lines of alternating iambic hexameter and heptameter – the "poulter's measure" that achieved popularity in the sixteenth century.

Dowriche's version of du Bourg's final oration follows closely the content and language in Tymme, emphasizing, for instance, his strong denial of a Protestant rebellion against the state: "Is this a rebel's part when men to princes give / Their bodies, goods, and all things else without repine and grief?" More than Protestant innocence, however, Dowriche's constantly reiterated theme is the evil of tyranny. Asserting that Henry II always intended to kill the Reformers in the Senate, Dowriche shows him abusing the constitutional process to achieve his ends. Debate in the Senate is simply used to smoke out Reformers. From her providential perspective, Dowriche likens Henry II to ill-fated enemies of God in the Bible – Ahab, Amaziah, and Zedekiah – a comparison supported by the king's accidental death shortly after condemning du Bourg. While du Bourg's martyrdom and Henry's death support her providential scheme, du Bourg is also a model of active political resistance to the tyrant.

In the final section of the poem, Dowriche brings to a dramatic climax many of the themes and images initiated earlier. In her account of the St. Bartholomew's Day Massacre in 1572, the verse is assured and the characters believable and fully in the grip of their passions and beliefs. Satan is prominently featured, urging on the Queen Mother, the Guises, and "the rest of the Papists." The heroic Huguenots – led by the king of Navarre, the prince of Condé, and especially by the admiral Gaspard de Coligny – are slowly and fatally enmeshed in a net of hatred and perfidy, yet always ready with a ringing declamation of faith. Guided by her source, the tenth book of the *The Three Parts of Commentaries,* Dowriche sets the scene for the Queen Mother to advocate murdering all the Huguenots gathered in Paris for the wedding of her daughter Marguerite to the Protestant Henry of Navarre:

> The captains being slain, the soldiers will be faint;
> So shall we quickly on the rest perform our whole intent.
> Pluck up therefore your sprites, and play your manly parts;
> Let neither fear nor faith prevail to daunt your warlike hearts.
> What shame is this that I (a woman by my kind)
> Need thus to speak, or pass you men in valor of the mind?
> For here I do protest, if I had been a man,
> I had myself before this time this murder long began.

The marginal gloss for this speech implicates Machiavelli, the "devil of Florence," of whom the queen is said to be "a good scholar." Dowriche embellishes the role of the stage Machiavel even further in the duke of Guise, who gloats over the barbaric murder of the admiral and asks his followers for more:

> Let nothing now prevail to daunt your hardy mind;
> No, though with tears they pity crave, let them no mercy find.
> Have no remorse unto the young nor yet the old;
> Without regard to anyone, to kill them all be bold.

> Now sanctify your swords, and bathe them in the blood
> Of these religious rebels, which do mean the king no good.

Demonic bloodthirstiness was a standard feature of anti-Catholic propaganda, although Dowriche never forgets her political theme in this section of the poem, as speakers on both sides question the role of the king. From the king's own Captain of the Guard, de Nance, who asks whether he should "consent to do this fearful thing / To shed this blood, because I am commanded by the king," to the doomed Monsieur de Pilles, who denounces the breaking of a "solemn kingly oath" and "a prince's faith," Dowriche continually draws her readers' attention to the consequences of bonds broken between ruler and people: civil war and war against God.

Constantly interweaving her providential framework and her political credo, Dowriche ends the poem with the French exile praying for peace in England where religious "Truth" is ensconced, and for "that noble Queen Elizabeth" who will "hunt with perfect hate / The popish hearts of fained friends before it be too late." Finally, then, the poem is part of the outpouring of pamphlets of the late 1580s, all of which give "news" from Europe and decry an international Catholic conspiracy. It also advocates political activism on behalf of God's law to which the monarch must also adhere. Dowriche reflects grassroots Puritan fears that intensified even after the Armada. Living in the southwest counties might also have contributed to her urgency about the Catholic threat. In *Richard Carew of Antony's The Survey of Cornwall* (1969) Halliday notes that after 1588, "there were constant alarms in Cornwall . . . as more Armadas, real or imaginary, were sighted in the Channel approaches." In *The Elizabethan Puritan Movement* (1967) Patrick Collinson quotes the diary of Richard Rogers for July 1589: "There is little hope of any better state to the Church. Sudden dangers are greatly to be feared. We are generally so secure and so little dreaming of them." Dowriche's poem expresses fundamental Puritan fears and warnings: unless Scripture becomes the highest law, obeyed by ruler and people alike; unless the English church is purged and reformed; unless God's enemies are punished, England might repeat the disastrous history of France.

Further work on Anne Dowriche is needed, including primary biographical research and an investigation of possible contexts for her poem. To what specific Puritan circles, whether literary, religious, or political, did the Dowriches belong? How does *The French History* relate to other historical poems and to letters, treatises, and news reports? What are its political roots in the late 1580s and what are its regional connections? Analysis of Dowriche's text and contexts may also clarify the role of women writers in sixteenth-century Protestant polemic and historiography.

References:

Elaine V. Beilin, *Redeeming Eve: Women Writers of the English Renaissance* (Princeton: Princeton University Press, 1987), pp. 101–107;

Beilin, "Writing Public Poetry: Humanism and the Woman Writer," *Modern Language Quarterly,* 51 (1990): 249–271;

Natalie Zemon Davis, "Gender and Genre: Women as Historical Writers, 1400–1820," in *Beyond Their Sex: Learned Women of the European Past,* edited by Patricia H. Labalme (New York: New York University Press, 1984), pp. 153–182;

W. H. Edgcumbe, *Records of the Edgcumbe Family* (Plymouth: W. Brendon & Son, 1888);

G. E. Trease, "Dowrich and the Dowrich Family of Sandford," *Devon and Cornwall Notes and Queries,* 33 (1974): 208–211.

John Florio
(1553? – 1625)

Konrad Eisenbichler
University of Toronto

BOOKS: *Florio His First Fruites . . . Also a Perfect Intro-duction to the Italian, and English Tongues* (London: Printed by T. Dawson for Thomas Woodcocke, 1578);

Florios Second Frutes . . . to Which Is Annexed His Gardine of Recreation (London: Printed by T. Orwin for Thomas Woodcock, 1591);

A Worlde of Wordes, or Most Copious, Dictionarie in Italian and English (London: Printed by Arnold Hatfield for Edward Blount, 1598); revised and enlarged as *Queen Anna's New World of Words, or Dictionarie Newly Much Augmented. Whereunto Are Added Rules for the Italian Tongue* (London: Printed by M. Bradwood for Edward Blount & William Barret, 1611); revised and enlarged by Giovanni Torriano as *Vocabolario Italiano et Inglese: A Dictionary Italian and English* (London: Printed by T. Warren for John Martin, James Allestry & Thomas Dicas, 1659); revised and enlarged by J. Davis as *Vocabolario Italiano et Inglese: A Dictionary, Italian and English* (London: Printed by R. Holt & W. Horton for R. Chiswell, T. Sawbridge, G. Wells & R. Bentley, 1688).

OTHER: Jacques Cartier, *A Short and Brief Narration of the Two Navigations and Discoveries to the North-West Parts Called New France . . . Now Turned into English by John Florio* (London: H. Bynneman, 1580);

A Letter Lately Written from Rome by an Italian Gentleman . . . Newly Translated out of Italian into English by J. F. (London: John Charlewoode, 1585);

Michel de Montaigne, *The Essays,* translated by Florio (London: Printed for Edward Blount, 1603);

Traiano Boccalini, *The New-found Politic,* translated by Florio and others (London: Printed for Francis Williams, 1626);

The Italian Tutor (London: Thomas Paine, 1640) — includes *Dialogues,* possibly printed from a manuscript by Florio.

John Florio; engraving by William Hole

Editions: Michel de Montaigne, *The Essayes . . . Translated by John Florio* (London: Oxford University Press, 1910);

Jacques Cartier, *Navigations to New France* (New York: Readex Microprint, 1966).

John Florio's reputation rests primarily on his 1603 translation of Michel de Montaigne's *Essais* (1572–1580) and his compilation of *A World of Words* (1598), an Italian-English dictionary. He worked for the French embassy in London; served

Queen Anne, the wife of James I, as a Groom of the Privy Chamber; and tutored some of the royal children in Italian. Florio's political connections were extensive and included Cecil, Southampton, Leicester, Rutland, and Bedford. His literary connections included Samuel Daniel, John Eliot, Thomas Nashe, Gabriel Harvey, and William Shakespeare – though not all were favorable to him. His work as a lexicographer and translator places him among the significant contributors to Renaissance English language and literature.

John Florio was born in London in 1553. His early education was at the hands of his father, Michael Angelo Florio. The elder Florio, Italian by birth, was a former Franciscan friar obliged to flee Italy because of his reformist views. He eventually settled in England, where in 1550 he was appointed pastor to the Italian Protestant church in London, founded and supported by Archbishop Thomas Cranmer and William Cecil, Lord Burghley. He served his congregation with mixed success, composed a short work on the Italian language, and was tutor in Italian to some members of the English nobility, foremost among whom was Lady Jane Grey. On the accession of Mary Tudor, the Florios left England and settled in Soglio, a small village in the Grisons canton of Switzerland. The younger Florio was sent to the University of Tübingen in 1563 (through arrangements put in place by Pier Paolo Vergerio, the former bishop of Capodistria who had turned Protestant) but seems not to have graduated. The elder Florio died sometime between 1566 and 1572. John Florio returned to England sometime after Elizabeth's accession to the throne in 1558 and before his father's death. On the basis of the *Returns of Aliens,* he may have been back in London in 1571.

Shortly after his return to England, Florio commenced his career as a teacher of Italian. He attended Oxford, where he finally matriculated from Magdalen College in 1581. At Oxford he met the Welsh doctor Matthew Gwinne, who became his lifelong friend, contributing under the pseudonym "Il Candido" congratulatory poems for Florio's publications. Florio compares their relationship to that of Montaigne and de la Boëtie in the dedication to his translation of the *Essays.* At Oxford, Florio also met Richard Hakluyt, who paid him to translate Giovanni Battista Ramusio's Italian version of Jacques Cartier's first two voyages, *A Short and Brief Narration of the Two Navigations and Discoveries to the North-West Parts called New France* (1580), later incorporated into Hakluyt's *Principal Navigations* (1589). Florio's prefatory epistle "To All Gentlemen, Merchants, and Pilots" is of interest as one of the earliest documents to advocate colonization. Hakluyt, who probably instilled such concepts in Florio, voiced similar views two years later in the dedication to his *Divers Voyages.*

Florio's most important work in these years was the Italian conversation and grammar book *First Fruits* (1578), dedicated to Robert Dudley, Earl of Leicester, by whose family the elder Florio had once been employed. The work is divided into two sections: a series of forty-four elementary dialogues and a grammar of Italian. The dialogues, given in both Italian and English, are printed in facing parallel columns on the same page and arranged according to increasing difficulty. The nameless, generic interlocutors (a man, a woman, a servant) exchange information and opinions. Although their conversations reflect contemporary interests and activities, they are superficial and stilted. The general effect is that of a series of simple sentences laced together to suggest dialogue. The grammar section begins with general rules on pronunciation and proceeds through the parts of speech and standard grammatical constructs. The grammatical model is Latin – Italian nouns, for example, are grouped into four declensions and declined according to the six Latin cases.

Florio periodically exhibits feelings of discontent in *First Fruits,* as when he notes "the reluctance of many English parents to have their children properly grounded in modern languages." This insular attitude would, understandably, have concerned Florio, whose livelihood depended to a large extent on teaching Italian language and conversation. The discontent may also reflect a patronizing attitude on the part of resident Italians and English Italophiles toward the "barbarous" English who had not yet assimilated or fully appreciated the artistic, commercial, political, or social refinements of the Italian Renaissance. The English language comes under fire from Florio, who describes it as confused and remarks that it "will do you good in England, but pass Dover, it is worth nothing." He also criticizes English dress and morals. Florio's views on amatory literature are exemplified in the comment that "it were labor lost to speak of love," a phrase that has become well known because of its resemblance to the title of one of Shakespeare's comedies. It is not a coincidence that the dialogue following this remark is titled "A Discourse upon Lust and the Force Thereof."

Several dialogues seem to contain a moral agenda, drawn in part from the works of the Spanish moralist Antonio de Guevara and the Italian

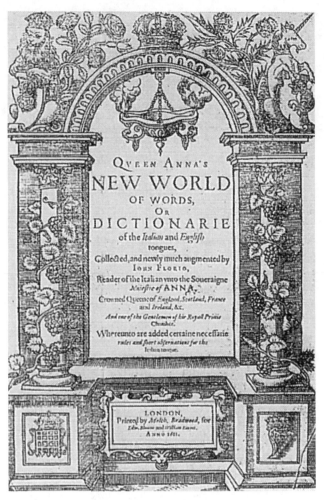

*Title page for the enlarged edition of Florio's
Italian-English dictionary*

statesman Lodovico Guicciardini. Florio's agenda suggests an outlook also fostered by contemporary religious debates and his own upbringing as a reform minister's son. The Puritanism evident in the dialogues may be a stance purposely assumed in order to counterbalance the current view of things Italian as wicked and their influence on sober English society as detrimental.

Such moralistic overtones are not present, however, in the *Second Fruits* (1591), a collection of twelve dialogues. It was jointly published with the *Gardine of Recreation,* Florio's alphabetical listing of some six thousand Italian proverbs culled from the best examples of Italian writing. Florio is not without pride in his compilation, comparing it in his preface to John Heywood's 1562 English collection and to Desiderius Erasmus's 1500 compilation of Greek and Latin proverbs. Florio also points out the importance of proverbs, claiming they are "the pith, the proprieties, the proofs, the purities, the elegan-

cies, as the commonest so the commendablest phrases of a language. To use them is a grace, to understand them a good, but to gather them a pain to me, though gain to thee." Such is Florio's interest in Italian proverbs that the dialogues presented in the *Second Fruits* become, at a certain point, an exercise in their use. Florio even marks the appearances of proverbs in the dialogues with asterisks, drawing them to his reader's attention.

The dialogues are printed with Italian and English versions on facing pages. Instead of generic interlocutors, as had been the case in the *First Fruits,* these dialogues introduce named speakers, some of whom are drawn from Florio's contemporaries. The character of "Nolano" (dialogue 1), for example, is clearly drawn from Giordano Bruno, the Italian philosopher and renegade Franciscan whom Florio had come to know when they were both employed by the French embassy in London.

Letter in Italian from Florio, probably to Robert Cotton, written circa 1600 (British Library, Ms. Cott. Jul. C. III, fol. 174ᵃ)

Second Fruits provides a fuller insight into Florio's world and views than its predecessor. It also shows that his outlook had changed. The moralism of the 1570s is toned down in favor of an excited, inquiring attitude to the world around him. Florio voices his enthusiasm in the first sentence of the dedicatory epistle, saying that "in this stirring time and pregnant prime of invention, when every bramble is fruitful, when every mole-hill hath cast off the winter's mourning garment, and when every man is busily working to feed his own fancies . . . I could not chose but apply myself in some sort to the season." In the preface, he cites verbatim Roger Ascham's dictum from *The Schoolmaster* (1570), "Inglese italianato è diavolo incarnato" (the Italianate Englishman is a devil incarnate) and responds to his xenophobic critics by pointing out the value of knowing several languages and being able to draw upon original sources. Translators and translations are to be encouraged, he adds, for they assist in the dissemination of knowledge: "Had they not known Italian, how had they translated it? Had they not translated it, where were now thy reading?" The fear of moral contamination is raised and refuted by Florio: "But thou wilt urge me with their manner and vices (not remembering that where great vices are, there are infinite virtues), and ask me whether they be good or bad?" He points out that good and evil exist in every nation. His Italian proverbs have been "selected and stamped for the wise . . . who will kindly accept of them." Confident of the value of his contribution, Florio seeks the gratitude of his countrymen for having brought them "Italian words and phrases that yet never saw Albion's cliffs."

Florio's changed attitude is partly attributable to the changed cultural climate of Elizabethan England, now more accepting of Italian influences, and also to his new circle of patrons and friends. His horizons, in fact, had expanded significantly. In the 1580s he had been employed by the French embassy, where he had the opportunity to meet and work with Bruno. Regular contact with the cosmopolitan world of international affairs and with foreign intellectuals who nurtured his inquisitive mind reinforced his own self-esteem as "an Englishman in Italian," as he writes in *Second Fruits*.

The self-confidence of the author – as a writer as well as an observer of his society – is reflected in the situations presented in the twelve dialogues. Organized in sequence from morning to night, they constitute a progression of vignettes that illustrate a day in the life of well-to-do, elegant Englishmen (there are no female interlocutors). As the day progresses, the speakers discuss clothes, soccer, riding, card and table games, food, table manners, social manners, arms, commerce, attractive and unattractive women, and news from the court, until finally, while walking with the night guard, they talk of love. These discussions belie Florio's earlier comment that "it were labor lost to speak of love." His English gentlemen no longer reflect an attitude toward love as a subject not worthy of a serious-minded person, but illustrate the manners of well-accomplished gentlemen for whom the ability to converse on the topic was a necessary accomplishment.

In the preface to the reader, Florio had mentioned that he would "shortly send into the world an exquisite Italian and English dictionary, and a compendious grammar." The promise was partly fulfilled in 1598 with the appearance of *A World of Words,* expanded in 1611 as *Queen Anna's New World of Words.* The dictionary established Florio's reputation among his contemporaries as a scholar and, with Giovanni Torriano's later revisions, remained the standard dictionary throughout the seventeenth century and formed the basis of later such works. Florio was aware of its importance, so much so that in the preface he compares his dictionary favorably to those of Thomas Elyot, Thomas Thomas, John Rider, and of the Stephanuses, *père et fils.* He also points out with pride that his dictionary reveals the wealth of the English language, which, for every Italian word, can provide several English equivalents. English, which in *First Fruits* was discounted because it could not pass Dover, is here praised for the richness of its lexicon.

The preface includes a long denunciation of "H.S.," a critic who had attacked Florio's earlier works. Henry Salisbury, the compiler of a Welsh dictionary, has been suggested as the object of Florio's wrath, but Frances Yates more convincingly identifies the critic as Hugh Sanford, William Herbert's tutor and the editor of the 1593 edition of Philip Sidney's *Arcadia.* The Sanford-Florio controversy was part of a much larger debate that embroiled some of the more eminent names in the contemporary literary circuit — Eliot, Nashe, Harvey, and Daniel — and touched upon the unauthorized first editions of Sidney's *Arcadia* (1590) and *Astrophil and Stella* (1591).

The years between the publication of the dictionary and the translation of Montaigne saw significant changes in the political situation in England. Essex's rebellion and his demise should have had severe repercussions for Florio since most of his patrons — Southampton, Rutland, the Danvers, the Bedfords, the Haringtons, and Lady Rich — were either implicated in the events or personally tied to Essex. Florio, however, survived unscathed. He continued to carry out his diplomatic work at the French embassy and his Italian tutoring for noble households. He may have been a spy planted by Cecil to observe the Essex camp, but the evidence is tenuous.

Currently the only tenable conclusion is that a network of patrons and friends gave Florio the support, not to say the encouragement, necessary to carry out the work that would most make his mark on English letters — the translation of Montaigne's *Essays.* This support came, in particular, from Lucy Russell, Countess of Bedford, who urged him to carry out the translation; Lady Anne Harington, her mother, who provided him with accommodations; his lifelong friend Matthew Gwinne, who researched Montaigne's quotations for him; his fellow Anglo-Italian Theodore Diodati, who assisted in translating difficult passages; and his brother-in-law Samuel Daniel, who read the translation and provided a long introductory poem for it.

The preface is an apology for translations. Recalling that Bruno had taught that "from translation all science had its offspring," Florio points out that translations make learning accessible to all, and "learning cannot be too common, and the commoner the better." Translating, however, is no easy venture: "Seven or eight of great wit and worth have assayed, but found these essays no attempt for French apprentices." Florio's efforts, on the contrary, have produced the first full translation of the *Essays* in English.

The Montaigne translation is not a precise rendering of the French into English. There are major differences, for example, in rhetorical style, with Montaigne's lean and direct prose being replaced by Florio's expansive elaborations. Florio's political and religious biases occasionally refashion Montaigne's. There are also many inaccuracies and outright errors in translation, the best known of which involves an unfortunate slipup between the French words for fish (*poisson*) and poison (*poison*). Nonetheless, his work stands with the best of his age. Among his contemporaries, Florio's translation was an immediate success. Writers such as Shakespeare, Ben Jonson, and Robert Burton drew upon it. Sir

Walter Ralegh took it with him into the Tower. In addition, the essay form became popular in England as a result.

A second edition of the Montaigne was published in 1611, dedicated this time to Queen Anne, in whose service Florio had entered in 1604 as a tutor in Italian and Groom of her Privy Chamber, with responsibilities akin to those of a private secretary. He may also have been tutor in Italian and French to Prince Henry and Princess Elizabeth. He participated in court life, taking a lively part in the festivities and literary activities of Queen Anne's circle. He was also tangentially involved in the various marriage proposals for the Stuart children. He frequented, for example, the house of the representative of the grand duke of Tuscany, Ottaviano Lotti, who was in London to advance a match with the Medicis. During these years Florio expanded the dictionary from about forty-six thousand to about seventy-four thousand definitions. His engraved portrait by William Hole — bearing his emblem (the sun with rays), motto ("Chi si contenta gode"), and age (58) — was included in the 1613 edition, an indication of the author's growing prestige and position. As Florio's importance as a courtier and scholar grew, he received the dedication of works by Nicholas Breton and Thomas Thorpe. He was also cited by Jonson in *Volpone* (1605–1606).

Queen Anne's death marked the end of Florio's success. Although theoretically the recipient of a sizable government pension, he never received payment for reasons of financial duress at the Exchequer. He retired to Fulham, where he carried out work toward a third, enlarged edition of the dictionary, published posthumously in 1659. He also translated twenty-eight chapters from Traiano Boccalini's *Ragguagli di Parnaso,* published by William Vaughan as the first part of *The Newfound Politic* (1626). Such work, however, did not provide significant financial rewards. Florio died, destitute, in late 1625.

Florio had at first been married to Daniel's sister, whose name is not known. They had at least three daughters, only one of whom, Aurelia, survived him. Widowed sometime in the 1610s, Florio married Rose Spicer in 1617, who survived him. Rose may have been Florio's only wife, whom he married after many years of concubinage and several children.

Florio was at the forefront of contemporary linguistic and stylistic developments. In the *First Fruits* he recommends an exact euphuism before John Lyly's *Euphues* (1578) was published. The *Second Fruits* inculcated an important principle of Elizabethan rhetoric by its insistence upon the use of *sententiae* ("sentences" — sententious, wise sayings) and proverbs. The dedications to his translation of Montaigne show that Florio had moved with the times and had taken up "Arcadianism." He was also a well-known figure in the literary world of the time, occasionally spoofed by his contemporaries for his grandiloquent ways. Shakespeare apparently drew upon him for such figures as Falstaff, Parolles, Landulpho, and Armado, and possibly Holofernes. The canon of Florio's works is still not closed — he may be the anonymous translator who produced the first (1620) English version of Giovanni Boccaccio's *Decameron* (1349–1351). Florio may perhaps have wished to be chiefly remembered for his untiring work as a collector of words and proverbs, a personal passion that contributed significantly to the richness of the English lexicon.

Biography:

Frances Yates, *John Florio: The Life of an Italian in Shakespeare's England* (Cambridge, Mass.: Harvard University Press, 1934).

References:

Arthur Acheson, *Shakespeare's Last Years* (New York: Brentano's, 1920);

Tom Conley, "Institutionalizing Translation: On Florio's Montaigne," in *Demarcating the Disciplines: Philosophy, Literature, Art,* edited by Samuel Weber (Minneapolis: University of Minnesota Press, 1986), pp. 45–58;

David O. Frantz, "Florio's Use of Contemporary Italian Literature in *A Worlde of Wordes*," *Dictionaries,* 1 (1979): 47–56;

Francis Otto Matthiessen, *Translation: An Elizabethan Art* (Cambridge, Mass.: Harvard University Press, 1931), pp. 103–168;

Herbert G. Wright, *The First English Translation of the "Decameron" (1620)* (Cambridge, Mass.: Harvard University Press, 1953).

Papers:

"James I, King of England," an unpublished manuscript translation in John Florio's hand of James I's Basilikon *Doron* (1603), is extant (British Library, Royal Mss. 14.A.v); it is his only rendering of this work from English into Italian.

William Fulbecke

(1560 – 1603?)

D. R. Woolf
Dalhousie University

BOOKS: *A Booke of Christian Ethicks or Moral Philosophie: Containing, the True Difference of Vertue, and Voluptuousnesse* (London: R. Jones, 1587);

A Direction or Preparative to the Study of the Lawe: Wherein Is Shewed, What Ought to Be Observed, and What Avoyded (London: Printed by A. Islip for T. Wight, 1600);

An Historicall Collection of the Continuall Factions, Tumults, and Massacres of the Romans and Italians. Selected and Handled in Three Bookes. Beginning where Livius Doth End, and Ending Where Tacitus Doth Begin (London: Printed by R. Field for W. Ponsonby, 1601); republished as *An Abridgement, or Rather, A Bridge of Roman Histories, to Passe the Neerest Way from Titus Livius to Tacitus* (London: Printed by T. East for M. Lownes, 1608);

A Parallele or Conference of the Civill Law, the Canon Law, and the Common Law of England. In Sundry Dialogues. [With] a Table of the Principall Points (London: Printed by A. Islip for T. Wight, 1601);

The Second Part of the Parallele. In Seaven Dialogues (London: Printed by A. Islip for T. Wight, 1602);

The Pandectes of the Law of Nations (London: Printed by A. Islip for T. Wight, 1602).

OTHER: *The Misfortunes of Arthur,* by Fulbecke, Nicholas Trotte, Francis Flower, Christopher Yelverton, Francis Bacon, John Lancaster, and Penruddock, in *Certaine Deuises and Shewes Presented by the Gentlemen of Grayes-Inn,* by Thomas Hughes (London: R. Robinson, 1587), sig. Gir–iir.

Although he wrote relatively little by Elizabethan standards and his life remains obscure, William Fulbecke was an important legal writer and historian of the late sixteenth century whose significance derives principally from his influential comparative approach to the study of law in an era during which common-law study remained largely impervious to other legal systems. He was also one of the earliest authors of works in English on the canon and civil laws, previously composed in Latin or French. As literature, his work is of interest for its application of a dramatic, frequently euphuistic prose style both to the narration of ancient history and to the discussion of relatively dry matters of jurisprudence, a style that would soon pass out of fashion with the advent in the early seventeenth century of a taste for the more clipped and terse prose epitomized by Tacitus and represented among legal authors by his older contemporary, the equally forceful but considerably less florid Sir Edward Coke.

Little is known about William Fulbecke's life. He was born in 1560 in the parish of St. Benedict, Lincoln, and was a younger son of Thomas Fulbecke, who died in 1566 during his term as mayor of Lincoln. After matriculating in 1577 at St. Alban Hall, Oxford (whence he was admitted a scholar at Christ Church on 6 February 1579), he took his B.A. in 1581, becoming a probationer fellow in October 1582. He then moved to Gloucester Hall, where he was exposed to the learned classicist, mathematician, and antiquary Thomas Allen. Fulbecke took his M.A. in 1584. After a brief period of study at Staple Inn, one of the Inns of Chancery, he was admitted to Gray's Inn to pursue studies in the common law and was called to the bar in 1591. He appears to have remained at Gray's Inn throughout most of his career, except for some time probably spent on the Continent studying civil law; Anthony Wood records in *Athenae Oxonienses* (1813–1820) that Fulbecke attained the title of doctor of laws, but this claim has not been verified.

Fulbecke's first book was the brief *Book of Christian Ethics or Moral Philosophy* (1587), wherein the author signed himself "master of arts and student of the laws of England." The work illustrates the euphuistic strain that marks most of Fulbecke's

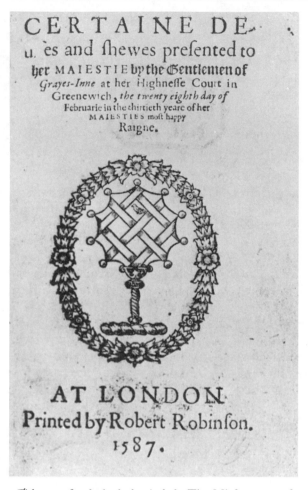

CERTAINE DE-
u. es and fhewes prefented to
her MAIESTIE by the Gentlemen of
Grayes-Inne at her Highneffe Court in
Greenewich, *the twenty eighth day of*
Februarie in the thirtieth yeare of her
MAIESTIES moft happy
Raigne.

AT LONDON
Printed by Robert Robinfon.
1587.

Title page for the book that includes The Misfortunes of
Arthur, *a masque to which Fulbecke contributed
two speeches*

writing, whereby example is piled upon example, and the same point is made in seven or eight different ways within a single sentence:

> In seeking the favor of noble men, in getting and retaining the friendship of equals, in the ambitious laboring for honors and dignities, in the hoarding of coin and scraping of commodity, in closing and disclosing, digging and delving, turning arable into pasturable and pasturable into arable, woods into wastes and wastes into woods, in building and battering, in turning square into round and triangles into quadrangles is such an infinite labor and a world of business, that he which weigheth in a balance both the care and the commodity shall find an ounce of commodity for a pound of care.

Though a typical example of the late-Tudor moral tract, *A Book of Christian Ethics* is interesting in its use of legal analogies and its author's unusual attitude toward romance literature, which at the time was being widely condemned by preachers such as Edward Dering. Fulbecke's tone reflects an Elizabethan godly intolerance of all vices (along with a pronounced hostility to dissimulation, deceit, and flattery – "Machiavellian" arts of statecraft that would come to be accepted and praised in the next century), and it also indicates his assumption, early in his career, of a Roman sternness that would figure in his later writings.

Fulbecke's remarks on romance are interesting because of his argument that the potential harm in such fictional works as the Trojan history lay in the attitude and intelligence of the reader rather than in the contents of the text: "Let the Trojan history be delivered to a sober, wise, and discreet scholar, he reaps much nonny [pleasure], much delight, much commodity by the reading thereof"; such a story placed before an ill-prepared mind, however, may produce "a second Catiline." (Catiline was a rebellious young noble of the first century B.C. whose unsuccessful coup, thwarted by Cicero, was recounted by Sallust, Fulbecke's favorite historian throughout his career.) Finally, the *Christian Ethics* also reveals Fulbecke's contempt for popular rule, citing the Roman civil wars of the first century as proof of the instability of a regime based on the people's favor.

Late in 1587 or early in 1588 Fulbecke was invited to contribute two speeches to the beginning (I.i) and conclusion (V.ii) of a masque generally known as *The Misfortunes of Arthur,* which was written and performed by eight members of Gray's Inn for Queen Elizabeth at Greenwich on 8 February 1587/1588 and published twenty days later under the name of its principal author, Thomas Hughes. Fulbecke's speeches are filled with classical allusion and the stock legal analogies of the time: the Furies are described as if they were judges from a "dreadful bench," and they provide an interesting foretaste of the Roman history he would write thirteen years later. For Hughes's heavy allusions to Virgil's fourth eclogue, complete with the coming of the Virgin Queen and references to the Tudor "stem of Brutus," Fulbecke substituted a harder-edged speech by Alecto emphasizing the need to restrain the twin evils of rebellion and tyranny. It draws on Virgil's *Aeneid* and the histories of Sallust and makes analogies between the civil wars of ancient Britain (depicted in the masque) and episodes in Roman history. It also warns of "the bastard covey of Italian birds," suggesting Fulbecke's embracing of the stock image of Italians as conspiratorial and turbulent, having sprung from the "seminary of lewd Catiline."

It was probably in the following years that Fulbecke acquired his learning in civil law, and in 1600 he published his first legal book, *A Direction or Preparative to the Study of the Law.* This work, which he had completed by the late summer of 1599, would prove successful enough to warrant republication by the Company of Stationers in 1620. Beginning with a brief overview of the importance of law to all human society, most of its ninety-five leaves are taken up with specific suggestions for legal study. The reader detects in it a strong preference, undoubtedly derived from Fulbecke's recent civil law training, for the clarity and rigidity of codified written law, as opposed to the ambiguity of custom. While Fulbecke nowhere declares himself in favor of adopting civil law in England (where at the time it was used almost exclusively in ecclesiastical courts), he does ask rhetorically "whether commonweals were better governed by written laws, or by the present and voluntary conceit of the magistrate." This statement is not, as one might suppose, an appeal for Roman-style absolutism. On the con-

trary, one of the recurring themes of Fulbecke's writings is that what he terms "convenient liberty" is best protected by strong laws, which can provide a balance between the power of principal magistrates and the unruliness of the multitude. Again, Rome serves as his test case, since its paradigmatic legal code, the Twelve Tables, was created precisely because too much freedom of decision had been left in the hands of kings and consuls.

One further point deserves emphasis. In the *Direction or Preparative* and elsewhere Fulbecke reveals the strength of late-Renaissance Aristotelianism in his method of presentation and his choice of logical categories for the organization of material (so far as legal study is concerned, he is explicitly hostile to the educational reforms of the Spaniard Juan-Luis Vives). A major influence on him in this regard is the writing of the great civilian Alberico Gentili, who had lived in England for twenty years and been professor of civil law at Oxford since 1587. Fulbecke had been exposed to humanism and elsewhere refers favorably to certain Italian humanist writers of the late quattrocento, most notably the Neoplatonists Marsilio Ficino — "a man of excellent learning" — and Giovanni Pico della Mirandola. But Gentili's attack on the *mos gallicus* and humanist law studies in his *De Juris interpretibus dialogi sex* (1582) clearly weighed heavily with Fulbecke. Nevertheless, his book is balanced in its recommendation of authorities, instructing the student to read both older authors, such as Bartolus and Baldus, and the newer writers of the *mos gallicus,* Guillaume Budé, Jacques Cujas, and François Hotman. In the search for general principles of law, however, Fulbecke was closer to Bartolus and to his own contemporary Jean Bodin than to the scholarship of Cujas: in many ways Fulbecke can be counted the first English "neo-Bartolist."

Fulbecke comments in the *Direction or Preparative* that, unlike history, which is ever in a state of debate and uncertainty, the law is never opposed to itself. It was precisely to resolve the apparent contradictions among historical authorities over a key episode, the fall of the Roman republic, that Fulbecke turned from Rome's law to its history. By the autumn of 1600 he had completed his *Historical Collection of the Continual Factions, Tumults, and Massacres of the Romans and Italians,* which was dated from his chamber at Gray's Inn and entered at the Stationers' Company on 10 October, though it did not appear in print until 1601. The work is an attempt to bridge the gap between the end of Livy's history of the republic and Tacitus's account of the early empire. Fulbecke wrote it at a time when Tacitus was

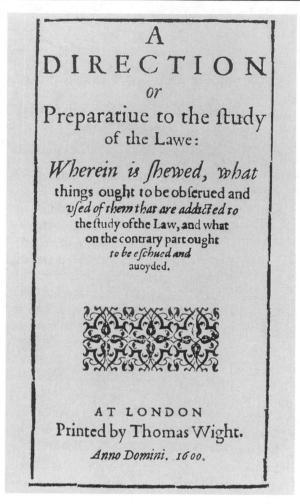

A
DIRECTION
or
Preparatiue to the ſtudy
of the Lawe:

Wherein is ſhewed, what
things ought to be obſerued and
vſed of them that are addicted to
the ſtudy of the Law, and what
on the contrary part ought
to be eſchued and
auoyded.

AT LONDON
Printed by Thomas Wight.
Anno Domini. 1600.

Title page for Fulbecke's first book on civil law

becoming – through the influence of both an English edition of the *Histories* by Sir Henry Savile and English versions of works of the Flemish scholar Justus Lipsius – a potent influence both on historical writing and political thinking. Much of what Tacitus described as useful tools for statecraft were similar to those recommended by Niccolò Machiavelli but did not carry the baggage of Machiavelli's evil reputation (a myth to which Fulbecke fully subscribed).

The *Historical Collection* is an interesting attempt to present a continuous narrative from the different and often contradictory sources of Dio Cassius, Dionysius of Halicarnassus, Lucius Florus, and Sallust, from whose works Fulbecke drew his detailed summary of the rebellion of Catiline, which was doubtless intended to evoke in readers thoughts of the recent tragedy of that latter-day Catiline, the earl of Essex, executed in February 1601; Fulbecke even dedicated the book to an archfoe of Essex, Thomas Sackville, Lord Buckhurst. His purpose was twofold: first, to provide readers with a historically accurate account of the events described, thereby to resolve the "great prolixity and the too exceeding brevity of the Roman historiographers." Second, he wished to demonstrate – as he states in a passage which well illustrates the strengths and weaknesses of his prose style – "the mischiefs of discord and civil dissension, in which the innocent are proscribed for their wealth, noble men dishonored, cities become waste by banishment and bloodshed; nay (which is more) virgins are deflowered, infants are taken out of their parents' arms and put to the sword, matrons do suffer villainy, temples and houses are spoiled, and every place is full of armed men, of carcasses, of blood, of tears." Like so many writers of the last years of Elizabeth's reign, Fulbecke's thoughts were running ahead to the daunting prospect of a disputed succession and a resumption of fifteenth-century instability, a specter that haunts much of the historical drama and poetry of the 1590s. His dramatic sense served him well here: the history is divided into three books (each named after one of the three Fates) and presents a compelling description of the collapse of the Roman republic.

A Parallel or Conference of the Civil Law, the Canon Law, and the Common Law of England and its second part, *The Second Part of the Parallel,* appeared in 1601 and 1602 respectively, and in some ways remains Fulbecke's most important and interesting work, one of the earliest English texts in comparative jurisprudence. Written in the time-honored form of a dialogue, between a great patron and three lawyers (a canonist, a civilian, and a barrister), it is an erudite and thoughtful attempt to reconcile the differing treatments in three legal systems of such matters as treason, theft, homicide, property, tenures, and debt. "It is observed by Seneca," he remarks in the preface to the first part, "that in one and the same plot of ground, the hound seeketh for a hare, the ox for good grass, and the stork for a snake or lizard. . . . It seemed strange unto me that these three laws should not as the three Graces have their hands linked together, and their looks directly fixed the one upon the other." Fulbecke believed that all laws derived ultimately from the law of nature and from a putative law of nations, though the precise character of the legal heritage of any people differed from others largely through the intrusion of national and local custom.

He also held that law was an organic creation, developing by accretion rather than in sudden leaps; thus he tends to be rather confusing on matters of canon law, which he simply equated with all religious-based law going back to the Druids and Egyptians, not specifically with the law of the medieval church. Fulbecke's more thorough knowledge of civil law, however, allowed him to transcend the "common law mind," as it has been called, of some of his contemporaries. He recognized, for example, that the Norman Conquest represented a sharp break in English legal development, since William I had introduced many customs of Normandy; on the other hand, he also acknowledged that much of the law codes of Ina, Alfred, and other Anglo-Saxon kings, as codified in the supposed laws of Edward the Confessor, had survived 1066 to be adapted to use in Norman England.

As in his earlier works, Fulbecke was concerned to defend a powerful monarchy nevertheless hemmed in by law; in this he anticipates Jacobean authors such as Samuel Daniel and the lawyer John Selden. In a work that to some degree is an abstraction from and extension of the *Parallel,* his *Pandects of the Law of Nations* (1602), Fulbecke endorsed on the one hand the notion that conquest of territory permits the abrogation of old laws and their replacement with those pleasing to the conqueror. On the other, he also pointed out that William I, though absolute in power, had exercised political wisdom and virtue in choosing to preserve and modify, rather than utterly abrogate, much of Anglo-Saxon law.

Fulbecke's career after 1602 and the date of his death remain obscure, though the Augustan scholar and bishop White Kennett believed that the lawyer had taken holy orders and become vicar of the parish of Waldeshare in Kent. Fulbecke enjoyed a modest reputation in his time; though he never achieved the stature of Gentili in civil law or that of John Selden or Coke in the common law, he was indisputably among the most learned legal minds of his age. His influence over modern legal thinking, relative to Selden, Coke, or Sir Matthew Hale, has been slight but deserves note, since he was one of the first common lawyers to stand back from the morass of custom, precedent, and statute that made up English law and to think, like a civilian, about general principles that English law shared with other legal systems. His literary style, moreover, is generally a pleasant one; though at times overburdened with classical images and examples and too given to periphrasis, it is more lively and clearer than that of many contemporary lawyer-writers. Although not especially original, Fulbecke nevertheless provided an important conduit for the works of continental and English civilians to English students of the common law who might otherwise have had little exposure to them.

References:

Brian P. Levack, *The Civil Lawyers in England, 1603–1641* (Oxford: Clarendon Press, 1973);

J. G. A. Pocock, *The Ancient Constitution and the Feudal Law,* second edition (Cambridge: Cambridge University Press, 1987);

Richard J. Terrill, "The Application of the Comparative Method by English Civilians: The Case of William Fulbecke and Thomas Ridley," *Journal of Legal History,* 2 (September 1981): 169–185;

D. R. Woolf, *The Idea of History in Early Stuart England* (Toronto: University of Toronto Press, 1990), pp. 178–181.

Stephen Gosson

(April 1554 – 13 February 1624)

Arthur F. Kinney
University of Massachusetts – Amherst

BOOKS: *The Schoole of Abuse, Conteining a Plesaunt Inuectiue against Poets, Pipers, Plaiers, Iesters, and Such Like Caterpillers of the Cõmonwealth* (London: Printed by T. Dawson for Thomas Woodcock, 1579);

The Emphemerides of Phialo, Deuided into Three Bookes. (London: Thomas Dawson, 1579);

Playes Confuted in Fiue Actions, Prouing That They Are Not to Be Suffred in a Christian Common Weale (London: Printed for Thomas Gosson, 1582);

The Trumpet of Warre. A Sermon Preached at Paules Crosse the Seuenth of Maie 1598 (London: Printed by V. Simmes for J. Oxenbridge, 1598).

Editions: *The School of Abuse,* in *Markets of Bawdrie: The Dramatic Criticism of Stephen Gosson,* edited by Arthur F. Kinney, Elizabethan Studies 4 (Salzburg: Institut für Englische Sprache und Literatur, 1974), pp. 69–118;

An Apology of The School of Abuse, in *Markets of Bawdrie: The Dramatic Criticism of Stephen Gosson,* pp. 121–135;

Plays Confuted in Five Actions, in *Markets of Bawdrie: The Dramatic Criticism of Stephen Gosson,* pp. 138–197.

OTHER: "Speculum humanum," in *The Mirror of Mans Lyfe,* by Pope Innocent III, translated by H. Kirton (London: Henry Bynneman, 1576);

Lopez de Gomara, *The Pleasant Historie of the Conquest of the Weast India,* translated by Thomas Nicholas (London: Henry Bynneman, 1578) – includes Gosson's commendatory verses "Stephen Gosson in Praise of the Translator" and "In Thomae Nicholai occidentalem Indiam St. Gosson";

"Stephen Gosson in Prayse of the Booke," in *Florio His First Fruits,* by John Florio (London: Printed by Thomas Dawson for Thomas Woodcock, 1578).

Along with the English dramatic criticism of Sir Philip Sidney and George Puttenham, that of Stephen Gosson was the most significant in the sixteenth century, and there is considerable evidence that it was more popular and at least as widely known. Gosson's criticism is important to intellectual and literary history, partly because he argued as coherently, concisely, and forcefully as any the reasons why many Elizabethans were dissatisfied with drama and in general distrusted all poetry, and partly because in isolating all the basic issues in his day he initiated one of the central critical debates in all of English literature. Writing a year or two after Richard Burbage opened his Theater in Southwark – where Gosson had his own plays staged – he attacked plays so decisively that his *School of Abuse* (1579) went through several editions, each in fifteen hundred copies, and called forth many plays and pamphlets in response. Even though Sidney felt moved to reply, perhaps privately, Gosson's attacks and those of his imitators and successors continued to prevail; indeed, his attacks were so comprehensive that no critic who succeeded him, including Sidney, found a major argument that did not grow directly out of his position. Thus even before William Shakespeare, Gosson founded the direct line of attack that would eventually, in 1642, close the theaters for several years and so preclude any unbroken descent in drama from the plays of Christopher Marlowe, Ben Jonson, and John Webster. Gosson's career had begun with literary connections from Oxford who commissioned from him commendatory poems and continued with a prose romance that won the praise of John Lyly as a "pretty discourse," but it was his criticism of poetry and plays that overshadowed everything else he did.

Stephen Gosson was baptized the second child and eldest son of Cornelius and Agnes Oxenbridge Gosson in the church of St. George the Martyr, Canterbury, on 17 April 1554. His father had emigrated from the Low Countries; he was a joiner who earned his freedom and later distinguished

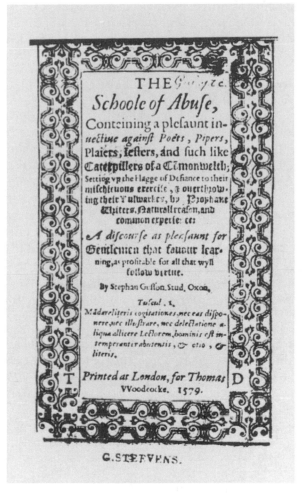

THE *Gosgte.*
Schoole of Abuse,
Conteining a plesaunt in-
uectiue against *Poëts*, *Pipers*,
Plaiers, Iesters, and such like
Caterpillers of a Cõmonwelth;
Setting vp the Flagge of Defiance to their
mischieuous exercise, & ouerthrow-
ing their Bulwarkes, by Prophane
Writers, Naturall reason, and
common experie: ce:

*A discourse as plesaunt for
Gentlemen that fauour learning, as profitable for all that wyll
follow virtue.*

By Stephan Gosson. Stud. Oxon.

*Tusul . 1,
Mãdareliteris cogitationes, nec eas dispo-
nere, nec illustrare, nec delectatione a-
liqua allicere Lectorem, hominis est im-
temperanter abutensis, & otio, &
literis.*

Printed at London, for Thomas
VVoodcocke. 1579.

G. STEEVENS.

Title page for Stephen Gosson's first book, an attack on the misuses of art

himself as a leading city craftsman: when Elizabeth I made her first visit to Canterbury as queen, the city asked him to fashion a huge wooden cross to be placed in the center of town for ceremonies in her honor. Agnes was the daughter of Thomas Oxenbridge (or Oxynbregge), a grocer who by redemption was named a freeman of the city in 1519. They were married on 18 July 1546 and in time had six children: Agnes in 1551, Stephen in 1554, William in 1558, the twins John and Joan in 1560, and Dorothy in 1563. Three children died in their youth, Joan when she was only a few days old.

The family lived over Cornelius's shop in the parish of St. George, a crowded section of Canterbury housing about eighty families along the southeast side of the great cathedral close. Apparently Stephen's father expected him to be a joiner, since he did not enter the cathedral school, then known as the Queen's School, until he was fourteen, as a scholar, his way paid for him. Although he contin-

ued to live with his family, the moral tone of all his written work and the religious learning especially apparent in *Plays Confuted* (1582) clearly derive from his period at Queen's School and, later, at Oxford. All grammar schools in Tudor England urged moral instruction, but none was more rigorous than the school at Canterbury. Sessions began at six o'clock each morning with prayers and responsive readings from the Psalms, followed by the customary drills and translations of Virgil, Horace, Cicero, Sallust, Ovid, Isocrates, Desiderius Erasmus, and part of the Greek New Testament. In addition, twice each day all of the students would file into the great stone cathedral to sit on cold benches through religious services, attending High Mass at the elevation of the Host and saying the Psalms and meditating through the Agnus Dei. Gosson's schoolmaster was John Gresshop, an M.A. from Christ Church, Oxford, known for his extraordinary personal library of 450 volumes, but students were also under the close supervision of Archbishop Matthew Parker. But while this model Christian humanist grammar school emphasized religious instruction, drama was also used for lessons. Stephen's later interest in plays may have begun as well with the frequent stage performances in the city itself. During his early years in Canterbury, Leicester's Men visited at least six times, Worcester's Men came at least twice, and there were fifteen other companies that performed locally.

Gosson went to Corpus Christi, Oxford, in 1572, two years after another Canterbury boy, John Lyly, had entered Magdalen College there. Gosson's appointment filled one of two openings for boys from Kent – openings not always filled, and so perhaps not especially competitive – and it was likely this that determined his choice and date of entrance. Once at Corpus Christi, though, he found another Christian humanist center of education that was vigorously religious in its curriculum and outlook, having been founded in 1516 by Richard Foxe, Bishop of Winchester. Among Gosson's classmates at Corpus Christi were Richard Hooker, subsequently the author of the *Laws of Ecclesiastical Polity* (1593, 1597, 1648); John Barefoot, later Archdeacon of Lincoln; Samuel Beck, later Canon of Exeter; Henry Parry, later Bishop of Gloucester, Bishop of Worcester, and eventually chaplain to Elizabeth I; and many others who later made careers less distinguished in the church, among whom Gosson would be one. It is no surprise that Corpus Christi has been called "the fountain head of pure Canterbury doctrine." Again, Gosson enjoyed access to a large and impressive library; the contemporary catalogue of books at Corpus Christi shows more than half of them were Bibles, biblical commentary, and patristic writings. But Gosson also learned manner as well as matter: he first encountered the euphuistic style that would later characterize much of his work in the lectures of John Rainoldes (who also taught John Lyly and George Pettie).

The poverty of a joiner's son and sizar seems to have hampered him, however. While he made a request to graduate on 31 October and was granted supplication on 17 December 1576, he was admitted to the degree of bachelor of arts provided he could determine (that is, pass an examination of public disputations) during the following Lent; he never signed the matriculation book and never made his final disputations. Later in *Plays Confuted* he would complain that he was "pulled from the University before I was ripe" – and in the dedicatory letter to that work he confesses a sense of inferiority to

scholars from Oxford, Cambridge, and the Inns of Court. Lack of funds, illness, or family deaths commonly caused students to postpone determinations but not preclude them, so it is possible that the lure of London and a career in writing caused Gosson to leave Corpus Christi. His serious training, however, is seen more and more as his work develops; his first important work, *The School of Abuse,* makes the schoolroom its central metaphor and moral instruction the primary function by which all literature is to be judged.

At first Gosson wrote poetry, and the poems that remain – "Speculum humanum," "Stephen Gosson in Praise of the Translator," "In Thomas Nicholai occidentalem Indiam St. Gosson" – were all commissioned to appear in the works of others and are, for the most part, heavily didactic, frequently commonplace, and almost totally lacking in a lively imagination. At the same time he attempted to write plays. In *The School of Abuse* he refers to *Catiline's Conspiracies,* written to teach good government and to demonstrate the evils of tyranny, clearly what was known as a moral or allegorically oriented work; in *Plays Confuted* he speaks of *The Comedy of Captain Mario,* which he calls "a cast of Italian devices," and *Praise at Parting,* another moral allegory; in his reply to Gosson, Thomas Lodge refers to a fourth play with "*Muscovian* strangers" and "*Scythian* monsters" and "one *Eurus* brought upon one stage in ships made of sheepskins." None of Gosson's dramas survives; nor is there evidence that any were published; and if it were not for these references to them, scholars would not even know the names of any of his plays.

By the summer of 1579 Gosson was beginning *The Ephemerides of Phialo* (1579), a prose romance that centers on moral disputations following the successful model of Lyly's *Euphues* (1578). Like *Euphues,* the *Ephemerides* (Greek for "daily occurrences," that is, a journal) has a slight narrative line. Phialo, a young student at Siena (perhaps representing Oxford), is cheated of his inheritance and, without funds to complete his studies, goes to Venice (perhaps echoing Gosson's trip to London). There his former friend Philotimo, who has become a young courtier, criticizes him for leaving the university. Phialo lectures him on the proper method for rebuking a friend, and they retire to Philotimo's lodgings for an evening of discussion and debate. The next day they visit Jeraldi, a gentleman, and Phialo lectures on the qualifications of a courtier. In the afternoon, visiting the streets of Venice, Philotimo falls in love with Polyphile at first sight, although Jeraldi warns him that she is not a virtuous lady. The third day all three go to Jeraldi's house, where Phialo lectures so eloquently on virtue that Polyphile confesses her hedonism and converts to a life of virtue, while Jeraldi and Philotimo at last are sufficiently impressed by Phialo's skills that they promise him patronage at court so he can continue his studies.

The romance is, on the surface, a tribute to the euphuistic style of Rainoldes and Lyly, with its balanced phrases and clauses, its simple and transverse alliterations, its use of parallelism and antithesis, and its employment of sententiae. It is also a hybrid of the courtier's handbook – Guazzo's *Civil Conversation* (1579) may also be a model – and a series of philosophical and religiously tinged disputations such as the ones Gosson heard and practiced both at Queen's School and Corpus Christi. Beneath the surface, however, Phialo is clearly meant to suggest Gosson and his plight; and since the romance was dedicated to Philip Sidney – whose own works were then unpublished and perhaps unknown but whose patronage for poetry, perhaps Protestant and thoughtful poetry, was widely known – the *Ephemerides* seems equally Gosson's own urgent request for the necessary patronage for his career, or perhaps for his return to Corpus Christi.

The *Ephemerides* was published in November 1579; but in September or early October, Gosson broke off work on this romance and wrote, fairly quickly, his first attack on the misuse of art, *The School of Abuse*. In this, then and now his best-known (and most misunderstood) work, he argues that good art (proper art) instructs men in virtue by presenting models of virtuous action while poor art corrupts man by suggesting such evil tendencies as immoderation. Art, he claims, is always enjoyable because it appeals to the emotions. But this can be dangerous: "Poets, either with fables to show their abuses, or with plain terms to unfold their mischief . . . disperse their poison through all the world." Poetry for Gosson thus subjugates reason and destroys man's special nature. Just as there is a right use of all art forms, there is the proper, instructive use of poetry, but until that special function is restored, it is best for men and women to remain home to avoid temptation. Gosson's essay is corrective and educative, meant to "school" the reader as well as art. Practical application follows his theory in two recommendations: that the lord mayor of London refuse all letters patent to players and that potential spectators at plays practice passive resistance: "The patient that will be cured, of his own accord, must seek the mean."

Gosson's intention is clearly artful, not simply admonitory. His seven-part essay follows Rainoldes's lectures on the formal oration or declamation, but Gosson so arranges his presentation that he combines all three forms of Aristotelian argumentation taught at Canterbury and Oxford. Thus his *School of Abuse* is an epideictic argument in which he censures certain practices and forms of art and sport in and around London and urges all citizens to react similarly; it is also a forensic argument, in the appended letter to Sir Richard Pipe, in which Gosson condemns past laxity and proposes certain legislation; and it is a deliberative argument, which in the appended letter to the gentlewomen of London warns of future dangers and argues for voluntary self-control. Following Aristotle, *The School of Abuse* means to teach, to delight, and to persuade; and the letters are meant as illustrations of what is argued in the main body of the work.

To aid in his artfulness, Gosson adds to his logical structure a rhetorical and metaphorical substructure. With clusters of metaphors and a shifting persona, Gosson argues that criticism must attract to awaken thoughtful response; teach right and wrong and point out correct behavior; expose vice, for only then is correction possible; and warn of future difficulty by pointing out hidden present dangers. To achieve these ends, he repeatedly insists that the critic must play the roles of (that is, act as if in a play as) host, teacher, doctor, and military leader. To keep this artfulness attractive, or "pleasant," his tone and stance shift as well as his roles, requiring a shifting relationship rhetorically with his audience. Thus he is a man of wisdom as well as a man of the people; he himself once sinned, but he has reformed and so is now a reliable moral guide; he is both cordial and stern.

While the apparent haste in composition causes Gosson's euphuistic, formal prose to jangle alongside direct, colloquial expressions, he is always careful to show that his criticism is about *abuse,* wrong uses of art, and not art itself. His attack is partial, not absolute. There are still good plays to be seen; not all poetry is bad: "The *Jew* [perhaps a source for *The Merchant of Venice*] and *Ptolomy,* shown at the Bull [Inn Theater], the one representing the greediness of worldly choosers and bloody minds of usurers; the other very lively describing how seditious estates with their own devices, false friends with their own swords, and rebellious commons [common people] in their own snares are overthrown." Such remarks are supported by classical allusions, and the fact that some of them are slightly erroneous, suggesting that Gosson relied on mem-

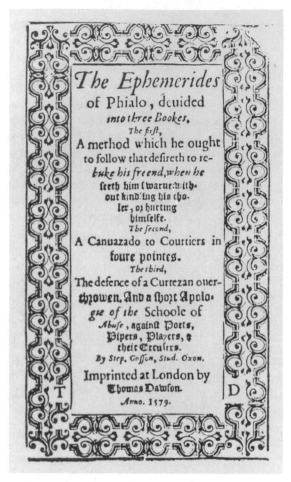

The Ephemerides
of Phialo, deuided
into three Bookes.
The first,
A method which he ought
to follow that desireth to rebuke his freend, when he
seeth him swarue with-
out kind'ting his cho-
ler, or hurting
himselfe.
The second,
A Canuazado to Courtiers in
foure pointes.
The third,
The defence of a Curtezan ouer-
throwen. And a short Apologie of the Schoole of
Abuse, against Poets,
Pipers, Players, &
their Excusers.
By Step. Gosson, Stud. Oxon.

Imprinted at London by
Thomas Dawson.
Anno. 1579.

*Title page for Gosson's prose romance, which was
influenced by John Lyly's* Euphues *(1578)*

ory, also suggests his haste for the occasion along-side the more considered artfulness of the style.

The School of Abuse, like the *Ephemerides,* was dedicated to Sidney, but Sidney did not respond either with money or other favors. Instead he was annoyed at this impertinence from a stranger. In a letter to Gabriel Harvey, Spenser notes Sidney's "scorn," suggesting that Sidney, like others, read the work of their contemporary as an ill-measured, ill-suited attack. Actors were also angered. They attacked Gosson on the stage and in scurrilous pamphlets, as he relates in *An Apology of The School of Abuse* (1579). None of these attacks is extant, but one, *Strange News Out of Affrick,* which Gosson calls a "Libell," was apparently circulated only in secrecy. Another work, Thomas Lodge's full-scale defense, survives only in an edition without a title page and is known as *Lodge's Defense* (circa 1580) or by a phrase in it, "Honest Excuses." This outcry prompted Gosson to write an even swifter, impromptu *Apology,* which he published with his *Ephe-*

merides. Here the argument seems only a shadow of the substance that preceded it. In the *Apology* he argues that plays pervert their rightful ends by arousing the senses, aided by poetic language and music. They are an offense against reason, undermining man's special nature and so rendering him unmanly. The fault arises from an unholy union between the playwright's temptation and the playgoer's inclination. While he means still to be a teacher like Demosthenes, Gosson's argument is grounded in authority that comes with common experience, and his test is still the utilitarian one of results.

Yet the apparent similarity conceals important shifts away from a moderate Christian humanism. Gosson expands here his charge that poets lie by pointing out that gods are characterized onstage by immoral acts and are therefore not good models to emulate; if players defend them as allegories, they are still dissembling, for there can be no truth at the basis of such allegories as these. Imitation in poetry and plays is based in images; and what Gosson is saying is that these images are not potentially instructive but in fact blasphemous. Players who counterfeit as gods are not only perpetuating idols, they are themselves idols or false gods. Thus players are no longer merely misguided; they are the devil's agents dancing in waistcoat pockets, and their acts are acts of sinful commission.

The argument has shifted to a position that is, finally, theologically conservative (although not Puritan, as Gosson will in time make clear) and antihumanist. It may therefore be the *Apology,* rather than the *School,* which first prompted Sidney's *Defense of Poetry* (1595). But there can be no doubt that the *School* lies directly behind Sidney's *Defense* as well: the form of the *Defense,* the judicial oration, is written in reply to another argument; the four charges Sidney lists in the *negatavio* are precisely those in Gosson's *School;* and Sidney maintains his geniality and wit in part, from the opening anecdote of the horsemaster Pugliano, by parodies of Gosson as a host, teacher, doctor, and soldier. But there is another, deeper reason why Sidney answers Gosson by means of parody: it is because in many ways Sidney agrees with Gosson that art should be moral and instructive and can be misused, and, moreover, he is unable to respond directly to Gosson's fundamental charge that man's nature is inherently corruptible. Before Gosson's statement that man once confronted with good and evil may choose evil — and that he must be careful not to and that there is no guarantee he will not — Sidney falls silent.

At the age of twenty-four Gosson had become famous — and to some notorious. He began work on a Latin treatise, but seeing how seriously his work was misunderstood, he retired to the country as a tutor. But he could not escape criticism and calumny. His own plays were staged to undermine his credibility and honesty. In late 1580 he received a copy of Lodge's rebuttal, which was not only a response to his position but an assassination of his character. He seems not to have hastened back to the city; rather, he spent fourteen more months reading Plato, patristic commentary, and Juan Luis Vives's work on Augustine and mastering a new concise Attic style that he no doubt thought would be more decisive. He was right. The work that resulted, *Plays Confuted in Five Actions,* has little metaphor except for the "actions" that are meant to be the new parts condemning the five-act plays of his day. Where the *School* had been euphuistic and rhetorical and the *Apology* impromptu and even blunt, *Plays Confuted* is logical and relentlessly Aristotelian.

Plays Confuted in Five Actions is Gosson's most significant and accomplished work, as it is the single most significant attack on plays in the entire Tudor period. Syllogistic constructs alone control the argument, and the five Aristotelian causes — one for each act of a standard play — control Gosson's presentation, displacing the schemes and tropes of *The School of Abuse.* Gosson defines plays by the four Aristotelian causes found in the *Physics* — efficient, material, formal, and final — and adds a fifth, the organic unity of the four shown as a single cause for arousing emotion (just as Aristotle argued for a fifth, organic statement of cause). But if Gosson turns to the humanists' Aristotle for his method, he turns to the New Logic and Attic prose of Peter Ramus for his style. The basis of his new and potent position in *Plays Confuted* is that all plays are by nature "addle eggs"; in concept and actuality, they are rotten before they are performed because they are the creations of the devil. Actors become the devil's agents, parodying and so blaspheming God. Thus Gosson's proposition — "that stage plays are not to be suffered in a Christian common weal" — is here demonstrated scientifically. Through inductive and deductive logic, Gosson means to show his statement is one of fact, not judgment.

The efficient cause of plays (action 1), their origin in the devil, establishes the important, fundamental dichotomy of true and false worship, of righteousness and apostasy on which Gosson's entire argument is systematically and conscientiously built. To profess God while upholding plays is simple hypocrisy; this is not a matter of values but a matter of properties. The natural enemies of plays are not the common people but rather preachers and the servants of God. By contrasting pagan ceremonies at which plays originated with later Christian celebrations, Gosson is able to show both the evil produced by drama and the nature of sin to perpetuate itself.

The material cause (action 2) calls for an agency to judge values and locates this, for plays, in the individual conscience. Here Gosson judges both dramatized actions and the players themselves; by choosing examples easily open to denigration, he (inductively) discredits all plays by association. In addition, agency itself is condemned. In presenting both good and bad actions, Gosson contends, actors must necessarily counterfeit. They are thus false, and what is so patently false must be ultimately false.

The third action deals with the conveyance of the effect, or the formal cause. The performance of plays is the act of counterfeiting: it is thus a violation of nature (and of God), the disowning, at least temporarily, of one's self for another self, and a dead or imaginary being — a human creation — at that. This violation of nature not only breaks divine law and parodies God's act of forming human nature, it also destroys the harmonious, stable, and singular order of things through multiplicity and fluidity.

Action 4 (the final cause or purpose of plays) is the overflow of affection. While this hearkens back to *The School of Abuse,* it is no longer the bald assertion that it was there but, conceptually framed by the three other anterior causes, is the natural and logical outcome that both consolidates and summarizes Gosson's argument. The conclusion to *Plays Confuted* (action 5) verifies the preceding four actions and shows their interdependence. Delight (action 4) appeals to the sight (action 3), arousing senses (action 4), making man subrational and consequently subhuman (for example, the actors, action 2). This appeal violates God's nature and His harmony and is therefore a concentrated union of forces inimical to Him (action 1). The final cause thus gives purpose to the formal cause in action 3; the material cause is used in arguing the efficient cause in action 1. The formal cause is the theoretical basis for testing the efficient cause in the first action.

Plays Confuted gains much of its undeniable power and cogency not from the progression of the argument but rather from the way in which issues are consistently made to interlock and reinforce. Gosson's position is made absolute because it rests

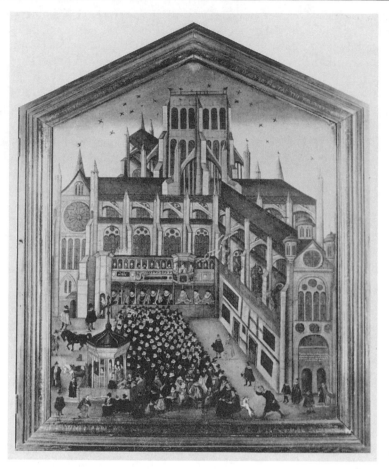

St. Paul's Cross, where Gosson preached The Trumpet of War *in 1596
and 1598, from* Farley's Dream *(circa 1616) by*
John Gipkyn

not on the humanist allusions to antiquity as the earlier attacks on drama had done, but to the certainty found in God's Word, Paul's letters, and the advice of church fathers — such as the notorious attack on men playing in women's clothing and becoming effeminate. Plays offer him only two responses: acceptance or rejection. Given his understanding of the sinful nature of drama, Gosson's demand for total abolition is credible, logical, and unavoidable.

This pious rigidity, new for Gosson but a natural outgrowth of what he had been taught since childhood by schools imbued with the faith of Elizabeth's Established Church, effectively ended any possibility of his returning to poetry and drama himself. It may also have had its effects on his teaching, for the next extant record of him is dated 15 April 1584, when he registered in the Pilgrim Book of the English College at Rome, the Jesuit training ground for Catholic students and converts meant to carry the mission of the Catholic Church through

Europe and into England. This may seem odd; it may seem odder still that within two months he resigned, being dispensed by Cardinal Severinus and then departing for reasons of bad eyesight. The reason is suspiciously weak and not borne out by later facts; the only interpretation that does work is that Gosson, like many others, had entered the international espionage system of Sir Francis Walsingham and was spying on Jesuit activities in Rome on behalf of the Church of England.

This seems confirmed by the remainder of Gosson's life. Shortly after his return to England at the age of thirty, he accepted an ecclesiastical appointment as lecturer, a preacher without cure of souls, at St. Martin's Church, Ludgate, London, a few hundred yards from St. Paul's Cathedral and the outdoor pulpit controlled by the bishop of London, St. Paul's Cross, where later he would be called many times to deliver the message of Elizabeth's church. By then he must have been ordained and may have completed a course in theology. Hard upon this appointment came others; he rose swiftly in the church. In February 1585 he was made lecturer at St. Dunstan's, Stepney, a far wealthier parish just east of London between Mile End Road and the Thames, where the parson, his patron, was Humphrey Cole, Gosson's classmate at Corpus Christi. In October 1586 Gosson was appointed vicar of St. Alban's Church, Sandridge, in Hertfordshire, by Thomas Jennings, at the extraordinary annual salary of eighty pounds. While St. Dunstan's was clearly Protestant but not Puritan, as the connection with Corpus Christi attests, there are records from St. Alban's that he was decidedly anti-Puritan in his priestly practices: there he was loyal to the Book of Common Prayer of 1559; he wore a surplice in church, used the sign of the cross at baptism, and conducted this service at a proper font at the front of the church. Moreover, he saw that the catechism was universally practiced, that his congregation bowed their heads at the name of Jesus, and that the ring was used in holy matrimony. While *Puritan* has been loosely used to characterize Gosson's position on poems and plays, it is clear that he was not a Puritan in any literal or authentic sense but that his moral sense came directly from the centers of the Anglican settlement at Canterbury and Oxford.

Gosson left St. Alban's in December 1591 to take up an appointment as parson of Great Wigborough in Essex, at the bestowal of the queen, at a church appropriately dedicated to St. Stephen. The parish, about seven miles from Colchester, came with a great deal of land as well as an annual wage. In 1596 Gosson was called to Paul's Cross to preach a sermon he was invited to deliver once more in 1598: *The Trumpet of War*. Under the recurring threat of Spanish invasion, his London congregation must have taken courage in his return to the militant metaphor he used in *The School of Abuse* and taken solace in his attack on the Puritans, for in this sermon he warns that men must be armed with stout faith to fight their chief enemies, the Spanish and the Presbyterians: "The new *Presbytery* [is] couching down at the gates of great persons, with her belly full of barking libels to disgrace the persons of the best men, and the labors of the best learned in the Church of England." He angrily views Presbyterian practices and beliefs concerning vestments, ceremonies, and the position of the altar. He can in fact see the day when

> God's altar [is] environed with a company of proud mules, striking at it with their heels, the altar itself battered by violence and beaten down, holy things trodden on and trampled with foul feet.... All those miseries springing from a wrangling humor of the *Presbytery* that hath brought religion into contempt.... It is a sign that religion decays, and devotion grows cold among us.

The danger is imminent, he claims, because of the powerful actions on the Continent that daily threaten the Englishman who is unwary.

This sermon, and others like it, doubtless led to Gosson's final appointment: on 8 April 1600 he was inducted as rector of St. Botolph's without Bishopsgate, then (and until early in the twentieth century) one of the wealthiest livings in England, second in London only to St. Paul's. The church had been fully restored by Sir William Allen during his year as lord mayor in 1571–1572. It served the Moorfields stretching north and east of the city, and to it Gosson devoted the last quarter century of his life. But this success did not come at the cost of diminishing his sense of morality. Countless records in the ecclesiastical courts of London show him a tireless litigant in his later years, pursuing the tithes and debts of his parishioners. The most famous member of Gosson's final parish was Edward Alleyn, who upon retiring as one of the most popular actors in the theater set up a charity at Dulwich College, in part with three poor brethren Gosson chose for him. There was also at least one notable marriage at St. Botolph's in those years — the marriage of Archibald Campbell, Earl of Argyll, in 1609.

Gosson wed Elizabeth Acton of London on 25 April 1587 at St. Dunstan's, Stepney; they had two sons and a daughter. Elizabeth Gosson died on 2 December 1615 at the age of sixty and was buried in the choir of old St. Botolph's Church. Their daughter, Elizabeth, who married Paul Bassano, died a little more than a year later, on 23 March 1617. Nothing more is known of Gosson's sons, suggesting they too predeceased him. Gosson continued alone for another ten years, dying, according to the registers of St. Botolph, Bishopsgate, in February 1624, "about 5 of the clock on Friday, in the afternoon being the 13th of this month, and buried in the night of the 17th, age 69." He was buried at his request in the chancel of his church, near his wife and daughter — and at night to save costs.

Gosson was survived by a sister, a niece, and a cousin, as well as by his brother, William, by then a gentleman and drum major to King James I. He left them all bequests, the largest to William, but he also remembered his curate, his maidservant, his parish clerk, his sexton, and the poor of each parish he had served — St. Martin's, Ludgate; St. Dunstan's; St. Alban's, Sandridge; Great Wigborough; and St.

Botolph's. His grave was destroyed when St. Botolph's was demolished in 1724 to make way for the new church, but his name remains inscribed as a memorial on the list of rectors placed within the door of the west front.

In addition to the immediate replies of Sidney, Lodge, and others, Gosson's criticism continued to influence other opponents of drama and the stage for more than fifty years. In 1580 Anthony Munday, considering *The School of Abuse* "the first blast," published his *Second and Third Blast of Retreat from Plays and Theaters,* repeating some of Gosson's arguments. In 1583 Philip Stubbes, in his *Anatomy of Abuses,* copied a third of his essay word for word from *Plays Confuted.* Henry Crosse, in *Virtue's Commonwealth* (1603), devoted twelve pages to Gosson. In *A Refutation of the Apology for Actors* (1615), "J. G." replies closely to Thomas Heywood's *Apology for Actors;* his last part, devoted to the efficient, material, formal, and final causes of plays, uses Gosson's topics and several details from his arguments. *The School of Abuse* and *Plays Confuted* are frequently cited by William Prynne in *Histrio-Mastix* (1633), the most encyclopedic attack of the seventeenth century: like Gosson, Prynne divides his arguments into acts. Citations are frequent – Gosson is in fact Prynne's chief authority – but this is the last use that was directly made of Gosson's arguments. By the time of Jeremy Collier's *Short View of the Immorality and Profaneness of the English Stage* (1698), Gosson had dropped from view. His work did not survive the Interregnum but was, in due course, discovered by editors in the nineteenth and twentieth centuries. In recent years his description of the Elizabethan public playhouse audience (partly in imitation of Ovid) as compared to an open market has attracted Marxist scholars, while his attack on cross-dressing has attracted social and theater historians. Because of the editors and scholars of the past two centuries, Gosson has now taken his place irrevocably in the history of dramatic criticism, if not in panegyric and romance.

References:

Jean-Christophe Agnew, *Worlds Apart: The Market and the Theater in Anglo-American Thought, 1550–1750* (Cambridge: Cambridge University Press, 1986);

Jonas Barish, *The Antitheatrical Prejudice* (Berkeley & Los Angeles: University of California Press, 1981);

Russell Fraser, *The War against Poetry* (Princeton: Princeton University Press, 1970);

Andrew Gurr, *Playgoing in Shakespeare's London* (Cambridge: Cambridge University Press, 1987);

Stephen S. Hilliard, "Stephen Gosson and the Elizabethan Distrust of the Effects of Drama," *English Literary Renaissance,* 9 (Spring 1979): 225–239;

Arthur F. Kinney, *Markets of Bawdrie: The Dramatic Criticism of Stephen Gosson,* Elizabethan Studies 4 (Salzburg: Institut für Englische Sprache und Literatur, 1974), pp. 1–67;

Kinney, "Parody and Its Implications in Sidney's *Defense of Poesie,*" *Studies in English Literature 1500–1900,* 12, no. 1 (1972): 1–19;

Kinney, "Stephen Gosson's Art of Argumentation in *The School of Abuse,*" *Studies in English Literature 1500–1900,* 7 (Winter 1967): 41–54;

Kinney, "Two Unique Copies of Stephen Gosson's 'Schoole of Abuse' (1579): Criteria for Judging Nineteenth-Century Editing," *Papers of the Bibliographical Society,* 59, no. 4 (1965): 425–429;

Laura Levine, "Men in Women's Clothing: Anti-Theatricality and Effemitization from 1579 to 1642," *Criticism,* 28 (Spring 1986): 121–143;

Edwin Haviland Miller, *The Professional Writer in Elizabethan England: A Study of Nondramatic Literature* (Cambridge, Mass.: Harvard University Press, 1959);

William Ringler, *Stephen Gosson: A Biographical and Critical Study* (Princeton: Princeton University Press, 1942);

Phoebe Sheavyn, *The Literary Profession in the Elizabethan Age,* second edition, revised by J. W. Saunders (Manchester: Manchester University Press, 1967);

Elbert N. S. Thompson, *The Controversy between the Puritans and the Stage,* Yale Studies in English 20 (New Haven: Yale University Press, 1903);

S. P. Zitner, "Gosson, Ovid, and the Elizabethan Audience," *Shakespeare Quarterly,* 9 (Spring 1958): 206–208.

Fulke Greville, First Lord Brooke

(3 October 1554 – 30 September 1628)

John Gouws
Rhodes University, South Africa

See also the Greville entry in *DLB 62: Elizabethan Dramatists.*

BOOKS: *The Tragedy of Mustapha* (London: Printed by J. Windet for N. Butter, 1609);

Certaine Learned and Elegant Workes (London: Printed by E. Purslowe for H. Seyle, 1633) — comprises *A Treatise of Humane Learning, An Inquisition upon Fame and Honour, A Treatise of Wars, Alaham, Mustapha, Caelica, A Letter to an Honorable Lady,* and *A Letter of Travel;*

The Life of the Renowned Sr Philip Sydney (London: Printed for Henry Seile, 1652);

The Remains of Sir Fulk Grevill Lord Brooke: Being Poems of Monarchy and Religion: Never Before Printed (London: Printed by T. N. for H. Herringman, 1670) — comprises *A Treatise of Monarchy* and *A Treatise of Religion.*

Editions: *Poems and Dramas of Fulke Greville, First Lord Brooke,* 2 volumes, edited by Geoffrey Bullough (Edinburgh: Oliver & Boyd, 1939; New York: Oxford University Press, 1945) — comprises *Caelica, A Treatise of Humane Learning, An Inquisition upon Fame and Honor, A Treatise of Wars, Mustapha,* and *Alaham;*

The Remains: Being Poems of Monarchy and Religion, edited by G. A. Wilkes (London: Oxford University Press, 1965) — comprises *A Treatise of Monarchy* and *A Treatise of Religion;*

The Prose Works of Fulke Greville, Lord Brooke, edited by John Gouws (Oxford: Clarendon Press, 1986) — comprises *A Dedication to Sir Philip Sidney* ("The Life of the Renowned Sir Philip Sidney") and *A Letter to an Honorable Lady.*

Fulke Greville, first Lord Brooke, survived most of his contemporaries. His active literary life of almost fifty years (the late 1570s to the 1620s) makes him the principal courtly writer of the Elizabethan and Jacobean eras (apart from his short-lived friend Sir Philip Sidney). Although some attention has been paid to him as a writer of short poems, the main interest in Greville has been focused not on his closet dramas *Alaham* (1633) and *Mustapha* (1609), his sonnet sequence *Caelica* (1633), nor on his verse treatises *An Inquisition upon Fame and Honor* (1633), *A Treatise of Humane Learning* (1633), *A Treatise of Wars* (1633), *A Treatise of Monarchy* (1670), and *A Treatise of Religion* (1670), but on his relationship with the Sidney circle, especially as it emerged from the biographical material on Sidney in Greville's *Dedication to Sir Philip Sidney* (originally published as *Life of the Renowned Sir Philip Sidney,* 1652). The principal anecdotal material of Sidney mythography derives from this work, and posterity has in consequence tended to accept Greville's presentation of himself as a secondary rather than a principal figure, or, to use Greville's own terms, as an adjective rather than a substantive.

Fulke Greville was born on 3 October 1554, the only son of an influential landowning Warwickshire family with aristocratic connections: his father, Sir Fulke Greville, de jure Lord Willoughby de Broke, married Ann Neville, daughter of the earl of Westmoreland. From childhood Greville had a sense of his own great, though perhaps unrecognized, worth; but it was only in middle age that he managed to achieve some sense of real autonomy. Born when his father was eighteen years old, he had to wait until the elder Greville's death in 1606 before coming into his inheritance. Only in 1621, after much petitioning and bargaining, was he accorded the title of Lord Brooke.

In 1564, at the age of ten, Greville was sent to join the young Philip Sidney at the newly founded school at Shrewsbury in the neighboring county of Shropshire. The friendship of the two boys was cemented by the three years they spent together at this school and was to influence Greville for the rest of his life. In 1568 the friends were parted: Greville entered Jesus College, Cambridge, while Sidney pursued his studies at Christ Church, Oxford. As was common for someone of his standing, Greville left Cambridge after three or four years without tak-

Portrait by an unknown artist (collection of Lord Willoughby de Broke)

ing a degree. Nothing is known of his activities in England during the period of Sidney's extended continental travels from 1572 to 1575.

Partly because he had been imbued with the humanist notion of service to one's prince, partly because he undoubtedly wished to keep company with his brilliant friend, and partly because he realized that he would probably be an old man before he came into his inheritance, Greville had by 1575 determined on a career at court, where he attached himself to the radical Protestant faction headed by Sidney's uncle, Robert Dudley, Earl of Leicester. Sidney was a member of this faction, but his political ambitions were frustrated by his failure to secure any significant office. Greville discovered that the distrust of the queen and her advisers, William

Cecil, Lord Burghley, and his son Sir Robert, was extended to him, so that any of his own more modest forays into conduct that could possibly be construed as having political significance were frustrated.

In 1585 Greville and Sidney were prevented from joining Sir Francis Drake's expedition to the West Indies. Greville's account of these events is particularly revealing. Drake, in order to facilitate the equipping of the expedition, may have secretly agreed to allow Sidney, frustrated by inactivity, to accompany him. He might even have fostered in Sidney the belief that he would have the standing of a joint commander. But it is clear that he had no intention of sharing the command, and it is probable that he never intended Sidney and Greville to leave the shores of England in his company. The skeptical and observant Greville soon discerned that Drake's conduct lacked candor and that his delaying tactics were intended to invite a royal order forbidding Sidney's attempt at independent action. Sidney's own forthright nature would not credit such duplicity, and he refused to heed his less-trusting companion's advice. In due course, the peremptory prohibition arrived, forcing Greville and Sidney to return to the court in disgrace. An account such as this reveals Greville as a willing seconder rather than initiator of action, but also as someone capable of distancing himself from events by a profound distrust of the apparent motives of human actions.

The chronology of Greville's literary works is by no means certain. It is clear that his earliest writing was undertaken in collaboration with Sidney, and to a lesser extent with Sir Edward Dyer. Sonnets 1 through 76 and 83 of *Caelica* appear to have been written after 1577, when the three friends were experimenting with verse forms. Many of Greville's poems can be seen as responses to rather than imitations of those of Sidney. The nature of this friendly rivalry is revealed by the titles of their sonnet sequences: Sidney's mistress is a single star (Stella); Greville addresses his poems to the entire sky (Caelica). Greville's poems thus need to be read in the context of his friend's. Sonnet 6 of *Caelica*, for example, his only poem in quantitative verse (rhymed sapphics), gains by being set against one of Sidney's generally less successful attempts to write in classical meters, "If Mine Eyes Can Speak to Do Hearty Errand."

But Greville's early poems cannot be treated simply as the poetic exercises of a young courtier bent on establishing a name for himself by initiating a new vernacular literature. In many ways, both he and Sidney can be seen as responding to the challenges presented by the literary practice of Petrarchan love. Sidney's sequence fails to resolve the conflicting demands of selfless adoration and physical desire in the lover, while Greville, from an initial exploration of the psychological consequences of these conflicting demands, turns to a cynical denial of the possibility of ideal love in this world, because women are unfaithful and the men who worship them are duped by self-deception.

The personal relationship between Sidney and Penelope Rich that underlies *Astrophil and Stella* (1591) should also be treated as part of the context of *Caelica*. Given the skepticism and disenchantment Greville expresses about the nature and possibility of love as his sequence progresses, he is the obvious candidate for the admonishing friend in sonnets 14,

21, and 69 of *Astrophil and Stella;* it is clear that even poems as late as sonnets 66 and 76 of *Caelica* are critical responses to the situation in songs 2 and 8 of *Astrophil and Stella.*

Greville's seventy-seven poems on human love are markedly different from Sidney's. They are not organized in the form of a narrative of a single passionate relationship. Instead, *Caelica* is more like a miscellany of predominantly short, often introspective poems in which no fewer than three mistresses are named: Caelica, Myra, and Cynthia. On the occasions when Greville writes sonnets, he prefers the English form to the Italian. Unlike Sidney, whose poems typically move from an abstraction to passionate attention to the beloved, Greville wrote poems throughout his career that turn from a particular experience to a generalized philosophical observation.

In the years following Sidney's death in 1586, Greville found no way of advancing his political career apart from representing the county of Warwickshire in all the remaining Parliaments of Elizabeth's reign and continuing to hold the lucrative office of secretary to the Council of the Marches of Wales. However, he naturally attached himself to Sidney's political heir, Robert Devereux, Earl of Essex, who had inherited Sidney's sword and married his widow. After many years of submitting, often unwillingly, to the queen's restraint of his activities, Greville eventually obtained, with Essex's support, the office of treasurer of the navy. This was his first significant appointment, one that he retained despite his patron's disgrace and subsequent execution in 1601. Greville had had the foresight to distance himself timeously from Essex. The queen, moreover, had come to take the measure of his capacity for independent action and knew that his loyalties lay with her. In this way, he avoided the immediate retaliation of Essex's great enemy, the ever-distrustful Sir Robert Cecil. Although Greville was knighted at the accession of King James in 1603, Cecil saw to it that he was forced from office because of the embarrassment Greville suffered when he refused to connive at the corruption of his fellow naval administrators. At the age of forty-nine, he retired to Warwickshire, seemingly at the end of his career.

The shock of Sidney's death did not prevent Greville from stopping the unauthorized publication of Sidney's *Arcadia* and, with the aid of Matthew Gwinne and John Florio, seeing the first authorized edition through the press in 1590. This publication was Greville's first significant contribution to Sidney mythography. In his own writing, he produced

Page from Greville's manuscript for a sonnet sequence written after 1577 (British Library, Add. Ms. 54570, fol. 68ª) no more poems of human love; and the handful of poems written between 1577 and 1603, *Caelica* sonnets 77–81, turn to the political and religious concerns that were to preoccupy him in the writing of his poetic closet dramas, *Alaham, Mustapha,* and the lost *Antony and Cleopatra,* during the last five years of the century.

In the extant plays Greville's immediate concern is with the dangers and evils of power and intrigue in an absolute monarchy. In addition to the examination of the public vices of tyranny, ambition, and intrigue, however, there is a somberly pessimistic view of the bewildered individual as radically incapable of escaping the consequences of political corruption. As such, the plays embody Greville's Protestant acceptance of the necessity of living in the world while yet being convinced of the irremediable fallibility and degeneracy of human nature since the Fall. The complexity of this view, which does not entail withdrawal from the world, is encapsulated in a remark of Greville in a letter to Sir John Coke dated 1 February 1613: "I know the world and believe in God."

It is likely that Greville's unfinished prose work, *A Letter to an Honorable Lady,* was composed during the period 1595–1601. Written in the literary tradition of the *consolatio* and of the Senecan epistle, the work attempts to persuade a virtuous aristocrat who has been ill-treated by her husband to lead a life of stoic, Christian patience. The material is deployed according to the rules of deliberative oratory. Chapter 1 constitutes the introductory *exordium,* followed by the *narratio,* which states the fact of the marriage as starting with love and ending in neglect and ill-treatment of the wife. The *refutatio* of chapter 2 dismisses the possibility of remedying the situation by reforming the husband. The succeeding three chapters provide the positive advice, or *confirmatio:* chapter 3 advocates turning inward in the face of the uncertainties of this life; chapter 4 suggests that the only proper response to the husband's authority is patience, stoic *apathia;* and in chapter 5 the advantages of this approach are asserted, since the wife retains her integrity and might even attain the reputation of a good wife. Where one would expect a concluding *peroratio,* in the unfinished chapter 6 there is a digressive extension of the *confirmatio,* in which Greville adds a specifically Christian dimension to the argument by suggesting the possibility of a spiritual augmentation, though not a replacement, of stoic ideas. The new ideas of chapter 6 disrupt the overall design of the work, and this might be the reason Greville left it incomplete.

The addressee of *A Letter to an Honorable Lady* has not been identified, though the circumstances of Margaret Clifford, Countess of Cumberland, match those assumed by the work. Lady Cumberland's plight is also touched on in two poems by Greville's protégé, Samuel Daniel: "A Letter from Octavia to Marcus Antonius" (1599) and "To Lady Margaret, Countess of Cumberland" (1603). The evidence is not decisive, however, and Greville could simply be exploring a favorite idea: the wife's secondary relation to her husband is figured as that between a subject and monarch. As such, the *Letter* has a great deal in common with the plays Greville was writing in the 1590s and also with *Caelica* sonnet 86, which advocates patience in the face of the vicissitudes of life and trust in the consolation of Heaven. In this work one can see Greville coming to terms with a central issue in his life and writings, the frustration at the lack of personal autonomy.

Greville was neither impoverished nor idle in his retirement. With an annual income of between £5,000 and £7,000, he was able to maintain six residences, and he spent a great deal of time overseeing the practical affairs connected with them. A major project was the refurbishment, at a cost of £10,000 over several years, of Warwick Castle, his seventh residence, which he acquired in 1604. These matters did not distract him from writing. In fact, the loss of office led directly to his most productive period.

A Treatise of Monarchy, Greville's first discursive poem, was written early in his retirement. According to his account in the *Dedication to Sir Philip Sidney,* the poem had its origin in the choruses of his plays. He might thus have begun work on it some time before 1599, at the time he was encouraging Daniel to write philosophical verse, and when the *Caelica* poems began to show a preference for the six-line stanza that was to be the standard form of his long poems. By 1610, after several major revisions, *A Treatise of Monarchy* took its final form. The 664 stanzas are divided into fifteen sections. The first five sections focus on the problematic nature of wielding monarchal power, with Greville not distinguishing between kingship and tyranny, or attempting to exempt monarchs from human fallibility. Sections 6–12 deal with the monarch's responsibility in the spheres of religion, law, the nobility, commerce, revenue, peace, and war. His main concern is with the practicalities of cautious but effective political government. In the last three sections, where the traditional alternatives of aristocracy and democracy are compared with monarchy, monarchy is upheld as the best hope against disorder.

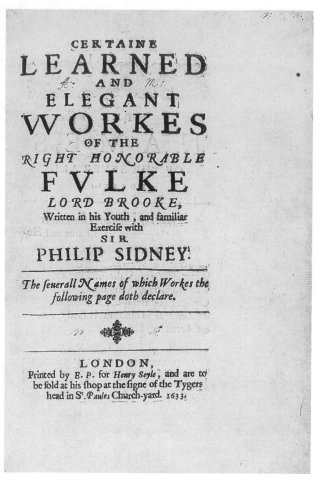

Title page for the earliest collected edition of Greville's works

The advice offered by Greville in *A Treatise of Monarchy* is that of a retired but committed politician. The same stance underlies the *Dedication to Sir Philip Sidney*, composed in its final form between 1610 and 1612. The first part of the work consists of a laudatory biography of Sidney as an ideal subject, hence the commonly misleading title "The Life of Sidney." The second part is an encomiastic history of Queen Elizabeth's reign, which by indirections makes clear Greville's opinion of the reign of her successor, James I. The awkward structure of the *Dedication* disappears once it is realized that the work was most likely intended for the eyes of Henry, Prince of Wales. By 1610 Henry had established a measure of independence from his father and had become the center of a circle advocating a vigorously anti-Catholic foreign policy that ran counter to that of James I. Given Henry's independence, his patronage would have been ideally suited to someone out of favor and office. Unfortunately for Greville, Henry died suddenly in November 1612, though by then it looked as if Greville's polit-

ical fortunes would change. His old enemy Cecil had died in May. The rancor that fuels so much of the *Dedication* no longer had an object, while the prospect of once again attaining office and so of being able to influence political decisions made advice to a potential patron irrelevant. Though Greville had to wait until October 1614 before returning to office, he appears to have abandoned the work. This possibility might explain the absence of the *Dedication* from the collection of manuscript fair copies of his works that Greville had prepared under his supervision.

The material on Sidney is written from within the rhetorical tradition of the panegyric biography and is the sole source of three anecdotes central to the Sidney myth: the tennis-court quarrel with the earl of Oxford, the high-minded abandoning of leg armor at the battle of Zutphen, and the resignation of some water to a fellow casualty in the battle with the words "Thy necessity is yet greater than mine." Greville was present at the quarrel but was not in the Netherlands to witness his beloved friend's last days. The idealization of Sidney during the succeeding centuries was focused particularly in terms of the story of what came to be known as the cup of water. In more-recent times the story has become a subject of controversy.

The second part of the *Dedication* is an essay in the new civil history being pioneered by Greville's friend and client, William Camden. Greville indicates how his ambition to write a history of Elizabeth was frustrated by Cecil, who was only too aware of the political uses to which such a history could be put in the reign of James. But the material on Elizabeth in the *Dedication* cannot be regarded as the torso of this failed project, for Greville simply translated material from Camden's original Latin manuscript of his *Annals* (1625). This use of Camden's unpublished material is not as predatory as it might appear, since it is more than likely that Camden's friendship with Greville allowed him access to material that would otherwise have been unavailable.

The *Dedication*, which survives in four manuscripts, was not published until 1652 under the cumbersome title of *The Life of the Renowned Sir Philip Sidney, with the True Interest of England as It Then Stood in Relation of All Foreign Princes, and Particularly for Suppressing the Power of Spain Stated by Him, His Principal Actions, Counsels, Designs, and Death, Together with a Short Account of the Maxims and Policies Used by Queen Elizabeth in Her Government. Written by Sir Fulke Greville, Knight, Lord Brook, a Servant to Queen Elizabeth, and His Companion and Friend.* From the lengthy subtitle it would seem as if the publication was motivated by an attempt to use the reputations of Sidney and Elizabeth to influence foreign-policy decisions in Commonwealth England.

Greville's collaboration with Camden indicates the nature of the tradition of patronage which he had inherited from Sidney. Through Greville, Camden had obtained the position of Clarenceux, King of Arms in the Herald's Office, which freed him to undertake his historical research. Another historian, John Speed, also received support from Greville. It is clear from Bishop Joseph Hall's dedication in *Epistles and Contemplations upon the Principal Passages of the Holy Bible* (1610), however, that Greville's patronage was valued more for his capacity for intellectual exchange with his clients than for material and social benefits that could arise from association with him: "The world hath long and justly both noted and honored you for eminence in wisdom and learning, and I above the most; I am ready with the awe of a learner to embrace all precepts from you: you shall expect nothing from me but tes-

timonies of respect and thankfulness." Certainly in his retirement Hall was in no position to exercise the kind of influence by which, in the last years of Elizabeth's reign, he was able to gain the deanships of Westminster and St. Paul's for Lancelot Andrewes and John Overall, respectively. As with Camden, the client-patron relationship could develop into one of friendship. This seems to have happened also in the case of Daniel, whose writing career was profoundly influenced by his relationship with Greville.

Four other writers' names have been linked with Greville. Francis Bacon, with whom he exchanged ideas about the nature and methods of writing history, is unlikely to have been in need of Greville's support during his early career. With Bacon's disgrace in 1620, the ever-cautious Greville severed all contact with him. The young William Davenant was a member of Greville's household, but there is no evidence to show that the aging Greville took an interest in his writing. The two remaining authors were linked to Greville in David Lloyd's *Statesmen and Favorites of England since the Reformation* (1670). According to Lloyd, Greville was known for "his respect of the worth of others, desiring to be known to posterity under no other notion than of Shakespeare's and Ben Jonson's Master." There is no evidence to substantiate this tantalizing suggestion, though the obvious Warwickshire connection with William Shakespeare and Ben Jonson's connection with Camden do lend it some plausibility. The greatest instance of Greville's political patronage is his friend Sir John Coke, whom he met when he was secretary to the navy. Coke subsequently looked after Greville's affairs and later rose to the office of secretary of state during the reign of Charles I.

During the period between the death of Prince Henry and his return to office as chancellor and treasurer of the exchequer and as privy councillor in October 1614, Greville composed *An Inquisition upon Fame and Honor*. The poem goes beyond his earlier preoccupation with merit and its implied neglect during James's reign. Although he brings to bear the double perspective of the temporal and divine in terms of which he tends to view all human conduct, the overall strategy is what one would expect from a revisionary metaphysician: Greville spends the first seventy-two stanzas undermining what he takes to be the commonly understood conceptions of fame and honor, and then in stanzas 73–86 offers virtue grounded in faith as the only possible alternative to the delusive idols of opinion (Fame) and worth (Honor). His Calvinist assumption is that in a spiritually degenerate and mutable world, human beings are deluded by pride in their own worth, by pride in their rank or office, and by vanity (stanzas 60–68). From a Christian perspective, stoic apathia, consisting of a withdrawal from worldly concerns, is therefore dismissed in the orthodox fashion: it is a manifestation of human pride, since, in not affirming human fallibility and human dependence on the divine, it attempts to establish the individual self as God. *An Inquisition upon Fame and Honor* thus provides an outright rejection of the stoic ideas espoused in the first five chapters of *A Letter to an Honorable Lady*.

Greville's concerns with the nature of merit, reward, and recognition (and with the human desire for them) are characteristic of a man coming to terms with a sense of his own unrecognized merit. If the *Caelica* poems are indeed arranged in roughly chronological order, then those that take up the concern with fame and honor can be used to trace his self-understanding during this period of his life. In *Caelica* sonnet 91, titles of honor are seen as being used by rulers to maintain their own power, while fame is merely the rationalization of evil. In the companion poem, *Caelica* sonnet 92, ennoblement is seen not as a recognition of merit but as a concealment of evil, and one is tempted to think of Robert Carr, Earl of Somerset's rise from obscurity and his subsequent disgrace. The possibility of contemporary reference is further enhanced when, in *Caelica* sonnet 101, Greville seemingly returns to an earlier perspective: in his warning against kings who fail to recognize merit and instead indulge their own pleasures in the distribution of honor, he appears to be responding to James I's advancement of young Scots favorites, which so scandalized Greville and his contemporaries. *Caelica* sonnets 104 and 105 place the preoccupation with fame and honor in a divine, consolatory perspective.

Other poems in *Caelica* following the "farewell to love" of sonnet 84 either enjoin or enact a renunciation of the values of the fallen world for inner dependence on divine grace. Of these, the most telling is a pair of poems whose modulated refrains represent an altered spiritual perspective or state. In sonnet 98 the refrain of the first two stanzas, "Lord, I have sinned, and mine iniquity, / Deserves this hell; yet Lord deliver me," is transformed in the third and last stanza to the reassurance of "Lord, from this horror of iniquity, / And hellish grave, thou would'st deliver me." In sonnet 99, a poem brought to prominence by Yvor Winters's discussion of it, the refrain undergoes a double transformation. "Deprived of human graces, and divine, / Even there

appears this saving God of mine" of the first two stanzas is first modified to reflect a realistic acceptance of the human condition, "Deprived of human graces, not divine, / Even there appears this saving God of mine." Only then can the assurance of salvation be asserted in the fourth and last refrain: "Deprived of human graces, not divine / Thus has His death raised up this soul of mine." It is on the basis of poems such as these that claims have been advanced for Greville as a religious poet comparable with John Donne.

Ronald Rebholz argues in *The Life of Fulke Greville, First Lord Brooke* (1971) that Greville experienced a major religious conversion sometime before 1614. Although this assumption allows Rebholz a plausible narrative in terms of which he can organize Greville's writings, there is no external evidence of a spiritual crisis in Greville's life at this time. Moreover, Rebholz's theory depends on two questionable assumptions. The first of these is the anachronistic post-Romantic myth that an author's works are a direct expression of his spiritual and psychological being. The second is that for works for which no separate versions are extant there is a single temporal moment of composition that can be tied to the inner life of the author. Given that Greville was an inveterate reviser, and given his self-presentation as a Calvinist throughout his writings, there are insufficient grounds for pressing selective literary evidence to underpin a supposition as to a specific religious experience.

The date of composition of the three remaining philosophical poems is uncertain, but it is thought to be after Greville's return to office. In the two-year period after his creation as Lord Brooke, and his loss of the chancellorship of the exchequer in 1621, he attended few Privy Council meetings. It is possible that in the absence of public duties and commitments he once again devoted his energies to writing.

In the first four stanzas of *A Treatise of Humane Learning*, Greville reveals the extent of his commitment to the tradition of Renaissance skepticism. Like Michel de Montaigne and Bacon, he acknowledges the human incapacity for accurate perception and intellectual conception, which results in universal disagreement and lack of self-knowledge. Unlike them, however, his views are grounded in his convictions about original sin. Montaigne's delight in relativism and Bacon's humanistic optimism hold no attractions for him.

Although *A Treatise of Humane Learning* has much in common with Bacon's *Advancement of Learning* (1605), it has even been seen as a response to

Part of a page from Greville's manuscript for A Treatise of Religion *(from Alexander B. Grossart, ed.,* The Works in Verse and Prose Complete of the Right Honorable Fulke Greville, Lord Brooke, *volume 4, 1870)*

that work, since Greville never endorses the project for redeeming the consequences of the Fall through learning. Instead he follows his initial dismissal of all human learning as vanity with an assertion of the double perspective of the temporal and the eternal: thus ignorance is the nurse and mother of lust, and learning is "A bunch of grapes sprung up among thorns, / Where, but by caution, none the harm can miss."

Setting aside the Elect, whose only concern is obedience to God, Greville presents a program for the reform of learning. His target is the same as Bacon's: scholastic speculation conducted in terms of the deductive method. The branches of learning he discusses are those of the university faculties. Theology should not meddle with the mysteries of divinity, but should be concerned with the relationship between humans and God. Law should be based on divine injunctions, protect the individual citizen, and maintain royal authority. Both medicine and moral philosophy must be concerned with practical and ethical matters, while political philosophy should enable kings to avoid impediments to their authority.

The "instrumental arts" of the traditional trivium (grammar, rhetoric, and logic) must be simplified. Of the "Arts of Recreation," music should properly enhance worship and inspire martial valor; poetry, based on truth "while it seemeth but to please, / Teacheth us order under pleasure's name."

Arithmetic, geometry, and astronomy are all to have a practical application. Conversely, the use of knowledge for evil ends is to be condemned. Turning then from these "vanities" to the Elect, Greville suggests that the faithful should obey willingly their temporal prince as part of their submission to God's providential scheme, since the only human obligation is to come to terms with the spiritual degradation precipitated by the Fall.

The two remaining treatises seem to be much more the work of an aging, disillusioned statesman and politician. In the first five stanzas of *A Treatise of Wars,* the benefits of peace to fallen mankind are celebrated. This is followed by a representation of war as "the perfect type of hell." In the remaining thirty-eight stanzas Greville treats his subject from a providential perspective. Rather than seeing war as an instrument of monarchal power (as in *A Treatise of Monarchy* and the *Dedication*), or as a means to personal honor (as in the *Dedication* or *Caelica* sonnet 108), he sees it primarily as a divine scourge of human wickedness, as a trial of the Elect, as a purge for the excesses of peace, and as an instrument for sustaining the vicissitudes of the fallen condition.

Greville then turns from the causes to the varieties of war. He distinguishes between human war and divine war (by which he appears to mean not holy wars such as the Crusades but something like the angelic wars against Satan). Of human wars, the only ones in which the Elect may participate are those having the divine sanctions of prophecies and angelic wonders, and then only on condition that they are conducted mercifully and charitably by lawfully constituted authorities. That being the case, there can be justification neither for involvement in war in order to attain honor or power, nor for rebellion or its suppression. War thus has value only to those whose undertakings are limited by this world. For this reason, the Elect must not be like nominal Christians and Mohammedans in being unable "to leave the world for God, nor God for it." Any superstitious compromise as to the benefits of war merely augments the evil of war. What is required is an absolute commitment: war will be brought to an end only when humans "begin / For God's sake to abhor this world of sin."

In *A Treatise of Religion* Greville writes directly about the topic that has dominated most of his thinking. The first four stanzas establish the assumption that fallen human nature can be redeemed only by grace through Christ; neither human passion nor reason is capable of redeeming us. Nevertheless, human beings naturally have such a sense of the need for redemption that if human nature were not radically corrupt, they would "grow happily adorers of the good." Instead, human affection and reason lead people to find external remedies for their condition in superstition and hypocrisy, respectively. True religion, however, is not external, but is manifested initially in virtue attained through grace.

By insisting that this virtue is not the pagan self-sufficiency of stoicism, Greville rejects the equanimity he advocated in *A Letter to an Honorable Lady.* He now maintains that regeneration is possible only through supernatural grace, by means of which the faithful, the "Church invisible," must devote themselves to prayer and obedience, not to the "book-learning" of a subservient external church professing faith in God but not obeying Him. In maintaining that the Elect are those who accept, and are regenerated by, grace, and so persevere in faith and good works, Greville implicitly rejects the Calvinistic doctrine of predestination. For him, humans are not eternally either redeemed or reprobate. Instead, they can either devote themselves to God, as Abel did, or seek some external manifestation of divinity and so fail in their obedience, as did Cain. Those who seek peace through other than heavenly things — rulers, the learned, and the clergy of an outward church — will all be brought to desolation, a vision of which is presented in the appropriately apocalyptic concluding poem of *Caelica,* sonnet 109. The

Elect, who are such by their faith in and devotion to Christ the Redeemer, will find peace and joy.

Greville obviously considered *A Treatise of Religion* the most important of his shorter philosophical poems. In a note in one of the volumes of the fair copies of his works prepared for him between 1619 and 1625, he indicates the order in which the poems are to be placed: "1. Religion. 2. Humane learning. 3. Fame and Honor. 4. War." However, when his works were put through the press by Coke and Sir Kenelm Digby, *A Treatise of Religion* ran afoul of the censors. All copies of *Certain Learned and Elegant Works* (1633) lack the pages that should have contained it, and it has generally been assumed that someone like William Lord, then bishop of London, would have taken exception to the slur on episcopacy in stanza 92 and to the criticism of an Established Church in stanzas 30–31 and 68–69. Two other works are also absent from the 1633 volume.

If in the case of the *Dedication* the work still survived among the manuscript fair copies, Greville's literary executors might have foreseen the difficulties that implicit criticism of James I could raise during his son's reign. They certainly did not even consider publication of *A Treatise of Monarchy,* with its notion of kingship as a product of human fallibility. With the absolute powers claimed by Charles I, the poem would have lent support to the increasingly vehement opposition to the king. Moreover, Coke and Digby would have recalled that Greville's plans for a lectureship in history at Cambridge had failed because of Laud's objection to the similar views of monarchy expressed by the first appointee, Isaac Dorislaus. The two potentially subversive treatises thus had to wait until 1670, when they were published in a volume titled *The Remains of Sir Fulke Greville: Being Poems of Monarchy and Religion.*

Greville's death followed shortly after the assassination on 23 August 1628 of George Villiers, Duke of Buckingham, the despised favorite of James I and Charles I. The attack on Greville by a servant, Ralph Hayward, on 1 September does not seem to have been politically motivated. Hayward appears to have been discontented with the terms of his employer's will and stabbed Greville in the stomach while he was assisting his master to fasten his breeches. There is no indication that the stabbing was occasioned by anything untoward happening while Hayward performed these personal services for his master, who prevented anyone from pursuing his assailant. Greville died of gangrene on 30 September, after physicians had replaced the depleted natural fatty membrane around their patient's intestines with animal fat. His corpse was transported from London to Warwick, where it was buried in the family crypt in St. Mary's Church. Nearby, now enclosed in a small room, stands the monumental tomb Greville had prepared for himself, bearing the inscription, "Fulke Greville / Servant to Queen Elizabeth / Councillour to King James / and Friend to Sir Philip Sidney. / Trophaeum Peccati." With its claims of only secondary fame and its awareness of the wages of sin, the inscription reveals much of Greville's complexity, while the location of the tomb aptly underscores the dominant mode of his life, frustration.

Greville's reputation has never stood as high as it does in the twentieth century. In the United States his standing as a poet of the "plain style" can in large measure be attributed to the critical writing of Winters, who regards him not only as a pivotal figure in literary history, but as a poet who "should be ranked with Jonson as one of the two great masters of the short poem in the Renaissance." Winters's estimation has not met with general critical assent, but it is clear that it has encouraged others to take Greville seriously. Much of the recent British writing on Greville has been from the perspective of cultural materialism, and it is likely that those interested in the poetics of culture and power in Renaissance England will find Greville's works central to their project. They will, however, find themselves hampered by the lack of recently edited scholarly texts: editions of the poems and dramas by G. A. Wilkes of Sydney University and of the letters by Norman K. Farmer of the University of Texas at Austin have been long awaited.

Bibliography:

Paula Bennet, "Recent Studies in Greville," *English Literary Renaissance,* 2 (Winter 1972): 376–382.

Biographies:

Ronald Rebholz, *The Life of Fulke Greville, First Lord Brooke* (Oxford: Clarendon Press, 1971);

Joan Rees, *Fulke Greville, Lord Brooke, 1554–1628* (London: Routledge & Kegan Paul, 1971; Berkeley: University of California Press, 1971).

References:

John Gouws, "Fact and Anecdote in Fulke Greville's Account of Sidney's Last Days," in *Sir Philip Sidney: 1586 and the Creation of a Legend,* edited by Jan van Dorsten and others (Leiden: E. J. Brill/Leiden University Press, 1986), pp. 62–82;

Gouws, "The Nineteenth-Century Development of the Sidney Legend," in *Sir Philip Sidney's Achievements,* edited by M. J. B. Allen and others (New York: AMS Press, 1990), pp. 251–260;

W. Hilton Kelliher, "The Warwick Manuscripts of Fulke Greville," *British Museum Quarterly,* 34 (1970): 107–121;

Charles Larson, *Fulke Greville* (Boston: Twayne, 1980);

David Norbrook, "Voluntary Servitude: Fulke Greville and the Arts of Power," in his *Poetry and Politics in the English Renaissance* (London: Routledge & Kegan Paul, 1984), pp. 157–174;

Richard Waswo, *The Fatal Mirror: Themes and Techniques in the Poetry of Fulke Greville* (Charlottesville: University of Virginia Press, 1972);

G. A. Wilkes, "The Sequence of the Writings of Fulke Greville, Lord Brooke," *Studies in Philology,* 56 (July 1959): 489–503;

Yvor Winters, "Aspects of the Short Poem in the English Renaissance," in his *Forms of Discovery: Critical and Historical Essays on the Forms of the Short Poem in English* (Chicago: Swallow Press, 1967), pp. 1–120;

Blair Worden, "Friend to Sir Philip Sidney," *London Review of Books,* 3 July 1986, pp. 19–22;

Michael B. Young, *Servility and Service: The Life and Work of Sir John Coke* (London: Boydell Press for the Royal Historical Society, 1986).

Papers:

The principal repository for Fulke Greville's papers is the British Library (the literary works are to be found in Add. Mss. 54566–71, the Warwick Manuscripts; there are also many letters in the as-yet uncatalogued Earl Cowper mss.). Individual manuscripts of the *Dedication to Sir Philip Sidney* are to be found in Headington, Oxford (the private collection of Dr. B. E. Juel-Jensen); Trinity College, Cambridge (Mss. R.7.32 and 33); and Shrewsbury Public Library (Ms. 295).

Bartholomew Griffin

(flourished 1596)

L. M. Storozynsky
University College of the Fraser Valley

BOOK: *Fidessa, More Chaste Then Kinde* (London: Printed by Widow Orwin for Matthew Lownes, 1596).

Editions: *Fidessa; A Collection of Sonnets,* edited by Philip Bliss (Chiswick: C. Whittingham, 1815);

The Poems of Bartholomew Griffin, edited by Alexander B. Grosart (Manchester, 1877).

Bartholomew Griffin is one of many minor poets whose works are generally dismissed as having little value compared with those of their better-known contemporaries. He produced only a single, mediocre collection of sonnets that has attracted little critical attention, and not favorable at that. Nevertheless, his modest contribution to Elizabethan literature is a characteristic example of the sixteenth-century practice of imitation, as well as an indication of just how popular and widespread the sonneteering fashion became. The fact that Griffin and others like him attempted to emulate poets such as Sir Philip Sidney, Edmund Spenser, and William Shakespeare reveals the true extent of the major poets' influence, while expanding the context in which the work of all Elizabethan poets should be considered.

Bartholomew Griffin may have been related to the Griffins of Dingley, Northamptonshire, but he is probably not the Bartholomew Griffin of Coventry buried at Holy Trinity Church, Coventry, on 15 December 1602. John Izon reports that a Bartholomew Griffin, a schoolmaster ordained in holy orders, was employed as a tutor by Sir Thomas Lucy of Charlecote, Warwickshire, around 1600. Even those meager details survive only because the tutor became involved in a scandal within his employer's family, resulting in a lawsuit for which there are extant records. The possibility of a connection between the schoolmaster and the poet obviously appeals to Izon, for that would place the sonneteer in the heart of Shakespeare's home county, but the evidence he cites is unsatisfactory. Griffin's sonnet se-

quence is dedicated to a William Essex of Lamborne, Berkshire, and addressed to "The Gentlemen of the Inns of Court," but these epistles yield no clues to his identity. Indeed, he asserts in the former that he is "so little known unto" his patron and in the latter that he is "a poor stranger." No Bartholomew Griffin is recorded in the registers of the inns.

Griffin's *Fidessa, More Chaste Than Kind* (1596) is a collection of sixty-two sonnets addressed to a probably fictional Fidessa. With the exception of sonnet 62, all are quatorzains. However, in his second preliminary epistle Griffin announces "a pastoral yet unfinished, that my purpose was to have added (for variety's sake) to this little volume of sonnets: the next term you may expect it." The promised poem seems never to have been finished, or at least printed, and readers can only speculate on how the "pastoral" might have complemented or even changed the nature of the volume. Had he published it, Griffin's work might then have been analogous to Richard Lynche's *Diella* (1596) and other collections of sonnets accompanied by long narrative poems.

The sonnets are conventional in subject matter, but, heavily influenced by the Song of Solomon, they include an unusual amount of description. Griffin is overly fond of rhetorical devices such as series of questions answered by a couplet (hypophora); the repetition of key words; ending each line of a poem with the same word (antistrophe); and exclamation, which when overused becomes hyperbole, resulting in an artificial intensity of emotion. Indeed, Griffin has been accused of achieving fine verbal and aural effects where there is little or no meaning. He is considerably more successful in his use of rhyme and meter than many of the minor Elizabethan sonneteers. Less interested in experimenting with the sonnet form, he rarely strays from the limits of the quatorzain and the English rhyme scheme. Regularity of rhyme and meter are achieved thanks to his ample, but fairly conven-

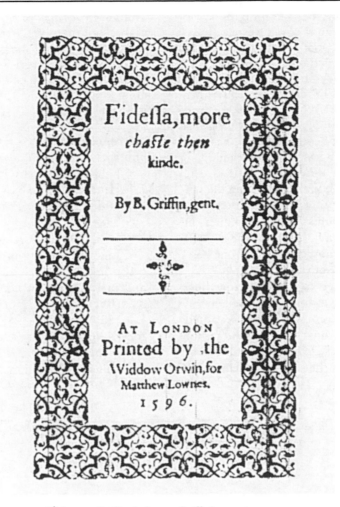

Title page for Bartholomew Griffin's sonnet sequence

tional, vocabulary. Unlike several of his contemporaries, he does not resort to coining words, adopting new spellings, or employing foreign words. On the other hand, in the few instances when he tentatively moves away from his set pattern, Griffin's caution can be tedious. His most ambitious departures consist of simple antistrophe, as in sonnets 23 and 62; in the latter the single rhyme also takes care of the poem's extra line. The final poem in the volume is an unusual summing up of the main themes treated throughout, but Griffin's attempt at combining anaphora and antistrophe (each line begins "Most true that" and ends with the word *love*) succeeds only in bringing the sequence to an anticlimactic close.

Several of Griffin's poems may have enjoyed modest success in his own time, for sonnet 3 from *Fidessa,* albeit in a variant version, was published by William Jaggard as poem 11 in *The Passionate Pilgrim* (1599), a collection published as if its contents were written entirely by Shakespeare. The reputation of

more than one minor poet has been made through this type of association with a well-known writer. It has been suggested that poems 4, 6, and 9 in *The Passionate Pilgrim* may also be Griffin's, given their similarity to 11.

More recently the reception of *Fidessa* has been decidedly cool. The sonnet sequence was republished in 1815 by Philip Bliss, who offers little commentary other than pointing out a few similarities between several of the sonnets and some passages in Shakespeare. Edward Arber included the sequence in *An English Garner* (1882), and Martha Foote Crow edited it for *Elizabethan Sonnet Cycles* (1897). While Crow has mixed feelings about Griffin, gently criticizing his borrowing from other poets, her opinion of the poetry is by far the most favorable: "His sonnets, while showing versatility and ingenuity, lack spontaneous feeling and have serious defects in form; yet these defects are in part offset by their conversational ease and dramatic vividness."

Sidney Lee included Arber's edition in *Elizabethan Sonnets* (1904), sharing Crow's reservations: "He had some genuine poetic faculty, but plagiarised with exceptional boldness." Lee claims that sonnets 15, 33, and 43 are simply reworkings of Samuel Daniel's sonnet 49 from *Delia* (1594), Michael Drayton's sonnet 16 in *Idea* (1594), and Thomas Watson's sonnet 52 from *Hekatompathia* (1582), respectively. Janet Scott, however, believes Sidney to be Griffin's strongest influence, and Daniel to a lesser extent; but, like other readers, she feels that any potential originality is lost in the frequent and blatant borrowing from many sonneteers. Lu Emily Pearson sums up these opinions in her *Elizabethan Love Conventions* (1933): "the work is such a mixture of various borrowings that one hesitates to name any definite source."

One might be tempted to argue that mediocrity such as Griffin's deserves to be forgotten, but in today's critical climate the commonplace is valued as a context for the extraordinary. As a showcase for rhetorical tropes and figures, *Fidessa* has found favor with at least one modern rhetorician (Richard A.

Lanham in *A Handlist of Rhetorical Terms,* 1991) and might legitimately be studied as an imitation of Watson's *Hekatompathia,* which is a veritable handbook on sonnet rhetoric. A critical edition of *Fidessa* would contribute to the much-needed recovery of minor works to render them more readily accessible for further study.

References:

John Erskine, *The Elizabethan Lyric* (New York: Columbia University Press, 1903), pp. 162–163;

C. J. Hindle, "The 1815 Reprint of Bartholomew Griffin's *Fidessa,*" *Notes and Queries* (5 May 1934): 308–310;

John Izon, "Bartholomew Griffin and Sir Thomas Lucy," *Times Literary Supplement,* 15 April 1957, p. 245;

Lu Emily Pearson, *Elizabethan Love Conventions* (Berkeley: University of California Press, 1933), pp. 126–128;

Janet G. Scott, *Les Sonnets Elisabéthains: Les sources et L'apport Personnel* (Paris: Librairie Ancienne Honoré Champion, 1929), pp. 191–194.

James VI of Scotland, I of England

(19 June 1566 – 27 March 1625)

Jenny Wormald
St. Hilda's College, Oxford

See also the King James entry in *DLB 151: British Prose Writers of the Early Seventeenth Century.*

BOOKS: *The Essayes of a Prentise, in the Divine Art of Poesie* (Edinburgh: Printed by Thomas Vautroullier, 1584);

Ane Frvtfvll Meditatioun Contening ane Plane and Facill Expositioun of ye 7.8.9 and 10 Versis of the 20 Chap. of the Reuelatioun in Forme of ane Sermon, edited by Patrick Galloway (Edinburgh: Printed by H. Charteris, 1588);

Ane Meditatioun vpon the xxv., xxvi., xxvii., xxviii., and xxix. Verses of the xv. Chapt. of the First Buke of the Chronicles of the Kingis, edited by Galloway (Edinburgh: Printed by H. Charteris, 1589);

His Maiesties Poeticall Exercises at Vacant Houres (Edinburgh: Printed by Robert Walde-graue, 1591);

Daemonologie, in Forme of a Dialogue, Diuided into Three Bookes (Edinburgh: Printed by Robert Walde-graue, 1597);

The Trve Lawe of Free Monarchies: or The Reciprock and Mutuall Dvtie Betwixt a Free King, and His Naturall Subiectes (Edinburgh: Printed by Robert Walde-graue, 1598);

ΒΑΣΙΛΙΚΟΝ ΔΩΡΟΝ. *Deuided into Three Books* (Edinburgh: Printed by Robert Walde-graue, 1599); revised as ΒΑΣΙΛΙΚΟΝ ΔΩΡΟΝ. *Or His Maiesties Instructions to His Dearest Sonne, Henry the Prince* (Edinburgh: Printed by Robert Walde-graue, 1603);

A Covnter-Blaste to Tobacco, anonymous (London: Printed by Robert Barker, 1604);

Triplici Nodo, Triplex Cuneus. Or, An Apologie for the Oath of Allegiance, against the Two Breves of Pope Pavlvs Qvintvs, and the Late Letter of Cardinal Bellarmine to G. Blackwel, the Arch-priest (London: Printed by Robert Barker, 1607; enlarged, 1607);

Declaration dv Serenissimie Roy Iacqves I. Roy de la Grand' Bretaigne France et Irlande, Defenseur de la Foy. Pour le droit des rois & independance de leurs Couronnes, contre la Harangve de L'Illustrissime

James VI of Scotland, I of England, circa 1620; portrait by Paul van Somer (collection of Her Majesty the Queen)

Cardinal du Perron pronouncée en la chambre du tiers Estat le XV. de Ianuier 1615 (London: Printed by John Bill, 1615); translated by Richard Betts as *A Remonstrance of the Most Gratious King James I. King of Great Brittaine, France, and Ireland, Defender of the Faith, &c. for the Right of Kings, and the Independence of Their Crownes. Against an Oration of the Most Illustrious Card. of Perron, Pronounced in the Chamber of the Third Estate. Ian. 15. 1615. Translated out of His Maiesties*

119

French Copie (Cambridge: Printed by Cantrell Legge, printer to the University of Cambridge, 1616);

The Workes of the Most High and Mightie Prince, James, by the Grace of God, King of Great Britaine, France and Ireland, Defender of the Faith, &c. Published by James, Bishop of Winton, and Deane of His Maiesties Chappel Royall (London: Printed by Robert Barker & John Bill, 1616; enlarged, 1620);

A Meditation vpon the Lords Prayer, Written by the Kings Maiestie, for the Benefit of All His Subjects, Especially of Such as Follow the Court. Ioh. 16.23. (London: Printed by Bonham Norton & John Bill, 1619);

A Meditation Vpon the 27, 28, 29, Verses of the XXVII. Chapter of S^t. Matthew. Or a paterne for a Kings inauguration (London: Printed by John Bill, 1620).

Editions: *New Poems of James I of England, from a Hitherto Unpublished Manuscript (Add. 24195) in the British Museum,* edited by Allan F. Westcott (New York: Columbia University Press, 1911; reprinted, New York: AMS Press, 1966);

The Political Works of James I, Reprinted from the Edition of 1616, edited by Charles Howard McIlwain (Cambridge, Mass.: Harvard University Press, 1918; New York: Russell & Russell, 1965);

The Basilicon Doron of King James VI, 2 volumes, edited by James Craigie (Edinburgh & London: Printed for the Scottish Text Society by W. Blackwood & Sons, 1944, 1950);

The Poems of James VI of Scotland, 2 volumes, edited by Craigie (Edinburgh: Printed for the Scottish Text Society by W. Blackwood, 1955, 1958);

Minor Prose Works of King James VI and I, edited by Craigie and Alexander Law (Edinburgh: Scottish Text Society, 1982);

King James VI and I: Political Writings, edited by Johann P. Sommerville (Cambridge: Cambridge University Press, 1994).

OTHER: *The Psalmes of King David, Translated by King James* (Oxford: Printed by William Turner, 1631).

Early Modern English and Scottish monarchs were expected to be cultured creatures, presiding over distinguished courts, patronizing writers, and even, in some cases, demonstrating their learning by writing their own poems or translating classical authors in addition to invoking the rhetoric of power in their speeches and letters. Most of them

James at the age of eight; portrait by R. Lockey after Arnold van Brounckhorst (National Portrait Gallery, London)

measured up to that expectation; one went far beyond it. The literary output of James VI of Scotland and I of England is unparalleled by any monarch in the British Isles. In quantity and range it is quite staggering: James the political polemicist, James the new David (with his translation of the Psalms), James the theologian, James the noted author of political theory as well as practicing politician, James the speech- and letter-writer on a vast scale, and James the poet-king and writer of poetic theory.

All of these features naturally attracted the attention of contemporaries. In particular, his poetry was the subject of extensive comment. In 1586 one of the tracts written about the disposition of the Scottish nobility for the information of the English government recorded the fact that the Scottish king loved not only hunting but also "enditing poesie." Ben Jonson's epigram is well known:

How, best of Kings, dost thou a scepter bear!
How, best of Poets, dost thou laurel wear!

Jonson was not the first to appeal to the idea of the double crown. One of the group of Scottish court poets whom James drew round him in the early 1580s, John Stewart of Baldynneis, gave the king as a New Year's gift in 1584 "a laurel tree formed of gold"; and indeed, James – following the example of Petrarch – seems actually to have been crowned with laurel, according to Stewart's poem "To His Majestie the Day of His Coronation with Laurell," which lauded him as "Deserving now ane doubill croune and moir." Sir Philip Sidney and John Taylor were among other English writers who paid tribute to the poet king. In *Pierce's Supererogation* (1593) Gabriel Harvey calls James "a Homer in himselfe," "the soveraine of the divine art"; rather more prosaically, Richard Barnfield recorded – according to his friend Francis Meres in *Palladis Tamia* (1598) – that "The King of Scots (now living) is a Poet / As his *Lepanto* and his *Furies* show it." Such comments were surely more than flattery to the probable future king of England. James's royalty may have sometimes gained him more praise than his poetry necessarily merited; but what was not in doubt was that he was a genuine poet of note and, in so being, a king of distinctive quality, directly contributing to as well as presiding over the literary culture of his age.

James's early years were not auspicious. He was born in Edinburgh Castle on 19 June 1566, the son of the politically inept Mary, Queen of Scots, and the irresponsible drunkard Henry, Lord Darnley. A year later, his father was dead, strangled as he tried to escape from the gunpowder that blew up his residence at Kirk o' Field, Edinburgh, on 9 February; his mother, widely suspected of complicity in the murder, had finally destroyed her reputation and position on the throne by her marriage in May to the other chief suspect, James Hepburn, Earl of Bothwell, and had been defeated and imprisoned by the sizable proportion of the Scottish political nation now ranged against her. In July 1567 she was forced to abdicate. Her bastard half brother James Stewart, Earl of Moray, became regent, and her son, James, aged thirteen months, was crowned king on 29 July 1567. Royal minorities were nothing new to Scotland; every reign since 1406 had opened with one. What was unusual was that the previous monarch was alive, and, from 1568, after her second defeat in Scotland, living in England where she would threaten Elizabeth's life

and complicate Scottish, English, and European politics for nineteen more years.

The early years of the minority were dominated by civil war in Scotland, which lasted until 1573, by which time three of James's regents were dead, two by violence; the fourth, the ruthless James, Earl of Morton, lasted until 1578, when he was ousted by a coup d'état and subsequently executed in 1581, ostensibly for his part in the murder of Darnley fifteen years earlier.

While these violent political events thundered outside, James was being educated in the relative seclusion of Stirling Castle. His principal tutor was the formidable and ferocious George Buchanan, the noted European humanist and political theorist who had been used to provide justification for deposing Mary; he had done so on the basis of an invented ancient Scottish constitution whereby "the people" had the right to elect and depose kings. He had also depicted James's mother as a whore, adultress, and murderess in his scurrilous *Detection of Mary Stuart* (1571). It is not surprising that James viewed his tutor with terror and was to have nightmares about him to the end of his life, nor that one of the earliest acts as he emerged from his minority was to have Buchanan's political writings banned in 1584. Yet especially once he was freed from Buchanan's tutelage, there were other things James could remember and speak of with pride; his tutor had been famed for his classical scholarship and his poetry.

James's education was, from an early age, exhaustive and exhausting. "They gar me speik Latin ar I could speik Scotis" (They made me speak Latin before I could speak Scots) is his revealing comment recorded by his second tutor, Peter Young, who described the king's daily routine. "Cleansed through prayer" and Greek readings and grammar came before breakfast; Latin – classical authors and Scottish and foreign historians – occupied him until dinner; and then came arithmetic, cosmography, dialectics, and rhetoric. Somehow he also found the time to become fluent in French and to develop an interest that was to remain with him for life: theology.

The gentler Young was responsible for building up James's library; beginning with what were recovered of Mary's books in Holyrood – 150 or less – it had reached 600 volumes by 1578 through purchase and gift. It was a comprehensive collection of classical, theological, historical, cosmographical, and mathematical works, as well as the medieval romances and books of poetry, many of which were inherited from his mother; it included also Buchanan's metrical Latin Psalter (bought, not given by the tutor) and two works of political theory far more to James's taste than that of Buchanan, Budé's *L'Institution du Prince* (1518–1519) and Bodin's *République* (1576). But Young's catalogue of his library as it existed between 1573 and 1583 shows also that the young scholar was not always at his books. The earl of Argyll gave him a French poem about hunting and a book on falconry, appropriate enough for a king with a lifelong passion for the chase; and bows, arrows, a shooting glove, and two golf clubs appear among the gifts. Young himself, much more amenable to James than Buchanan, was to accompany the king to England, where he became royal librarian, an office in which he was succeeded by his son, Dr. Patrick Young. The collection for which they were responsible was to form the important nucleus of the Royal Library, which was moved to the British Museum in 1759.

For all its rigors, James's early education gave him a genuine love of scholarship on which he was to pride himself throughout his life. During his state visit to Oxford in 1605 his enthusiasm for the Bodleian Library prompted him to exclaim that "were I not a King I would be a University-man; and if it were so that I must be a prisoner, if I might have my wish, I would have no other prison than this library, and be chained together with these good authors." It was no mere politeness. Godfrey Goodman, Bishop of Gloucester, described him as a man who "did love solitariness, and was given to his study." More sourly, Lord Thomas Howard, writing to John Harrington in 1611, provides an early example of elitist English obsession with the "right" accent, when he comments that the king would do better if he taught English to his Scottish favorite, Robert Carr, instead of spending each morning teaching him Latin. In addition, the table talk — often theological — that was noted in Scotland continued in England; as one commentator described it, "that King's table was a trial of Wits."

Meanwhile, in 1579 the young scholar was beginning to emerge from the study. He came from Stirling accompanied by several of the leading nobility and a vast train, and on 17 October he made his first state entry into Edinburgh, where — neatly encapsulating the tensions in Scottish society between the sacred and the profane — he was met by Dame Music and her scholars as well as by Dame Religion. A sermon and the singing of the twentieth psalm were followed by a meeting with Bacchus, sitting with his puncheons of wine at the market cross. But what was there when he had passed by the shows and pageants, and arrived at Holyrood? One court poet, Patrick Hume of Polwarth, languishing alone in the bardic chair in the chimney nook; for

court life in Scotland had come to an end with the downfall of Mary, Queen of Scots. The transformation was rapid and dramatic. James's first favorite, Esmé Stuart, came to Edinburgh from France, bringing with him the most distinguished of the Jacobean poets, Alexander Montgomerie; and James himself judged the flyting with which Montgomerie and Polwarth re-created the great age of the court of James IV, and the renowned flyting of William Dunbar and Walter Kennedy, when Montgomerie challenged Polwarth for pride of place and was declared by the king to be the winner.

From then on, Montgomerie was the focal point of a circle of poets — one of whom was the king. Buchanan's pupil gave way to the self-styled "Prentise in the Divine Art of Poesie"; and in the early years of the 1580s, James displayed a talent for sheer lighthearted enjoyment, which is deeply attractive and was never repeated. In "Ane Admonition to the Maister Poete" (composed before 1584), he teases his greatest poet:

> gif patient eire to sumthing i man saye
> Belovit sandirs maister of oure airt
> the mous did help the lyon on a daye
> so I protest ye tak it in guid pairt
> my admonition cumming from a hairt
> that wishis veill to you and all your craft
> quha vald be sory for to see you smairt
> thocht uther poetes trowes ye be gain daft[.]

He also warns Montgomerie that Polwart "countis ye done and hopes but anie mair / his tyme about, to winn the chimnay nuik" and that all the other poets "hope for to outflyte you." All of which was because

> ye was crakking crouslie of youre broune
> (gif robert lye not) all the other nicht
> that thaire was ony lyke hime in this toune
> apon the grounde ye vald not latt it licht
> he vas so firie spedy yauld and vicht
> for to be short he was an A per se —

which is, that Montgomerie was boasting all night of his brown horse, but when the test came, poet and horse were left so far behind in the race that they were not even spattered by the mud thrown up by the horses in front. Bacchus appears again when the young poet confesses that he had, after supper, "with pen and drinke compiled yow this propine / I gatt it ended long before the dawin / Such pith hade Bacchus ou'r me God of wine." He is invoked finally in "O mightie Gods" (1584), that begins as a serious address to the gods, runs into trouble, and saves itself by turning to Bac-

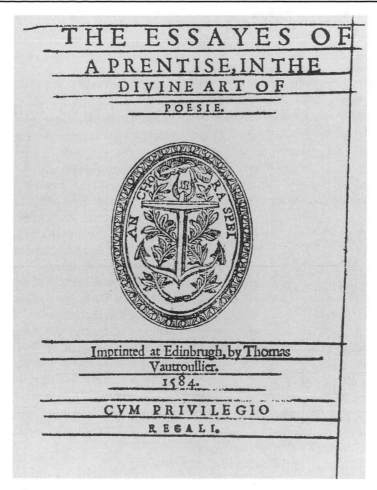

THE ESSAYES OF
A PRENTISE, IN THE
DIVINE ART OF
POESIE.

Imprinted at Edinbrugh, by Thomas
Vautroullier.
1584.

CVM PRIVILEGIO
REGALI.

Title page for James's first book, a collection of poems that includes Some
Reulis and Cautelis to Be Observit and Eschewit in Scottish
Poesie, *the first critical treatise on Scottish poetry*

chus, who had helped Alexander the Great and now
has ensnared "our maister poete" of the same name,
whose epitaph would be: "Here lyis whome Bacchus by his wyne / Hath trapped first, and made
him render syne."

The art of which Montgomerie was the master
was, of course, far more than flyting or teasing. The
king's court poets called themselves the Castalian
Band, the name taken from the spring on Mount
Parnassus dedicated to the Muses; the king himself
represented Apollo. They exchanged sonnets, using
them as introductory compliments to the work of
others; James's *Poeticall Exercises at Vacant Houres*
(1591), the cycle containing the major poem *Lepanto*
and his translation of Guillaume de Salluste, Seigneur du Bartas's *Les Furies,* for example, was prefaced by several admiring sonnets by William
Fowler and others.

They also wrote longer works; the other
major collection of James's poetry, *The Essayes of a*

Prentise, in the Divine Art of Poesie (1584), included,
along with sonnets and other short pieces, another translation of du Bartas, the *Uranie,* in
which he experimented with heroic couplets, and
what was probably the best and most moving of
his poems, the *Phoenix,* a long allegory on the exile
and death of Esmé Stuart, from whose "ashes"
would come the new Phoenix, his son Ludovic.
James's translations broke his own rule, which
was to advise against translation because it denied "Inventioun." His poets followed his example rather than his advice; Stewart of
Baldynneis produced a version of Ludovico
Ariosto's *Orlando Furioso* (1516, 1532), Thomas
Hudson of du Bartas's *Judith* (1572), and
Fowler of Petrarch's *Trionfi* (circa 1346–1374),
as well as the first translation into "English" –
Scots – of Niccolò Machiavelli's *Il Principe*
(1513). The impact of what was happening in
the Scottish court can be seen in the fact that du

Bartas himself paid James the great compliment of translating his *Lepanto* (1585).

It is easy to sense the confidence and pleasure James derived from his Castalian band, fellow poets and gentlemen of the court, men who shared also in his political life as royal servants. He was profoundly aware of the weaknesses of his position, describing himself in an incomplete poem on his journey to Denmark in 1589:

> As I being a King by birth . . .
> and laiking parents, brethren, bairns or any neir of kinn
> inkaice of death or absence to suplee my place thairin
> and chieflie in so kittill [difficult to manage] ane lande quhaire feu remember can
> for to have seine governing thaire a king that vas a man [a reference to the period going back to the death of James V in 1542].

Now, he was emerging as a man who could take pride in his kingship.

King and scholar as well as poet: it is not surprising that the "Prentise" in poetry also showed an early taste for being master. Thus, *The Essayes of a Prentise, in the Divine Art of Poesie* included one prose work: *Some Reulis and Cautelis to Be Observit and Eschewit in Scottish Poesie* (Some Rules and Regulations to Be Observed and Avoided in Scottish Poetry). This work was not a plagiarism of the English *Certain Notes of Instruction* (1575) by George Gascoigne, as has been dismissively suggested. James's library showed a huge preponderance of French over English works, and much more probably the *Reulis and Cautelis* drew on Pierre de Ronsard and Joachim du Bellay, whose works on poetry were on his bookshelves. But the most important point about it is that it was a work – the only work – intended to lay down rules for the glory of *Scottish* poetry, an assertion, in other words, of the importance and value of Scottish culture, as exemplified by the court of James VI. He justified his work on two grounds. First, "lyke as the tyme is changeit sensyne, sa is the ordour of Poesie changeit . . . Thairfore, quhat I speik of Poesie now, I speik of it, as being come to mannis age and perfectioun, quhair as then [in the past], it was bot in the infancie and chyldheid." Second, "that as for thame that hes written in it of late, there has never ane of thame written in our language. For albeit sindrie hes written of it in English, quhilk is lykest to our language, yit we differ from thame in sindrie reulis of Poesie, as ye will find be experience." Thus, he offers his work not

To ignorants obdurde, quhair wilfull errour lyis,
Nor yit to curious folkis, quhilkis carping dois deject thee,
Nor yit to learned men, quha thinkis thame onelie wyis,
But to the docile bairns of knawledge I direct thee.

In other words, those willing to follow the king's rules would create, with him, the Scottish Renaissance.

Thus, formal rules were laid down for the writing of Scots poetry, using terms unique to James: *Troilus Verse* to be used "for tragicall materis, complaintis, or testamentis"; *Rouncefallis,* or *Tumbling Verse,* "for flyting or Invectives"; *Ballad Royal,* for "any heich and grave subjectis, specially drawn out of learnit authouris"; *Commoun verse,* "in materis of love"; and each of these was illustrated by the king's own verse, or those of his Castalians. He also used *literall* (French *lettrisé*) instead of the English *alliterative, section* for *cæsura* and *flowing* for *rhythm,* by which he meant the counting and arranging of syllables in a line in a way pleasing to the ear, which previous poets had failed to do. Thus,

> I remit to the judgement of the same [the ear], quhilk of thir twa lynis following flowis best

> Into the Sea then Lucifer upsprang

> In the Sea then Lucifer to upsprang

> I doubt not bot your eare makkis yow eaislie to persave that the first lyne flowis weil, and the uther nathing at all.

"The verie twichestane [of flowing] is Musique," he continues, and the need for it meant that "a lang rable of mennis names, or names of tounis, or sik uther names" must be avoided, for they would not "flow weill."

Above all were the rules for the new form being taken up by James and his poets, the sonnet. It came late to Scotland, but the seven hundred examples written between the 1580s and 1630 show its popularity and its endurance. In subject matter, it was to be much more wide-ranging than the English sonnet:

> For compendious praysing of any bukes, or the authouris thairof, or ony argumentis of uther historeis, quhair sindrie sentences, and change of purposis are requyrit, use *Sonet* verse, of fourtene lynis and ten fete in every lyne.

Part of a letter dated 26 January 1586 [1587] from James to Queen Elizabeth, interceding on behalf of his mother, Mary, Queen of Scots

Love was not even mentioned in the list, though love sonnets were of course written. And under Montgomerie's influence, the sonnet form consistently used by James, as illustrated in his two introductory sonnets in the *Reulis and Cautelis* and prescribed for his poets, was that normally associated with Edmund Spenser, but in fact anticipating his works: *ababbcbccdcdee*.

In form and range of subject matter, James's poets followed the king's rules – from philosophy and religious themes to Montgomerie's use of the sonnet to demand a pension from the king. The *Reulis and Cautelis* did indeed provide the guidelines for the new culture of the Scottish court. What other king in Europe could rival the king who was the motivating force for that culture, not by buying, importing, and commissioning artists and architects, but by creating it – and "legislating" for it? That kings came before parliaments, and were the first lawmakers, would be a note sounded by the mature King James in his *Trve Lawe of Free Monarchies* (1598). The first law he made, when emerging from his minority in 1584, was the law for Scottish poesie.

Yet from the mid 1580s the beginnings of change are detectable. James continued for another decade and more to write poetry on a wide variety of subjects, from sonnets addressed to Anne of Denmark, which were fairly flat, to rather more lively satires on women to sonnets addressed to Tycho Brahe and du Bartas or about the attack on him in Holyrood by the earl of Bothwell. Thereafter, he wrote rarely, although he continued to the end of his life with his translation of the Psalms. His poems after 1603 include a complaint about the cold in January 1616, into which not even the most industrious literary critic could read anything other than frustration with weather that, as the last line says, "kills all creaturs and doth spoile our sport"; a dignified but again uninspired work on the death of Queen Anne; a poem to his greatest favorite, the duke of Buckingham; and little else, apart from a long and bitter political diatribe in 1623. The change may be significant. The teenager who had come out of his study to enjoy the new poetic life of his court inevitably became the king caught up in politics.

Thus, in the later 1580s the luxury of the writing game was increasingly overtaken by political events: the threat posed by the extreme Presbyterians in the kirk, the final crisis over his mother, and the Spanish Armada. Montgomerie left Scotland in 1586, on a mission that has never been properly explained. When he returned in 1590, it was not to royal favor; there was no place for this strenuous Catholic and cryptosupporter of Mary, although on his death in the late 1590s James wrote a genuinely moving epitaph for him. Other influences were coming in. To his religious poetry the king added theology, with his first biblical commentary, on Revelation, published in 1588, and having as its imprimatur not a sonnet by a fellow Castalian, but a preface by a minister of the kirk. It introduces a problem as it launches into a vitriolic attack on the Antichrist:

> hee shall bee head of a false and hypocriticall Church; hee shall claime a supreme power in earth; he shall usurp the power of God; he shall deceive men with abusing locusts; he shall persecute the faithfull. . . . In the end, feeling his kingdome decay, and the trew Church beginning to prosper, he shall by a new sort of deceiving spirits, gather together the Kings of the earth . . . and by joyning or at least suffering of that other great open enemy, he shall . . . encompasse the campes of the faithfull.

The interest of this diatribe lies not in that it says anything novel, but in the identification James made. The Antichrist was the Pope; his new deceiving spirits were the Jesuits; the great enemy was the Turk, with whom the Pope was now at truce. Within twenty years, James would be writing his attacks on Robert Bellarmine and the theory of the indirect deposing power of the papacy in equally flamboyant language and sending his *Premonition* round the crowned heads of Europe – Catholic and Protestant alike.

By that time, however, James had fallen naturally and habitually into the role of the king who himself provided the defense for kingly power; and Bellarmine and Paul V were an all-too-obvious target. These works do not, therefore, necessarily conflict with the image of James the nonpersecutor of Catholics, expressed dramatically in a letter to Cecil proclaiming that "I protest to God I reverence their Church as our mother church, though clogged with many infirmities and corruptions, besides that I ever did hold persecution as one of the infallible notes of a false church," an attitude that the kirk in Scotland complained about, but which the Catholics in England after the Gunpowder Plot welcomed with immense relief – though James had some very fiery things to say about the plot in his writings.

But the choice of the verses in Revelation that produced the impassioned antipapalism of 1588 cannot be so readily explained. Politically, it was not particularly appropriate; indeed, if anything, it was inappropriate for a king keeping open diplomatic options that would enable him to indulge in some fairly shady negotiations with Philip II of Spain and the papacy in the mid

1590s. Surely it marks the moment when James began to carve out a new role for himself: the most cultured king in Europe was beginning the ascent to becoming the most Protestant king in Europe; the poet-king was becoming the theologian-king. Catholics might be tolerated, provided they kept quiet; Jesuits – the Antichrist's minions – were more to be feared, as indeed was noted when in 1600–1601 his attitude against them was observed to harden; and the Pope was the great enemy of God and the king.

Even the poet played his part. James's *Lepanto,* the great epic of the decisive victory by the Christian over the Turkish fleet in 1571, was clearly a poem in which he took distinct pride. It is not in fact a great work, though it sweeps along in a lusty narrative, showing the king who was "Rex Pacificus" caught up and excited by the drama of battle. But he was very careful not to leave it as a victory for a Catholic hero over the infidel Turk. It was God who joined forces against Satan. In his preface, he pointedly asserts that, unlike Virgil and Aeneas, he was not writing an epic in praise of a hero; any praise for the victor of Lepanto, Don John, was "onely as of a particular man when hee falles in my way to speak the truth of him." And the final "Chorus Angelorum" gives the praise to God, who "doth mercie shew to all that do professe the same":

> And not alanerlie to them Professing it aright
> But even to them that mixe therewith Their own intentions slight
> As speciallie this samin time most plainlie may appear
> In giving them such victorie That not aright Him fears;
> For since He shewes such grace to them That thinks themselves are just
> What will He more to them that in His mercies only trust.

By the time *Lepanto* was published in 1591, Satan had not only been defeated in the East. He was a very present figure in Scotland, for in 1590 the coven of witches at North Berwick had confessed to James that their diabolical pact was aimed directly against him, the king whom Satan regarded – with some flattery – as "the greatest enemie he hath in the world." This began the first of the great Scottish witch hunts, which lasted until 1597, the particularly intensive periods being 1590–1592 and 1596–1597. James was undoubtedly fascinated and terrified, and he took a prominent part in the trials.

But in 1597 he did two things: he revoked the standing commissions of the Privy Council that had provided the judicial machinery for the persecution;

and he wrote his tract on witchcraft, the *Daemonologie*. It is a short work, much shorter than those of the great skeptics Johann Weyer and Reginald Scot, whom James was setting out to refute; it is almost entirely unoriginal; it is unusually turgid for a man who would show himself in later writings to be a master of vivid and compelling prose. And it was done in a hurry, as the fragments of the first draft indicate; they are much cleaner than James's usual first drafts, which are full of erasures and rewriting. Almost certainly it was written for self-reassurance by a king who still believed in witchcraft and diabolical power, but who found it increasingly impossible to believe that the hundreds of women condemned in the 1590s were all witches. The preface tells us that his intention was to resolve doubting hearts. Perhaps the most doubting heart was that of the author. Certainly William Shakespeare's compliment in *Macbeth* (1606) to the royal demonologist was misplaced; as the English found when they brought witches to James's attention after 1603, he was no longer interested.

What did interest him in the late 1590s was political theorizing. By then he was well on the way to winning his battle for control of the kirk with the followers of the presbyterian Andrew Melville, whose strenuous assertion of the separation of church and state and denial of royal control had made them his most dangerous opponents in the 1590s. If the *Daemonologie* was written for reassurance, the next two works, *Basilikon Doron* (1599) and *The Trve Lawe of Free Monarchies,* are a clear and confident statement of the kingship he was exercising. He was using his writing to demystify and explain his kingship so that the hidden should be open, as he says in his preface to *Basilikon Doron.*

The explanation is certainly comprehensive. There is a vast difference between the two works. *The Trve Lawe,* setting out the theory of divine right kingship, is a full-scale demolition of the contractual and resistance theory of the Huguenots and James's own tutor George Buchanan, and of the Melvillian theory of the two swords, church and state. *Basilikon Doron,* by contrast, is a practical manual of kingship, written for James's son Henry. Its scathing diatribes against the Puritans gave no more comfort to the Melvillians than *The Trve Lawe,* and predictably they howled about it; but there was much less in it to upset secular politicians. The Scottish nobility might have felt collectively affronted by the assertion that "The naturall sicknesse that I have perceived this estate subject to in my time, hath

been, a fectlesse arrogant conceit of their greatnes and power," or the comment on their feuding: "(without respect to God, King, or Commonweale) to bang it out bravelie, hee and all his kinne, against him and all his." But at least they had the consolation that the king advised his son that it was to his honor to make use of them, and to "consider that vertue followeth oftest noble blood." For the "phanaticke spirits," the Puritans, "verie pestes in the Church and Common-weale," there was no such compensation.

Basilikon Doron was to make far more impact than the more theoretic *Trve Lawe,* perhaps because it was clearly the book in which James took most pride; as late as 1619, two decades after he had written and revised it, he was dragging it into his *Meditation vpon The Lords Prayer,* when describing the care he took with dedications: *Basilikon Doron* had been Henry's, now dead, and must therefore belong to Charles. The king's own enthusiasm for this splendid, fast-moving, witty piece of prose had its effect in the vast number of copies that flooded the London market in the spring of 1603 and the frequent translations that followed; *The Trve Lawe* was a poor second best.

Theology, demonology, and political writing did not, however, crowd out the culture of the court; a distinguished court, as much as the need to overcome his Presbyterian opponents and rid his land of witches, was the basis for a kingship that would impress Europe, but there was another consideration. James's *Reulis and Cautelis* extolled Scottish poetry; and it had its postscript when after 1603 he unfairly trounced Sir William Alexander, Earl of Stirling, one of the younger Castalians who followed him to England, and followed his lead in Anglicizing his writings, for his "harshe vearses after the Inglishe fasone."

James was the future king of England, however, and not wholly averse to English culture, despite the heavy Scottish emphasis on French influence. He had indeed tried to bring French influence to bear not just on his present but on his future kingdom, explaining his translation of du Bartas's *Uranie* on the grounds that "I could not do so well, as by publishing some work of his to this yle of Brittain (swarming full of quick ingynes,) aswell as they ar made manifest already to France." But equally some of these "quick ingynes" from south Britain were being invited to make an impact in the north. He had inherited an English family of musicians, the Hudsons, from his mother; but they had become absorbed into the Castalian band.

James and his wife, Anne of Denmark; engraving by Renold Elstrack

In 1589, however, there was a new departure. There is some evidence that in 1588 he himself had written a masque, which has only partially survived, for the wedding of his second great favorite, George, Earl of Huntly, to the daughter of his first, Esmé Stuart, and apparently took a leading part in it. But when turning to the preparations for his own forthcoming marriage, he sent a request to Elizabeth for six maskers and six torchbearers, and for English actors. English actors – comedians – seem to have been invited again in 1594, presumably for the baptism of his first son, Henry; certainly Laurence Fletcher was known to the king by this time. Fletcher and his men were back in 1599, causing a furious row between James and the Edinburgh clergy – which the king won. They may, indeed, have stayed on in Scotland, for they turn up again in 1601, when they went on tour to Dundee and Aberdeen. Fletcher's name heads the list, with Shakespeare's second, in the Letters Patent to the King's Men in May 1603. Scottish culture had begun it all; British culture was being introduced in the north well before James became king of Britain.

In 1603, therefore, England got a king who, from very uncertain and even weak beginnings, had built up a confidence and expertise of unusual range. As king, as poet, as theologian, and as political theorist, he had made his emphatic mark. He could justifiably take pride in his achievements and look forward to the future when the successful king of Scotland would bring two nations long hostile to one another together in peace as the new kingdom of Great Britain.

There were two basic problems, however. First, the English did not share their new king's enthusiasm for extending the personal union of the crowns to a political union of the kingdoms. James's proclamation of 1604 asserting his new style of king of Great Britain served only to stir up English hostility, especially as he was using a proclamation to insist on what the English Parliament of 1604 had refused to endorse; and his second proclamation of 1606, which brought into being the British flag –

the Union Jack – fared little better. His speeches to the English Parliament in 1604 and 1607 pleading for union were equally ineffective. Yet the passion in these speeches, especially in that of 31 March 1607, is unmistakable; the 1607 speech is a deeply moving appeal to his new subjects on behalf of his old, whom he rightly saw were threatened with neglect; "London," he said, "must bee the Seate of your King, and Scotland joyned to this kingdome by a Golden conquest, but cymented with love. . . . Judge mee charitably, since in this I seeke your equall good." He was not judged charitably. By 1607 his vision of union was dead, destroyed by English indifference and opposition.

Part of this failure rested on Anglo-Scottish antagonism and English assumptions of superiority, but it was also bound up with the second problem: suspicion of the king himself and his dangerous ideas about the nature of his kingship. He was already the author of noted books that left no doubt about his belief in kingship by divine right. So also had Elizabeth believed in divine right; but she had been "mere English," bound by English tradition and constitutional procedure. The Scottish James was a European theorist. Throughout his English reign, he upset and disturbed English members of Parliament and common lawyers by his refusal to be pinned down on that most thorny of constitutional questions, the relationship between the king and the law. Sometimes he could speak acceptably on king-in-Parliament as the legislator; but English sighs of relief were no sooner heard than dispelled by claims such as "Rex est lex loquens." The unease, even suspicion, shown by his English subjects led to alienation on the part of the English king.

Alienation went beyond the forum of Parliament and the formal statements in speeches and proclamations. The formality of the English court, the excessive flattery that courtiers had been trained to offer the old queen, were much less appropriate for the new king. The Scottish court, where James had so visibly been at ease, was far more informal than its English counterpart, the public appearances less elaborate and more manageable. James was capable of dramatic outbursts of royal rage; he could put on the cloak of excessive royal dignity. But in Scotland, he had shown a talent for friendly conviviality, commented on by the English visitor Sir Henry Wotton in 1601 and reflected in, among other things, his passion for nicknames. His childhood friend John, Earl of Mar, was "Jock o' the sclaittis" (slates – referring to his mathematical

ability). That was clearly much more acceptable than "my little beagle," "my little wiffe waffe," with which this prolific letter-writer addressed his great English servant Robert Cecil, Earl of Salisbury.

The clash of cultural styles and its effect on the king were notably demonstrated in James's dislike of public appearances, which produced a quick and hostile reaction from his English subjects. Yet that well-known fact, long taken for granted, requires some explanation. For in Scotland, James had certainly been observed to like solitude. But equally he had taken part with no lack of enthusiasm in public spectacles, acting in his masque, taking the part of one of the Christian knights who fought in the tournament during the baptism celebrations for Prince Henry in 1594, appearing publicly in procession in Edinburgh. Indeed, his own devising of appropriate robes for members of the Scottish parliament to process through Edinburgh does not suggest a king unaware of the importance of royal show. His journey south in 1603 was a joyous, even – on occasion – a riotous success.

What went wrong was that this king with a long record of successful rule suddenly found that the sheer scale of the English court and its culture, and indeed the sheer scale of English government, were not amenable to the control he had imposed on his Scottish kingdom and to the easy and confident mastery of his Scottish court. The state entry into London in 1604 was far more glorious than anything devised in Scotland; it was also infinitely more chaotic – and it is a nice irony that the same would be true of King James's own funeral. The surviving Castalians came south with him; but there was no longer the pleasure and security of the Castalian band. Instead, there was only the flattery of English poets; and as they extolled the man who had united Britain, that flattery rang increasingly hollow. The sureness of touch of *Basilikon Doron* and *The Trve Lawe* gave way to rhetorical jostling, as the man grounded in resistance theory came up against the unrealistic ideal of harmonious politics, and as the king was told by English common lawyers how to play by the rules.

In time, James did impose his intellectual and scholarly tastes on the English court. Pride of place in recognizing the genius of Ben Jonson goes to Anne of Denmark, who first gave him patronage. But the king took over, and scholar-king developed a relationship with scholar-poet that underpinned the glories of the Jonsonian masque. Even if the king never acted himself, and on one notorious oc-

Page from the manuscript for Basilikon Doron, *the book of instructions on regal duties that James wrote for his son Prince Henry (British Library)* casion in 1618 grumpily pronounced himself bored with *Pleasure Reconciled to Virtue,* the Jacobean masque that came to portray the ideal of kingship with wit, style, and elegance; the sets, costumes, and texts devised by Jonson and Inigo Jones combined to raise the culture of the court to a level never achieved under the Tudors and hardly matched in the reign of Charles I.

Equally, the Jacobean court not only offered opportunities for English scholars such as Robert Cotton, William Camden, and Francis Bacon, but became a focal point for European ones. Johannes Kepler was among those who dedicated his book to the king, as a leading Protestant and noted intellectual. Isaac Casaubon and Hugo Grotius came to England, attracted by a king who sought to aid the cause of religious conciliation. He even attempted, with some success, to break the monopoly of Oxford and Cambridge by establishing a college of divinity at Chelsea, though lack of adequate endowment and changing political circumstances meant that it lasted only until the middle of the seventeenth century.

James's contribution to theological debate was his attack on the Dutch Arminian Vorstius; having shown his belief in debate as the way forward by presiding over the Hampton Court Conference in 1604 in an effort to resolve English ecclesiastical tensions, he moved the idea onto the European stage with the Synod of Dort, the great confrontation between Calvinists and Arminians in 1618. Above all, he brought from Scotland an unrealized dream of a new translation of the Bible. After Hampton Court it became reality, and the Authorized Version remains to this day a masterpiece of English learning and English prose. It is a fitting monument to King James.

Much of the European attention that James attracted arose from his new political works, which brought the king and the theologian together. His Scottish analysis of divine-right kingship was expanded into direct confrontation with the papacy and its claims over secular rulers; James began defending European kingship. He began in 1608 with *Triplici nodo, Triplex Cuneus. Or, An Apologie for the Oath of Allegiance,* directed against Paul V and Cardinal Bellarmine. "Now let us heare the words of [the Pope's] thunder," he wrote, and he rushed to demolish them. The issue here was the papal attempt to insist that English Catholics should not attend "the Churches of Heretikes" and should not take the oath of allegiance to the king, introduced after the Gunpowder Plot.

Attacked for this work by Bellarmine, James raised the stakes and in 1609 addressed the crowned heads of Europe in *A Premonition to All Most Mightie Monarches, Kings, Free Princes and States of Christendome,* arguing passionately against papal pretensions to superiority over kings. Finally, in 1615, he produced *A Remonstrance for the Right of Kings, and the Independance of Their Crownes,* which was a broadside against Cardinal Perron and the French clergy for rejecting the oath proposed by the Third Estate in the uncertain period after the assassination of Henry IV, on similar lines to the English oath of allegiance; thanks to the clergy, the French would remain bewitched "of this pernicious opinion; That Popes may tosse the French King his Throne like a tennis ball, and that killing of Kings is an acte meritorious to the purchase of the crowne of Martyrdome."

Clearly James had not lost his ability to produce the effective phrase, but the writings after 1603 lack the force and certainty of touch that characterize the earlier works. He wrote less in England – certainly less for recreation and pleasure. Tiredness and disillusion had their part. His Epistle Dedicatorie to his 1620 *Meditation Vpon the 27, 28, 29, Verses of the XXVII Chapter of S*^t *Matthew* quite explicitly paints the picture of a king "being grown in yeeres . . . weary of controversies," who had found the account of the soldiers decking Christ with the trappings of kingship so compelling "that my head hammered upon it divers times after, and specially the croune of thornes went never out of my mind, remembering the thorny cares, which a King . . . must be subiect unto." The theme of ennui is sustained by the appearance of the greatest and most notorious of the Jacobean favorites, George Villiers, Duke of Buckingham, in an unfamiliar light; for Buckingham "humbly and earnestly desired mee that he might have the honour to bee my amanuensis in this worke, First because it would free me from the paine of writing, by sparing the labour both of mine eyes and hand . . . And indeed my granting of this request to Buckingham hath much eased my labor, considering the slowness, ilnesse and uncorrectnesse of my hand."

The self-portrait in these lines is a sad and far cry from the vigorous intellectual whose manuscript of *Basilikon Doron,* written some twenty years earlier, creates such a vivid image – with its vigorous scorings-out and rewritings – of the furious impatience with the difficulty of finding the right words to express the ideas swarming in the brain. The slowness of the prose marks it out even from the previous year's *Meditation vpon the Lord's Prayer*. Here, there is something of the old sharpness. Again Buckingham appears, this time as dedicatee, "for it is made upon a very short and plaine Prayer, and therefore the fitter for a Courtier"; courtiers have little leisure, and especially Buckingham, who has time only for a short work because of his continual service to his king and "the uncessant swarme of suitors importunately hanging upon you." But if this sounds sympathetic, there is nothing mild about the next sentence: "and that it is plaine, it is the fitter for you, since you were not bred a scholler."

Nevertheless, such phrases appear as sudden interruptions to the general decline so evident in the works of James's last years. He had never been a really great poet; but he had been a master of taut, pithy prose. Now, he rambled, shoving great and small matters together in an increasingly ill-judged mishmash. Even in 1604 his preface to the *Covnter-Blaste to Tobacco* had been far too grand for a treatise on what he himself called mere smoke. The *Meditation vpon The Lord's Prayer* (1619) wanders. The old bite might flash out when phrases such as "And lead us not into temptation" produced "The Arminians cannot but mislike the frame of this Petition; for I am sure they would have it, *And suffer us not to be ledde into temptation,* and Vorstius would adde, *as farre, Lord, as is in thy power, for thy power is not infinite.*" But the work begins with a vitriolic digression on Puritans and Brownists, which takes him far from their attitude to prayer; and it includes a couple of hunting stories, a pious reference to his father-in-law, and an attack on "Tobacco-drunkardes" as the epitome of sinners.

The same rambling mars the *Meditation Vpon . . . Matthew.* The passion of Christ was indeed an amazing choice of subject on which to create a discourse on the inauguration of kings and their grievous burdens. James justifies it by claiming that he was not discussing the horror and blasphemy of it, "but what use it hath pleased the Almighty and All-mercifull God to draw out of their wickednesse, and turne it to his glorie." But the insistent and lengthy linking of Christ's suffering to the suffering of kings, brought together by the symbol of the crown of thorns, is not only tedious but on occasion comes very close to toppling over into a kind of blasphemy. He is frankly boring on the difficulty of plaiting a crown of thorns, on the etymology of the Greek word *diadema,* on the lost recipe for the purple dye of the ancients, and much else besides – and it comes as a shock to find King James a bore. There is a loss of judgment in these works. Perhaps it symbolizes a king trapped and floundering in the excessive complexity of English ideology, English style, English government.

James's three last poems were written in 1622–1623. The title of the first, the "Elegie . . . Concerning His Counsell for Ladies and Gentlemen to Departe the Citie of London According to His Majesties Proclamation," suggests that it was a poetic version of a theme close to his heart, the subject of proclamations in 1615 and 1622 and of part of his speech to the Star Chamber in 1616: that the aristocracy and gentry should make themselves deaf to the siren song of London and return to the country to fulfill their traditional obligations of hospitality, especially at Christmas, and of keeping order in the localities. In fact, its target is "You women that doe London love so well" but whose "husbands will as kindly you embrace / without your jewels or your painted face" back in the simpler life of the country. A subtext of the Star Chamber speech now became the main text; women were to blame for the rush to London and the court, and women must take their husbands and themselves home: "And you good men its best you gett you hence / least honest Adam paie for Eves offence."

This poem retains some of the old vigor – James could still be quite amusing in his attitude to women – and the final poem, appealing for the safe return of Jack and Tom, has a certain grace and pathos. But his lengthy "Answere to the Libell called the Comons teares," written in late 1622 or early 1623, is tragic. Like the much earlier poem on his journey to Denmark, it shows his strong sense of the peculiar nature of his kingship, and the background that had dictated so much of his struggle for success: "Tis true I am a cradle king." It contains one of the most effective lines he ever wrote: "God and Kings doe pace together." He had little else left to pace with. As the foreign policy he had followed so consistently (as Rex Pacificus) throughout his reign in England was falling apart, with Spanish procrastination over the Anglo-Spanish marriage, and increasingly insistent calls for the leading Protestant king to defend the Protestants of Europe, he invoked not the language of love, but of threat: "If once I bend my angry brow. . . . Hold you the publique beaten way / wonder at kings and them obey." Royal love would be given only for obedience.

It was an extremely unequal contract. It was also the despairing cry of a man whose style of kingship had changed, had been impoverished by the demands made on him in England. Eleven

Title page, engraved by Renold Elstrack, for the collected edition of James's prose works

her in 1567 as his was doing in 1624: the whine that her subjects did not appreciate her.

How, then, does one assess King James? He was himself a paradox. On occasion his writing directly illumines policy; there is, for example, a link between *Lepanto* and his refusal after 1603 to have dealings with the sultan, with predictable effect on the frenzied Cecil and the Levant Company. His belief in the importance of authorship is not in doubt. But he was a very private man, and his writings are not translucent. The paradox is heralded in the first verse of his first poem, written probably when he was about fifteen:

Since thought is free, thinke what thou will
O troubled hart to ease thy pain
Thought unrevealed can do no evill
Bot wordes past out, cummes not againe
Be cairfull aye for to invent
The way to gett thy owen intent.

In the course of his life, he passed many words out. At first they brought pleasure. Increasingly they reflected pain.

James died on 27 March 1625. It was a loss felt keenly by his circle of Scottish friends and politicians who could remember the days of his kingship in Scotland before 1603 and who were now faced for the first time with the chill of absentee monarchy under a king with whom there was no such personal relationship. In England, the world was Charles I's and Buckingham's. Jacobean dreams of closer union had not been realized, and efforts to keep England out of war in Europe had failed. Yet after his death, men looked back on James as the king of scholarship and wit. Even the hostile critic and avid parliamentarian Anthony Weldon said that he was "very witty, and had as many ready witty jests as any man living, at which he would not smile himselfe, but deliver them in a grave and serious manner."

His table talk was recorded and published, under the somewhat variant titles of the sixty "Wittie observations Gathered from our Late Soveraign King James in His Ordinarie Discourse" and the two hundred "Flores Regii, or Proverbs and Aphorisms, Divine and Morall, as They Were . . . Spoken by His Most Excellent Majestie James of Famous Memory." They are not a hilarious read; indeed, they are somewhat heavy, though some have a certain enjoyably pithy flavor: "Alexander was not thanked and commended for Conquering the World, but for doing it before thirty years old." There were also the flashes of antifemale comment: "It hath like operation to make women learned as to

years earlier, he had been described in the hostile letter by Howard to Harington as talking "of his subjects fear and subjection," where the old queen had talked of their love; as early as 1611 the pressures and the scale of English rule had had their effect on a king known for intimate dealings and affection in Scotland. This last poem looks forward also to the last speech he made, to Parliament in 1624, when he complained that he had been presented with two scrolls of grievances, "wheras I expected you rather should have presented your thankes unto me that you had soe little cause of grevance, for I dare bouldly say never commons had lesse." This is not the bouncy confidence that had prompted him to write, in *Lepanto,* that "it becomes not the honour of my estait lyk a hyrling to penn the praise of any man." In these last words of a king of such ability and such achievement, one suddenly hears the sad echo of the dreadful whining of his mother when her world had crashed about make Foxes tame, which teacheth them only to steal more cunningly; the possibilitie is not equall, for where it doth one good, it doth twenty harm."

More generally, King James's impact on the culture of his two courts and on his political world was surely remarkable. For some forty-five years, he shaped and dominated the cultural scene, presiding over the flowering of poetry in Scotland and of the masque in England. Through his extensive political and theological writings, he had a political and intellectual influence that went far beyond the practical pursuits of kings.

Undoubtedly James's happiest period was his reign in Scotland. In England his prose works were collected and published in 1616 by the flattering and admiring James Montagu, Bishop of Winchester, a second and extended edition following in 1620; some of these writings, notably *Basilikon Doron,* were extensively translated. But he never recreated the sheer pleasure of being at the center of a group of poets, engaged in a heady cooperative enterprise, which had been such a marked feature of his Scottish rule. James's relationship with Jonson was deeply rewarding to both. But other poets felt excluded and frustrated by the towering success of Jonson; thus, the heirs and admirers of Sir Philip Sidney and Spenser began to look back to an Elizabethan age that sat very oddly with the reality Sidney and Spenser themselves had criticized, and Elizabeth's reputation, in the hands of men like Fulke Greville, first Lord Brooke, became infinitely higher after death than in the later years of her life.

As time went on, James's own literary reputation went into sad decline. It became all too easy to assume that it was only his position as king that had given him any place as poet and scholar, an assumption seized on by hostile critics of King James in the nineteenth and twentieth centuries, from Sir Walter Scott to David Harris Willson. In the early twentieth century, his political works, edited by Charles Howard McIlwain, made sufficient impact for historians to use and analyze them in elucidating the political figure of King James. But the literary figure was rescued from its dismal obscurity only in the middle of the century, thanks to the efforts of one man, James Craigie, who was responsible for editing his poems, his psalms, and some of his prose works.

Modern literary scholars now take the Scottish works seriously, although so far their comments on the whole still tend to show an ingrained reluctance to move away from the idea that it was his royalty and patronage that gave him his importance, and the ready distinction between Mont-

gomerie the great poet and James the unoriginal scribbler of verse remains inherent in their critique. Nevertheless, his writing cannot now be ignored; questions are being asked, and there are signs that as more attention is given to his works, so his reputation in the world of scholarship and literature, about which he cared so much and in which he probably found his deepest pleasure, is beginning to revive. It deserves to. He was, after all, a unique phenomenon.

Letters:

Letters of Queen Elizabeth and King James VI of Scotland, edited by John Bruce, old series 46 (London: Camden Society, 1849);

Correspondence of King James VI of Scotland with Sir Robert Cecil and Others, edited by Bruce (London: Camden Society, 1861).

Biographies:

David Harris Willson, *King James VI and I* (London: Cape, 1956);

Robert Ashton, *James I by His Contemporaries* (London: Hutchinson, 1969);

The Reign of James VI and I, edited by Alan G. R. Smith (London: Macmillan, 1973);

Maurice Lee Jr., *Great Britain's Solomon: James VI and I in His Three Kingdoms* (Urbana: University of Illinois Press, 1990).

References:

Arthur Melville Clark, *Murder under Trust: The Topical Macbeth and Other Jacobean Matters* (Edinburgh: Scottish Academic Press, 1981);

Jonathan Goldberg, *James VI and the Politics of Literature* (Baltimore: Johns Hopkins University Press, 1983);

R. D. S. Jack, "Poetry under King James VI," in *The History of Scottish Literature. Volume 1: Origins to 1660,* edited by Jack (Aberdeen: Aberdeen University Press, 1988), pp. 125–139;

R. J. Lyall, "'A new maid channoun?' Redefining the Canonical in Medieval and Renaissance Scottish Literature," *Studies in Scottish Literature,* 26 (1991): 1–18;

J. Derrick McClure, "'O Pheonix Escossois': James VI as Poet," in *A Day Estivall: Essays on the Music, Poetry and History of Scotland and England in Honour of Helena Mennie Shire,* edited by Alisoun Gardner-Medwin and Janet Hadley Williams (Aberdeen: Aberdeen University Press, 1990), pp. 97–111;

McClure, "Translation and Transcreation in the Castalian Period," *Studies in Scottish Literature,* 26 (1991): 185–198;

David Norbrook, *Poetry and Politics in the English Renaissance* (London: Routledge & Kegan Paul, 1984);

Graham Parry, *The Golden Age Restor'd: The Culture of the Stuart Court, 1603–42* (Manchester: Manchester University Press, 1981);

Linda Levy Peck, ed., *The Mental World of the Jacobean Court* (Cambridge: Cambridge University Press, 1991);

Walter Scott, ed., *A Secret History of the Court of James I,* 2 volumes (Edinburgh, 1811);

Kevin Sharpe, "Private Conscience and Public Duty in the Writings of James VI and I," in *Public Duty and Private Conscience in Seventeenth-Century England: Essays Presented to G. E. Aylmer,* edited by John Morrill, Paul Slack, and Daniel Woolf (Oxford: Oxford University Press, 1993), pp. 77–100;

Sharpe and Peter Lake, eds., *Culture and Politics in Early Stuart England* (London: Macmillan, 1994);

Sharpe and Steven N. Zwicker, eds., *The Politics of Discourse: The Literature and History of Seventeenth Century England* (Berkeley: University of California Press, 1987);

Helena Mennie Shire, *Song, Dance and Poetry at the Court of Scotland under King James VI* (Cambridge: Cambridge University Press, 1969);

R. Malcolm Smuts, *Court Culture and the Origins of a Royalist Tradition in Early Stuart England* (Philadelphia: University of Pennsylvania Press, 1987);

G. F. Warner, "The Library of James VI, in the Hand of Peter Young, His Tutor, 1573–1583," in *Miscellany of the Scottish History Society,* edited by Warner (Edinburgh: Scottish History Society, 1893), I: x–lxxv;

Jenny Wormald, "James VI and I: Two Kings or One?," *History,* 68 (June 1983): 187–209.

Papers:

Manuscripts of King James's prose and poetry and his letters and speeches (including holograph versions and corrected copies) are located in the Scottish Record Office, Edinburgh; the National Library of Scotland, Edinburgh; the Public Record Office, London; the British Library, London; the Bodleian Library, Oxford; the Cambridge University Library; Hatfield House, Hatfield, Hertfordshire; the Folger Shakespeare Library, Washington D.C.; and the Huntington Library, San Marino, California.

Thomas Lodge

(1558 – September 1625)

Charles Whitworth
University of Montpellier

BOOKS: [*Honest Excuses*] (London?, 1579) – both surviving copies lack title page;

An Alarum against Usurers (London: Printed by T. Este for Sampson Clarke, 1584) – includes *Forbonius and Prisceria* and *Truth's Complaint over England*;

Scillaes Metamorphosis (London: Printed by Thomas Orwin for Richard Jhones, 1589);

Rosalynde. Euphues Golden Legacie (London: Printed by Thomas Orwin for Thomas Gubbin & John Busbie, 1590);

Catharos. Diogenes in His Singularitie (London: Printed by William Hoskind & John Danter for John Busbie, 1591);

The Famous, True and Historicall Life of Robert Second Duke of Normandy (London: Printed by Thomas Orwin for Nicholas Ling & John Busbie, 1591);

Euphues Shadow. The Battaile of the Sences (London: Printed by Abel Jeffes for John Busbie, 1592);

The Life and Death of William Long Beard (London: Printed by Richard Yardley & Peter Short, 1593);

Phillis: Honoured with Pastorall Sonnets, Elegies, and Amorous Delights (London: Printed by James Roberts for John Busbie, 1593);

A Looking Glasse for London and England. Made by Thomas Lodge Gentleman, and Robert Greene (London: Printed by Thomas Creede, sold by William Barley, 1594);

The Wounds of Civill War (London: Printed by John Danter, 1594);

A Fig for Momus: Containing Pleasant Varietie, Included in Satyres, Eclogues, and Epistles (London: Printed by Joan Orwin for Clement Knight, 1595);

The Divel Conjured (London: Printed by Adam Islip for William Mats, 1596);

A Margarite of America (London: Printed by Abel Jeffes for John Busbie, 1596);

Prosopopeia: Containing the Teares of the Holy, Blessed, and Sanctified Marie, the Mother of God (London: Printed by Thomas Scarlet for Edward White, 1596);

Wits Miseries, and the Worlds Madnesse: Discovering the Devils Incarnat of This Age (London: Printed by Adam Islip, sold by Cuthbert Burby, 1596).

Editions: *The Works of Thomas Lodge,* 4 volumes, edited by Edmund Gosse (Glasgow: Hunterian Club, 1883);

Rosalynde, edited by W. W. Greg (London: Chatto & Windus, 1907);

The Wounds of Civil War, edited by John Dover Wilson (Oxford: Oxford University Press, 1910);

A Margarite of America, edited by G. B. Harrison (Oxford: Blackwell, 1927);

A Looking Glass for London and England, edited by Greg (Oxford: Oxford University Press, 1932);

The Wounds of Civil War, edited by Joseph W. Houppert (Lincoln: University of Nebraska Press, 1969);

A Margarite of America, edited by J. C. Addison (Salzburg: Universitat Salzburg, 1980);

William Longbeard, edited by Allan H. Findlay (Copenhagen: University of Copenhagen, 1983).

PLAY PRODUCTIONS: *The Wounds of Civil War,* London, The Theatre(?) and/or The Rose(?), circa 1586–1587;

A Looking Glass for London and England, by Lodge and Robert Greene, London, The Theatre(?), circa 1591.

OTHER: *The Phoenix Nest,* edited by R. S. (London: Printed by J. Jackson, 1593) – includes sixteen poems by Lodge;

England's Helicon, edited by Nicholas Ling (London: Printed by J. Roberts for J. Flasket, 1600) – includes fourteen poems by Lodge.

TRANSLATIONS: *The Flowers of Lodowicke of Granado. The First Part* (London: Printed by James Roberts for Thomas Heyes, 1601);

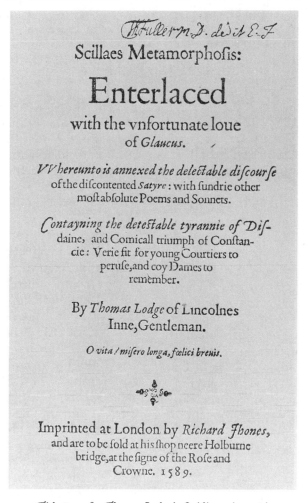

Scillaes Metamorphofis:

Enterlaced

with the vnfortunate loue
of *Glaucus.*

VVhereunto is annexed the delectable difcourfe
of the difcontented *Satyre* : with fundrie other
moſt abfolute Poems and Sonnets.

Contayning the detestable tyrannie of Dif-
daine, and Comicall triumph of Conftan-
cie : Verie fit for young Courtiers to
perufe, and coy Dames to
remèmber.

By *Thomas Lodge* of Lincolnes
Inne, Gentleman.

O vita ! mifero longa, fœlici breuis.

Imprinted at London by *Richard Jhones,*
and are to be fold at his fhop neere Holburne
bridge, at the figne of the Rofe and
Crowne. 1589.

Title page for Thomas Lodge's Ovidian minor epic

The Famous and Memorable Workes of Josephus (London: Printed by Peter Short for G. Bishop, S. Waterson, P. Short & Thomas Adams, 1602);

François Vallériole, *A Treatise of the Plague* (London: Printed by Thomas Creede & Valentine Simmes for Edward White & Nicholas Ling, 1603);

The Workes Both Morall and Natural of Lucius Annæus Seneca (London: Printed by William Stansby, 1614; revised, 1620);

A Learned Summary upon the Famous Poeme of William of Saluste Lord of Bartas (London: Printed by George Purslowe for John Grismand, 1621).

Thomas Lodge remains, nearly four centuries after his death, an ill-defined figure among many illustrious Elizabethans. Although a good deal is known about his multifaceted life, as a literary personality he continues to be a "minor Elizabethan." But his output was more varied and more copious than that of most of his contempo-

raries. He outlived most of the writers of his generation. His lifetime spans exactly the reigns of Elizabeth and James, and for almost thirty years after his career as an Elizabethan author ended, he practiced his other vocation, medicine. He was the son of a lord mayor of London who disinherited him. He was an Oxford graduate and a member of Lincoln's Inn who also knew a debtors' prison from the inside. He was a devout Catholic who suffered exile for his faith. He was an adventurer who went on at least two voyages, one of them the circumnavigation attempt of George Cavendish in 1591–1592: Lodge returned; Cavendish did not. He was embroiled in a virtually endless series of litigations, some of them with members of his own family; his elder brother once organized an ambush of him in Nottinghamshire.

He was also an author of dozens of lyric poems, some of which were set to music by prominent Elizabethan composers; prose romances, one of which was dramatized by William Shakespeare; plays, one of which influenced Christopher Marlowe; sonnets; narrative poems; satires in verse and prose; assorted pamphlets; medical treatises; and translations. His poems, in widely various genres, forms, and lengths, number almost two hundred. He was a prominent contributor to major poetical miscellanies, *The Phoenix Nest* (1593) and *England's Helicon* (1600). In the former, Lodge, with sixteen poems, was by far the chief contributor. He published the first English collection of verse satires and epistles on the classical model.

In *Scilla's Metamorphosis* (1589) Lodge's free treatment of the story of Glaucus and Scilla from Ovid's *Metamorphoses* pointed the way for his followers, including Shakespeare, in the genre of the *epyllion,* or minor epic. The stanza of *Scilla's Metamorphosis* is the iambic pentameter sixain, rhymed *ababcc,* the stanza used by Shakespeare in *Venus and Adonis* (1593). Lodge was the first to employ it for a long narrative piece. In "The Discontented Satyre," one of seventeen poems appended to the title piece, is the first explicit identification in English poetry of satire with the Satyr, the mythological man-goat; in the same year George Puttenham gave formal expression to the concept in his *Art of English Poesie* (1589).

Lodge's best-known work, the prose romance *Rosalynde* (1590), ran to ten editions by 1642. His final romance, *A Margarite of America* (1596), outdoes almost anything in Matteo Bandello, Robert Greene, or Thomas Nashe in decadent horror and sheer bloodiness, yet it contains no fewer than twenty-five poems, some of them among Lodge's most polished lyrics. Nashe boasted in 1592 that he had written "in all sorts of humors privately . . . more than any young man of my age in England." Lodge could certainly have claimed legitimately, had he been so inclined, at the end of his long life, to have written and published in more "humors" than any of his contemporaries. Despite Lodge's oar being "in every paper boat," as the anonymous authors of the play *The Return from Parnassus* (1602) said of him, literature was only one of his vocations, and not, he would no doubt have insisted, the most important. It is because he was a writer that Lodge is remembered at all today; yet his well-documented life has received as much attention as his works, perhaps precisely because it is well documented and because none of his works, individually or taken as a whole, is quite outstanding enough to win him a place among the greats of Elizabethan literature.

Many of the allusions to Lodge in modern works of criticism or literary history occur in the context of a discussion of other authors: he is one of a cluster of "University Wits" but is outshone by the likes of John Lyly, Marlowe, Nashe, and Greene; he is one of many "minor" sonneteers, lyric poets, prose romancers, satirists, narrative poets, translators, and dramatists. In all of these genres it is other names that first come to mind. It is almost as if, try as he might, Lodge never succeeded in securing a place for himself in posterity. Whatever genre or style he assayed, he appears now to have been a pedestrian among gods and other highfliers. When he pioneered or had a rare success, it was surpassed or appropriated and relegated to the minor ranks by greater contemporaries or followers – often Shakespeare: Lodge was the author of *Rosalynde* (the source for *As You Like It,* circa 1599–1600), of *Scilla's Metamorphosis* (the model for *Venus and Adonis*) and of *The Wounds of Civil War* (circa 1586–1587) – a precursor of the Roman plays. In *Wit's Miseries and the World's Madness* (1596) Lodge makes a well-known reference to a performance of a *Hamlet* – several years before Shakespeare wrote his play of that title. Even when Lodge appears to fit a description neatly, he is, as it were, shouldered aside by a more visible, more assertive figure. Greene's allusion in 1592 to "young Juvenal, that biting satirist, that lastly with me together writ a comedy," has almost always been taken to refer to Nashe – despite the comedy that Lodge wrote with Greene (*A Looking Glass for London and England,* circa 1591) and several satiric works by Lodge in prose and verse published prior to 1592.

Unlike many of his literary fellows, Lodge came from a prominent family of the London merchant-gentry class, one that left its own records and figured in the records of others. Furthermore, Lodge was a recorded member of institutions and professions, and he was engaged in affairs that occasioned correspondence or produced legal records. Even had he left no literary legacy, scholars would be able to compile a fairly full biographical account of him. In addition, Lodge lived a long time: sixty-seven years. There was more time for records to accumulate and traces to be left. Many of the writers of his generation died relatively young: George Peele at forty, Edmund Spenser at forty-seven, Lyly at about fifty, and Shakespeare at fifty-two.

Thomas Lodge was born in 1558. He was the second son of Thomas and Anne Lodge. The elder Thomas, of Shropshire stock, was a member of the Grocers' Company who became master of the company. He was sheriff and then, in 1562, lord mayor of London; he was knighted that year, an honor customarily bestowed upon lord mayors. His second wife, Anne, came from another family of grocers: her first husband, William Lane, and her stepfather, Sir William Laxton, the founder of Oundle School, were both members of the company. Laxton had been lord mayor in 1544. Sir Thomas Lodge plunged from zenith to nadir: he went bankrupt in the year of his mayoralty. The scandal was recorded by John Stow in his *Survey of London* (1598).

Young Thomas served in the household of Henry Stanley, Earl of Derby, at some time during his childhood, a fact to which he alluded years later in the dedication of his verse collection *A Fig for Momus* (1595) to William Stanley, the sixth Earl of Derby. It may have been at this period that Lodge first became attracted to Roman Catholicism, for the Stanleys were a prominent Catholic clan. Lodge was sent to the Merchant Taylors' School in 1571 and came under the tuition of the renowned schoolmaster Richard Mulcaster. After only two years Lodge went to Trinity College, Oxford, where he was tutored by the brilliant young scholar Edward Hoby. In the dedication to *Rosalynde* Lodge speaks of having been a "scholar in the university under that learned and virtuous knight." In 1577 he was admitted bachelor of arts. It is reasonable to assume that he began writing verse and perhaps plays at Oxford; the universities produced many of the writers who made the late 1580s and 1590s such an extraordinary "Golden Age." In 1578 he was registered as a clerk of Lincoln's Inn. Although this association was proudly announced from 1584 to 1595 on the title pages of at least five of Lodge's publications, he never entered the legal profession for which the Inns of Court were the training schools.

Lodge's literary career is usually dated from 1579, when he published an epitaph (now lost) on his mother, Lady Anne Lodge. She died in December, leaving her son a handsome legacy in the form of property. It was probably a few months earlier, though, that Lodge emerged onto the professional scene with a pamphlet defending literature, and particularly plays, from an attack by the sometime playwright Stephen Gosson in his *School of Abuse* (1579). Gosson's diatribe was entered in the Stationers' Register on 22 July. On 7 November he entered another work called *An Apology of the School of Abuse.* In the *Apology* Gosson speaks of "certain honest ex-

cuses" that some players had commissioned in response to his earlier attack. Taking a hint from Gosson's phrase, John Dover Wilson suggested that Lodge's defense may have been called *Honest Excuses.* The absence of title pages and the poor quality of the printing in the two surviving copies may indicate that the work was published clandestinely as well as hurriedly and was suppressed by hostile authorities, who may have commissioned Gosson. Lodge's defense is bookish: it reads like the work of a young graduate eager to make an impression on the London scene, with its new theaters: The Theatre (built in 1576), the First Blackfriars (opened the same year by the Children of the Chapel Royal), and the Curtain (1577). The main interest of this flyting between two Oxford graduates, continued by Gosson in *Plays Confuted in Five Actions* (1582) and wittily concluded by Lodge in 1584, is historical: in it occur the earliest salvos in a war that raged until the closing of the theaters in 1642.

Apart from a brief prefatory verse to Barnabe Riche's romance *Don Simonides* (1581), there is a hiatus of several years between Lodge's first modest ventures into publication in 1579 and his first significant work, *An Alarum against Usurers,* a 1584 collection of pieces in prose and verse. Lodge's lines in Riche's volume reveal hints of personal difficulties and conclude: "I leave thee now, my Muse affords no more, / A doleful dump pulls back my pleasant vein." These lines and the address to the readers of *An Alarum against Usurers,* beginning "Let it not seem strange unto you that he which hath long time slept in silence, now beginneth publicly to salute you," have led biographers to surmise that Lodge may have been in debtors' prison.

Lodge's life around this time certainly seems to have been unsettled. Sir Thomas Lodge and his executor Sir William Cordell agreed that the property Lady Anne left her son should not revert to him, because of his "disordered" lifestyle. Sir Thomas died in February 1594, a few weeks after his son published his first major book. The young poet may have been his mother's favorite, but he was clearly not his father's: the younger Thomas is not mentioned in the elder's will. Whether or not the account of the usurers' tactics for ensnaring young gentlemen — related with a wealth of detail in *An Alarum* — is autobiographical, it is fascinating documentary material. One biographer, E. A. Tenney, finds the fervor of bitter experience in Lodge's warnings against the depredations of the moneylenders, asserting, "The lines glow with personal indignation."

Lodge's probable birthplace, his family's country residence in Plaistow, West Ham

The usurer in Greene and Lodge's play, *A Looking Glass for London and England,* echoes in his speech of repentance the chief villain of Lodge's tale. The volume was dedicated to Sir Philip Sidney, in anticipation of his "undoubted protection," a rash claim were Lodge not sure of it. His reasons for writing, he says in *An Alarum,* were "first that the offender, seeing his own counterfeit in this mirror might emend it, and those who are like by overlavish profuseness to become meat for their mouths, might be warned by this caveat to shun the scorpion ere she devoureth." Lady Anne's will withheld Lodge's legacy until he was twenty-five, that is, until 1583. It is not improbable that he borrowed against that promised inheritance denied him by his father, so that he fell into debt and the usurers' clutches.

The 1584 volume also includes Lodge's first attempt at prose fiction in a pastoral vein, *The Delectable History of Forbonius and Prisceria,* and an allegorical poem in a late-medieval vein, *Truth's Complaint over England.* Sidney's influence is immediately evident in the former, a sort of adumbration, in a mere thirty-two pages, of parts of the Musidorus and Pamela plot from *Arcadia* (1591). The heroine Prisceria is the granddaughter of Theagenes and Chariclea, hero and heroine of Heliodorus's *Æthiopian History,* a work singled out for praise by Sidney in his *Apology for Poetry* (1595), and Lodge borrows names of minor characters from Heliodorus as well. If Lodge knew Sidney's work, it would have been in the original version, the "old" *Arcadia,* and in manuscript; this is not at all unlikely, as it seems to have circulated widely from about 1580. Sidney remained a major influence on Lodge. His tacit avowal of this influence in the form of *Forbonius* and indeed his dedication of the volume to the renowned courtier and poet may, however, have been late decisions on Lodge's part: the catchword on the last page of the text of *An Alarum* is "Truths," suggesting that his verse complaint was originally intended to follow and that *Forbonius* was inserted belatedly.

This promising beginning was not followed up for several more years. In the interval between 1584 and 1589, the year of his next publication, Lodge was presumably trying to make a living by writing and trying to obtain some financial benefit from his inheritance. Subsequent lawsuits

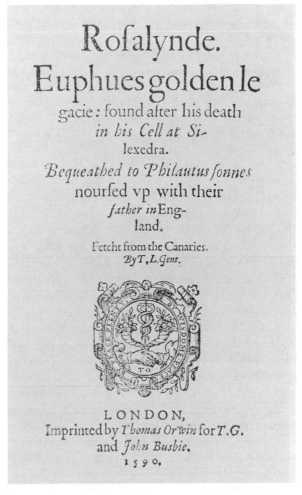

Title page for Lodge's best-known work, a prose romance that was the source for William Shakespeare's As You Like It *(circa 1599–1600)*

with his elder brother, William, suggest that Lodge may have sold some or all of the interest in the inherited property to his brother and that the cash realized in the transaction was insufficient to his needs or expectations. The one play certainly attributable to Lodge alone, *The Wounds of Civil War,* though not published until 1594, was probably written in 1586 or early 1587; it was performed by the Admiral's Men, according to the quarto title page. The Throckmorton plot had been uncovered in 1583. The Babington conspiracy in the summer of 1586 and the execution of Mary Stuart in February 1587 were part of the immediate, highly charged political context in which Lodge's play about civil war was written. His sources were Appian and Plutarch, his subject the Roman civil wars between Marius and Sulla (Lodge calls him Scilla). N. Burton Paradise demonstrates in *Thomas Lodge: The History of an*

Elizabethan (1931) that Marlowe, who was also writing for the Admiral's Men in the late 1580s, knew and borrowed from Lodge's play in both *Tamburlaine* (1590) and *Edward II* (1594).

Besides his literary activities in this period, Lodge probably made the first of his two sea voyages. There has been much speculation about the date and circumstances of this voyage. The little that Lodge relates about it is in the preface to *Rosalynde.* His most recent and thorough biographer, the French scholar Eliane Cuvelier, believes that the conjunction of references to the Carey (or Carew) family and to "Captain Clark" in the dedication and preface points to a privateering venture of 1585 backed by Sir George Carey, Lord Hunsdon, and not, as earlier biographers had surmised, to Sir Richard Grenville's Virginia expedition later the same year in which Capt. John Clark took part nor to Tenney's proposal, a Clark voyage of 1586–

1587. There were other Clark voyages, however, such as the one in the spring of 1590, when he captained Cavendish's *Galleon Dudley* and sank a Flemish vessel loaded with salt; this voyage fits the chronology of the publication of *Rosalynde,* written, Lodge claims, during the voyage in the autumn of that year.

But the choice of any of these dates leaves unanswered questions: if the voyage were as early as 1585 or 1586, why was it so long before Lodge published the book he claimed he had written while at sea, "rough, as hatched in the storms of the ocean, and feathered in the surges of many perilous seas," and why is there no allusion to such an adventure in the prefatory material of the verse collection published in 1589? If, on the other hand, he both sailed with Clark and wrote the romance as late as 1590, why did he fail to give Edmund Carey, son of his dedicatee, Lord Hunsdon, his proper title? Carey had been knighted in 1587, but Lodge calls him only "Master." It could have been mere oversight or carelessness, of course, and in any case the language of the passage in question leaves open the possibility that Lodge was naming Hunsdon's sons Edmund and Robert as he had known them when they were students together at Oxford.

H. C. Hart suggested as long ago as the nineteenth century that Lodge's friend and sometime collaborator Greene may have retouched *Rosalynde* and seen it through the press. Some modern stylistic studies also claim to have detected Greene's hand in the romance. The assertive Greene is unlikely to have allowed the work to appear, however, without some acknowledgment of his contribution if it were in any way substantial. Like much else in Lodge's biography, the date of his first sea voyage, and thus the date of composition of his best-known work, remain uncertain.

In 1589 appeared a verse collection that, whatever its intrinsic merits, was to mark the beginning of the short but rich period that may be considered Lodge's literary career proper. In the brief span between 1589 and the end of 1596, when he left England to study medicine in Avignon, he produced the body of work that entitles him to the modest recognition that he has received as a contributor to the Golden Age of English literature. It was as a narrative and lyric poet that Lodge returned to the scene in 1589, and it was poetry, primarily, and prose fiction that were to be his chief modes in the productive years that followed. *Scilla's Metamorphosis* includes not only the title piece, a major early example of the Elizabethan epyllion, or Ovidian minor epic; it is followed by a veritable poet's portfolio – a collection of seventeen pieces in a variety of forms and styles. In the title piece as well as in several of the appended poems, Lodge exploits the device he had used in *Truth's Complaint over England:* presenting himself as a solitary, pensive, earnest poet-reporter figure, reminiscent of Geoffrey Chaucer's poet-dreamers. In "The Discontented Satyre" the narrator overhears the Satyr's apostrophe to Discontent. As Louis Lecocq observes, Lodge's grumpy Satyr seems to be the first incarnation of the Elizabethan fin de siècle satirist persona. Here is another example of Lodge's apparently beginning something that others were to develop. He never really wrote "biting satyre" in the vein of John Donne, John Marston, or Joseph Hall. Other pieces in the collection, such as "In Praise of the Country Life" and "In Commendation of a Solitary Life," strike the gentler pastoral and Horatian tones Lodge preferred.

Scilla's Metamorphosis is far more significant than the slight pieces appended to it in the 1589 collection. Among the literary genres that flourished briefly but brilliantly in the last decade of the century, the epyllion, whether based on Ovidian subjects or on legendary history, attracted almost as many writers as the sonnet. Dozens of works appeared by well-known figures such as Marlowe, Shakespeare, Michael Drayton, Marston, Thomas Heywood, George Chapman, and Francis Beaumont and by virtually unknown ones such as Thomas Edwards, Dunstan Gale, William Barksted, and Henry Petowe. They are not translations but rewritings of Ovid's familiar tales. Lodge's poem is doubly surprising for its doleful-narrator frame, resembling that of the earlier allegorical complaints, and the appearance of such psychological abstractions as Fury, Rage, and Wanhope. In *English Literature in the Sixteenth Century, Excluding Drama* (1954) C. S. Lewis speaks of its "mediæval frame," and in a 1967 edition of the work, Nigel Alexander invokes "*The Romance of the Rose* and other mediæval allegorical love-visions."

Scilla's Metamorphosis may be Ovidian, but it is Ovid anglicized, as the melancholy narrator sees the sea-god Glaucus rise from the Isis (Thames). While the main story is that of Glaucus and his unrequited love for the nymph Scilla, the narrator remains visible, even accompanying Glaucus in his pursuit of Scilla, mounted upon a dolphin helpfully provided by the god. Several modern critics have felt that Lodge's tongue was firmly in his cheek and that it is impossible not to read the poem from a comic-ironic point of view. Certainly the envoi addressed to the ladies, admonishing them to take note of the dis-

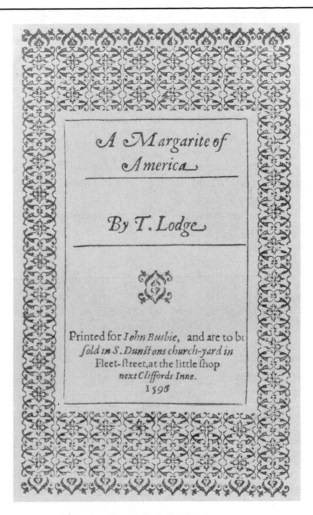

Title page for Lodge's final prose romance

dainful nymph's ghastly fate, can hardly be taken "straight." Irony, humor, and eroticism are present in abundant measure in the minor epics, not least those by Marlowe, Shakespeare, and Marston.

Forbonius and Prisceria had been a first slight effort at narrative romance writing in prose. The year 1590 saw the first of five further works of prose fiction produced by Lodge, a series culminating with *A Margarite of America;* four of these prose works were produced in successive years from 1590 to 1593. This substantial prose output — there was nonfiction as well — coincided with the production of a remarkable quantity of shorter verse: lyrics, sonnets, satires. Dozens of those poems were incorporated in the prose tales themselves: twenty-one in *Rosalynde,* thirteen in *William Longbeard* (1593), twenty-five in *Margarite,* and a further eleven shared between *Robert, Second Duke of Normandy* (1591) and *Euphues' Shadow* (1592). In addition there were the sonnet sequence *Phillis* (1593), a principal contribution to the anthology *The Phoenix Nest* in the same

year, and Lodge's original collection of verse satires, epistles, and eclogues, *A Fig for Momus.* A just analysis of Lodge's literary achievement must focus on those few years in the first half of the 1590s and must take account of both his prose fiction and his nonnarrative poetry. Not that his efforts during those years were limited to those genres: in 1591 he also wrote *Catharos. Diogenes in His Singularity,* a generalized moral complaint in dialogue form, and probably wrote, with Greene, the biblical drama *A Looking Glass for London and England.*

If *Rosalynde* remains Lodge's best-known work, it is largely because Shakespeare adopted it as the source for *As You Like It.* But the work enjoyed its own success: it had reached a fourth edition by 1598, before Shakespeare took it up. It went on to a further six editions by 1642. *Rosalynde* seems to embody an essential late-Elizabethan fondness for the particular combination of chivalric adventure narrative, pastoralism, and lyric poetry that only Sidney's *Arcadia* had provided in English before; Sidney's work, too, was first published, in its partly revised form, in 1590.

Lodge's source, for the first part of his tale at least, was the fourteenth-century verse romance *The Tale of Gamelyn,* once attributed to Chaucer. This swashbuckling narrative in the Robin Hood vein provided the Elizabethan author with his plot of a younger brother oppressed by his elder, who flees for safety to the greenwood with a faithful family retainer for company. The old servant Adam retains his name in both Lodge and Shakespeare. For the medieval tale's denouement of bloody revenge and gloating triumph, Lodge substitutes pastoral romance, multiple love plots, forgiveness, and reconciliation. A kindly, philosophizing old shepherd, Coridon, gives shelter to the fugitive heroines, one of whom is disguised as a page, Ganymede; the reconciled brothers Rosader and Saladyne marry Rosalynde and Alinda; the mournful young shepherd Montanus gets his Phoebe; the deposed king Gerismond, Rosalynde's father, is restored to his throne. The usurper Torismond, Alinda's father (who is nowhere said to be the rightful king's brother), is killed in a battle at the end.

Lodge retains some of the hardness of true romance but sprinkles it with songs and other verses; the prominence of songs in *As You Like It* – it has more than any other Shakespeare play – recalls the lyricism of its main source in this as in other respects. Some of Lodge's best lyrics, including Rosalynde's often-anthologized "Love in my bosom like a bee," are among the twenty-one poems. Another is the "Wooing Eclogue," a series of sonnets divided into dialogue, in which Rosader woos Rosalynde in her disguise as Ganymede; Shakespeare borrowed the episode virtually whole. Much has been said about what Shakespeare did to *Rosalynde,* but as C. S. Lewis points out, Lodge did a great deal to *Gamelyn,* transforming it utterly into the most "golden" of Elizabethan romances.

None of Lodge's other pieces of prose fiction survived a single printing, and it was the nineteenth century before any of them were republished or edited. *Robert, Second Duke of Normandy,* or "Robert the Devil," has analogues in medieval homiletic romances such as *Robert of Sicily* and *Sir Gowther,* and there are many French versions, in verse and prose, of the legend of *Robert le Diable.* Lodge seems to have worked from the medieval French *Croniques de Normandie,* first printed at Rouen in 1487; a later edition of 1578 was reprinted in 1581 and 1589. The addition of euphu-

istic soliloquies and several poems, including love lyrics – incongruous as they are in the context of the grim medieval legend about a diabolically sired maniac who rapes and murders nuns and then repents and becomes a Crusader champion – was calculated to sell it to an Elizabethan popular readership. Here is revealed the uneasy cohabitation of Lodge's sober moralism and the exigencies of the new literary professionalism of the 1590s.

Euphues' Shadow is the nearest imitation of Lyly's *Euphues* that has survived. Lodge adumbrates Lyly's two-part work. The main curiosity is its appearance twelve years after Lyly's sequel, *Euphues and His England* (1580), when the euphuistic vogue was decidedly on the wane. Perhaps Lodge had written it years before and brought it out belatedly to raise cash; the work was seen through the press by Greene during Lodge's absence on the Cavendish voyage. Lyly's Euphues and Philautus reappear as Philamis and Philamour, but the reconciliation of the two friends takes place only after many misadventures and magical interventions. In the end Philamour marries Harpaste as his counterpart Philautus married Camilla, and the friend, Philamis, retreats from the world as Euphues retired to Mount Silexedra. Eurinome rejects Philamis, then dies of remorse, unlike Lyly's unrepentant Lucilla.

Robert, Second Duke of Normandy and *Euphues' Shadow* include far fewer poems than *Rosalynde* or the two prose tales that followed; the latter has only four. One of them, "Philamis' Barginet," is a charming lyric in Lodge's best delicate and wistful manner; it has never been reprinted. One of the seven inset poems in *Robert* is an impressive, somber piece on the carpe diem theme, "Pluck the fruit, and taste the pleasure."

William Longbeard, published in 1593 following Lodge's return from the Cavendish expedition, is a much shorter piece than *Robert* or *Euphues' Shadow.* The volume is fleshed out with a dozen ministories from one to six pages in length, translated from a 1587 Italian collection by Giglio. The title piece is a mere thirty pages long and is stuffed with poems. The historical twelfth-century rabble-rouser and petty criminal William Fitzosbert, about whose brief and turbulent career Lodge read in Fabyan's chronicle, becomes in Lodge's treatment a romantic swain, inditing sonnets to his "lemman" Maudline.

More strikingly than in *Robert,* Lodge was trying to fit moralistic chronicle material into a fashionable mold. He seems aware of the incongruity and excuses the excess of lyrics as the effusions of William's dissolute youth. The hero is another in

Lodge's family of repentant villains, following Saladyne in *Rosalynde,* Robert the Devil, and Philamis. This time though, there is no happy ending: William is executed for his crimes, leaving behind a handful of meditative exhortations in verse. In its portrayal of a career of wickedness and the villain's grim fate and its incongruous juxtaposition of such a narrative with the trappings of a love story and lyrical interludes, it anticipates Lodge's last and strangest production in the prose fiction genre, *A Margarite of America.*

In the meantime, Lodge published his sonnet sequence *Phillis,* to which he appended a long narrative in verse based on legendary history, *The Complaint of Elstred,* following the example of Samuel Daniel, whose *Delia* (1592), with *The Complaint of Rosamund,* had appeared the previous year. *Phillis* is one of the few Elizabethan sonnet collections to announce itself as pastoral, although two "eclogues" are the only true pastorals in it. One of them, "Muses help me, sorrow swarmeth," was republished twice, in *The Phoenix Nest* and *England's Helicon,* the only one of Lodge's nearly sixty fourteen-line sonnets to be republished in a contemporary collection.

Lodge's poor reputation as a sonneteer has rested on *Phillis,* but he was always at his best in freer lyric forms than the rigid quatorzain that modern critics have designated as the sonnet proper. The Elizabethans were not so exclusive in their use of the term: twelve- and eighteen-line poems and others of various lengths were designated "sonnets" indiscriminately. Furthermore, most of Lodge's best efforts in that strict form are to be found elsewhere, scattered through the prose fiction; barely half his sonnets are contained in *Phillis.*

The Phoenix Nest, a collection of poems dedicated to Sidney's memory, also appeared in 1593. Lodge's sixteen poems, only three of which had been published elsewhere (in *Phillis* earlier in the year) make him by far the major contributor – ahead of Sir Walter Ralegh (with eight poems), Nicholas Breton (with five), the earl of Oxford, Sir Edward Dyer, Peele, Greene, and others. The collection is thus an important item in the Lodge canon. His contributions exhibit remarkable assurance and dexterity; he uses couplets, quatrains, sixains, rhyme royal, the sonnet, and various complex metrical patterns. Among the pieces are some of his finest lyrics: "My Bonny Lass, Thine Eye," "For Pity, Pretty Eyes, Surcease," "Accursed Be Love and They That Trust His Trains," and "Fain to Content, I Bend Myself to Write," in which Lodge reverts to the *ababcc* stanza.

Lodge's life about this time seems to have been particularly troubled. He returned from his eventful voyage with Cavendish to find his brother William lying in wait for him. Lodge's Star Chamber affidavit, in which he claims that William's men ambushed him near Rolleston in Nottinghamshire in February 1593, proves that he was back in England by then. The voyage had been a disaster for all concerned, and Lodge was probably even more financially distressed than before. The spate of publications in that year looks like a desperate bid for quick cash. He must have begun thinking seriously about a new profession at this time. His one publication of 1595 has something of a valedictory air about it, and in 1596 he cleaned out his desk, publishing four books, before setting off to study medicine in Avignon.

A Fig for Momus, Lodge's last verse collection, was something completely new. It is not lyric or pastoral verse, nor sonnets, nor narratives, but fifteen secular meditative pieces in couplets, divided, numbered, and carefully identified by Lodge as satires, epistles, and eclogues. He adopts a fractious, "satyrical" tone in the preface but soon drops it, going on to explain to the reader what is novel in his collection, claiming particular originality for his epistles: "they are in that kind wherein no Englishman of our time hath publicly written." He evokes indirectly the Roman satirists; it is the spirit of Horace rather than of Juvenal that pervades the collection, though the latter's influence has been demonstrated, with Spenser hovering in the background.

Each of the four eclogues is a dialogue on some such topic as youth and age, art and arms, or writers and patrons. The first is addressed to "Reverend Colin," that is, Spenser; others are to Daniel and Drayton, who is also addressed in epistle 5. Epistle 4 is to "H. L.," perhaps Lodge's brother Henry; in it the poet refers to himself, for the only time in his entire corpus, as "Tom." In eclogue 3 Lodge represents himself by the anagram *Golde:* the topic, significantly, is the difficulty of finding a literary patron. The epistles reflect Lodge's medical and scientific reading at the time. Overall, the poems in *A Fig for Momus,* whether Lodge calls them satires, epistles, or eclogues, are closer in tone to the satiric work of Sir Thomas Wyatt and Spenser, and Ben Jonson's verse epistles than to the ostensible "satyres" of Donne, Hall, and Marston: tolerant, even amused at times, reprov-

Lodge's memorial tablet in Rolleston Church

ing but somewhat detached. Indeed, the "satyr" figure is nowhere to be seen in Lodge's collection. It simply was not his role.

The year 1596 marks the end of Lodge's literary career proper. The satiric-admonitory stance is maintained in the prose pamphlets *The Devil Conjured* and *Wit's Misery and the World's Madness*. The former begins as a tale, with three philosophers seeking out a famous hermit, Anthony, in his desert retreat. The snarling Cynic Diogenes of *Catharos* gives way to the saintly Christian sage; the text soon settles down to a monologue on vanity, free will, devils, and so forth. *Wit's Misery* is much livelier, thanks to the influence of Nashe's *Pierce Penniless*, published in 1592. The Nashean bits are the best; in between are expanses of flat prose, mostly translated from a French treatise. Lodge uses a framework of the Seven Deadly Sins, as Nashe had done, but maintains it throughout, giving a clear structure to the lengthy work. It is in his description of Hate-Virtue, son of Beelzebub, that he makes the famous allusion to the *Ur-Hamlet:* "You shall know

him by this: he is a foul lubber, his tongue is tipped with lying, his heart steeled against charity; he walks for the most part in black under color of gravity, and looks as pale as the vizard of the ghost which cried so miserably at the theater like an oyster-wife, 'Hamlet, revenge!'"

Another pamphlet of the same year is overtly Catholic, beginning with the title: *Prosopopeia: Containing the Tears of the Holy, Blessed, and Sanctified Mary, the Mother of God.* It seems that prior to leaving the country, Lodge had resolved to "come out" where his faith was concerned; the former was probably the anticipated consequence of the latter. Two further tracts in the same vein, translated from Spanish, were published in 1601.

The most striking product in this year of endings in Lodge's career is without doubt the last of his prose romances, *A Margarite of America*. Lodge claims in the preface that he had found the Spanish original in the Jesuit library at Santos, Brazil, where his ship put in on the outward leg of the Cavendish expedition. There is evidence that Lodge was there, for he brought back a book that he later donated to the Bodleian Library in Oxford, but of the original for *Margarite* there is no longer any trace.

The tale is an extraordinarily bleak and bloody one of human depravity and motiveless malignity, interspersed with no fewer than twenty-five poems. The incongruity is greater than in *Robert, Second Duke of Normandy* and *William Longbeard*. Here there is no repentance and redemption, no reward for virtue. Twelve named characters die, all but two of them "on stage." The villain-protagonist Arsadachus is responsible for ten of the deaths, including, at last, his own, to the relief of the reader.

Lewis finds that, while it resembles the romances of Heliodorus and Sidney, it is "harsher and (in some ways) more splendid than either"; he describes it as "hard romance." Its world is that of Jacobean tragedy – cruel, cold, its brilliance steely rather than golden, "replenished," in Lodge's words, "with all vice and impoverished of all virtue." The reader – and Lodge – is a long way from the pastoral mellowness of *Rosalynde*.

The inset poems include some of Lodge's best: "With Ganymede Now Joins the Shining Sun," "I Pine Away Expecting of the Hour," "O Shady Vales, O Fair Enrichèd Meads," and "'Twixt Reverence and Desire How Am I Vexed"; fourteen of the twenty-five are sonnets, overlooked by anthologizers, except for one ("O Shady Vales") anthologized in *England's Helicon* a few years later. In that outstanding collection of pastorals, as in *The Phoenix Nest,* Lodge's contribution was substantial. Fourteen poems by him, all but two of them printed previously, are included, a figure exceeded only by the twenty-five poems selected from Bartholomew Young's 1598 translation of Montemayor's *Diana* (1559) and the fifteen pieces by Sidney. In this colection Lodge was in truly impressive company: Drayton; Peele; Marlowe; Ralegh; Shakespeare; Spenser; Fulke Greville, first Lord Brooke; and a host of others, as well as Sidney. This was a final, belated – if resounding – echo of Lodge's career as a poet and pastoralist, and it is unlikely that he was directly responsible for his prominent place in the collection: the editor, Nicholas Ling, had previously published *Rosalynde* (from which seven of the poems were taken) and *Robert, Second Duke of Normandy* and may have had access to Lodge's manuscripts.

In the beginning of 1597 Lodge was in Avignon, enrolled in the Faculty of Medicine. His full-time literary career was over, just eighteen years or so after it had begun. His career as a physician would last somewhat longer. After a period

of voluntary exile on the Continent – Elizabeth's England was not a comfortable place for devout Roman Catholics in the last decade of her reign – he established a medical practice in London, and he is mentioned by Thomas Heywood in his *Troia Britannica* (1609) as among the prominent physicians of the city. He was appointed official medical officer by the city authorities during the plague of 1625; he was presumably carrying out his duty when he died in September.

Despite his busy medical practice, he continued to write after 1596: the devotional tracts of 1601 (fervent pieces of jesuitic orthodoxy); and a treatise on the plague translated from French in 1603, fascinating as evidence of the state of medical knowledge at the time (Lodge probably knew the author's son at the medical faculty at Avignon). He contributed an introduction to *The Countess of Lincoln's Nursery* (1622), on child rearing. Another medical treatise, "The Poor Man's Talent," was written near the end of his life (probably 1623) but not published.

There were also the monumental translations. The works of Flavius Josephus, first published in 1602, had been entered in the Stationers' Register as early as 1591; Lodge seems to have been engaged on it for some time, and there are traces of the Jewish historian's work in his play *A Looking Glass for London and England*. A folio of nearly 850 pages, it went through seven editions by 1670, making it Lodge's most popular work after *Rosalynde*. It may, ironically in view of his Roman allegiance, have been a new interest in early church history fostered by Puritanism that maintained demand for Lodge's translation for much of the century. An even larger and more handsome folio of more than 950 pages, dedicated to Thomas Egerton, Baron Ellesmere, appeared in 1614, containing translations of the prose works of Seneca. It was clearly the work of many years: there is an entry in the Stationers' Register of 1600 for what is almost certainly Lodge's translation. Revised and improved by Lodge himself – the only one of his works of which that is true – it was republished in 1620 and remained the sole English translation of Seneca's complete prose until modern times. The massive volume includes also Lodge's translation of the Latin life of Seneca by Justus Lipsius. A third large-scale work in folio appeared in 1621: a translation of the standard commentary by the Calvinist Simon Goulart on Salluste du Bartas's religious epic *La Semaine* (1578). At the end of a long and remarkably full life, an English Roman Catholic poet turned physician translates a commentary by a Genevan theologian on an epic poem by a French Huguenot soldier-poet – a fitting finale to the multiple careers of Thomas Lodge.

His posthumous career has hardly been remarkable. Few of his works had been edited before Edmund Gosse produced under the auspices of the Hunterian Club of Glasgow in 1883 an old-spelling, type-facsimile edition of his works in four volumes, in which all of the misprints of the Elizabethan originals are carefully retained. There is still no collected scholarly edition of even his major works. A few individual titles – *Rosalynde, Scilla's Metamorphosis, A Margarite of America*, the plays, and the miscellanies *The Phoenix Nest* and *England's Helicon* – have received scholarly treatment in twentieth-century editions. A few of the shorter poems have appeared in anthologies. No substantial work on Lodge in English has appeared for more than half a century, and the spate of monographs published in the 1930s by Charles J. Sisson, Tenney, Paradise, and Alice Walker were mostly biographical. The only major piece of published research since then has been Cuvelier's 1984 French *thèse d'état*, which must be considered the definitive study. It places Lodge firmly in his age, using a wealth of documentation. Occasional chapters in studies of Elizabethan fiction or poetry deal with Lodge; the most extensive in recent years is in Arthur F. Kinney's *Humanist Poetics: Thought, Rhetoric, and Fiction in Sixteenth-Century England* (1986). Articles occasionally appear, mainly on *Rosalynde* or *Margarite*, but the profile of this unique, richly various Elizabethan author remains low. Despite the preponderance of poetry, especially lyrics, among Lodge's purely literary writings, it is primarily the prose fiction that attracts modern critics with an interest in narrative. But unless a publisher can be found who is willing to undertake a serious scholarly edition of the major narrative works and the sizable body of verse – making them accessible again – Lodge will probably not benefit from a critical revaluation. All those paper boats of his will continue to bob unregarded and undisturbed on the blurred horizon, neither receding entirely from view nor advancing into clearer focus.

Bibliographies:

A. F. Allison, *Thomas Lodge 1558–1625: A Bibliographical Catalogue of the Early Editions (to the end of the seventeenth century)*, Pall Mall Bibliographies 2 (Folkestone & London: Dawson's of Pall Mall, 1973);

Joseph W. Houppert, "Thomas Lodge," in *The Predecessors of Shakespeare: A Survey and Bibliography of Recent Studies in English Renaissance Drama*, edited by Terence P. Logan and Denzell S. Smith (Lincoln: University of Nebraska Press, 1973), pp. 153–160;

Kevin J. Donovan, "Recent Studies in Thomas Lodge (1969–1990)," *English Literary Renaissance*, 23 (Winter 1993): 201–211.

Biographies:

N. Burton Paradise, *Thomas Lodge: The History of an Elizabethan* (New Haven: Yale University Press, 1931);

Charles J. Sisson, "Thomas Lodge and His Family," in *Thomas Lodge and Other Elizabethans*, edited by Sisson (Cambridge, Mass.: Harvard University Press, 1933), pp. 1–164;

Alice Walker, "The Life of Thomas Lodge," *Review of English Studies*, 9 (October 1933): 410–432; 10 (January 1934): 46–54;

E. A. Tenney, *Thomas Lodge*, Cornell Studies in English 26 (Ithaca: Cornell University Press, 1935);

Pat M. Ryan Jr., *Thomas Lodge, Gentleman* (Hamden, Conn.: Shoe String Press, 1958);

James George, "Additional Materials on the Life of Thomas Lodge between 1604 and 1613," in *Papers Mainly Shakespearian*, edited by G. I. Duthie (Edinburgh: Oliver & Boyd, 1964), pp. 90–105;

Joseph W. Houppert, "Thomas Lodge's Letters to William Trumbull," *Renaissance News*, 18 (1965): 117–123;

Eliane Cuvelier, *Thomas Lodge: témoin de son temps* (Paris: Didier, 1984).

References:

Douglas Bush, *Mythology and the Renaissance Tradition in English Poetry* (Minneapolis: University of Minnesota Press, 1932);

Walter R. Davis, *Idea and Act in Elizabethan Fiction* (Princeton: Princeton University Press, 1969);

Simone Dorangeon, *L'eglogue anglaise de Spenser à Milton* (Paris: Didier, 1974);

Esther Garke, *The Use of Songs in Elizabethan Prose Fiction* (Bern: Francke, 1972);

Richard Helgerson, *The Elizabethan Prodigals* (Berkeley: University of California Press, 1976), pp. 105–123;

William Keach, *Elizabethan Erotic Narratives: Irony and Pathos in the Ovidian Poetry of Shakespeare, Marlowe, and Their Contemporaries* (East Brunswick, N.J.: Rutgers University Press, 1977);

Arthur F. Kinney, *Humanist Poetics: Thought, Rhetoric, and Fiction in Sixteenth-Century England* (Amherst: University of Massachusetts Press, 1986);

Louis Lecocq, *La Satire en Angleterre de 1588 à 1603* (Paris: Didier, 1969);

Wesley D. Rae, *Thomas Lodge* (New York: Twayne, 1967);

Paul Salzman, *English Prose Fiction 1558–1700: A Critical History* (Oxford: Clarendon Press, 1985);

Hallett Smith, *Elizabethan Poetry* (Cambridge, Mass.: Harvard University Press, 1952);

Charles W. Whitworth, "Thomas Lodge, Elizabethan Pioneer," *Cahiers Elisabéthains,* 3 (April 1973): 5–15.

Papers:

A letter (dated 1610) from Thomas Lodge to Sir Thomas Edmondes is preserved among the Edmondes papers in the British Library (Stowe Ms. 171, fol. 352); it is reproduced by W. W. Greg in *English Literary Autographs 1550–1650,* Part I (Oxford: Oxford University Press, 1925), No. XIX. Other letters, to Edmondes's secretary, William Trumbull, are in the same collection.

Richard Lynche

(flourished 1596 – 1601)

L. M. Storozynsky
University College of the Fraser Valley

BOOK: *Diella, Certaine Sonnets, Adioyned to the Amorous Poeme of Dom Diego and Gineura* (London: Printed by James Roberts for Henry Olney, 1596).

Editions: *Diella: Certaine Sonnets,* edited by E. V. Utterson (Beldornie, Isle of Wight: Privately printed at the Beldornie Press, 1841);

Poems by Richard Lynche, Gentleman, edited by Alexander B. Grosart (Manchester: Charles E. Simms, 1877);

The Love of Dom Diego and Gynevra, in *Seven Minor Epics of the English Renaissance,* edited by Paul Miller (Gainesville, Fla.: Scholars' Facsimiles & Reprints, 1967), pp. 61–102.

TRANSLATIONS: Vincenzo Cartari, *The Fountain of Ancient Fiction* (London: Printed by Adam Islip, 1599);

Giovanni Nanni, *An Historical Treatise of the Travels of Noah into Europe: Containing the First Inhabitation and Peopling Thereof* (London: Printed by Adam Islip, 1601).

Regarded as a minor poet and translator, Richard Lynche has received almost no critical attention, yet his sonnet sequence is one of only half a dozen Elizabethan sonnet sequences that were originally printed accompanied by a long narrative poem. *Diella* and *The Love of Dom Diego and Ginevra* (1596) therefore must be considered in the context of Samuel Daniel's *Delia* and *The Complaint of Rosamond* (1592), Thomas Lodge's *Phillis* and *The Complaint of Elstred* (1593), Giles Fletcher the Elder's *Licia* and *Richard III* (1593), Edmund Spenser's *Amoretti* and *Epithalamion* (1595), and William Shakespeare's *Sonnets* and *A Lover's Complaint* (1609).

Nothing is known of Lynche other than his name, and even that is sometimes spelled Linche. It is tempting to believe that a sonnet in Richard Barnfield's *Poems in Divers Humors* (1598) dedicated "to his friend Master R. L." might be addressed to Lynche, but there is no evidence to support such an identification. Unfortunately, no clues can be gleaned from the dedications and addresses prefacing Lynche's own works. The lack of biographical data, indeed the poet's uncertain identity, are frustrating; on the other hand, the sheer number of anonymous and nearly anonymous early printed works appears to confirm the widely held belief that sixteenth-century writers viewed the printing trade with some disdain. Anonymity shielded the poet from the consumer. Paradoxically, many texts were produced with great care, the printers often inserting apologies to the reader for any perceived carelessness and lists of errata to compensate for outright mistakes but rarely apologizing for the absence of the author's name.

Diella, Certain Sonnets, Adjoined to the Amorous Poem of Dom Diego and Ginevra identifies its author only as "R. L., Gentleman." The volume is dedicated to Lady Anne Glemnham by the bookseller Henry Olney, who refers to the author of *Diella* as "a gallant gentleman" but does not name him. A suggestion that *Diella* might be attributed to Richard Lylesse, a scholar of King's College, Cambridge, has received no support, and Richard Lynche is generally accepted as the author. Alexander B. Grosart in his 1877 edition of Lynche's poems bases his acceptance of Lynche's authorship on his readings of the two prose translations in which Lynche's name appears in full and suggests that the classical name "Lynceus" in sonnet 22 of *Diella* may be a clue to the poet's identity.

The thirty-nine sonnets of *Diella* are fairly conventional love poems, but several (such as the two numbered 13) experiment with the form. The repetition of a sonnet number, not a usual practice, seems deliberate here, as the two poems are linked by punctuation and the second continues to explore the

Diella,
Certaine Sonnets, adioy-
ned to the amorous Poeme of
Dom Diego and *Gineura.*
(∵)

By R. L. Gentleman.

Ben balla, á chi fortuna fuona,

AT LONDON,
Printed for *Henry Olney,* and are
to be fold at his fhop in Fleetftreete,
neer the Middle-temple gate.
1 5 9 6.

Title page for Richard Lynche's sonnet sequence

same theme as the first, forming an expanded or double sonnet. As the second 13 has only twelve lines and its rhyme scheme follows from the previous poem, the two form, in effect, a single twenty-six-line poem.

Lynche has been criticized for expressing too explicitly the frustrated sonneteer's sexual desire in sonnets 3, 4, 31, and 32. Number 3 is, in fact, a catalogue of the mistress's "rare-shaped parts," a series of strictly conventional metaphors leading to a commonplace conclusion in the couplet: "Her other parts so far excel the rest, / That wanting words, they cannot be expressed." Number 4 is just as innocuous. The other two form a linked pair, lines 1 and 3 of the second repeating lines 14 and 13 of the first, respectively, and the same theme and imagery are explored throughout, resulting in an expanded catalogue, or blazon. The problem for some readers seems to be that of the itemized charms, the poet clearly preferring

those lily rounds which ceaseless hold their moving,
From whence my prisoned eyes would ne'er be gone
which to such beauties are exceeding loving;
O, that I might but press their dainty swelling,
and thence depart to which must now be hidden,
And which my crimson verse abstains from telling,
because by chaste ears I am so forbidden;
There in the crystal-paved vale of pleasure,
Lies locked up a world of richest treasure.

However, like the couplet in number 3, this pair of sonnets terminates in ideas that finally "cannot be expressed." Decorum ultimately intercedes, resulting in images that may be tantalizing, even titillating, but hardly obscene. Without these occasional refreshingly honest expressions of desire, most of the sonnets in *Diella* might be scarcely distinguishable from hundreds of other Elizabethan love sonnets.

Another redeeming feature is Lynche's use of language: his extensive and varied vocabulary, as well as his frequent use of compound epithets and unusual words – particularly in the early sonnets – lends interest to what otherwise would be trite. Like many sonneteers, Lynche draws upon classical mythology for parallels to illustrate the unhappy situation of the poet-lover, but his allusions are heavy-handed, consisting mainly of a generous sprinkling of the names of mythological characters throughout the sequence. Two sonnets more skillfully recall certain tales: the fire and flood metaphors of sonnet 1 and the chaotic state of the world of sonnet 14 bring to mind stories such as Ovid's account of the gods' destruction of humankind in the first book of *Metamorphoses.*

The final sonnet in *Diella,* which prefaces *Dom Diego and Ginevra,* is a rare example of a deliberate and direct link between a sonnet sequence and its narrative companion piece. It can be no coincidence that in *Diella,* whose title clearly recalls Samuel Daniel's *Delia,* the sonneteer beseeches his loved one to hear a narrative that might move her, much as Delia is appealed to by the ghostly narrator of Daniel's *Complaint of Rosamond.* The circumstances are different, Diella being invited to listen to a story of requited love, but the device linking the poems in each case is similar. However, Lynche's effort to create a suitable link is not as subtle as Daniel's, and the result is rather artificial in light of the previous sonnet, which ends in despair and was no doubt originally the final sonnet in the sequence:

> Never did one account of woman more,
>   than I of her, nor ever woman yet,
> Respected less, or held in lesser store
>   her lover's vows, than she by mine doth set.
> What resteth then, but I despair and die,
> That so my death may glut her ruthless eye.

After these lines the reader does not expect anything more; thus the sudden reversal of mood and renewed hope in sonnet 38 sound like a last desperate effort to persuade the mistress, a technique Michael Drayton so elegantly employs in his best-known sonnet, "Since There's No Help" (in *Idea,* 1619). The octave of sonnet 38, in fact, is a synopsis of the story the poet asks Diella to hear or read. This final sonnet is also the first in which Diella's name occurs, as if Lynche realized that the poem needed to be linked back to the sonnet sequence as well as to *Dom Diego and Ginevra:*

> Harken awhile (Diella) to a story,
>   that tells of beauty, love, and great disdain,
> The last, caused by suspect; but she was sorry

> that took that cause, true love so much to pain,
> For when she knew his faith to be unfeigned,
>   spotless, sincere, most true, and pure unto her,
> She joyed as if a kingdom she had gained,
>   and loved him now as when he first did woo her.
> I ne'er incurred suspicion of my truth,
>   (fairest Diella) why wilt thou be cruel?
> Impose some end to undeserved ruth,
>   and learn by others how to quench hate's fuel.
> Read all, my dear, but chiefly mark the end,
> And be to me, as she to him, a friend.

Diella has attracted little critical attention, and only Grosart is at all enthusiastic, maintaining that "the finest and most noticeable things are inspired by an undoubtedly real and not merely poetical 'passion.'" He praises Lynche's use of colors and the picturesque quality of his images, although he finds the frankness of some sonnets to "cross the border of modesty." Most readers, such as Sidney Lee in *Elizabethan Sonnets* (1904), find the poems entirely conventional: "R. L.'s sonnets are typically servile in their repetition of well-worn phrases and imagery." Lu Emily Pearson assesses *Diella* as "a strange jumble of inarticulate ideas," half praising, half criticizing Lynche's attempt to move into new areas of sonneteering while maintaining old conventions in awkward juxtaposition. She also criticizes what she perceives to be "frank and lustful praise of physical charms for their own sake . . . the other side of love poetry, the coarse, the obscene."

The sonnets are immediately followed by *The Love of Dom Diego and Ginevra.* The amorous narrative is a verse translation of one of Matteo Bandello's novellas (circa 1554), either from the original or earlier translations. Paul Miller offers the fullest account of possible sources, also suggesting that Lynche's poem imitates Thomas Lodge's *Scilla's Metamorphosis* (1589). Perhaps the fact that *Dom Diego and Ginevra* is even less original than *Diella* contributes to the general lack of interest in this poem. However, Lynche's efforts both to follow and innovate sonneteering fashion must be acknowledged. In transforming the prose narrative into verse, Lynche renders the story a suitable companion piece for his sonnet sequence. In addition, while he borrowed the story, he can be credited with the refreshing addition of a narrative that is not a complaint but which provides a happy ending, at least for Diego and Ginevra. Only Spenser's *Amoretti* leads to the same kind of conclusion in *Epithalamion,* a narrative defined by its title as a celebration of a marriage. Finally, it should be noted that Lynche's narrative is unique among those annexed to a sonnet sequence in that it falls into the category of the minor epic for its erotic subject matter, its length, and Lynche's use of rhetorical devices associated with the genre. The poem is written in sixains, with the exception of the final stanza, to which a couplet is added. This couplet and a concluding sonnet refer to *Diella,* strengthening the link between the narrative and the sonnet sequence.

At the same time, Lynche's narrative serves much the same purpose as a complaint. The adventures of Diego, his requited love for Ginevra, and their quarrel and reconciliation are told mostly in the poet's voice, although the voices of Diego, Ginevra, and several minor figures are often heard directly or indirectly. But the poet-narrator uses the story of this pair of lovers in the hope that Diella will be moved to return his love, as Ginevra returns Diego's. A final appeal to Diella is made in the couplet added to the last stanza, which sums up the "happy ever after" conclusion while referring briefly to the earlier ups and downs of the relationship:

These, whilst they lived, did live in all content,
    contending who should love each other most,
To which pure love, proud Fame her ears down lent,
    and through the world, of it doth highly boast.
O happy he to whom love comes at last,
That will restore what hate before did waste.
    Then (dearest love) Gynevryze at the last,
    And I shall soon forget what ere is past.

Lynche's transformation of a proper noun into a verb is probably unique among sonneteers, but not even such a compliment moves the stony-hearted Diella, as the reader learns from the sonnet printed at the end of the narrative poem:

And now farewell, when I shall fare but ill,
    flourish and joy, when I shall droop and languish,
All plenteous good await upon thy will,
    when extreme want shall bring my soul death's anguish
Forced by thee (thou mercy-wanting maid)
    must I abandon this my native soil,
Hoping my sorrow's heat will be allayed
    by absence, time, necessity, or toil.
So, now adieu; the winds call my depart.
    Thy beauty's excellence, my rudest quill
Shall never-more unto the world impart,
    so that it know thy hate, I have my will;

And when thou hear'st that I for thee shall perish,
Be sorrowful. And henceforth true love cherish.

Lynche's poems were not republished in his own time, nor have they been satisfactorily edited. E. V. Utterson in his 1841 edition and Sidney Lee in his anthology *Elizabethan Sonnets* omit *Dom Diego and Ginevra.* Edward Arber's *An English Garner* (1883) offers the entire collection. E. and G. Goldsmids' *The Bookworm's Garner* (1887) essentially reprints Utterson, and Paul Miller's 1967 edition includes a facsimile of only the narrative poem. Grosart alone provides a critical introduction and some notes and is the first to draw attention to the fact that the sonnets and narrative are deliberately linked. There is no recent edition of the entire work, and few of the sonnets are ever anthologized.

Lynche also translated two Italian prose works that have nothing in common with his poetry. The first is *The Fountain of Ancient Fiction* (1599), subtitled "Wherein is lively depictured the images and statues of the gods of the ancients, with their proper and particular expositions." Lynche's dedication to M. Peter Davison, Esquire, expresses gratitude for "courtesies received" while apologizing for offering him "a subject so much disagreeing with your own disposition" and dismissing his work as "a poetical and vain fiction . . . not altogether beseeming the countenance of so grave and worthy a personage." In his address to the reader Lynche claims that he had not intended the work to be printed, that it was "penned and translated for my own exercises and private recreations." He apologizes for the hasty preparation of the work, for errors it might contain, and even for the "shallowness in the not proper understanding of the first author's meaning." But despite this self-deprecation — a common feature of sixteenth-century dedications and addresses — Lynche's translation may have been well received, for his next work appeared two years later. *An Historical Treatise of the Travels of Noah into Europe: Containing the First Inhabitation and Peopling Thereof* (1601) is dedicated to Peter Manwood, Esquire, described by Lynche as an "assured friend" to whom he is grateful for "many kindnesses." The volume offers "a brief recapitulation of the kings, governors, and rulers commanding in the same, even until the first building of Troy by Dardanus."

Because minor Elizabethan poets are generally overshadowed by their better-known and more talented contemporaries, the historical value and literary merit of their work are often ignored. Richard Lynche's career was brief and his work mediocre, but his sonnets and narrative poem make an unusual and innovative contribution to the genre of the Elizabethan sonnet sequence and deserve recognition in their own right as well as for the light they may shed on conventional practices of Renaissance imitation and translation. A critical edition of Lynche's poetry would secure it a place in the genre currently monopolized by the works of Spenser, Shakespeare, Daniel, Lodge, and Fletcher while simultaneously expanding the context in which those poets are studied and conventions are defined.

References:

John Erskine, *The Elizabethan Lyric* (New York: Columbia University Press, 1903), pp. 160–162;

Jeanette Fellheimer, "The Source of Lynche's 'Amorous Poeme of Dom Diego and Gineura,' " *PMLA,* 58 (1943): 579–580;

Paul Miller, Introduction to *Seven Minor Epics of the English Renaissance* (Gainesville, Fla.: Scholars' Facsimiles & Reprints, 1967), pp. vii–xxvii;

Lu Emily Pearson, *Elizabethan Love Conventions* (Berkeley: University of California Press, 1933), pp. 136–138;

René Pruvost, *Matteo Bandello and Elizabethan Fiction* (Paris: Librairie Ancienne Honoré Champion, 1937), pp. 96–97;

Janet G. Scott, *Les Sonnets Elisabéthains: Les Sources et L'apport Personnel* (Paris: Librairie Ancienne Honoré Champion, 1929), pp. 194–197.

John Marston

(7 October 1576 – 25 June 1634)

James P. Bednarz
Long Island University

See also the Marston entry in *DLB 58: Jacobean and Caroline Dramatists.*

BOOKS: *The Metamorphosis of Pigmalions Image. And Certaine Satyres* (London: Printed by J. Roberts for E. Matts, 1598);

The Scourge of Villanie. Three Bookes of Satyres (London: Printed by J. Roberts & sold by J. Buzbie, 1598; revised and enlarged edition, London: J. Roberts, 1599);

Jacke Drums Entertainment: Or, The Comedie of Pasquill and Katherine (London: Printed by T. Creede for R. Olive, 1601);

Loves Martyr: or, Rosalins Complaint, by Marston, Ben Jonson, William Shakespeare, and George Chapman (London: Printed for E. B., 1601);

The History of Antonio and Mellida (London: Printed by R. Bradock for M. Lownes & T. Fisher, 1602);

Antonios Revenge (London: Printed by R. Bradock for T. Fisher, 1602);

The Malcontent (London: Printed by V. Simmes for W. Aspley, 1604);

Eastward Hoe, by Marston, Chapman, and Jonson (London: Printed by G. Eld for W. Aspley, 1605);

The Dutch Courtezan (London: Printed by T. Purfoote for J. Hodgets, 1605);

Parasitaster, or The Fawne (London: Printed by T. Purfoote for W. Cotton, 1606);

The Wonder of Women, or The Tragedie of Sophonisba (London: Printed by J. Windet, 1606);

What You Will (London: Printed by G. Eld for T. Thorppe, 1607);

Histrio-mastix: Or, The Player Whipt (London: Printed by G. Eld for T. Thorp, 1610);

The Insatiate Countesse, by Marston and William Barksted (London: Printed by T. Snodham for T. Archer, 1613);

*The Workes of M*ʳ*. J. Marston* (London: Printed by A. Mathewes for W. Sheares, 1633); republished as *Tragedies and Comedies* (London: Printed by A. Mathewes for W. Sheares, 1633);

Comedies, Tragi-comedies; & Tragedies, Nonce Collection (London, 1652);

Lust's Dominion, or The Lascivious Queen (presumably the same play as *The Spanish Moor's Tragedy*), by Marston, Thomas Dekker, John Day, and William Haughton (London: Printed for F. K. & sold by Robert Pollard, 1657).

Editions: *The Plays of John Marston,* 3 volumes, edited by H. Harvey Wood (Edinburgh: Oliver & Boyd, 1934–1939);

The Poems of John Marston, edited by Arnold Davenport (Liverpool: Liverpool University Press, 1961);

The Malcontent, edited by M. L. Wine, Regents Renaissance Drama Series (Lincoln: University of Nebraska Press, 1964);

Antonio and Mellida: The First Part, edited by G. K. Hunter, Regents Renaissance Drama Series (Lincoln: University of Nebraska Press, 1965);

Antonio's Revenge: The Second Part of Antonio and Mellida, edited by Hunter, Regents Renaissance Drama Series (Lincoln: University of Nebraska Press, 1965);

The Dutch Courtesan, edited by Wine, Regents Renaissance Drama Series (Lincoln: University of Nebraska Press, 1965);

The Fawn, edited by Gerald A. Smith, Regents Renaissance Drama Series (Lincoln: University of Nebraska Press, 1965);

The Malcontent, edited by Bernard Harris, New Mermaids Series (London: Benn, 1967);

The Malcontent, edited by Hunter, Revels Plays (London: Methuen, 1975);

Antonio's Revenge, edited by W. Reavley Gair, Revels Plays (Manchester: Manchester University Press / Baltimore: Johns Hopkins University Press, 1978);

The Fawn, edited by Davis A. Blostein, Revels Plays (Manchester: Manchester University Press /

Baltimore: Johns Hopkins University Press, 1978);

The Wonder of Women or The Tragedy of Sophonisba, edited by William Kemp (New York: Garland, 1979);

The Insatiate Countess, edited by Giorgio Melchiori, Revels Plays (Manchester: Manchester University Press, 1984).

PLAY PRODUCTIONS: *Histriomastix,* London, Paul's theater, 1599;

Antonio and Mellida, London, Paul's theater, 1599–1600;

Lust's Dominion, by Marston, Thomas Dekker, John Day, and William Haughton, London, Rose theater, Spring 1600;

Jack Drum's Entertainment, London, Paul's theater, 1600;

Antonio's Revenge, London, Paul's theater, 1600;

What You Will, London, Paul's theater, 1601;

The Malcontent, London, Blackfriars theater, 1603–1604;

Parasitaster, or The Fawn, London, Blackfriars theater, 1604;

Eastward Ho, by Marston, George Chapman, and Ben Jonson, London, Blackfriars theater, 1604–1605;

The Dutch Courtesan, London, Blackfriars theater, 1605;

The Wonder of Women, or The Tragedy of Sophonisba, London, Blackfriars theater, 1606;

The Spectacle Presented to the Sacred Majesties of Great Britain, and Denmark as They Passed through London, London, 31 July 1606;

The Entertainment of the Dowager-Countess of Darby, Ashby-de-la Zouch in Leicester, 1607;

The Insatiate Countess, by Marston and William Barksted, London, Whitefriars theater, 1608?.

OTHER: Robert Chester, *Loves Martyr; or, Rosalins Complaint* (London: Printed by Richard Field for E. Blount, 1601) – includes four lyrics by Marston;

"Amicis, amici nostri dignissimi, dignissimis," in *Sejanus His Fall,* by Ben Jonson (London: Printed by George Eld for Thomas Thorpe, 1605).

John Marston's current reputation as one of the foremost poet-playwrights of the English Renaissance rests primarily on the strength of *The Malcontent* (1603–1604), the one masterpiece among his comedies that continues to be reprinted in anthologies of Renaissance drama. In his own time, how-ever, Marston made his greatest impact on the London literary scene at the beginning of his career, as a writer of verse satire noted for its stylistic and emotional excess. It was in this medium, first with *Certain Satires* (1598) and soon after with *The Scourge of Villainy* (1598), that he established a literary voice of violent disaffection that shifted through registers of rage, self-justification, melancholy, sadism, and self-doubt. In an age when satirists were generally expected to cultivate an acerbic tone – to adopt the persona of the malcontent in railing against contemporary abuses – *The Scourge of Villainy* distinguished itself in rendering the most truculent, hysterical, and, some would say, obscene voice of late-Elizabethan invective. The most powerful effect that Marston's writing had on nondramatic satire was to elicit condemnation from his peers. The more balanced Horatian tone developed by Ben Jonson would have a far greater impact on the development of formal verse satire in the seventeenth century. Nevertheless, the language of unreconciled alienation that Marston first perfected in verse served as a precedent for the development of satiric rhetoric in both late Elizabethan and early Jacobean drama. The rage of William Shakespeare's Hamlet, King Lear, and Timon, as well as the malice of Thersites and Iago, are generally seen as having been foreshadowed in the language of Marston's *Scourge of Villainy*.

The son of a Coventry landowner and lawyer (after whom he was named) and Marie Guarsi Marston, the daughter of an Italian physician, John Marston was christened on 7 October 1576, born into a world of privilege. In 1594 he received a bachelor's degree from Brasenose College, Oxford, after which he was admitted to the Middle Temple of the Inns of Court, where, residing with his father (a reader), he studied law. A year before his father's death at the end of 1599, however, Marston had already begun to neglect legal studies in order to devote himself to writing literature, first poetry and then drama. Indeed, the main body of his verse appeared in 1598, when his two collections, *The Metamorphosis of Pygmalion's Image and Certain Satires* and *The Scourge of Villainy,* were published anonymously. Thus, while Marston regularly composed plays until about 1608, he published only a few nondramatic poems after 1598: "Satire Nova" – an attack on Joseph Hall, a rival satirist – added to the expanded *Scourge* in 1599; the four short Neoplatonic love lyrics he contributed (along with Jonson, Shakespeare, and George Chapman) to *Love's Martyr* in 1601; and his commendation of Jonson's neoclassical tragedy *Sejanus,* in its first edition of 1605.

Recent scholarship has had a difficult time trying to establish an exact chronology for the inception of Marston's career from 1598 to 1599. In an influential essay titled "John Marston's *Histriomastix* as an Inns of Court Play: A Hypothesis" (1966), Philip J. Finkelpearl argues that Marston had completed his first comedy by the end of 1598, so that he had, from the beginning of his career, simultaneously written poetry and drama. But in "Representing Jonson: *Histriomastix* and the Origin of the Poets' War" (1991), James P. Bednarz seems to confirm, instead, the traditional hypothesis that *Histriomastix* was composed at the end of 1599 for the private theater at St. Paul's.

This theory, in turn, supports the corollated assumption that Marston changed the primary focus of his literary activity from poetry to drama in the second half of 1599, in a move that coincided with the suppression of *Pygmalion's Image* and *The Scourge* by the so-called Order of Conflagration issued in June of that year by John Whitgift, Arch-Bishop of Canterbury, and Richard Bancroft, Bishop of London — the official censors of the Elizabethan press. Evidently angered by what they perceived to be the contentious and salacious tone of contemporary literature, the bishops on 1 June ordered the Stationers' Company (the monopoly of licensed printers) to confiscate from its members about a dozen works by major London writers. These prohibited works included both of Marston's recent volumes; *Skialetheia* (1598), by his cousin Everard Guilpin; the *Satires* (1597) of his rival Joseph Hall; *The Elegies* (1598) of Christopher Marlowe bound up with *The Epigrams* (1598) of John Davies of Hereford; the "snarling satires" of Thomas Middleton's *Micro-Cynicon* (1599); and the controversial pamphlets of Thomas Nashe and Gabriel Harvey. The order also explicitly banned any further publication of "Satires or Epigrams." An official announcement, dated three days later, subsequently gave pride of place to *Pygmalion's Image* and *The Scourge* in its list of books that had been "presently . . . burnt" in the Stationers' Hall.

If Marston had not already anticipated shifting from print to drama as part of an inevitable evolution, the bishops' ban would have furnished him with a concrete incentive to change genres. Consequently, three months after the ban, in September 1599, the impresario Philip Henslowe recorded a payment to Marston, "the new poet," for his collaboration on an unnamed play for the Admiral's Men. Before the year was out, Marston had not only found temporary employment with Henslowe but had also then moved on to write *Histriomastix* (1610)

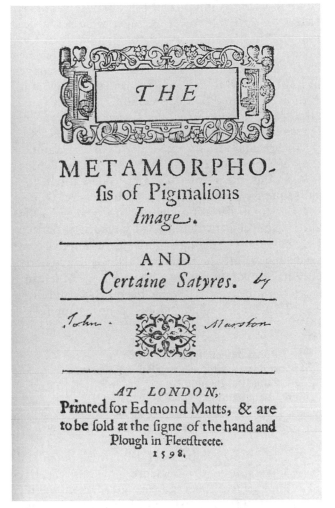

Title page for John Marston's first book, which, along with
The Scourge of Villainy (1598), was suppressed by
John Whitgift's "Order of Conflagration" in June 1599

and *Antonio and Mellida* (1602) for the Boys of St. Paul's.

Although Marston quickly secured a reputation for being a "snarling satirist," he had initially presented himself in a far more ambivalent manner in his first publication, *The Metamorphosis of Pygmalion's Image and Certain Satires,* where he assumes the self-contradictory persona of both a sexual libertine and a severe moralist, whose criticism centers on the denunciation of pleasure. The volume is divided, generically and conceptually, between an erotic mythological narrative in which sexual fantasy is extravagantly rewarded and a collection of five verse satires that characterize pleasure in terms of moral transgression. As a whole, the volume indulges in a sexual fantasy that is then rejected in guilt by its author, who claims he never intended to vindicate pleasure. As Samuel Schoenbaum notes in

"The Precarious Balance of John Marston" (1952), "Marston is unable to countenance what is physical in man, but he cannot avoid contemplating it. This divided response of attraction and revulsion reaches its culmination in the desecration motif, in images of noble or lovely things besmirched and reviled." Although uncited by Schoenbaum, Marston's own attack on *Pygmalion's Image* in *Certain Satires* is a perfect example of this impulse to desecrate the erotic.

Pygmalion's Image expands Ovid's account in the tenth book of *The Metamorphoses* of how Pygmalion sculpts the statue of a girl, Galatea, which is subsequently brought to life by his desire. One of the principal differences between *Pygmalion's Image* and its source is its heightened voyeurism, particularly evident in the long ecphrastic (descriptive) passage cataloguing the parts of Galatea's naked body. Having finished carving her image, Marston's Pygmalion begins to admire his creation and finds what John Donne might call his "centric happiness":

> his eye descended so far down
> That it descried Love's pavillion:
> here Cupid doth enjoy his only crown,
> And Venus hath her chiefest mansion:
> There would he wink, and winking look again,
> Both eyes and thoughts would gladly there remain.

The difference between Marston's poem and its Ovidian source is underscored in a self-reflective joke that surfaces three stanzas later, when, having viewed the "fair proportion of her thigh," Pygmalion is made to cry out to his original creator: "O Ovid . . . Did ere Corinna show such Ivory / When she appeared in Venus' livery?" Pygmalion is here apparently asking for the kind of explicit physical detail that distinguishes Marston from Ovid. To further titillate his readers, Marston even invents an episode in which Pygmalion strips himself naked and takes the statue to bed with him, where,

> fondly doting, oft he kissed her lip.
> Oft would he dally with her ivory breasts.
> No wanton love-trick would he over-slip,
> But full observed all amorous behests,
> Whereby he thought he might procure the love
> Of his dull image, which no plaints could move.

Whatever irony the poem possesses is directed toward a criticism of those who, like Pygmalion, foolishly attempt to escape passion and, as a consequence, suffer the return of the repressed. The poem is thus an indictment of Petrarchan love in favor of what can only be called naturalism. Pygmalion, "whose chaste mind all beauties in Cyprus could not ensnare," is comic only to the extent that he unsuccessfully seeks to resist physical desire and, ironically, as a result fixates on the "dull image" of his own erotic fantasy. Having recognized the "fond dotage" of falling in love "with his own workmanship," his prayer to Venus "to inspire life into his love" is answered in a manner that celebrates the naturalization of desire and simultaneously engages in an act of extreme wish fulfillment that obliterates the difference between fantasy and truth, the imagined and the empirical, the ideal and the real.

Modern critics have, nevertheless, been polarized in their readings of *Pygmalion's Image,* uncertain as to whether or not it contains subtle ironies that negate Marston's libertine stance. One group (including Douglas Bush and Anthony Caputi) has maintained that the poem is a generic burlesque that deconstructs its advocacy of sexual desire by canceling, through irony, whatever superficial concessions it makes to a putative romance narrative. Another group (including Arnold Davenport, C. S. Lewis, and Finkelpearl) has rejected this premise, arguing instead that even though Marston's poem contains ironic elements, its final effect is to sanction rather than censure libido. It was for this reason, they conclude, that the poem conforms to, rather than parodies, an Ovidian norm.

It is certainly not difficult to understand why some readers have interpreted *Pygmalion's Image* as a literary burlesque or mock-epyllion, or minor epic, since this opinion was first set forth by Marston himself. First, in an ironic epilogue titled "The Author in Praise of His Precedent Poem," Marston preempts criticism by refusing to be lashed by "the whips of epigrammatists" for having constructed an Ovidian narrative, because, he states, they have misunderstood the "dissembling shifts" he uses to expose vice. These shifts would apparently include parody, and he consequently mocks those who assume "I . . . thought my poem good, when I see / My lines are froth." Then, in the sixth satire of *The Scourge,* he again bluntly states that only a gullible faultfinder could assume that he wrote "Such nasty stuff as is *Pygmalion*" in a state of "sad seriousness":

> Thinkst thou, that I, which was create to whip
> Incarnate fiends
> . . . .
>   will lisp (sweet love)
> Or pule (aye me) some female soul to move?
> Thinkst thou, that I in melting poesy
> Will pamper itching sensuality?
> (That in the body's scum all fatally
> Intombs the soul's most sacred faculty.)
>   Hence, thou misjudging Censor, know I wrote

Those idle rhymes to note the odious spot
And blemish that deforms the lineaments
Of modern Poesy's habiliaments.

Reading *Pygmalion's Image* in this way has the advantage of providing a unified interpretation of Marston's first volume of poems that places him among the vanguard of a new generation of writers who dismissed the romantic culture of their immediate predecessors as being both emotionally and philosophically unsatisfying.

The only problem with this reading of *Pygmalion's Image* is that it distorts the poem's meaning. The primary emphasis of the work's Ovidian irony dwells on the folly of attempting to resist desire. By no stretch of the imagination does it illustrate how "the body's scum . . . / Intombs the soul's most sacred faculty." In fact, one of the most agreeable aspects of Marston's narrative is the manner in which he scrupulously redeems the pleasure principle – so crucial to Ovid's account – from the anti-sexual imposed allegories of the medieval *Ovide moralisé* tradition. Marston's *Pygmalion's Image* participates in the Renaissance drive to free Ovid from the encrustations of the stultifying and often absurd layer of didactic theory that the classical text had acquired. In stanza 14 Pygmalion is not mocked for feeling desire, only for preferring the fantasy of "his own art" to the substance of living woman:

> Look how the peevish papists crouch, and kneel
> To some dumb idol with their offering,
> As if a senseless carved stone could feel
> The ardor of his bootless chattering,
>   So fond he was, and earnest in his suit
>   To his remorseless image, dumb and mute.

Critics have noticed an undercurrent of mockery and jocularity in Marston's poem, but irony is absent from the final scene of sexual gratification, when Pygmalion is granted the distinction of having his sexual fantasy realized. One could argue that Marston's view of sexuality is defective, since it tends to reduce women conceptually to the status of a male fantasy. Galatea's name does not appear even once in the entire poem; she is merely an "image," or a figment of Pygmalion's imagination. Rather than concentrating on a pattern of reciprocal and mutually realized desire, Marston creates an adolescent fantasy – a perfect sex object – and then describes the summit of pleasure as being the moment in which that fantasy comes to life. Aside from this problem with the enunciation of desire, what is refreshing about Marston's poem, however, is its relative lack of guilt in a society dominated by sex-

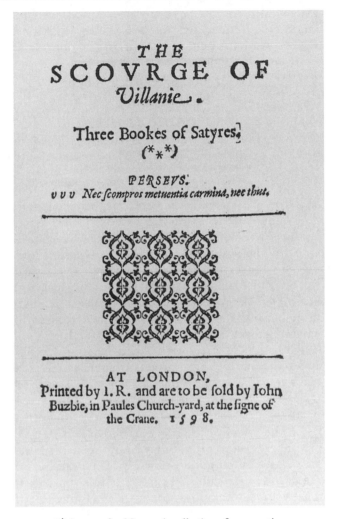

Title page for Marston's collection of verse satires

ual repression. In this regard alone Marston's poem surpasses its two important precedents by Marlowe and Shakespeare and might be seen as challenging the limitations they place on desire.

Unlike Marlowe's *Hero and Leander* (1598) or Shakespeare's *Venus and Adonis* (1593), which explore the tension between erotic fantasy and a tragic reality that negates desire, *Pygmalion's Image* celebrates the absolute triumph of libido. Pygmalion is ridiculous only to the extent that he believes he can be satisfied by a lifeless ideal, by a figure analogous to the typical Petrarchan mistress. It would be an exaggeration to state that *Pygmalion's Image* is pornographic, although Marston does devote considerable space to describing female anatomy and concludes by encouraging his male readers to imagine what they would do if they had the opportunity "to let one pair of sheets contain / The willing bodies of those loving twain." Then he asks, "Who knows not what ensues?" before apologizing both to those who would like to hear more and to those who might be offended by "the loose lines" that have slipped from his pen, in a poem that he defends as "wanton" but "not obscene." Marston, in other words, was far more implicated in romantic culture than he was willing to admit, but he neutralized the repressed guilt he felt in writing *Pygmalion's Image* by adopting a high moral tone, voicing disgust for the paradigm of sexuality he had, in fact, sanctioned. In order to write *Pygamlion's Image,* Marston had also to repress it.

It is only in the latter half of the volume that Marston assumes, for the first time, his even more notorious voice of moral indignation. *Certain Satires* comprises five poems, the first three of which provide a synoptic survey of satiric stereotypes. Following the loosely organized structure of classical Roman satire – established by Horace, Juvenal, and Persius – Marston's satires usually consist of a narrator haranguing a series of straw men accused of various moral crimes. A thematic format is established by having each of the satires begin with references to interlocking Latin tags such as *Quaedam videntur, et non sunt* (What is seen and is not) or *Quaedam sunt, et no videntur* (What is, and is not seen).

The effect of the first three satires is to give the impression of providing a comprehensive overview of contemporary society. The shape of Marston's verse satire, like much of this genre written by his contemporaries, such as Donne, Hall, and John Weever, is fluid and elusive. The one serious attempt to define its literary pattern – Mary Claire Randolph's "The Structural Design of Formal Verse Satire" (1942) – remains unconvincing. Taken as a group, however, late-Renaissance satirists did have favorite satiric stereotypes that distinguished them from their predecessors. As Alvin Kernan asserts in *The Cankered Muse: Satire of the English Renaissance* (1959), "Where the standard targets of medieval satire had been the clergy and professional men who were more concerned for their individual welfare than the good of the Christian commonwealth, the common butts of the new satire are the members of the rising middle class, the new-made knights, the yeomen's sons come to London to the Inns of Court, the merchant adventurer who buys a great estate and a coat-of-arms."

Despite the wide variety of specimens showcased in *Certain Satires,* they are for the most part drawn from Marston's own social class, the gentry. He is particularly caustic toward the young men he identifies as "gallants," especially those who try to advance themselves through fraud, indulge in con-

spicuous consumption, or submit to the "circuity" of sexual desire. It is in this context, for instance, that we find "the absolute Castilio," a man of fashion, "famous for his revelling" (satire 3.41), whose "queer substance" stripped of "ceremonious compliment" is called worthless and absurd. "O age!" Marston complains, "in which our gallants boast to be / Slaves unto riot and rude luxury!" Outside of the gallants, who would presumably comprise the majority of his readers, Marston concentrates on several divergent types to which the gentry were exposed, such as the pretentious parasite and the lecherous soldier.

The fourth satire ("Reactio") breaks this continuity by posing a personal attack on Hall's literary criticism, as the social parody of *Certain Satires* is broadened by the inclusion of specific literary invective. Many of the vices that Marston had earlier evoked involve either abuses of language or literature; for example, he constantly amuses himself by citing the absurdity of hyperbolic love poetry. Luscus, for instance, is ridiculed in satire 11 of *The Scourge of Villainy* because he can speak "Naught but pure *Juliet* and *Romeo*" after having seen Shakespeare's play performed at the Curtain Theater. But it is only one rival – the satirist Hall, who had claimed to be the first man to publish English satires in his *Virgidemiae* of 1597 – that Marston identifies as his principal target. Hall had begun *Virgidemiae* with a critique of contemporary poetry, and Marston moves through Hall's satire, point by point, to support his own position: that the only defect to be found in modern English poetry is Hall's lack of judgment. "Who cannot rail? – what dog but dare to bark," Marston asks, "'Gainst Phoebus' brightness in the silent dark?"

A movement toward closure, based on self-contradiction, is made in the fifth satire, which concludes the volume with a mythological poem citing the moral transgressions of the classical gods, especially their acts of fraud and sexual perversion, to show how "odious villainy" is "rewarded with high dignity." The final satire consequently serves to invalidate the norm of Ovidian eroticism presented in *Pygmalion's Image,* as Marston engages in a final act of self-cancellation.

The Scourge of Villainy, Marston's second and last volume of poems, published several months later, recapitulates the basic satiric concerns of *Certain Satires.* Yet there are subtle differences between the two collections. The tone of *The Scourge* is slightly more defiant and embattled, and the poet adds even more defensive material, justifying both his subject matter and its dark style. Where his first publication had been offered, perhaps ironically, to "good opinion," the source of honor, the second is sardonically dedicated "To his most esteemed and best beloved Self" and presented "To Detraction":

> Foul canker of fair virtuous action,
> Vile blaster of the freshest blooms on earth,
> Envy's abhored child, Detraction.
> I here expose, to thy all-tainting breath,
>   The issue of my brain: snarl, rail, bark, bite.

In the ten satires of *The Scourge,* Marston also expands the treatment of topics he covers, so that, for instance, the range of his religious satire is more fully developed into coordinated attacks on both Catholics and Puritans in satire 2. "Democritus," he urges, "sport at the madness of that hotter clime, / Deride their frenzy, that for policy / Adore wheat dough as real deity." But, he adds, "I am vexed" as well "by lewd precisians, / Who, scorning Church-rites, take the symbol up / As slovenly as careless courtiers slurp / Their mutton gruel!"

The Scourge also exhibits an increased interest in the taboo subject of sexual perversion, which Marston includes to shock his readers further. Here, the reader encounters the astronomer whose "whore / And sister are all one" (satire 1); dissolute gentlemen who frequent brothels where they account it "royal, to be last in thirtieth slime" (satire 2); and Luscus, who feeds "his monstrous lust" at (the suddenly allegorical) Hogsdon, where he keeps "a bawdy-house of beasts" (satire 3).

But the social and literary criticism of *The Scourge* is, for the most part, indistinguishable from that of its predecessor. With the exception of satire 6, "Hem nostri'n" (a defense of *Pygmalion's Image and Certain Satires*), and "Satire Nova" (placed between verses nine and ten in the second edition of 1599), which are specific in their critiques, the new poems are similarly arranged as a loosely united series of satires, outlined under general rubrics – such as *Fronti nulla fides* (appearances cannot be trusted), which prefaces the first satire, and, from Juvenal, *Difficile est satyram non scribere* (it is difficult not to write satire), which begins the second.

Among the poems of *The Scourge,* one is perhaps his best work: "Satire 7: A Cynic Satire." The poem assumes the shape of a conversation between a narrator convinced that not a single human being can be found alive and a second interlocutor who insists that the streets are teeming with them:

> A man, a man, a kingdom for a man!
> Why, how now currish, mad Athenian?
> Thou Cynic dog, see'st not the streets do swarm

> With troops of men? No, no: for Circe's charm
> Hath turned them all to swine. . . .
>   For that same radiant shine –
> That luster wherewith Nature's nature decked
> Our intellectual part – that gloss is soiled
> With staining spots of vile impiety,
> And muddy dirt of sensuality.
> These are no men, but apparitions,
> *Ignes fatui,* glowworms, fictions,
> Meteors, rats of Nilus, fantasies,
> Colosses, pictures, shades, resemblances.

Taking on the voice of Shakespeare's Machiavellian Richard III and the cynic philosopher Diogenes (who walked through the marketplace with a lantern, in daylight, looking for an honest man), Marston resists the theory that moral integrity can be discovered in the contemporary world. Anticipating Donne's similar analysis of universal transgression in "The Anatomy of the World," Marston ends satire 7 in even greater despair, afraid that "the slime, that from our souls do flow," might have made it impossible for humanity to regain its lost "cognisance." Satire 7 documents the point at which Renaissance satire, under pressure from Renaissance skepticism, negates its putative teleology of reforming society and loses its way in an abyss of agonizing self-doubt.

Marston had initially referred to himself as "Epictetus," after the ancient Greek Stoic philosopher, at the end of *Certain Satires.* Now, in a slightly more aggressive mode, he names himself "the scourge of villainy," which he defines as a surrogate to Rhamnusia (the goddess of retributive justice). But *The Scourge* simultaneously fractures this identity into the multiple (but apparently indistinguishable) roles of "Theriomastix" (the whipper of beasts), and "Don Kinsayder" (the "kinser," or castrator, of stray dogs).

Still, whatever he calls himself, the narrative voice Marston projects remains fundamentally unstable, because his justification for engaging in satire continually gives way to sadism, cynicism, and despair. Again, the reader is verbally assaulted by an abusive, alienated speaker who derives sadistic gratification from punishing others. "I bear the scourge of just *Rhamnusia,* / Lashing the lewdness of *Britania,*" he boasts in the proem to the first book; "my vexed thoughtful soul, / Takes pleasure, in displeasing sharp control." Again, the basic self-contradictions concerning his own poetic authority persist. Marston periodically insists on his own moral superiority:

> Know that the Genius, which attendeth on,
> And guides my powers intellectual,

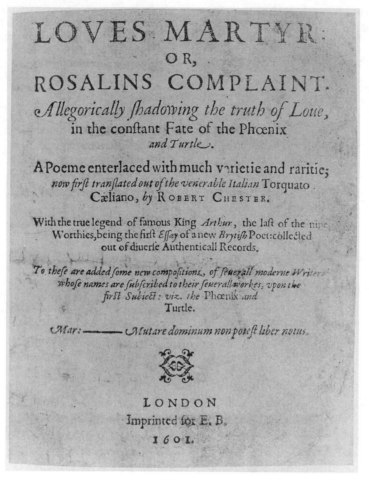

LOVES MARTYR:
OR,
ROSALINS COMPLAINT.
Allegorically shadowing the truth of Loue,
in the constant Fate of the Phœnix
and Turtle.

A Poeme enterlaced with much varietie and raritie;
now first translated out of the venerable Italian Torquato
Cæliano, by ROBERT CHESTER.

With the true legend of famous King Arthur, the last of the nine
Worthies, being the first Essay of a new Brytish Poet: collected
out of diuerse Authenticall Records.

To these are added some new compositions, of seuerall moderne Writers
whose names are subscribed to their seuerall workes, vpon the
first Subiect: viz. the Phœnix and
Turtle.

Mar:――― Mutare dominum non potest liber notus.

LONDON
Imprinted for E. B.
1601.

*Title page for the anthology that includes Marston's final
collection of poems*

Holds in all vile repute Detraction,
My soul an essence metaphysical,
    That in the basest sort scorns Critic's rage,
    Because he knows his sacred parentage. . . .
    Spite of despite, and rancor's villainy,
    I am my self, so is my poesy.

But, having emphasized his mind's "sacred parentage," he nonetheless continues to denounce himself for being as flawed as those he opposes. "He that thinks worse of my rhymes than my self, I scorn him, for he cannot," Marston writes ("To the Judicial Peruser"), and "he that thinks better, is a fool." The same poet who speaks of his readers as being wholly depraved – "I prostitute my Muse, / For all the swarm of idiots to abuse" – also imagines an audience of understanders, an elite group of "diviner wits, celestial souls, / Whose free-born minds no kennel-thought controls."

Apart from the bishops' ban of 1599, Marston's satires were greeted with considerable acri-mony from several contemporary writers. If what he relates in "Satira Nova" is true, Hall, whom he had previously rebuked in *Certain Satires,* was the first critic to travesty Marston, when he caused an epigram characterizing the satirist as a stray dog in need of castration to be pasted into the copies of *Pygmalion's Image and Certain Sonnets* delivered to the Cambridge stationer. This assault was continued by Weever in *The Whipping of the Satyr* (1601), which reprimands Marston at length for his hypocrisy, rage, obscenity, and pretense. "Is it not villainy," Weever asks, "That one should live by reckoning up of vice, / And be a sin-monger professedly, / Involuming offenses for a price?" He continues, "There's no estate but vilely you impeach, / And loudest lies report in lewdest speech." Instead of knowledge, Weever writes, Marston offers a strained philosophical vocabulary, comprised of obscure language, employed only to "filch some praise out of the vulgar's mouth." The anonymous author of *The Return from Parnassus,* a student play produced at

Cambridge during the Christmas festivities of the same year, offered an identical assessment:

> What Monsier Kinsayder, lifting up your leg and piss-
>   ing against the world. . . .
> Methinks he is a ruffian in his style,
> Without band's or garter's ornament,
> He quaffs a cup of Frenchman's Helicon.
> Then roister doister in his oily terms,
> Cuts, thrusts, and foins at whomsoever he meets. . . .
> Tut, what cares he for modest close-couched terms,
> Cleanly to gird our looser libertines. . . .
>   Aye, there is one that backs a paper steed
> And . . .
> Brings the great battering ram of terms to towns
> And at first volley of his cannon shot,
> Batters the walls of the old fusty world.

Marston's odd style, which blends ruffian street language with obscure philosophical diction, seems to have bothered his detractors as much as his obscenity and anger. It was his most persistent critic, Jonson, who first analyzed these stylistic flaws in a systematic manner during the Poets' War, when, after having taken offense with Marston's depiction of him as "Chrisoganus" in *Histriomastix,* Jonson drew three caustic caricatures of Marston as "Clove" in *Every Man Out of His Humour* (1599), "Hedon" in *Cynthia's Revels* (1600), and "Rufus Laberius Crispinus" in *Poetaster* (1601). In an infamous scene at the conclusion of Poetaster (V.iii), Crispinus/ Marston is found guilty of slandering Horace/Jonson and is fed purgative pills that force him to vomit choice specimens of Marston's vocabulary from his poetry and plays. The sole piece of evidence that convicts him is a parody of Marston's verse that combines echoes of *The Scourge* and *Antonio's Revenge* (1602):

> Ramp up, my genius; be not retrograde:
> But boldly nominate a spade a spade.
> What, shall thy lubrical and glibbery Muse
> Live, as she were defunct, like punk in stews?
> Alas! That were no modern consequence,
> To have cothurnal buskins frighted hence.
> No; teach thy incubus to poetize;
> And throw abroad thy spurious snotteries.

Marston published little poetry after *The Scourge,* and what he did print was radically different from his earlier work. The final phase of his poetic career is strangely serene: the bitterness had gone, and his tone had become oddly conciliatory. His last published poem is, ironically, a tribute to Jonson published in the first edition of *Sejanus,* in which the man who might well have been his worst enemy is temporarily embraced as his closest friend.

This period of reconciliation began with Marston's compliment to Jonson in the epilogue to *The Malcontent,* printed in 1604, and ended (after both writers had been imprisoned for collaborating on *Eastward Ho,* 1605) with Marston's snub of Jonson as a slavish imitator in the preface to *Sophonisba,* published in 1606.

In 1601, at the climax of the Poets' War, Marston, Jonson, Shakespeare, and Chapman submitted a series of Neoplatonic lyrics to *Love's Martyr,* a strange compendium of prose and poetry designed to elucidate the iconology of the phoenix as a symbol of transcendence. One measure of the fame Marston had achieved at the turn of the century is found in this volume's reference to him and the three aforementioned poets as the "best and chiefest of our modern writers." Within three years of active writing, he was considered Shakespeare's equal or, at least, to be among the few writers who could bear comparison. Marston himself, however, viewed Shakespeare's writing at this time with particular deference.

Indeed, Marston's first poem, "A Narration and Description of a Most Exact Wondrous Creature, Arising out of the Phoenix and the Turtle Dove's Ashes," is an appreciation of and sequel to Shakespeare's brilliant allegory, "The Phoenix and Turtle," which immediately precedes it in the volume. "O 'twas a moving Epicedium!" Marston begins, after which he goes on to praise both the symbol of the phoenix and Shakespeare's poem: "never came / So strong amazement on astonished eye / As this, this measureless pure rarity." But what, Marston asks, is the meaning of Shakespeare's vision? What does the union of the phoenix and the turtle represent? In the three subsequent poems – "The Description of This Perfection," "To Perfection," and "Perfectioni Hymnus" – Marston provides a complex but redundant answer. The phoenix, he explains in "The Description," is nothing less than perfection itself:

> To this, Earth's purest was unclean
>   Which virtue even instructed.
>
> By it all Being's decked and stained,
> *Ideas* that are idly fained
>   Only here subsist invested.
>
> Dread not to give strained praise at all,
> No speech is hyperbolical,
>   To this perfection blessed.

What then is perfection? Does it somehow adhere to physical reality or is it, instead, a mental con-

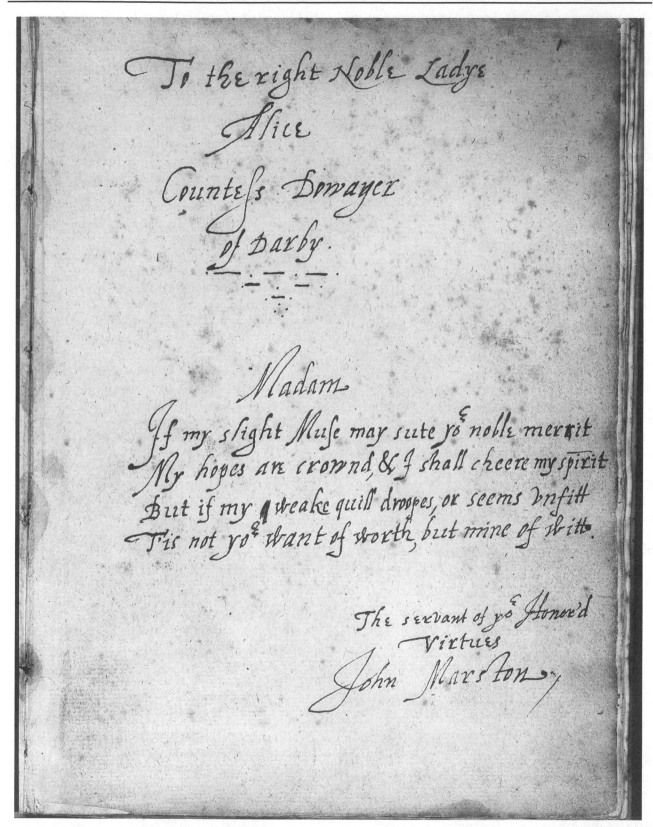

The presentation address and first page of the concluding eclogue, in Marston's hand, from the manuscript for the 1607 Entertainment of the Dowager-Countess of Darby *(Henry E. Huntington Library and Art Gallery, E. L. 34. B9)*

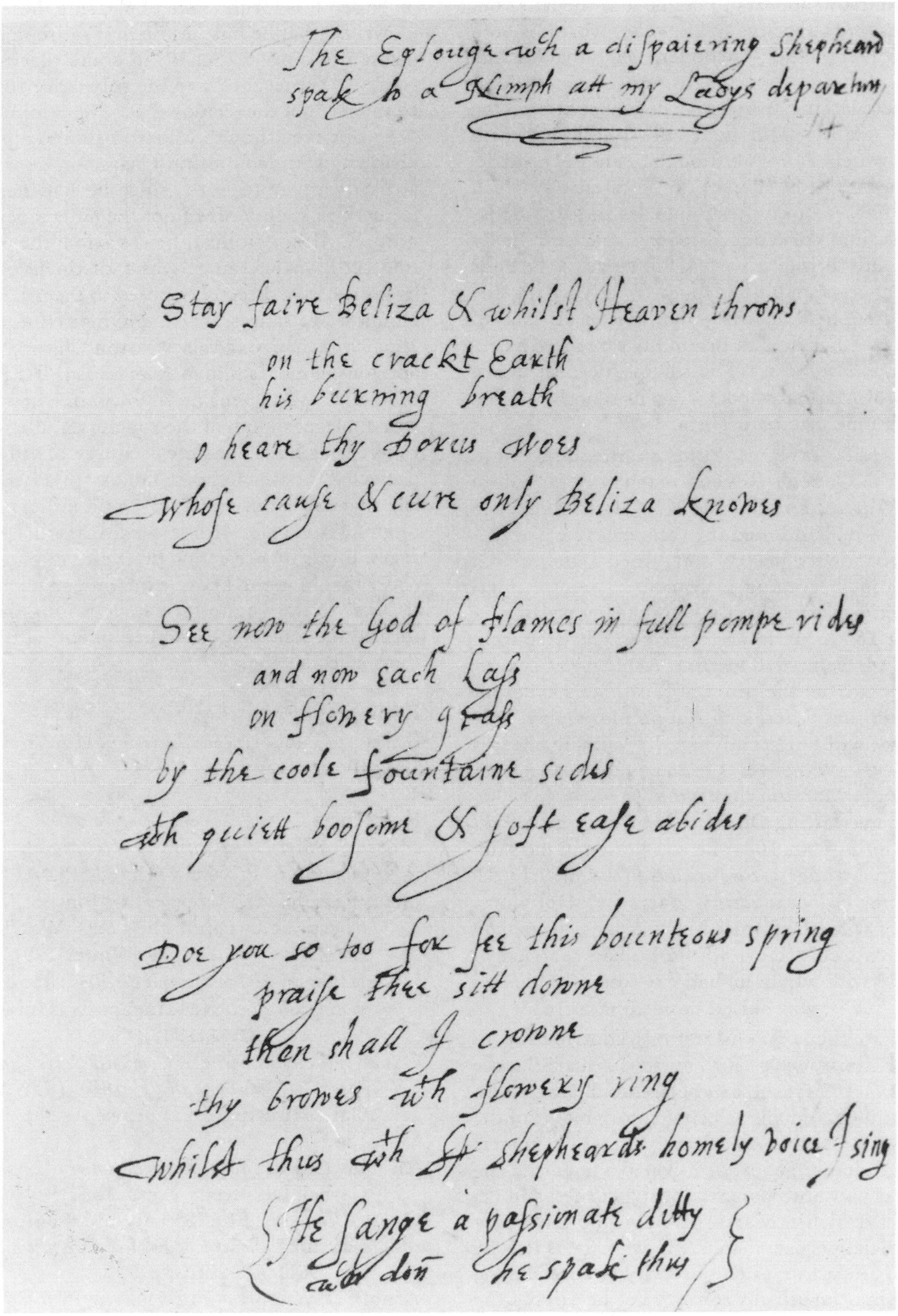

The Eglouge wch a dispairing Shepheard
spake to a Nimph att my Ladys departure

Stay faire Beliza & whilst Heaven throws
on the crackt Earth
his burning breath
o heare thy Dorus woes
Whose cause & cure only Beliza knowes

See now the God of flames in full pompe rides
and now each Lass
on flowery grass
by the coole fountaine sides
wth quiett boosome & soft ease abides

Doe you so too for see this bounteous spring
praise thee sitt downe
then shall I crowne
thy browes wth flowery ring
whilst thus wth ye shepheards homely voice I sing

{He sange a passionate ditty
wch don he spake thus}

struct? Marston appears to define it as the latter but then goes on to specify, ambiguously, that it is both "Deep contemplation's wonder" *and* "that boundless *Ens,* that amplest thought transcendeth." Marston's Neoplatonic perspective defines it as both the essential quality of thought and the hidden truth toward which rational thought can only inadequately aspire. It is, at any rate, an essence in which "all is *Mind, /* As far from spot, as possible defining." His final collection of poems in *Love's Martyr* consequently brings his work full circle, as he ends his career as a published poet by advocating the kind of nonphysical love – the love of an idea of perfection – that he had begun his career by mocking in *Pygmalion's Image.* The restless, deconstructive energies of Marston's poetry again cancel its original commitment to naturalism.

In 1608, having sold his shares in the Children of the Queen's Revels, a company for whom he had written plays since 1604, Marston at the age of thirty-two abandoned the theater (as he had previously abandoned poetry) and turned to the Church of England, becoming a deacon in Stanton Harcourt, Oxfordshire, shortly before being ordained a priest in 1609. He later resided at Christchurch, Hampshire, from 1616 to 1631. A measure of his estrangement from literature at this time is apparent in the fact that when a collection of his plays was published, without permission, by William Sheares in 1633, he forced Sheares to remove his name from the volume. Marston dedicated *The Scourge of Villainy* "To everlasting Oblivion," and after he died in London on 25 June 1634, he was buried in the Middle Temple under a tombstone that similarly declared him *Oblivioni Sacrum* (Sacred to Oblivion). Marston's wife, the former Mary Wilkes, the daughter of a church rector, whom he had married in 1605 (and with whom he had one son, who died an infant in 1624), was buried beside him in 1657.

What, then, was Marston's contribution to English Renaissance poetry, outside of his influence on drama? At best, he can be credited, along with Donne and Chapman, as being an originator of the metaphysical style. All three writers are coterie poets who simultaneously cultivated a linguistic medium that was both ostentatiously learned and deliberately difficult. Marston's note "To those that seem judicial perusers" in *The Scourge* states that he hates "to affect too much obscurity and harshness, because they profit no sense." Yet he admits the pressure he feels to make his style even more recondite, from readers who term all satires "bastard" that "are not palpable dark, and so rough writ, that the hearing of them read, would set a man's teeth on edge." It is for the sake of pleasing these readers, he writes, that he has, in the first satire, mistakenly written in a style that is "in some places too obscure." "Yet let me have the substance rough," he counters, "not the shadow."

But even though Marston shared a poetics of obscurity with Donne and Chapman, he was still at a disadvantage to both, since he had neither the former's flexibility of wit nor the latter's depth of erudition. Although his tone is varied, the one thing that set his work apart was a distinctive voice of hysterical rage directly opposed to the urbane wit of Donne's five satires. The anonymous author of *The Return from Parnassus* calls Marston "Furor Poeticus," and Jonson mocks him in *Poetaster* as a "HERCULES in poetry" who "pens high, lofty, in a new stalking strain, bigger than half the rhymers in the town." In reinventing himself as the "scourge of villainy," he projected the Renaissance fantasy of a heroic nihilism that exists only to receive and inflict pain in an ongoing struggle with a world against which it rages. It was by perfecting this voice of bitter melancholy that Marston became infamous as a main contributer to the vogue for satiric railing that transformed the tone of Elizabethan poetry at the end of the sixteenth century.

Bibliography:

Kenneth Tucker, *John Marston: A Reference Guide* (Boston: Twayne, 1985).

References:

Morse S. Allen, *The Satire of John Marston* (Columbus, Ohio: Privately printed, 1920);

James P. Bednarz, "Representing Jonson: *Histriomastix* and the Origin of the Poets' War," *Huntington Library Quarterly,* 54 (Winter 1991): 1–30;

Douglas Bush, *Mythology and the Renaissance Tradition in English Poetry* (Minneapolis: University of Minnesota Press, 1932);

Oscar James Campbell, *Comicall Satyre and Shakespeare's "Troilus and Cressida"* (San Marino, Cal.: Huntington Library, 1938), pp. 135–184;

Anthony Caputi, *John Marston, Satirist* (Ithaca, N.Y.: Cornell University Press, 1961);

Gustav Cross, "The Retrograde Genius of John Marston," *Review of English Literature,* 2 (October 1961): 19–27;

Arnold Davenport, "The Quarrel of the Satirists," *Modern Language Review,* 37 (April 1942): 123–130;

Davenport, ed., *The Whipper Pamphlets* (Liverpool: Liverpool University Press, 1951);

Jonathan Dollimore, *Radical Tragedy* (Chicago: University of Chicago Press, 1986), pp. 29–49;

T. S. Eliot, "John Marston," in his *Elizabethan Essays* (London: Faber & Faber, 1934);

Philip J. Finkelpearl, "From Petrarch to Ovid: Metamorphosis in John Marston's *Metamorphosis of Pygmalion's Image*," *English Literary History*, 32 (September 1965): 333–348;

Finkelpearl, *John Marston of the Middle Temple: An Elizabethan Dramatist in His Social Setting* (Cambridge, Mass.: Harvard University Press, 1969);

Finkelpearl, "John Marston's *Histriomastix* as an Inns of Court Play: A Hypothesis," *Huntington Library Quarterly*, 29 (May 1966): 223–234;

David O. Frantz, " 'Lewd Priapians' and Renaissance Pornography," *Studies in English Literature*, 12 (Winter 1972): 157–172;

Richard Hardin, "Marston's Kinsayder: The Dog's Voice," *Notes and Queries*, 29 (April 1982): 134–135;

R. C. Horne, "Voices of Alienation: The Moral Significance of Marston's Satiric Strategy," *Modern Language Review*, 81 (January 1986): 18–33;

R. W. Ingram, *John Marston* (Boston: Twayne, 1978);

Alvin Kernan, *The Cankered Muse: Satire of the English Renaissance*, Yale Studies in English 142 (New Haven: Yale University Press, 1959), pp. 81–140;

Richard A. McCabe, "Elizabethan Satire and the Bishops' Ban of 1599," *Yearbook of English Studies*, 2 (1981): 188–193;

Lynette McGrath, "John Marston's Mismanaged Irony: The Poetic Satires," *Texas Studies in Literature and Language*, 18 (Fall 1976): 393–408;

David G. O'Neill, "The Commencement of Marston's Career as a Dramatist," *Review of English Studies*, new series 22 (November 1971): 442–445;

John Peter, *Complaint and Satire in Early English Literature* (Oxford: Clarendon Press, 1956), pp. 157–168;

Mary Claire Randolph, "The Structural Design of Formal Verse Satire," *Philological Quarterly*, 21 (October 1942): 368–384;

Samuel Schoenbaum, "The Precarious Balance of John Marston," *PMLA*, 67 (December 1952): 1069–1078;

Steven R. Shelburne, "Principled Satire: Decorum in John Marston's *The Metamorphosis of Pygmalion's Image* and *Certain Satires*," *Studies in Philology*, 86 (Spring 1986): 198–218;

Roscoe Addison Small, *The Stage-Quarrel between Ben Jonson and the So-Called Poetasters* (Breslau: M. & H. Marcus, 1899);

Arnold Stein, "The Second English Satirist," *Modern Language Review*, 38 (October 1943): 273–278;

Elizabeth M. Yearling, "'Mount Tufty Tamburlaine': Marston and Linguistic Excess," *Studies in English Literature*, 20 (Winter 1980): 257–269;

Paul M. Zall, "John Marston, Moralist," *English Literary History*, 20 (September 1953): 186–193.

Elizabeth Melville, Lady Culross

(circa 1585 – 1640)

Carolyn R. Swift
Rhode Island College

BOOK: *Ane Godlie Dreame* (Edinburgh: R. Charteris, 1603); translated by the author into English as *A Godly Dream* (Edinburgh: R. Charteris, 1604?).

Editions: "Ane Godlie Dreame," in *Early Metrical Tales,* edited by David Laing (Edinburgh: W. D. Laing / London: J. Duncan, 1826), pp. 147–169; revised and enlarged by W. Carew Hazlitt in *Early Popular Poetry of Scotland and the Northern Border* (London: Reeves & Turner, 1895), II: 279–301.

OTHER: "A Sonnet Sent to Blackness," in *Early Metrical Tales,* edited by David Laing (Edinburgh: W. D. Laing / London: J. Duncan, 1826), p. xxxii.

Elizabeth Melville first published *Ane Godlie Dreame* in 1603 in Scottish. She translated it into English in an undated edition, probably the next year, and may have revised some of its seventeenth-century editions. Although written in the tradition of medieval dream visions, the poem describes the uniquely personal religious experience of a woman active in the Scottish Reformation. Defining the spiritual quest that governed her whole life, it reveals a Reformation woman's confidence in her theological understanding and manifests her belief (endorsed in her letters as well) that the purpose of poetry is to serve religion. Although no complete twentieth-century edition exists in English, this poem's importance to seventeenth-century Scottish Presbyterians is witnessed by its multiple seventeenth- and eighteenth-century English editions (1606, 1620, 1644, 1680, 1686, 1692, 1698, 1718, and 1737) – more than any other single volume by a British woman who lived before 1640. Letters written to Melville by the Reverend Samuel Rutherford and John Livingstone's references to her in *Memorable Characteristics* (1759) testify to her importance in the struggle with King James VI of Scotland, I of England, leading to the Covenant of 1638, which founded the Presbyterian Church.

Elizabeth Melville was the daughter of Sir James Melville of Halhill, a statesman in the courts of Mary, Queen of Scots, and King James VI of Scotland. His *Memoirs of His Own Times* (first printed in 1683) do not mention his daughter, but his references to poems and his contact with the French statesman and poet Guillaume de Salluste, Seigneur du Bartas, reveal that she was reared in a home that valued poetry as well as statesmanship. She married John Colville of Wester-Cumbrae, who inherited the title and fiscal advantages and responsibilities of commendator of the Abbey at Culross. Since he refused the peerage in 1609, probably because of financial difficulties, Melville's titles of Lady Comrie and Lady Culross were purely honorary. Although modern bibliographers often refer to her by her husband's last name, Colville, she always signed her letters "E. Melvill," using her birth name, as was typical of sixteenth- and seventeenth-century Scottish women. Her letters reveal that she bore at least six children: Alexander, Samuel, James, Robert, John, and a daughter (whose name she does not mention) who had recently died at the time of her mother's correspondence. Only Alexander, Samuel, and James survived their parents. The eldest, Alexander, became a professor of Hebrew and theology at the University of Sedan in France and later at St. Andrews. Samuel may be the Samuel Colville who wrote *The Whig's Supplication; or, The Scots Hudibras* (1681), in which a verse castigates those who cannot find "the jewel" in Lady Culross's dream. Her letters refer to James as serving Sir Robert Ker. As is true of many women of her century, no record exists of either her birth or death.

Eleven letters from 1625 to 1631 are all that remains of Melville's prose: eight written to the minister John Livingstone, two to her son James Colville, and one to Lady Eglinton (among her papers at the University of Edinburgh). These epistles

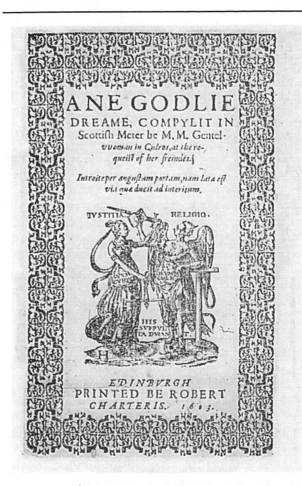

Title pages for the first edition, in Scottish, and the English translation of Elizabeth Melville's religious poem

reflect Melville's efforts to maintain family ties and her concern for her own spiritual well being as well as that of her children and friends. A letter to James reveals tensions in her marriage as she tried to prevent her husband's selling of family land that should have been inherited by their eldest son, Alexander; she yielded only when it became clear that her husband might otherwise be imprisoned for indebtedness. Even so, she vigorously refused to sell until the transaction stipulated Alexander's right to buy the property again. Her husband's financial hardship meant that in middle age Melville traveled extensively by foot or on borrowed horses over rough terrain in difficult weather to take part in Presbyterian gatherings in 1629 and 1630. Even so, Livingstone describes her as the center of prayer and spiritual experiences at the Communion at Shotts in 1630. These and earlier travels influenced her imagery. The hell that she describes in her vision resembles Scottish mountain glens that drop steeply into perilous rivers. Her image of heaven resembles the turreted castles that can still be seen heading glens that she may have struggled to climb

in her home county of Fife and neighboring Stirlingshire.

Besides *A Godly Dream*, the only other extant poetic work by Melville is her "Sonnet Sent to Blackness," written to encourage the minister John Welsh (the son-in-law of John Knox) while he endured the horrors of imprisonment in Blackness Castle in 1605. First printed in 1826, its skillful use of alliteration and internal rhyme furthers its intense evocation of Christ's presence. It confirms the talent revealed in her longer poem, and suggests our loss of the other works she might have published in an age more encouraging to women writers:

My dear Brother, with courage bear the cross;
Joy shall be joined with all thy sorrow here;
High is thy hope; disdain this earthly dross!
Once shall you see the wished day appear.
Now it is dark, thy sky cannot be clear;
After the clouds, it shall be calm anon;
Wait on His will, whose blood hath bought you dear;
Extol His name, though outward joys be gone.
Look to the Lord, thou art not left alone.
Since He is there, what pleasure canst thou take!

He is at hand, and hears thy heavy moan;
End out thy faught [fight], and suffer for his sake!
A sight most bright thy soul shall shortly see,
When store of glore thy rich reward shall be.

The Scottish first edition of *Ane Godlie Dreame* cites its author as "M. M." (presumably, "Mistress Melville"), but the title pages in other early editions name the author "Elizabeth Melville, Lady Culross the Younger." The title pages of all editions explain that the volume was "compiled . . . at the request of a friend" or "friends." This customary apology protected the author's modesty in an age when publication would have been a breach of chastity. At the same time, it acknowledges interest of her friends, and like its many editions, proclaims the poem's importance to Scottish Calvinists.

The sixty stanzas of *A Godly Dream,* each eight lines in iambic pentameter, divide into three sections. In the first stanza the poet as pilgrim mourns "full sore," grieving her spiritual failures, a common early Protestant religious practice. Depicting the heaviness that "so mischieved" her heart, Melville vividly describes a religious melancholy such as that Robert Burton later defined in *Anatomy of Melancholy* (1621). Like a modern depressive, she "loathed" her life; she was unable to eat, sleep, or speak, "but mused alone."

In the second, prophetic section, beginning in the twelfth stanza, Melville finds consolation after she falls asleep and dreams that Jesus becomes her close companion: "through ditches deep . . . / Through pricking thorns, through water and through fire, / Through dreadful dens which made my heart aghast, / He bare me up." On the journey Jesus also grants the poet a view of the heaven she will someday gain when her trials on earth end. "I looked up unto that castle fair, / Glistering like gold and shining bright: / The stately towers did mount above the air, / They blinded me they cast so great a light." Elated at seeing the heavenly castle, she runs to climb its steps alone. She does not even ask the way "because I thought [I] kenned it." Angered at her pride, Jesus warns, "Without my help thinkst thou to climb so high? / Come down again, thou yet must suffer more / If thou desirest that dwelling place to see." Together they enter "a pit most black," which causes the poet to question, "Is this . . . the Papist's purging place?" Jesus answers with the Protestant Reformation view that greed caused "the brain of man" to invent Purgatory; instead, "This pit is Hell." Terrified by the sight of "Poor damned souls tormented sore for sin, / In flaming fire . . . frying wonder fast," her "faith grew weak," and she "begouth [began] to fall." Her nightmare startles her awake, "crying aloud, Lord Jesus, come again." In the conclusion of this visionary section, Melville recognizes her own spiritual authority as she determines "to write the same, and keep it still in mind."

Aware that her vision might benefit other struggling Christians, Melville explicates its theological significance in her concluding section. These final eighteen stanzas suitably complete her several roles in the poem: pilgrim, prophet, and preacher. Throughout, Melville takes upon herself the Christian duty of imitating Jesus and draws her words and images from Thomas Sternhold and John Hopkins's *Whole Book of Psalms* (1562) and from the Basandyne Bible of 1576.

On the last page of all early editions of *A Godly Dream* is a short lyric, "Away, Vain World." It is preserved among the manuscript poems of Alexander Montgomerie (donated by Drummond of Hawthornden to the University of Edinburgh Library in 1627) and was later printed with Montgomerie's collected *Poems* (1821). Because it was common for Renaissance poets to copy each other's poems for their own use, it is as reasonable to conjecture that Montgomerie copied Melville's text as that she copied his. Even if this poem is by Montgomerie, its inclusion with Melville's vision demonstrates her connection with the Scottish poets of her age.

Critical comment on Melville has been both rare and disparate. Her contemporary Alexander Hume dedicated to her his *Hymns or Sacred Songs wherein the Right Use of Poesy May Be Espied* (1599); he describes her as "a tender youth, solitaire, and sanctified" and praises her "compositions so copious, so pregnant, so spiritual, that I doubt not but it is the gift of God in you." John Armstrong asks in his *Miscellanies* (1770) about Melville's "old composition, now I am afraid lost, perhaps because it was almost *too terrible for the ear*." He describes its "dreadful wild expressions of distraction and melancholy." But John Pinkerton responds vigorously in *Scottish Tragic Ballads* (1781) that "this composition is neither lost, nor is it too terrible for the ear. On the contrary, a child might hear it repeated, in a winter night, without the smallest emotion." He recognizes that "the [dread] and melancholy of this production are solely of the religious kind, and may have been deeply affecting to the enthusiastic at the period in which it was wrote." Pinkerton justifies his ad-

Last page of a letter from Melville to her brother (University of Edinburgh Library, Ms. La III 347)

miration by quoting *A Godly Dream* at length. In "Lady Culross's Dream" (1859) Rosina Bulwer-Lytton conjectures that Armstrong had mistaken Melville's work for an earlier ballad; a scholar identified only as "T. G. S." also responds to Armstrong by extolling Melville's *Godly Dream* as "one of the books of the people," recognizing that she was expressing her "longing to be at rest" through "brooding over her sins and the wretchedness of this world." David Laing suggests in *Early Metrical Tales* (1826) that Melville's dream-pilgrimage may have influenced John Bunyan's *Pilgrim's Progress* (1678). It is also possible that her descriptions of nature influenced William Wordsworth, since the great Romantic poet's signature is on the title page of an edition of Laing's *Metrical Tales* at the Houghton Library at Harvard University. Laing viewed *A Godly Dream* as a poem of "considerable beauty and imagination" and blamed its current invisibility on critics' prejudice or their "want of taste and discernment." Alexander Lawson comments in his 1902 edition of Alexander Hume's poetry that *A Godly Dream* "used not a little art. It is singularly vivid and in parts picturesque, and it shows keen religious insight, deep spiritual conviction, and a feeling of the terrible which is never monotonous."

Even after the women's liberation movement, with its development of feminist criticism, led to renewed interest in women as writers, too little attention has been paid to Melville. Anthologies by Betty Travitsky in 1981 and Germaine Greer in 1988 include brief comments on *A Godly Dream* as religious verse. In *Redeeming Eve: Women Writers of the English Renaissance* (1987), Elaine Beilin more extensively examines the poem as part of the Renaissance tradition of women's responses to Christian condemnation of Eve. For Beilin, Melville expresses "the faith of her sect: an almost overwhelming sense of human depravity coupled with the infinitely sustaining mercy of God which will guide the chosen to immortal life." She praises Melville's "poetic confidence" and recognizes her as establishing a woman's "persona at the center of her poem, whether as poet, Christian pilgrim, recipient of God's grace, exemplum, or teacher." Melville's early Protestant poem of abiding, melancholy beauty deserves more recognition in the future than it has had in the past.

Letters:

"Letters from Lady Culross, Etc.," in *Select Biographies,* edited by W. K. Tweedie (Edinburgh: Wodrow Society, 1845), I: 349–370.

References:

James Anderson, *Ladies of the Covenant: Memoirs of Distinguished Scottish Female Characters, Embracing the Period of the Covenant and the Persecution* (New York: A. C. Armstrong, 1880), pp. 49–62;

Elaine Beilin, *Redeeming Eve: Women Writers of the English Renaissance* (Princeton: Princeton University Press, 1987), pp. 107–110;

Rosina Bulwer-Lytton, "Lady Culross's Dream," *Notes and Queries,* second series 8 (24 September 1859): 247–248;

David Laing, ed., *Early Metrical Tales* (Edinburgh: W. D. Laing / London: J. Duncan, 1826), pp. xxix–xxxvi;

James Melville, *Memoirs of His Own Life 1549–1593* (Edinburgh: Bannatyne Club, 1827);

T. G. S., "Lady Culross's Dream," *Notes and Queries,* second series 8 (15 October 1859): 311–313;

Betty Travitsky, ed., *The Paradise of Women: Writings by English Women of the Renaissance,* Contributions in Women's Studies 22 (Westport, Conn. & London: Greenwood Press, 1981), pp. 25–29.

Papers:

Manuscripts of Elizabeth Melville's extant letters are in the University of Edinburgh Library (shelf mark La III 347).

Anthony Munday

(October 1560 – August 1633)

Richard H. Branyan
Grace–St. Luke's Episcopal School, Memphis

See also the Munday entry in *DLB 62: Elizabethan Dramatists.*

BOOKS: *The Mirrour of Mutabilitie, or Principall Part of the Mirrour for Magistrates* (London: Printed by J. Allde, sold by R. Ballard, 1579);

The Paine of Pleasure, attributed to Munday (London: Printed by J. Charlewood for H. Car, 1580);

A View of Sundry Examples. Reporting Many Straunge Murthers (London: Printed by J. Charlewood for W. Wright, sold by J. Allde, 1580);

Zelauto. The Fountaine of Fame (London: Printed by J. Charlewood, 1580);

A Courtly Controuersie betweene Looue and Learning (London: Printed by J. Charlewood for H. Carre, 1581);

The Araignement and Execution of a Wilfull and Obstinate Traitor, named E. Ducket, alias Hauns (London: Printed by J. Charlewood for E. White, 1581);

A Breefe Discourse of the Taking of Edmund Campion (London: Printed by J. Charlewood for W. Wright, 1581);

A Discouerie of Edmund Campion and His Confederates (London: Printed by J. Charlewood for E. White, 1582);

A Breefe Aunswer Made vnto Two Seditious Pamphlets (London: Printed by J. Charlewood, 1582);

A Breefe and True Reporte, of the Execution of Certaine Traytours at Tiborne (London: Printed by J. Charlewood for W. Wright, 1582);

The English Romayne Lyfe (London: Printed by J. Charlewoode for N. Ling, 1582);

A Watch-Woord to Englande to Beware of Traytours (London: Printed by J. Charlewood for T. Hacket, 1584);

Fedele and Fortunio. The Deceites in Loue, translation and adaptation, attributed to Munday, of an Italian play by Luigi Pasqualigo (London: Printed by J. Charlewood [?] for T. Hacket, 1585);

A Banquet of Daintie Conceits (London: Printed by J. Charlewood for E. White, 1588);

The First Part of the True and Honorable Historie, of the Life of Sir J. Oldcastle, by Munday, Michael Drayton, Richard Hathway, and Robert Wilson (London: Printed by V. Simmes for T. Pavier, 1600);

The Downfall of Robert, Earle of Huntington, Afterward Called Robin Hood of Merrie Sherwoode, by Munday, revised by Henry Chettle (London: Printed by R. Bradock for W. Leake, 1601);

The Death of Robert, Earle of Huntington, by Munday and Chettle (London: Printed by R. Bradock for W. Leake, 1601);

The Triumphes of Re-United Britania. Performed in Honor of Sir L. Holliday Lorde Mayor. 1605 (London: Printed by W. Jaggard, 1605);

Camp-Bell, or The Ironmongers Faire Field (London: Printed by E. Allde, 1609);

Londons Love, To the Royal Prince Henrie, Meeting Him at His Returne from Richmonde (London: Printed by E. Allde for N. Fosbrooke, 1610);

A Briefe Chronicle of the Successe of Times, from the Creation (London: Printed by W. Jaggard, 1611);

Chruso-Thriambos. The Triumphes of Golde. At the Inauguration of Sir J. Pemberton, in the Dignity of Lord Maior (London: Printed by W. Jaggard, 1611);

Himatia-Poleos. The Triumphes of Old Draperie. At the Enstalment of S. T. Hayes in the High Office of Lord Maior (London: Printed by E. Allde, 1614);

Metropolis Coronata, The Triumphes of Ancient Drapery. In Honour of the Advancement of Sir J. Jolles, to the High Office of Lord Maior (London: Printed by G. Purslowe, 1615);

Chrysanaleia: The Golden Fishing: Or, Honour of Fishmongers. Applauding the Advancement of J. Leman, to Lord Maior (London: Printed by G. Purslowe, 1616);

Sidero-Thriambos. Or Steele and Iron Triumphing. Applauding the Advancement of Sir S. Harvey, to the Dignitie of Lord Maior (London: Printed by N. Okes, 1618);

A Suruay of London, by John Stow, continued and enlarged by Munday (London: Printed by G. Purslow, 1618); completed by Munday, Humphrey Dyson, and others (London: Printed by E. Purslow, sold by N. Bourne, 1633);

The Triumphs of the Golden Fleece. For the Enstaulment of M. Lumley in the Maioraltie (London: Printed by T. Snodham, 1623).

Editions: *The Life of Sir John Oldcastle,* by Munday, Michael Drayton, Richard Hathway, and Robert Wilson; edited by Percy Simpson (London: Printed for the Malone Society, 1908);

Fidele and Fortunio, translation and adaptation, attributed to Munday, of an Italian play by Luigi Pasqualigo; edited by Simpson (London: Printed for the Malone Society, 1909); supplement, edited by W. W. Greg (London: Printed for the Malone Society at Oxford University Press, 1933?);

The Book of Sir Thomas More, by Munday, with revisions by Thomas Dekker and Henry Chettle, probably William Shakespeare, and perhaps Thomas Heywood; edited by Gregg (London: Printed for the Malone Society at Oxford University Press, 1911);

Zelauto: The Fountain of Fame, edited by Jack Stillinger (Carbondale: Southern Illinois University Press, 1963);

The Downfall of Robert, Earl of Huntingdon, by Munday, revised by Chettle; edited by John C. Meagher (Oxford: Printed for the Malone Society at Oxford University Press, 1965);

The Death of Robert, Earl of Huntingdon, by Munday and Chettle; edited by Meagher (Oxford: Printed for the Malone Society at Oxford University Press, 1967);

The English Roman Life, edited by Philip J. Ayres (Oxford: Clarendon Press, 1980);

An Edition of Anthony Munday's "John a Kent and John a Cumber," edited by Arthur E. Pennell (New York: Garland, 1980).

TRANSLATIONS: Anonymous, *The Famous, Pleasant, and Variable Historie, of Palladine of England,* translated by Munday from Claude Colet's French translation of part 1 of the romance *Florando de Inglaterra* (London: Printed by E. Allde for J. Perrin, 1588);

Palmerin de Oliva, *The Mirrour of Nobilitie,* part 1 (London: Printed by J. Charlewoode for W. Wright, 1588); parts 1 and 2 (London: Printed by T. Creede, 1597);

François de la Noue, *The Declaration of Lord de la Noue, vpon His Taking Armes* (London: Printed by J. Woolfe, 1589);

Francisco de Moraes, *The Honorable, Pleasant and Rare Conceited Historie of Palmendos* (London: Printed by J. Charlewood for S. Watersonne, 1589);

Anonymous, revised by Garci Ordóñez or Rodríguez Montalvo, *The First Book of Amadis of Gaule,* translated by Munday from Nicholas de Herberay's French translation of the original Spanish (London: Printed by E. Allde, 1590?); books 3 and 4 (London: Printed by N. Okes, 1618);

L. T. A., *The Masque of the League and the Spanyard Discovered* (London: Printed by J. Charlewoode for Richard Smyth, 1592);

Etienne de Maisonneuve, *Gerileon of England. The Second Part* (London: Printed by T. Scarlet [?] for C. Burbie, 1592);

Guillaume Telin, *Archaioplutos. Or the Riches of Elder Ages. Proouing that the Ancient Emperors Were More Rich than Such Liue in These Daies* (London: Printed by J. Charlewood for R. Smith, 1592);

Ortensio Landi, *The Defence of Contraries. Paradoxes against Common Opinion, Debated in Forme of Declamations to Exercise Yong Wittes,* translated by Munday from the French translation, usually attributed to Charles Estienne, of *Paradossi* (London: Printed by J. Windet for S. Waterson, 1593);

Primaleon of Greece, *The First Booke of Primaleon of Greece* (London: Printed by J. Danter for C. Burby, 1595); *The Second Booke of Primaleon of Greece* (London: Printed by J. Danter for C. Burby, 1596); books 1–3 published as *The Famous and Renowned Historie of Primaleon of Greece* (London: Printed by T. Snodham, 1619);

de Moraes, *The First and Seconde Parts, of the No Lesse Rare, Historie of Palmerin of England* (London: Printed by T. Creede, 1596); *The Third and Last Part of Palmerin of England* (London: Printed by J. Roberts for W. Leake, 1602);

Anonymous, *A Breefe Treatise of the Vertue of the Crosse* (London: E. Allde for E. White, 1599);

José Teixeira, *The Strangest Adventure That Ever Happened. Containing a Discourse of the King of Portugall Dom Sebastian, from 1578. unto 1601. First Done in Spanish, Then in French, and Now into English* (London: Printed by R. Field for F. Henson, 1601);

Philippe de Mornay, *The True Knowledge of a Mans Owne Selfe* (London: Printed by J. Roberts for W. Leake, 1602);

Woodcut depicting "The true and perfect manner of the execution of one Richard Atkins, Englishman at Rome," from Anthony Munday's The English Roman Life *(1582)*

François Citois, *A True and Admirable Historie, of a Mayden of Confolens, that for Three Yeeres Hath Lived, without Receiving either Meate or Drinke,* translated by Munday from Marc Lescarboux's French translation (London: Printed by J. Roberts, 1603);

Jacopo Affinati d'Acuto, *The Dumbe Divine Speaker . . . A Treatise, in Praise of Silence* (London: Printed by R. Bradock for W. Leake, 1605);

Charlotte Brabantine of Nassau, *The Conversion of a Most Noble Lady of Fraunce. Madame Gratiana, Wife to Claudius, Duke of Thouars. Written by Her, to the Ladyes of Fraunce* (London: Printed by T. Purfoot for N. Butter, 1608).

PLAY PRODUCTIONS: *Fedele and Fortunio,* translation and adaptation, attributed to Munday, of an Italian play by Luigi Pasqualigo, London, at court, circa 1584;

John a Kent and John a Cumber, London, Rose theater, December 1594(?);

Mother Redcap, by Munday and Michael Drayton, London, Rose theater, 1597–1598;

The Downfall of Robert, Earl of Huntingdon, London, Rose theater, licensed 28 March 1598;

The Death of Robert, Earl of Huntingdon, by Munday and Henry Chettle, London, Rose theater, licensed 28 March 1598;

Richard Coeur de Lion's Funeral, by Munday, Chettle, Drayton, and Robert Wilson, London, Rose theater, June 1598;

Valentine and Orson, by Munday and Richard Hathway, London, Rose theater, July 1598;

Sir Thomas More, by Munday, with revisions by Thomas Dekker, Chettle, probably William Shakespeare, and perhaps Thomas Heywood, probably not produced, circa 1598;

The True and Honorable History of Sir John Oldcastle, parts 1 and 2, by Munday, Drayton, Hathway, and Wilson, London, Rose theater, October–December 1599;

Fair Constance of Rome, part 1, by Munday, Dekker, Drayton, Hathway, and Wilson, London, Rose theater, June 1600;

Fair Constance of Rome, part 2, by Munday, Hathway, and others, London, Rose theater, summer 1600;

The Rising of Cardinal Wolsey, by Munday, Chettle, Drayton, and Wentworth Smith, London, Fortune theater, August–November 1601;

Jephthah, by Munday and Dekker, London, Fortune theater, 1602;

Caesar's Fall, or The Two Shapes, by Munday, Dekker, Drayton, Thomas Middleton, and John Webster, London, Fortune theater, May 1602;

The Set at Tennis, London, Fortune theater, December 1602;

The Triumphs of Reunited Britannia, streets of London, 29 October 1605;

Camp-Bell, or The Ironmongers Fair Field, streets of London, 29 October 1609;

London's Love to Prince Henry, streets of London, 31 May 1610;

Chruso-Thriambos, streets of London, 29 October 1611;

Himatia Poleos, streets of London, 29 October 1614;

Metropolis Coronata, streets of London, 30 October 1615;

Chrysanaleia, streets of London, 29 October 1616;

Siderothriambos, streets of London, 29 October 1618;

The Triumphs of the Golden Fleece, streets of London, 29 October 1623.

The long career of Anthony Munday almost embarrassingly typifies the profession of letters in Elizabethan and Jacobean England. In an age when literary hackwork enslaved many an embittered poet, Munday eagerly generated an astonishing variety of such writing. His canon includes prose fiction, translations of prose romances, sensational news, plays, possibly a pamphlet attacking plays, political and moral pamphlets, and city pageants. He also wrote ballads and lyric poems, and he updated John Stow's city chronicle. Nor did he confine this mercenary tendency to his writing. He worked as a printer, studied at a Jesuit seminary, spied against Catholics, and took part in the doomed search for the Martin Marprelate pamphleteer, all while holding the title of draper. With such a life, it is hardly surprising that amid a largely mediocre canon Munday's most entertaining book should be *The English Roman Life* (1582), which recounts his own continental adventures. The work has value as prose, as history, and as travel literature. *Zelauto* (1580), his only original work of prose fiction, has importance in the early development of the novel, and Munday's prose, at its best, displays a clarity and economy of expression remarkable for the period.

The exact date of Munday's birth remains unknown, but he was probably born a few days before 13 October 1560, the date of his baptism, in the parish of St. Gregory. His father, Christopher Munday, a freeman of the Draper's Company who worked as a stationer, died young. His mother, Jane, died soon after, and Anthony was apprenticed in 1576 to the stationer John Allde.

While in Allde's employment Munday made an unpromising literary debut with a commendatory poem, "See, Gallants, See This Gallery of Delights," which appeared in the unsuccessful miscellany titled *Gorgeous Gallery of Gallant Inventions* (1578). A moral pamphlet, *The Defense of Poverty* (now lost), soon followed, and in September 1578 Richard Jones licensed *The Pain of Pleasure* (1580), a dreary set of poems almost certainly by Munday, describing the horrid consequences of all pleasures. Allde, who had published none of those books, perhaps thought he could profit from his young apprentice's talent: he was fined that year for printing without a license "Munday's Dream," perhaps one of the ballads that later earned Munday the ridicule of Ben Jonson and John Marston.

Apparently stricken with wanderlust and a desire to improve his language skills, Munday suddenly canceled his indentures with Allde in the autumn of 1578 and traveled to Rome. He feigned conversion to Catholicism in order to enter the English College, where he stayed from February to May 1579. While there, he took part in a student insurrection that left the college, a Roman Catholic seminary, firmly in the hands of Jesuits. That experience and more gave Munday material for his best book, *The English Roman Life.*

After returning to London, Munday contributed some verses to *An Excellent Discourse of John Fox,* a 1579 pamphlet version of *The Admirable Deliverance of 266 Christians by J. Reynard* (1608), in which he falsely claims to have met the hero, John Fox ("Reynard"), in Rome in 1577. (Munday was nowhere near Rome that year, which probably explains the deletion of his verses from the 1608 edition of the book.) He then completed his *Mirror of Mutability* (1579), modeled after the enormously successful editions of the *Mirror for Magistrates* (1559–1587). Munday's version, dedicated to Edward de Vere, seventeenth Earl of Oxford (whom Munday in the introduction claims suggested his trip to Rome), presents tragic biblical and apocryphal stories to complement the classical and historical tales of the earlier volumes. The unreliability of a personified Fortune thus takes a theological turn, perhaps to please puritanical, middle-class readers more comfortable with an avenging god than a capricious goddess. Judas, that most treacherous of biblical

¶A Difcouerie of *Edmund Campion*, and his Confederates, their moft horrible and traiterous practifes, againft her Maiefties moft royall perfon, and the Realme.

Wherein may be feene, how thorowe the whole courfe of their *Araignement: they were miferably* conuicted of euery caufe.

VVhereto is added., *the Execution of* Edmund Campion, Raphe Sherwin, *and* Alexander Brian, *executed at Ti-* borne the 1. of *December*.

Publifhed by *A. M.* fometime the Popes Scholler, allowed in the Seminarie at *Roome* amongft them : a Difcourfe needefull to be read of euery man, to beware how they deale with fuch fecret feducers.

Seene, and allowed.

☞Imprinted at London for *Edwarde VVhite*, dwelling at the little North doore of Paules, at the figne of the Gunne, the 29. of Ianua. 1582.

Title page for the published version of Munday's testimony at Edmund Campion's trial for treason

traitors, elicits predictably harrowing treatment, as he laments "with a currish countenance, his paunch torn out, and round about beset with dreadful flames of fire." The work's narratives are belabored by heavy-handed retribution and relentlessly mediocre verse, and a promised second edition never appeared.

Munday's next book, also dedicated to the earl of Oxford, reveals another attempt to cash in on a proven literary commodity, in this case John Lyly's *Euphues* (1578) and its sequel, *Euphues and His England* (1580). At the time Munday could have been in the service of de Vere (he apparently had enough leisure time to enroll in language classes), as was Lyly, whom he may have wished to flatter or rival. Lyly had just published the second Euphues book; Munday quickly followed with his euphuistic *Zelauto. The Fountain of Fame* which made him the first Elizabethan novelist without university train-

ing, a distinction of some significance to *Zelauto,* for its style has more vigor and clarity than its highly refined model, contains fewer superfluous allusions, and hence is more readable today than Lyly's books.

The title character, a Venetian duke's son on a quest for fame, encounters the usual pageant, tournament, hostile hermit, and amorous innkeeper's wife. A mildly interesting episode set in England has an armed lady put down an insolent suitor to the maiden queen, though for the most part Zelauto's adventures seem ordinary enough. Likewise the several poems in *Zelauto* are undistinguished, though they do not long outstay their welcome as in Munday's previous endeavors.

Zelauto impresses most in its stylistic departures from euphuism and in its narrative structure. Spoken passages have a directness alien to Lyly: "Ah Sir (quoth Cornelia) is the wind in that door now? Are you sea-sick so soon, and not half a mile over? Well, well, this little sparkle will flame to so fierce a fire, that perhaps all the wit you have is not able to quench it." Munday seems to be perfecting the relaxed, conversational style that so well serves *The English Roman Life.* Colloquial, jestbook-style humor also adds a sentience often lacking in his more elegant and academic rivals: "The old whoreson would needs be lusty, and to cheer up his churlish carcass, would get him a wanton wife. And though I say it, he was as well made a man, and as curious in his qualities as ever an old horse in this town, when he is nibbling on a thistle."

Perhaps most important, the narrative of *Zelauto* boasts unprecedented complexity, uniquely juxtaposing elements of chivalric romance, pastoralism, and courtesy literature with its euphuism. For its unusual structure, the book deserves more attention from historians of the novel than it gets, and it would get more had Munday's skill matched his apparently ambitious design (though a case could be made that, given Munday's obscure background and education, the hybrid character of the text could just as well indicate a lack of design). The connection between various episodes can seem haphazard, and the story ends abruptly. Munday's dedicatory epistle blames "the brevity of time and speediness in the imprinting" for its incompleteness. No sequel appeared; either the book sold poorly or the subsequent avalanche of Lyly imitations rendered a sequel superfluous.

If Munday sought to impress the earl of Oxford with *Zelauto,* he courted an altogether different sort of audience with *A View of Sundry Examples* (1580). It consists of a series of sensational news stories involving murder and suicide, with plenty of somber commentary on the wages of sin and God's inescapable wrath. Perhaps Munday, who probably had acted on the stage, scared even himself into upright behavior, for soon after there appeared a ballad attributed to him attacking plays and players, and he may have written *A Second and Third Blast of Retreat from Plays and Theaters* (1580), a more substantial attack on drama. He obviously found the moral high ground congenial, for he remained dissociated from the theater for at least two years, by which time he had found an even worthier podium of bourgeois respectability in his conspicuous anti-Catholicism.

In the meantime he licensed in February 1581 his first translation, *Palmerin of England,* of which no copy survives, and *A Courtly Controversy between Love and Learning* (1581). The latter work, another attempt at euphuism, portrays a debate between Palunor, a misogynistic scholar, and Caliphia, a lovely "prize of Padua," on "whether Learning may live without Love, or Love without Learning." Caliphia wins what becomes a stuffy contest of secondhand classical allusions.

A Brief Discourse of the Taking of Edmund Campion (1581) marks the beginning of Munday's controversial stint as an anti-Catholic propagandist. Campion, formerly in the English Church, came to England on a Jesuit mission accompanied by some young priests from the English College in Rome, some of whom Munday knew during his term there. With anti-Catholic sentiment spreading, Munday's quick conversion to the cause could have resulted as much from nervousness about his past as from his usual opportunism. Whatever his motive, he acted quickly, publishing his sensational octavo version of Campion's arrest scarcely a week after it occurred. He singled out his old confessor at Rome, Robert Parsons, who accompanied Campion to England, for making treasonous statements. Other of Munday's continental companions would receive similar treatment during the next few years. Clearly Munday, in trying to inflate his reputation as a patriot, damaged his character and credibility.

Munday's haste in preparing the *Brief Discourse* also hurt him, for George Elliot, the man who arrested Campion, exposed its inaccuracies in *A Very True Report of the Apprehension of E. Campion.* A second pamphlet by Munday, *The Arraignment and Execution of . . . E. Duckett, alias Hauns* (1581), was similarly discredited. With such pamphlets circulating, few believed Munday when he testified at Campion's trial, especially since he had never before met Campion. He published his testimony, largely hearsay

about traitorous remarks, in *A Discovery of Edmund Campion and His Confederates* (1582), in which he also claimed that he attended the Roman seminary to "undermine them and sift out their purposes." Intent upon being known as a patriotic Protestant at any cost, he further damaged his reputation by revealing in his *Brief and True Report of the Execution of Certain Traitors* (1582) that Luke Kirby, whose execution his testimony had assured, had assisted him with friendship and money in Rome, even while knowing that Munday was not really a Catholic.

Some impressive invective against Munday came in a Catholic priest's *True Report of the Death and Martyrdom of Master Campion,* (1582) which charges, among other things, that Munday deceived his printing master John Allde, turned to writing pamphlets against the theater after having been hissed off the stage, and was never admitted to the English College at Rome. Some charges Munday answered in *A Brief Answer Made unto Two Seditious Pamphlets* (1582), but soon afterward he published his final word to the skeptical, *The English Roman Life,* which gives an engaging account of his travels on the Continent, his term at the English College, the daily routine there, and the treasonous statements of the English exiles.

The book is, compared to Munday's other works, believable. Too richly detailed and interesting to have been imagined by the author of *Zelauto,* much in the book can be confirmed by other documents, and Munday, true to form, eagerly reveals his own dubious activities. He takes a schoolboy's pride in describing his cozening of generous Catholics and his incessant breaking of seminary rules. He pokes sardonic fun at the various "rotten relics" and pieties of Catholics, then displays unctuous horror whenever the exiles denounce Elizabeth or her church. A likable rogue, at once naive, duplicitous, ironic, and smug, emerges from his self-portrayal, and the superbly detailed narrative is disarmingly chatty and readable:

> As for their fare, trust me it is very fine and delicate, for every man hath his own trencher, his manchet, knife, spoon, and fork laid by it, and then a fair white napkin covering it, with his glass and pot of wine set by him. And the first mess, or the *antepast* as they call it, that is brought to the table is some fine meat to urge them to have an appetite, as sometime the Spanish anchovies, and sometime stewed prunes and raisins of the sun together, having such fine tart syrup made to them as I promise you a weak stomach would very well digest them.

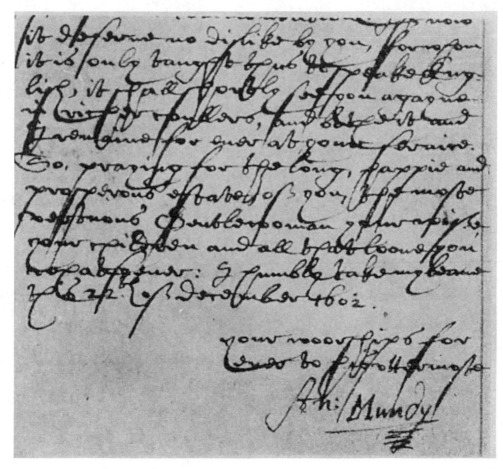

Part of the dedication page from Munday's unpublished tract "Heaven of the Mind," a translation of
a work by Isabella Sforza (British Library, Ms. Add. 33384, fol. 2ᵇ)

With its strong characterization, familiar tone, and engrossing detail, *The English Roman Life* suggests that Munday could have become a prose writer of genuine stature.

But Munday sought more-immediate rewards, and his willingness to assist the government in its trumped-up charges against Campion paid off. He worked as a government agent until 1592, rooting out suspected recusants for Richard Topcliffe, and became a "Messenger of Her Majesty's Chamber" with power to arrest and serve warrants. He also worked from 1588 to 1590 as one of John Whitgift's chief agents in pursuit of the people behind a series of pamphlets by the pseudonymous "Martin Marprelate," attacking the Established Church and arguing for a Presbyterian system.

Munday continued to publish prolifically but wrote no more original nondramatic literature of note. An exception would be the excellent "Shepherd Tonie" poems in *England's Helicon* (1600), but there remains no proof that Munday wrote them, and the lackluster poetry of *A Banquet of Dainty Con-*ceits (1588), as well as the overall mediocrity of his poetic oeuvre, does little to advance his case. Translations of prose fiction, most notably the Palmerin romances, occupied his pen during the years of government service; though they contain some decent poetry, none stands out today. After *The English Roman Life* he reserved his best efforts for the stage, collaborating on many plays in the 1590s and devising pageants until 1623. Old and ailing, he then worked on his expanded edition of John Stow's *Survey of London* (1633). He died and was buried on 9 August 1633, an old man to be sure but well shy of the eighty years claimed for him on his tombstone (quoted in the *Survey of London*).

Jonson parodied Munday as Antonio Balladino in *The Case Is Altered,* (1597), and Marston ridiculed him as Posthaste in *Histriomastix* (1610), but Munday had admirers. Henry Chettle, whose "old Anthony Now Now" in *Kind-Heart's Dream* (1592) could be a good-natured if not quite flattering portrait of Munday, befriended him. In *Palladis Tamia* (1598) Francis Meres hailed him as "our best plotter" (perhaps a loaded compliment, given Munday's extraliterary activities) and one of "the best for comedy amongst us." William Webbe in his *Discourse of English Poetry* (1586) describes Munday's *Sweet Sobs* (1583), a lost volume of love lyrics, as "well worthy to be viewed, and to be esteemed as very rare poetry." Munday's posthumous reputation as a hack writer has remained remarkably consistent, as it rests on an enormous, undeniably ephemeral canon. Though latent displays of talent suggest that, given an artistic conscience, Munday could have wielded considerable influence as a prose stylist, he remains a shadowy character whose name most often turns up in discussions of his sometime collaborators, Chettle, Thomas Dekker, Michael Drayton, Thomas Middleton, and William Shakespeare. Munday criticism begins in earnest with Muriel St. Clare Byrne's brilliant if unconvincing case for Munday's authorship of the "Shepherd Tonie" poems. Celeste Turner's critical biography remains the only full-length study of Munday's career and, though excellent for its time, needs updating in light of recent critical editions of *Zelauto* and *The English Roman Life.*

References:

Philip J. Ayres, Introduction to Munday's *The English Roman Life* (Oxford: Clarendon Press, 1980), pp. xiii–xxviii;

Muriel St. Clare Byrne, "Anthony Munday and His Books," *Library,* fourth series 1 (1921): 225–256;

Mark Eccles, "Anthony Munday," in *Studies in the English Renaissance Drama,* edited by J. W. Bennett and others (New York: New York University Press, 1959), pp. 95–105;

Mary Patchell, *The Palmerin Romances in Elizabethan Prose Fiction* (New York: Columbia University Press, 1947);

Paul A. Scanlon, "Munday's *Zelauto:* Form and Function," *Cahiers Élisabéthains,* 18 (October 1980): 11–15;

Jack Stillinger, Introduction to Munday's *Zelauto: The Fountain of Fame* (Carbondale: Southern Illinois University Press, 1963), pp. vii–xxix;

Celeste Turner, *Anthony Munday: An Elizabethan Man of Letters* (Berkeley: University of California Press, 1928).

Papers:

"The Heaven of the Mind," a manuscript of an unpublished translation by Anthony Munday, is at the British Library, as is the manuscript for his play *Sir Thomas More.* The manuscript for the play *John a Kent and John a Cumber* is at the Huntington Library.

Edward de Vere, Seventeenth Earl of Oxford

(2 April 1550 – 24 June 1604)

Dennis Kay
University of North Carolina at Charlotte

PUBLICATIONS: "The Labouring Man That Tilles the Fertile Soyle," in *Cardanus Comforte Translated into Englishe,* by Girolamo Cardano, translated by Thomas Bedingfield (London: T. Marshe, 1573);

The Paradyse of Daynty Deuises, Aptly Furnished, with Sundry Inuentions: Written for the Most Part, by M. Edwards, the Rest, by Sundry Gentlemen (London: [Printed by H. Jones for] H. Disle, 1576) – includes six poems by Oxford;

"In Pescod Time," in *A Pleasaunte Laborinth Called Churchyardes Chance, Framed on Fancies,* by Thomas Churchyard (London: J. Kyngston, 1580);

William Byrd, *Psalmes, Sonets & Songs of Sadnes & Pietie, Made into Musicke of Fiue Parts: Whereof, Some Are Heere Truly Corrected, and th'other Newly Composed, Are Heere Published* (London: T. East, at the assign of W. Byrd, 1588) – includes "My Mind to Me a Kingdome Is" and "If Woemen Could Be Fayre and Yet not Fonde";

T. W., *The Teares of Fancie. Or, Loue Disdained* (London: [Printed by J. Danter for] W. Barley, 1593) – includes one poem by Oxford;

"What Cunning Can Expresse," in *The Phoenix Nest. Built vp with the Most Rare and Refined Workes of Noble Men. Set Foorth by R. S. of the Inner Temple* (London: J. Jackson, 1593).

Editions: *The Poems of Thomas, Lord Vaux; Edward, Earl of Oxford; Robert, Earl of Essex; and Walter, Earl of Essex. For the First Time Collected,* edited by Alexander B. Grosart (Blackburn, 1872);

"The Poems of Edward de Vere, Seventeenth Earl of Oxford," edited by Steven W. May, *Studies in Philology,* Texts and Studies 77 (1980): 1–132;

Steven W. May, ed., *The Elizabethan Courtier Poets: The Poems and Their Contexts* (Columbia & London: University of Missouri Press, 1991).

Edward de Vere, seventeenth Earl of Oxford, was a significant poet at the court of Queen Elizabeth I. Though few works can be authoritatively attributed to him, it is clear that he enjoyed high esteem as a poet in his day. The subject matter, style, and tone of his writings identify him with the newer, younger generation of poets, and he was one of the first of Elizabeth's courtiers to establish a reputation as a writer of vernacular lyric. He was a patron of literature, receiving the dedication of a wide range of works, and the sponsor of a dramatic troupe. His most significant protégé was John Lyly. Since the 1920s there has been some speculation that he was also the author of works more conventionally attributed to William Shakespeare.

When Edward de Vere was born on 2 April 1550, the only son of John de Vere, sixteenth Earl of Oxford, and Margaret Golding, he was given the title Lord Bulbeck. His father died in 1562, and the young man succeeded to the earldom, and to the title lord great chamberlain on 3 August of that year. As was the case with others of his age, class, and circumstances (such as the young earl of Southampton), he became a royal ward in the household of William Cecil, Lord Burghley. Burghley drew up an elaborate and detailed program of study and recreation for the young man, designed to furnish him with a variety of accomplishments of mind and body. Oxford accidentally killed his manservant during rapier practice in 1567 at Burghley's house. In later life he kept a large group of armed and liveried retainers.

Oxford was a prominent figure at Elizabeth's court from about 1564 to 1582, although there were significant periods of absence and loss of favor throughout that time. He had a turbulent and unsettled life as a courtier, making many enemies. He was impetuous and extravagant, and even his allies found him distinctly erratic in his political judgment and behavior. All the poems that can be reliably attributed to him seem to date from his time at court. In August 1564 he was one of a group of courtiers accompanying the queen on her progress to Cambridge, and he was made an M.A. of that university.

Edward de Vere, seventeenth Earl of Oxford; portrait by an unknown artist
(collection of the Duke of Portland, Welbeck Abbey)

He was made an M.A. of Oxford University in a similar fashion during the queen's progress of September 1566.

In May 1571 Oxford is recorded as a challenger (along with Sir Henry Lee, Christopher Hatton, and Charles Howard) in a tournament held at court. In June he was involved in organizing a parade of harquebusiers before the ambassador of France. In December he married Anne Cecil, the daughter of his guardian, who had been recently ennobled as Lord Burghley. Queen Elizabeth was present at the dinner held to mark the union.

Foreign ambassadors were able to report in May 1573 that Oxford was one of the queen's chief favorites. In 1572 he was displeased at the prosecution of the duke of Norfolk, withdrew for a time from the court, and spent some months in Flanders. His travels also included a period in Italy during 1575–1576. On 14 July 1575, during his absence, Queen Elizabeth stood as godmother to his daughter. He is recorded as exchanging New Year's gifts

with the queen in 1575, 1579, 1580, and 1581. Oxford's hereditary office as lord great chamberlain was largely ceremonial. It did not necessarily involve him in the daily life of the court and gave no assurance of a place there. When he is registered in a list of court lodgings (as he was in 1574), or when his name appears in a list of the court establishment (as it does on a "Bouge de Curia" list of 20 January 1575), such records testify to periods of particular favor with the queen. The records of the late 1580s, the period when his relationship with Elizabeth was cooler, indicate a falling off in his attendance, and his name is no longer found in the lists of those officially fed and housed.

Oxford's return to England in the mid 1570s coincided with the reorganization of the theatrical companies. He became the patron of a company of players known as Oxford's Men. In the spring of 1578 Oxford performed in a Shrovetide pageant along with Philip Howard (Earl of Surrey, then Lord Arundel), Thomas Howard, and Lord Windsor. He was also credited with writing plays that were performed at court. In 1579 he was involved in a celebrated public quarrel at the tennis court with Sir Philip Sidney; the queen was obliged to intervene.

As the next decade began, Oxford's star waned. He was at least a Catholic sympathizer, and probably a convert. His reputation at court suffered increasingly because of his erratic conduct and bouts of uncontrolled temper. He was disgraced when Queen Elizabeth discovered that he had been conducting a sexual relationship with one of the maids of honor, Anne Vavasour (later to be the mistress of Sir Henry Lee), who gave birth to Oxford's child at court in March 1581. In the aftermath of this birth, there was a violent vendetta between Oxford and his supporters and Thomas Knyvett, Anne's self-styled "patron." A cycle of retributive murders was allowed to run its course, as the queen was anxious neither to intervene nor to allow the scandal of a public trial. Oxford was formally reconciled with his wife in 1582. A son, born in 1583, died in infancy. Thereafter two daughters were born and brought up by their grandfather, who found husbands for them.

Of Oxford's activities in later years there is relatively little record, although he retained his status as lord great chamberlain, and in 1583 some rapprochement with the queen was brokered by Sir Walter Ralegh (years later, during Ralegh's disgrace in 1592 following his secret marriage to Elizabeth Throckmorton, Oxford's low standing with the queen meant that his capacity to reciprocate was negligible). Oxford backed unsuccessful foreign ventures to the tune of thousands of pounds. On his own foreign journeys he spent profligately: in fourteen months in 1575–1576 he had managed to spend £4,561. He was predictably cavalier with his associates' money. In 1591 Thomas Churchyard hired lodgings for him but was then compelled to seek sanctuary when confronted with the huge bill Oxford had run up before leaving town. He was obliged to sell off much of the property he had inherited.

In 1586 Oxford sat, by virtue of his rank and office, as one of the judges of Mary, Queen of Scots, and in the same year Queen Elizabeth offered some relief to his financial problems by granting him a £1,000 annuity paid out of revenues from the unfilled bishopric of Ely. He was involved in the action against the Spanish Armada in 1588. In the same year his wife died and was buried in Westminster Abbey. Still Oxford's money troubles persisted, and family property continued to be sold. He con-

tracted a second marriage, to Elizabeth Trentham, in 1592. A son and heir was born the following year. In 1595 he unsuccessfully sought his father-in-law's support to secure the preemption of tin in Cornwall. In 1601 he sat as a judge at the trial of Essex and Southampton after the Essex rebellion. In 1603 he subscribed his name to the proclamation of the acccession of James I and later officiated at the new monarch's coronation in his capacity as lord great chamberlain. Toward the end of his life he moved from his house in Cannons Row, Westminster, to Newington in Middlesex, where he died on 24 June 1604. He was buried in Hackney on 6 July of that year and was succeeded by his son Henry, born in 1593.

Oxford's verse appears to date exclusively from his period of prominence at Elizabeth's court. It circulated fairly widely in manuscript, and one or two of his pieces remained popular with compilers of miscellanies for several generations – up to the 1630s. In addition, no fewer than eighteen poems that are attributed to him had appeared in printed books before 1593, nine of them by 1576. Alexander B. Grosart's collected edition of Oxford's works appeared in 1872, but the most important editorial studies of his writings are a 1969 doctoral thesis by L. G. Black and Steven W. May's 1980 edition of the poems, published in *Studies in Philology*. May's numbering of the poems is employed throughout the following discussion.

Oxford was a courtier. For centuries such status was confined to those who resided at the ruler's court, held some kind of office there, and probably received the "Bouge of Court," the daily allowance of food, in addition to lodging. Oxford fitted that definition from time to time throughout his career. In *The Elizabethan Courtier Poets: The Poems and Their Contexts* (1991) May demonstrates just how few allegedly courtly writers were in receipt of the Bouge of Court. In the strict sense, Sidney, for example, was not formally a courtier, and his exclusion from the queen's favor is an important aspect of his career. On the other hand, the conditions of the centralized early modern court encouraged everyone in public or official life to don the rhetorical mantle of the courtier, transforming whole populations into what Shakespeare would call "dwellers on form and favor." As a young man Oxford wrote a preface to Bartholomew Clerke's 1571 Latin translation of Castiglione's *Il libro del cortegiano* (The Book of the Courtier, 1528) that suggests he was aware of these new developments. Secrecy, allegory, and obliquity were the key features of courtly discourse. What was said or written had to be defensible.

*Anne Vavasour, one of Queen Elizabeth's maids of honor. After
an affair with Oxford, she bore his child in March 1581
(portrait ascribed to Marcus Gheeraerts; collection
of Francis Howard).*

Oxford had family and high rank but little money, power, or influence. Elizabeth's court was dominated by the new establishment, most of whose members owed everything to the Tudors and were bound by ties of kinship. The great old aristocratic dynasties such as the de Veres enjoyed hereditary dignities but rarely held high office in government. Oxford's position, then, obliged him to covet a position of responsibility, but his rank made it inconceivable that he should beg. His writings almost constitute a refusal to play the conventional games of courtiers seeking advancement. Where they were earnest, he was playful.

Oxford and Sir Edward Dyer were the first of Elizabeth's courtiers to woo her, to "court" her in verse. In *The Art of English Poesie* (1589) George Puttenham refers to the "new crew of courtly makers." In this situation as in many others, Oxford was a self-conscious setter of trends. The introduction of the vogue for Italianate lyric poetry seems to have been as studied as the introduction of

Italian gloves. There is a significant degree of self-conscious display about the lyrics of Oxford and Dyer, a deliberate distancing of themselves from their graver humanist contemporaries. "When we see one gay and gallant," asserts Thomas Wilson in *The Art of Rhetoric* (1553), "we use to say, he courts it." Oxford and Dyer challenged the orthodox view of the older generation that verse — other than occasional or reflective poetry — was a morally suspect activity. Their example elevated the status of poetry, to the point where the flamboyant display of eloquence, especially in the medium of love lyrics, was a valued courtly skill whose practitioners derived prestige from their virtuosity. Puttenham suggests that such writers, if their achievement became generally known, would also confer luster on the court. He claims, "And in her Majesty's time are sprung up another crew of courtly makers, noble men and gentlemen of her Majesty's own servants, who have written excellently well as it would appear if their doings could be found out and made public with the rest, of which number is first that noble gentleman, Edward, Earl of Oxford."

Oxford's earliest datable printed poem is not a love lyric; it is instead an occasional piece, a wholly conventional literary gesture for a courtier of the period. In 1573 Thomas Bedingfield, a gentleman-pensioner who was later to share the playing-card monopoly, brought out a translation of Girolamo Cardano, titled *Cardanus Comfort*. Oxford furnished commendatory verse for the volume. His choice of the vernacular as a medium for composition is perhaps significant. The poem's twenty-six lines list instances where the worker does not enjoy the fruits of his toil ("Who worketh most, to their share least doth fall"). Thus the greyhound does not eat the hares it catches; the mason builds a stone house for his lord but lives in a cottage with paper walls; the bees work for the drone; and "the landlord doth possess the finest fare." This is then applied to Bedingfield's work:

> So he that takes the pain to pen the book
> Reaps not the gifts of goodly golden Muse,
> But those gain that who on the work shall look,
> And from the sour the sweet by skill doth choose.

Oxford's verses offer the buyer of the book a certain profit from the investment and hold out a promise of social advancement, as readers are placed in the position of lords and patrons. They also reveal a relish for similes, soon to be gratified by John Lyly and his imitators.

May and others have argued that many courtly verses are allegories to which the key has been lost, and that they are capable of being unlocked by chance discoveries of salient facts. Yet this perhaps underestimates the extent to which Elizabeth presided over and actively encouraged a culture of institutionalized obliquity. The present-day reader should recall Thomas Wilson's observation in *The Art of Rhetoric* that "the miseries of the courtier's life" were best described obliquely, by the use of "similitudes, examples, comparisons of one thing to another, apt translations, and heaping of allegories." While some of Oxford's poems could be related to what was generally known or believed about him, most are much more reticent in their method. Through indirection his verses reveal and reflect upon the life of the courtier. By virtue of their date, their visibility, the prominence of their author, and their variety, they almost define the mode. He paints a picture of a world of secret hopes and fears, of feelings "that within which passes show," concealed behind an imperturbable and urbane public mask.

Several poems are attributed to Oxford in *The Paradise of Dainty Devices* (1576). The first, "Even as the Wax Doeth Melt," employs several of the same comparisons that had been used in the dedicatory poem, so it is perhaps roughly contemporary with it. Oxford's contribution to the *Paradise* is characterized, as is the rest of his writing, by his mastery of a wide variety of styles and evident technical accomplishment. In the first place, his authorship of love lyrics (poems 2, 3, 5, and 9) was novel and striking. He depicts the lover's condition from several distinct viewpoints and in different verse forms. There is a constant striving for innovation, as when his version of Petrarch's *Rime* 102 ("Cesare, poi che 'l traditor d'Egitto") begins by throwing its spotlight directly on its speaker:

> I am not as I seem to be,
> Nor when I smile, I am not glad;
> A thrall although you count me free,
> I most in mirth, most pensive sad.
> I smile to shade my bitter spite.

Poem 4 is a forceful dramatic monologue by a courtly speaker whose good name has been lost — "past all recovery, / I stayless stand t'abide the shock of shame and infamy." Other poems represent the rejected courtly lover: sometimes in the more traditional alliterative style, employing poulter's measure (poem 3) or allegory (poem 8), and sometimes in a more adventurous modern style (poems 6 and 9). Several poems depict the speaker in the torn, antithetical predicament of the Petrarchan lover. Poem 12 seems to anticipate many later courtly lyrics:

> A malcontent yet seem I pleased still,
> Bragging of heaven yet feeling pains of hell.
> But Time shall frame a time unto my will,
> Whenas in sport this earnest will I tell;
> Till then (sweet friend) abide these storms with me,
> Which shall in joys of either fortunes be.

The speaker occasionally fights back against the blows of fortune — "I am no sott to suffer such abuse" — and depicts himself in fiercely dramatic terms as a revenger — "My 'mazed mind in malice so is set / As death shall daunt my deadly dolors long" (poem 10). Perhaps the most celebrated of Oxford's poems is poem 11, a version of a poem by Panfilo Sassi and singled out by Puttenham for praise as the work of "a most noble and learned gentleman" who wrote "an emblem of desire otherwise

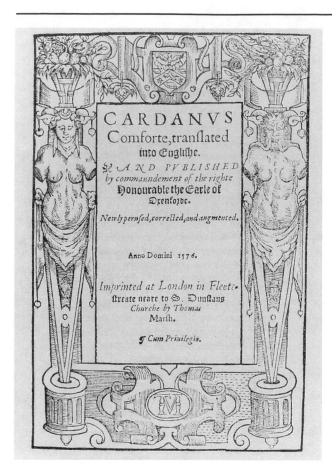
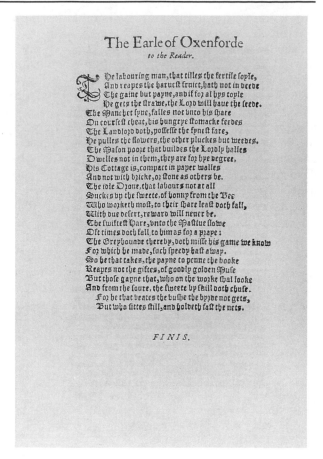

Title page and Oxford's commendatory poem in Thomas Bedingford's translation of a work by Girolamo Cardano. The poem is Oxford's earliest datable printed verse.

called *Cupid,* which for his excellency and wit, I set down some part of the verse."

Oxford's various speakers create a picture of a courtly culture that prizes secrecy: "I like in heart, yet dare not say I love / . . . With feigned joy I hide my secret grief." The court is also a place where there is a strong parallel between sex and power, where courtiers are driven by desire for love and for advancement (poems 8 and 11) and delighted by the failure of their rivals: "Desire can have no greater pain, / Than for to see another man, that he desireth to obtain, / Nor greater joy can be than this, / Than to enjoy that others miss" (poem 8).

Oxford was the first Elizabethan courtier to make a name as a published writer. Like Ralegh, he achieved even greater fame as a literary personality. In each case individual poems circulated because they confirmed the celebrated author's reputation. Whether he or Dyer wrote it cannot be conclusively determined, but attributing to Oxford the manuscript of "My Mind to Me a Kingdom Is" is characteristic of this process. With Oxford's name at-

tached to it, it becomes more than a general reflection on privacy and self-sufficiency. It gains ironies similar to those identified in some of John Donne's *Songs and Sonnets* in depicting a speaker making the best of a situation not entirely to his liking. The only kingdom he can rule is in his mind; the avenues to more-conventional power are blocked. The manuscript tradition likewise draws on the scandal of Oxford's liaison with Anne Vavasour to provide a situation, a context, for his verses: the Bodleian manuscript Rawl. Poet. 85 is titled "Verses made by the Earl of Oxford and Mrs Ann Vavesor" and includes "Sitting Alone upon My Thought."

One of Oxford's better-known poems, which compares love to a game of tennis, enjoyed a predictable popularity among scribes after his quarrel with Sidney. The poem is itself unremarkable:

Whereas the Heart at tennis plays and men to gaming fall,
Love is the court, Hope is the house, and Favor serves the Ball.

> The ball itself is True Desert, the line which measure shows
> Is Reason, whereon Judgment looks how players win or lose.

Surviving manuscript copies date from the 1580s, and the poem continued to be popular with compilers of poetical miscellanies into the 1630s. It first saw print in 1655 in Thomas Cotgrave's *Wit's Interpreter* (1665) and was later printed in *The School of Recreation* (1684). The poem's abiding celebrity was intimately connected with Oxford's reputation, particularly to the story of his public quarrel with Sidney over the use of a tennis court in 1579. This event was more than a personal squabble between two imperious hotheads roused to fury when Oxford insisted Sidney should yield the court to him and called the younger man a *puppy*. Clearly, Oxford was standing on his rank, but he was also explicitly distancing himself from the strongly Protestant views of the Leicester-Sidney faction and challenging their ascendancy. Sidney, as subsequently interpreted by Fulke Greville, first Lord Brooke, was making the point that "place was never intended for privilege to wrong." The poem's popularity indicates the continuing relevance of the clash in the political culture of Stuart England and testifies to Oxford's abiding reputation as a literary figure, a courtly "character."

The influence of Oxford can be seen in the writings of his younger successors such as Ralegh (a poet chiefly in the manuscript tradition), Sir Arthur Gorges, and Sidney, whose career as a poet began with imitations of Oxford and Dyer. His "Dialogue between Two Shepherds" seems to echo Oxford's poem 11; song 5 of *Astrophil and Stella* recalls Oxford's complaint (poem 9), and May considers *Old Arcadia* sonnet 73 a substantial reworking of Oxford's dream vision (poem 8). Sidney's problematic relationship with the queen is expressed through the medium of Petrarchan conceits and conventions, and the wide circulation of his works continued the process begun by Oxford of disseminating the pose and the culture of courtliness to articulate a wide range of the frustrations and discontent of modern life.

The range of Oxford's activities as a patron may be suggested by a brief and selective survey of published works dedicated to him beginning in his teens. Some of these books merely reflect moments of his public prominence, as when his presence at the head of the royal entourage led to his being one of the four dedicatees of Gabriel Harvey's *G. Harveii Gratulationum Valdinensium libri quatuor*

(1578). Among the earliest works dedicated to him were Arthur Golding's translation of Pompeius Trogus, *The Abridgement of the Histories Collected by Justine* (1564), and Thomas Underdowne's translation of Heliodorus, *An Æthiopian History* (1569). As time went by, authors and publishers began to connect him with particular spheres of activity. Dedications include many scientific and medical works, such as George Baker's *Composition or Making of the Oil Called Oleum Magistrale* (1574); Leonardo Fioravanti's *Short Discourse upon Surgery,* translated by J. Hester (1580); and Conrad Gesner's *Practice of the New and Old Physic,* translated by George Baker (1599).

Dedications to Oxford include many translations, which suggests more than the range of his known interests or the enterprising propositions of impecunious translators. There may be a sense in which Oxford's famed eloquence gave him something of the status of a champion of the vernacular (a similar status was enjoyed by Sidney), thereby making his an especially suitable name for translators to evoke. Until Sidney's writings burst onto the literary scene in the early 1590s, Oxford's name had possessed unique commercial cachet. No other prominent courtier was so well known as an author of published English verse. He was regularly praised both as a potential protector and as an accompished writer himself. Edmund Spenser dedicated the 1590 edition of *The Faerie Queene* to him as follows:

> Receive most Noble Lord in gentle gree,
>   The unripe fruit of an unready wit:
>   Which by thy countenaunce doth crave to bee
>   Defended from foule Envies poisnous bit.
> Which so to doe may thee right well besit,
>   Sith th'antique glory of thine auncestry
>   Under a shady vele is therein writ,
>   And eke thine owne long living memory,
> Succeeding them in true nobility:
>   And also for the love, which thou doest beare
>   To th'*Heliconian* ymps, and they to thee,
>   They unto thee, and thou to them most deare:
> Deare as thou art unto thy selfe, so love
>   That loves and honours thee, as doth behove.

There were also several translations of significant religious works, including Arthur Golding's translation of *The Psalms of David and Others. With J. Calvin's Commentaries* (1571). The puritanical Golding's half sister Margaret was Oxford's mother, and Golding was associated with Leicester and the Sidney circle. Other similar dedications included T. Stocker's translation of John Calvin's *Divers Sermons Concerning Jesus Christ* (1581) and J. Brooke's translation of the Huguenot writer Guido's *Staff of Christian Faith* (1577). Other noteworthy works dedicated to him included the antiquarian M. P. Humphrey Llwyd's *Breviary of Britain* (1573), Geoffry Gates's *Defense of Military Profession* (1579), and Angel Day's *English Secretary* (1586).

While Oxford was a champion of Lyly and of the vogue for euphuism, many other works of fiction were dedicated to him, including Edmund Elviden's *Most Pleasant History of Peristratus and Catanea* (1570), Anthony Munday's *Mirror of Mutability* (1579), Lyly's *Euphues and His England* (1580), Munday's *Zelauto, the Fountain of Fame* (1580), Robert Greene's *Gwydonius: The Card of Fancy, etc.* (1584), and Munday's translations of *Palmerin d'Olivia Turned into English by A. M.* (1588) and of *The First Book of Primaleon of Greece* (1595). Significant works of poetry and music dedicated to Oxford include Thomas Watson's *Hekatompathia, or Passionate Centuries of Love* (1582), John Soowthern's *Pandora: The Music of the Beauty of His Mistress Diana* (1584), and John Farmer's *Forty Several Ways of Two Parts in One Made upon a Plain Song* (1591).

It is not clear what role, if any, Lyly played in Oxford's chaotic household, where servants and secretaries must have spent much of their time shielding their employer from angry creditors. Documents connect the earls of Oxford with expensive performances of drama at least as far back as 1492, and their retainers had a well-established tradition of playing. It was probably through Burghley that Lyly came into the service of his son-in-law in the early 1580s. Compared to the way the earl of Leicester had used pageants and stage plays to seek to influence the queen personally and politically, Oxford and Lyly adopted less-direct strategies. The plays (especially *Endimion* and *Midas*) evidently address contemporary political issues, but they do so with courtly obliquity and ambiguity that make them suggestive and generally applicable, rather than allegorical. The Oxford's Men's best players were taken into the Queen's Men in the great reorganization of the companies in 1594 after the plague. After that, the remnants of his company survived as a touring entity in the provinces, but its status and resources were much reduced.

Oxford's verse has appeared in influential modern collections, such as *The Oxford Book of Sixteenth Century Verse* (1932), edited by E. K. Chambers, who singled out Oxford as the "most hopeful" of the writers whose works appeared in the anthologies of the 1570s and 1580s; Chambers summed him up as "a real courtier, but an ill-conditioned youth, who also became mute in later life." Cham-

bers, perhaps playfully, placed Oxford between Queen Elizabeth and Sidney and included poems 16, 11, and 14, while attributing the well-known "My Mind to Me a Kingdom Is" to Dyer. Oxford's works continue to appear in anthologies of Renaissance verse. Emrys Jones, in *The New Oxford Book of Sixteenth-Century Verse* (1992), takes his texts from L. G. Black (1969). He includes texts of four poems accepted by May into the canon (numbers 1, 8, 11, and 14) and two classed by May as "possibly" by Oxford (numbers I and III). He also includes a lyric beginning "Though I be strange, sweet friend, be thou not so," which Black classes as dubious and suggests may be by Anne Vavasour. In addition, Jones prints a piece sometimes attributed to Oxford in later centuries, beginning "When I was fair and young, then favor graced me," as well as "My Mind to Me a Kingdom Is," tentatively attributed to Dyer. Oxford features less prominently in *The Penguin Book of Renaissance Verse* (1992), which includes only May's poem 16, "Were I a King I Could Command Content."

In *English Literature in the Sixteenth Century, Excluding Drama* (1954), C. S. Lewis concludes that Oxford's work "shows, here and there, a faint talent, but is for the most part undistinguished and verbose." Thanks to the labors of Black, May, and others who have advanced present-day understanding and knowledge of Elizabethan court culture and of the splendors and miseries of the courtier's life, Oxford can now be seen as a significant figure at a crucial time. Both his writing and reputation played important roles in making skill in writing vernacular verse an accomplishment to be prized and admired.

Oxford was an important court poet. His writing was a part of the life he led at the center of Elizabeth's court. When removed by scandal from that environment, and perhaps when confronted with the extraordinary innovations of the next generation, led by Sidney and Spenser, the conditions that formerly nourished his talent seem to have vanished. Or perhaps, as some have speculated, they merely found another outlet.

Oxford probably had a wider range of literary skills than the surviving evidence demonstrates. He may have written plays. Puttenham unambiguously praises "the Earl of Oxford and Master Edwards of Her Majesty's Chapel for comedy and interlude." According to Francis Meres in *Palladis Tamia* (1598), Oxford was to be celebrated among the "best for comedy," along with William Gager and Richard Edwards. The first person to promote the idea that Oxford was the author of works traditionally attrib-

Letter from Oxford to William Cecil, Lord Burghley, dated 31 October, probably 1572 (British Library, Ms. Lansd. 14, fol. 187)

uted to Shakespeare was J. Thomas Looney, an English schoolmaster from Gateshead, who related how years of teaching *The Merchant of Venice* to his schoolboys persuaded him that its author must have traveled to Italy and moved in the best society. The glover's son from Stratford seemed to fall short on both counts. This led Looney to list a series of general features the real author of the plays must have possessed (such as being an enthusiast for drama and the habitual associate of educated people). To these he added special characteristics, some of which are hardly controversial: he would have been an enthusiast for Italy and a lover of sports and music, and would have had Catholic sympathies and complicated attitudes toward women. Other characteristics narrow the field considerably: he would have been a supporter of the Lancastrian cause in the Wars of the Roses, had involvement with the feudal system, and been a member of the higher aristocracy.

Looney began his search with Francis Turner Palgrave's *Golden Treasury* (1864) and the *Dictionary of National Biography*. He found that Oxford used the six-line stanza of *Venus and Adonis* in "If Women Could Be Fair, and Yet Not Fond." He also found reference to Puttenham and Meres, who praised Oxford extravagantly: he read that Oxford wrote plays, that he was the patron of a dramatic troupe, and that only a small part of his literary output had survived. He glossed over the fact that Meres also praised Shakespeare, to whom he attributed twelve plays, two narrative poems, and some sonnets.

These discoveries were the start of a work of detection in which Shakespeare's works were scoured for clues. From the early plays it was clear to Looney that Oxford had used Shakespeare as a convenient front, a mask, to enable him to settle old scores (such as attacking Gabriel Harvey as Holofernes in *Love's Labor's Lost*) as well as pleading his own case in *Hamlet* and as Bertram in *All's Well That Ends Well*. An apparent problem for the Oxfordian theory is, of course, the death of Oxford in 1604. Looney dealt with this by suggesting that all the later plays had been left in some sort of draft, to be completed by less-accomplished writers. In this analysis, *The Tempest* was judged an inferior work.

Looney acknowledged his own lack of literary sophistication and had to fight skepticism from publishers (not least because he refused to consider adopting a pseudonym). Yet his work sent more ingenious sleuths on the trail of disguise, ciphers, conspiracies, and the rest. Always the starting point is the same: the man from Stratford was disqualified by education, life experience, and class from consideration as the possible author of the immortal plays and poems. Academics offered no help: they had their positions to consider. So it was left to individual men and women to crack the mystery. The Shakespeare Fellowship was founded as early as 1922, and their *Newsletter* became a forum for Oxfordian speculation. Sigmund Freud was an early convert, and the 1930s saw a great deal of energy spent in elaborating the theory, notably in a series of four books by Gerald H. Rendall. As time went by, the theories became more elaborate. To Charlton Ogburn the texts, once decoded, proclaimed their message clearly. Oxford was speaking to modern readers: he could not speak in his own day, when he was forced to leave his works of genius to fall into lesser hands, so that they became merely "a tale told by an idiot." The Oxfordian movement gained added impetus from the support of Oxford's collateral descendant the earl of Burford from the late 1980s, and the anti-Stratfordian case was granted substantial publicity in a media culture steeped in ideas of conspiracy and cover-up.

It is perhaps surprising, at a time when the academic study of Shakespeare has become more historicized, that the challenge to the Oxfordian hypotheses has not been mounted more clearly. At the most basic level, the contemporaneity of the post-1604 Shakespeare plays has been conclusively demonstrated in works such as Leah Marcus's *Puzzling Shakespeare* (1988). The evidence for Shakespeare's authorship of the plays and poems is much stronger than is commonly conceded, and many recent studies have closely examined his relation to the circumstances of publication and reception during his lifetime. Much of the Oxfordian speculation is based on anachronistic beliefs about the way life and art are related, and on highly selective reading of Renaissance culture. Much of it takes pride in its independence of formal educational structures and yet dismisses Shakespeare for lacking what they repudiate. Perhaps the remote inaccessibility of much academic writing is partly to blame, as is the shrill and scornfully condescending tone in which the Oxford

claims have frequently been dismissed. The snobbery of some Oxfordian writing has collided with the equally intense inverse snobbery of the academy, and the clash of views all too easily descends into name-calling. During this century periods of heightened Oxfordian activity have tended to coincide with periods of increased abstruseness within the academy. There may be a connection.

The evidence for Shakespeare's authorship is strong, stronger in some ways than for many of his most famous contemporaries, and Dennis Kay, in *William Shakespeare: His Life, Works, and Era* (1992) and *William Shakespeare: Life and Times* (1995) connects Shakespeare's life with his writings in such a way as to support this claim. There are gaps in the evidence, but they are consistent with the nature of Elizabethan publishing and records. It was not a conspiracy, for example, that keeps Shakespeare's name off title pages until 1598; it was merely the commercial reality of the publishing business. Elizabethan publishers were agreed that scriptwriters' names did not sell copies – until, that is, Ben Jonson showed it could be done in 1597, and was followed by Shakespeare. If Oxford's plays were so cryptic and allegorical, it is surely likely that expert decoders of allegory (such as all those readers of Spenser, for example) would have cracked it. The elaborate system of censorship and control was part of a culture in which plenty of ingenuity was spent looking for hidden meanings. In addition, the assumptions of the Oxfordians – that it is possible to derive from the plays and poems an image of the man who could have written them – need to be considered in the light of the period (1914–1940) and the distinctly elitist, antidemocratic culture from which they sprang. Nevertheless, as with any long-established conspiracy theory, the Oxfordian view is now sufficiently robust to withstand several direct factual hits. Every refutation spawns a new explanation, and so it is likely to continue. Writings in this field are indexed in the annual bibliography published in the *Shakespeare Quarterly,* which annotates specialist journals, such as the *Shakespeare Oxford Society Newsletter.*

The earl of Oxford's brief and brilliant career as a court poet constituted a challenge to the extraordinary younger generation of courtiers that followed him. In addition, his status and visibility established him as a model to writers outside the court and also contributed to the growing prestige and ambition of vernacular poetry and poets. Yet even those few surviving works that may reliably be attributed to him attest to a talent of more than merely historical importance. His achievement as a writer is notable. His poems are not merely innovative and eloquent; they are also, with their subtle interplay of the personal and the political, among the most revealing and at times moving documents from the heart of Queen Elizabeth's court.

Biography:

B. M. Ward, *The Seventeenth Earl of Oxford* (London: John Murray, 1928).

References:

L. G. Black, "Studies in Some Related Poetical Manuscript Miscellanies of the 1580's," dissertation, Oxford University, 1969;

Katherine V. Chiljan, ed., *Dedication Letters to the Earl of Oxford* (N.p.: Katherine V. Chiljan, 1994);

Mark Eccles, "Brief Lives: Tudor and Stuart Authors," *Studies in Philology,* Texts and Studies 79 (Fall 1982): 1–135;

H. N. Gibson, *The Shakespeare Claimants* (London: Methuen, 1962);

Dennis Kay, *William Shakespeare: His Life, Works, and Era* (New York: Morrow, 1992);

J. Thomas Looney, *"Shakespeare" Identified in Edward de Vere, the Seventeenth Earl of Oxford* (New York: Stokes, 1920);

Leah Marcus, *Puzzling Shakespeare* (Berkeley: University of California Press, 1988);

Irvin Leigh Matus, *Shakespeare, In Fact* (New York: Continuum, 1994);

Steven W. May, "The Authorship of 'My Mind to Me a Kingdom Is,'" *Review of English Studies,* new series 26 (1975): 385–394;

May, *The Elizabethan Courtier Poets: The Poems and Their Contexts* (Columbia: University of Missouri Press, 1991);

Winifred Maynard, "*The Paradise of Dainty Devices* Revisited," *Review of English Studies,* new series 24 (1973): 295–300;

J. G. McManaway, *The Authorship of Shakespeare* (Washington, D.C.: Folger Shakespeare Library, 1962);

Charlton Ogburn, *The Mysterious William Shakespeare,* second edition (McLean, Va.: EPM, 1992);

Peter Sammartino, *The Man Who Was William Shakespeare* (New York: Cornwall Books, 1990);

Samuel Schoenbaum, *Shakespeare's Lives,* revised edition (Oxford: Clarendon Press, 1991);

Lawrence Stone, *The Crisis of the Aristocracy, 1558–1641* (Oxford: Clarendon Press, 1965);

Gary Taylor, *Reinventing Shakespeare: A Cultural History from the Restoration to the Present* (London: Hogarth Press, 1989);

Richard F. Whalen, *Shakespeare – Who Was He? The Oxford Challenge to the Bard of Avon* (Westport, Conn.: Greenwood Press, 1994);

Frank Whigham, *Ambition and Privilege: The Social Tropes of Elizabethan Courtesy Theory* (Berkeley: University of California Press, 1984).

Papers:

The following libraries hold manuscripts of Edward de Vere, seventeenth Earl of Oxford's poems: the British Library, London: Add. Ms. 22583 (poem 16); Harleian Ms. 7392(2) (poems 8, 11, 15, IV); the Bodleian Library, Oxford: Ms. Douce e 16 (poem 4); Ms. Rawl. Poet. 85 (poems 12, III); Ms. Tanner 306 (poem 10); the Folger Shakespeare Library, Washington, D.C.: Ms. V.a. 89 (poem I); Inner Temple Library, London: Petyt Ms. 538.10 (poem II); Marsh's Library, Dublin: Ms. 183 (poem 13).

Henry Peacham the Elder

(September 1547 – September 1634)

Michael McClintock
University of Toronto

BOOKS: *The Garden of Eloquence Conteyning the Figures of Grammer and Rhetorick* (London: Printed by H. Jackson, 1577; revised and enlarged edition, London: Printed by R. Field for H. Jackson, 1593);

A Sermon upon the Three Last Verses of the First Chapter of Job (London: Printed by R. Jones and E. Aggas, 1591).

Edition: *The Garden of Eloquence (1593),* edited by William G. Crane (Gainesville, Fla.: Scholars' Facsimiles and Reprints, 1954).

Frequently overshadowed by the fame of the son who shares his name, the elder Henry Peacham is remembered today as the author of *The Garden of Eloquence,* which was first published in 1577 and then republished in a significantly altered form in 1593. *The Garden of Eloquence* is one of the most comprehensive collections of rhetorical figures produced in the Renaissance. Although the work has had its fair share of critics, such as Wilbur S. Howell, who in his *Logic and Rhetoric in England, 1500–1700* (1956) describes it as an "interminable enumeration of stylistic devices" that appears "more concerned with the husks than with the kernels of style," some recent attempts have been made to present the work in a more favorable light, such as Brian Vickers's "'The Power of Persuasion': Images of the Orator, Elyot to Shakespeare" (1983) and *In Defence of Rhetoric* (1988). Peacham had a successful career in the church, which left its mark on his works: most of the examples of figures in *The Garden of Eloquence* are drawn from the Bible, and in 1591 he published a sermon that he had recently preached on the Book of Job. His literary works, for their part, helped to advance his religious career, as a shrewd choice of patrons led him to further benefices.

Henry Peacham was born in September 1547 in Burton Latimer, Northamptonshire. No record exists of his attendance at university, although ecclesiastical documents indicate that he received both his B.A. and his M.A. In 1574 he was ordained deacon and made the curate of North Mymms, Hertfordshire. In 1578 he was ordained priest, and later in that year he was appointed rector of North Leverton, Lincolnshire. In 1595 Peacham increased his holdings further when he received the living of South Leverton.

Peacham's major work, *The Garden of Eloquence,* is a collection of rhetorical figures, or, as the 1593 title page calls them, the "Most Excellent Ornaments, Exornations, Lights, Flowers, and Forms of Speech, Commonly Called the Figures of Rhetoric." A figure, as defined by Peacham, is "a form of words, oration, or sentence, made new by art, differing from the vulgar manner and custom of writing or speaking." Each figure in the collection is defined, and then illustrated by several examples taken chiefly from the Bible and classical literature. In the second edition Peacham adds two sections, "The Use" and "The Caution," to each definition, perhaps having become more aware of the potential for abuse in the figures after publishing the 1577 edition.

Peacham's discussion of anaphora, taken from the 1593 edition, is typical of the entries in *The Garden of Eloquence.* He begins by offering a definition: "Epanaphora, or Anaphora, is a form of speech which beginneth diverse members still with one and the same word" and then provides several examples of the figure's correct use, such as this passage from Psalm 29: "The Lord sitteth above the water floods. The Lord remaineth a king for ever. The Lord shall give strength unto his people. The Lord shall give his people the blessing of peace." After these examples Peacham outlines the proper way to employ the figure and warns against potential abuses. The purpose of anaphora "is chiefly to repeat a word of importance and effectual signification, as to repeat the cause before his singular effects, or contrariwise the effect before his several causes, or any other word of principal account. It serveth also pleasantly to the ear, both in the respects of the repetition, and also of the variety of the new clause." He then lists three potential problems that may occur when the figure is used. First, there is the danger of overuse: "Although this figure be an exornation of great use, yet it may be too often used in an oration." Second, there is the possibility that a word may be repeated too many times: "the repetition ought not to be many; I mean, the word ought not to be repeated too oft, as some do use it, in a most wearisome tautology." Finally, the orator needs to choose the right word for repetition: "heed ought to be taken, that the word which is least worthy or most weak be not taken to make the repetition, for that were very absurd."

As the dedicatory epistles to the two editions of *The Garden of Eloquence* make clear, a knowledge of rhetorical figures offers a path to the humanist virtues of wisdom and eloquence. By using figures well, one achieves eloquence, and through eloquence one can give voice to wisdom. Without rhetoric to join them, these two virtues can become vices:

> Many not perceiving the nigh and necessary conjunction of these two precious jewels do either affect fineness of speech, and neglect the knowledge of things, or contrariwise covet understanding and condemn the art of eloquence . . . the one sort of these speak much to small purpose, and the other (though they be wise) are not able aptly to express their meaning.

But when eloquence brings forth wisdom, the two virtues form a complementary pair,

> for even as by the power of the sunbeams the nature of the root is shewed in the blossom and the goodness of the sap tasted in the sweetness of the fruit, even so the precious nature and wonderful power of wisdom is by the commendable art and use of eloquence produced and brought into open light.

As far as his own treatise was concerned, Peacham hoped to redress an imbalance. He notes that while wisdom and philosophy were well represented in published works, few English works on eloquence were available:

> I was of a sudden moved to take this little garden in hand, and to set therein such figurative flowers, both of grammar and rhetoric, as do yield the sweet savor of eloquence, and present to the eyes the goodly and beautiful colors of elocution, such as shine in our speech like the glorious stars in firmament.

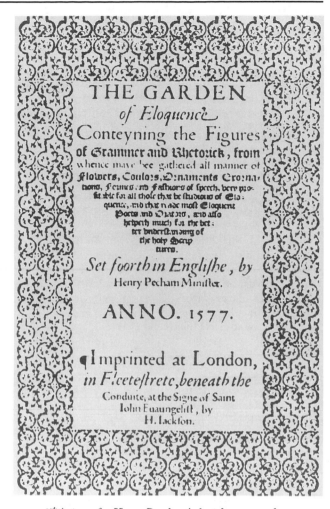

Title page for Henry Peacham's best-known work, a comprehensive collection of rhetorical figures

By publishing his work in the vernacular, Peacham suggests that the virtue of eloquence is as readily attainable in English as it is in Latin.

Peacham follows his chief classical sources — Cicero, Quintilian, and the anonymous *Ad Herennium* (which he attributes to Cornificius) — and divides his figures into two main groups: figures of thought, or tropes, and figures of diction, or schemes. Tropes are those figures that affect the meaning of a word rather than the word itself; Peacham defines a trope as "an artificial alteration of a word or a sentence from the proper and natural signification to another not proper, but yet nigh, and likely." Familiar tropes that Peacham deals with include metaphor, metonymy, and synecdoche (tropes of words), as well as allegory, hyperbole, and irony (tropes of sentences). Schemes are those figures that alter a word or a sentence in some way without changing its literal sense. The greater part of the figures treated in *The Garden of Eloquence* are classified as schemes, which Peacham defines as "those figures or forms of speaking, which do take away the wearisomeness of our common speech, and do fashion a pleasant, sharp, and evident kind of expressing our meaning, which by the artificial form doth give unto matters great strength, perspicuity, and grace." Some common schemes he defines include anaphora, apostrophe, and antithesis.

For Peacham, the most important aspect of the figures is their power to move an audience. His clearest expression of this idea is in the dedicatory epistle to the 1593 edition, in which he describes the orator's power of persuasion in the highest terms:

> so mighty is the power of this happy union (I mean of wisdom and eloquence) that by the one the orator forceth, and by the other he allureth, and by both so worketh that what he commendeth is beloved, what he dispraiseth is abhorred, what he persuadeth is obeyed, and what he disuadeth is avoided: so that he is in a manner the emperor of men's minds and affections, and next to the omnipotent God in the power of persuasion, by grace and divine assistance.

In the 1593 edition this concern with persuasion appears in Peacham's arrangement of the schemes, which he organizes into three orders, according to their emotional force. The schemes of the first order are "those figures which do make the oration plain, pleasant, and beautiful," providing "a musical proportion wherein the mind and wit of man even by a natural instinct taketh pleasure and delight." The more forceful second-order schemes "do attend upon affections as ready handmaids at commandment, to express most aptly whatsoever the heart doth affect or suffer," and they "are such as do make the oration not only pleasant and plausible, but also very sharp and vehement, by which the sundry affections and passions of the mind are properly and elegantly uttered." The third order covers figures of amplification, which Peacham defines as "a certain affirmation very great and weighty, which by large and plentiful speech moveth the minds of the hearers, and causeth them to believe that which is said." Figures for Peacham are clearly more than decorative devices.

Peacham's work provided the most complete English collection of figures produced in the Renaissance: the 1577 edition defines 191 figures, while the 1593 edition reduces this slightly to 157. Despite its comprehensiveness, Peacham's work was not the first of its kind in English. In 1550 Richard Sherry published *A Treatise of Schemes and Tropes,* which was revised in 1555 as the *Treatise of the Figures of Grammar and Rhetoric.* Peacham clearly knew Sherry's work: even though Sherry's name is not mentioned in *The Garden of Eloquence,* several of Peacham's entries are copies of entries in Sherry. Both Peacham and Sherry modeled their works on Johannes Susenbrotus's Latin collection of figures, the *Epitome Troporum ac Schematum,* first published in Zurich in 1540 and republished throughout the rest of the century. Susenbrotus's treatise became the standard Renaissance collection of schemes and tropes and was used in Elizabethan grammar schools. The ultimate Renaissance source for Peacham, Sherry, and Susenbrotus was Desiderius Erasmus, especially his *De Copia* (1512). More than any other writer, Erasmus provided the theoretical underpinnings for Peacham's philosophy of eloquence. Other sixteenth-century English works treating figures include the third book of George Puttenham's *Art of English Poesie* (1589), Abraham Fraunce's *Arcadian Rhetoric* (1588), and Angel Day's *The English Secretary* (1586), which included a catalogue of tropes and schemes beginning with the 1592 edition.

A look at Peacham's career as a whole displays a pragmatic choice of patrons. The 1577 edition of *The Garden of Eloquence* was dedicated to John Aylmer, Bishop of London. In March 1578 Peacham was ordained a priest by Aylmer, and later in the year he received the living of North Leverton, an appointment in which Aylmer may have had some influence. In 1591 Peacham decided to publish his *Sermon upon the Three Last Verses of the First Chapter of Job,* a work that argues for a moderate response to affliction, neither too passionate nor too unconcerned. He had recently preached this sermon before Margaret Clifford, Countess of Cumberland, and her sister, Anne Dudley, Countess of Warwick. His dedication of the published work to the two countesses may have been a factor in his receipt of the living of South Leverton in March 1595. Only the dedication of the 1593 edition of *The Garden of Eloquence* to Sir John Puckering, Lord Keeper of the Great Seal, had no apparent profit for Peacham.

Little is known about Peacham after the publication of his sermon in 1591 and the republication of *The Garden of Eloquence* in 1593, apart from routine references in ecclesiastical records and his involvement in a long-running land dispute in the Chancery court. Although he lived well into the seventeenth century, he published nothing further. His clerical work was recognized in the seventeenth century by his son, Henry Peacham, in a collection of emblems titled *Minerva Britanna; or, A Garden of Heroical Devices* (1612). The younger Peacham dedicates the emblem "Zelus in Deum" (Zeal in God), "To my Father, Mr. Henry Peacham, of Leverton in Holland, in the county of Lincolnshire," and the subtitle of the collection may derive from the elder Peacham's *The Garden of Eloquence*. Henry Peacham the Elder died in September 1634 at the age of eighty-seven and was presumably buried, as his will requested, in the chancel of St. Helena's Church in Leverton.

Peacham's major work, *The Garden of Eloquence,* marks the high point for the figured, copious approach to language that characterizes Elizabethan writing in a variety of genres. Since there are no contemporary references to the work, it is hard to gauge influence. The fact that a second edition of *The Garden of Eloquence* appeared in 1593 argues that it achieved some popularity, but the general taste for figured language in this period, as seen in writers such as John Lyly, makes it impossible to trace Peacham's direct influence. The growth of rational and scientific discourse in the seventeenth century promoted the virtues of a plain style, and increasingly the figures that for Peacham created eloquence came to be seen as unnecessary ornaments, interfering with the clear correspondence of word and thing. It is this suspicion, perhaps, that lies behind many dismissals of *The Garden of Eloquence*. As more is discovered about the attitudes toward language on which Peacham's work is based, however, more-understanding treatments of it may surface in the future.

References:

Joseph X. Brennan, "The *Epitome Troporum Ac Schematum:* The Genesis of a Renaissance Rhetorical Text," *Quarterly Journal of Speech,* 46 (February 1960): 59–71;

William G. Crane, *Wit and Rhetoric in the Renaissance: The Formal Basis of Elizabethan Prose Style* (New York: Columbia University Press, 1937), pp. 104–106, 237–240;

Wilbur S. Howell, *Logic and Rhetoric in England, 1500–1700* (Princeton, N.J.: Princeton University Press, 1956), pp. 116–137;

Brian Vickers, *In Defence of Rhetoric* (Oxford: Clarendon Press, 1988), pp. 324–327;

Vickers, "'The Power of Persuasion': Images of the Orator, Elyot to Shakespeare," in *Renaissance Eloquence: Studies in the Theory and Practice of Renaissance Rhetoric,* edited by James J. Murphy (Berkeley: University of California Press, 1983), pp. 416–422;

Alan R. Young, "Henry Peacham, Author of 'The Garden of Eloquence' (1577): A Biographical Note," *Notes and Queries,* new series 24 (December 1977): 503–507.

William Percy

(1575 – May 1648)

L. M. Storozynsky
University College of the Fraser Valley

BOOKS: *Sonnets to the Fairest Coelia* (London: Printed by Adam Islip for W. P[onsonby?], 1594);

The Cuck-Queanes and Cuckolds Errants or The Bearing Downe the Inne. A Comaedye. The Faery Pastorall or the Forrest of Elves, edited by William Nicol (London: Shakespeare Press, 1824).

Editions: *Coelia; Containing Twenty Sonnets,* edited by Sir Egerton Brydges (Lee Priory, Kent: John Warwick, 1818);

The Sonnets of William Percy, in *Occasional Issues of Unique or Very Rare Books,* volume 4, edited by Alexander B. Grosart (Manchester: Charles Simms, 1877).

William Percy, minor poet and dramatist, is an obscure figure who might have been long forgotten were it not for the historical interest of his connection with another, better-known Elizabethan poet, Barnabe Barnes. In addition, Percy's plays, while most remain unpublished, offer details of Elizabethan stage practices that have attracted the attention of theater and stage historians.

Although Percy was born into an aristocratic family, the recorded details of his life are far from clear, particularly as he has often been confused with other people with the same or similar names. He was the third son born to Henry Percy, eighth Earl of Northumberland, and Catherine Neville Percy. His date of birth is usually given as 1575, and his birthplace was probably in or near Durham. He appears to have had an unsettled childhood, living as he did in troubled, turbulent times. In 1583 he may have been sent to France with two of his brothers, possibly for their own safety. Their father, suspected of involvement in the rising of the North in 1576 and later of plotting in support of Mary Stuart, was imprisoned in the Tower in 1584. On 20 June 1585 the earl was discovered shot dead, and William's older brother Henry became the ninth earl. Henry participated in the hiring and arming of ships against the Armada in 1588, and William may have sailed with him; there is a blank-verse description of the Armada in one of his manuscript plays. Two younger brothers were later involved in the Essex rebellion, and Thomas Percy, kinsman and steward in the Percy household, was implicated in the Gunpowder Plot. Henry, too, was involved in the latter and imprisoned for fifteen years.

William remained quietly and unobtrusively on the fringes of these events, and little is known of his early years until he went to Oxford, where he probably studied Latin and Italian language and letters; his name appears in the matriculation registers of Gloucester Hall for 13 June 1589. At Oxford, Percy and Barnes, who may have known each other previously in Durham, formed a lasting friendship. There, too, Percy belonged to a small literary circle whose members included Thomas Campion, Charles Fitzgeoffrey, and three brothers, Edward, Lawrence, and Thomas Mychelbourne. Apparently Percy was looked upon as the group's patron, and his praises were sung by Campion in an ode, "Ad Nobiliss. virum Gul. Percium" (1595), and by Fitzgeoffrey in a Latin epigram printed in a collection titled *Affaniae* (1601). A manuscript epigram by Percy is dedicated to the three brothers. Another contemporary reference to him is found in William Covell's catalogue of poets, *Polimanteia* (1595). Later in London, Percy's circle of literary friends may have expanded to include the dramatists John Ford and John Webster. Meanwhile, Barnes dedicated his *Parthenophil and Parthenophe* (1593) to "M. William Percy, Esquire, his dearest friend," who in turn addressed a madrigal to Barnes at the end of his own sonnet sequence in 1594. Barnes's fictional Parthenophe may have been modeled on Percy's sister, Eleanor; but given the salacious nature of Barnes's poems, it is unlikely that either she or her brother would have taken kindly to such a "compliment." Barnes's *Four Books of Offices* (1606) includes the only other known printed poem by Percy, another madrigal.

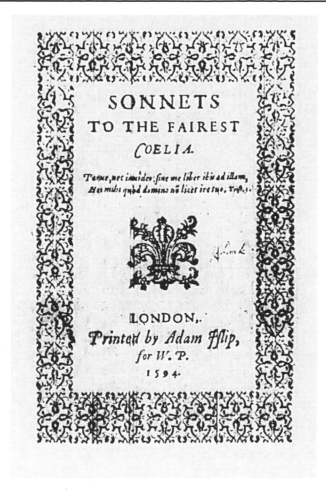

Title page for William Percy's sonnet sequence

Percy's Oxford student days were probably the calmest and happiest period of his life, but they were all too brief. By 1596 he is known to have been in London, where in a duel he apparently wounded one Henry Dennye, who died shortly thereafter. The records of this event are confused, but Percy appears not to have suffered any consequences. His friend Barnes was twice accused of attempted murder, but in each case the evidence was inconclusive. Percy incorporated details from these events into his play *A Forest Tragedy* (1602). The reasons for the rapid decline of his fortunes are unclear; but in about 1606 he withdrew to Oxford, where he remained for the rest of his life, living in the house of a Mr. Nicholls in Pennyfarthing Street, St. Ebbs parish, and possibly spending some time in prison in Oxford Castle for unpaid debts. In 1638 a G. Garrard of Oxford described Percy thus, "He lives obscurely in Oxford and drinks nothing but ale." Percy died in Oxford in May 1648 and was buried there on 28 May in Christ Church Cathedral.

Percy's *Sonnets to the Fairest Coelia* (1594) is a collection of twenty poems that may well have survived thanks to the final item in the volume, the madrigal addressed "To Parthenophil upon His Laya and Parthenophe," for the historical interest of this connection between Percy and Barnes is the high point of the volume. Percy's introductory address to the reader is an amusing example of the kind of disclaimer written by many sixteenth-century poets in response to the supposedly unauthorized printing of their work:

Courteous Reader, whereas I was fully determined to have concealed my sonnets, as things privy to myself, yet of courtesy having lent them to some, they were secretly committed to the press, and almost finished, before it came to my knowledge. Wherefore making, as they say, virtue of necessity I did deem it most convenient to propose mine epistle, only to beseech you to account of them as of toys and amorous devices, and ere long, I will impart unto the world another poem, which shall be both more fruitful and ponderous. In the mean while I commit these as a pledge unto your indifferent censures.

The most convenient aspect of all this alleged secrecy and abuse of courtesy is that the resulting epistle draws attention and lends importance to a group of otherwise unremarkable sonnets. The announcement of a forthcoming work is, again, not unlike promises made by other poets (for example, Thomas Watson in the headnote to *Hekatompathia* (1582) and Bartholomew Griffin in the second dedication of *Fidessa* (1596), but the world is still awaiting Percy's next "poem" (the parallel with others again suggests itself).

Percy's sonnets are conventional love sonnets, all quatorzains, three of which are given titles: "Mysterie" (number 10), "To Polyxena" (number 11), and "Echo" (number 15, an echo poem). *Coelia* appears to have been inspired by *Parthenophil and Parthenophe* (in addition to the poem addressed to Barnes, there are similarities between Percy's tenth sonnet and Barne's tenth madrigal), but it falls far short of anything Barnes achieved. Lu Emily Pearson comments in *Elizabethan Love Conventions* (1933) on the absurdity of Percy's expressions, which are indeed reminiscent of the extreme hyperbole in the anonymous *Zepheria* (1594).

Percy makes no attempt to experiment with the sonnet form other than in the echo poem, which is one of the least imaginative examples of its kind. His sonnets are linked and sometimes paired by a continuation and development of the main theme, occasional repetition of last and first lines (as in sonnets 2 and 3, 17, 18, and 19), and recurring references to the eponymous Coelia. Direct speech and dialogue, especially Coelia's replies, are featured in some of the poems (sonnets 2, 4, and 17). Although a loose chronology can be discerned, the poems cannot be said to tell a story. Percy does make one attempt to narrate what should be a charming anecdote – Coelia accidentally steps on the poet's foot (sonnet 5). It might have relieved the conventionality of the sequence, but it is handled with so little skill that the amusing personal incident becomes a poetic blunder, drawing disproportionate attention to itself especially as Percy, not content to let the matter rest, alludes to it again in sonnets 6 and 9. With the same lack of subtlety, the names of figures from classical mythology are simply inserted into the poems; no attempt is made to rework the myths or to incorporate them into a meaningful subtext. Finally, the eleven-line madrigal addressed to Barnes has nothing to do with Percy's sonnets, although it takes the form of a warning from one hopeless lover to another. Its real function, surely, is to draw attention to *Coelia* by reinforcing the connection between Percy and Barnes.

Extant copies of the original *Coelia* are rare, but the work has been republished four times since its first appearance. Sir Egerton Brydges, in his rather carelessly printed edition of 1818, acknowledges that he worked from a transcription of the poems made by a Mr. Park; he also reports Park's opinion that "Percy's Sonnets have scarcely any plea for reproduction except their rarity. They are void of natural thought, of pleasing sentiment, of graceful metre, or even of grammatical propriety." Brydges finds Percy's "thoughts and expressions quaint and laboured and obscure," attributing this partly to the "fashion of the day." Alexander B. Grosart expresses a much more favorable opinion in his 1877 edition of *Coelia* but offers little commentary on the poems. Edward Arber's edition in *An English Garner* (1883) is reprinted by Sidney Lee in his anthology *Elizabethan Sonnets* (1904), but Lee is at his most unflattering in his brief discussion of the sequence, which he lists under the heading "Poetae Minimi." He finds Percy's poetry "invariably grotesque and at times coarse, while his rhymes constantly strike the most discordant notes." Percy and *Coelia* have been virtually ignored since Lee.

Percy's plays have fared little better than his sonnets. All six survive in autograph manuscripts, and only two have been published. In 1824 Joseph Haslewood, once the owner of the manuscript volume and the first to identify Percy as the author, printed *The Cuck-queene and Cuckolds Errants; or, The Bearing Down the Inn,* a prose comedy, and *The Fairy Pastoral; or, Forest of Elves,* in blank verse. The remaining unpublished plays are *Arabia Sitiens; or, A Dream of a Dry Year* (1601); *The Aphrodisial; or, Sea Feast* (1602); *A Forest Tragedy in Vacuniam; or, Cupid's Sacrifice* (1602); and *Necromantes; or, The Two Supposed Heads,* a comic piece acted by the children of St. Paul's theater company in about 1602. These plays are of interest to theater and stage historians as they contain unusually clear indications of Elizabethan stage practice. All the plays seem to have been written for the children of St. Paul's, but changes are noted in the event that adult actors should perform. Each piece contains a list of theatrical properties required, and several offer detailed stage directions.

As a minor, mediocre poet, Percy has understandably attracted little interest in recent times. But as an Elizabethan, a member of an aristocratic family, an observer of momentous historic events, and the friend and patron of contemporary poets, he merits reconsideration. It is especially unfortunate that his dramatic works have received so little critical attention, as it is possible that the manuscripts containing them and the plays themselves might reveal much more about Percy and his world. A critical edition of the plays would make a valuable contribution to the ongoing task of reexamining and reevaluating early works, particularly in the present critical climate, in which aesthetic quality is only one of the values by which literature is judged.

References:
John Erskine, *The Elizabethan Lyric* (New York: Columbia University Press, 1903), pp. 150–151;

Caroline E. Jameson, Introduction to "An Edition of *A Forrest Tragedye in Vacunium* by William Percy," M.A. thesis, University of Birmingham, 1972;

John H. Long, "The Music in Percy's Play Manuscripts," *Renaissance Papers* (1980): 39–44;

Lu Emily Pearson, *Elizabethan Love Conventions* (Berkeley: University of California Press, 1933), pp. 122–123;

Janet G. Scott, *Les Sonnets Elisabéthains: Les Sources et L'apport Personnel* (Paris: Librairie Ancienne Honoré Champion, 1929), pp. 181–184.

Papers:
William Percy's plays survive in three autograph manuscripts. Two are kept at Alnwick Castle, Alnwick, Northumberland: one contains four plays and two poems (Ms. 508); the second contains all six plays, songs written for one of the plays, and a collection of epigrams (Ms. 509). The third, a copy of Alnwick Ms. 509, is in the Henry E. Huntington Library (HM 4).

Sir Walter Ralegh

(1554? – 29 October 1618)

Jerry Leath Mills
University of North Carolina at Chapel Hill

BOOKS: *A Report of the Truth of the Fight about the Iles of Açores, This Last Sommer. Betwixt the Revenge, one of her Maiesties Shippes, And an Armada of the King of Spaine* (London: Printed for William Ponsonbie, 1591);

The Discoverie of the Large, Rich and Bewtiful Empire of Guiana, with a Relation of the Great and Golden City of Manoa (Which the Spaniards call El Dorado) And the Provinces of Emeria, Arromaia, Amapaia and Other Countries, with Their Rivers, Adjoyning. Performed in the Yeare 1595 (London: Printed by Robert Robinson, 1596);

The History of the World (London: Printed for Walter Burre, 1614);

The Prerogative of Parliaments in England: Proved in a Dialogue (pro & contra) betweene a Councellour of State and a Justice of Peace. Written by the Worthy (Much Lacked and Lamented) Sir Walter Raleigh Knight, Deceased. Dedicated to the Kings Maiestie, and to the House of Parliament Now Assembled (Midelburge [London: printed by T. Cotes], 1628);

Sir Walter Raleighs Instructions to His Sonne and to Posterity. Whereunto Is Added a Religious and Dutifull Advice of a Loving Sonne to His Aged Father (London: Printed for Benjamin Fisher, 1632);

To Day a Man, To Morrow None: or, Sir Walter Rawleighs Farewell to His Lady, The Night before Hee Was Beheaded: Together with His Advice Concerning Her, and Her Sonne (London: Printed for R. H., 1644);

Sir Walter Rawleigh His Apologie for his Voyage to Guiana (London: Printed by T. W. for Humphrey Moseley, 1650);

A Discourse of the Originall and Fundamentall Cause of Naturall, Customary, Arbitrary, Voluntary and Necessary Warre. With the Mistery of Invasive Warre. That Ecclesiasticall Prelates, Have Alwayes Beene Subject to Temporall Princes, And That the Pope Had Never Any Lawfull Power in England, Either in Civill or Eccesiasticall

Sir Walter Ralegh and his elder son, Wat; portrait by an unknown artist (National Portrait Gallery, London)

Businesse, after Such Time, as Brittaine Was Won from the Roman Empire (London: Printed by T. W. for Humphrey Moseley, 1650);

Excellent Observations and Notes, Concerning the Royall Navy and Sea-service. Written by Sir Walter Rawleigh and by Him Dedicated to the Most Noble and Illustrious Prince Henry Prince of Wales (London: Printed by T. W. for Humphrey Moseley, 1650);

Ralegh's wife, Lady Elizabeth Throckmorton; portrait by an unknown artist (National Portrait Gallery of Ireland)

Maxims of State (London: Printed by W. Bentley, 1651);

Remains of Sir Walter Raleigh; Viz. Maxims of State. Advice to His Son: His Sons Advice to His Father. His Sceptick. Observations Concerning the Causes of the Magnificency and Opulency of Cities. The Prerogative of Parliaments in England, Proved in a Dialogue between a Councellour of State and a Justice of the Peace. His Letters to Divers Persons of Quality (London: Printed for William Sheares, Junior, 1657; enlarged, 1661).

Editions and Collections: *The Works of Sir Walter Ralegh, Kt., Now First Collected: To Which Are Prefixed the Lives of the Author,* 8 volumes, edited by William Oldys and Thomas Birch (Oxford: Oxford University Press, 1829; New York: Franklin, 1965);

The Poems of Sir Walter Ralegh, edited by Agnes M. C. Latham (London: Constable, 1929; Boston & New York: Houghton Mifflin, 1929; revised edition, London: Routledge & Kegan Paul, 1951; Cambridge, Mass.: Harvard University Press/The Muses' Library, 1951);

Advice to a Son: Precepts of Lord Burghley, Sir Walter Ralegh, and Francis Osborne, edited by Louis B. Wright (Ithaca, N.Y.: Published for the Folger Shakespeare Library by Cornell University Press, 1962);

"The Poems of Sir Walter Ralegh: An Edition," edited by Michael Rudick, dissertation, University of Chicago, 1970;

The History of the World (selections), edited by C. A. Patrides (London: Macmillan, 1971; Philadelphia: Temple University Press, 1971);

A Choice of Sir Walter Ralegh's Verse, edited by Robert Nye (London: Faber & Faber, 1972);

Sir Walter Ralegh: Selected Writings, edited by Gerald Hammond (Manchester, U.K.: Carcanet Press, 1984).

OTHER: George Gascoigne, *The Steele Glas* (London: Printed for Richard Smith, 1576) – includes prefatory poem, "Walter Rawely of the Middle Temple, in Commendation of the Steele Glasse";

Edmund Spenser, *The Faerie Queene,* Books I–III (London: Printed for William Ponsonby, 1590) – includes Ralegh's sonnets "Methought I Saw the Grave Where *Laura* Lay" and "The prayse of meaner wits this worke like profit brings";

Nicholas Breton, *Brittons Bowre of Delights* (London: Printed by Richard Jhones, 1591) – includes Ralegh's poems "Like to a Hermite poore in place obscure" and "Hir face, Hir tong, Hir Wit";

The Phoenix Nest (London: Printed by John Jackson, 1593); edited by Hyder Edward Rollins (Cambridge, Mass.: Harvard University Press, 1931) – includes "Praisd be Dianas Faire and Harmles Light" and other poems attributed to Ralegh;

Englands Helicon (London: Printed by J. R. for John Flasket, 1600; enlarged, 1614); edited by Hugh Macdonald (London: Etchells & Macdonald, 1925; Cambridge, Mass.: Harvard University Press, 1950) – includes "The Nimphs Reply to the Sheepheard" and other poems attributed to Ralegh.

For all the opportunism, self-promotion, misjudgment, and personal failure that undeniably mark his long career, Sir Walter Ralegh remains the most credible embodiment that Tudor-Stuart England has to offer of the ideal of the Renaissance man. By turns a soldier, privateer, explorer, and projector for colonization, he was as well a courtier, poet, scientist, and historian. Almost all his own poetry was written for self-advancement at court, yet he promoted unselfishly the fortunes of Edmund Spenser and facilitated the publication of Spenser's epic, *The Faerie Queene* (1590, 1596). Though obviously cultivating a personal stake in his projects for colonization of the two Americas, he fixed those projects firmly in a larger perspective of advancing England's well-being in a world increasingly dominated by Spain; and his colonization plan, unlike the purely economic undertakings of the Spanish, included permanent settlement of families, the development of a nautical academy, and the learning of aboriginal languages, such as the Algonquian that his assistant, Thomas Harriot, remained on Roanoke Island for nearly a year to acquire. During his long imprisonment in the Tower of London his achievements included the production of a million-word history of the world (up to 131 B.C.) and the invention of a medical remedy ("Balsam of Guiana"), both of which sold vigorously for a hundred years.

Ralegh was born, probably in 1554, in Devonshire on the southern coast of England to a family long and intimately involved with the sea. The youngest son of Walter Ralegh of Budleigh and Katherine Champernown, he had two half siblings by his father's first marriage to Joan Drake and four by his mother's to Otho Gilbert. The paternal name, like many in that age of extremely unstable orthography, is on record in a large number of variant spellings – including "Raleigh," "Rawleigh," "Rauleygh," "Rauley," "Raullygh," and "Raulligh" – but Sir Walter seems to have settled on "Ralegh" after his knighthood was conferred in 1585.

Ralegh's early education is nowhere described in any detail; but it may safely be assumed that it was Protestant, in keeping with the family religion, and classical in emphasis, in keeping with the expectations of boys of his class for eventual university training. By that time William Lyly's Latin grammar held sway in English grammar-school education; the book illustrated points of grammar and composition with quotations from the best Roman authors to ensure that pupils not only learned the mechanics but also acquired an admiration for elegance of style. In prose, this style meant almost exclusively the balanced, oratorical style of Cicero, a personalized and flexible form of which Ralegh wrote, with considerable effect, for the rest of his life.

Judging from his lifelong intellectual curiosity and his quickness to master and digest information, Ralegh was no doubt an able student. Attraction to active pursuits must have outweighed the delights of study in his middle teens, however, for he set out to France, perhaps as early as 1569, to fight with Huguenot forces under his kinsman Henry Champernown. Such service was a popular but risky course of volunteer action for English Protestants, who could expect the tacit approval but not the overt support of a sovereign wary of applying too much pressure at any one point of the delicate interrelation of religious powers in Europe. Years later, in *The History of the World* (1614), Ralegh recalled in vivid detail some of the action he saw in France, including smoking enemy troops out of underground entrenchments with smoldering bales of hay.

On his return in 1572 he entered Oriel College, Oxford. Although based solidly on the Greek and Roman classics, humanistic education at Oxford was no ivory-tower experience but rather a course of preparation for public service in the military, clergy, law, or the governmental complex that had its center in the royal court. Since all these pursuits required facility in expression and persuasion, a rhetorical education was deemed appropriate. Students studied logic, rhetoric, and other aspects of style on the premise that since we think in words, a balanced and elegant style was important in providing a framework for lucid and reasonable thought. The great Roman historians were studied not simply for historical and political principles but also in order to analyze and appreciate the orations they often attribute to generals and statesmen. Students put on dramatic performances to develop forensic skills, and school recitations involved a great deal of debate, often on paradoxes, ingenious dilemmas, and unanswerable questions, such as "Which is better, day or night?" (an exercise John Milton professionalized in a later age with his paired poems *L'Allegro* and *Il Penseroso* [circa 1631]). In debate the premium was on cleverness, wit, and rhetorical adroitness – excellent preparation for future careers in the web of clientage, patronage, and competition that made up the daily business of life at court.

Sixteenth-century universities also valued the study and composition of poetry. Students were required, as prescribed by the humanist "doctrine of imitation," to memorize long passages of Latin verse, analyze their grammatical and rhetorical structures, and then re-create them in English, with variations conceived by the young scholars themselves. Ralegh's remembrance of these exercises is probably attested in his lyric poem beginning "Now Serena Be Not Coy," an adaptive paraphrase and expansion of a Latin poem by Catullus. Contemporary poetry was not formally taught, but students were encouraged, by peer pressure as much as anything, to become knowledgeable about it, and it was an unmotivated pupil who could not quote extensively from French and Italian masters of recent ages.

Ralegh left Oxford in 1574 without a degree. In London he entered first Lyon's Inn and then the Middle Temple, institutions where one studied law and – more important for many of the aspirant courtiers who attended – formed contacts with people and institutions capable of furthering one's ambitions for public life. The latter, rather than preparation as a barrister, seems to have been Ralegh's intent (although – despite his protestation that he knew little of the law – he was to show considerable legal sophistication at his trial for treason in 1603). Probably the earliest extant example of his poetry

dates from this period, a set of commendatory verses written to his fellow templar George Gascoigne on the publication of Gascoigne's satire *The Steel Glass* (1576) and published as a preface to that work. This poem reflects, as was no doubt intended, the aphoristic, generally nonmetaphorical plain style favored by Gascoigne himself. It is uncertain how well Ralegh knew the older poet; but he must have seen in him something of his own disposition, since Gascoigne, too, was a soldier as well as a poet and had served with Ralegh's half brother Sir Humphrey Gilbert in the Low Countries. Ralegh later adopted Gascoigne's motto *Tam marti quam mercutio* as one of his own, declaring a temperament as indebted to Mars for strength and vigor as to Mercury for intellectual and artistic powers.

After sea duty with Gilbert in an unsuccessful search for a northwest passage in 1578–1579 and a brief period of association with the entourage of Edward de Vere, seventeenth Earl of Oxford, Ralegh embarked on an important phase of his military career in 1580 when he took charge of a company of soldiers under Arthur, Lord Grey, in Ireland. He soon distinguished himself – dubiously so, in some modern eyes – as the leader, on Lord Grey's orders, of a massacre of disarmed Spanish and Italian troops at Smerwick. It was in Ireland – although precisely when is not known – that he first met Spenser, who was Lord Grey's secretary, and there also that he defeated the ambush by Irish troops that Spenser was to turn into an episode in *The Faerie Queene*.

Soon after his return to England as something of a war hero in December 1581, Ralegh was called into personal consultation with the queen about affairs in Ireland. He thus began, through a combination of personal charm and astuteness of political and military opinion, his phenomenal rise in Elizabeth's favor and in prominence at her court. (The well-known story that Ralegh first attracted the queen's attention by spreading his cloak before her so that she could cross a puddle is almost certainly apocryphal.) By 1582 he was a well-established courtier, recipient of the lucrative privileges Elizabeth was disposed to grant her most cherished assistants. In 1583 he received a profitable commission to license the sale of wines. In 1584 Elizabeth granted him the customs receipts on imported woolens; he became the warden of the stannaries and was admitted to Parliament in the same year. In 1585, the year he was knighted, he was appointed vice admiral for his home region of Devon and Cornwall. The Crown provided him lodgings at Durham House in London, and in 1587

Letter from Ralegh to Sir Walter Cope, dated 5 October 1610 (Pierpont Morgan Library) he was appointed captain of the queen's personal guard.

During this period Ralegh exploited his standing with his sovereign to further his interests, first stimulated by Gilbert, in exploration and colonization. He sent settlers to a large area in Ireland, and with another Gilbert, his half brother Adrian, he obtained the letters patent necessary for the project on Roanoke Island in present-day North Carolina that became famous as the Lost Colony. (Ralegh named the whole area Virginia, in honor of his virgin queen.) The product of a series of voyages beginning in 1584, the colony *planted* (to use the terminology of the time) on Roanoke in 1587 vanished mysteriously, probably through a combination of massacre and absorption into the Indian nation of Chief Powhatan in coastal regions to the north. Ralegh's plan to search for the colonists was stifled by the Spanish Armada's attempted invasion of England in 1588. All English naval resources were required at home, and Ralegh himself was put into service as a supervisor of preparations on the southern coast; he also contributed a ship, the *Bark Ralegh,* to the war effort. During 1589 his rivalry with Robert Devereux, second Earl of Essex, who threatened to diminish Ralegh's influence with the queen, may have been a factor in his giving up his formal interests in North America, although he retained colonization rights to South America and was no doubt already contemplating the expedition to Guiana that he was to undertake personally in 1595. (Although Ralegh did not, as is often claimed, introduce American tobacco into England, he did popularize the smoking of it.)

To the years of Ralegh's association with the court can probably be attributed the majority of his poems. The word *probably* deserves special emphasis, however, because the poetry as a body, as Steven W. May observes in *The Elizabethan Courtier Poets* (1991), "presents one of the most difficult editorial problems of the English Renaissance." Although several of his verses circulated freely in manuscript during the 1580s, exact dating is in most cases impossible. The canon, too, remains quite unstable, because Ralegh made no apparent attempt to preserve his poems and because his name sometimes appears as an attention getter in association with poems he almost surely did not write. In the various modern editions the number ascribed to him varies from forty-one (plus twelve others assigned conjecturally) in Agnes M. C. Latham's 1951 edition to a niggardly twenty-three (plus fragments of translation and seven "possible" works) in the conservative edition of Michael Rudick (1970). De-

tailed discussions of the problem of authenticity of individual poems are given in the apparatus in Rudick's edition, in Pierre Lefranc's *Sir Walter Ralegh, écrivain* (1968), and in May's *Sir Walter Raleigh* (1989).

Many of Ralegh's court poems involved stylized descriptions of his relationship with Queen Elizabeth, and most of those involve his imaginative adaptation of themes and conventions from the literary mode established by the great Italian Francesco Petrarca, or, as he was known in England, Francis Petrarch. Although Petrarch had lived and written in the Italy of two centuries earlier, Elizabethans of poetic inclination considered him a contemporary in spirit. His popularity during the Renaissance derived in large part from the formula he devised for a group of more than three hundred sonnets and other lyrical poems written to or about Laura, a lady whom he idealized as a paradigm of earthly beauty and spiritual inspiration during the twenty-one years between his first glimpse of her – an experience he claimed made him instantly a poet – and her death. In this formula, sex and spirituality find mutual accommodation and, indeed, interdependence. In its conventionalized form the Petrarchan experience takes something like the following pattern: the poet is overwhelmed at first sight of his lady with an admiration of her physical beauty that leads, in turn, to appreciation of her mind, then of her spiritual beauty, and finally to the realization that not only this beauty but also the poet's ability to appreciate it comes ultimately from the goodness of God.

For the Petrarchan, then, what begins as attraction to concrete, sensory phenomena ends in religious understanding. Laura's beauty eventually recedes into philosophical perspective as simply one stage in a continuum of increasingly refined levels of perspectivity, linking the sensual with the divine and thus reconciling the amatory and philosophical instincts with the personality of Renaissance man.

But for most workers in the Petrarchan literary vein, what proved of most frequent interest in this idealistic scheme was the midrange of the process, the stage at which the lover's burning desire and the lady's chaste refusal of his advances interact to create tension and stress. The posture of the despairing lover, who must suffer the agonies of his unrequited passion with fever, chills, and mental distraction before advancing to a higher stage of awareness, is a familiar one in Elizabethan literature. It occurs, for example, with great seriousness in Spenser's *Amoretti* (1595) sonnet sequence and, as the object of indulgent satire, in William Shakespeare's *As You Like It* (circa 1600). With Ralegh its uses become complexly political.

If Ralegh did not actually invent what A. D. Cousins calls "political Petrarchism," he certainly developed it to new levels of self-serving appropriateness. Leonard Tennenhouse has argued that Ralegh exploits the fact that much of what was metaphorical in the imagined relationship between lover and lady in the sonnet tradition became, when transposed to the relationship between courtier and queen, literally true. The Petrarchan accorded his lady the power of life and death, banishment and acceptance, enchainment and freedom. Elizabeth – as Ralegh would be painfully reminded during his imprisonment in 1592 – possessed these powers in a very real way. Her disdain could indeed be deadly, her approbation a shower of manna. "Praised be Diana's fair and harmless light" (1593) provides a detailed example of the way in which Ralegh manipulated convention for results that are both flattering to the queen and assertive of his own material interest:

Praised be Diana's fair and harmless light,
Praised be the dews, wherewith she moists the ground;
Praised be her beams, the glory of the night,
Praised be her power, by which all powers abound.

Praised be her Nymphs, with whom she decks the
    woods,
Praised be her knights, in whom true honor lives,
Praised be that force, by which she moves the floods,
Let that Diana shine, which all these gives.

In Heaven Queen she is among the spheres,
In aye she Mistress-like makes all things pure;
Eternity in her oft change she bears,
She beauty is, by her the fair endure.

Time wears her not, she doth his chariot guide,
Mortality below her orb is placed;
By her the virtue of the stars down slide,
In her is virtue's perfect image cast.

   A knowledge pure it is her worth to know;
   With Circes let them dwell that think not so.

One can imagine how phrases such as "Time wears her not" must have reverberated in the imagination of the notoriously vain Elizabeth, advanced in years when the poem was probably written and so conscious of the passage of time that she forbade any public discussion of her "grand climacteric," or sixty-third birthday, when it occurred in 1596. But there is also an elaborate subtext of petition and solicitation in the poem, established by allusion. Ralegh often addressed the Virgin Queen (as did Spenser, who follows his lead in this regard) with the names of goddesses associated with the virtue of chastity: Diana, Cynthia, or Phoebe (in Ralegh's poetic coinage, Belphoebe). All of these figures are connected in classical myth with the moon, as Diana is in Ralegh's poem. But the heavenly body most frequently used by poets and politicians alike as a symbol of kingship was the sun – partly because of its primacy in the sky and partly because of its traditional symbolism of the virtue of justice. These symbolic relations have biblical precedents: "For behold, the day cometh, that shall burn as an oven; and all the proud, yea, all that do wickedly, shall be stubble: and the day that cometh shall burn them up" (Malachi 4:1–2). Ralegh draws on these precedents in the central section of "The Ocean to Scinthia," when he wants to represent the severity of Elizabeth's royal displeasure. But the moon, dominant in its own temporal sphere, is soft and feminine, a better vehicle for the image of monarchy that Ralegh wants to develop in his petitions to the queen. In contrast with the sun's evocation of justice, the moon evokes consolation, mercy, and love. By what Ralegh calls its "harmless" light, human failings are overlooked and romance is allowed to flourish. Thus, a somewhat cynical but essentially accurate reading of the first line might be simply "Please keep on giving the honors and rewards to which your petitioner is joyfully accustomed."

"Like to a Hermit poor in place obscure" (1591) is another Petrarchan exercise, this time in the presentation of the lover in despair, seeking isolation and obscurity (situations that never appealed to Ralegh) as a response to his lady's neglect. Given Ralegh's propensity for sartorial splendidness and show, his contemporaries must have taken special note of the irony in his promise that "A gown of gray my body shall attire." But he knew what he was doing, and, presumably, so did the queen. Although to the modern ear these poems may sound overwrought or even fulsome (Henry David Thoreau thought Ralegh's genius was "warped by the frivolous society of the court"), it is possible to see them as part of a stylized, sophisticated discourse that brought grace and a measure of blitheness to the otherwise mundane power brokering that characterized the workings of the Tudor court.

Among the most memorable and possibly most successful of Ralegh's adaptations of the Petrarchan mode is the fine sonnet he contributed to the group of congratulatory verses printed with the first three books of *The Faerie Queene,* whose publication in 1590, if one is to believe Spenser's ac-

*Engraved title page for the work Ralegh wrote to please Prince
Henry, the young son of James I*

count in *Colin Clouts Come Home Againe* (1595), owed
something to Ralegh's encouragement, as its favorable reception by Elizabeth owed something to
Ralegh's recommendation. Ralegh, to whom Spenser addresses his preface to *Colin Clouts Come Home
Againe,* in the form of an epistle, manages to eulogize the epic, flatter Elizabeth, and perhaps develop
implications of his own feelings of neglect, all in
fourteen lines:

> Methought I saw the grave, where *Laura* lay,
> Within that temple, where the vestal flame
> Was wont to burn, and passing by that way,
> To see that buried dust of living fame,
> Whose tomb fair love, and fairer virtue kept,
> All suddenly I saw the Fairy Queen:
> At whose approach the soul of *Petrarch* wept,
> And from thenceforth those graces were not seen.
> For they this Queen attended, in whose stead
> Oblivion laid him down on *Laura's* hearse:
> Hereat the hardest stones were seen to bleed,

> And groans of buried ghosts the heavens did pierce.
> Where *Homer's* sprite did tremble all for grief,
> And cursed th' access of that celestial thief.

Ralegh's ostensible purpose is to celebrate
Spenser's achievement by holding that his poem
will outgo all earlier accomplishments in verse — especially those of Petrarch, whose Laura will be
dimmed in favor of Spenser's Gloriana, who by
Spenser's own assertion represents Elizabeth.
Homer and other poets of antiquity will lament in
their afterlife to see Spenser stealing from them reputations once thought secure. Elizabeth, of course,
whose virtues make the depiction possible, shares
with the artist the glory that is now England's. But,
as Peter Ure and Cousins have pointed out, most of
the sonnet concentrates on the theme of displace-
ment, on the abandonment and despair of those dis-
lodged from former prominence. Ralegh's emotional identification with these figures may perhaps

be explained by his anxieties throughout 1589 over competition for Elizabeth's favor with the young and powerful earl of Essex. Ralegh had, in fact, felt obliged literally to displace himself for a while to his Irish estates to avoid violent conflict and the royal anger that would have surely ensued (Ralegh and Essex had agreed on one occasion to a duel, but the queen's counselors prevented it). Being overshadowed, then, was more than merely a literary motif in Ralegh's mind at the time of composition.

In his sonnet on *The Faerie Queene* Ralegh has been seen as formulating an early literary statement of a theme that was also to figure largely in his historiographical musings in *The History of the World:* that all joy and all monuments lack permanence, and humanity is forever destined to watch its greatest achievements fade and die. An extremely poignant expression of this idea – among the most forceful expressions of it that the Elizabethan period has to offer – is Ralegh's "Nature that washed her hands in milk," a poem that turns again to the Petrarchan tradition, but this time with a clear-minded assertion of the way that time and mutability render futile the attempts of human beings, with their idealizing philosophies, to find permanence on earth. Ralegh begins with the poet idealizing his lady in good Petrarchan form, then moves on to the predictable lack of responsiveness of the proud and tyrannizing beauty, who plays the game with all the aloofness and stoniness of heart that the role of "cruel fair" requires. Yet Time is not impressed, nor tolerant of the self-deluding attitude of either party:

> But Time which nature doth despise,
>   And rudely gives her love the lie,
> Makes hope a fool, and sorrow wise,
>   His hands do neither wash, nor dry,
> But being made of steel and rust,
> Turns snow, and silk, and milk to dust.
>
> The light, the belly, lips and breath
>   He dims, discolors, and destroys;
> With those he feeds, but fills not death,
>   Which sometimes were the food of joys;
> Yea Time doth dull each lively wit,
> And drys all wantonness with it.
>
> Oh cruel Time which takes in trust
>   Our youth, our joys and all we have,
> And pays us but with age and dust;
>   Who in the dark and silent grave,
> When we have wandered all our ways
> Shuts up the story of our days.

Ralegh's notice of the human propensity for self-delusion is registered again, in a witty and sardonic vein, in his reply (1600) to Christopher Marlowe's poem of invitation, "The Passionate Shepherd to His Love" ("Come live with me, and be my love," 1600). There Marlowe had indulged in a conventional pastoral escapist fantasy that the proper antidote to human problems is withdrawal from social complexity into a natural setting whose beauty transcends all the distractions of life in the city or court. To this attitude of neoprimitivism Ralegh does what he does to Petrarchism in "Nature that washed her hands in milk": he subjects it to the pressure of a rationalism based firmly on awareness of the power of time. To Marlowe's persuasive shepherd, Ralegh's "nymph" replies that the promise of a paradise requiring permanent youth and joy is a promise no mortal can fulfill:

> Time drives the flocks from field to fold,
> When rivers rage, and rocks grow cold,
> And Philomell becometh dumb,
> The rest complains of cares to come.

The skepticism evident in poems such as these has perhaps contributed to a tendency, once widespread but now generally discredited, to magnify some charges hinted at by Ralegh's enemies in his own time into a full-blown philosophical conspiracy, whereby Ralegh is seen as heading, throughout much of the 1590s, an antireligious and philosophically occult "School of Night" that included such men as George Chapman, Thomas Harriot, Sir Henry Percy (the "Wizard Earl" of Northumberland), and, in some accounts, Marlowe – all of whom are assumed to have been interested in such pursuits as occult science and necromancy and in defying conventional Christianity on every hand. These notions found full expression in two books published in 1936, M. C. Bradbrook's *The School of Night* and Frances Yates's *A Study of "Love's Labour's Lost."* These works differ in emphasis but find in Shakespeare's play a satiric attack on Ralegh's group and a repudiation of its supposed premium on contemplation and abstract theory over active life. Although little factual evidence exists for these theories, they still come up occasionally in popular biographies. Ernest A. Strathmann's *Sir Walter Ralegh: A Study in Elizabethan Skepticism* (1951) and John W. Shirley's biography of Thomas Harriot (1983) provide authoritative rebuttals.

Had Ralegh ever entertained any delusions about the permanence of status and power, it is unlikely that they could have survived the events of 1592, a year that witnessed his precipitous decline from privilege and command to a cell in the Tower of London. Chiefly through material from the diary of Ralegh's brother-in-law, published by A. L. Rowse in *Sir Walter Ralegh, His Family and Private Life* (1962), what seems to be the full story of his fall is now known. Possibly as early as 1588 Ralegh had married Elizabeth Throckmorton, an honorary attendant in the royal privy chamber. Because of the queen's well-known hostility to marriage on the part of her favorites, whose undivided loyalties her vanity required, the union had to be kept secret. A child, Damerei Ralegh, died soon after his birth on 26 March 1592, and although Elizabeth Ralegh returned to court in April as though nothing had happened, the queen discovered the true state of affairs and committed the couple to separate confinement in the Tower in July. In September, however, Ralegh was released to supervise the removal of captured Spanish goods from a ship whose crew could be kept in check only by the force of his personality and the respect in which they held him. Although she allowed him to keep Sherborne, the fine estate she had granted him only months before the scandal erupted, the queen removed Ralegh from his captainship of the guard and essentially exiled him from court. Lady Ralegh was never again admitted to the royal presence, even after her husband's restoration to favor in 1597.

Although these happenings were widely known and much talked about in their time, their chief literary consequences had to wait almost three hundred years for entry into public view. Discovered in 1870 among some papers relating to Ralegh at Hatfield House, the family seat of Elizabeth's lord treasurer, William Cecil, Lord Burghley, are four poems that all but a few modern critics read as Ralegh's sustained lament to the queen during his imprisonment: a seven-line poem beginning "If Synthia be a Queen, a princess, and supreme"; a sonnet, "My Body in the Walls Captived"; a 522-line poem in interlocking couplets, "The 21st: and Last Book of the Ocean to Scinthia"; and a 22-line fragment, "The End of the Books of the Ocean's Love to Scinthia, and the Beginning of the 22nd Book, Entreating of Sorrow," which breaks off in the middle of a line. The last two poems, or parts of poems, are generally spoken of by critics collectively as "The Ocean to Cynthia." Some editors, Agnes M. C. Latham among them, read the numerals as "11th" and "12th"; but in 1985 Stacy M. Clanton confirmed in a detailed paleographic study of the manuscript (which is in Ralegh's own hand) the readings "21st" and "22nd."

Readers who appreciate neatness in literary history have found little comfort in the maze of problems surrounding these verses, problems involving the date, the exact nature of the events alluded to, and the possibility of a larger structure, either lost or unwritten, of which the surviving fragments may have been intended as parts. Because Spenser mentions in *Colin Clouts Come Home Againe* (written in some form in 1589 though not printed until 1595) that Ralegh, whom he calls the Shepherd of the Ocean, had written a "lamentable lay" about hard usage at the hands of his lady, Cynthia, many early critics assumed that the overall structure was at least conceived and partially executed prior to the exposure of Ralegh's marriage, then continued to include later events. And because of their fragmentary appearance, some writers have even assumed that they are parts of a vast epic, possibly planned for twelve books on the model of Virgil's *Aeneid*. The bulk of scholarly opinion now, however, is that the poems date from 1592 and were probably composed with the hope that they would reach the queen (Katherine Duncan-Jones is in a distinct minority in her belief that "The Ocean to Cynthia" dates from Ralegh's second imprisonment, under King James, and that it mourns Elizabeth's death), and that what survives is almost surely all that was written, the unfinished appearance either resulting from Ralegh's release, which would have made further composition redundant, or constituting a literary effect in which the speaker's distracted state of mind is mirrored in the broken form of the poem itself.

That these poems exist as an intentionally unfinished structure may be argued on grounds of their possible organization in terms of "topomorphic composition," a compositional strategy common in the Renaissance. Topomorphic composition denotes the way in which poems achieve symmetrical or otherwise significant internal structures through repetition of motifs, images, numerical patterns, and even rhymes to achieve balance and internal cross-referencing related to the main ideas. Beginnings and ends of poems are frequently linked in this way, and the central idea or image often occurs in the exact center of the poem. (Spenser accomplishes such a structure in each of the first three books of *The Faerie Queene*.)

Regarded in light of topomorphic practice, "The Ocean to Cynthia" can be seen as possessing an internal completeness of structure that underlies the apparent fragmentation that first meets the eye. The "21st Book" begins and ends with the development of a winter pastoral scene (reminiscent of the setting in Thomas Sackville's induction to the 1563 edition of *A Mirror for Magistrates*), the landscape serving as a symbolic restatement of the motif of

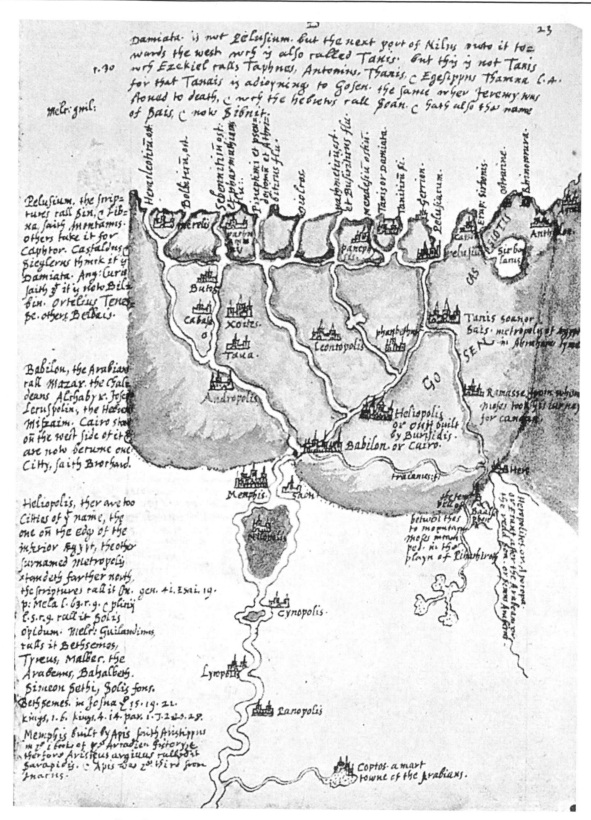

Page from Ralegh's notes for The History of the World *(British Library)*

desolation and withering that exists inside the speaker's heart and mind. The first thirty-six and the last fifty-two lines develop this mood, echoing several central images — withered leaves, dryness, impending storms, sheep in the fields. The opening and closing lines share certain specific words, concepts, and rhyming sounds — *complain, again, mean* (pronounced "main") — to suggest a kind of circularity and closure:

> Sufficeth it to you my joys interred,
> In simple words that I my woes complain,
> You that then died when first my fancy erred,
> Joys under dust, that never live again.
> . . . .
> To God I leave it, who first gave it me,
> And I her gave, and she returned again
> As it was hers. So let his mercies be,
> Of my last comforts, the essential mean.
> > But be it so, or not, th' effects, are past.
> > Her love had end; my woe must ever last.

"Woes" in the opening section is echoed in the "woe" of the closing; the "joys" of line 4 corresponds to the "comforts" of line 520; and the image of death dominates both sections.

Most of the poem consists of lament for a time when the speaker enjoyed the bounty of his sovereign and love and for the fact that the gentle Belphoebe of former times (here, as usual, identified with the moon) has been supplanted by the blazing sun of justice, as the speaker's one thoughtless indiscretion has earned him perpetual grief. At the center of the poem falls a passage that contains the biblical image of justice burning away the stubble of a fallow field:

> And as a field wherein the stubble stands
> Of harvest past, the plowman's eye offends,
> He tills again or tears them up with hands,
> And throws to fire as foiled and fruitless ends,
>
> And takes delight another seed to sow. . . .
> So doth the mind root up all wonted thought
> And scorns the care of our remaining woes;
> The sorrows, which themselves for us have wrought,
>
> Are burnt to cinders by new kindled fires,
> The ashes are dispersed into the air,
> The scythes, the groans of all our past desires
> Are clean outworn, as things that never were.

Other indications that the work is organized to achieve a subtext of significant form may be gleaned from the manuscript, which bears marks of Ralegh's plans for revision. The overall structure is a series of verse modules of varying lengths, devel-

oping the main ideas and related associationally, though not always in the sequence of a plot, with each other. Several such sections are written in lighter-colored ink than the rest of the manuscript and tick-marked to the left of each line. Since these passages are rhetorical exercises, or elaborations, of rhetorical topoi rather than advancements of the narrative, it seems reasonable to conclude that Ralegh left a certain number of lines uncomposed and places marked for later inclusion during the progress of the first draft but clearly knew how many lines or modular units he wanted in the completed poem: that is, he was engaged in some form of numerical composition, working toward a predetermined proportionality that may or may not lie hidden in the work as it exists. Also to the point is that the "22nd Book" breaks off in the middle of its twenty-second line; the number 22, in Spenser's works, usually symbolizes chastity, virginity, and self-denial, all qualities appropriate to the virgin queen who is the stimulus for Ralegh's poem.

It is not known whether Queen Elizabeth ever saw "The Ocean to Cynthia," or whether the remorse that Ralegh expresses there was a factor in her decision to free him from the Tower. But if she read Spenser's *The Faerie Queene* she must have recognized another, extended story of her relationship with Ralegh continued allegorically through several books of Spenser's epic in the ongoing story of Arthur's squire, Timias, whom Spenser had created to represent Ralegh in Book 3 (published in 1590) and to whom he returned in Books 4 and 5 (published in 1596). In Book 3 Timias falls in love with Belphoebe, one of several representations of the queen in Spenser's poem; but in the later section the story goes on to chronicle the complications of 1592. In Book IV, Canto vii, Timias's betrayal of the trust of Belphoebe by succumbing to the attractions of Amoret refers specifically to the Throckmorton marriage. A reconciliation begins in the following canto, as Spenser evidently hoped it would in real life; and the epic poet may be seen as taking Ralegh's part, although he does acknowledge the wrong done through human frailty. In Book 6 Ralegh and his wife may be found again in the episodes with Timias and Serena (Serena is a name used by Ralegh in one of his lyric poems).

With characteristic resilience Ralegh took as active a part in national affairs as his fortunes permitted throughout 1593. Serving his third session in the House of Commons, he sponsored several measures favorable to the queen and continued his advocacy of an aggressive policy toward Spain. In the summer of that year he attended a dinner party with the Reverend Ralph Ironside, with whom he argued, evidently in a friendly way, some points of divinity. The exchange became the subject of much gossip and popular speculation, which attributed to Ralegh's unorthodox, even heretical, beliefs, and a commission was formed to investigate. Although Ralegh was cleared of the allegations and his case was dismissed without formal charges, the affair contributed to the perennial rumors about his atheistic and occult interests.

For some time Ralegh had been interested in a project of exploration and colonization in regions along the Orinoco River in Guiana, a part of what is today Venezuela, both for the wealth such a project might bring and for the hedge it might provide against Spanish power in the New World. Having obtained a measure of support from the Crown, he set forth in February 1595 with hopes of finding El Dorado, the supposed interior capital of Guiana, a city rich beyond conception. He, of course, found no such city; but his explorations in Guiana provided, when he recorded them in *The Discovery of the Large, Rich and Beautiful Empire of Guiana* (1596), what one critic has termed one of the most fascinating adventure stories ever written.

Ralegh's talents as a prose stylist were great — in fact, up until the twentieth century his literary reputation rested chiefly on prose. In 1591 his rousing defense of Sir Richard Grenville's conduct in a naval encounter with Spanish forces, *A Report of the Truth of the Fight about the Isles of Açores, This Last Summer. Betwixt the Revenge, One of Her Majesty's Ships, And an Armada of the King of Spain,* had been widely admired and had succeeded admirably in its intent. The Guiana tract embodies, with great skill, the combination of propagandistic sophistication and understanding of literary effect that invigorates most of Ralegh's prose. Ralegh always wrote with immediate purpose, with persuasion as his goal. In his main works he favors the first-person point of view, and his reader is consistently aware of a dominating personality behind the page. *The Discovery of the Large, Rich, and Beautiful Empire of Guiana* is an example of Ralegh's prose at its best.

Having presumably been trained, like most Elizabethan pupils, on rhetorical principles deriving ultimately from Aristotle, Ralegh had learned the basic criteria of persuasive writing and oratory: the ethical, pathetic, and logical avenues of appeal. The ethical appeal, or the criterion of ethos, prescribes the speaker's establishment of his own authority to speak — his command of the facts and the legitimacy of his purposes. He must gain the audience's confidence in his character. Ralegh's attention to the narrator's persona is careful and deliberative, because he is attempting to promote interest in further exploration and exploitation — managed, of course, by himself. Thus, he is at pains to establish himself as a clear and practical thinker and planner, a man with a scientific mind and a capacity for retaining details — not some romantic visionary following the lead of idealism and an overactive imagination. Passages such as this establish practical authority: "The great river of *Orenoque* or *Baraquan* hath nine branches which fall out on the north side of his own main mouth: on the south side it hath seven other fallings into the sea, so it disemboketh by 16 arms in all, between islands and broken ground, but the islands are very great, many of them as big as the Isle of *Wight* and bigger, and many less. From the first branch on the north to the last of the south it is at least 100 leagues, so as the river's mouth is no less than 300 miles wide at his entrance into the sea. . . . all those that inhabit in the mouth of this river . . . are these *Tivitivas,* of which there are two chief lords which have continual wars one with the other."

The pathetic approach, or the criterion of pathos, requires appeal to the reader's emotions and capacity to imagine the sensory experience evoked by a scene such as one in which Ralegh draws on pastoral traditions in literature as well as on his own experience to depict Guiana as potentially an Eden of natural beauty and resources: "On both sides of this river, we passed the most beautiful country that ever mine eyes beheld: and whereas all that we had seen before was nothing but woods, prickles, bushes, and thorns, here we beheld plains of beauty miles in length, the grass short and green, and in divers parts groves of trees by themselves, as if they had been by all the art and labor in the world so made of purpose: and still as we rowed, the deer came down feeding by the water's side, as if they had been used to a keeper's call."

The criterion of *logos,* the logical approach, gets to the deliberative purpose of it all. Having prepared his audience by building trust in the speaker and re-creating the emotional context of his experience, Ralegh turns to the reasons and the means. Guiana, he argues, will be a source of national treasure as well as a defense against Spain in the very heart of its empire: "Now although these reports may seem strange, yet if we consider the many millions which are daily brought out of *Peru* into Spain, we may easily believe the same, for we find that by the abundant treasure of that country, the Spanish king vexeth all the princes of Europe, and is become in a few years from a poor king of *Castile* the greatest monarch of this part of the world, and likely

Ralegh's burial site, south side of altar at St. Margaret's Church, Westminster

every day to increase, if other princes forslow the good occasions offered, and suffer him to add this empire to the rest, which by far exceedeth all the rest: if his gold now endanger us, he will then be unresistable."

Ralegh's tract, for all the attention it elicited, succeeded more as a literary work than as an immediate incentive to investors or statesmen. It was not until twenty years later that he was able to go back to the Orinoco regions, and then it was on the final, calamitous expedition that precipitated his execution. Among the literary descendants of *The Discovery of the Large, Rich and Beautiful Empire of Guiana* can be counted such works as Shakespeare's *The Tempest* (circa 1611) and Daniel Defoe's *The Life and Strange Surprising Adventures of Robinson Crusoe* (1719).

By 1597 Ralegh had regained the queen's favor and was reappointed Captain of the Guard. No small factor in his recovery of status was his participation in 1596 with Lord Admiral Thomas Howard and Ralegh's former antagonist, the earl of Essex, on a daring raid against the Spanish at Cadiz. In 1598 he spoke prominently in the House of Commons, and in 1600 he was appointed governor of the Isle of Jersey, a post whose duties he executed conscientiously, though chiefly in absentia. The following year he helped put down Essex's rebellion and attended, in his capacity as the captain of the guard, the earl's execution, a function that

earned him some accusations of callousness because he had supposedly smoked his pipe as Essex prepared to die.

During these years Ralegh wrote voluminously on many topics in prose — treatises on ship building, agriculture and economics, the waging of war, the nature of the soul. Most of these works defy precise dating, and several, such as the Machiavellian political treatise "Cabinet-Council," have been convincingly banished from his canon. Most of his writings display the qualities of trenchancy, logical force, and a capacity for the startlingly apt phrase that led Thoreau to describe him as a man who gave the impression of writing with a pen in one hand and a sword in the other. The most impressive result of these abilities was *The History of the World,* another literary product of the Tower of London.

After the queen's death in 1603 Ralegh's lack of favor with the new monarch, James I, was readily apparent. James feared war with Spain, which Ralegh had long supported, and generally represented the opposite of Ralegh in most aspects of personality. Furthermore, his opinion of Ralegh had been soured by Lord Henry Howard and Sir Robert Cecil, both of whom feared Ralegh's ability to sway public opinion and wished to prevent him from obtaining the kind of influence he had enjoyed during Elizabeth's reign. James began dismantling Ralegh's major holdings almost immediately, removing him from the captaincy of the guard, lifting his patent to license wines, and evicting him from his London residence, Durham House. On 17 November 1603 Ralegh was tried for high treason.

Specifically, Ralegh was charged with participation in the so-called Main Plot of Lord Cobham (Henry Brooke) and others, possibly with the assistance of Spain, to assassinate the royal family and place people of their own choosing in power. Ralegh seems to have had some inkling that schemes were afoot but shared no complicity in them. His conviction was guaranteed by James's desire and that of Ralegh's influential enemies; and despite his eloquent self-defense throughout the proceedings, he was sentenced to death, with execution scheduled for 9 December. In a last-minute reprieve the sentence was commuted to imprisonment at the pleasure of the king. Ralegh's confinement was to last for thirteen years.

In prison Ralegh was allowed regular visits from his wife and friends (his second son, Carew Ralegh, was begotten in the Tower) and allowed to develop interests in chemistry and other sciences, sometimes in the company of the earl of Northumberland, another prisoner of rank who was interested in the New Science. Among other achievements in the laboratory Ralegh produced his "Balsam of Guiana," a medicine that achieved considerable notice. Not long after his imprisonment began he apparently decided that his main hope for release lay in the young Prince Henry, his frequent visitor in the Tower. Prince Henry had selected Ralegh as a mentor or surrogate father, an attractive alternative to his own neglectful father. It was for Prince Henry that *The History of the World* was begun. When Henry died of typhoid fever in 1612 Ralegh gave up the project, writing a long, majestic preface before allowing the huge fragment to be printed in 1614.

In that preface his bitterness toward the king is everywhere apparent. Stressing the vanity of human pomp, the transitory nature of earthly rule, and the proposition that no monarch stands above the law of God, he thoroughly embarrassed James, who remarked that Ralegh was "too saucy in the censuring of princes" and ordered that Ralegh's name and portrait be excised from all copies before further distribution. Ralegh argued, according to a providential view of history common in Christian thought since it was formulated by Saint Augustine in the fifth century, that history is a map of God's will, that God intervenes in the course of history to punish and reward human rulers, either by immedi-

ate action or by consequences deferred to later generations in the same dynastic line. In history God is the First Cause, generating a plan decreed at the Creation and continuing to the Day of Judgment.

On the other hand, in the preface and throughout the body of the book Ralegh also shows an interest in the more recent, "politic" historians such as Jean Bodin, Niccolò Machiavelli, and Francis Bacon, who concentrated on the secondary causes constituted by human psychology, motives, and politics. These writers generally considered history and what is now called political science in a context apart from theology, believing that human beings to a large degree operate in a world of their own making and with consequences incurred or avoided by their own ability to plan and manipulate.

If Ralegh hoped to assimilate these two perspectives into a single coherent view, he was — in the opinion of most modern students of historiography — unsuccessful. But as a literary monument *The History of the World* retains its appeal. Ralegh illustrates points about ancient conflicts with vivid, concrete details from his own experiences at war, advising his reader how similar situations were handled when he met them during his service in France or Ireland or at sea. Biblical nations are compared in various respects with the native populations of Guiana and the North American Outer Banks. As a result of his own botanical study, he determines that the Tree of Life in Eden was a variety of *Ficus indica,* the Indian fig. On the whole, his history is less a map of God's will than a mirror of his own mind, in all its richness of imagination and its command of effect.

Ralegh seems ultimately to doubt that people are willing to learn much from history. Human pride and stubbornness probably ensure that people will recommit the crimes and errors of their forebears. The sonorous conclusion to the preface, written after the death of Prince Henry and of Ralegh's best hopes, extols Death as the one superior teacher whom no one can ignore: "O eloquent, just and mighty Death! whom none could advise, thou hast persuaded; that none hath dared, thou hast done; and whom all the world hath flattered, thou only hast cast out of the world and despised: thou hast drawn together all the far stretched greatness, all the pride, cruelty, and ambition of man, and covered it all over with these two narrow words, *Hic jacet.*"

After two strokes, confiscation of his estate at Sherborne by the king, and other discommodities attendant upon being a perpetual prisoner, Ralegh at last persuaded James, who was short on funds, to accept his proposal to establish a gold industry with mines in Guiana, which he claimed gave almost certain promise of an abundance of precious metals. James may have been persuaded in part by his queen, Anne, who remained well disposed toward Sir Walter. It is not possible at this remove to know Ralegh's true intent, but many scholars believe that he knew quite well there was little hope of finding gold in Guiana but a good chance of taking lucrative Spanish prizes on the high seas in the old privateering style of Elizabethan days. Could enough Spanish gold be taken, Ralegh may have believed, James would find it impossible not to be appeased.

The expedition was a disaster. With more than a dozen ships and a thousand men, Ralegh left England in June 1617, unaware that the Crown had covertly supplied his itinerary to the Spanish ambassador — either through fear of offending Spain or with direct intent to ruin Ralegh. Encountering Spanish troops near Santo Tomé in Guiana, Ralegh's forces attacked, and his eldest son was killed in battle. After some fruitless exploration the company returned to England, with Ralegh in grief and resigned to his fate. Captured after a half-hearted attempt to gain asylum in France, he was returned to the Tower for execution under the reinvoked sentence of 1603. He was beheaded, after a moving scaffold speech, on 29 October 1618, outside the Palace of Westminster.

For three centuries after his death Ralegh was represented as a man of letters chiefly by his prose writings. *The History of the World,* with its assertion that no monarch stood above the laws and judgments of God, appealed strongly to Oliver Cromwell and contributed in no small measure to the intellectual climate that made possible the revolution of 1649 and the execution of Charles I. *The Discovery of . . . Guiana* remained current as a remarkable adventure story well into Victorian times. Ralegh's poetry, in contrast, was generally neglected until recent times, when scholars and critics — mainly those interested in Ralegh's relationship with Edmund Spenser — began a revival of interest in his poems both for their own sake and for the insight they provide into the interrelationship of political and literary realms during the time of Elizabeth I. Ralegh today is generally regarded as a poet of occasional brilliance and consistent understanding of the literary currents of his age, an author who wrote memorably and effectively when occasion presented itself, but for whom the writer's art was but one of the many accomplishments of a life pledged equally to Mercury and Mars.

Bibliographies:

T. N. Brushfield, *A Bibliography of Sir Walter Ralegh Knt. Second Edition with Notes Revised and Enlarged with Portraits and Facsimiles* (Exeter, U.K.: Commin, 1908; New York: Franklin, 1968);

Jerry Leath Mills, "Recent Studies in Ralegh," *English Literary Renaissance,* 15 (Spring 1985): 225–244;

Mills, *Sir Walter Ralegh: A Reference Guide* (Boston: G. K. Hall, 1986);

Christopher M. Armitage, *Sir Walter Ralegh: An Annotated Bibliography* (Chapel Hill: University of North Carolina Press, 1987).

Biographies:

Edward Edwards, *The Life of Sir Walter Ralegh,* 2 volumes (London: Macmillan, 1868);

Willard M. Wallace, *Sir Walter Ralegh* (Princeton: Princeton University Press, 1959; Oxford: Oxford University Press, 1959);

J. H. Adamson and H. F. Folland, *The Shepherd of the Ocean: An Account of Sir Walter Ralegh and His Times* (Boston: Gambit, 1969; London: Bodley Head, 1969).

References:

James P. Bednarz, "Ralegh in Spenser's Historical Allegory," *Spenser Studies,* 4 (1984): 49–70;

Stacy M. Clanton, "The 'Number' of Sir Walter Ralegh's *Booke of the Ocean to Scinthia,*" *Studies in Philology,* 82 (Spring 1985): 200–211;

A. D. Cousins, "The Coming of Mannerism: The Later Ralegh and the Early Donne," *English Literary Renaissance,* 9 (Winter 1979): 86–107;

Cousins, "Ralegh's 'A Vision upon this Conceipt of the Faery Queen,' " *Explicator,* 41 (Spring 1983): 14–16;

Donald Davie, "A Reading of 'The Ocean's Love to Cynthia,'" in *Elizabethan Poetry,* edited by John Russell Brown and Bernard Harris (London: Arnold, 1960), pp. 71–89;

Katherine Duncan-Jones, "The Date of Ralegh's '21st: and Last Booke of the Ocean to Scinthia,' " *Review of English Studies,* new series 21 (May 1970): 143–158;

Philip Edwards, *Sir Walter Ralegh* (London: Longmans, Green, 1953);

Stephen J. Greenblatt, *Sir Walter Ralegh: The Renaissance Man and His Roles* (New Haven: Yale University Press, 1973);

Frank Wilson Cheney Hersey, "Sir Walter Ralegh as a Man of Letters," *Proceedings of the State Literary and Historical Association of North Carolina,* no. 25 (1918): 42–54;

Christopher Hill, "Ralegh – Science, History, and Politics," in his *The Intellectual Origins of the English Revolution* (Oxford: Clarendon Press, 1965), pp. 131–224;

Joyce Horner, "The Large Landscape: A Study of Certain Images in Ralegh," *Essays in Criticism,* 5 (July 1955): 197–213;

Michael L. Johnson, "Some Problems of Unity in Sir Walter Ralegh's *The Ocean's Love to Cynthia,*" *Studies in English Literature,* 14 (Winter 1974): 17–30;

Pierre Lefranc, *Sir Walter Ralegh, écrivain* (Paris: Librairie Armand Colin, 1968);

F. J. Levy, *Tudor Historical Thought* (San Marino, Cal.: Huntington Library, 1967), pp. 286–294;

Steven W. May, *The Elizabethan Courtier Poets: The Poems and Their Contexts* (Columbia & London: University of Missouri Press, 1991);

May, *Sir Walter Raleigh* (Boston: Twayne, 1989);

Jerry Leath Mills, "Sir Walter Ralegh as a Man of Letters," in *Ralegh and Quinn: The Explorer and His Boswell,* edited by H. G. Jones (Chapel Hill: North Caroliniana Society, 1987), pp. 165–179;

Walter Oakeshott, *The Queen and the Poet* (London: Faber & Faber, 1960);

John Racin, *Sir Walter Ralegh as Historian: An Analysis of "The History of the World"* (Salzburg, Austria: Universität Salzburg, 1974);

A. L. Rowse, *Sir Walter Ralegh, His Family and Private Life* (New York: Harper & Row, 1962);

John W. Shirley, *Thomas Hariot: A Biography* (Oxford: Clarendon Press, 1983);

Ernest A. Strathmann, *Sir Walter Ralegh: A Study in Elizabethan Skepticism* (New York: Columbia University Press, 1951);

Leonard Tennenhouse, "Sir Walter Ralegh and the Literature of Clientage," in *Patronage in the Renaissance,* edited by Guy Fitch Lytle and Stephen Orgel (Princeton: Princeton University Press, 1981), pp. 235–258;

Henry David Thoreau, *Sir Walter Ralegh,* edited by Henry Aiken Metcalf (Boston: Bibliophile Society, 1905; reprinted, New York: Gordon Press, 1976);

Peter Ure, "The Poetry of Sir Walter Ralegh," *Review of English Literature,* 1 (July 1960): 19–29;

Arnold Williams, *The Common Expositor: An Account of the Commentaries on Genesis, 1527–1633* (Chapel Hill: University of North Carolina Press, 1948);

J. W. Williamson, *The Myth of the Conqueror: Prince Henry Stuart. A Study of Seventeenth-Century Personation* (New York: AMS Press, 1978), pp. 56–60, 87–90.

Papers:
Ralegh's letters and other manuscripts are widely dispersed. The most important collection relating to his literary career is the material constituting the "Cynthia" poems in the Cecil Papers at Hatfield House. Many letters and other documents repose in the Bodleian Library, the British Library, and the Harry Ransom Humanities Research Center, University of Texas at Austin. The most complete and useful guide to these materials is Pierre Lefranc, *Sir Walter Ralegh, écrivain* (cited above).

William Shakespeare

(circa 23 April 1564 – 23 April 1616)

Dennis Kay

University of North Carolina at Charlotte

See also the Shakespeare entry in *DLB 62: Elizabethan Dramatists.*

BOOKS: *Venus and Adonis* (London: Printed by Richard Field, sold by J. Harrison I, 1593);

The First Part of the Contention betwixt the Two Famous Houses of Yorke and Lancaster [abridged and corrupt text of *Henry VI*, part 2] (London: Printed by Thomas Creede for Thomas Millington, 1594);

Lucrece (London: Printed by Richard Field for John Harrison, 1594); republished as *The Rape of Lucrece. Newly Revised* (London: Printed by T. Snodham for R. Jackson, 1616);

The Most Lamentable Romaine Tragedie of Titus Andronicus (London: Printed by John Danter, sold by Edward White & Thomas Middleton, 1594);

A Pleasant Conceited Historie, Called The Taming of a Shrew [corrupt text] (London: Printed by John Danter, sold by Edward White & Thomas Middleton, 1594; London: Printed by Peter Short, sold by Cuthbert Burbie, 1594);

The True Tragedie of Richard Duke of Yorke, and the Death of Good King Henrie the Sixt [abridged and corrupt text of *Henry VI*, part 3] (London: Printed by Peter Short for Thomas Millington, 1595);

The Tragedy of King Richard the Third (London: Printed by Valentine Simmes & Peter Short for Andrew Wise, 1597);

The Tragedie of King Richard the Second (London: Printed by Valentine Simmes for Andrew Wise, 1597);

An Excellent Conceited Tragedie of Romeo and Juliet [corrupt text] (London: Printed by John Danter [& E. Allde?], 1597); republished as *The Most Excellent and Lamentable Tragedie of Romeo and Juliet. Newly Corrected, Augmented,* *and Amended* (London: Printed by Thomas Creede for Cuthbert Burby, 1599);

A Pleasant Conceited Comedie Called, Loues Labors Lost (London: Printed by William White for Cuthbert Burby, 1598);

The History of Henrie the Fourth [part 1] (London: Printed by Peter Short for Andrew Wise, 1598);

The Passionate Pilgrime, attributed to Shakespeare (London: William Jaggard, 1599);

A Midsommer Nights Dreame (London: Printed by R. Bradock for Thomas Fisher, 1600);

The Most Excellent Historie of the Merchant of Venice (London: Printed by James Roberts for Thomas Heyes, 1600);

The Second Part of Henrie the Fourth, Continuing to His Death, and Coronation of Henrie the Fift (London: Printed by Valentine Simmes for Andrew Wise & William Aspley, 1600);

Much Adoe about Nothing (London: Printed by Valentine Simmes for Andrew Wise & William Aspley, 1600);

The Cronicle History of Henry the Fift [corrupt text] (London: Printed by Thomas Creede for Thomas Mullington & John Busby, 1600);

The Phoenix and Turtle, appended to *Loves Martyr: or, Rosalins Complaint,* by Robert Chester (London: Printed by Richard Field for E. Blount, 1601);

A Most Pleasaunt and Excellent Conceited Comedie, of Syr John Falstaffe, and the Merrie Wives of Windsor [corrupt text] (London: Printed by Thomas Creede for Arthur Johnson, 1602);

The Tragicall Historie of Hamlet Prince of Denmark [abridged and corrupt text] (London: Printed by Valentine Simmes for Nicholas Ling & John Trundell, 1603); republished as *The Tragicall Historie of Hamlet, Prince of Denmarke. Newly Imprinted and Enlarged to Almost as Much Againe as It Was, According to the True and Perfect Coppie* (London: Printed by James Roberts for Nicholas Ling, 1604);

*The Flower Portrait of William Shakespeare, which came into the
possession of Mrs. Charles Flower in 1895 (Royal Shakespeare
Theater, Stratford-upon-Avon, Picture Gallery); the portrait is
now generally believed to be after the engraving on the title
page of the 1623 First Folio of Shakespeare's plays.*

*M. William Shak-speare: His True Chronicle Historie of
the Life and Death of King Lear and His Three
Daughters* (London: Printed by N. Okes for
Nathaniel Butter, 1608);

The Historie of Troylus and Cresseida (London:
Printed by G. Eld for R. Bonian & H.
Walley, 1609);

Shake-speares Sonnets (London: Printed by G. Eld for
Thomas Thorpe, sold by W. Aspley & John
Wright, 1609);

*The Late, and Much Admired Play, Called Pericles,
Prince of Tyre* (London: Printed by W. White
for Henry Gosson, 1609);

The Tragædy of Othello, The Moore of Venice (London:
Printed by Nicholas Okes for Thomas
Walkley, 1622);

*Mr. William Shakespeares Comedies, Histories, & Trage-
dies. Published according to the True Originall Cop-
ies* (London: Printed by Isaac Jaggard & Ed-
ward Blount, 1623) — comprises *The Tempest;
The Two Gentlemen of Verona; The Merry Wives of
Windsor; Measure for Measure; The Comedy of Er-
rors; Much Ado About Nothing; Love's Labor's Lost;
A Midsummer Night's Dream; The Merchant of
Venice; As You Like It; The Taming of the Shrew;
All's Well That Ends Well; Twelfth Night; The
Winter's Tale; King John; Richard II; Henry IV,*

parts 1 and 2; *Henry V; Henry VI,* parts 1–3; *Richard III; Henry VIII; Troilus and Cressida; Coriolanus; Titus Andronicus; Romeo and Juliet; Timon of Athens; Julius Caesar; Macbeth; Hamlet; King Lear; Othello; Antony and Cleopatra; Cymbeline;*

The Two Noble Kinsmen, by Shakespeare and John Fletcher (London: Printed by Thomas Cotes for John Waterson, 1634);

Poems. Written by Wil. Shake-speare, Gent. (London: Thomas Cotes & John Benson, 1640).

Editions: *A New Variorum Edition of Shakespeare,* 29 volumes to date, volumes 1–15, 18, edited by Horace Howard Furness; volumes 16–17, 19–20, edited by Horace Howard Furness Jr. (Philadelphia & London: Lippincott, 1871–1928); volumes 1–25, general editor, Joseph Quincey Adams; volumes 26–27, general editor, Hyder Edward Rollins (Philadelphia & London: Lippincott for the Modern Language Association of America, 1936–1955); volumes 28– , general editors, Robert K. Turner Jr. and Richard Knowles (New York: Modern Language Association of America, 1977–);

The Works of Shakespeare, The New Cambridge Shakespeare, 39 volumes, edited by J. Dover Wilson, Arthur Quiller-Couch, and others (Cambridge: Cambridge University Press, 1921–1967);

The Complete Works of Shakespeare, edited by George Lyman Kittredge (Boston: Ginn, 1936); revised by Irving Ribner (Waltham, Mass.: Ginn, 1971);

Shakespeare Quarto Facsimiles, 14 volumes, edited by W. W. Greg and Charlton Hinman (Oxford: Clarendon Press, 1939–1966);

William Shakespeare: The Complete Works, edited by Peter Alexander (London & Glasgow: Collins, 1951; New York: Random House, 1952);

The Arden Shakespeare, 38 volumes to date, general editors, Harold F. Brooks and Harold Jenkins (London: Methuen, 1951–);

The Complete Works of Shakespeare, edited by Hardin Craig (Chicago: Scott Foresman, 1961); revised by Craig and David Bevington (Glenview, Ill.: Scott Foresman, 1973); revised again by Bevington (Glenview, Ill.: Scott Foresman, 1980); revised again by Bevington (New York: Longman, 1997);

The New Penguin Shakespeare, general editor, T. J. B. Spencer, 33 volumes to date (Harmondsworth: Penguin, 1967–);

The Norton Facsimile: The First Folio of Shakespeare, edited by Hinman (New York: Norton, 1968);

William Shakespeare: The Complete Works, The Complete Pelican Shakespeare, general editor, Alfred Harbage (Baltimore: Penguin, 1969);

The Complete Signet Classic Shakespeare, general editor, Sylvan Barnet (New York: Harcourt Brace Jovanovich, 1972);

The Riverside Shakespeare, general editor, G. Blakemore Evans (Boston: Houghton Mifflin, 1974);

Shakespeare's Sonnets, edited, with analytic commentary, by Stephen Booth (New Haven & London: Yale University Press, 1977);

Shakespeare's Plays in Quarto: A Facsimile Edition of Copies Primarily from the Henry E. Huntington Library, edited by Michael J. B. Allen and Kenneth Muir (Berkeley: University of California Press, 1982);

The Complete Works: Original-Spelling Edition, general editors, Stanley Wells and Gary Taylor (Oxford: Clarendon Press, 1986);

The Poems. Venus and Adonis, The Rape of Lucrece, The Phoenix And the Turtle, The Passionate Pilgrim, A Lover's Complaint, The New Cambridge Shakespeare, edited by John Roe (Cambridge: Cambridge University Press, 1992).

PLAY PRODUCTIONS: *Henry VI,* part 1, London, unknown theater (perhaps by a branch of the Queen's Men), circa 1589–1592;

Henry VI, part 2, London, unknown theater (perhaps by a branch of the Queen's Men), circa 1590–1592;

Richard III, London, unknown theater (perhaps by a branch of the Queen's Men), circa 1591–1592;

The Comedy of Errors, London, unknown theater (probably of Lord Strange's Men), circa 1592–1594; London, Gray's Inn, 28 December 1594;

Titus Andronicus, London, Rose or Newington Butts theater, 24 January 1594;

The Taming of the Shrew, London, Newington Butts theater, 11 June 1594;

The Two Gentlemen of Verona, London, Newington Butts theater or the Theatre, 1594;

Love's Labor's Lost, perhaps at the country house of a great lord, such as the earl of Southampton, circa 1594–1595; London, at court, Christmas 1597;

Sir Thomas More, probably by Anthony Munday, revised by Thomas Dekker, Henry Chettle, Shakespeare, and possibly Thomas Heywood, evidently never produced, circa 1594–1595;

King John, London, the Theatre, circa 1594–1596;

Richard II, London, the Theatre, circa 1595;

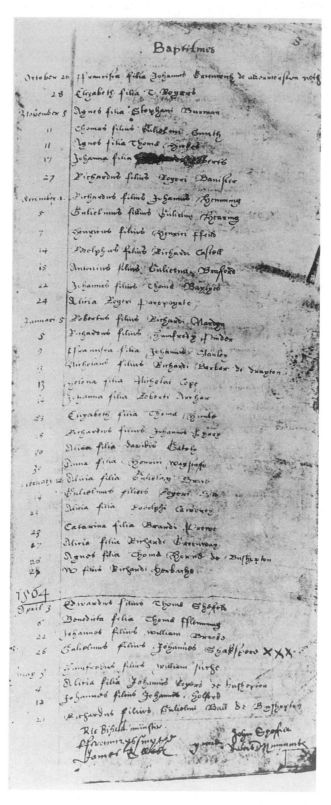

Page from the baptismal register of Holy Trinity Church, Stratford-upon-Avon, recording Shakespeare's christening on 26 April 1564 (Shakespeare's Birthplace Trust Records Office, Stratford-upon-Avon)

Romeo and Juliet, London, the Theatre, circa 1595–1596;

A Midsummer Night's Dream, London, the Theatre, circa 1595–1596;

The Merchant of Venice, London, the Theatre, circa 1596–1597;

Henry IV, part 1, London, the Theatre, circa 1596–1597;

Henry IV, part 2, London, the Theatre, circa 1597;

The Merry Wives of Windsor, Windsor, Windsor Castle, 23 April 1597;

Much Ado About Nothing, London, the Theatre, circa 1598–1599;

Henry V, London, Globe theater(?), between March and September 1599(?);

Julius Caesar, London, Globe theater, 21 September 1599;

As You Like It, London, Globe theater, circa 1599–1600;

Hamlet, London, Globe theater, circa 1600–1601;

Twelfth Night, London, at court(?), no earlier than 6 January 1601(?); London, Globe theater(?), circa 1601–1602(?); London, Middle Temple, 2 February 1602;

Troilus and Cressida, London, Globe theater(?), circa 1601–1602(?);

All's Well That Ends Well, London, Globe theater, circa 1602–1603;

Measure for Measure, London, Globe theater(?), 1604(?); London, at court, 26 December 1604;

Othello, London, Globe theater(?), 1604(?); Westminster, Whitehall, 1 November 1604;

King Lear, London, Globe theater(?), by late 1605 or early 1606; London, at court, 26 December 1606;

Timon of Athens (possibly unperformed during Shakespeare's lifetime); possibly London, Globe theater, circa 1605–1608;

Macbeth, London, Globe theater(?), 1606(?); London, at court, probably 7 August 1606;

Antony and Cleopatra, London, Globe theater, circa 1606–1607;

Pericles, possibly by Shakespeare and George Wilkins, London, at court, between January 1606 and November 1608; London, Globe theater, probably circa 1607–1608;

Coriolanus, London, Globe theater, circa 1607–1608;

Cymbeline, London, Blackfriars theater or Globe theater, 1609;

The Winter's Tale, London, Globe theater, 15 May 1611;

The Tempest, London, at court, 1 November 1611;

Cardenio, probably by Shakespeare and John Fletcher, London, Globe theater(?), circa 1612–1613;

Henry VIII, possibly by Shakespeare and Fletcher, London, Globe theater, 29 June 1613;

The Two Noble Kinsmen, by Shakespeare and Fletcher, London, probably Blackfriars theater (possibly Globe theater), 1613.

William Shakespeare's reputation is based primarily on his plays. With the partial exception of the *Sonnets* (1609), quarried since the early nineteenth century for autobiographical secrets allegedly encoded in them, the nondramatic writings have traditionally been pushed to the margins of the Shakespeare industry. Yet Shakespeare first achieved celebrity as a writer through his narrative poems, and the study of his nondramatic poetry generally can illuminate Shakespeare's activities as a poet emphatically of his own age, especially in the period of extraordinary literary ferment in the last ten or twelve years of the reign of Queen Elizabeth.

Shakespeare's exact birth date remains unknown. He was baptized in Holy Trinity Church in Stratford-upon-Avon on 26 April 1564. He was his mother's third child, but the first to survive infancy. Of five further siblings, only one, his sister Joan, outlived him. His mother, Mary Arden, came from a farming family in Wilmcote that claimed kinship with Ardens who traced their line back to pre–Norman Conquest times. His father, John Shakespeare, moved to Stratford in about 1552 and rapidly became a prominent figure in the town's business and politics. His business activities were based on making and selling gloves, but included trading in wool, moneylending, and other enterprises. He rose to be bailiff, the highest official in the town, but then in about 1575–1576 his prosperity declined markedly and he withdrew from public life. In 1596, thanks to his son's success and persistence, he was granted a coat of arms by the College of Arms, and the family moved into New Place, the grandest house in Stratford.

Speculation that William Shakespeare traveled, worked as a schoolmaster in the country, was a soldier and a law clerk, or embraced or left the Roman Catholic Church continues to fill the gaps left in the sparse records of the so-called lost years. It is conventionally assumed (though attendance registers do not survive) that Shakespeare attended the King's New School in Stratford, along with others of his social class. At the age of eighteen, in November 1582, he married Anne Hathaway, daughter of a local farmer. She was pregnant with Susanna Shakespeare, who was baptized on 26 May 1583. The twins, Hamnet and Judith Shakespeare, were baptized on 2 February 1585. There were no further children from the union.

William Shakespeare had probably been working as an actor and writer on the professional stage in London for four or five years when the London theaters were closed by order of the Privy Council on 23 June 1592. The authorities were concerned about a severe outbreak of the plague and alarmed at the possibility of civil unrest (Privy Council minutes refer to "a great disorder and tumult" in Southwark). The initial order suspended playing until Michaelmas and was renewed several times. When the theaters reopened in June 1594, the theatrical companies had been reorganized, and Shakespeare's career was wholly committed to the troupe known as the Lord Chamberlain's Men until 1603, when they were reconstituted as the King's Men.

By 1592 Shakespeare already enjoyed sufficient prominence as an author of dramatic scripts to have been the subject of Robert Greene's attack on the "upstart crow" in *Greene's Groatsworth of Wit*. Such renown as he enjoyed, however, was as transitory as the dramatic form. Play scripts, and their authors, were accorded a lowly status in the literary system, and when scripts were published, their link to the theatrical company (rather than to the scriptwriter) was publicized. It was only in 1597 that Shakespeare's name first appeared on the title page of his plays — *Richard II* and a revised edition of *Romeo and Juliet*.

While the London theaters were closed, some actors tried to make a living by touring outside the capital. Many of them were forced to give up, and costumes, props, and scripts were sold off as companies disbanded. Meanwhile, Shakespeare turned from the business of scriptwriting to the pursuit of art and patronage; unable to pursue his career in the theatrical marketplace, he adopted a more conventional course.

Shakespeare's first publication, *Venus and Adonis* (1593), was dedicated to the eighteen-year-old Henry Wriothesley, third Earl of Southampton. The dedication reveals a frank appeal for patronage, couched in the normal terms of such requests, if perhaps slightly less servile than some:

> Right Honorable, I know not how I shall offend in dedicating my unpolished lines to your Lordship, nor how the world will censure me for choosing so strong a prop to support so weak a burden. Only if your Honor seem but pleased, I account myself highly praised, and vow to take advantage of all idle hours, till I have honored you

with some graver labor. But if the first heir of my invention prove deformed, I shall be sorry it had so noble a godfather, and never after ear so barren a land, for fear it yield me still so bad a harvest. I leave it to your honorable survey, and your Honor to your heart's content, which I wish may always answer your own wish, and the world's hopeful expectation.

It is signed, "Your Honor's in all duty, William Shakespeare."

Much about this passage is highly conventional. The novice poet calling the poem the "first heir of my invention" classifies it as his first proper publication, his first substantial work. He offers it as a nobleman's recreation to read, as it had been his to write in "all idle hours"; he promises to follow up with something graver, more substantial. The image of the text as offspring is standard Elizabethan usage — Sir Philip Sidney presented *Arcadia* (1590) as "this child I am loth to father" — as is the element of nonchalant self-deprecation, or *sprezzatura*. The tone argues no intimacy: it was quite common for such dedications to be essentially speculative.

Richard Field, Shakespeare's printer, was professionally accomplished (warden of the Stationers in 1605, master in 1619 and 1622), as well as a Stratford neighbor. Their fathers knew each other well. Field was apprenticed to Thomas Vautrollier, whose printing shop was in Blackfriars. When Vautrollier died in 1587, his widow married Field, only recently out of his apprenticeship. The firm had specialized in high-quality work, including Richard Mulcaster's *Elementary* (1582) and Thomas North's *Plutarch's Lives* (1579). In 1591 they had printed Sir John Harington's translation of Ludovico Ariosto's *Orlando Furioso* (1532), and in 1598 they would produce the handsome folio *Arcadia* plus other collected works by Sidney. Field himself published books under his own imprint from 1589, including George Puttenham's *Arte of English Poesie* (1589), the 1596 edition of Edmund Spenser's *The Faerie Queene,* as well as his *Daphnaïda* and *Fowre Hymnes* (1591, 1596). *Venus and Adonis* is of a piece with Field's normal output.

Shakespeare's choice of printer indicates an ambition to associate himself with unambiguously high-art productions, as does the quotation from Ovid's *Amores* on the title page: "Vilia miretur vulgus: mihi flavus Apollo / Pocula Castalia plena ministret acqua" (Let worthless stuff excite the admiration of the crowd: as for me, let golden Apollo ply me with full cups from the Castalian spring, that is, the spring of the Muses). Christopher Marlowe's contemporary version was more imperious: "Let base conceited wits admire vile things; / Fair Phoebus lead me to the Muses' springs." Such lofty repudiation of the vulgar was calculated to appeal to the teenage Southampton. It also appealed to a sizable slice of the reading public. In the midst of horror, disease, and death, Shakespeare was offering access to a golden world, showing the delights of applying learning for pleasure rather than pointing out the obvious morals to be drawn from classical authors when faced with awful catastrophe.

With *Venus and Adonis* Shakespeare sought direct aristocratic patronage, but he also entered the marketplace as a professional author. He seems to have enjoyed a degree of success in the first of these objectives, given the more intimate tone of the dedication of *Lucrece* to Southampton in the following year. In the second objective, his triumph must have outstripped all expectation. *Venus and Adonis* went though fifteen editions before 1640 and was clearly still regarded as a sufficiently profitable literary property in that year for John Benson to be unable to include it (or, indeed, *Lucrece*) in his 1640 edition of Shakespeare's poetry.

Venus and Adonis was entered in the Stationers' Register on 18 April 1593. It is a fine and elegantly printed book, with a text over which a great deal of care had been taken, although it is not known how closely Shakespeare was involved in the publication. It consists of 1,194 lines in 199 six-line stanzas rhymed *ababcc*. The verse form was a token of social and literary ambition on Shakespeare's part. Its aristocratic cachet derived from its popularity at court, being favored by several courtier poets, such as Sir Walter Ralegh; Sir Arthur Gorges; Robert Devereux, second Earl of Essex; Edward de Vere, seventeenth Earl of Oxford; Sir Edward Dyer; Sir Thomas Heneage; and Ferdinando Stanley, Lord Strange. Some of this courtier verse was circulating in manuscript, and some had been published in anthologies such as *Britton's Bower of Delights* (1591) and *The Paradise of Dainty Devices* (1576). Eight poems in Sir Philip Sidney's *Arcadia* use the form, as do the January and December eclogues of Spenser's *Shepheardes Calender* (1579) and his *Astrophel* (1595). In 1589 it had been used by Thomas Lodge in his Ovidian poem entitled *Scilla's Metamorphosis,* the title page of which claims it is "very fit for young courtiers to peruse and young dames to remember."

Venus and Adonis is unquestionably a work of its age. In it a young writer courts respectability and patronage. At one level, of course, the poem is a traditional Ovidian fable, locating the origin of the inseparability of love and sorrow in Venus's reaction to the death of Adonis: "lo here I prophesy, / Sor-

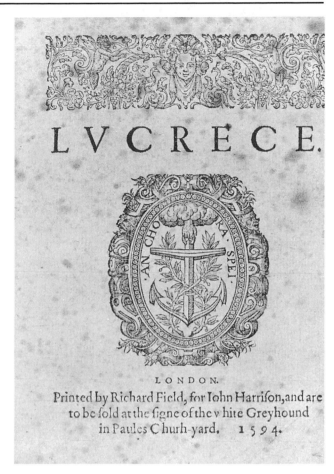

Title page for Shakespeare's long narrative poem, later republished as The Rape of Lucrece *(1616)*

row on love hereafter shall attend /. . . all love's pleasure shall not match his woe." It invokes a mythic past that explains a painful present. Like so many texts of the 1590s, it features an innocent hero, Adonis, who encounters a world in which the precepts he has acquired from his education are tested in the surprising school of experience. His knowledge of love, inevitably, is not firsthand ("I have heard it is a life in death, / That laughs and weeps, and all but with a breath"). There is a staidly academic quality to his repudiation of Venus's "treatise," her "idle over-handled theme."

Shakespeare's literary and social aspirations are revealed at every turn. In his Petrarchism, for example, he adopts a mode that had become a staple of courtly discourse. Elizabethan politicians figured themselves and their personal and political conditions in Petrarchan terms. The inescapable and enduring frustrations of the courtier's life were habitually figured via the analogy of the frustrated, confused, but devoted Petrarchan lover. Yet Shakespeare's approach to this convention typifies the

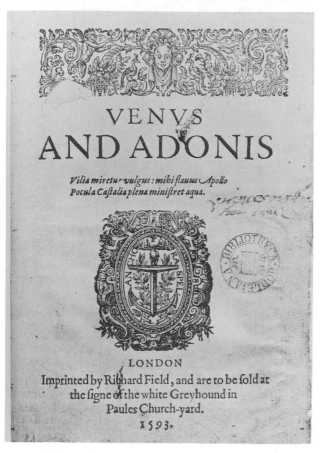

Title page for Shakespeare's Ovidian narrative poem

1590s younger generation's sense of its incongruity. Lines such as "the love-sick queen began to sweat" are understandably rare in Elizabethan courtly discourse. Power relations expressed through the gendered language of Elizabeth's eroticized politics are reversed: "Her eyes petitioners to his eyes suing / . . . Her eyes wooed still, his eyes disdain'd the wooing." It is Venus who deploys the conventional carpe diem arguments: "Make use of time / . . . Fair flowers that are not gath'red in their prime, / Rot, and consume themselves in little time"; she even provides a *blason* of her own charms: "Thou canst not see one wrinkle in my brow, / Mine eyes are grey, and bright, and quick in turning."

The poem's Petrarchism is so crude as to be almost comic at times. Thus, the reader learns that Venus "bathes in water, yet her fire must burn," and Adonis had earlier been summed up as "red for shame, but frosty in desire." The most obvious instance is the reiterated white/red figure. It starts with Venus praising Adonis as "More white and red than doves or roses are." His oscillating between "crimson shame and anger ashy-pale" pleases Venus: "Being red, she loves him best, and being white, / Her best is better'd with a more delight." The narrator describes Venus and the "fighting conflict of her hue, / How white and red each other did destroy" and later uses similar terms to indicate her reaction to the news that Adonis plans to hunt the boar: "a blushing pale, / Like lawn being spread upon the blushing rose, / Usurps her cheek." These terms are fatally transferred to the dreaded boar, "Whose frothy mouth bepainted all with red, / Like milk and blood being mingled all together," and then finally to the flower that springs up from Adonis's blood.

Shakespeare signals indebtedness to Sidney by providing Venus with the *joy/annoy* rhyme whereby Astrophil epitomizes his predicament in *Astrophil and Stella* sonnets 44 and 108. First "life was death's annoy / . . . death was lively joy." The rhyme recurs at the numerical center of the poem – as Geoffrey Chaucer had placed the physical union of Troilus and Criseyde at the numerical center of his romance, so Shakespeare does in the stanza beginning "Now is she in the very lists of love." Like most Elizabethan treatments of love, it is characterized by paradox ("She's love, she loves, and yet she is not lov'd"), by narrative and thematic diversity, and by attempts to render the inner workings of the mind, exploring the psychology of perception ("Oft the eye mistakes, the brain being troubled"). The poem addresses such artistic preoccupations of the 1590s as the relation of poetry to painting and the possibility of literary immortality, as well as social concerns such as the phenomenon of "masterless women," and the (to men) alarming and unknowable forces unleashed by female desire, an issue that for a host of reasons fascinated Elizabeth's subjects.

Like other successful works of the 1590s, *Venus and Adonis* flirts with taboos, offering readers living in a paranoid, plague-ridden city a fantasy of passionate and fatal physical desire, with Venus leading Adonis "prisoner in a red-rose chain." In its day it was appreciated as an erotic fantasy glorying in the inversion of established categories and values, with a veneer of learning and the snob appeal of association with a celebrated aristocrat. In June 1593 Richard Stonely, an elderly civil servant at the Exchequer, recorded in his notebook the purchase of three books for a shilling, including "the Venus & Adhonay p^r Shakspear." The remarkable letters of the first recorded reader of Shakespeare's poem, William Reynolds, have been shown by Katherine Duncan-Jones to be part of the powerful immediate impact of Shakespeare's poem. She cites Thomas Edwards's *Cephalus and Procris* in addition to *Narcissus,* entered on 22 October 1593; Michael Drayton's

Piers Gaveston, entered in the Register on 3 December; and Thomas Heywood's large-scale imitation in *Oenone and Paris* (1594). Drayton's *Matilda* (1594), in turn, would refer to *Lucrece* soon after its publication.

Since the Romantic period the frank sexuality of Shakespeare's Venus has held less appeal for literary critics and scholars than it had to Elizabethan and Jacobean readers. Male embarrassment since the time of Samuel Taylor Coleridge conceded grudging praise to the description of the horse and other natural details and the supposition that the poem was comically grotesque. C. S. Lewis concludes in *English Literature in the Sixteenth Century, Excluding Drama* (1954) that "if the poem is not meant to arouse disgust it was very foolishly written." In more recent years a combination of feminism, cultural studies, renewed interest in rhetoric, and a return to traditional archival research has begun to reclaim *Venus and Adonis* from such prejudice.

The elevated subject of Shakespeare's next publication, *Lucrece,* suggests that *Venus and Adonis* had been well received, as does its dedication to Southampton:

> The love I dedicate to your Lordship is without end: whereof this pamphlet without beginning is but a superfluous moiety. The warrant I have of your honorable disposition, not the worth of my untutored lines, makes it assured of acceptance. What I have done is yours; what I have to do is yours; being part in all I have, devoted yours. Were my worth greater, my duty would show greater; meantime, as it is, it is bound to your Lordship, to whom I wish long life still lengthened with all happiness.

Like *Venus and Adonis, Lucrece* was printed by Richard Field, but the publisher was John Harrison, to whom Field also transferred the earlier poem. There were no fewer than eight editions of *Lucrece* before 1640; it was with the sixth quarto edition in 1616 that the title *The Rape of Lucrece* was used, although the words had been used as a running title as early as the first edition. The poem was cited in the Cambridge Parnassus plays and is referred to in *Willobie His Avisa* (1594), whose prefatory verses include the lines "Yet Tarquin plucked his glistering grape, / And Shake-speare paints poor Lucrece's rape." This is the earliest printed naming of Shakespeare as a poet.

Shakespeare took his story from Ovid's *Fasti,* from Livy's *Historia,* from Chaucer's *The Legend of Good Women,* and from William Painter's version of Livy in his *Palace of Pleasure* (1566). A more contemporary model was Samuel Daniel's *Complaint of Rosamund* (spoken by the ghost of Rosamund, the neglected mistress of Henry II), published at the end of his sonnet sequence *Delia* (1592). In Livy and Ovid the Lucrece story begins, as does Shakespeare's "Argument," with Roman noblemen boasting about the virtue of their wives and then testing that virtue for a wager; all versions indicate that it was the wager that inflamed Tarquin's lust. The "Argument" of *Lucrece* – which differs in emphasis and some points of substance from the poem – presents the story in the context of Roman political history. It stresses the significance of Tarquin's act as the final outrage that causes the Romans to "root out the whole hated family of the Tarquins," after which "the state government changed from kings to consuls." At first sight, the ensuing poem may appear less politically risqué, but the "Argument" adds an ominous weight to the narrative's conclusion.

Lucrece comprises 1,855 lines, disposed in 265 stanzas. The stanza (as in *Complaint of Rosamund*) is the seven-line rhyme royal (*ababbcc*) immortalized in Chaucer's *Troilus and Criseyde* (circa 1385) and thereafter considered especially appropriate for tragedy (as in Thomas Sackville's induction to the 1559 edition of *The Mirror for Magistrates*), complaint (as in Spenser's *Ruines of Time,* 1591), and philosophical reflection (as in Spenser's *Fowre Hymnes*). Sidney associated the form with antiquity and political allegory, as in Gynecia's lament from the *Old Arcadia* (written circa 1581) and the pastoral allegory "As I my little flock on Ister bank" from the same work. Gabriel Harvey observed in marginalia written between 1598 and 1601 that Shakespeare's "Lucrece, and his tragedy of Hamlet, Prince of Denmark, have it in them, to please the wiser sort."

The "wiser sort" evidently relished *sententiae* such as "The old bees die, the young possess their hive" or "Poor women's faces are their own faults' books." Several sententious passages are indicated typographically in quarto 1; double inverted commas occur before lines 87, 88, 460, 528, 530, 560, 831–832, 867–868, and 1109–1118. In places the narrator explicitly highlights the various rhetorical set pieces ("Here she exclaims against repose and rest"). Lucrece herself comments on her performance after the apostrophes to "comfort-killing Night, image of Hell," Opportunity, and Time. Elizabethan readers would have appreciated the plentiful wordplay ("to shun the blot, she would not blot the letter"; "Ere she with blood had stain'd her stain'd excuse") and verbal dexterity, as in the antithetical he/she passage following the rape.

Tarquin is an exemplary tyrant from ancient history. Yet his inner debate features the conventional 1590s conflict between willful youthful prodigality and sententious experience ("My part is youth, and beats these from the stage"). The arguments in his "disputation / 'Tween frozen conscience and hot burning will" are those of the Petrarchan lover: "nothing can affection's course control," and "Yet strive I to embrace mine infamy." But the context of this rhetorical performance is crucial throughout. Unlike *Venus and Adonis, Lucrece* is not set in a mythical golden age, but in a fallen, violent world. This is particularly apparent in the rhetorical and ultimately physical competition of their debate – contrasting Tarquin's speeches with Lucrece's eloquent appeals to his better nature.

The combination of ancient and contemporary strengthens the political elements in the poem. It demonstrates tyranny in its most intimate form, committing a private outrage that is inescapably public; hence the rape is figured in terms both domestic (as a burglary) and public (as a hunt, a war, a siege). It also reveals the essential violence of many conventional erotic metaphors. The poem begins with the "Lust-breathed" Tarquin speeding from the siege of Ardea to Lucrece. The notion of rape is latent in the image of the attacked city, and vice versa, of course. This context adds urgency to Tarquin's otherwise conventional conflation of military and erotic metaphors, with his "drumming heart" beating as he attacks the citadel of Lucrece's body and honor. Shakespeare draws on the powerful Elizabethan myth of the island nation as a woman: although Tarquin is a Roman, an insider, his journey from the siege of Ardea to Lucrece's chamber connects the two assaults. His attack figures a society at war with itself, and he himself is shown to be self-divided.

Tyranny, lust, and greed translate the metaphors of Petrarchism into the actuality of rape, which is figured by *gradatio,* or climax: "What could he see but mightily he noted? / What did he note but strongly he desired?" Notwithstanding the virtuoso rhetoric, the reader is instructed to focus on the visual aspects of the poem ("Imagine her as one in dead of night") and directed, as in the frequent use of *thus.* This is the state of mind – "To see sad sights moves more than hear them told" – in which Lucrece begins her interaction with the image of the Trojan War: "Certain sorrow, writ uncertainly." Tarquin's blason of Lucrece is the act of a spectator "Rolling his greedy eyeballs in his head," whose wonder arouses lust: "With more than admiration he admired / Her azure veins, her alablaster skin, / Her coral lips, her snow-white dimpled chin."

Lucrece's colors are figured as Petrarchan red and white – "This heraldry in Lucrece' face was seen, / Argued by beauty's red and virtue's white." To Tarquin her face stages a "silent war of lilies and of roses" and transforms the colors to the white of terror and the red of shame. Lucrece and her maid gaze with ashen faces on each other: Lucrece blushes with shame when the blushing groom comes to her. Collatine bathes his pale face in Lucrece's blood. The image of Sinon, the embodiment of duplicity, has cheeks "neither red nor pale, but mingled."

The poem abounds with images of predation. Tarquin is a hunter ("Into the chamber wickedly he stalks") and a bird of prey ("The dove sleeps fast that this night-owl will catch"). Elsewhere he is like a "grim lion" fawning over his prey. Before the rape Lucrece trembles "Like to a new-killed bird," like a fowl that hears the falcon's bells "with trembling fear," like a "weak mouse" grabbed by a "vulture," and like "the poor unseasonable doe" taken by a poor sportsman. At the rape itself ("The wolf hath seiz'd his prey, the poor lamb cries"), Tarquin is compared to a "full-fed hound or gorged hawk." The poem concludes with Lucrece as "this pale swan in her wat'ry nest."

Although the narrator defines Tarquin as "this lustful lord" and his victim as "harmless Lucretia" and "Lucrece the chaste," the poem actually begins with uncertainty about Tarquin's motivation; the reader learns that Tarquin resembles insomniacs with "troubled minds" and in his "inward mind doth much debate." Crucially, the rape itself is unseen, passed over in two stanzas, whose focus is on darkness, on the covering of Lucrece's eyes, and Tarquin's muffling her cries. The narrator silences her, too. Her first speech is merely reported as "vehement prayers," and later "With untun'd tongue she hoarsely calls her maid." When Lucrece and Collatine gaze amazedly at each other, his voice is "damn'd up by woe" when he hears her story. When Lucrece writes her letter to Collatine, she "dares not . . . make discovery" of what has happened to her. Instead "Here folds she up the tenure of her woe, / Her certain sorrow, writ uncertainly." The articulation of her final monosyllabic words is depicted as a heroic struggle: "'He, he,' she says, / But more than 'he' her poor tongue could not speak." This reduces Collatine to silence: "The deep vexation of his inward soul / Hath serv'd a dumb arrest upon his tongue."

Lucrece raises important issues of reputation, reading, and interpretation. Interpretation is shown to be a complex business in a wilderness of parallels

*Portrait of Shakespeare formerly attributed to Richard Burbage,
but now believed to have been painted in the eighteenth
century (National Portrait Gallery, London)*

and comparisons, where the story of Troy, combining rape and siege, also raises the idea of empire, of the role of Brutus, which connects Troy to Rome and inescapably to Britain. After the rape Lucrece imagines herself becoming, like Criseyde, a watchword for faithlessness — "The orator to deck his oratory / Will couple my reproach to Tarquin's shame." She proclaims herself a speaking picture ("the illiterate that know not how / To cipher what is writ / . . . Will quote my loathsome trespass in my looks") and a text in which is "character'd in my brow, / The story of sweet chastity's decay." Lucrece speaks a complaint in the character of Hecuba, whose silent image in a painting provokes her to comment on the artist: "he did her wrong, / To give her so much grief, and not a tongue." As she "feelingly . . . weeps Troy's painted woes," she echoes Britomart's *planctus,* "O lamentable fall of famous towne" (from *Faerie Queene* III.ix.38–39). But when she is moved to scratch the image of Sinon, who recalls Tarquin, she acknowledges the futility of her response: "his wounds will not be sore." The references in the poem to Philomel are more than formulaic, in that they argue for an irrepressible voice eternally proclaiming rape and injustice. In this context Lucrece's meditation on suicide shows a woman trapped ("What is the quality of my offense, / Being constrained with dreadful circumstance?") by the values of a patriarchal society. Her death arouses amazement and initiates yet another debate, between her father and husband, over who owns her and who has more right to mourn. The fatal dagger becomes an instrument of personal vengeance and political transformation and connects Lucrece's death with that process.

The historically validated interpretation — for Shakespeare's readers, descendants of Brutus in New Troy — is figured by Brutus, who "pluck'd the knife from Lucrece' side." He steps forward, casting off his reputation for folly and improvising a ritual (involving kissing the knife) that transforms grief and outrage at Lucrece's death into a determination to "publish Tarquin's foul offense" and change the political system. Brutus emerges from the shadows, reminding the reader that the poem, notwithstanding its powerful speeches and harrowing images, is also remarkable for what is unshown, untold, implicit. In the painting of Troy, Achilles is "left unseen, save to the eye of mind"; a weapon, a fragment of his body "Stood for the whole to be imagined."

Until recently few commentators have taken up the interpretative challenge posed by Brutus. Traditionally *Lucrece* has been dismissed as a bookish, pedantic dry run for Shakespeare's tragedies, in William Empson's phrase, "the Bard doing five-finger exercises," containing what F. T. Prince in his 1960 edition of the poems dismisses as defective rhetoric in the treatment of an uninteresting story. Misogyny abounds: J. C. Maxwell in his New Cambridge edition of the poems (1965) condemns Lucrece's lament as formless and confused, while John Roe in his 1992 edition grudgingly concedes that compared to Thomas Kyd's play *The Spanish Tragedy* (1592) Lucrece's speeches are "not at all excessive." Many critics have sought to define the poem's genre, which combines political fable, female complaint, and tragedy within a milieu of self-conscious antiquity. Maurice Evans, for example, in his Penguin edition of *The Narrative Poems* (1989), defines the poem in terms of its interplay of tragic theme and moral narrative, the first half of which is the tragedy – in the Chaucerian/Boethian sense – of Tarquin, and whose second half is the planctus, or complaint – on Samuel Daniel's model – of Lucrece.

Perhaps the most significant recent developments have been the feminist treatments of the poem, the reawakening interest in rhetoric, and a dawning awareness of the work's political engagement. *Lucrece,* like so many of Shakespeare's historical tragedies, problematizes the categories of history and myth, of public and private, and exemplifies the bewildering nature of historical parallels. The self-conscious rhetorical display and the examination of representation is daringly politicized, explicitly, if inconclusively, connecting the aesthetic and the erotic with politics both sexual and state. At the time of its publication, *Lucrece* was Shakespeare's most profound meditation on history, particularly on the relations between public role and private morality and on the conjunction of forces – personal, political, social – that creates turning points in human history. In it he indirectly articulates the concerns of his generation and also, perhaps, of his young patron, who was already closely associated with the doomed earl of Essex.

In 1598 or 1599 the printer William Jaggard brought out an anthology of twenty miscellaneous poems. The title page of the first edition is lost: the volume, discovered in 1920, survives in an incomplete form in the Folger Shakespeare Library. A second edition, titled *The Passionate Pilgrime* appeared in 1599. This edition was to be sold by William Leake, who was also selling the 1599 Quarto 5 and Quarto 6 of *Venus and Adonis.* In 1612 Jaggard brought out a third edition, titled *The Passionate Pilgrime. Or Certaine Amorous Sonnets, betweene Venus and Adonis, Newly Corrected and Augmented. By W. Shakespere.* The Bodleian copy of this edition features a cancel title page, which omits *"By W. Shakespere."* That there was a disagreement between Jaggard and Shakespeare is supported by Thomas Heywood's protest at the 1612 edition, where some of his own poems had been printed without acknowledgement and with the implication that they had been written by Shakespeare. In his *Apology for Actors* (1612), Heywood refers to "the author I know much offended with M. Jaggard (that altogether unknown to him) presumed to make so bold with his name." Shakespeare's name first appeared on the title pages of *Richard III* and *Richard II* in 1597. The second quarto of *Henry IV,* part I, like *The Passionate Pilgrim* published in 1599, was advertised as having been "Newly corrected by W. Shakespeare." Jaggard's volumes testify to the rapidity with which Shakespeare's name acquired commercial value.

At least five of the twenty poems are demonstrably Shakespearean. Poem 1 is a version of Sonnet 138 ("When My Love Swears that She Is Made of Truth"), poem 2 of Sonnet 144 ("Two Loves I Have, of Comfort and Despair"), and the rest are sonnets that appear in act 4 of *Love's Labor's Lost* (1598): poem 3 is Longaville's sonnet to Maria ("Did Not the Heavenly Rhetoric of Thine Eye"); poem 5 is Berowne's "If Love Make Me Forsworn"; and poem 16 is Dumaine's song "On a Day (Alack the Day)." Poems 8 and 20 are by Richard Barnfield, and poem 19 is a version of the Marlowe/ "Ralegh" exchange "The Passionate Shepherd." Poems 4, 6, 9, and 11 are based on the story of Venus and Adonis, to which some of the others may also refer (poems 10 and 12–14). Because Poem 11 also appears in Bartholomew Griffin's *Fidessa* (1596), commentators have tended to assume that Griffin wrote it and that Griffin wrote the other three Venus and Adonis poems. Neither may be correct. There has been speculation from Edmond Malone's time that Shakespeare was the author of some of these pieces. Perhaps these were Shakespeare's "sugared sonnets" circulated "among his private friends"; they certainly harmonize with Francis Meres's praise of Shakespeare in *Palladis Tamia* (1598) as an Ovidian writer and might offer insight into Jaggard's sense of the Ovidian taste of his market.

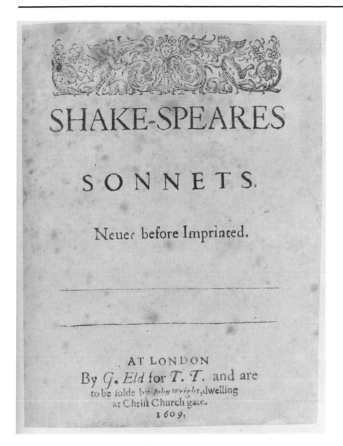

SHAKE-SPEARES

SONNETS.

Neuer before Imprinted.

AT LONDON
By G. Eld for T. T. and are
to be folde by John Wright, dwelling
at Chrift Church gate.
1609.

TO.THE.ONLIE.BEGETTER.OF.
THESE.INSVING.SONNETS.
Mr. W. H. ALL.HAPPINESSE.
AND.THAT.ETERNITIE.
PROMISED.

BY.

OVR.EVER-LIVING.POET.

WISHETH.

THE.WELL-WISHING.
ADVENTVRER.IN.
SETTING.
FORTH.

T. T.

Title page and dedication page for the most important of Shakespeare's nondramatic writings. Since the nineteenth century, the sonnets have been examined for autobiographical content, and the identity of the "Mr. W. H." of printer Thomas Thorpe's dedication has been the source of much speculation.

Investigation of Jaggard's volume has yielded and will continue to yield insight into such matters as the relationship of manuscript to print culture in the 1590s, the changing nature of the literary profession, and the evolving status of the author. It may also, as with *The Phoenix and Turtle* (1601), lead to increased knowledge of the chronology and circumstances of Shakespeare's literary career, as well as affording some glimpses of his revisions of his texts.

During the centuries attempts have regularly been made to augment the canon of Shakespeare's poems. Stanley Wells and Gary Taylor's edition of Shakespeare's works (1986) makes cases for several poems that have some traditional association with Shakespeare's name. No attribution is contemporary, though some have circumstantial and traditional claims to authenticity. It would be surprising if Shakespeare had not written occasional verses. He was paid forty-four shillings in March 1613 for providing the words and Richard Burbage was paid the same amount for making the painted image for the earl of Rutland's *imprese* worn at the king's Ac-

cession Day tilt on 24 March. In 1594 the widower Alexander Aspinall, master of the Grammar School at Stratford-upon-Avon (from 1582 to 1624 – too late to have taught Shakespeare), married the widow Anne Shaw (one of whose sons, July, or Julius, witnessed Shakespeare's will in 1616). In the seventeenth century Sir Francis Fane of Bulbeck recorded in his commonplace book a "posy" alleged to have been given by Aspinall to Mistress Shaw to accompany a present of a pair of gloves, and the lines – "The gift is small: / The will is all: / Asheyander Asbenall" – are attributed to Shakespeare, supposedly written "upon a pair of gloves that master sent to his mistress." From a similar Stratford milieu are two epitaphs said to be on Shakespeare's friend John Combe. The better known, "Ten in the Hundred," had a wide manuscript circulation, was connected with a variety of businessmen, and was attributed to Shakespeare in 1634. The second, "How E'er He Liv'd," was attributed to him in 1650, in a manuscript owned by Nicholas Burgh. Burgh's manuscript also attributes to Shakespeare a mock-epitaph on Ben Jonson, allegedly composed in a tavern exchange of repartee. The Oxford edition attributes to Shakespeare a poem in praise of King James printed on the frontispiece of the king's *Works* (1616), as well as (following the lead of Dowdall in 1693) the epitaph on his own grave, beginning "Good friend, for Jesus' sake forbear," in Stratford.

Of particular interest to scholars investigating the early years of Shakespeare's career, and especially his connections with the family of Ferdinando Strange, Earl of Derby, are two epitaphs at Tong Church in Shropshire, attributed to Shakespeare in William Dugdale's *Visitation of Shropshire* (1664). The epitaphs are on Sir Thomas Stanley (died 1576) and on his son Sir Edward, who was two years older than Shakespeare and died in 1632. Dugdale reports the verses were "made by William Shakespeare, the late famous tragedian." If genuine, the poems reinforce the suggestion that Shakespeare had been associated with Lord Strange's Men (Lord Strange was Sir Thomas's nephew and Sir Edward's cousin).

One of Shakespeare's partners in the purchase of the Blackfriars gatehouse in 1613 was John Jackson. Jackson was related by marriage to the brewer Elias James, who had premises at the foot of Puddle Dock Hill, close to Blackfriars. A poetical manuscript miscellany from the 1630s includes an epitaph on James, "When God was pleased (the world unwilling yet) / Elias James to Nature paid his debt," attributed to Shakespeare. The second Shakespeare attribution in the miscellany, a lyric in nine short stanzas beginning "Shall I die?," has proved more controversial. The attribution was recorded but ignored until accepted by Gary Taylor prior to the publication of the Oxford edition. In the course of the sometimes bitter debate that followed, a second manuscript copy dated 1638–1639, without attribution, was identified at Yale. The matter has not been resolved. The defense of the canon has traditionally been mounted with all the vigor of an ambitious *advocatus diaboli* at the Vatican scrutinizing the claims of a candidate for sainthood, though the presence of these poems in the Oxford and Penguin editions is likely to influence some readers in favor of their acceptance.

The Phoenix and Turtle is Shakespeare's contribution to *Loves Martyr: or, Rosalin's Complaint, Allegorically Shadowing the Truth of Love, in the Constant Fate of the Phoenix and Turtle* (1601), a volume of poems compiled by Robert Chester and associated with Sir John Salisbury. Appended to this work are "Some new compositions, of several modern writers whose names are subscribed to their several works, upon the first subject: viz., the Phoenix and Turtle."

These writers are "Ignoto" (possibly John Donne), Shakespeare, John Marston, George Chapman, and Ben Jonson. Shakespeare's poem appears without a title. Chester's *Love's Martyr* is an allegorical poem (treating the myth of the phoenix's rebirth from its own ashes) whose occasion and meaning remain obscure. Given the importance of the phoenix in Elizabeth I's cult, connections with the queen have been proposed; many scholars have claimed to find an allegory of her relationship with the earl of Essex, executed in 1601. Others have located the poem firmly in the circumstances of Salisbury's wedding in 1586. E. A. J. Honigmann goes further and argues, as part of his "early-start" view of Shakespeare's writing career, that Shakespeare's poem is contemporary with the Salisbury nuptials.

Shakespeare's poem owes something in setting and subject to Matthew Roydon's elegy on Sidney, published in *The Phoenix Nest* (1593). The first of two marked sections consists of thirteen four-line stanzas rhymed *abba*. It is followed by the "Threnos," consisting of five three-line stanzas. The first section is in two parts, namely an invocation of five stanzas followed by the explicit announcement "Here the anthem doth commence."

The Phoenix and Turtle connects with the end of Chester's piece, where from the funeral pyre of the phoenix and turtle rises up a new phoenix, in whose heart lives "a perpetual love / Sprong from the bosom of the turtle dove." The invocation, in the tradition of bird-masses (such as John Skelton's *Philip Sparrow*), summons to the service the "bird of loudest lay," the swan, the crow, and the presiding eagle, and banishes the screech owl. The congregation sings its anthem on the unity in diversity of the lovers:

> So they loved as love in twain
> Had the essence but in one,
> Two distincts, division none:
> Number there in love was slain.

Shakespeare uses the languages of academic logic and philosophy paradoxically, in the service of metaphor and ambiguity: "How true a twain / Seemeth this concordant one!" The implication that love can be so powerful as to overwhelm logic and reason is a Shakespearean commonplace. The final threnos, also attributed to Reason, concludes that the unique union of the phoenix and turtle, their logic-defying conjunction of "two distincts," beauty and truth, has left the world. Some critics view the conclusion as tragic, as a recognition of the gulf separating mortal comprehension — which sees only "dead birds" — from the essential nature of the creatures and their union. Others find that the phoenix and turtle have bequeathed to mortals an image of ideal love to which they may aspire.

There is no substantial tradition of criticism before the mid twentieth century, when the poem's inclusion in Helen Gardner's anthology *Metaphysical Poets* (1957) stimulated academic interest. Since then it has enjoyed a rarefied acclaim. The tradition of biographical/historical reading has continued and remains vigorous. The vogue for treating the poem as almost abstract "pure poetry" may have passed, but there is still life in the Neoplatonic school of interpretation. There is a tendency for (usually male) critics to wax rhapsodic about the poem, which seems to engender less embarrassment than the sonnets or the narrative poems.

"With this key / Shakespeare unlocked his heart," wrote William Wordsworth in "Scorn not the Sonnet" (1827) of the *Sonnets*. "If so," replied Robert Browning in his poem "House" (1876), "the less Shakespeare he." None of Shakespeare's works has been so tirelessly ransacked for biographical clues as the 154 sonnets, published with *A Lover's Complaint* by Thomas Thorpe in 1609. Unlike the narrative poems, they enjoyed only limited commercial success during Shakespeare's lifetime, and no further edition appeared until Benson's in 1640. The title page, like Jaggard's of *The Passionate Pilgrim,* relies upon the drawing power of the author's name and promises "SHAKE-SPEARES / SONNETS / Never before Imprinted." The poems are preceded by the poet's elegant dedications to Southampton; here Thorpe provides an enigmatic text, perhaps echoing Shakespeare's *Lucrece* dedication ("I wish long life still lengthened with all happiness"): "TO. THE. ONLIE. BEGETTER. OF. / THESE INSUING. SONNETS. / Mr. W. H. ALL. HAPPINESSE. / AND THAT ETERNITIE. / PROMISED. / BY. / OUR. EVER-LIVING. POET. / WISHETH. / THE. WELL-WISHING. / ADVENTURER. IN. / SETTING. FORTH. / T.T."

"T.T." was obviously Thorpe, an established and reputable publisher responsible for the book publication of Jonson's *Sejanus* (1605) and *Volpone* (1607). His title page introduces a collection of 154 numbered sonnets, two of which (138 and 144) had appeared in print before, followed by *A Lover's Complaint.* Full title pages survive intact in eleven of the thirteen extant copies. All indicate that the book was printed by George Eld (who had printed *Sejanus*): seven were "to be sold by John Wright, dwelling at Christ Church gate," the other four "to be sold by William Aspley." Presumably Thorpe was spreading the investment risk.

Some features of the dedication are straightforward. The "ever-living poet" is Shakespeare, the term perhaps alluding to his reiterated treatment of poetic immortality (in sonnets 15, 18, 19, 55, 60, 63, 81, and 101) and to his evident aspiration to emulate Ovid and Sidney (whose recent acquisition of immortality through verse had already become a cultural cliché). Presumably the "well-wishing adventurer" is Thorpe himself, both explorer and entrepreneur who sets forth on a journey, setting out his wares as his printers set type. Other aspects pose more problems. Most commentators take the "onlie begetter" to be the "chief inspiration" rather than the "sole supplier" of the text of the sonnets. The identity of "Mr. W. H." is unknown and has been the subject of much speculation. Even though the title "Master" would appear to rule them out, the candidates most frequently advanced are Shakespeare's two celebrated aristocratic patrons – Henry Wriothesley, Earl of Southampton, dedicatee of the narrative poems, and William Herbert, Earl of Pembroke, dedicatee of the First Folio.

The 154 sonnets are conventionally divided between the "young man" sonnets (1–126) and the "dark lady" sonnets (127–152), with the final pair often seen as an envoy or coda to the collection. There is no evidence that such a division has chronological implications, though the volume is usually read in such a way. Shakespeare employs the conventional English sonnet form: three quatrains capped with a couplet. Apart from the obvious error in 146, where Thorpe opens a hypermetric second line with the repeated last three words of line one, there are just three formally irregular sonnets: 99 has fifteen lines; 126, the farewell to the young man of the preceding sonnets, has twelve pentameters rhymed in couplets (with two line spaces indicated typographically by the use of open brackets); and 145 uses octosyllabics. Drama is conjured within individual poems, as the speaker wrestles with some problem or situation; it is generated by the juxtaposition of poems, with instant switches of tone, mood, and style; it is implied by cross-references and interrelationships within the sequence as a whole.

There remains a question, however, of how closely Shakespeare was involved in preparing the text of the sonnets for publication. Some commentators – from a variety of ideological perspectives – have advocated skepticism about all attempts to recover Shakespeare's intention. Others have looked more closely at Thorpe, at Benson, and at the circulation of Shakespeare's verse in the manuscript culture: these investigations have led to a reexamina-

Frontispiece to Poems. Written by Wil. Shake-speare, Gent. *(1640), the earliest collected edition of Shakespeare's poetry*

tion of the ideas of authorship and authority in the period. Although scholarly opinion is still divided, several influential studies and editions in recent years have argued, on a variety of grounds, for the authority, integrity, and coherence of Thorpe's text, an integrity now regarded as including *A Lover's Complaint.*

The subsequent history of the text of the sonnets is inseparable from the history of Shakespeare's reputation. John Benson's *Poems: Written by Wil. Shake-speare. Gent* (1640) was part of an attempt to "canonize" Shakespeare, collecting verses into a handsome quarto that could be sold as a companion to the dramatic folio texts ("to be serviceable for the continuance of glory to the deserved author in these his poems"). Benson dropped a few sonnets, added other poems, provided titles for individual pieces, changed Thorpe's order, conflated sonnets, and

modified some of the male pronouns — though not as many as is usually asserted — thereby making the sequence seem more unambiguously heterosexual in its orientation. In recent years there has been increasing study of Benson's edition as a distinct literary production in its own right.

Benson's attempt to make fashionable verses of the 1590s palatable to the taste of 1640 achieved little success. The vogue for sonnets was long over. For the next century and a half, the sonnets were regularly excluded from editions of Shakespeare (such as those of Nicholas Rowe in 1709 and Alexander Pope in 1723–1725). After 1780, however, everything changed when Edmond Malone published a critical edition of the *Sonnets* based on Thorpe's quarto, with Malone's learned introduction and commentary. Ten years later he included them in his great edition of the *Plays and Poems;* thus, the sonnets became "literature" in the heyday of the Romantic poets and the new vogue for literary biography. Thereafter, they were assumed to be highly personal writings.

The Romantic compulsion to read the sonnets as autobiography inspired attempts to rearrange them to tell their story more clearly. It also led to attempts to relate them to what was known or could be surmised about Shakespeare's life. Some commentators speculated that the publication of the sonnets was the result of a conspiracy by Shakespeare's rivals or enemies, seeking to embarrass him by publishing love poems apparently addressed to a man rather than to the conventional sonnet-mistress. The five appendices to Hyder Edward Rollins's Variorum edition document the first century of such endeavors. Attention was directed toward "problems" such as the identity of Master W. H., of the young man, of the rival poet, and of the dark lady (a phrase, incidentally, never used by Shakespeare in the sonnets). The disappearance of the sonnets from the canon coincided with the time when Shakespeare's standing as the nation's bard was being established. The critics' current fascination is just as significant for what it reveals about contemporary culture, as the "Shakespeare myth" comes under attack from various directions.

The sonnets were apparently composed during a period of ten or a dozen years starting in about 1592–1593. In *Palladis Tamia* Meres refers to the existence of "sugared sonnets" circulating among Shakespeare's "private friends." This remark is corroborated in part by the poems included in *The Passionate Pilgrim.* Other individual poems evidently had an independent existence before 1609, notably the popular Sonnet 2, as well as 8,

106, and 128. Surviving manuscript texts of 2 and 128 in particular appear to derive from 1590s originals. Stylometric examination also suggests that several sonnets may be from that decade. *The Passionate Pilgrim* suggests that Shakespeare initially planned to write a "Venus and Adonis" sequence. Yet some of the sonnets can be no less plausibly dated as contemporary with Shakespeare's Jacobean writings, and research indicates a date shortly after 1600 for *A Lover's Complaint*. The reexamination of the manuscript tradition is a comparatively recent scholarly phenomenon, and further discoveries can be anticipated.

The fact of prior circulation has important implications for the sonnets. While single poems were transcribed into miscellanies from memory or from commonplace books, it was more normal for foliated paper to be used, which suggests that clusters of poems would have been circulated (perhaps on the same theme, or groups self-evidently connected, such as 33 and 34, 82 and 83). Yet the particular poems that were in circulation suggest that the general shape and themes of the *Sonnets* were established from the earliest stages.

Evidence suggesting a lengthy period of composition is inconvenient for commentators seeking to unlock the autobiographical secret of the sonnets. An early date (1592–1594) argues for Southampton as the boy and Marlowe as the rival poet; a date a decade later brings George Herbert and George Chapman into the frame. There are likewise early dark ladies (Lucy Negro, before she took charge of a brothel) and late (Emilia Lanier, Mary Fitton). There may, of course, have been more than one young man, rival, and dark lady, or in fact the sequence may not be autobiographical at all.

No Elizabethan sonnet sequence presents an unambiguous linear narrative, a novel in verse. Shakespeare's is no exception. Yet neither are the *Sonnets* a random anthology, a loose gathering of scattered rhymes. While groups of sonnets are obviously linked thematically, such as the opening sequence urging the young man to marry (1–17), and the dark lady sequence (127–152), the ordering within those groups is not that of continuous narrative. There are many smaller units, with poems recording that the friend has become the lover of the poet's mistress (40–42), or expressing jealousy of the young man's friendship with a rival poet (78–86). Sonnet 44 ends with a reference to two of the four elements "so much of earth and water wrought," and 45 starts with "The other two, slight air and purging fire." Similarly indivisible are the two "horse" sonnets 50 and 51, the "Will" sonnets

135 and 136, and 67 and 68. Sonnets 20 and 87 are connected as much by their telling use of feminine rhyme as by shared themes. Dispersed among the poems are pairs and groups that amplify or comment on each other, such as those dealing with absence (43–45, 47–48, 50–52, and 97–98).

The sonnet sequence was a highly self-conscious form, a cumulative, aggregative genre. Even in Dante Alighieri's *Vita Nuova* (written 1290–1294) the sequence was a showcase for vernacular virtuosity, a work of confessional introspection, and a treatise on poetry and on the relationships between writing and life, art and truth. In the culture of Protestant England, the sonnet sequence participated in the secularization of introspection. Like King David in the Penitential Psalms, the sonnet speaker was an example – partly to be repudiated, partly to be admired, partly to be emulated – whose eloquence permitted him to articulate the stages of some emotional or personal crisis. Shakespeare's speaker, however much he may recall David, Ovid, Horace, or Petrarch, is steeped in the English tradition. Readers in 1609 would have recognized points of congruity and divergence from the sonneteering performances of Sidney, Daniel, Spenser, Thomas Watson, and Drayton.

"My name is Will," declares the speaker of 136. Sonnet 145 apparently puns on Anne Hathaway's name ("I hate, from hate away she threw"). Elizabethan sonneteers, following Sidney, conventionally teased their readers with hints of an actuality behind the poems. Sidney had given Astrophil his own coat of arms, had quibbled with the married name of the supposed original for Stella (Penelope Rich) and with the Greek etymology of his own name (Philip, "lover of horses") in *Astrophil and Stella* sonnets 41, 49, and 53. Shakespeare's speaker descends as much from Astrophil as from Daniel's more enigmatic persona, most obviously in the deployment of the multiple sense of *will* in 135 and 136. He also produces equestrian sonnets (50–51, for example). Sidney's punning on *rich* is echoed in a dozen of the sonnets: thus, the young man is "most rich in youth before my sight" (sonnet 15), and the speaker claims, "So am I as the rich" (52), or later, "That love is merchandiz'd whose rich esteeming / The owner's tongue doth publish every where" (102). He even refers to the "star that guides my moving" (26) and calls love "the star to every wand'ring bark" (116). Sonnet 8 (based in part on an episode in the *Arcadia*) duplicates the *joy / annoy* rhyme that concludes *Astrophil and Stella*.

Shakespeare's monument and grave in Holy Trinity Church, Stratford-upon-Avon. Popular tradition ascribes the verses on the gravestone to Shakespeare.

Shakespeare's sequence is unusual in including sexual consummation (Spenser's *Amoretti* led to the celebration of marriage in *Epithalamion,* 1595) and unique in its persuasion to marry. There is evidence that some contemporary readers were disturbed by the transgressive and experimental features of 1590s erotic writing. Works by Marston and Marlowe were among those banned in 1599 along with satires and other more conventional kindling. Benson's much-discussed modification of the text of the *Sonnets* indicates at least a certain level of anxiety about the gender of the characters in the poems. Benson retained Sonnet 20 but dropped 126 ("O Thou My Lovely Boy") and changed the direct address of 108 ("Nothing, Sweet Boy") to the neutral "Nothing, Sweet Love."

The speaker sums up his predicament in 144, one of the *Passionate Pilgrim* poems:

Two loves I have of comfort and despair,
Which like two spirits do suggest me still:
The better angel is a man right fair,
The worser spirit a woman color'd ill.

The speaker's attraction to the "worser spirit" is figured in harsh language throughout the sequence: Cupid's "heart-inflaming brand" in sonnet 154, "Till my bad angel fire my good one out" in 144,

"My love is as a fever, longing still / For that which longer nurseth the disease" in 147, and, above all, "Th'expense of spirit in a waste of shame . . . none knows well / To shun the heaven that leads men to this hell" in 129. In fact, the brutal juxtaposition of lyricism and lust is characteristic of the collection as a whole. The consequent disjointedness expresses a form of psychological verisimilitude by the standards of Shakespeare's day, where discontinuity and repetition were held to reveal the inner state of a speaker.

The anachronism of applying modern attitudes toward homosexuality to early modern culture is self-evident. Where Shakespeare and his contemporaries drew their boundaries cannot be fully determined, but they were fascinated by the Platonic concept of androgyny, a concept drawn on by the queen herself almost from the moment of her accession. Sonnet 53 is addressed to an inexpressible lover, who resembles both Adonis and Helen. Androgyny is only part of the exploration of sexuality in the sonnets, however. A humanist education could open windows onto a world very different from post-Reformation England. Plato's praise of love between men was in marked contrast to the establishment of capital punishment as the prescribed penalty for sodomy in 1533.

In the *Sonnets* the relationship between the speaker and the young man both invites and resists definition, and it is clearly presented as a challenge to orthodoxy. If at times it seems to correspond to the many Elizabethan celebrations of male friendship, at others it has a raw physicality that resists such polite categorization. Even in sonnet 20, where sexual intimacy seems to be explicitly denied, the speaker's mind runs to bawdy puns. The speaker refers to the friend as "rose," "my love," "lover," and "sweet love," and many commentators have demonstrated the repeated use of explicitly sexual language to the male friend (in 106, 109, and 110, for example). On the other hand, the acceptance of the traditional distinction between the young man and the dark lady sonnets obscures the fact that Shakespeare seems deliberately to render the gender of his subject uncertain in the vast majority of cases.

For some commentators the sequence also participates in the so-called birth of the author, a crucial feature of early modern writing: the liberation of the writer from the shackles of patronage. In Joel Fineman's analysis, Shakespeare creates a radical internalization of Petrarchism, reordering its dynamic by directing his attention to the speaker's subjectivity rather than to the ostensible object of the speaker's devotion: the poetry of praise becomes poetry of self-discovery.

Sidney's Astrophil had inhabited a world of court intrigue, chivalry, and international politics, exemplifying the overlap between political and erotic discourse in Elizabethan England. The circumstances of Shakespeare's speaker, in contrast, are not those of a courtier but of a male of the upwardly mobile "middling sort." Especially in the young man sonnets, there is a marked class anxiety, as the speaker seeks to define his role, whether as a friend, a tutor, a counselor, an employee, or a sexual rival. Not only are comparisons drawn from the world of the professional theater ("As an unperfect actor on the stage" in sonnet 23), but also from the world of business: compared to the prodigal "Unthrifty loveliness" of the youth (sonnet 4), "Making a famine where abundance lies" (1), the speaker inhabits a bourgeois world of debts, loans, repayment, and usury. Sonnet 6 portrays marriage as an investment whose dividend is offspring:

> That use is not forbidden usury
> Which happies those that pay the willing loan –
> That's for thyself to breed another thee,
> Or ten times happier be it ten for one.

A foolish investor pins hopes on noble favor (126):

> Have I not seen dwellers on form and favor
> Lose all, and more, by paying too much rent,
> For compound sweet forgoing simple savor,
> Pitiful thrivers, in their gazing spent?

To the dark lady he speaks a similar language – "I myself am mortgaged to thy will" (134).

Yet Shakespeare's linguistic performance extends beyond the "middling sort." He was a great popularizer, translating court art and high art – John Lyly, Sidney, Spenser – into palatable and sentimental commercial forms. His sequence is remarkable for its thematic and verbal richness, for its extraordinary range of nuances and ambiguities. He often employs words in multiple senses (as in the seemingly willfully indecipherable resonance, punning, polysemy, implication, and nuance of sonnet 94). Shakespeare's celebrated verbal playfulness, the polysemy of his language, is a function of publication, whether by circulation or printing. His words acquire currency beyond himself and become the subject of reading and interpretation.

This linguistic richness can also be seen as an act of social aspiration: as the appropriation of the ambiguity axiomatically inherent in courtly speech. The sequence continues the process of dismantling traditional distinctions among rhetoric, philosophy, and poetry begun in the poems of 1593–1594. The poems had dealt in reversal and inversion and had combined elements of narrative and drama. The *Sonnets* occupy a distinct, marginal space between social classes, between public and private, narrative and dramatic, and they proceed not through inverting categories but rather through interrogating them. Variations are played on Elizabethan conventions of erotic discourse: love without sex, sex without love, a "master-mistress" who is "prick'd . . . out for women's pleasure" as the ultimate in unattainable ("to my purpose nothing," 20) adoration. Like Spenser's *Amoretti,* Shakespeare's collection meditates on the relationships among love, art, time, and immortality. It remains a meditation, however, even when it seems most decided. Thus, the young man is conventionally told "So long as men can breathe or eyes can see, / So long lives this, and this gives life to thee" (18); but though the verses have survived, the young man's name has not.

The speaker is alert to the consequences of such publication, whereby he has made himself "a motley to the view" (110), allowing his reputation to be stained "preposterously" (109). As he puts it in sonnet 111, "my name receives a brand, / And almost thence my nature is subdu'd / To what it works in, like the dyer's hand."

The consequences of love, the pain of rejection, desertion, and loss of reputation are powerful elements in the poem that follows the sequence. Despite Thorpe's unambiguous attribution of the piece to Shakespeare, *A Lover's Complaint* was rejected from the canon, on distinctly flimsy grounds, until quite recently. It has been much investigated to establish its authenticity and its date. It is now generally accepted as Shakespearean and dated at some point between 1600 and 1609, possibly revised from a 1600 first version for publication in Thorpe's volume. Forceful arguments for its authenticity were crowned by John Kerrigan's edition of *The Sonnets and A Lover's Complaint* (1986), which has played a valuable role in restoring its visibility, as did numerological studies such as that of Thomas Roche.

The poem comprises 329 lines, disposed into forty-seven seven-line rhyme-royal stanzas. It draws heavily on Spenser and Daniel and is the complaint of a wronged woman about the duplicity of a man. It is in some sense a companion to *Lucrece* and to *All's Well That Ends Well* (circa 1602–1603) as much as to the sonnets. Its connections with the narrative poems, with the plays, and with the genre of female complaint have been thoroughly explored. The woman is a city beseiged by an eloquent wooer ("how deceits were gilded in his smiling"), whose essence is dissimulation ("his passion, but an art of craft"). There has been a growing tendency to relate the poem to its immediate context in Thorpe's *Sonnets* volume and to find it a reflection or gloss or critique of the preceding sequence.

Interest in Shakespeare's nondramatic writings has increased markedly in recent years. They are no longer so easily marginalized or dismissed as conventional performances or reserved to the delight of an elite cognoscenti. Curiosity about Shakespeare's engagement with his own age in all its features has stimulated much excellent work on these most characteristically contemporary of his works. They may never regain the exceptional popularity they enjoyed in his lifetime, but they are coming to be seen as central to an understanding of his age. The more present-day readers see how Shakespeare was a writer of his age, the better they can understand why his contemporaries found him, in Jonson's words, a writer "for all time."

Bibliographies:

Walter Ebish and Levin L. Schucking, *A Shakespeare Bibliography* (Oxford: Clarendon Press, 1931);

Larry S. Champion, *The Essential Shakespeare: An Annotated Bibliography of Major Modern Studies* (Boston: G. K. Hall, 1986);

See also the annual bibliographies in *Shakespeare Quarterly,* plus the reviews of current scholarship and criticism in the annuals *Shakespeare Survey* and *The Year's Work in English Studies.*

References:

Marie Axton, *The Queen's Two Bodies: Drama and the Elizabethan Succession* (London: Royal Historical Society, 1978);

Philippa Berry, "Women, Language and History in *The Rape of Lucrece,*" *Shakespeare Survey,* 44 (1992): 33–39;

John Buxton, "Two Dead Birds," in *English Renaissance Studies Presented to Helen Gardner,* edited by John Carey (Oxford: Oxford University Press, 1980), pp. 44–55;

Margreta De Grazia, "The Scandal of Shakespeare's Sonnets," *Shakespeare Survey,* 46 (1994): 35–50;

Ian Donaldson, *The Rapes of Lucretia: A Myth and Its Transformations* (Oxford: Oxford University Press, 1982);

Heather Dubrow, *Captive Victors: Shakespeare's Narrative Poems and Sonnets* (Ithaca, N.Y.: Cornell University Press, 1987);

Katherine Duncan-Jones, "Much Ado with Red and White: The Earliest Readers of Shakespeare's *Venus and Adonis* (1593)," *Review of English Studies,* new series 44 (1993): 479–501;

Duncan-Jones, "Was the 1609 *Shake-speares Sonnets* Really Unauthorized?," *Review of English Studies,* new series 34 (1983): 151–171;

Robert Ellrodt, "Shakespeare the Non-dramatic Poet," in *The Cambridge Companion to Shakespeare Survey,* edited by Stanley Wells (Cambridge: Cambridge University Press, 1986), pp. 105–125;

William Empson, "*The Phoenix and the Turtle,*" *Essays in Criticism,* 16 (June 1966): 147–153;

Anne Ferry, *The "Inward Language"* (Chicago: University of Chicago Press, 1983);

Joel Fineman, *Shakespeare's Perjured Eye: The Invention of Poetic Subjectivity in the Sonnets* (Berkeley: University of California Press, 1986);

Thomas M. Greene, "Pitiful Thrivers: Failed Husbandry in the Sonnets," in *Shakespeare and the Question of Theory,* edited by Patricia Parker and Geoffrey Hartman (London: Methuen, 1985), pp. 230–244;

A. Kent Hieatt, "*Cymbeline* and the Intrusion of Lyric into Romance Narrative: Sonnets, 'A Lover's Complaint,' Spenser's *Ruins of Rome,*" in *Unfolded Tales: Essays on Renaissance Romance,* edited by George M. Logan and Gordon Teskey

(Ithaca, N.Y.: Cornell University Press, 1989), pp. 98–118;

C. H. Hobday, "Shakespeare's Venus and Adonis Sonnets," *Shakespeare Survey,* 26 (1973): 103–109;

E. A. J. Honigmann, *Shakespeare: The Lost Years* (Manchester: Manchester University Press, 1985);

Clark Hulse, *Metamorphic Verse: The Elizabethan Minor Epic* (Princeton, N.J.: Princeton University Press, 1981);

Anthea Hume, "*Love's Martyr,* 'The Phoenix and the Turtle,' and the Aftermath of the Essex Rebellion," *Review of English Studies,* new series 40 (1989): 48–71;

Coppelia Kahn, "The Rape in Shakespeare's *Lucrece,*" *Shakespeare Survey,* 9 (1976): 45–72;

Dennis Kay, *William Shakespeare: His Life, Works, and Era* (New York: Morrow, 1992);

William Keach, *Elizabethan Erotic Narratives* (New Brunswick, N.J.: Rutgers University Press, 1977);

John Kerrigan, *Motives of Woe: Shakespeare and the "Female Complaint"* (Oxford: Oxford University Press, 1991);

Arthur F. Marotti, "'Love is not Love': Elizabethan Sonnets and the Social Order," *ELH,* 49 (Summer 1982): 396–428;

Marotti, "Shakespeare's Sonnets as Literary Property," in *Soliciting Interpretation: Literary Theory and Seventeenth-Century English Poetry,* edited by Elizabeth D. Harvey and Katharine Eisaman Maus (Chicago: University of Chicago Press, 1990), pp. 143–173;

Katherine E. Maus, "Taking Tropes Seriously: Language and Violence in *Lucrece,*" *Shakespeare Quarterly,* 37 (Spring 1986): 66–82;

Georgio Melchiori, *Shakespeare's Dramatic Meditations: An Experiment in Criticism* (Oxford: Oxford University Press, 1979);

Joseph Pequigney, *Such Is My Love: A Study of Shakespeare's Sonnets* (Chicago: University of Chicago Press, 1985);

Thomas P. Roche Jr., *Petrarch and the English Sonnet Sequences* (New York: AMS Press, 1989);

Bruce R. Smith, *Homosexual Desire in Shakespeare's England: A Cultural Poetics* (Chicago: Chicago University Press, 1991);

Peter Stallybrass, "Editing as Cultural Formation: The Sexing of Shakespeare's Sonnets," *Modern Language Quarterly,* 54 (March 1993): 91–103;

Gary Taylor, "Some Manuscripts of Shakespeare's Sonnets," *Bulletin of the John Rylands Library,* 68 (1985): 210–246;

Nancy M. Vickers, "'The Blazon of Sweet Beauty's Best': Shakespeare's *Lucrece,*" in *Shakespeare and the Question of Theory,* pp. 95–115;

Linda Woodbridge, "Palisading the Elizabethan Body Politic," *Texas Studies in Language and Literature,* 33 (Fall 1991): 327–354.

Papers:

The Booke of Sir Thomas More (a play probably written principally by Anthony Munday, with revisions by Thomas Dekker, Henry Chettle, William Shakespeare, and possibly Thomas Heywood) is preserved in a manuscript at the British Library (Harleian Ms. 7368). Most scholars now concur that two brief passages were written by Shakespeare circa 1594–1595, and that one of them represents the only surviving example of a literary or dramatic manuscript in Shakespeare's hand. Shakespeare's autograph signature occurs in three places in his will, dated 25 March 1616, located in the Public Records Office (PROB 1/4). His signature is also on a deposition given to the Court of Requests in 1612 (Public Records Office, REQ 4/1), and in two documents relating to the mortgage purchase of a property in Blackfriars (one in the Guildhall Library, the other in the British Library, Egerton Ms. 1787).

Robert Tofte

(January 1561 or 1562 – January 1619 or 1620)

L. M. Storozynsky
University College of the Fraser Valley

BOOKS: *Laura. The Toyes of a Traueller. Or the Feast of Fancie* (London: Printed by Valentine Simmes, 1597);

Alba. The Months Minde of a Melancholy Lover, Diuided into Three Parts: by R. T. Gentleman (London: Printed by Felix Kingston for Matthew Lownes, 1598).

Editions: *Alba. The Month's Minde of a Melancholy Lover,* edited by Alexander B. Grosart (Manchester: Charles E. Simms, 1880);

Laura, The Toys of a Traveller: or The Feast of Fancy, in *An English Garner,* volume 8, edited by Edward Arber (Westminster, 1896), pp. 267–340;

Laura, The Toys of a Traveller: or The Feast of Fancy, in *Elizabethan Sonnets,* volume 2, edited by Sidney Lee (Westminster: Archibald Constable, 1904), pp. 351–424;

The Poetry of Robert Tofte, 1597–1620: A Critical Old-Spelling Edition, edited by Jeffrey N. Nelson (Hamden, Conn.: Garland, 1994).

TRANSLATIONS: Ludovico Ariosto, *Two Tales Translated out of Ariosto* (London: Printed by Valentine Simmes, 1597);

Matteo Maria Boiardo, *Orlando Inamorato* (London: Printed by Valentine Simmes, 1598);

Ercole Tasso and Torquato Tasso, *Of Marriage and Wiving* (London: Printed by Thomas Creede for John Smethwick, 1599);

Anonymous, *The Bachelors' Banquet,* attributed to Antoine de La Sale, probably translated by Tofte (London: Printed by Thomas Creede for Thomas Pavier, 1603);

Ariosto, *Ariosto's Satires in Seven Famous Discourses* (London: Printed by Nicholas Okes for Roger Jackson, 1608); revised and enlarged as *Ariosto's Seven Planets Governing Italy, or His Satires,* containing three elegies probably by Tofte (London: Printed by William Stansby for Roger Jackson, 1611);

Nicolas de Montreux, *Honour's Academy* (London: Printed by Thomas Creede, 1610);

Benedetto Varchi, *The Blazon of Jealousy* (London: Printed by Thomas Snodham for John Busby, 1615).

Robert Tofte, an Elizabethan poet, translator, and annotator, has attracted the attention of readers of both English and continental Renaissance literature, although he is by no means a well-known figure and his work remains neglected. His contribution is small but valuable: his two collections of poetry have many affinities with contemporary sonnet sequences; he is responsible for the earliest allusion to William Shakespeare's *Love's Labor's Lost* (1594–1595); and his translations and annotations provide insights into the practice and process of Renaissance translation and the life and interests of an Elizabethan gentleman. Furthermore, as translator and annotator, Tofte experimented with a curious form of autobiography.

The few certain details of Tofte's life form a disappointingly incomplete picture. His father, William Tofte, thought to have been from Guildford, Surrey, became a fishmonger in the parish of St. Magnus Martyr, Bridge Ward, London, where he married Mary Cowper, daughter of John Cowper, a fishmonger and alderman. Robert was born in January of either 1561 or 1562; the parish register for 15 January 1561–1562 reports, "Was Robert son of Mr. Tofte baptized." Tofte had an elder brother, John, and a younger half brother and two half sisters from his mother's second marriage. Nothing is known of his youth or education; although the matriculation register for Exeter College, Oxford, contains an entry for "Robert Tafte of London, Gent." dated 24 November 1581, it is not certain that this is the poet. Tofte is always designated "gentleman," and there is no indication that he entered into any type of business or profession. The St. Magnus parish register for 18 November 1582 records the marriage of a Robert Tofte to Brygget Redwood, but no other evidence suggests that Tofte ever married.

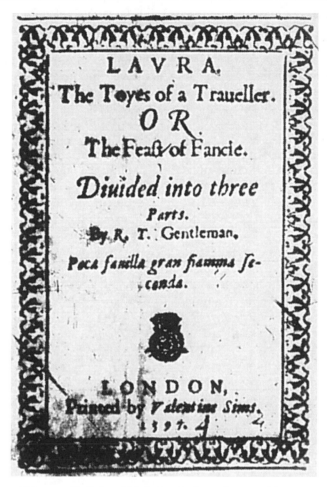

Title page for Robert Tofte's first book, a collection of forty-one love poems

As an adult Tofte lived in Holborn; although his residence was not far from two of Shakespeare's London addresses, it appears that the two never met. Indeed, the few documented events in Tofte's life are disappointingly mundane: the probate of his grandfather John Cowper's will on 18 August 1584; a lawsuit brought against a London merchant in 1594; his appearance as a witness at a trial in 1613; the signing of his own will on 30 March 1618; the probate of his will on 3 January 1620; and his burial on 24 January 1619 or 1620. The parish register of the Church of St. Andrew, Holborn, records, "Robert Tofte, gent., out of Widow Goodall's house near Barnard's Inn, was buried the 24." The nineteenth-century scholar Alexander B. Grosart, a specialist in the retrieval of ancient documents, reproduces Tofte's will in the introduction to his 1880 edition of a selection of Tofte's poetry, but the document is typical of its time and offers little to interest either the biographer or the literary scholar. Tofte died financially well-off and debt-free. Passages of the will

indicate kindness and generosity in his legacies to the poor and his release of certain debtors from their obligations.

Tofte was a traveler, and, while few precise details are available, the evidence for his sojourns in France and Italy prior to the publication of any of his works seems reliable. If he kept journals or diaries, they apparently have not survived. According to Franklin B. Williams, on at least one occasion he may have been commissioned to carry official government dispatches, but the document recording this service, like the university register, names one Robert Tafte. Tofte's brother John is said to have made plans to join the last voyage of Sir Francis Drake, but whether he actually sailed is not known. The fleet sailed in August 1595, returning the following year after a series of disasters including Drake's death; John Tofte lived until 1599. Both Leslie Hotson and C. A. O. Fox suggest, on rather flimsy evidence, that Robert may have traveled to America shortly before his death. Tofte's European travels are confirmed by his own declaration that many of his poems were "conceived in Italy," by several poems with city names indicating their place of conception (they may have been written abroad or the cities may have provided inspiration, although location is not important to the content or context of the poems), and by the enumeration in his will of items acquired in Italy. Several of his poems play upon the theme of absence from the loved one, admittedly a common motif in love poetry of the period. Finally, Tofte's command of French and Italian, evident from the nature and quality of his translations, suggests that he had the opportunity to practice and perfect his skills abroad.

Tofte's earliest printed works include two long collections of his own poems. Although not always considered examples of the genre, both collections have much in common with contemporary Elizabethan sonnet sequences. *Laura: The Toys of a Traveller; or, The Feast of Fancy* (1597) is dedicated to Lady Lucy Percy, sister of Lord Henry, Earl of Northumberland; their brother William Percy was also a sonneteer. A poem prefacing the collection is addressed "Alla bellissima sua Signora. E. C.," whose identity has given rise to much speculation but has yet to be established. Nowhere in the preliminary items are the poems in *Laura* referred to as sonnets; Tofte calls the poems in the dedication "toys" and "trifles" and in the poem to E. C., "verses." However, the final item in the volume is a curious disclaimer signed "R. B.," supposedly a friend of Tofte's, who refers to the volume as "this poem" and to individual poems as "sonnets," as if they were stanzas making up a single work:

> Without the author's knowledge, as is before said by the printer, this poem is made thus publicly known; which . . . the gentleman himself (suspecting what is now proved too true) . . . earnestly entreated me to prevent. But I came at the last sheets' printing, and find more than thirty sonnets not his, intermixed with his: helped it cannot be but by the well-indulging reader, who will with less pain distinguish between them, than I on this sudden possibly can.

Given the flexible Renaissance understanding of the term *sonnet, Laura* can be regarded as a sequence or collection of love sonnets and one that is carefully arranged, despite Tofte's supposed lack of participation in its printing. As the title page announces, the book is divided into three parts, each comprising forty-one poems, or sonnets: twenty of twelve lines and twenty of ten, one of each per page, plus a concluding poem of twenty-four lines. Most

of the poems, although ending with a rhymed couplet, simply develop the argument from first to last line, following a less-demanding rhyme scheme (maintained with only minor variations throughout the volume) than a quatorzain requires. The symmetry of the poems and the design of the volume cast doubt on R. B.'s statement concerning the thirty sonnets not written by Tofte: how can he claim there are thirty "alien" sonnets when he himself is unable to "distinguish between them"? The longer poems, added as conclusions to each section and meant to bring each to a close, if not resolution, would be just as appropriate as introductions. The first two employ the same conceit (likening parts 1 and 2 to the first and second courses at a banquet), but the conceit is dropped in the third poem, which, in spite of its position at the end, humbly offers the work to the lady addressed.

The second collection, *Alba: The Month's Mind of a Melancholy Lover* (1598), offers preliminary poems addressed to Lady Anne Herne and her brothers, Sir Calisthines Brooke and Sir John Brooke. Four poems, whose authors have not been conclusively identified, are addressed to Tofte, who supplies a verse reply to each. *Alba,* like *Laura,* is divided into three parts, but it is not so readily accommodated by even the most flexible definition of a sonnet sequence. Each part, with its own title page, contains what is really a single long, narrative, Petrarchan-style love poem in sixains. Following *Alba,* a new title page introduces "Certain Divine Poems"; this, too, is a long narrative in sixains, apparently having nothing to do with *Alba* except that the poet, who now styles himself "a convert from vain love," has turned his thoughts away from Alba to heaven. The final item in the collection is titled "A Most Excellent Pathetical and Passionate Letter of Duke D'Epernoun," which the volume title page explains is a letter sent by the duke "unto the late French King, Henry the 3. of that name, when he was commanded from the court and from his royal company." The letter has no apparent connection with either *Alba* or "Certain Divine Poems."

Neither *Laura* nor *Alba* has received much critical attention, and each work has been edited only once. Edward Arber's 1896 edition of *Laura* was reprinted in 1904 by Sidney Lee, who points out that "the rules of the sonnet form are for the most part ignored." *Alba* has been edited by Grosart (1880), who includes in his introduction selections from *Laura,* finding it inferior to *Alba;* the fact that thirty of the *Laura* poems are said not to be by Tofte de-

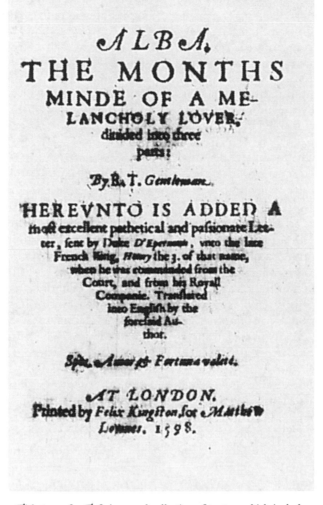

Title page for Tofte's second collection of poetry, which includes the earliest printed allusion to William Shakespeare's Love's Labor's Lost *(circa 1594–1595)*

ters him from printing the whole work, and *Alba* has not met Grosart's optimistic expectation that it would make its way into "after-Anthologies of our 'sweet singers.'" Later scholars who even mention either collection find they have little literary merit, although *Alba* is generally considered superior because it includes the earliest allusion to Shakespeare's *Love's Labor's Lost:*

Loves Labor Lost, I once did see a play,
Ycleped so, so called to my pain.
Which I to hear to my small joy did stay,
Giving attendance on my froward dame:
    My misgiving mind presaging to me ill,
    Yet was I drawne to see it 'gainst my will.
Each actor played in cunning wise his part,
But chiefly those entrapped in Cupid's snare;
Yet all was feigned, 'twas not from the heart,
They seemed to grieve, but yet they felt no care:

'Twas I that griefe (indeed) did bear in breast;
The others did but make a show in jest.

Like the work of many Elizabethan sonneteers, *Laura* and *Alba* have provoked much biographical speculation and are sometimes regarded as accounts of an unhappy love affair. They and Tofte's other works contain frequently recurring references that are cited as "internal evidence" pointing to the real name of the fictional Laura and Alba (thought to be the same woman) and identifying Tofte with the love-stricken poet-narrator. Anagrams suggest the name E. Caril of Warington; continental place-names suggest Tofte's real travels; and the uppercase letters R and T and the nickname "Robin Redbreast" are taken to be references to Tofte himself. Some of his poems are signed R. T., possibly the author's way of subtly identifying himself with the poet-lover, although the initials may have been added by the printer.

Tofte's earliest translations are contemporary with *Laura* and *Alba,* and throughout his career he seems deliberately to have chosen works whose subject matter reflects the conflicting passions, disappointments, and bitterness found in his own poetry. His apparent obsession with the themes of unrequited love and fickle women has led modern readers to view him as a misogynist. Most of his translations and certainly his annotations reveal personal experience, provide useful references to his travels, and become progressively more subjective in tone and content.

Two Tales Translated out of Ariosto (1597) presents episodes from canto 43 of *Orlando Furioso* (1532), translated in heroic verse, or ottava rima. A printer's note states that Tofte prepared the work "in the year 1592, he being then in Italy," and Tofte dates one tale from Siena, 28 July 1592, the other from Naples, 27 March 1593. *Orlando Inamorato* (1598), also in heroic verse, claims to be a translation of the three first books of Matteo Maria Boiardo's lengthy 1487 work but in fact includes only the first three cantos of book 1. To the original Tofte adds a few verses of his own, as well as five explanatory stanzas. The story and characters bear some resemblance to those of Shakespeare's *Midsummer Night's Dream* (circa 1595–1596) and *As You Like It* (circa 1599–1600) and there are references to Tofte's *Alba. Of Marriage and Wiving* (1599), a mainly prose translation of Ercole and Torquato Tasso's *Torquato and Hercules,* was burned with other books by order of the archbishop of Canterbury as part of a campaign to suppress satire. *The Bachelors' Banquet* (1603), a translation of *Les Quinze Joyes de Mariage* (attributed to Antoine de La Sale), was thought to be by Thomas Dekker but is now attributed, albeit inconclusively, to Tofte. *Ariosto's Satires* (1608), with Tofte's first annotations – historical, literary, biographical, cultural, and geographical commentary – was first published as by Gervase Markham, but Tofte's later claim to the first and the second edition (1611) is undisputed. The second edition is more heavily annotated and includes three elegies generally thought to be written by Tofte.

Honour's Academy (1610) is a translation of Nicolas de Montreux's *Cinquieme et Dernier Livre des Bergeries de Julliette* (1598), itself an imitation of Jorge de Montemayor's *Diana* (1559). The text is in prose and verse, and Tofte provides marginal glosses and summaries of the story; but the translation, apparently done hastily and not revised, is not up to Tofte's usual standards. Fox, who sees frequent allusions to Shakespeare's *Sonnets* (1609) and plays in *Laura* and *Alba,* draws attention to the description of a shipwreck and the characters of the Old Magician and "the monster foul" in *Honour's Academy,* arguing that Shakespeare must have been familiar with the work when writing *The Tempest.*

Finally, *The Blazon of Jealousy* (1615), a translation of *Lettura di M. Benedetto Varchi, sopra un sonetto Della Gelosia di Mons. Dalla Casa,* is for a variety of reasons Tofte's most important translation. It is in this work that Tofte claims the translation of Ariosto's satires as his own. The dedication to Sir William Dymoke, hereditary champion of the English court, recalls Tofte's time in Italy: "not my self alone, but divers other gentlemen, as well English as strangers, were beholding for the kind entertainment you gave us at our being in Italy together." Through Dymoke, Tofte may have met Samuel Daniel, who was in Italy with the former. However, Tofte's claims of friendship with poets such as Henry Constable and Thomas Watson are not corroborated elsewhere. In *Blazon* his annotations take on new dimensions, adding much autobiographical and other material. Finally, appended to *Blazon,* the poem "The Fruits of Jealousy," generally ascribed to Tofte, brings to a close the poet-translator's lengthy preoccupation with the theme of jealousy.

It must be said that Tofte's annotations offer a sometimes deceptive impression of the extent of his learning. Although he clearly consulted original sources, his references to Greek authors must have been to secondary sources in translation, since he did not read Greek; his apparent familiarity with contemporary English works and writers is belied by his extensive and often inaccurate use of anthologies such as *England's Parnassus, Belvedere,* and *The Phoenix Nest.* However, his translations reveal a keen interest in continental, especially Italian, life and letters. It is difficult to assess the popularity of his work in his own time, and none of his translations has been edited, but he is generally regarded as a talented translator who corrected, elaborated, augmented, and illustrated the texts while infusing his work with personal experience and sentiment.

Three manuscripts by Tofte also deserve mention. In "A Discourse of the Five Last Popes" (1597), dedicated to Bishop Richard Bancroft, Tofte mentions being in Rome in June 1593 and records observations clearly made firsthand. Inserted into the document are several illustrations and a health certificate issued to him in Loreto, dated 27 February 1594. "The Loves of Armide" is an undated translation from *Les Amours d'Armide* (1597) by

Pierre Joulet. It is notable for its preliminary verses by Tofte, full of allusions to contemporary poets such as Sir Philip Sidney, Sir John Harington, Edmund Spenser, Daniel, and Michael Drayton. A third, untitled work includes verses that Hotson and Fox cite as proof of Tofte's voyage to America. Finally, several autograph annotations, Tofte's initials, and his full signature appear in the copy of Geoffrey Chaucer's works that he once owned.

The current revival of interest in Elizabethan sonnet sequences is marked by a flexible and far less exclusive definition of the genre than that previously used; scholars now recognize affinities among them and other collections of poetry, such as miscellanies and commonplace books. In light of these new approaches, a timely project would be a modern critical edition of Tofte's poetry aimed at placing him within the context of both major and minor contemporary love poets. Further scholarship might include the editing of his manuscripts and the reexamination of both his poems and translations in the hopes of extracting a fuller version of their subtext: Tofte's autobiography.

References:

John Erskine, *The Elizabethan Lyric* (New York: Columbia University Press, 1903), pp. 164–165;

C. A. O. Fox, *Notes on William Shakespeare and Robert Tofte* (Swansea: C. A. O. Fox, 1957);

Leslie Hotson, *I, William Shakespeare* (London: Cape, 1937), pp. 234–236;

Lisle Cecil John, *The Elizabethan Sonnet Sequences: Studies in Conventional Conceits* (New York: Russell & Russell, 1964), pp. 109–110;

George Morrow Kahrl, "Robert Tofte's Annotations in *The Blazon of Iealousie*," *Harvard Studies and Notes in Philology and Literature,* 18 (1935): 47–67;

Robert C. Melzi, "Un Contributo Alla Storia Del Petrarchismo In Inghilterra: Robert Tofte E Il Blazon Of Iealousie," *Il Lettore di Provincia,* 17 (1986): 17–40;

Lu Emily Pearson, *Elizabethan Love Conventions* (London: Allen & Unwin, 1966), pp. 131–135;

Glyn Pursglove, "Robert Tofte, Elizabethan Translator of Boiardo," in *The Renaissance in Ferrara and Its European Horizons,* edited by J. Salmons and W. Moretti (Cardiff: University of Wales Press, 1984), pp. 111–122;

Janet G. Scott, *Les Sonnets Elisabéthains: Les Sources et L'apport Personnel* (Paris: Librairie Ancienne Honoré Champion, 1929), pp. 201–202;

Franklin B. Williams, "Robert Tofte," *Review of English Studies,* 13 (1937): 282–296, 405–424;

F. P. Wilson, *"The Bachelors' Banquet": An Elizabethan Translation of "Les Quinze Joyes de Mariage"* (Oxford: Oxford University Press, 1929).

Papers:

The autograph manuscripts of Robert Tofte's "A Discourse of the Last Five Popes" and "The Loves of Armide" are held at Lambeth Palace (Lambeth Ms. 1112) and the Bodleian Library (Ms. Rawlinson D 679), respectively. Another containing verses that some readers cite as evidence for Tofte's journey to America is also at the Bodleian (Ms. Malone 16).

William Warner

(1558 – 9 March 1609)

Ursula F. Appelt
State University of New York at Stony Brook

BOOKS: *Pan His Syrinx, or Pipe, Compact of Seuen Reedes: Including in One, Seuen Tragical and Comicall Arguments* (London: Thomas Purfoote, 1584); revised as *Syrinx, or a Seauenfold Historie. Newly Perused* (London: Thomas Purfoote, 1597);

Albions England. Or Historicall Map of the Same Island, 4 books (London: Printed by George Robinson for Thomas Cadman, 1586); revised and enlarged as *The First and Second Parts of Albions England,* 6 books (London: Printed by Thomas Orwin for Thomas Cadman, 1589); revised and enlarged again as *Albions England; the Third Time Corrected and Augmented,* 9 books (London: Thomas Orwin, 1592); revised and enlarged again as *Albions England: a Continued Historie of the Same Kingdome,* 12 books (London: Printed by Widow Orwin for J. B., 1596); enlarged again, 13 books and epitome (London: Printed by Edm. Bollifant for George Potter, 1602); books 14–16 published separately as *A Continuance of Albions England* (London: Printed by Felix Kyngston for George Potter, 1606); complete edition, 16 books (London: Printed by W. Stansby for George Potter, 1612).

Editions: *The Poems of William Warner,* in *The Works of English Poets,* volume 4, edited by Alexander Chalmers (London, 1810), pp. 499–658 – includes books 1–12 of *Albion's England* and *Aeneidos,* a prose recension of Caxton's version of Virgil's *Aeneid* combined with the Brut legend;

William Warner's "Syrinx or a Sevenfold History," edited by Wallace Bacon (Evanston, Ill.: Northwestern University Press, 1950; reprinted, New York: AMS Press, 1970);

"William Warner's *Albions England,*" 2 volumes, edited by David W. Becker, dissertation, Rutgers University, 1954;

Albions England. A Continued Historie of the Same Kingdome (Hildesheim: Olms, 1971).

OTHER: Plautus, *Menaecmi. A Pleasant and Fine Conceited Comaedie, Taken out of Plautus,* translated by Warner (London: T. Creede, 1594);

"Argentile and Curan," in *Specimens of the British Poets,* volume 2, edited by Thomas Campbell (London: John Murray, 1819), pp. 272–279.

In *Palladis Tamia* (1598) Frances Meres called William Warner "our English Homer." For Gabriel Harvey, Thomas Nashe, and Michael Drayton, among others, Warner was the equal both of classical writers such as Homer, Virgil, Horace, and Ovid and of contemporary writers such as Edmund Spenser, William Shakespeare, and Sir Philip Sidney. In *England's Parnassus* (1600) Robert Allott champions Warner for his sententious coinings and quotes passages from his work extensively, citing only Spenser and Drayton more frequently. This immense popularity was based on his major work, the verse chronicle *Albion's England* (1586–1612). For modern readers these comparisons and the excessive praise seem uncalled for, since Warner is almost a cipher, a forgotten, or at best unsuccessful, author. Even though his prose romance *Syrinx* (1584) was influential, his masterpiece did not stand the test of time. However, Warner does not deserve oblivion. *Albion's England* is a precursor of Drayton's *Polyolbion* (1605–1629); it combines the storytelling and allegorical techniques of Spenser's *Faerie Queene* (1590) with the material of world and British history; and it contains the most diverse collection of stories available in sixteenth-century literature. As an ambitious and popular failure, *Albion's England* reveals something about the tastes and popular beliefs of Elizabethan England.

Little is known about Warner's life. He was an attorney of the Common Pleas and died suddenly in Great Amwell, Hertfordshire, on 9 March 1609. Apart from these two facts, the biographer must turn to *Albion's England.* Warner was born in London in 1558, the year of Elizabeth's accession to the throne. In book 11 he mentions that his father participated in Richard Chancellor's expedition to Russia in 1553, and in book 12 he refers to his father's death during William Towerson's voyage of exploration to Guinea in 1577. Warner's extensive use of Richard Hakluyt's voyages in these two books attests to his interest in the topic and is an attempt both to honor and to commemorate these voyages. Warner received his education at Cambridge, became an attorney, and settled in Hertfordshire in the neighborhood of his patrons, the Lords Hunsdon. He was married and had several children. It is possible that he married a second time, to a widow, and had a son.

His choice of the queen's cousins as patrons seemed propitious, but his relations with Henry and George Carey did not lead to reward or advancement. Both Careys held the position of Lord Chamberlain and were thus linked to Shakespeare's theater company. The connection between Warner, the Careys, and Shakespeare tempted early readers to make Warner the translator of Plautus's *Menaechmi,* Shakespeare's source for *The Comedy of Errors* (circa 1592–1594). However, the styles of Warner's works and of the translation are different. Because Warner changed his dedication of *Albion's England* from George and Henry Carey to Sir Edward Coke in 1606 and complained about "thanks-starved dedications" in the address to the reader of the 1602 edition, it is safe to assume that there was a break between patrons and poet.

His two works belong to radically different genres. *Syrinx* was an example of the emerging, popular prose narrative that Sidney, Nashe, and John Lyly shaped into inimitable and complex form. *Albion's England,* an offshoot of the sixteenth-century craze for all things historical, was a mixture of chronicle, epic, romance, fable, and love story. Even though Warner seemed to be on the cutting edge of literary fashion, his choices of genre reflect literary movements that either took time to develop (the prose romance) or were short-lived experiments (the verse chronicle, which even Samuel Daniel abandoned). Warner's poor literary judgment was equaled by the quality of his execution.

Warner took the title for his prose romance *Syrinx* from Ovid's story of Pan, as he tells the reader in the preface. Chased by Pan, Syrinx was turned into the reeds out of which Pan fashioned the pipe that bears her name. Warner divided his romance into seven *calami,* or tales. Both the first edition, of 1584, and the second, of 1597, are dedicated to George Carey, second Lord Hunsdon. In printing the second edition Thomas Purfoote was probably capitalizing on the popularity of Warner,

or of the genre, for Warner holds him responsible for publishing "an imperfection of my non-age." He limited his revisions to pruning the stylistic excesses of Lyly's euphuism, which is recognizable in most prose narratives of the time, including Sidney's *Arcadia.* These devices emerged from translations of Italian novellas and of Heliodorus's *Aethiopica.* Robert Greene popularized the genre and borrowed from Warner, who, as he says in the preface to the second edition, felt flattered by such plagiarism. In the seventeenth century Thomas Dekker and Robert Daborne, among others, drew on Warner's tales for their plays.

Syrinx bears all the marks of a Greek prose romance: lost parents and children, love stories, confused identities, shipwrecks, surprise denouements, and spectacular reunions – plot elements that generate a confusing and twisted story line. It is full of speeches with moralistic, doleful, or edifying intent, as in Abraces' speech about his endured hardships: "But hope overcoming despair, for that in the one is possibility, in the other no remedy, knowing that as the gods have power by justice to punish, so they have will by mercy to pardon, we have made necessity a virtue, continuance a custom, and patience our protector."

The frame of the story deals with the family of Abraces and Dricilla, who were separated during the wars between Media and Assyria. Abraces spends most of his long life, more than two hundred years, abandoned on a desolate island, while Dricilla governs and brings culture to another, almost paradisal island. Their son, Sorares, separated from his mother while an infant and later reared by the hostile Assyrian king Ninus, is shipwrecked on Abraces' island. After Abraces and a companion steal Sorares' ship and return to safety, they decide to rescue the Assyrians. Meanwhile, Sorares' sons Atys and Abynados set out in search of their father. After many adventures they all finally land on Dricilla's island but, except for Sorares and his sons, do not know each other's fates. To guard her island from invasion, especially from the monstrous Assyrians, Dricilla has established a rule that all potential invaders be put to death. The execution of her relatives is narrowly averted by the islanders' pity for the condemned, which forces Dricilla to explain and justify her harsh rule. In the ensuing spectacular reunion, three generations are brought together.

Interpolated tales make up the bulk of *Syrinx:* stories about lovers, the sons and daughters of kings caught in the midst of wars, or star-crossed lovers of unequal social status. One gruesome tale involves a

Title page for William Warner's major work, a history in verse
that combines elements of chronicle, epic, romance,
and fable traditions

cruelty, and the uncertainty of their world. However, Warner imposes Christian ideas onto his pre-Christian world. The resulting contradiction between providentialism and arbitrary fortune cannot be resolved. Since this world is one of injustice, corruption, and hardship, he allows at least his main characters to escape from the world altogether. After the islanders burn their ships, they live happily ever after on Dricilla's hermetically sealed island.

For his major work Warner turned away from the world of prose romance and to British history, where his skill in telling a good story and in writing impressive speeches served him almost as well as in the earlier work. *Albion's England* is encyclopedic in scope, digressive in plot, and innovative in its insertion of speeches and intermixtures of genres. In other words, Warner imposes romance techniques onto historical subject matter. He managed to please all popular tastes by including in his verse history stories from various other genres, such as beast fable, burlesque, fabliau, and romance. Thus, the work partakes of many genres, aspiring to both history and epic while reading like a collection of instructive and amusing stories.

History was one of the most prestigious and popular genres of the Renaissance, and the proliferation of chronicles during the Tudor era attests to a growing interest in history and to an emerging nationalism in the reading public. Warner's glorification of British history, anti-Catholic diatribes, and satiric treatment of mythological characters helped to make his masterpiece not only popular but also patriotic. It was republished three times from 1619 through 1621. Like Spenser in *The Faerie Queene* and many other Tudor writers, Warner warns against the dangers of internal stife and foreign intervention. Throughout the course of English history, the reader can recognize the unfolding of God's providence that made England a great nation.

The publication history of *Albion's England* reveals that Warner added material to the work incessantly, but he he did not revise or research his poetic version of British history. In the first edition he tells world and British history from the time of Noah to the Norman Conquest. To these four books he appended the *Aeneidos,* a prose abridgment of Virgil and Geoffrey of Monmouth, which covers the events from the *Aeneid* to the coming of Brutus to Britain. The next installment, of 1589, brings his history up to Richard III. By 1592 the book has caught up with Mary Tudor's reign. The enlarged edition of 1596 deals with the main events of Elizabeth's reign: the queen's foreign policy in re-

faithless woman, Thetis, who has been discovered with her lover, the enemy of her husband. Her husband kills the lover and forces his wife to drink from the dead man's skull and eat his flesh. The husband's narrative to Atys and Abynados includes a diatribe against the fickleness, falseness, and insatiability of women: "Of her two extremes, love and hate, her love is a minute but her hate a monument. As readily doth she leave as rashly she doth love, being as prone to mutability as desirous of variety, changing for pleasure but choosing for profit." But this negative and terrifying example of the female character is counterbalanced by many tales about faithful women.

In such a tumultuous world, man's actions often have little or no effect. Greed, ambition, and the vicissitudes of war cause morally corrupt people to rise to power and destroy the lives of upright rulers and citizens. Even though the evildoers meet their deserved ends or repent and reform, Warner's characters know that they are subject to fortune, gard to Rome, Spain, France, and the Low Countries and the English voyages of exploration. In book 13 Warner indulges in a rehashing of religious debates about the existence of God. This book and a prose "Epitome of the Whole History of England" constitute the two new features of the 1602 edition. Once James I became king of England, Warner added chapters on Scottish and Welsh history that repeat material already covered in book 3 without altering the negative presentation of Scotland.

For his compilation of British history, Warner drew on well-known chronicles and a host of other sources. What he lacked in originality he made up for by breadth of reading and industry. For the early part he used William Caxton's translation of Raoul Lefevre plus the *Brut* and Ralph Higden's, Robert Fabyan's, and Thomas Cooper's chronicles. After book 5 he turned to Richard Grafton's and Raphael Holinshed's chronicles and William Camden's *Britannia* (1586); for the story of Rosamund and Henry II he relied on John Stow's *Annales* (1592). John Hooker, John Calvin, and Saint Augustine provided the basis for the theological book 13. Some of the digressive tales, as in book 8, chapter 43, are based on Giovanni Boccaccio's *Decameron* (1349–1351) and Marguerite of Navarre's *Heptameron*. For his account of the voyages, Warner condensed Hakluyt, often verbatim. There are also allusions to the Bible and to classical authors, especially Ovid – like all chroniclers, Warner uses euhemerism to transform the pagan gods into mighty emperors of antiquity.

Even though Warner derived his material from known sources and did not contribute anything new to English history, his versatility in writing orations and the "variety of inventive and historical intermixtures" (as the title page of the 1596 edition proclaims) raise *Albion's England* above the level of both verse and prose chronicles. One of the stories that enjoyed a long afterlife is the pastoral tale of Curan and Argentile in book 4, chapter 20. Argentile's uncle denies her rightful claim to the throne and tries to marry her off to a peasant. Curan, a Danish prince disguised as a kitchen servant, is in love with Argentile, who rejects him and runs away from the court. When they meet again in pastoral disguise, Curan falls in love with the unknown shepherdess and laments his faithlessness toward Argentile. Once the confusion of identities is cleared up, he helps Argentile claim her throne, and both rule successfully. Warner got his story from the *Brut* (where Argentile simply marries the kitchen hand Curan) but added the pastoral exile.

Owen Tudor's wooing of Henry V's widow Kate provides a striking example of Warner's use of declamatory speeches. Owen justifies their courtship by pointing out that the gods themselves often loved below their rank. His portrayal of the gods' debates about love culminates in a prophecy in which the first letters of each line spell "Elizabeth Tuderr," concluding:

Those changes not withstanding they a people shall remain
Unchased thence, and of that strain shall five at length rereign.
Dread terrene Gods, the fifth of those, a terrene Goddesse, she
Even at the fiery region shall our chief ascendant be:
Right *Phoebe*-like (*Phoebe* may like a compeer like to her)
Retrieve her name, here named, to time the trial we refer.

This daring version of the origin of the Tudor house and its apotheosis represents one of the curious mixtures of mythology, providentialism, and nationalism that Warner employed in complimenting his queen.

The best known of the moralistic tales in *Albion's England* is the story of Henry II's mistress, Rosamund. Warner emphasizes the moral about jealous wives by moving the story out of its chronological context into the reign of Mary Tudor, who is plagued by doubts about the fidelity of her husband, King Philip of Spain. A courtier tells Mary about Queen Eleanor's pursuit and poisoning of the beautiful Rosamund. Despite Eleanor's success at eliminating her rival, Henry II takes revenge and imprisons her so that she loses his love forever. In a counterbalancing story, the courtier provides the more positive example of a lady who simply lets her beguiled husband know that she knows about his affair. Through her patience she regains his love. Warner's Mary Tudor, however, does not take heed of these tales and is consumed by her jealousy.

At times Warner tries his hand at political allegory, as in the long beast fable that a gentleman tells Perkin Warbeck's faithful wife in book 7, chapter 37. This convoluted fable about an owl, a bat, and a weasel could be an allegory, though not a precise one, for the history of three generations of the Dudley family. The moral of the story concerns pride, greed, and the rise and fall of fortunes.

It is difficult to classify *Albion's England*. The historical trajectory of Holinshed combined with the moralizing of *A Mirror for Magistrates* and the variety of genres combined with Ovidian storytelling make Warner's work unique, but its strengths become its weaknesses. The ambition of its conception is hampered by the weakness of its execution. Digressions take up more space than the history itself, and often the links between main story line and interpolations are forced, as in the case of the alternations between the voyages and the tale of Sir John Mandeville:

> Now let us say the lands, the seas, the people, and their lore
>   This knight did see, whom, touching which, not story shall we more:
>   But to our *English* voyages, even in our times, let's frame.
>   Our muse, and what you hear of those of his the like do aim.
>   Yet interlace we shall among the love of her and him:
>   Meanwhile about the world our muse is stripped now to swim.

The only connection is the common theme – travel. On the whole, the last four books seem patched together, as if Warner ran out of material and stretched his story wherever possible. In addition, Warner could not master the fourteener meter that gave significant problems even to better poets, such as George Chapman. Its unwieldy repetitiveness and lumbering flow often get in the way of the story.

In 1606, three years after the queen's death, Warner expressed his bitterness toward ungrateful and ungracious readers. Given the praise his contemporaries heaped on him, his complaint probably arose from the neglect of patrons and, more generally, from a lack of regard for historical poetry in his age. For present-day critics it is clear that a comparison between Warner and Homer is utterly out of place. At the same time, however, it is not so much an indication of Renaissance confusion about genres and history as it is an indication of what Warner was trying to do for English literature and England. That he tried to do too much is one of the reasons why he does not attract critical attention today. The height of his reputation lasted only about a generation, and then he plunged into oblivion. However deserved this state of affairs might be

in regard to the quality of his work compared with Spenser's, for example, critical neglect does a disservice to an understanding of the age. The beast fables, for example, might harbor curious political commentary. There is still the possibility that in the current broadening of the scope of critical attention Warner will find a place among his canonical superiors.

References:

Wallace A. Bacon, Introduction to *William Warner's "Syrinx, or a Sevenfold History"* edited by Bacon (Evanston, Ill.: Northwestern University Press, 1950), pp. xi–lxxxv;

David W. Becker, "William Warner of Cambridge," *Notes and Queries,* new series 1 (November 1954): 463–465;

Robert Birley, "William Warner: *Albions England,*" in his *Sunk without a Trace* (London: Hart-Davis, 1962), pp. 11–39;

Friedrich Brie, "Zu Warners 'Albion's England,' " *Archiv für das Studium der neueren Sprachen und Literaturen,* 127 (1911): 328–335;

Douglas Bush, "A Note on William Warner's Medievalism," *Modern Language Notes,* 44 (January 1929): 40–41;

Robert Ralston Cawley, "Warner and the Voyages," *Modern Philology,* 20 (November 1922): 113–147;

Savoia Dianella, "William Warner's Absolute Albion," *Quaderni di lingue e letterature,* 8 (1983): 43–69;

Nancy A. Gutierrez, "An Allusion to 'India' and Pearls," *Shakespeare Quarterly,* 36 (Summer 1985): 220;

John William Mahon, "A Study of William Warner's 'Albions England,' " dissertation, Columbia University, 1980;

John O'Connor, "William Warner and Ford's 'Perkin Warbeck,' " *Notes and Queries,* new series 2 (June 1955): 233–235;

William Irving Zeitler, "The Life, Works, and Literary Influence of William Warner," dissertation, Harvard University, 1926.

Elizabeth Jane Weston

(circa 1582 – 23 November 1612)

Donald Cheney
University of Massachusetts, Amherst

BOOKS: *Poemata Elisabethae Joannae Westoniae Anglae, virginis nobilissimae, poetriae celeberrimae, linguarum plurimarum peritissimae, studio ac opera G. Martinii a Baldhofen Silesii collecta et amicis communicata* (Frankfurt am Oder: Eichorn, 1602);

Parthenicon Elisabethae Joannae Westoniae, virginis nobilissimae, poetriae florentissimae, linguarum plurimarum peritissimae, liber I opera ac studio G. Martinii a Baldhoven Silesii collectus et nunc denuo amicis desiderantibus communicatus (Prague: Paulus Sessius, circa 1608).

In her lifetime the Anglo-Latin poet Elizabeth Jane Weston (Elisabetha Joanna Westonia) enjoyed considerable fame on the Continent: she is one of seven English authors included by Thomas Farnaby in his *Index Poeticus* (1634) and the only woman to appear in his entire list of distinguished Latin writers, past and present. Although her subsequent obscurity was the result of declining interest in Neo-Latin literature and her lifelong residence outside England, she provides fascinating evidence of a British presence at the court of Rudolph II in Prague and of one talented woman's ability to flourish within the international republic of letters constituted by the humanists of her time.

An explanation for Weston's presence in Prague was provided by Karel Hrdina in 1928, when he reported on a unique copy of her poem on the death of her mother; not until 1988 was this information made available to English readers by Susan Bassnett. It now appears that when Weston's father (about whom nothing is known) died shortly after her birth, her mother (née Jane Cooper) almost immediately married Edward Kelley, an associate of Dr. John Dee, and the Dee and Kelley households (including Elizabeth and her brother, John Francis, born in 1580) left England in 1583 on travels to Poland and Bohemia. Although Dee returned to his homeland, Kelley remained to pursue a career of some eminence as court alchemist to Rudolph, acquiring considerable wealth and an

imperial knighthood in 1589 (at which point he took the title de Imany in reference to an alleged Irish noble origin). From 1591 onward, however, his fortunes declined, partly as a result of a duel in which he killed a member of the court. In late 1597 he died in prison under circumstances that remain obscure.

With Kelley dead and his property either confiscated or heavily encumbered by creditors, Elizabeth emerged as the most articulate representative of the destitute family; her brother, a student at Ingolstadt, was in poor health and died three years later. In composing appeals to the emperor and to anyone who might have access to him, Weston revealed a graceful command of Latin verse (typically in the form of elegiac distichs) and an increasingly sure instinct for the rhetoric of self-presentation. Although it is difficult to date her verses, except when they are clearly associated with a dated letter, the poetry written up to the time of the 1602 *Poemata* is chiefly devoted to awakening sympathy for the impoverished widow and her orphaned daughter. True nobility, she implies, can best be shown by a magnanimous response to undeserved suffering such as theirs. Further, if Caesar has not yet made such a response, it must be that envious courtiers keep him in ignorance.

An example of Weston's command of the strategies of praise and petition is her poem in praise of the private gardens of the emperor's secretary, Johann Barvitius. She praises their calm and order as an emblem of the cultivated mind of their owner. Barvitius finds rest here when he is wearied by his duties at court; and here he receives "the prayers of widows and the petitions of clients," like the ancient Roman patrician whose style the Holy Roman Empire mimics. In praying that "he not be bruised at court by that Envy which always seems to accompany Virtue," Weston implies that Barvitius should favor her cause if he wishes his cause to be favored in turn by the emperor. Rather like Ben Jonson's poem about Penshurst (the Sidney estate), Weston's piece insinuates her mother and herself into this private setting in a way that suggests she has thereby enabled her patron to enjoy a civilized pleasure that will earn him imperial favor in return.

Weston's principal patron and editor, a Silesian nobleman named Georg Martinius von Baldhoven – who was four or five years her senior – was apparently instrumental in bringing her literary talents to other European humanists, who praised her extravagantly in their letters and verses. The librarian at Heidelberg, Paul Melissus, mailed her a laurel wreath, and the physician Oswald Croll solicited dedicatory verses from her for his *Basilica chymica* (1609). The terms in which she was praised acknowledged the peculiar role she had created for herself: lacking any possibility of an official position within the court bureaucracy, she proved that a helpless orphan could bear witness to the *humanitas* of the Rudolphine circle and that a specifically English maiden could bear witness to its imperial scope as well. It is possible, too, that the coincidence of her given name may have helped to suggest that she was a kind of embassy or icon of the authentic *Virgo Angla* who ruled a sister kingdom across the seas.

In April 1603, within a month of Queen Elizabeth's death, Weston's personal circumstances underwent a definitive alteration when she married Johannes Leo, a German jurist and an agent of Christian von Anhalt to the imperial court: during the next nine years she was to bear him seven children. Yet, although she was no longer the destitute orphan whose plight inspired generous aristocrats to sympathetic efforts on her behalf, no clear alternative to the role of "English Maiden" seems to have emerged as Weston's public persona. Baldhoven continued to collect letters and poems written to and by her; and when he published these sometime around 1608, he gave them the title *Parthenica* (Maidenly Writings) and published them under

Weston's maiden name with only glancing reference to her marriage some years previously.

That this edition did not meet with Weston's full approval is evident from a manuscript poem that appears in two copies of the volume, dated 1610 and signed with her married name. In it she complains of the confused disorder of the poems, their many printing errors, as well as the fact that some poems she wrote as a married woman are referred to as "maidenly." She concludes with a hope that a subsequent edition of her poems will be more accurate and representative of her full career; but her death in 1612 left her without such an edition, or indeed any coherent record of her later career. Poems that she addressed to King James I of England in 1603 and King Matthew II of Hungary and Bohemia in 1612, however, make clear that her literary career was not limited to the "virginal" phase that her humanist friends and patrons were so eager to celebrate.

Bibliography:

Jan Martínek, "Westonia," *Rukověť Humanistického Básnictví* (Prague), 5 (1982): 470–477.

References:

Susan Bassnett, "Elizabeth Jane Weston – The Hidden Roots of Poetry," in *Prag um 1600,* edited by Eliška Fučíková (Freren/Emsland: Luca Verlag, 1988), pp. 9–15;

Bassnett, "Revising a Biography: A New Interpretation of the Life of Elizabeth Jane Weston (Westonia), Based on Her Autobiographical Poem on the Occasion of the Death of Her Mother," *Cahiers Élisabéthains,* 37 (April 1990): 1–8;

Donald Cheney, "Westonia on the Gardens of Barvitius," *American Notes and Queries,* new series 5, no. 2–3 (1992): 64–67;

Karel Hrdina, "Dvě práce z dějin českého humanismu," *Listy filologické,* 55 (1928): 14–19.

Zepheria

L. M. Storozynsky
University College of the Fraser Valley

Renaissance Edition: *Zepheria* (London: Printed by the widow Orwin for Nicholas Ling & John Busby, 1594).

Modern Editions: *Zepheria,* edited by E. V. Utterson (Beldornie, Isle of Wight: Privately printed at the Beldornie Press, 1842);

Zepheria, edited by T. Corser (Manchester: Charles Simms, 1869);

Zepheria, in *An English Garner,* volume 5, edited by Edward Arber (Birmingham, 1882), pp. 61–86.

The sonnet sequence *Zepheria* (1594) offers no clues to the identity of its author, whose anonymity remains undisturbed. The collection itself has received no serious critical attention since its first printing, although it must have attracted notice in its own time, given the existence of three contemporary references to it. The poems can hardly be described as great or even good poetry, and several do not conform to the generally accepted definition of a sonnet. However, the recent revival of interest in Elizabethan sonnet sequences is characterized by an increasingly flexible understanding of the structure and nature of the poems they comprise, and *Zepheria,* the neglected work of an unknown Elizabethan sonneteer, merits reexamination within the context of both its well-known and lesser-known contemporaries. Even mediocre texts may shed light on the conventions they seek to imitate and innovate. *Zepheria* is highly self-referential: both conventional and written in an unusually comic vein, the work is parodic, mocking the very fashion to which it belongs. In addition, its anonymity may be a challenge to researchers attempting to reconstruct the literary and social context of the time: does anonymity reflect careless printing practices or the poet's indifference?

Zepheria is prefaced by a twenty-one-line poem in English but addressed "Alli veri figlioli delle Muse" (To the true sons of the Muse), which serves as an introductory poem as well as a dedication to earlier and contemporary poets, although only "Roman Naso" (Ovid) and "Tuscan Petrarch" are named directly, while Samuel Daniel and Sir Philip Sidney are alluded to in the phrases "Delian sonnetry" and "high-mused Astrophil." In spite of the classical and Italian references, the poem is principally addressed to "The modern Laureates of our Western Isle." In the last lines the poet conventionally expresses modesty about his own poetic offering:

Oh pardon, for my artless pen too much
Doth dim your glories through his infant skill,
Though may I not with you the spoils divide
(You sacred offspring of Mnemosyne)
Of endless praise which have your pens achieved,
(Your pens the trumps to immortality);
Yet be it lawful that like maims I bide,
Like brunts and scars in your love's warfare,
And here though in my home-spun verse of them declare.

The sequence consists of forty love poems, which the author calls *canzoni*. The majority are quatorzains in the form of the English sonnet, although seven vary in length from fifteen to twenty-seven lines. The *canzoni* are highly conventional in subject matter and treatment, but *Zepheria* is perhaps not as trivial an effort as most critics believe. It is true that the sequence abounds in bad rhymes and startling neologisms, but the poet's use of legal terminology (especially in *canzoni* 5, 6, 20, 21, 37, and 38) is an expanded and well-crafted metaphor, distinguishing these poems from most other early sequences. Barnabe Barnes and William Shakespeare employ similar language in *Parthenophil and Parthenophe* (1593) and the *Sonnets* (1609), respectively, but it is not commonly or extensively used by other sonneteers. Although often noted, little attention has been given to the allusion to *Zepheria* made by Sir John Davies in the eighth poem of his *Gulling Sonnets* (circa 1594–1596). Readers have assumed that Davies singled out *Zepheria* as a specific example of the kind of literature he parodies in all of the *Gulling Sonnets,* but it may well be that *Zepheria* is parodic and that Davies recognized it as such.

Although scorning other love poets in his first *canzone,* the anonymous poet employs and exagger-

(Though was I slain by your artillery.)
  The blithsome stars, (like Leda's lovely twins,
When clear they twinkle in the firmament,
Promise esperance to the Seamen's wanderings)
So have your shine made ripe mine heart's content:
  Or as the light which Sestyan Hero showed,
Arm-finned Leander to direct in waves,
When through the raging Hellespont he rowed,
Steering to Love's port: so by thine eyes' clear rays
  Blest were my ways: but since no light was found,
  Thy poor Leander in the deep is drowned.

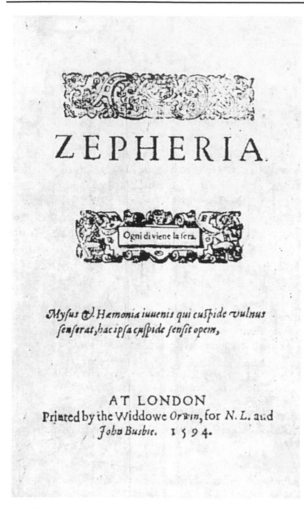

Title page for the parodic sonnet sequence written by an unknown Elizabethan writer

ates all the techniques used by his contemporaries. He particularly favors hyperbole of all kinds: far-fetched description and comparison; apostrophe, which, overused, imparts a frenzied or breathless pace to some poems, creating a sense of urgency; and vocabulary that mocks the reader's expectations. Expressions such as "hyperbolized trajections" (*canzone* 2), "thesaurize" (*canzone* 6), and "matriculated" (*canzone* 25) may be suitable for the conceits developed in *Zepheria,* but they are discordant and ridiculous in the context of love poetry, and laughter seems to be the response the poet attempts to provoke – unlike John Soowthern, for example, a poet whose extravagances are clearly meant to be taken seriously. *Canzone* 8 illustrates Zepherian hyperbole, while managing to say absolutely nothing of significance:

  Illuminating lamps, the orbs' crystal light,
Transparent mirrolds, globes divining beauty,
How have I joyed to wanton in your light?

While it is not uncommon for Elizabethan love poets and dramatists to parody the Petrarchan lover (Shakespeare's Romeo and Orlando, for example), the author of *Zepheria* is intent on highlighting the wretched condition of the lover instead of making the beloved the focus of the poems. Although her name is frequently repeated and there are occasional hints of happier moments in the relationship (*canzoni* 11, 23, 16, and 30), such references, mostly to physical contact, may reflect wishful thinking rather than reality. The lovelorn narrator seems to be addressing himself with the motto printed below the final *canzone:* "Troppo sperar inganna" (to hope too much is to be deceived), but, cunningly placed at the end of the volume, it may be addressed to the readers of *Zepheria,* giving them a belated clue to the spirit of parody in which the work was written and in which it should be read. *Canzoni* 10 and 11 mention other works by the poet, his "comic poesies" and a "pastoral ode," but whether these had an existence outside the fiction of the sonnet sequence is impossible to determine.

Two other contemporary references suggest that although *Zepheria* was read, its reception was not enthusiastic. William Covell, in his *Polimanteia* (1595), remarks rather ambiguously, "then should not *Zepheria, Cephalus and Procris* (works I dispraise not) like watermen pluck every passenger by the sleeve: then every brainless toy should not usurp the name of poetry: then should not the Muses in their tinsel habit be so basely handled by every rough swain." A marginal gloss suggests the possible unauthorized publication of the works cited, which Covell declares are "by the greedy printers so made prostitute that they are condemned." Of course, many a poet blamed the printer for premature printing or for errors in their works. However, there is a list of errata on the verso of the title page of the original 1594 edition of *Zepheria,* and while it is not always possible to determine whether such additions were inserted by the author after proofreading or by the printer, it is an indication that the book was treated with care. On the other hand, one might ask how and why the author's name was omitted from a carefully printed book, but such omissions were frequent. Finally, William Drummond of Hawthornden, who owned a copy of *Zepheria* attributed the work to "some uncertain writer" (the volume is listed in a catalogue of Drummond's library, *Auctarium bibliothecae,* 1627).

Zepheria has been republished four times in modern editions and anthologies, but without critical commentary. E. V. Utterson, in his privately published edition (1842), remarks only on the use of legal terminology in the poems. Of greater interest perhaps is his reference to the sequence as a single poem, as if he reads the *canzoni* as stanzas rather than as individual poems. In his introduction to a Spenser Society edition of 1869, T. Corser offers little more than bibliographical information. Edward Arber's edition, included in his anthology *An English Garner* (1882), is a modernized text with that editor's characteristic alterations in spelling and punctuation. Sidney Lee, although known to prefer "regular" fourteen-line sonnets, in this instance chooses to ignore irregularities and condescends to include the whole of *Zepheria* (Arber's edition) in his collection *Elizabethan Sonnets* (1904), although he characterizes the work of the "anonymous poetaster" in disparaging terms: "*Zepheria* limps clumsily along a most cacophonous path. The author was a law-student who mistook legal technicalities for poetic imagery. To help out his rhyme he invented a vocabulary of his own."

Janet G. Scott, the only scholar to have read the sequence with an eye to detail, finds that in spite of the Italian and Latin mottos that punctuate the volume, *Zepheria* probably owes little to any contemporary influences, with the possible exception of Barnes. She comments on the themes and frequent use of apostrophe common to both *Zepheria* and Barnes's *Parthenophil and Parthenophe,* and more precisely on the recurrent linking of the poet's "endless grief" and the mistress's "matchless beauty." But of course these are motifs found in all Elizabethan sonnet sequences. Otherwise, the author of *Zepheria* stands largely alone in his failure to imitate successfully any earlier or contemporary poet. Although Scott finds some small merit in the poet's attempts at originality and his use of legal language, his multiple failures lead her to dismiss the sequence thus: "La perte de ces sonnets ne serait pas un très grand malheur pour la litterature" (the loss of these sonnets would not be a great misfortune for literature). Lu Emily Pearson seems to share Utterson's reading of *Zepheria* as a single poem: she refers to its "stanzas of irregular length." Otherwise, her opinion of the anonymous sonneteer is much the same as Lee's: "one is not sure whether he intended to write sheer nonsense or whether he was only trying to 'be different.'"

The author of *Zepheria* will never receive the "endless praise" achieved by the poets he himself admired, but his admittedly "home-spun" verse, too readily dismissed as having little or no value, is one of many minor sonnet sequences that display as much complexity and diversity in content, structure, and form as those sequences that are generally considered the best examples of the genre. Further study of *Zepheria* might include a critical edition that would put the work back into circulation, bringing it to the attention of researchers seeking to recuperate, reexamine, and recontextualize early literature.

References:

John Erskine, *The Elizabethan Lyric* (New York: Columbia University Press, 1903), pp. 151–152;

Sidney Lee, ed., *Elizabethan Sonnets,* volume 1 (Westminster: Archibald Constable, 1904), pp. ci–cii;

Lu Emily Pearson, *Elizabethan Love Conventions* (Berkeley: University of California Press, 1933), pp. 138–140;

Janet G. Scott, *Les Sonnets Elisabéthains: Les Sources et L'apport Personnel* (Paris: Librairie Ancienne Honoré Champion, 1929), pp. 181–184;

Andrew Stott, "From *Voi Che* to *Che Vuoi?:* The Gaze, Desire, and the Law in the *Zepheria* Sonnet Sequence," *Criticism,* 36 (1994): 329–358.

Appendix

Documents on Sixteenth-Century Literature

Stephen Gosson, *The Schoole of Abuse* (1579)

The Syracusans used such varietie of dishes in their banquets, that when they were set, and their bordes furnished, they were many times in doubt which they should touch first, or taste last. And in my opinion the worlde geveth every writer so large a fielde to walke in, that before he set penne to the booke, he shall find him selfe feasted at Syracusa, uncertayne where to begin, or when to end: this caused Pindarus to question with his Muse, whether he were better with his art to discifer the life of Nimpe Melia, or Cadmus encounter with the dragon, or the warres of Hercules at the walles of Thebes, or Bacchus cuppes, or Venus jugling? He saw so many turnings layde open to his feete, that hee knew not which way to bende his pace.

Therefore, as I cannot but commend his wisdom which in banquetting feedes most uppon that that doth nourishe best, so must I dispraise his methode in writing which, following the course of amarous poets, dwelleth longest on those points that profit least, and like a wanton whelpe leaveth the game to runne riot. The scarabe flies over many a sweet flower, and lightes in a cowsherd. It is the custome of the flie to leave the sound places of the horse, and sucke at the botch: the nature of colloquintida to draw the worst humors to it selfe: the manner of swine to forsake the fayre fields and wallowe in the myre; and the whole practise of poets, either with fables to shewe their abuses, or with playne tearmes to unfolde their mischeefe, discover their shame, discredite themselves, and disperse their poison through the world. Virgil sweats in describing his gnatte; Ovid bestirreth him to paint out his flea: the one shewes his art in the lust of Dido; the other his cunning in the incest of Myrrha, and that trumpet of bawdrie, the Craft of Love.

I must confesse that poets are the whetstones of wit, notwithstanding that wit is dearely bought: where honie and gall are mixt, it will be hard to sever the one from the other. The deceitfull phisition geveth sweete syrroppes to make his poyson goe downe the smoother: the jugler casteth a myst to work the closer: the Syrens songue is the saylers wracke; the fowlers whistle the birdes death; the wholesome baite the fishes bane. The Harpies have virgin faces, and vultures talents: Hyena speakes like a friend, and devours like a foe: the calmest seas hide dangerous rockes: the woolfe jets in weathers felles. Manie good sentences are spoken by Davus to shadowe his knaverie, and written by poets as ornamentes to beautifie their woorkes, and sette their trumperie to sale without suspect.

But if you looke well to Epæus horse, you shall finde in his bowels the destruction of Troy: open the sepulchre of Semyramis, whose title promiseth suche wealth to the kynges of Persia, you shall see nothing but dead bones: rip up the golden ball that Nero consecrated to Jupiter Capitollinus, you shall see it stuffed with the shavinges of his bearde: pul off the visard that poets maske in, you shall disclose their reproch, bewray their vanitie, loth their wantonnesse, lament their folly, and perceive their sharpe sayinges to be placed as pearles in dunghils, fresh pictures on rotten walles, chaste matrons apparel on common curtesans. These are the cuppes of Circes, that turne reasonable creatures into brute beastes; the balles of Hippomenes, that hinder the course of Atalanta, and the blocks of the Devil, that are cast in our wayes to cut of the race of toward wittes. No marveyle though Plato shut them out of his schoole, and banished them quite from his common wealth, as effeminate writers, unprofitable members, and utter enimies to vertue.

The Romans were very desirous to imitate the Greekes, and yet very loth to receive their poets; insomuch that Cato layeth it in the dishe of Marcus, the noble, as a foule reproche, that in the time of his Consulshippe he brought Ennius, the poet, into his province. Tully accustomed to read them with great diligence in his youth, but when he waxed graver in studie, elder in yeers, ryper in judgement, hee accompted them the fathers of lyes, pipes of vanitie, and Schooles of Abuse. Maximus Tyrius taketh uppon him to defend the discipline of these doctors under the name of Homer, wresting the rashness of Ajax to valour, the cowardice of Ulisses to policie, the dotage of Nestor to grave counsell, and the battaile of Troy to the woonderfull conflicte of the foure elementes; where Juno, which is counted the ayre, settes in her foote to take up the strife, and steps boldly betwixt them to part the fray. It is a pageant woorth the sighte to beholde how he labors with mountaines to bring forth mice; much like to some of those Players, that come to the scaffold with drumme and trumpet to profer skirmishe, and when they have sounded Allarme, off goe the peeces to encounter a shadow, or conquere a paper monster. You will smile, I am sure, if you reade it, to see how this morall philosopher toyles to draw the lions skinne upon Æsops asse, Hercules shoes on a childes feet; amplifying that which, the more it is stirred, the more it stinkes, the lesser it is talked of the better it is liked; and as waiwarde children, the more they bee flattered the woorse they are, or as curste sores with often touching waxe angry, and run the longer without healing. Hee attributeth the beginning of vertue to Minerva, of friendshippe to Venus, and the roote of all handy crafts to Vulcan; but if he had broke his arme aswel as his legge, when he fell out of heaven into Lemnos, either Apollo must have plaied the bone setter, or every occupation beene layde a water.

Plato, when he saw the doctrine of these teachers neither for profit necessary, nor to bee wished for pleasure, gave them all Drummes for entertainment, not suffering them once to shew their faces in a reformed common wealth. And the same Tyrius, that layes such a foundation for poets in the name of Homer, overthrowes his whole building in the person of Mithecus, which was an excellent cooke among the Greekes, and asmuche honoured for his confections, as Phidias for his carving. But when he came to Sparta, thinking there for his cunning to be accompted a god, the good lawes of Licurgus, and custome of the countrey were too hot for his diet. The Governors banished him and his art, and al the inhabitants, folowing the steppes of their predecessors, used not with dainties to provoke appetite, but with labour and travell to whette their stomackes to their meate. I may well liken Homer to Mithecus, and poets to cookes: the pleasures of the one winnes the body from labour, and conquereth the sense: the allurement of the other drawes the minde from vertue, and confoundeth wit. As in every perfect common wealth there ought to be good laws established, right mainteined, wrong repressed, vertue rewarded, vice punished, and all manner of abuses thoroughly purged, so ought there such schooles for the furtherance of the same to be advaunced, that young men may be taught that in greene yeeres, that becomes them to practise in gray hayres.

Anacharsis being demaunded of a Greeke, whether they had not instrumentes of musicke or schooles of poetrie in Scythia? aunsweared, yes, and that without vice; as though it were eyther impossible, or incredible that no abuse should be learned where such lessons are taught, and such schooles mainteined.

Salust in describing the nurture of Sempronia commendeth her witte, in that shee coulde frame her selfe to all companies, to talke discretly with wyse men, and vaynely with wantons, takyng a quip ere it came to grounde, and returning it backe without a faulte. She was taught (saith he) both Greek and Latine; she could versifie, sing and daunce better then became an honest woman. Sappho was skilful in poetrie and sung wel, but she was whorish. I set not this down to condemne the giftes of versifying, daunsing or singing in women, so they bee used with meane and exercised in due time; but to shew you that, as by Anacharsis report the Scythians did it without offence, so one swallow brings not summer, nor one particular example is sufficient proofe for a generall precept. White silver drawes a black lyne; fyre is as hurtfull as healthie; water is as daungerous as it is commodious, and these qualities as harde to be wel used when we have them, as they are to be learned before wee get them. He that goes to sea must smel of the ship, and that which sayles into poets wil savour of pitch.

C. Marius in the assembly of the whole Senate of Rome, in a solemne oration, giveth an account of his bringing up: he sheweth that he hath beene taught to lye on the ground, to suffer all weathers, to leade men, to strike his fo, to feare nothing but an evill name; and chalengeth praise unto himselfe in that he never learned the Greeke tounge, neither ment to be instructed in it hereafter, either that he thought it too farre a jorney to fetch learning beyonde the fielde, or because he doubted the abuses of those schooles where poets were ever the head maisters. Tiberius, the emperour, sawe somewhat when he judged Scaurus to death for writing a tragedy; Augustus when hee banished Ovid, and Nero when he charged Lucan to put up his pipes, to stay his penne, and write no more. Burrus and Seneca, the schoolemaisters of Nero, are flowted and hated of the people for teaching their scholer the song of Attis: for Dion saith, that he hearing thereof wrounge laughter and teares from most of those that were then about him. Wherby I judge that they scorned the folly of the teachers, and lamented the frenzy of the scholer, who beeing emperour of Rome, and bearing the weight of the whole common wealth uppon his shoulders, was easier to bee drawen to vanitie by wanton poets, then to good government by the fatherly counsel of grave senators. They were condemned to dye by the lawes of the Heathens whiche inchaunted the graine in other mens grounds; and are not they accursed, thinke you, by the mouth of God, which having the government of young Princes, with poetical fantasies draw them to the schooles of their own abuses, bewitching the graine in the greene blade, that was sowed for the sustenance of many thousands, and poysoning the spring with their amorous layes, whence the whole common wealth should fetch water? But to leave the scepter to Jupiter, and instructing of Princes to Plutarch and Xenophon, I wil beare a lowe saile, and rowe neere the shore, least I chaunce to bee carried beyonde my reache, or runne a grounde in those coasts which I never knewe. My onely indevour shalbe to shew you that in a rough cast which I see in a cloude, loking through my fingers.

And because I have been matriculated my self in the schoole where so many abuses florish, I wil imitate the dogs of Ægypt, which comming to the bancks of Nylus to quench theyr thirste, syp and away, drinke running, lest they be snapt short for a pray to crocodiles. I shoulde tell tales out of schoole and bee ferruled for my fault, or hyssed at for a blab, yf I layde all the orders open before your eyes. You are no soner entred but libertie looseth the reynes and geves you head, placing you with poetrie in the lowest forme, when his skill is showne too make his scholer as good as ever twangde: he preferres you to pyping, from pyping to playing, from play to pleasure, from pleasure to slouth, from slouth to sleepe, from sleepe to sinne, from sinne to death, from death too the Divel, if you take your learning apace, and passe through every forme without revolting. Looke not to have me discourse these at large: the crocodile watcheth to take me tardie: whichesoever of them I touche is a byle: tryppe and goe, for I dare not tarry.

Heraclides accounteth Amphion the ringleader of poets and pipers: Delphus Philammones penned the birth of Latona, Diana and Apollo in verse, and taught the people to pype and daunce rounde aboute the Temple of Delphos. Hesiodus was as cunning in pipyng as in poetrye: so was Terpandrus, and after hym Clonas. Apollo, whiche is honoured of poets as the God of their art, had at the one syde of his idoll in Delos a bowe, and at the other the three Graces with sundrie instrumentes; and some writers doe affirme that he piped himself nowe and then.

Poetrie and piping have always been so united togither, that til the time of Melanippides pipers were poets hyerlings. But marke, I pray you, how they are now both abused.

The right use of auncient poetrie was to have the notable exploytes of worthy captaines, the holesome councels of good fathers and vertuous lives of predecessors set downe in numbers, and sung to the instrument at solemne feastes, that the sound of the one might draw the hearers from kissing the cup too often, the sense of the other put them in minde of things past, and chaulke out the way to do the like. After this maner were the Bæotians trained from rudenesse to civilitie, the Lacedæmonians instructed by Tyrtæus verse, the Argives by the melody of Telesilla, and the Lesbians by Alcæus odes.

To this end are instruments used in battaile, not to tickle the eare, but to teach every souldier when to strike and when to stay, when to flye and when to followe. Chiron by singing to his instrument quencheth Achilles fury: Terpandrus with his notes laieth the tempest, and pacifies the tumult at Lacedæmon: Homer with his musike cured the sick souldiers in the Grecians camp, and purgeth every mans tent of the plague. Thinke you that those miracles could bee wrought without playing of daunces, dumpes, pavins, galiardes, measures, fancyes, or newe streynes? They never came where this grew, nor knew what it ment.

Pythagoras bequeathes them a clokebagge, and condemnes them for fooles, that judge musike by sound and eare. If you will bee good scholers, and profite well in the arte of musike, shut your fidels in their cases and looke uppe to Heaven: the order of the spheres, the unfallible motion of the planets, the juste course of the yeere, the varietie of the seasons, the concorde of the elementes and their qualities, fyre, water, ayre, earth, heate, colde, moisture and drought concurring togeather to the constitution of earthly bodies, and sustenaunce of every creature.

The politike lawes in wel governed common wealthes, that treade downe the proude and upholde the meeke; the love of the king and his subjectes, the father and his chylde, the lorde and his slave, the maister and his man; the trophees and triumphes of our auncestours which pursued vertue at the harde heeles, and shunned vice as a rock for feare of shipwracke, are excellent maisters to shewe you that this is right musicke, this perfecte harmony. Chiron when he appeased the wrath of Achilles tolde hym the duetie of a good souldier, repeated the vertues of his father Peleus, and sung the famous enterprises of noble men. Terpandrus, when he ended the brabbles at Lacedemon, neither piped Rogero nor Turkelony; but reckoning up the commodities of friendship and fruits of debate, putting them in minde of Licurgus lawes, taught them to tread a better measure. When Homers musicke drove the pestilence from the Grecians campe, ther was no such vertue in his penne, nor in his pipe, but, if I might be umpier, in the sweete harmonie of divers natures, and wonderful concorde of sundry medicines. For Apolloes cunning extendeth it self aswel to phisick, as musicke or poetrie; and Plutarche reporteth that as Chiron was a wise man, a learned poet, a skilfull musition, so was hee also a teacher of justice by shewing what Princes ought to doe, and a reader of phisicke by opening the natures of many simples. If you enquire how many such poets and pipers we have in our age, I am perswaded that every one of them may creepe through a ring, or daunce the wilde morrice in an needles eye. We have infinit poets, and pipers, and suche peevishe cattel among us in Englande, that live by merrie begging, mainteyned by almes, and prively encroche upon every mans purse. But if they that are in auctority, and have the sworde in their handes to cut of abuses, should call an accompt to see how many Chirons, Terpandri and Homers are heere, they might cast the summe without pen or counters, and sit downe with Racha to weepe for her children, because they were not.

He that compareth our instruments with those that were used in ancient tymes shall see them agree like dogges and cattes, and meete as jump as Germans lippes. Terpandrus and Olimpus used instruments of 7 strings, and Plutarch is of opinion that the instruments of 3 strings, which were used before their time, passed all that have folowed since. It was an old law, and long kept, that no man should according to his own humor adde or diminish in matters concerning that art, but walk in the pathes of their predecessors. But when newfangled Phrynis becam a fidler, being somewhat curious in carping, and serching for moats with a paire of bleard eies, thought to amend his maisters, and marred al. Timotheus, a bird of the same broode, and a right hound of the same haire, took the 7 stringed harp, that was altogether used in Terpandrus time, and encreased the number of the strings at his owne pleasure. The Argives appointed by their lawes great punishments for such as placed above 7 strings upon any instrument. Pythagoras commaunded that no musition should go beyond his diapason. Were the Argives and Pythagoras nowe alive, and saw how many frets, how many stringes, how many stops, how many keyes, how many cliffes, howe many moodes, how many flats, how many sharpes, how many rules, how many spaces, how many noates, how many restes, how many querks, how many corners, what chopping, what

changing, what tossing, what turning, what wresting and wringing is among our musitions, I believe verily that they would cry out with the country man, *Heu, quòd tam pingui macer est mihi taurus in arvo.* Alas, here is fat feeding and leane beasts; or as one said at the shearing of hogs, great cry and litle wool, much adoe and smal help. To shew the abuses of these unthrifty scholers, that despise the good rules of their ancient masters, and run to the shop of their owne devises, defacing olde stampes, forging newe printes, and coining strange precepts, Phærecrates, a comicall poet, bringeth in Musicke with her clothes tottered, her fleshe torne, her face deformed, her whole bodie mangled and dismembred: Justice, viewing her well and pitying her case, questioneth with her howe she came in that plight? to whom Musicke replies that Melanippides, Phrynis, Timotheus, and such fantasticall heades had so disfigured her lookes, defaced her beautie, so hacked her and hewed her, and with manye stringes geven her so many woundes, that she is striken to death, in daunger to peryshe, and present in place the least part of her selfe. When the Sicilians and Dores forsooke the playn song that they had learned of their auncestours in the mountaynes, and practised long among theyr heardes, they founde out such descant in Sybaris instrumentes that by daunsing and skipping they fel into lewdnesse of life. Neither stayed those abuses in the compasse of that countrie; but like to ill weedes, in time spread so farre, that they choked the good grayne in every place.

For as poetrie and piping are cosen germaines, so piping and playing are of great affinitye, and all three chayned in linkes of abuse.

Plutarch complayneth that ignorant men, not knowing the majestie of auncient musike, abuse both the eares of the people, and the arte it selfe, with bringing sweet comfortes into Theaters, which rather effeminate the minde as prickes unto vice, then procure amendement of maners as spurres to vertue. Ovid, the high Martial of Venus feeld, planteth his mayn battell in publike assemblies, sendeth out his scoutes to Theaters to descrye the enimie, and in steede of vaunte curriers, with instruments of musick, playing, singing and dauncing gives the first charge. Maximus Tyrius holdeth it for a maxime, that the bringing of instrumentes to Theaters and playes was the first cuppe that poysoned the common wealth. They that are borne in Seriphos and cockered continually in those islandes, where they see nothing but foxes and hares, will never be persuaded that there are huger beasts. They that never went out of the champion in Brabant will hardly conceive what rocks are in Germany; and they that never goe out of their houses, for regarde of their credite, nor steppe from the university for love of knowledge, seeing but slender offences and smal abuses within their own walles, wil never beleeve that such rocks are abrode, nor such horrible monsters in playing places. But as (I speake the one to my comforte, the other to my shame, and remember both with a sorowful heart) I was first instructed in the University, after drawn like a novice to these abuses, so will I shew you what I see, and informe you what I reade of such affaires. Ovid saith that Romulus builte his theater as a horsfaire for hoores, made triumphes and set out playes to gather the faire women together, that every one of his souldiers might take where hee liked a snatch for his share: whereupon the amarous schoolmaister bursteth out in these wordes: —

Romule, militibus solus dare præmia nosti:
Hæc mihi si dederis commoda, miles ero.

Thou, Romulus, alone knowest how thy souldiers to reward:
Graunt me the like, my selfe will be attendant on thy gard.

It should seeme that the abuse of such places was so great, that for any chaste liver to haunt them was a black swan, and a white crow. Dion so streightly forbiddeth the ancient families of Rome, and gentlewomen that tender their name and honor, to com to Theaters, and rebuks them so sharply when he takes them napping, that if they be but once seene there, hee judgeth it sufficient cause to speake ill of them and thinke worse. The shadow of a knave hurts an honest man; the sent of the stewes a sober matron; and the shew of Theaters a simple gaser. Clitomachus the wrestler, geven altogether to manly exercise, if hee had hearde any talke of love, in what company soever he had ben, would forsake his seat and bid them adue.

Lacon, when hee sawe the Athenians studie so much to set out playes, sayde they were madde. If men for good exercise, and women for their credite, be shut from Theaters, whom shall we suffer to goe thither? Little children? Plutarche with a caveat keepeth them out, not so muche as admitting the litle crackhalter, that carrieth his masters pantables, to set foote within those doores; and alleageth this reason — that those wanton spectacles of light huswives drawing gods from the heavens, and young men from themselves to shipwracke of honesty, wil hurt them more then if at the epicures table they had burst their guts with over feeding. For if the bodie be overcharged, it may bee holpe, but the surfite of the soule is hardely cured. Here, I doubt not, but some archeplayer or other that hath read a

little, or stumbled by chance upon Plautus comedies, will cast me a bone or two to pick, saying that whatsoever these ancient writers have spoken against plaies is to be applied to the abuses in olde comedies, where gods are brought in as prisoners to beautie, ravishers of virgines, and servantes by love to earthly creatures. But the comedies that are exercised in our dayes are better sifted: they shewe no such branne. The first smelt of Plautus; these tast of Menander: the leudenes of the gods is altred and chaunged to the love of young men; force to friendshippe; rapes to mariage; woing allowed by assurance of wedding; privie meetinges of bachelours and maidens on the stage, not as murderers that devour the good name ech of other in their mindes, but as those that desire to bee made one in hearte. Nowe are the abuses of the worlde revealed: every man in a playe may see his owne faultes, and learne by this glasse to amende his manners. Curculio may chatte till his heart ake, ere any bee offended with his girdes. Deformities are checked in jeast, and mated in earnest. The sweetenesse of musicke, and pleasure of sportes temper the bitternes of rebukes, and mittigate the tartnes of every taunt according to this: —

Omne vafer vitium ridenti Flaccus amico
Narrat, et admissus circum precordia ludit.

Flaccus among his friends, with fawning muse,
Doth nippe him neere that fostreth foule abuse.

Therefore, they are either so blinde that they cannot, or so blunt that they will not see why this exercise shoulde not be suffered as a profitable recreation. For my part, I am neither so fonde a phisition, nor so bad a cooke, but I can allowe my patient a cuppe of wine to meales, althoughe it be hotte and pleasant sawces to drive downe his meate, if his stomacke be queasie. Notwithstanding, if people will bee instructed (God bee thanked) wee have divines enough to discharge that, and moe by a greate many then are well harkened to: yet sith these abuses are growne to heade, and sinne so ripe, the number is lesse then I would it were. Euripides holds not him onely a foole, that being well at home will gadde abrode, that hath a conduit within doore and fetcheth water without, but all such beside as have sufficient in themselves to make themselves merry with pleasaunt talke, tending to good and mixed with ευτραπελια, the Grecians glee, yet will they seeke, when they neede not, to be sported abrode at playes and pageantes. Plutarch likeneth the recreation that is gotte by conference to a plesaunte banquet: the sweete pappe of the one sustaineth the body, the savery doctrine of the other doth nourish the mind; and as in banquetting the wayter standes readye to fill the cuppe, so in all our recreations we shoulde have an instructer at our elbowes to feede the soule. If we gather grapes among thistles, or seeke for this foode at theaters, wee shall have a harde pyttaunce and come to short commons. I cannot think that city to be safe that strikes downe her percolleces, rammes up her gates, and suffereth the enimie to enter the posterne: neyther will I bee persuaded that hee is any way likely to conquere affection which breaketh all his instrumentes, burneth his poets, abandons his haunt, muffleth his eyes as hee passeth the streate, and resortes to theaters to be assaulted. Coockes did never shewe more crafte in their junketts to vanquishe the taste, nor paynters in shadowes to allure the eye, then poets in theaters to wounde the conscience.

There set they a broche straunge consortes of melodie to tickle the eare, costly apparrell to flatter the sight, effeminate gesture to ravish the sence, and wanton speache to whette desire to inordinate lust. Therefore of both barrelles I judge cookes and painters the better hearing, for the one extendeth his art no farther then to the tongue, palate and nose, the other to the eye, and both are ended in outwarde sense, which is common to us with brute beastes. But these by the privy entries of the eare sappe downe into the heart, and with gunshotte of affection gaule the minde, where reason and vertue shoulde rule the roste. These people in Rome were as pleasant as nectar at the first beginning, and caste out for lees when their abuses were knowen. They whome Cæsar uphelde were driven out by Octavian; whom Caligula reclaimed were cast of by Nero; whom Nerva exalted were throwne downe by Trajan; whom Anthony admitted were expelled agayn, pestred in gallies, and sent into Hellespont by Marcus Aurelius. But when the whole rabble of poets, pipers, players, jugglers, jesters and dauncers were received agayne, Rome was reported to bee fuller of fooles then of wise men. Domitian suffered playing and dauncing so long in theaters, that Paris ledde the shaking of sheetes with Domitia, and Mnester, the Treuchmouth, with Messalina. Caligula made so muche of players and dauncers, that he suffered them openly to kisse his lippes, when the senators might scarce have a licke at his feete. He gave dauncers great stipends for selling their hopps, and placed Apelles, the player, by his own sweete side. Besides that, you may see what excellent grave men were ever about him: he loved Prasinus the cocheman so wel, that for good wil to the master he bid

his horse to supper, gave him wine to drinke in cups of estate, set barly graines of gold before him to eate, and swore by no bugs that he would make him a Consul; which thing (saith Dion) had ben performed, but that he was prevented by suddein death; for as his life was abominable, so was his end miserable. Comming from dancing and playing, he was slayne by Chærea, a just reward and a fit catastrophe. I have heard some players vaunt of the credite they had in Rome, but they are as foolishe in that as Vibius Rufus, which bosted himselfe to be an Emperor, because he had syt in Cæsars chayre, and a perfect orator, because he was married to Tullies widow. Better might they say themselves to be murderers, because they have represented the persons of Thyestes, and Atreus, Achilles, and Hector; or perfect limme lifters for teaching the trickes of every strompet. Such are the abuses that I read of in Rome: such are the caterpillers that have devoured and blasted the fruit of Ægypt: such are the dragons that are hurtfull in Affricke: such are the adders that sting with pleasure and kill with payne; and such are the basiliskes of the world that poyson, as wel with the beame of their sight, as with the breath of their mouth.

Consider with thy selfe (gentle Reader) the olde discipline of Englande: marke what wee were before, and what we are now. Leave Rome a while, and cast thine eye backe to thy predecessours, and tell me howe woonderfully we have beene changed since we were schooled with these abuses. Dion saith that English men could suffer watching and labor, hunger and thirst, and beare of all storms with head and shoulders: they used slender weapons, went naked, and wer good soldiours: they fedde uppon rootes and barkes of trees: they would stande up to the chinne many dayes in marshes without victualles, and they had a kinde of sustenaunce in time of neede, of which if they hadde taken but the quantitie of a beane, or the weight of a pease, they did neither gape after meate, nor long for the cuppe a great while after. The men in valure not yeelding to Scythia; the women in courage passing the Amazons. The exercise of both was shooting and darting, running and wrestling, and trying such maisteries as eyther consisted in swiftnesse of feet, agilitie of bodie, strength of armes, or martiall discipline.

But the exercise that is nowe among us is banquetting, playing, pyping, and dauncing, and all suche delightes as may winne us to pleasure, or rocke us in sleepe. *Quantum mutatus ab illo!* Oh, what a wonderfull change is this! Our wrastling at armes is turned to wallowing in ladies lappes; our courage to cowardice; our cunning to riot, our bowes into bolles, and our dartes to dishes. Wee have robbed Greece of gluttony, Italy of wantonnes, Spayne of pride, France of deceite, and Duchland of quaffing. Compare London to Rome and England to Italy, you shall finde the theaters of the one, the abuses of the other, to bee rife among us. *Experto crede:* I have seene somewhat, and therefore I thinke I may say the more. In Rome when playes or pageants are shewne, Ovid changeth his pilgrims to creepe close to the Saintes whome they serve, and shewe their double diligence to lift the gentlewomens roabes from the ground for soyling in the duste, to sweepe moates from their kyrtles, to keepe their fingers in use, to lay their hands at their backes for an easie stay, to looke uppon those whome they beholde, to prayse that which they commende, to like everye thing that pleaseth them, to present them pomgranates to picke as they set, and when all is done to wayte on them mannerly to their houses. In our assemblies at playes in London, you shall see suche heaving and shooving, suche ytching and shouldering to sytte by women; suche care for their garments that they be not trode on; suche eyes to their lappes that no chippes lighte in them; such pillowes to their backes that they take no hurte; suche masking in their eares, I know not what; suche geving them pippins to passe the time; suche playing at foote saunt without cardes; such ticking, such toying, such smiling, such winking, and such manning them home when the sportes are ended, that it is a right comedie to marke their behaviour, to watch their conceates, as the catte for the mouse, and as good as a course at the game it selfe, to dogge them a little, or follow aloofe by the printe of their feete, and so discover by slotte where the deare taketh soyle.

If this were as well noted as il seene, or as openly punished as secretely practised, I have no doubt but the cause woulde be seared to drye up the effect, and these prettie rabbets verye cunningly ferretted from their borrowes. For they that lacke customers all the weeke, either because their haunt is unknowen, or the constables and officers of their parish watch them so narrowly that they dare not queatche, to celebrate the Sabboth flocke too theaters, and there keepe a generall market of bawdrie. Not that anye filthinesse, in deede, is committed within the compasse of that ground, as was once done in Rome, but that every wanton and his paramour, everye man and his mistresse, every John and his Joane, every knave and his queane are there first acquainted, and cheapen the marchandise in that place, which they pay for else where, as they can agree. These wormes, when they dare not nestle in the pescod at home, find refuge abrode and ar hidde in the eares of other mens corne.

Every vauter in one blind taverne or other is tenant at will, to which she tolleth resort, and playes the stale to utter their victuals, and helpe them to emptie their mustie caskes. There is she so entreated with woordes and received with curtesie, that every back roome in the house is at her commaundement. Some that have neyther land to mainteine them, nor good occupation to get their bread, desirous to strowte it with the best, yet disdayning to live by the sweat of their browes, have founde out this cast of ledgerdemayne to playe fast and loose among their neighbours. If any part of musicke have suffred shipwrecke and arived by fortune at their fingers endes, with shewe of gentility they take up faire houses, receive lusty lasses at a price for boordes, and pipe from morning till evening for wood and coale. By the brothers, cosens, uncles, great grandsiers, and suche like acquayntance of their gheastes, they drink the best, they syt rent free, they have their owne table spread to their handes without wearing the strings of their purse, or any thing else but housholde and honestie. When resort so encreaseth that they grow in suspition, and the pottes which are sent so often to the taverne gette such a knock before they come home, that they returne their maister a cracke to his credite, though hee bee called in question of his life, he hath shiftes yenough to avoyd the blank. If their houses bee searched, some instrumente of musicke is laide in sighte to dazell the eyes of every officer, and all that are lodged in the house by night, or frequent it by day, come thither as pupilles to be well schoolde. Other there are, which beyng so knowne that they are the bye word of every mans mouth, and pointed at commonly as they passe the streetes, eyther couch themselves in allies or blinde lanes, or take sanctuary in Frieries, or live a mile from the cittee, like Venus nunnes in a cloyster of Nuington, Ratliff, Islington, Hogsdon or some such place, where like penitentes they deny the world, and spende theire dayes in double devotion; and when they are weery of contemplation, to consort themselves and renue their acquaintance, they visit Theaters, where they make full accompt of a play before they depart.

Solon made no law for parricides, because he feared that he should rather put men in mind to commit such offences, then by any strange punishment geve them a bit to keep them under; and I intend not to shew you al that I see, nor half that I here of these abuses, lest you judge me more wilful to teach them, then willing to forbid them. I looke stil when Players shoulde cast me their gauntlettes, and challenge a combate for entring so farre into theyr possessions, as thoughe I made them Lordes of this Misrule, or the very schoolemaisters of these abuses: though the best clarks be of that opinion, they heare not mee saye so. There are more howses then parishe churches, more maydes then Maulkin, more wayes to the wood then one, and more causes in nature then efficientes. The carpenter rayseth not his frame without tooles, nor the Divell his woorke without instrumentes: were not Players the meane to make these assemblies, suche multitudes woulde hardly bee drawne in so narrowe a roome. They seeke not to hurte, but desire to please: they have purged their comedies of wanton speaches, yet the corne which they sell is full of cockle, and the drinke that they drawe overcharged with dregges. There is more in them then we perceive: the Divell standes at our elbowe when we see not, speaks when we heare him not, strikes when we feele not, and woundeth sore when he raseth no skinne nor rentes the fleshe. In those thinges that we lest mistrust the greatest daunger doeth often lurke: the countrieman is more afraid of the serpent that is hid in the grasse, than the wilde beaste that openly feedes upon the mountaines: the marriner is more endaungered by privye shelves then knowen rockes; the souldier is sooner killed with a little bullet then a long sworde. There is more perill in close fistuloes then outward sores, in secret ambushe then mayne batteles, in undermining then playne assaulting, in friendes then foes, in civill discorde then forrayne warres. Small are the abuses, and slight are the faultes that nowe in Theaters escape the poets pen; but tall cedars from little graynes shoote high: greate oakes from slender rootes spread wide: large streames from narrowe springes runn farre: one little sparke fiers a whole citie: one dramme of Elleborns raunsacks every vayne: the fishe Remora hath a small body, and great force to staye shippes agaynst winde and tide: Ichneumon, a little worme, overcomes the elephant: the viper slayes the bull; the weesell the cockatrice, and the weakest waspe stingeth the stoutest man of warre. The height of Heaven is taken by the staffe: the bottome of the sea sounded with lead: the farthest cost discovered by compasse: the secrets of nature searched by wit: the anotomy of man set out by experience; but the abuses of Plaies cannot be showen, because they passe the degrees of the instrument, reach of the plummet, sight of the minde, and for tryall are never broughte to the touchstone. Therefore, he that wil avoyde the open shame of privie sinne, the common plague of private offences, the greate

wrackes of little rockes, the sure disease of uncertaine causes, must set hande to the sterne, and eye to his steppes to shun the occasion as neere as he can; neither running to bushes for renting his clothes, nor rent his clothes for emparing his thrift, nor walke upon yse for taking of a fall, nor take a fall for brusing himselfe, nor go to Theaters for beeing allured, nor once bee allured for feare of abuse.

Bunduica, a notable woman and a Queene of Englande that time that Nero was Emperour of Rome, having some of the Romans in garrison heere against her, in an oration which she made to her subjects, seemed utterly to contemne their force and laugh at their folly. For shee accounted them unworthy the name of men, or title of souldiers, because they were smoothly appareled, soft lodged, daintely feasted, bathed in warme waters, rubbed with sweet oyntments, strewd with fine poulders, wine swillers, singers, dauncers and players. God hath now blessed England with a Queene, in vertue excellent, in power mighty, in glory renowned, in government politike, in possession rich, breaking her foes with the bent of her browe, ruling her subjects with shaking her hand, removing debate by diligent foresight, filling her chests with the fruites of peace, ministring justice by order of law, reforming abuses with great regarde, and bearing her swoord so even, that neither the poore are trode under foote, nor the rich suffred to looke to hye: nor Rome, nor France, nor tyrant, nor Turke dare for their lives to enter the list. But we, unworthy servants of so milde a mistresse, degenerate children of so good a mother, unthankful subjects of so loving a prince, wound her swete hart with abusing her lenitie, and stir Jupiter to anger to send us a storke that shal devoure us. How often hath her Majestie, with the grave advice of her whole Councel, set downe the limits of apparel to every degree, and how soone againe hath the pride of our harts overflowen the chanel? Howe many times hath accesse to theaters beene restrained, and howe boldely againe have we reentred? overlashing in apparel is so common a fault, that the verye hyerlings of some of our plaiers, which stand at reversion of vi shillings by the weeke, jet under gentlemens noses in sutes of silke, exercising them selves to prating on the stage, and common scoffing when they come abrode, where they looke askance over the shoulder at every man of whom the Sunday before they begged an almes. I speake not this as though every one that professeth the qualitie so abused him selfe, for it is wel knowen that some of them are sober, discreete, properly learned, honest housholders, and citizens well thought on amonge their neighbours at home, though the pride of their shadowes (I meane those hangbyes whome they succour with stipend) cause them to bee somewhat il talked of abrode.

And as some of the players are farre from abuse, so some of their playes are without rebuke, which are easily remembered, as quickly reckoned. The two prose bookes played at the Belsavage, where you shall finde never a woorde without witte, never a line without pith, never a letter placed in vaine. The Jew, and Ptolome, showne at the Bull; the one representing the greedinesse of worldly chusers, and bloody mindes of usurers; the other very lively describing howe seditious estates with their owne devises, false friendes with their owne swoords, and rebellious commons in their owne snares are overthrowne; neither with amorous gesture wounding the eye, nor with slovenly talke hurting the eares of the chast hearers. The Black Smiths Daughter, and Catilins Conspiracies, usually brought in at the Theater: the firste containing the trechery of Turks, the honourable bountye of a noble mind, the shining of vertue in distresse. The last because it is knowen to be a pig of mine owne Sowe, I will speake the lesse of it; onely giving you to understand that the whole mark which I shot at in that woorke was to showe the rewarde of traytors in Catiline, and the necessary government of learned men in the person of Cicero, which forsees every danger that is likely to happen, and forstalles it continually ere it take effect. Therefore I give these playes the commendation that Maximus Tyrius gave to Homers works – καλὰ μὲν γὰρ τὰ Ὁμήρου ἔπη, καὶ ἔπων τὰ κάλλιστα, καὶ φανώτατα, καὶ ἄδεσθαι μουσαῖσ πρέποντα ἀλλα οὐ πᾶσι καλὰ, οὐδὲ ἀεὶ καλά.

These playes are good playes and sweete playes, and of all playes the best playes, and most to be liked, woorthy to be soung of the Muses, or set out with the cunning of Roscius him self, yet are they not fit for every mans dyet: neither ought they commonly to be showen. Now, if any man aske me why my selfe have penned comedyes in time past, and inveigh so egerly against them here, let him knowe that *Semel insanavimus omnes:* I have sinned, and am sorry for my fault: he runnes far that never turnes: better late then never. I gave my selfe to that exercise in hope to thrive, but I burnt one candle to seeke another, and lost bothe my time and my travell when I had done.

Thus sithe I have in my voyage suffred wracke with Ulisses, and wringing-wett scambled with life to the shore, stand from mee Nausicaä with all thy traine, till I wipe the blot from my forhead, and with sweete springs wash away the salt froth that cleaves to my soule. Meane time, if players be called to account for the abuses that growe by these assemblyes, I woulde not have them to aunswere, as Pilades did for the theaters of Rome when they were complayned on, and Augustus waxed angrye: "This resorte, O Cæsar, is good for thee, for heere wee keepe thousandes of idle heds occupied, which else peradventure would brue some mischiefe." A fit cloude to cover their abuse, and not unlike to the starting hole that Lucinius founde, who like a greedy surveiour, beeing sent into Fraunce to governe the countrye, robbed them and spoyled them of all their treasure with unreasonable taskes: at the last, when his crueltie was so lowdely cryed out on that every man heard it, and all his packing did savour so stronge that Augustus smelt it, hee brought the good Emperour into his house, flapped him in the mouth with a smooth lye, and tolde him, that for his sake and the safetie of Rome, hee gathered that riches, the better to impoverish the countrie for rysing in armes, and so holde the poore Frenchmennes noses to the grindstone for ever after.

A bad excuse is better, they say, then none at all. Hee, because the Frenchman paid tribute every moneth, into xiiii moneths devided the yeere: these, because they are allowed to play every Sunday, make 4 or 5 Sundayes at least every weeke; and all that is doone is good for Augustus, to busy the wits of his people for running a wool-gathering, and emptie their purses for thriving to fast. Though Lucinius had the cast to plaister upp his credite with the losse of his money, I trust that they which have the swoorde in their hands among us to pare away this putrified flesh, are sharp sighted and wil not so easely be deluded.

Marcus Aurelius saith, that players falling from just labour to unjuste idlenesse doe make more trewands, and ill husbands, then if open schooles of unthrifts and vacabounds were kept. Who soever readeth his epistle to Lambert, the governour of Hellespont, when players were banished, shall finde more against them, in plainer termes, then I will utter.

This have I set downe of the abuses of poets, pipers and players, which bring us to pleasure, slouth, sleepe, sinne, and without repentaunce to death and the devill: whiche I have not confirmed by authoritie of Scriptures, because they are not able to stand uppe in the sight of God; and sithens they dare not abide the fielde, where the worde of God doth bid them battaile, but runne to antiquities (though nothing be more ancient than holy Scriptures) I have given them a volley of prophan writers to begin the skirmish, and doone my indevour to beate them from their holdes with their owne weapons. The patient that wil be cured of his owne accord must seeke the meane: if every man desire to save one, and drawe his own feete from Theaters, it shall prevaile as much against these abuses, as Homers Moly against witchcraft, or Plinies peristerion against the byting of dogges.

God hath armed every creature against his enemie: the lyon with pawes, the bull with hornes, the bore with tuskes, the vulture with tallents, harts, hindes, hares and such like with swiftnesse of feet, because they are fearefull, every one of them putting his gifte in practise; but man, which is lord of the whole earth, for whose service herbes, trees, rootes, plants, fish, foule and beasts of the fielde were first made, is farre worse then the brute beastes: for they, endewed but with sence, doe, *appetere salutaria et declinare noxia,* seeke that which helpes them, and forsake that which hurtes them.

Man is enriched with reason and knowledge; with knowledge to serve his maker and governe himselfe; with reason to distinguish good and ill, and chose the best, neither referring the one to the glory of God, nor using the other to his owne profite.

Fire and ayre mount upwardes, earth and water sinke downe, and every insensible body els never rests til it bring it selfe to his owne home. But we, which have both sense, reason wit and understanding, are ever overlashing, passing our bounds, going beyond our limites, never keeping our selves within compasse, nor once loking after the place from whence we came, and whither we must in spighte of our hartes. Aristotle thinketh that in greate windes the Bees carry little stones in their mouthes to peyse their bodies, leste they bee carryed away or kept from their hives, unto whiche they desire to returne with the fruites of their labour. The crane is said to rest uppon one leg, and holding uppe the other keeps a pebble in her claw, which as soone as the sences are bound by approche of sleepe falles to the grounde, and with the noyse of the knock against the earth makes her awake, whereby shee is ever ready to prevent her enemyes. Geese are foolish byrdes, yet when they flye over the mount Taurus they showe great wisdome in their own defence; for they stop their pipes ful of gravel to avoide gaggling, and so by silence escape the eagles. Woodcocks, though they lack witte to save them selves, yet they want not wit to avoyde hurte, when they thrust their heads in a bushe and thinke their bodyes out of danger. But wee, which are so brittle that we breake with every fillop, so

weake that we are drawne with every thread, so light that wee are blowen away with every blast, so unsteady that we slip in every ground, neither peyse our bodyes against the winde, nor stand uppon one legge for sleeping too much, nor close upp our lippes for betraying our selves, nor use any witte to garde our owne persons, nor shewe our selves willing to shunne our owne harmes, running most greedily to those places where wee are soonest overthrowne. I can not liken our affection better then to an arrowe, which, getting libertie, with winges is carryed beyonde our reach; kepte in the quiver it is still at commaundement: or to a dogge; let him slippe, he is straight out of sight; holde him in the lease, hee never stirres: or to a colte; give him the bridle, he flinges about; raine him hard and you may rule him: or to a ship; hoyst the sayles, it runnes on head; let fall the ancour, all is well: or to Pandoraes boxe; lift upp the lidde, out flyes the Devil; shut it up fast, it cannot hurt us.

Let us but shut uppe our eares to poets, pipers and players; pull our feete backe from resorte to theaters, and turne away our eyes from beholding of vanitie, the greatest storme of abuse will bee overblowne, and a faire path troden to amendment of life: were not we so foolish to taste every drugge and buy every trifle, players woulde shut in their shops, and carry their trash to some other country.

Themistocles in setting a peece of his ground to sale, among all the commodities which were reckoned uppe, straightly charged the cryer to proclaime this, that hee which bought it should have a good neighbour. If players can promise in woordes, and performe it in deedes, proclaime it in their billes, and make it good in their Theaters, that there is nothing there noysome to the body, nor hurtfull to the soule, and that every one which comes to buy their jestes shall have an honest neighbour, tagge and ragge, cutte and long tayle, goe thither and spare not, otherwise I advise you to keepe you thence: my selfe will beginne to leade the daunce.

I make just reckoning to bee helde for a Stoike in dealing so hardly with these people; but all the keyes hange not at one mans girdell, neither doe these open the lockes to all abuses. There are other which have a share with them in their schooles; therfore ought they to daunce the same rounde, and be partakers together of the same rebuke. Fencers, Dicers, Daunsers, Tumblers, Carders and Bowlers.

Daunsers and Tumblers, because they are dumbe Players, and I have glaunced at them by the way, shall be let passe with this clause, that they gather no assemblyes, and goe not beyonde the precincts which Peter Martyr in his Commentaryes uppon the Judges hath set them downe. That is, if they will exercise those qualityes, to doe it privilye for the health and agilitie of the body, referring all to the glorie of God.

Dycers and Carders, because these abuses are as commonly cryed out on as usually showen, have no neede of a needelesse discourse, for every manne seeth them, and they stinke almoste in every mans nose. Common bowling allyes are privy mothes, that eate uppe the credite of many idle citizens, whose gaines at home are not able to weigh downe their losses abroade; whose shoppes are so farre from maintaining their play, that their wives and children cry out for bread, and goe to bedde supperlesse ofte in the yeere.

I woulde reade you a lecture of these abuses, but my Schoole so increaseth that I cannot touch all, nor stand to amplifie every poynte. One worde of fencing, and so a *congé* to all kinde of playes. The knowledge in weapons may bee gathered to be necessary in a common wealth by the Senators of Rome, who in the time of Catilins conspiracyes caused Schooles of Defence to be erected in Capua, that teaching the people howe to warde, and how to locke, howe to thrust and howe to strike, they might the more safely coape with their enemyes. As the arte of logique was first sette downe for a rule by whiche wee might *confirmare nostra et refutare aliena,* confirme our owne reasons and confute the allegations of our adversaryes, the end being trueth, which once fished out by the harde incounter of eithers argumentes, like fire by the knockinge of flintes togither, bothe partes shoulde be satisfied and strive no more. And I judge that the craft of defence was first devised to save our selves harmelesse, and holde enimies still at advantage, the ende being right, which once throughely tryed out at handye stroakes, neither hee that offered injurie should have his wil, nor he that was threatened take any hurte; but both be contented and shake handes.

Those dayes are nowe changed: the skill of logicians is exercised in caveling; the cunning of fencers applied to quarrelling: they thinke themselves no schollers, if they be not able to finde out a knotte in every rushe; these no men, if for stirring of a strawe they prove not their valure uppon some bodies fleshe. Every Duns will bee a carper; every Dicke Swashe a common cutter. But as they bake, many times so they brue: selfe doe, selfe have: they whette their swordes against themselves, pull the house on their owne heades, returne home by Weeping Crosse, and fewe of them come to an honest ende; for the same water that drives the mil,

decayeth it: the wood is eaten by the worme that breedes within it: the goodnes of a knife cuts the owners finger: the adders death is her owne broode; the fencers scath his owne knowledge. Whether their harts be hardened which use that exercise, or God geve them over, I knowe not well: I have read of none good that practised it muche. Commodus, the Emperour, so delighted in it, that often times he slue one or other at home to keepe his fingers in use; and one day hee gathered all the sicke, lame, and the impotent people in one place, where hee hampred their feete with strange devises, gave them soft spunges in their handes to throwe at him for stones, and with a great clubbe knatched them all on the hed as they had been giauntes. Epaminondas, a famous captaine, sore hurte in a battayle, and carried out of the feelde halfe dead, when tydinges was broughte him that his souldiers gotte the day, asked presently what became of his buckler? whereby it appeareth that he loved his weapons, but I finde it not said that he was a fencer. Therefore I may liken them, which would not have men sent to the warre till they are taughte fencing, to those superstitious wisemen which would not take upon them to burye the bodies of their friendes, before they had beene cast unto wilde beastes. Fencing is growne to such abuse, that I may well compare the schollers of this schoole to them that provide staves for their owne shoulders; that foster snakes in their owne bosoms; that trust wolves to garde their sheepe, and the men of Hyrcania that keepe mastiffes to woorrye themselves.

Though I speake this to the shame of common fencers, I goe not aboute the bushe with souldiers. Homer calleth them the Sonnes of Jupiter, the images of God, and the very sheepeherds of the people: beeing the Sonnes of Jupiter, they are bountifull to the meeke, and thunder out plagues to the proude in heart: being the images of God, they are the welsprings of justice, which geveth to every man his owne: beeing accompted the shepheardes of the people, they fight with the woolfe for the safetie of their flock, and keepe of the enimie for the wealth of their countrie. Howe full are poets woorkes of bucklers, battels, launces, dartes, bowes, quivers, speares, javelins, swords, slaughters, runners, wrestlers, chariottes, horse and men at armes! Agamemnon, beyonde the name of a king, hath this title, that he was a souldier. Menelaus, because he loved his kercher better then his burgonet, a softe bed then a hard fielde, the sound of instrumentes then neighing of steedes, a fayre stable then a foule way, is let slippe without prayse. If Lycurgus, before hee make lawes for Sparta, take counsell of

Apollo whether it were good for him to teach the people thrifte, and husbandrie, he shalbe charged to leave those preceptes to the white liverd Hylotes. The Spartanes are all steele, fashioned out of tougher mettall, free in mind, valiant in heart, servile to none; accustoming their fleshe to stripes, their bodies to labour, their feete to hunting, their handes to fighting. In Crete, Scythia, Persia, Thracia, all the lawes tended to maintenance of martial discipline. Among the Scythians no man was permitted to drinke of their festivall cuppe, which had not manfully killed an enimy in fight. I coulde wish it in Englande, that there were greater preferment for the valiant Spartans, then the sottishe Hilotes; that our lawes were directed to rewarding of those whose lives are the first that must be hazarded to maineteyne the liberty of the lawes. The gentlemen of Carthage were not allowed to weare any more linkes in their chaynes, then they had seene battailes. If our gallantes of Englande might carry no more linkes in their chaynes, nor ringes on their fingers, then they have fought feelds, their neckes should not bee very often wreathed in golde, nor their handes imbrodered with precious stones. If none but they might be suffered to drinke out of plate, that have in skirmish slain one of her Majesties enimies, many thousands shoulde bring earthen pots to the table.

Let us learn by other mens harme to looke to our selves. When the Ægyptians were moste busy in their husbandrie, the Scythians overran them: when the Assyrians wer looking to their thrift, the Persians were in armes, and overcam them: when the Trojans thought themselves safest, the Greekes were nearest: when Rome was a sleepe, the Frenche men gave a sharpe assault to the Capitoll: when the Jewes were idle, their walles were rased and the Romans entred: when the Chaldees were sporting, Babilon was sacked: when the Senators were quiet, no garisons in Italy, and Pompey from home, wicked Catiline began his mischevous enterprise. We are like those unthankfull people which puffed up with prosperity forget the good turnes they received in adversity. The patient feeds his Phisition with gold in time of sicknes, and when he is wel, scarsely affoords him a cup of water. Some there are that make gods of soldiers in open warrs, and trusse them up like dogs in time of peace. Take heed of the foxeford night cap; I meane those schoolemen that cry out upon Mars, calling him the bloody god, the angry god, the furious god, the mad god, πολύδαχρυς, the teare thirsty god. These are but casts of their office and wordes of course. That is a vain brag, and a false allarme that Tullie gives to soldiers,

Cedant arma togæ, concedat laurea linguæ

Let gunns to gouns, and bucklers yeeld to bookes.

If the enimy beseege us, cut off our victuals, prevent forreine aide, girt in the city, and bring the ramme to the walles, it is not Ciceroes tongue that can peerce their armour to wound the body, nor Archimedes prickes, and lines, and circles, and triangles, and rhombus, and riffe raffe that hath any force to drive them backe. Whilst the one chats, his throte is cut; whilest the other syttes drawing mathematicall fictions, the enimie standes with a swoord at his breast. Hee that talketh muche and doeth little is like unto him that sailes with a side wind, and is borne with the tide to a wrong shore. If they meane to doe any goode in deede, bidde them follow Demosthenes and joyne with Phocion; when they have geven us good counsel in wordes, make muche of souldiers that are ready to execute the same with their swoordes. Bee not carelesse; plough with weapons by your sides; studie with a booke in one hand, a darte in the other; enjoy peace with provision for warre; when you have left the sandes behinde you, looke well to the rockes that lie before you; let not the overcomming one tempest make you secure, but have an eye to the cloud that comes from the south, and threateneth rayne. The least oversight in dangerous seas may cast you away: the least discontinuaunce of martiall exercise geve you the foyle. When Achilles loytered in his tent, geving eare to musicke, his souldiers were bidde to a hot breakefaste. Hannibals power received more hurte in one dayes ease at Capua, then in al the conflicts they had at Cannas. It were not good for us to flatter our selves with these golden dayes: highe floodes have lowe ebbes; hotte fevers could crampes; long daies shorte nightes, drie summers moyst winters. There was never fort so strong but it might be battered, never ground so fruitful but it might be barren, never countrie so populous but it might be wast, never monarch so mighty but he might be weakened, never realme so large but it might be lessened, never kingdom so flourishing but it might be decayed. Scipio before he levied his force to the walles of Carthage gave his souldiers the print of the cittie in a cake to be devoured: our enimies, with Scipio, have already eaten us with bread, and licked up our blood in a cup of wine. They do but tarry the tyde, watch opportunitie, and wayt for the reckoning, that with the shot of our lives shoulde paye for all. But that God that neither slumbreth nor sleepeth for the love of Israel, that stretcheth out his armes from morning to evening to cover his children (as the hen doth her chicken with the shadow of her wings) with the breath of his mouth shall overthrowe them, with their owne snares shall overtake them, and hang them up by the heare of their own devises.

Notwithstanding, it behoveth us in the mean season not to sticke in the myer, and gape for succour without using some ordinarye waye our selves; or to lye wallowing like lubbers in the ship of the common wealth, crying Lord, Lord! when we see the vessell toyle, but joyntly lay our hands and heads and helpes together to avoide the danger, and save that which must be the surety of us all. For as to the body ther are many members serving to severall uses, the eye to see, the eare to heare, the nose to smell, the tongue to tast, the hand to touch, the feet to beare the whole burden of the rest, and every one dischargeth his duety without grudging, so shoulde the whole body of the common wealth consist of fellow laborers, all generally serving one head, and particularly following their trade without repining. From the head to the foote, from top to the toe, there shoulde nothing be vaine, no body idle. Jupiter himself shall stand for example, who is ever in worke, still mooving and turning about the heavens: if he should pull his hand from the frame, it were impossible for the world to endure. All would be day, or al night; al Spring or al Autume; all Sommer or all Winter; al heate or al could; al moysture or al drowght; no time to til, no time to sow; no time to plant, no time to reape; the earth barren, the rivers stopt, the seas stayde, the seasons chaunged, and the whole course of nature overthrowne. The meane must labor to serve the mighty; the mighty must study to defend the meane. The subjects must sweat in obedience to their Prince; the Prince must have a care over his poore vassals.

If it be the duety of every man in a common wealth one way or other to bestirre his stoomps, I cannot but blame those lither contemplators very much, which sit concluding of sillogismes in a corner, which in a close studye in the Universitye coope themselves up xl yeres together, studying al things and professe nothing. The bell is knowen by his sounde, the birde by her voyce, the lion by his rore, the tree by the fruite, a man by his woorkes. To continue so long without mooving, to reade so much without teaching, what differeth it from a dumbe picture, or a dead body? No man is born to seek private profit; part for his countrie, parte for his freends, part for himselfe. The foole that comes into a faire garden likes the beawty of the flowers, and stickes them in his cap: the phisition considereth their nature, and puttes them in the pot: in the one they wither without profite; in the other they serve to the health of the bodie. He that readeth good writers, and pickes out their flowers for his owne nose is like a foole: hee that preferreth their vertue before their sweet smel is a good phisition. When Anacharsis travelled all over Greece to seeke out wise men, he found none in Athens, though no doubt there were many good schollers there; but comming to Chenas, a blind village in comparison of Athens, a Palcockes Inne, he found one Miso, well governing his house, looking to his grounde, instructing his children, teaching his family, making of marriages among his acquayntance, exhorting his neighbours to love and friendeship, and preaching in life; whom the philosopher, for his scarcitie of woordes, plenty of workes, accompted the onelye wiseman that ever he saw.

I speak not this to preferre Botley before Oxeford, a cottage of clownes before a colledge of Muses, Pans pipe before Apollos harp; but to shew you that poore Miso can reade you such a lecture of philosophie as Aristotle never dreamed on. You must not thruste your heades in a tubbe and say *Benè vixit, qui benè latuit,* hee hath lived well that hath loitred well. Standing streames geather filth; flowing rivers are ever sweet. Come foorth with your sicles, the harvest is greate, the laborers few: pul up the sluces, let out your springs, geve us drink of your water, light your torches and season us a little with the salt of your knowledge. Let Phœnix and Achilles, Demosthenes and Phocion, Pericles and Cimon, Lælius and Scipio, Nigidius and Cicero, the word and the sword, be knitte together. Set your talents a worke; lay not up your tresure for taking rust; teach early and late, in time and out of time; sing with the swan to the last houre. Follow the dauncing chaplens of Gradivus Mars, which chaunte the prayses of their god with voyces, and tread out the time with their feet. Play the good captaynes: exhort your souldiers with your tongues to fight, and bring the first ladder to the wall your selves: sound like bels and shine like lanternes; thunder in words and glister in workes; so shall you please God, profite your country, honor your prince, discharge your dueties, geve up a good accompt of your stewardship and leave no sinne untouched, no abuse unrebuked, no fault unpunished.

Sundry are the abuses, as well of Universityes as other places, but they are such as neither become me to touch, nor every idle head to understand.

The Thurines made a law that no common find fault should meddle with any abuse but adultery. Pythagoras bound all his schollers to five yeers silence, that as soone as ever they crept from the shel, they might not aspire to the house top. It is not good for every man to travell to Corinth, nor lawfull for all to talk what they list, or write what they please, least their tongs run before their wits, or their pennes make havock of their paper, and so wading too farre in other mens maners, whilst they fill their bookes with other mens faults, they make their volume no better then an apothecaries shop of pestilent drugges, a quackesalvers budget of filthy receites, and a huge chaos of fowle disorder. Cookes did never long more for great markets, nor fishers for large pondes, nor greedy dogs for store of game, nor soaring hawkes for plenty of foule, then carpers doe nowe for copye of abuses, that they might ever bee snarling, and have some flyes or other in the waye to snatche at.

As I would that offences should not be hid for going unpunished, nor escape without scourge for il example, so I wishe that every rebuker should place a hatch before the doore, keepe his quill within compasse. He that holdes not himselfe contented with the light of the sunne, but liftes his eyes to measure the bignes, is made blinde: he that bites every weede to searche out his nature may lighte uppon poyson, and so kill himselfe: he that loves to be sifting of every cloude may be strooke with a thunderbolt, if it chance to rent, and hee that taketh uppon him to shewe men their faults may wound his owne credite, if he go too farre. We are not angry with the Clarke of the Market, if he come to our stall and reproove our ballaunce when they are faultie, or forfeit our weightes when they are false: nevertheles, if he presume to enter our house and rigge every corner, searching more then belongs to his office, we lay holde on his locks, turne him away with his backe full of stripes, and his handes loden with his own amendes. Therefore, I will contente my selfe to shewe you no more abuses in my Schoole, then myself have seene, nor so many by hundreds as I have hearde off. Lyons folde uppe there nailes when they are in their dennes, for wearing them in the earth and nede not: eagles draw in their tallants as they set in their nestes, for blunting them there among drosse; and I will cast ancor in these abuses, reste my barke in this simple roade, for grating my wittes upon needlesse shelves. And because I accuse other for treading awry, which since I was borne never went right; because I finde so many faults abroade, which have at home more spottes on my body then the leopard, more staines on my coate then the wicked Nessus, more holes in my life then the open sive, more sinnes in my soule then heares on my head, if I have beene tedious in my lecture, or you be weary of your lesson, harken no longer for the clock, shut upp the Schoole, and get you home.

Thomas Lodge, from *Defence of Poetry* (1579)

Protogenes can know Apelles by his line though he se him not, and wise men can consider by the Penn of aucthoritie of the writer thoughe they know him not. The Rubie is discerned by his pale rednes; and who hath not hard that the Lyon is knowne by hys clawes? Though Æsopes craftie crowe be neuer so deftlye decked, yet is his double dealing esely desiphered: & though men neuer so perfectly pollish there wrytings with others sentences, yet the simple truth wil discouer the shadow of ther follies: and bestowing euery fether in the bodye of the right M. tourne out the naked dissembler into his owen cote, as a spectacle of follye to all those which can rightlye Iudge what imperfections be.

There came to my hands lately a litle (woulde God a wittye) pamphelct, baring a fayre face as though it were the scoole of abuse; but, being by me aduisedly wayed, I fynd it the oftscome of imperfections, the writer fuller of wordes then iudgement, the matter certainely as ridiculus as serius. Assuredly his mother witte wrought this wonder, the child to disprayse his father, the dogg to byte his mayster for his dainty morcell: but I se (with Seneca) that the wrong is to be suffered, since he disprayseth, who by costome hath left to speake well. But I meane to be short, and teach the Maister what he knoweth not, partly that he may se his own follie, and partly that I may discharge my promise, – both binde me: therefore I would wish the good scholmayster to ouer looke his abuses againe with me, so shall he see an ocean of inormities which begin in his first prinsiple in the disprayse of poetry. And first let me familiarly consider with this find faulte what the learned haue alwayes esteemed of poetrie. Seneca, thoughe a stoike, would haue a poeticall sonne, and, amongst the auncientest, Homer was no les accompted then *Humanus deus.* What made Alexander, I pray you, esteme of him so much? why allotted he for his works so curious a closset? was ther no fitter vnderprop for his pillow then a simple pamphelet? in all Darius cofers was there no iewell so costly? Forsoth, my thinks, these two (the one the father of Philosophers, the other the cheftaine of chiualrie) were both deceiued if all were as a GOSSON would wish them; yf poets paynt naughte but palterie toyes in vearse, their studies tended to foolishnesse, and in all their indeuors

they did naught els but *agendo nihil agere.* Lord, howe Virgil's poore gnatt pricketh him, and how Ouid's fley byteth him! he can beare no bourde, he hath raysed vp a new sect of serius stoikes, that can abide naught but their owen shadowe, and alow nothing worthye but what they conceaue. Did you neuer reade (my ouer wittie frend) that vnder the persons of beastes many abuses were dissiphered? haue you not reason to waye that whatsoeuer ether Virgil did write of his gnatt or Ouid of his fley was all couertly to declare abuse? but you are *homo literatus,* a man of the letter, little sauoring of learning; your giddy brain made you leaue your thrift, and your abuses in London some part of your honestie. You say that Poets are subtil; if so, you haue learned that poynt of them; you can well glose on a trifeling text. But you haue dronke perhaps of Lethe; your gramer learning is out of your head; you forget your Accidence; you remember not that vnder the person of Æneas in Virgil the practice of a dilligent captaine is discribed, vnder the shadow of byrds, beastes, and trees the follies of the world were disiphered; you know not that the creation is signified in the Image of Prometheus, the fall of pryde in the person of Narcissus; these are toyes, because they sauor of wisedome which you want. Marke what Campanus sayth: *Mira fabularum vanitas, sed quae si introspiciantur videri possunt non vanae.* The vanitie of tales is wonderful; yet if we aduisedly looke into them they wil seme and proue wise. How wonderful are the pithie poemes of Cato? the curious comedies of Plautus? how brauely discouereth Terence our imperfection in his Eunuch? how neatly dissiphereth he Dauus? how pleasauntly paynteth he out Gnatho? whom if we shoulde seeke in our dayes, I suppose he would not be farr from your parson.

But I see you would seeme to be that which you are not, and, as the prouerb sayth, *Nodum in scirpo quaerere.* Poetes, you say, vse coullors to couer their inconueniences, and wittie sentences to burnish their bawdery; and you diuinite to couer your knauerye. But tell mee truth, Gosson, speakest thou as thou thinkest? what coulers findest thou in a Poete not to be admitted? are his speeches vnperfect? sauor they of inscience? I think, if thou hast any shame, thou canst not but like and approue them: are their gods displesant vnto thee? doth Saturne in his maiesty moue thee? doth Iuno with her riches displease thee? doth Minerua with her weapon discomfort thee? doth Apollo with his harping harme thee? – thou mayst say nothing les then harme thee, because they are not, and, I thinke so to, because thou knowest them not. For wot thou that in the person of Saturne our decaying yeares are signified; in the picture of angry Iuno our affections are dissiphered; in the person of Minerua is our vnderstanding signified, both in respect of warre as policie. When they faine that Pallas was begotten of the braine of Iupiter, their meaning is none other but that al wisedome (as the learned say) is from aboue, and commeth from the father of Lights: in the portrature of Apollo all knowledge is denotated. So that, what so they wrot, it was to this purpose, in the way of pleasure to draw men to wisedome: for, seing the world in those daies was vnperfect, yt was necessary that they like good Phisitions should so frame their potions that they might be appliable to the quesie stomaks of their werish patients. But our studientes by your meanes haue made shipwrack of theyr labors; our schoolemaisters haue so offended that by your iudgement they shall *subire poenam capitis* for teaching poetry; the vniversitie is litle beholding to you, – al their practices in teaching are friuolus. Witt hath wrought that in you, that yeares and studie neuer setled in the heads of our sagest doctors. No meruel though you disprayse poetrye, when you know not what it meanes.

Erasmus will make that the path waye to knowledge which you disprayse; and no meane fathers vouchsafe in their seriouse questiones of deuinitie to inserte poeticall sensures. I think, if we shal wel ouerloke the philosophers, we shal find their iudgements not halfe perfect. Poetes, you saye, fayle in their fables, Philosophers in the verye secrets of Nature. Though Plato could wish the expulsion of Poetes from his well publiques, which he might doe with reason, yet the wisest had not all that same opinion: it had bene better for him to haue sercht more narowly what the soule was, for his definition was verye friuolus, when he would make it naught els but *Substantiam intellectu predictam.* If you say that Poetes did labour about nothing, tell me (I besech you) what wonders wroughte those your dunce Doctors in ther reasons *de ente, et non ente,* in theyr definition of no force, and les witt? how sweate they, power soules, in makinge more things then cold be? that I may vse your owne phrase, did not they spende one candle by seeking another? Democritus, Epicurus, with ther scholler Metrodorus, how labored they in finding out more worlds then one? Your Plato in midst of his pre-

sisnes wrought that absurdite that neuer may be redd in Poets, to make a yeartly creature to beare the person of the creator, and a corruptible substance an incomprehensible God! for, determining of the principall causes of all thinges, a made them naughte els but an Idea, which if it be conferred wyth the truth, his sentence will sauour of Inscience. But I speake for Poetes; I answeare your abuse; therefore I will disproue or disprayse naught, but wish you with the wise Plato to disprayse that thing you offend not in. Seneca sayth that the studdie of Poets is to make children ready to the vnderstanding of wisdom, and that our auncients did teache *artes Eleutherias, i. liberales,* because the instructed children by the instrument of knowledg in time became *homines liberi, i. Philosophye.* It may be that in reding of poetry it happened to you as it is with the Oyster, for she in her swimming receiueth no ayre, and you in your reding lesse instruction. It is reported that the shepe of Euboia want ther gale, and on the contrarye side that the beastes of Naxus have *distentum fel.* Men hope that scollers should have witt, brought vpp in the Vniuersite; but your sweet selfe, with the cattell of Euboia, since you left your College, have lost your learning. You disprayse Maximus Tirius pollicey, and that thinge that he wrott to manifest learned Poets mening you atribute to follye. O holy hedded man! why may not Iuno resemble the ayre? why not Alexander valour? why not Vlisses pollice? Will you have all for your owne tothe? must men write that you maye know theyr meaning? as though your wytt were to wrest all things? Alas! simple Irus, begg at knowledge gate awhile; thou haste not wonne the mastery of learning. Weane thy selfe to wisdome, and vse thy tallant in zeale, not for enuie; abuse not thy knowledge in dispraysing that which is pereles. I shold blush from a Player to become an enuiouse Preacher, if thou hadst zeale to preach; if for Sions sake thou coldst not holde thy tongue, thy true dealing were prayse worthy, thy reuolting woulde counsell me to reuerence thee. Pittie weare it that Poetrye should be displaced; full little could we want Buchanan's workes, and Boetius comfortes may not be banished. What made Erasmus labor in Euripides tragedies? Did he indeuour by painting them out of Greeke into Latine to manifest sinne vnto vs? or to confirme vs in goodness? Labor (I pray thee) in Pamphelets more prayse worthy: thou haste not saued a Senator, therefore not worthye a Lawrell wreth; thou hast not (in disprouing poetry) reproued an abuse, and therfore not worthy commendation.

Seneca sayth that *Magna vitae pars elabitur male agentibus, maxima nihil agentibus, tota aliud agentibus.* The most of our life (sayd he) is spent either in doing euill, or nothing, or that wee should not; and I would wish you weare exempted from this sensure. Geue eare but a little more what may be said for poetrie, for I must be briefe; you haue made so greate matter that I may not stay on one thing to long, lest I leaue another vntouched. And first, whereas you say that Tullie, in his yeres of more iudgement, despised Poetes, harke (I pray you) what he worketh for them in his Oration *pro Archia poeta:* but before you heare him, least you fayle in the incounter, I would wysh you to followe the aduise of the dasterdlye Ichneumon of Ægipt, who, when shee beholdeth the Aspis her enemye to drawe nighe, calleth her fellowes together, bismering herselfe with claye, agaynst the byting and stroke of the serpent; arme your selfe, call your witts together: want not your wepons, lest your imperfect iudgement be rewardede with Midas eares. You had neede play the night burd now, for your day Owl hath misconned his parte, and for "to who" now a dayes he cryes "foole you": which hath brought such a sort of wondering birds about your eares, as I feare me will chatter you out of your Iuey bush. The worlde shames to see you, or els you are afrayde to shew your selfe. You thought poetrye should want a patron (I think) when you fyrste published this inuectiue, but yet you fynd al to many, euen *preter expectationem;* yea, though it can speake for its selfe, yet her patron Tullie now shall tell her tale. *Haec studia* (sayth he) *adolescentiam alunt, senectutem oblectant, secundas res ornant, aduersis perfugium ac solatium praebent, delectant domi, non impediunt foris, pernoctant nobiscum, peregrinantur, rusticantur.* Then will you disp:rayse that which all men commend? you looke only vpon the refuse of the abuse, nether respecting the importance of the matter nor the weighte of the wryter. Solon can fayne himselfe madde, to further the Athenians. Chaucer in pleasant vein can rebuke sin vncontrold; and, though he be lauish in the letter, his sence is serious. Who in Rome lamented not Roscius death? and canst thou suck no plesure out of thy M. Claudian's writings? Hark what Cellarius a learned father attributeth to it; *Acuit memoriam* (saith he), it profiteth the memory. Yea and Tully atributeth it for prais to Archias that vpon any theame he cold versify extempory. Who liketh not of the promptnes of Ouid? who not vnworthely cold bost of himself thus, *Quicquid conabar dicere versus erat.* Who then doothe not wonder at poetry? who thinketh not that it procedeth from aboue? what made the Chians and Colophonians

fal to such controuersy? Why seke the Smirnians to recouer from the Salaminians the prais of Homer? Al wold haue him to be of ther city: I hope not for harme, but because of his knowledge. Themistocles desireth to be acquainted with those who could best discipher his praises. Euen Marius himselfe, tho neuer so cruel, accompted of Plotinus poems. What made Aphricanus esteme Ennius? Why did Alexander giue prais to Achilles, but for the prayses which he found written of him by Homer? Why estemed Pompie so muche of Theophanes Mitiletus? or Brutus so greatlye the wrytinges of Accius? Fuluius was so great a fauorer of Poetry, that, after the Aetolian warres, he attributed to the Muses those spoiles that belonged to Mars. In all the Romaine conquest, hardest thou euer of a slayne Poete? nay rather the Emperours honored them, beautified them with benefites, and decked their sanctuaries with sacrifice. Pindarus colledg is not fit for spoil of Alexander ouercome; nether feareth poetry the persecutors sword. What made Austin so much affectate that heauenly fury? not folly, for, if I must needes speake, *illud non ausim affirmare,* his zeale was in setting vp of the house of God, not in affectate eloquence; he wrot not, he accompted not, he honnored not so much that (famous poetry) whyche we prayse, without cause, for, if it be true that Horace reporteth in his booke *de Arte Poetica,* all the answeares of the Oracles weare in verse. Among the precise Iewes you shall find Poetes; and for more maicstie Sibilla will prophesie in verse, Beroaldus can witnes with me that Dauid was a poet, and that his vayne was in imitating (as S. Ierom witnesseth) Horace, Flaccus, and Pindarus; somtimes his verse runneth in an Iambus foote, anone he hath recourse to a Saphic vaine, and *aliquando semipede ingreditur.* Ask Iosephus, and he wil tel you that Esay, Iob, and Salomon voutsafed poetical practises, for (if Origen and he fault not) theyre verse was Hexameter and pentameter. Enquire of Cassiodorus, he will say that all the beginning of Poetrye proceeded from the Scripture. Paulinus, tho the Byshop of Nolanum, yet voutsafeth the name of a Poet; and Ambrose, tho he be a patriarke in Mediolanum, loueth versifing. Beda shameth not the science that shamelesse Gosson misliketh. Reade ouer Lactantius, his proofe is by poetry; and Paul voutsafeth to ouerlooke Epimenides: let the Apostle preach at Athens, he disdaineth not of Aratus authorite. It is a pretye sentence, yet not so pretty as pithy, *Poeta nascitur, Orator fit:* as who should say, Poetrye commeth from aboue, from a heauenly seate of a glorious God, vnto an excellent creature man; an Orator is but made by exercise. For, if we examine well what befell Ennius amonge the Romans, and Hesiodus among his contrimen the Grecians, howe they came by theyr knowledge, whence they receued their heauenly furye, the first will tell vs that, sleping on the Mount of Parnassus, he dreamed that he received the soule of Homer into him, after the which he became a Poete; the next will assure you that it commeth not by labor, nether that night watchings bringeth it, but that we must haue it thence whence he fetched it, which was (he saith) from a well of the Muses which Persius calleth Caballinus, a draught whereof drewe him to his perfection; so of a shephard he becam an eloquent Poet. Wel then you see that it commeth not by exercise of play making, nether insertion of gawds, but from nature, and from aboue: and I hope that Aristotle hath sufficiently taught you that *Natura nihil fecit frustra*. Persius was made a poete *Diuino furore percitus;* and whereas the poets were sayde to call for the Muses helpe, ther mening was no other, as Iodocus Badius reporteth, but to call for heauenly inspiration from aboue to direct theyr endeuors. Nether were it good for you to sette light by the name of a Poet, since the offspring from whence he commeth is so heauenly. Sibilla in her answers to Æneas against hir will, as the poet telleth vs, was possessed with thys fury; yea, wey consideratly but of the writing of poets, and you shal se that when ther matter is most heauenly their stile is most loftye, a strange token of the wonderfull efficacy of the same. I would make a long discourse vnto you of Platoes 4 furies, but I leue them: it pitieth me to bring a rodd of your owne making to beate you wythal.

But, mithinks, while you heare thys, I see you swallowe down your owne spittle for reuenge, where (God wot) my wryting sauoreth not of enuye. In this case I could wyshe you fare farre otherwyse from your foe; yf you please, I wyll become your frende, and see what a potion or receypt I can frame fytt for your diet. And herein I will proue myselfe a practiser; before I purdge you, you shall take a preparatiue to disburden your heuay hedde of those grose follis you haue conceued: but the receipt is bitter, therfore I would wysh you first to tasten your mouth with the Sugar of perseuerance: for ther is a cold collop that must downe your throate, yet such a one as shall chaunge your complection quit. I wyll haue you therfore to tast first of the cold riuer Phricus, in Thracia, which, as Aristotle reporteth, changeth blacke into white, or of Scamandar, which maketh gray yalow, that is of an enuious man a wel minded person, reprehending of zeale that wherein he hath sinned by folly; and so being prepard, thy purgation wyll worke more easy,

thy vnderstandinge wyll be more perfit, thou shalt blush at thy abuse, and reclaime thy selfe by force of argument; so wilt thou proue a clene recouered patient, and I a perfecte practiser in framing so good a potion. This broughte to passe, I with thee wil seeke out some abuse in poetry, which I wil seeke for to disproue by reason, first pronounced by no smal birde, euen Aristotle himselfe. *Poetae* (sayth he) *multa mentiuntur;* and to further his opinion seuer Cato putteth in his censure, *Admiranda canunt, sed non credenda, Poetae.* These were sore blemishes, if obiected rightly; and heare you may say the streme runnes a wronge; but, if it be so, by your leue, I wyll bring him shortly in his right chanel. My answere shall not be my owne, but a learned father shall tell my tale; if you wil know his name, men call him Lactantius, who, in hys booke *de diuinis institutionibus,* reesoneth thus. I suppose (sayth he) Poets are full of credit, and yet it is requisite for those that wil vnderstand them to be admonished that among them not onely the name but the matter beareth a show of that it is not; for if, sayth he, we examine the Scriptures litterallye, nothing will seeme more falls, and, if we way Poetes wordes and not ther meaning, our learning in them wilbe very mene. You see nowe that your Catoes iudgement is of no force, and that all your obiections you make agaynst Poetrye be of no valor; yet, lest you should be altogether discoraged, I wyll helpe you forwarde a little more. It pities me to consider the weaknes of your cause; I wyll therfore make your strongest reason more strong, and, after I have builded it vp, destroy it agayn. Poets you confesse are eloquent, but you reproue them in their wantonnesse: they write of no wisedom; you may say their tales are friuolus, they prophane holy thinges, they seeke nothing to the perfection of our soules, theyr practise is in other things of lesse force. To this obiection I answer no otherwise then Horace doeth in his booke *de Arte Poetica,* where he wryteth thus.

Siluestres homines sacer interpresque deorum
Caedibus et victu foedo deterruit Orpheus:
Dictus ob hoc lenire tigres, rabidosque leones:
Dictus et Amphion, Thebanae conditor vrbis,
Saxa mouere sono testudinis, et prece blanda
Ducere quo vellet: fuit haec sapientia quondam,
Publica priuatis secernere, sacra profanis;
Concubitu prohibere vago; dare iura maritis;
Oppida moliri; leges incidere ligno.

The holy spokesman of the Gods,
Wich heauenly Orpheus hight,
Did driue the sauage men from wods,
And made them liue aright;
And therefore is sayd the Tygers fierce

And Lyons full of myght
To ouercome: Amphion, he
Was sayd of Theabs the founder,
Who by his force of Lute did cause
The stones to part a sonder,
And by his speach them did derect,
Where he would haue them staye.
This wisedome this was it of olde
All strife for to allay;
To giue to euery man his owne;
To make the Gods be knowne;
To driue each lecher from the bed
That neuer was his owne;
To teach the law of mariage;
The way to build a towne;
For to engraue these lawes in woods –
This was these mens renowne.

I cannot leaue Tirtheus pollicy vntouched, who by force of his pen could incite men to the defence of theyr countrye. If you require of the Oracle of Apollo what successe you shal haue, *respondet bellicoso numine.*

Lo now you see your obiections [and] my answers; you behold or may perceiue manifestlye that Poetes were the first raysors of cities, prescribers of good lawes, mayntayners of religion, disturbors of the wicked, aduancers of the wel disposed, inuentors of laws, and lastly the very fot-paths to knowledge and vnderstanding; yea, if we shold beleue Hierome, he will make Plato's exiles honest men, and his pestiferous poets good preachers, for he accounteth Orpheus, Museus, and Linus Christians; therefore Virgil (in his 6 boke of Æneiados, wher he lernedly describeth the iourny of Æneas to Elisium) asserteneth vs that, among them that were ther for the zeale they beare toward their country, ther wer found *Quique pii Vates, et Phoebo digna loquuti:* but I must answer al obiections, I must fil euery nooke. I must arme myself now, for here is the greatest bob I can gather out of your booke, forsoth Ouid's abuses, in descrybing whereof you labour very vehementlye, terming him letcher, and in his person dispraise all poems: but shall one man's follye destroye a vniuersal commodity? what gift, what perfit knowledg hath ther bin among the professors of which ther hath not bin a bad one; the Angels haue sinned in heauen, Adam and Eue in earthly paradise, emong the holy Apostles vngratious Iudas. I reson not that al poets are holy, but I affirme that poetry is a heauenly gift, a perfit gift, then which I know not greater plesure. And surely, if I may speak my mind, I think we shal find but few Poets, if it were exactly wayd, what they oughte to be: your Muscouian straungers, your Scithian monsters wonderful, by one Eurus brought vpon one stage in ships made of Sheepe skins, wyll not proue you a poet, nether your life alow you to bee of that learning. If you had wisely wayed the abuse of poetry, if you had reprehended the foolish fantasies of our Poets *nomine non re* which they bring forth on stage, my self wold haue liked of you and allowed your labor. But I perceiue nowe that all red colloured stones are not Rubies, nether is euery one Alexander that hath a scare in his cheke; al lame men are not Vulcans, nor hooke nosed men Ciceroes, nether each professor a poet. I abhore those poets that sauor of ribaldry: I will with the zealous admit the expullcion of such enormities: poetry is dispraised not for the folly that is in it, but for the abuse whiche manye ill Wryters couller by it. Beleeue mee the magestrats may take aduise (as I knowe wisely can) to roote out those odde rymes which runnes in euery rascales mouth, sauoring of rybaldry. Those foolishe ballets that are admitted make poets good and godly practises to be refused. I like not of a wicked Nero that wyll expell Lucan, yet admit I of a zealous gouernour that wil seke to take away the abuse of poetry. I like not of an angrye Augustus which wyll banishe Ouid for enuy. I loue a wise Senator, which in wisedome wyll correct him, and with aduise burne his follyes: vnhappy were we, yf like poore Scaurus we shoulde find a Tiberius that wyll put vs to death for a tragedy making; but most blessed were we, if we might find a iudge that seuerely would amende the abuses of Tragedies. But I leaue the reformation thereof to more wyser than myselfe, and retourne to GOSSON, whom I wyshe to be fully perswaded in this cause; and therefore I will tell hym a pretty story, which Iustin wryteth in the prayse of poetrye. The Lacedemonians, when they had loste many men in diuers incountryes with theyr enemyes, soughte to the Oracles of Apollo requiring how they myght recouer theyr losses. It was answered, that they mighte ouercome if so be that they could get an Athenian gouernor: Whereupon they sent Orators vnto the Athenians, humbly requesting them that they woulde appoynt them out one of theyr best captaynes. The Athenians, owinge them old malice, sent them in steede of a *soldado vechio* a scholar of the Muses, in steede of a worthy warrior a poore poet, for a couragious Themistocles a silly Tirthetus, a man of great eloquence and singuler wytte, yet was he but a lame lymde captaine, more fit for the coche then the field. The Lacedemonians, trusting the Oracle, receued the champion, and, fearing the gouernment of a stranger, made him ther Citizen; which once don, and he obteining the Dukdome, he assended the theater, and ther very learnedly wyshing them to forget theyr folly and to thinke on victory, they, being acuate by his eloquence, waging battail, won the fielde.

Lo now you see that the framing of common welthes, and defence therof, proceedeth from poets, how dare you therfore open your mouth against them? how can you disprayse the preseruer of a countrye? You compare Homer to Methecus, cookes to Poetes, you shame your selfe in your vnreuerent similituds, you may see your follyes; *verbum sapienti sat*. Where as Homer was an ancient poet, you disalow him, and accompte of those of lesser iudgement. Strabo calleth poetry *primam sapientiam*. Cicero, in his firste of hys Tusculans, attributeth the inuencion of philosophy to poets. God keepe vs from a Plato that should expel such men: pittie were it that the memory of these valiant victours should be hidden, which haue dyed in the behalfe of ther countryes. Miserable were our state yf we wanted those worthy volumes of Poetry: could the learned beare the losse of Homer? or our younglings the wrytings of Mantuan? or you your volumes of Historyes? Belieue me, yf you had wanted your Mysteries of nature, and your stately storyes, your booke would haue scarce bene fedde wyth matter. If therefore you will deale in things of wisdome, correct the abuse, honor the science, renewe your schoole; crye out ouer Hierusalem wyth the prophet the woe that he pronounced; wish the teacher to reforme hys lyfe, that his weake scholler may proue the wyser; cry out against vnsaciable desyre in rich men; tel the house of Iacob theyr iniquities; lament with the Apostle the want of laborers in the Lords vineyards; cry out on those dume doggs that will not barke; wyll the mightye that they ouer mayster not the poore; and put downe the beggars prowde heart by thy perswasions. Thunder oute wyth the Prophete Micha the mesage of the Lord, and wyth him desyre the Iudges to heare thee, the Prynces of Iacob to hearken to thee, and those of the house of Israell to vnderstande; then tell them that they abhorre iudgement, and preuent equitie, that they iudge for rewardes, and that theyr priests teach for hyre, and the prophets thereof prophesie for money, and yet that they saye the Lorde is wyth them, and that no euil can befall them; breath out the sweet promises to the good, the cursses to the badde, tell them that a peace muste needes haue a warre, and that God can rayse vp another Zenacharib; shew them that Salamons kingdome was but for a season, and that aduersitie cometh ere we espye it. These be the songes of Sion, these be those rebukes which you oughte to add to abuses; recouer the body, for it is

sore; the appendices thereof will easely be reformed, if that we ar at a staye.

Well, I leaue this poynt til I know further of your mynde; mean while I must talke a little wyth you about the thyrd abuse, for the cater cosens of Pypers, theyr names (as you terme them), be Players, and I thinke as you doe, for your experience is sufficient to enforme me; but here I must loke about me, *quacunque te tetigeris vlcus est:* here is a task that requireth a long treatis, and what my opinion is of Players ye now shall plainly perceue. I must now search my wits; I see this shall passe throughe many seuere sensors handling; I must aduise me what I write, and write that I would wysh. I way wel the seriousnes of the cause, and regarde very much the iudges of my endeuor, whom, if I could, I would perswade that I woulde not nourish abuse, nether mayntaine that which should be an vniversall discomoditye. I hope they wil not iudge before they read, nether condemne without occasion. The wisest wil alwais carry two eares, in that they are to diserne two indifferent causes. I meane not to hold you in suspence (seuere Iudges): if you gredely expect my verdit, brefely this it is.

Demosthenes thoughte not that Phillip shoulde ouercome when he reproued hym, nether feared Cicero Anthonies force when in the Senate hee rebuked hym. To the ignorant ech thinge that is vnknowne semes vnprofitable, but a wise man can forsee and prayse by proofe. Pythagoras could spy oute in women's eyes two kind of teares, the one of grefe, the other of disceit; and those of iudgement can from the same flower suck honey with the bee, from whence the Spyder (I mean the ignorant) take their poison. Men that haue knowledge what comedies and tragedis be wil comend them, but it is sufferable in the folish to reproue that they know not, becaus ther mouthes will hardly be stopped. Firste therfore, if it be not tedious to GOSSON to harken to the lerned, the reder shal perceiue the antiquity of playmaking, the inuentors of comedies, and therewithall the vse and comoditye of them. So that in the end I hope my labor shall be liked, and the learned wil soner conceue his folly. For tragedies and comedies, Donate the gramarian sayth, they wer inuented by lerned fathers of the old time to no other purpose but to yeelde prayse vnto God for a happy haruest or plentiful yeere. And that thys is trewe the name of Tragedye doth importe, for, if you consider whence it came, you shall perceiue (as Iodocus Badius reporteth) that it drewe his original of *Tragos, Hircus, et Ode, Cantus* (so called), for that the actors thereof had in rewarde for theyr labour a gotes skynne fylled wyth wyne. You see then that the fyrste matter of Tragedies was to giue thankes and prayses to God, and a gratefull prayer of the countrymen for a happye haruest, and this I hope was not discommendable. I knowe you will iudge it farthest from abuse. But to wade farther, thys fourme of inuention being found out, as the dayes wherein it was vsed did decay, and the world grew to more perfection, so the witt of the younger sorte became more riper, for they leauing this fourme inuented an other, in the which they altered the nature but not the name; for, for sonnets in prayse of the gods, they did set forth the sower fortune of many exiles, the miserable fal of haples princes, the reuinous decay of many countryes; yet not content with this, they presented the liues of Satyers, so that they might wiselye, vnder the abuse of that name, discouer the follies of many theyr folish fellow citesens. And those monsters were then as our parasites are now adayes: suche as with pleasure reprehended abuse. As for Commedies, because they bear a more plesanter vain, I will leaue the other to speake of them. Tulley defines them thus: *Comedia* (saith he) is *imitatio vitae, speculum consuetudinis, et imago veritatis;* and it is sayde to be termed of *Comai* (emongste the Greekes), which signifieth *Pagos,* and *Ode, Cantus;* for that they were exercised in the fielde, they had theyr beginning with tragedies, but their matter was more plessaunt, for they were suche as did reprehend, yet *quodam lepore.* These first very rudly were inuented by Susarion Bullus and Magnes, two auncient poets, yet so that they were meruelous profitable to the reclamynge of abuse; whereupon Eupolis with Cratinus and Aristophanes began to write, and with ther eloquenter vaine and perfection of stil dyd more seuerely speak agaynst the abuses then they: which Horace himselfe witnesseth. For, sayth he, ther was no abuse but these men reprehended it; a thefe was loth to be seene [at] one [of] there spectacles, a coward was neuer present at theyr assemblies, a backbiter abhord that company; and I my selfe could not haue blamed you (Gosson) for exempting yourselfe from this theater; of troth I shoulde have lykt your pollicy. These therefore, these wer they that kept men in awe, these restrayned the vnbridled cominaltie; wherupon Horace wisely sayeth,

Oderunt peccare boni, virtutis amore:
Oderunt peccare mali, formidine poenae.

The good did hate al sinne for vertues loue:
The bad for feare of shame did sin remoue.

Yea, would God our realme could light vppon a Lucilius; then should the wicked bee poynted out from the good; a harlot woulde seeke no harbor at stage plais, lest she shold here her owne name growe in question, and the discourse of her honesty cause her to bee hated of the godly. As for you, I am sure of this one thing, he would paint you in your players ornaments, for they best becam you. But as these sharpe corrections were disanulde in Rome when they grewe to more licenciousnes, so I fear me if we shold practise it in our dayes the same intertainmente would followe. But in ill reformed Rome what comedies now? A poet's wit can correct, yet not offend. Philemon will mitigate the corrections of sinne by reprouing them couertly in shadowes. Menander dare not offend the Senate openly, yet wants he not a parasite to touch them priuely. Terence wyl not report the abuse of harlots vnder there proper stile, but he can finely girde them vnder the person of Thais. Hee dare not openly tell the Rich of theyr couetousnesse and seuerity towards their children, but he can controle them vnder the person of Durus Demeas. He must not shew the abuse of noble yong gentilmen vnder theyr owne title, but he wyll warne them in the person of Pamphilus. Wil you learne to knowe a parasite? Looke vpon his Dauus. Wyl you seke the abuse of courtly flatterers? Behold Gnato. And if we had some Satericall Poctes nowc a dayes to penn our commedies, that might be admitted of zcalc to discypher the abuses of the worlde in the person of notorious offenders, I knowe we should wisely ryd our assemblyes of many of your brotherhod.

But, because you may haue a full scope to reprehende, I will ryp vp a rablement of play makers, whosc wrightingcs I would wishe you ouerlooke, and seeke out theyr abuses. Can you mislike of Cecilius? or dispise Plinius? or amend Neuius? or find fault with Licinius? Wherein offended Atilius? I am sure you can not but wonder at Terence? Wil it please you to like of Turpilius? or alow of Trabea? You muste needs make much of Ennius; for ouerloke al thes and you shal find ther volums ful of wit if you examin them; so that, if you had no other masters, you might deserue to be a doctor, wher now you are but a folishe scholemaister: but I wyll deale wyth you very freendlye, I wil resolue eueri doubt that you find; those instrumentes which you mislike in playes grow of auncient custome, for, when Roscius was an Actor, be sure that as with his tears he moued affections, so the Musitian in the Theater before the entrance did mornefully record it in melody (as Seruius reporteth). The actors in Rome had also gay clothing, and euery mans aparel was apliable to his part and person. The old men in white, the rich men in purple, the parasite disguisedly, the yong men in gorgeous coulours, ther wanted no deuise nor good iudgement of the comedy, where I suppose our players both drew ther plaies and fourme of garments. As for the appointed dayes wherin comedies wer showen, I reede that the Romaynes appoynted them on the festiual dayes; in such reputation were they had at that time. Also Iodocus Badius will assertain you that the actors for shewing pleasure receued some profite. But let me apply those dayes to ours, their actors to our players, their autors to ours. Surely we want not a Roscius, nether ar ther great scarsity of Terence's profession, but yet our men dare not nowe a dayes presume so much as the old Poets might, and therfore they apply ther writing to the peoples vain; wheras, if in the beginning they had ruled, we should now adaies have found smal spectacles of folly. But (of truth) I must confes with Aristotle that men are greatly delighted with imitation, and that it were good to bring those things on stage that were altogether tending to vertue: all this I admit and hartely wysh, but you say vnlesse the thinge be taken away the vice will continue. Nay, I say if the style were changed the practise would profit, and sure I thinke our theaters fit that Ennius, seeing our wanton Glicerium, may rebuke her. If our poetes will nowe become seuere, and for prophane things write of vertue, you I hope shoulde see a reformed state in those thinges; which I feare me yf they were not, the idle hedded commones would worke more mischiefe. I wish as zealously as the best that all abuse of playinge weare abolished; but for the thing, the antiquitie causeth me to allow it, so it be vsed as it should be. I cannot allow the prophaning of the Sabaoth. I praise your reprehension in that; you did well in discommending the abuse, and surely I wysh that that folly wer disclaymed; it is not to be admitted, it maks those sinne, whiche perhaps, if it were not, would have binne present at a good sermon. It is in the Magistrate to take away that order, and appoynt it otherwyse. But sure it were pittie to abolish that which hath so great vertue in it, because it is abused. The Germanes, when the vse of preaching was forbidden them, what helpe had they I pray you? Forsoth the learned were fayne couertly in comedies to declare abuses, and by playing to incite the people to vertues, when they might heare no preaching. Those were lamentable dayes you will say, and so thinke I; but was not this, I pray you, a good help in reforming the decaying Gospel? You see then how comedies (my seuere iudges) are requesit both for ther antiquity and for ther commoditye, for the dignity of the wrighters, and the pleasure of the hearers. But, after your discrediting of playmaking, you salue vppon the sore somewhat,

and among many wise workes there be some that fitte your vaine: the practice of parasites is one, which I meruel it likes you so well, since it bites you so sore. But sure in that I like your iudgement, and for the rest to I approue your wit, but for the pigg of your owne sow (as you terme it) assuredly I must discommend your verdit. Tell me, GOSSON, was all your owne you wrote there? did you borow nothing of your neyghbours? Out of what booke patched you out Cicero's Oration? Whence fet you Catilin's Inuectiue. Thys is one thing, *alienam olet lucernam, non tuam;* so that your helper may wisely reply vpon you with Virgil —

Hos ego versiculos feci: tulit alter honores.

I made these verses, other bears the name.

Beleue me I should preferr Wilson's: Shorte and sweete, if I were iudge, a peece surely worthy prayse, the practice of a good scholler; would the wiser would ouerlooke that, they may perhaps cull some wisedome out of a player's toye. Well, as it is wisedome to commend where the cause requireth, so it is a poynt of folly to praise without deserte. You dislike players very much, theyr dealings be not for your commodity; whom if I myghte aduise, they should learne thys of Iuuenal.

Viuendum est recte, cum propter plurima, tum his
Praecipue causis, vt linguas mancipiorum
Contemnas. Nam lingua mali pars pessima serui.

We ought to leade our liues aright,
For many causes moue.
Especially for this same cause,
Wisedom doth vs behoue
That we may set at nought those blames
Which seruants to vs lay;
For why, the tongue of euel slaue
Is worst, as wisemen euer say.

Methinks I heare some of them verifiing these verses vpon you; if it be so that I hear them, I will concele it: as for the statute of apparrell and the abuses therof, I see it manifestly broken, and, if I should seeke for example, you cannot but offend my eyes. For, if you examine the statuts exactly, a simple cote should be fitted to your backe, we shold bereue you of your brauerye, and examine your auncestry, and by profession, in respect of that statute, we should find you cater cosens with a, (but hush) you know my meaning: I must for pitie fauor your credit, in that you weare once a scholler.

. . . .

And because I think my selfe to haue sufficiently answered that I supposed, I conclude wyth
this: God preserue our peaceable Princes, and confound her enemies: God enlarge her wisedom, that
like Saba she may seeke after a Salomon: God con-
founde the imaginations of her enemies, and perfit
his graces in her, that the daies of her rule may be
continued in the bonds of peace, that the house of
the chosen Isralites may be maynteyned in
happinesse: lastly, I frendly bid GOSSON farwell,
wyshinge him to temper his penn with more discretion.

King James VI of Scotland, *Ane Schort Treatise Conteining Some Reulis and Cautelis to Be Obseruit and Eschewit in Scottis Poesie* (1584)

THE PREFACE TO THE READER

The cause why (docile Reader) I haue not dedicat this short treatise to any particular personis (as commounly workis vsis to be) is, that I esteme all thais quha hes already some beginning of knawledge, with ane earnest desyre to atteyne to farther, alyke meit for the reading of this worke, or any vther, quhilk may help thame to the atteining to thair foirsaid desyre. Bot as to this work, quhilk is intitulit *The Reulis and cautelis to be obseruit and eschewit in Scottis Poesie,* ye may maruell parauenture quhairfore I sould haue writtin in that mater, sen sa mony learnit men, baith of auld and of late, hes already written thairof in dyuers and sindry languages: I answer that, nochtwithstanding, I haue lykewayis written of it, for twa caussis. The ane is: As for them that wrait of auld, lyke as the tyme is changeit sensyne, sa is the ordour of Poesie changeit. For then they obseruit not *Flowing,* nor eschewit not *Ryming in termes,* besydes sindrie vther thingis, quhilk now we obserue and eschew, and dois weil in sa doing: because that now, quhen the warld is waxit auld, we haue all their opinionis in writ, quhilk were learned before our tyme, besydes our awin ingynis, quhair as they then did it onelie be thair awin ingynis, but help of any vther. Thairfore, quhat I speik of Poesie now, I speik of it as being come to mannis age and perfectioun, quhair as then it was bot in the infancie and chyldheid. The vther cause is: That as for thame that hes written in it of late, there hes neuer ane of thame written in our language. For albeit sindrie hes written of it in English, quhilk is lykest to our language, yit we differ from thame in sindrie reulis of Poesie, as ye will find be experience. I haue lykewayis omittit dyuers figures, quhilkis are necessare to be vsit in verse, for twa causis. The ane is, because they are vsit in all languages, and thairfore are spokin of be *Du Bellay,* and sindrie vtheris, quha hes written in this airt. Quhairfore, gif I wrait of them also, it sould seme that I did bot repete that quhilk they haue written, and yit not sa weil as they haue done already. The vther cause is that they are figures of Rhetorique and Dialectique, quhilkis airtis I professe nocht, and thairfore will apply to my selfe the counsale quhilk *Apelles* gaue to the shoomaker, quhen he said to him, seing him find falt with the shankis of the Image of *Venus,* efter that he had found falt with the pantoun, *Ne sutor vltra crepidam.*

I will also wish yow (docile Reidar) that, or ye cummer yow with reiding thir reulis, ye may find in your self sic a beginning of Nature as ye may put in practise in your verse many of thir foirsaidis preceptis, or euer ye sie them as they are heir set doun. For gif nature be nocht the cheif worker in this airt, Reulis wilbe bot a band to nature, and will mak yow within short space weary of the haill airt; quhair as, gif Nature be cheif, and bent to it, reulis will be ane help and staff to Nature. I will end heir, lest my preface be langer nor my purpose and haill mater following: wishing yow, docile Reidar, als gude succes and great proffeit by reiding this short treatise as I tuke earnist and willing panis to blok it, as ye sie, for your cause. Fare weill.

I haue insert in the hinder end of this Treatise maist kyndis of versis quhilks are not cuttit or brokin, bot alyke many feit in euerie lyne of the verse, and how they are commounly namit, with my opinioun for quhat subiectis ilk kynde of thir verse is meitest to be vsit.

To knaw the quantitie of your lang or short fete in they lynes, quhilk I haue put in the reule quhilk teachis yow to knaw quhat is *Flowing,* I haue markit the lang fute with this mark — , and abone the heid of the shorte fute I haue put this mark ᴗ.

SONNET OF THE AVTHOVR
TO THE READER.

SEN for your saik I wryte vpon your airt,
Apollo, Pan, and ye O Musis nyne,
And thou, O Mercure, for to help thy pairt
I do implore, sen thou be thy ingyne,
Nixt efter Pan had found the quhissill, syne
Thou did perfyte that quhilk he bot espyit:
And efter that made Argus for to tyne

(Quha kepit Io) all his windois by it.
Concurre ye Gods, it can not be denyit,
Sen in your airt of Poësie I wryte.
Auld birds to learne by teiching it is tryit:
Sic docens discens, gif ye help to dyte.
  Then Reidar sie of nature thou haue pairt,
  Syne laikis thou nocht bot heir to reid the airt.

SONNET DECIFRING
THE PERFYTE POETE.

ANE rype ingyne, ane quick and walkned witt,
With sommair reasons, suddenlie applyit,
For euery purpose vsing reasons fitt,
With skilfulnes, where learning may be spyit,
With pithie wordis, for to expres yow by it
His full intention in his proper leid,
The puritie quhairof weill hes he tryit,
With memorie to keip quhat he dois reid,
With skilfulnes and figuris, quhilks proceid
From Rhetorique, with euerlasting fame,
With vthers woundring, preassing with all speid
For to atteine to merite sic a name:
All thir into the perfyte Poëte be.
Goddis, grant I may obteine the Laurell trie.

THE REVLIS AND CAVTELIS TO BE OBSERVIT AND ESCHEWIT IN SCOTTIS POESIE.

CHAP. I.

FIRST, ye sall keip iust cullouris, quhairof the cautelis are thir.

That ye rymc nocht twysc in ane syllabe. As for exemple, that ye make not *proue* and *reproue* ryme to gether, nor *houe,* for houeing on hors bak, and *behoue.*

That ye ryme ay to the hinmest lang syllabe (with accent) in the lyne, suppose it be not the hinmest syllabe in the lyne, as *bakbyte yow* and *out flyte yow.* It rymes in *byte* and *flyte,* because of the lenth of the syllabe, and accent being there, and not in *yow,* howbeit it be the hinmest syllabe of ather of the lynis. Or *question* and *digestion:* It rymes in *ques* and *ges,* albeit they be bot the antepenult syllabis, and vther twa behind ilkane of thame.

Ye aucht alwayis to note that, as in thir foirsaidis or the lyke wordis, it rymes in the hinmest lang syllabe in the lyne, althoucht there be vther short syllabis behind it, sa is the hinmest lang syllabe the hinmest fute, suppose there be vther short syllabis behind it, quhilkis are eatin vp in the pronounceing and na wayis comptit as fete.

Ye man be war likewayis (except necessitie compell yow) with *Ryming in Termis,* quhilk is to say, that your first or hinmest word in the lyne exceid not twa or thre syllabis at the maist, vsing thrie als seindill as ye can. The cause quhairfore ye sall not place a lang word first in the lyne is that all lang words hes ane syllabe in them sa verie lang, as the lenth thairof eatis vp in the pronouncing euin the vther syllabes quhilks ar placit lang in the same word, and thairfore spillis the flowing of that lyne. As for exemple in this word, *Arabia,* the second syllable (*ra*) is sa lang that it eatis vp in the prononcing (*a*), quhilk is the hinmest syllabe of the same word. Quhilk (*a*) althocht it be in a lang place, yit it kythis not sa, because of the great lenth of the preceding syllabe (*ra*). As to the cause quhy ye sall not put a lang word hinmest in the lyne, it is because that the lenth of the secound syllabe (*ra*), eating vp the lenth of the vther lang syllabe (*a*), makis it to serue bot as a tayle vnto it, together with the short syllabe preceding. And because this tayle nather seruis for cullour nor fute, as I spak before, it man be thairfore repetit in the nixt lyne ryming vnto it, as it is set doune in the first: quhilk makis that ye will scarcely get many wordis to ryme vnto it, yea nane at all will ye fine to ryme to sindrie vther langer wordis. Thairfore cheifly be warre of inserting sic lang wordis hinmest in the lyne, for the cause quhilk I last allegit. Besydis that, nather first nor last in the lyne, it keipis na *Flowing.* The reulis and cautelis quhairof are thir, as followis.

CHAP. II.

FIRST ye man vnderstand that all syllabis are deuydit in thrie kindes: That is, some schort, some lang, and some indifferent. Be indifferent I meane they quhilk are ather lang or short, according as ye place thame.

The forme of placeing syllabes in verse is this. That your first syllabe in the lyne be short, the second lang, the thrid short, the fourt lang, the fyft short, the sixt lang, and sa furth to the end of the lyne. Alwayis tak heid that the number of your fete in euery lyne be euin, and nocht odde: as four, six, aucht, or ten, and not thrie, fyue, seuin, or nyne, except it be in broken verse, quhilkis are out of reul and daylie inuentit be dyers Poetis. Bot gif ye wald ask me the reulis quhairby to knaw euerie ane of thir thre foir saidis kyndis of syllabes, I answer your eare man be the onely iudge and discerner thairof. And to proue this, I remit to the iudgement of the same quhilk of thir twa lynis following flowis best,

Into the Sea then Lucifer vpsprang,

In the Sea then Lucifer to vpsprang.

I doubt not bot your eare makkis you easilie to persaue that the first lyne flowis weil and the vther nathing at all. The reasoun is because the first lyne keips the reule abone written — to wit, the first fute short, the secound lang, and sa furth, as I shewe before — quhair as the vther is direct contrair to the same. Bot specially tak heid, quhen your lyne is of fourtene, that your *Sectioun* in aucht be a lang monosyllabe, or ellis the hinmest syllabe of a word alwais being lang, as I said before. The cause quhy it man be ane of thir twa is for the Musique, because that quhen your lyne is ather of xiiij or xij fete it wilbe drawin sa lang in the singing, as ye man rest in the middes of it, quhilk is the *Sectioun*: sa as, gif your *Sectioun* be nocht ather a monosyllabe, or ellis the hinmest syllabe of a word, as I said before, bot the first syllabe of a polysyllabe, the Musique sall make yow sa to rest in the middes of that word, as it sall cut the ane half of the word fra the vther, and sa sall mak it seme twa different wordis, that is bot ane. This aucht onely to be obseruit in thir foirsaid lang lynis: for the shortnes of all shorter lynis then thir before mentionat is the cause that the Musique makis na rest in the middes of thame, and thairfore thir obseruationis seruis nocht for thame. Onely tak heid that the *Sectioun* in thame kythe something langer nor any vther feit in that lyne, except the secound and the last, as I haue said before.

Ye man tak heid lykewayis that your langest lynis exceid nochte fourtene fete, and that your shortest be nocht within foure.

Remember also to mak a *Sectioun* in the middes of euery lyne, quhether the lyne be lang or short. Be *Sectioun* I mean, that gif your lyne be of fourtene fete, your aucht fute man not only be langer then the seuint, or vther short fete, but also langer nor any vther lang fete in the same lyne, except the secound and the hinmest. Or gif your lyne be of twelf fete, your *Sectioun* to be in the sext. Or gif of ten, your *Sectioun* to be in the sext also. The cause quhy it is not in fyue is because fyue is odde, and euerie odde fute is short. Or gif your lyne be of aucht fete, your *Sectioun* to be in the fourt. Gif of sex, in the fourt also. Gif of four, your *Sectioun* to be in twa.

Ye aucht likewise be war with oft composing your haill lynis of monosyllabis onely (albeit our language haue sa many as we can nocht weill eschewe it), because the maist pairt of thame are indifferent, and may be in short or lang place, as ye like. Some wordis of dyuers syllabis are likewayis indifferent, as

Thairfore, restore.
I thairfore, then.

In the first *thairfore*, (*thair*) is short and (*fore*) is lang; in the vther, (*thair*) is lang and (*fore*) is short; and

yit baith flowis alike weill. Bot thir indifferent wordis, composit of dyuers syllabes, are rare, suppose in monosyllabes commoun. The cause then quhy ane haill lyne aucht nocht to be composit of monosyllabes only is that, they being for the maist pairt indifferent, nather the secound, hinmest, nor *Sectioun* will be langer nor the other lang fete in the same lyne. Thairfore ye man place a word composit of dyuers syllabes, and not indifferent, ather in the secound, hinmest, or *Sectioun,* or in all thrie.

Ye man also tak heid that quhen thare fallis any short syllabis efter the last lang syllabe in the lyne, that ye repeit thame in the lyne quhilk rymis to the vther, even as ye set them downe in the first lyne: as for exempill, ye man not say

Then feir nocht
Nor heir ocht,

Bot

Then feir nocht
Nor heir nocht,

repeting the same *nocht* in baith the lynis: because this syllabe *nocht,* nather seruing for cullour nor fute, is bot a tayle to the lang fute preceding, and thairfore is repetit lykewayis in the nixt lyne quhilk rymes vnto it euin as it [is] set doun in the first.

There is also a kynde of indifferent wordis asweill as of syllabis, albeit few in number. The nature quhairof is that gif ye place thame in the begynning of a lyne they are shorter be a fute nor they are gif ye place thame hinmest in the lyne, as

Sen patience I man haue perforce,
I liue in hope with patience.

Ye se there are bot aucht fete in ather of baith thir lynis abone written. The cause quhairof is that *patience* in the first lyne, in respect it is in the beginning thairof, is bot of twa fete, and in the last lyne of thrie, in respect it is the hinmest word of that lyne. To knaw and discerne thir kynde of wordis from vtheris, your eare man be the only iudge, as of all the vther parts of *Flowing,* the verie twichestane quhairof is Musique.

I haue teachit yow now shortly the reulis of *Ryming, Fete,* and *Flowing.* There restis yet to teache yow the wordis, sentences, and phrasis necessair for a Poete to vse in his verse, quhilk I haue set doun in reulis, as efter followis.

CHAP. III

FIRST, that in quhatsumeuer ye put in verse, ye put in na wordis ather *metri causa* or yit for filling furth the nomber of the fete, bot that they be all sa necessare as ye sould be constrainit to vse thame in cace ye were speiking the same purpose in prose. And thairfore that your wordis appeare to haue cum out willingly, and by nature, and not to haue bene thrawin out constrainedly, be compulsioun.

That ye eschew to insert in your verse a lang rable of mennis names, or names of tounis, or sik vther names, because it is hard to mak many lang names all placit together to flow weill. Thairfore, quhen that fallis out in your purpose, ye sall ather put bot twa or thrie of thame in euerie lyne, mixing vther wordis amang thame, or ellis specifie bot twa or thre of them at all, saying (*With the laif of that race*), or (*With the rest in thay pairtis*), or sic vther lyke wordis: as for example,

> Out through his cairt, quhair Eous was eik
> With other thre, quhilk Phaëton had drawin.

Ye sie thair is bot ane name there specifeit, to scrue for vther thrie of that sorte.

Ye man also take heid to frame your wordis and sentencis according to the mater: As in Flyting and Inuectiues your wordis to be cuttit short, and hurland ouer heuch. For thais quhilkis are cuttit short, I meane be sic wordis as thir,

> *Iis neir cair,*

for

> *I sall neuer cair,* gif your subiect were

of loue, or tragedies. Because in thame your words man be drawin lang, quhilkis in Flyting man be short.

Ye man lykcwayis tak heid that ye waill your wordis according to the purpose: as in ane heich and learnit purpose to vse heich, pithie, and learnit wordis.

Gif your purpose be of loue, to vse commoun language, with some passionate wordis.

Gif your purpose be of tragicall materis, to vse lamentable wordis, with some heich, as rauishit in admiratioun.

Gif your purpose be of landwart effairis, to vse corruptit and vplandis wordis.

And finally, quhatsumeuer be your subiect, to vse *vocabula artis,* quhairby ye may the mair viuelie represent that persoun quhais pairt ye paint out.

This is likewayis neidfull to be vsit in sentences, als weill as in wordis. As gif your subiect be heich and learnit, to vse learnit and infallible reasonis, prouin be necessities.

Gif your subiect be of loue, to vse wilfull reasonis, proceding rather from passioun nor reasoun.

Gif your subiect be of landwart effaris, to vse sklender reasonis, mixt with grosse ignorance, nather keiping forme nor ordour. And sa furth, euer fram-

ing your reasonis according to the qualitie of your subiect.

Let all your verse be *Literall,* sa far as may be, quhatsumeuer kynde they be of, bot speciallie *Tumbling* verse for flyting. Be *Literall* I meane that the maist pairt of your lyne sall rynn vpon a letter, as this tumbling lyne rynnis vpon F.

> *Fetching fude for to feid it fast furth of the Farie.*

Ye man obserue that thir *Tumbling* verse flowis not on that fassoun as vtheris dois. For all vtheris keipis the reule quhilk I gaue before, to wit, the first fute short, the secound lang, and sa furth. Quhair as thir hes twa short and ane lang throuch all the lyne, quhen they keip ordour: albeit the maist pairt of thame be out of ordour, and keipis na kynde nor reule of *Flowing,* and for that cause are callit *Tumbling* verse: except the short lynis of aucht in the hinder end of the verse, the quhilk flowis as vther verses dois, as ye will find in the hinder end of this buke, quhair I giue exemple of sindrie kyndis of versis.

CHAP. IIII.

MARK also thrie speciall ornamentis to verse, quhilkis are *Comparisons, Epithetis,* and *Prouerbis.*

As for *Comparisons,* take heid that they be sa proper for the subiect that nather they be ouer bas, gif your subiect be heich, for then sould your subiect disgrace your *Comparisoun,* nather your *Comparisoun* be heich quhen your subiect is basse, for then sall your *Comparisoun* disgrace your subicct. Bot let sic a mutuall correspondence and similitude be betwix them as it may appeare to be a meit *Comparisoun* for sic a subiect, and sa sall they ilkane decore vther.

As for *Epithetis,* it is to descryue brieflie, *en passant,* the naturall of euerie thing ye speik of, be adding the proper adiectiue vnto it, quhairof there are twa fassons. The ane is to descryue it be making a corruptit worde, composit of twa dyuers simple wordis, as

> *Apollo gyde-Sunne.*

The vther fasson is be *Circumlocution,* as

> *Apollo, reular of the Sunne.*

I esteme this last fassoun best, because it expressis the authoris meaning als weill as the vther, and yit makis na corruptit wordis, as the vther dois.

As for the *Prouerbis,* they man be proper for the subiect, to beautifie it, chosen in the same forme as the *Comparisoun.*

CHAP. V

IT is also meit, for the better decoratioun of the verse, to vse sumtyme the figure of Repetitioun, as

> *Quhylis ioy rang,*
> *Quhylis noy rang. &c.*

YE sie this word *quhylis* is repetit heir. This forme of repetitioun, sometyme vsit, decoris the verse very mekle. Yea, quhen it cummis to purpose, it will be cumly to repete sic a word aucht or nyne tymes in a verse.

CHAP VI.

YE man also be warre with composing ony thing in the same maner as hes bene ower oft vsit of before. As in speciall, gif ye speik of loue, be warre ye descryue your *Loues* makdome, or her fairnes. And siclyke that ye descryue not the morning and rysing of the Sunne in the Preface of your verse; for thir thingis are sa oft and dyuerslie writtin vpon be Poëtis already, that gif ye do the lyke it will appeare ye bot imitate, and that it cummis not of your awin *Inuentioun,* quhilk is ane of the cheif properteis of ane Poete. Thairfore, gif your subiect be to prayse your *Loue,* ye sall rather prayse hir vther qualiteis, nor her fairnes or hir shaip; or ellis ye sall speik some lytill thing of it, and syne say that your wittis are sa smal, and your vtterance sa barren, that ye can not discryue any part of hir worthelie; remitting alwayis to the Reider to iudge of hir, in respect sho matches, or rather excellis, *Venus,* or any woman, quhome to it sall please yow to compaire her. Bot gif your subiect be sic as ye man speik some thing of the morning or Sunne rysing, tak heid that, quhat name ye giue to the Sunne, the Mone, or vther starris the ane tyme, gif ye happin to wryte thairof another tyme, to change thair names. As gif ye call the Sunne *Titan* at a tyme, to call him *Phœbus* or *Apollo* the vther tyme; and siclyke the Mone, and vther Planettis.

CHAP. VII.

BOT sen *Inuention* is ane of the cheif vertewis in a Poete, it is best that ye inuent your awin subiect your self, and not to compose of sene subiectis. Especially translating any thing out of vther language, quhilk doing, ye not onely essay not your awin ingyne of *Inuentioun,* bot be the same meanes ye are bound, as to a staik, to follow that buikis phrasis quhilk ye translate.

Ye man also be war of wryting any thing of materis of commoun weill, or vther sic graue sene subiectis (except Metaphorically, of manifest treuth opinly knawin, yit nochtwithstanding vsing it very seindil), because nocht onely ye essay nocht your

awin *Inuentioun,* as I spak before, bot lykewayis they are to graue materis for a Poet to mell in. Bot because ye can not haue the *Inuentioun,* except it come of Nature, I remit it thairvnto, as the cheif cause not onely of *Inuentioun* bot also of all the vther pairtis of Poesie. For airt is only bot ane help and a remembraunce to Nature, as I shewe yow in the Preface.

CHAP. VIII.

TUICHING THE KYNDIS OF VERSIS MENTIONAT IN THE PREFACE.

FIRST, there is ryme quhilk seruis onely for lang historeis, and yit are nocht verse. As for exemple,

> *In Maii when that the blissefull Phœbus bricht,*
> *The lamp of ioy, the heauens gemme of licht,*
> *The goldin cairt, and the etheriall King,*
> *With purpour face in Orient dois spring,*
> *Maist angel-lyke ascending in his sphere,*
> *And birds with all thair heauenlie voces cleare*
> *Dois mak a sweit and heauinly harmony,*
> *and fragrant flours dois spring vp lustely:*
> *Into this season, sweitest of delyte,*
> *To walk I had a lusty appetyte.*

And sa furth.

For the descriptioun of Heroique actis, martiall and knichtly faittis of armes, vse this kynde of verse following, callit *Heroicall,* as

> *Meik mundane mirrour, myrrie and modest,*
> *Blyth, kynde, and courtes, comelie, clene, and chest,*
> *To all exemple for thy honestie,*
> *As richest rose, or rubie, by the rest,*
> *With gracis graue, and gesture maist digest,*
> *Ay to thy honnour alwayis hauing eye,*
> *Were fassons fliemde, they micht be found in the:*
> *Of blissings all, be blyth, thow hes the best;*
> *With euerie berne belouit for to be.*

For any heich and graue subiectis, specially drawin out of learnit authouris, vse this kynde of verse following, callit *Ballat Royal,* as

> *That nicht he ceist, and went to bed, bot greind*
> *Yit fast for day, and thocht the nicht to lang.*
> *At last Diana doun her head recleind*
> *Into the sea. Then Lucifer vpsprang,*
> *Auroras post, whome sho did send amang*
> *The Ieittie cludds, for to foretell ane hour,*
> *Before sho stay her tears, quhilk Ouide sang*
> *Fell for her loue, quhilk turnit in a flour.*

For tragicall materis, complaintis, or testamentis, vse this kynde of verse following, callit *Troilus* verse, as

To thee, Echo, and thow to me agane,
In the desert, amangs the wods and wells,
Quhair destinie hes bound the to remane,
But company, within the firths and fells,
Let vs complein, with wofull youtts and yells,
A shaft, a shotter, that our harts hes slane:
To thee, Echo, and thow to me agane.

For flyting, or Inuectiues, vse this kynde of verse following, callit *Rouncefallis* or *Tumbling* verse.

In the hinder end of haruest, vpon Alhallow ene,
Quhen our gude nichtbors rydis (nou gif I reid richt),
Some bucklit on a benwod, and some on a bene,
Ay trottand into troupes fra the twylicht:
Some sadland a sho ape, all grathed into grene:
Some hotcheand on a hemp stalk, hovand on a heicht:
The king of Fary with the Court of the Elf quene,
With many elrage Incubus, rydand that nicht:
*   There ane elf on ane ape ane vnsell begat,*
*   Besyde a pot baith auld and worne:*
*   This bratshard in ane bus was borne:*
*   They fand a monster, on the morne,*
*   War facit nor a Cat.*

For compendious praysing of any bukes, or the authouris thairof, or ony argumentis of vther historeis, quhair sindrie sentences and change of purposis are requyrit, vse *Sonet* verse, of fourtene lynis, and ten fete in euery lyne. The exemple quhairof I neid nocht to shaw yow, in respect I haue set doun twa in the beginning of this treatise.

In materis of loue, vse this kynde of verse, quhilk we call *Commoun* verse, as

Quhais answer made thame nocht sa glaid
That they sould thus the victors be,
As euen the answer quhilk I haid
Did greatly ioy and confort me:
Quhen lo, this spak Apollo myne,
All that thou seikis, it sall be thyne.

Lyke verse of ten fete, as this foirsaid is of aucht, ye may vse lykewayis in loue materis: as also all kyndis of cuttit and brokin verse, quhairof new formes are daylie inuentit according to the Poëtes pleasour, as

Quha wald haue tyrde to heir that tone,
Quhilk birds corroborat ay abone
*   Throuch schouting of the Larkis!*
They sprang sa heich into the skyes,
Quhill Cupide walknis with the cryis
*   Of Naturis chapell Clarkis.*
Then, leauing all the Heauins aboue,
*   He lichted on the eard.*
Lo! how that lytill God of loue
*   Before me then appeard,*
So myld-lyke,
*   With bow thre quarters skant*
And chyld-lyke,
*   So moylie*
*   He lukit lyke a Sant.*
*   And coylie,*

And sa furth.

This onely kynde of brokin verse abonewrittin man of necessitie, in thir last short fete, as *so moylie and coylie,* haue bot twa fete and a tayle to ilkane of thame, as ye sie, to gar the cullour and ryme be in the penult syllabe.

And of thir foirsaidis kyndes of ballatis of haill verse, and not cuttit or brokin as this last is, gif ye lyke to put ane owerword till ony of thame, as making the last lyne of the first verse to be the last lyne of euerie vther verse in that ballat, [will] set weill for loue materis.

Bot besydis this kyndes of brokin or cuttit verse, quhilks ar inuentit daylie be Poetis, as I shewe before, there are sindrie kyndes of haill verse, with all thair lynis alyke lang, quhilk I haue heir omittit, and tane bot onelie thir few kyndes abone specifeit as the best, quhilk may be applyit to ony kynde of subiect, bot rather to thir quhairof I haue spokin before.

Francis Meres, from *Palladis Tamia, Wits Treasurie* (London: Printed by P. Short for C. Burbie, 1598)

POETRIE.

As in a Vine clusters of grapes are often hidde vnder the broade and spacious leaues: so in deepe conceited and well couched poems, figures and fables, many things verie profitable to be knowne, do passe by a yong scholler. *Plut.*

As, according to Philoxenus, that flesh is most sweete which is no flesh, and those the delectablest fishes which are no fishes: so that Poetrie dooth most delight which is mixt with Philosophie, and that Philosophie which is mixt with Poetrie. *Plutarchus in Commentario, quomodo adolescens Poetas audire debet.*

As a Bee gathereth the sweetest and mildest honie from the bitterest flowers and sharpest thornes: so some profite may bee extracted out of obscene and wanton Poems and fables. *idem.*

Albeit many be drunke with wine, yet the Vines are not to bee cut downe, as *Lycurgus* did, but Welles and Fountaines are to be digged neare vnto them: so although many abuse poetrie, yet it is not to bee banished, but discretion is to vsed, that it may bee made holesome. *idem.*

As Mandrake growing neare Vines doth make the wine more mild: so philosophie bordering vppon poetrie dooth make the knowledge of it more moderate. *idem.*

As poyson mixt with meate is verie deadlie: so lasciuiousnesse and petulancie in poetrie mixt with profitable and pleasing matters is very pestilent. *idem.*

As we are delighted in deformed creatures artificiallye painted: so in poetrie, which is a liuely adumbration of things, euil matters ingeniously contriued do delight.

As Phisitians vse for medicine the feete and wings of the flies *Cantharides,* which flies are deadly poyson: so we may gather out of the same poem that may quell the hurtfull venome of it; for poets do alwaies mingle somewhat in their Poems, wherby they intimate that they condemne what they declare. *idem.*

As our breath doth make a shiller sound being sent through the narrow channell of a Trumpet then if it be diffused abroad into the open aire: so the well knitte and succinct combination of a Poem dooth make our meaning better knowen and discerned then if it were deliuered at random in prose. *Seneca.*

As he that drinkes of the Well *Clitorius* doth abhorre wine: so they that haue once tasted of poetry cannot away with the study of philosophie. After the same maner holdes the contrarie.

As the Anabaptists abhorre the liberall artes and humane sciences: so puritanes and precisians detest poetrie and poems.

As eloquence hath found many preachers & oratours worthy fauourers of her in the English tongue: so her sister poetry hath found the like welcome and entertainment giuen her by our English poets, which makes our language so gorgeous & delectable among vs.

As Rubarbe and sugarcandie are pleasant & profitable: so in poetry ther is sweetnes and goodness. *M. John Haring.,* in his *Apologie for Poetry* before his translated *Ariosto.*

Many cockney and wanton women ar often sicke, but in faith they cannot tell where: so the name of poetrie is odious to some, but neither his cause nor effects, neither the summe that contains him nor the particularities descending from him, giue any fast handle to their carping dispraise. *Sir Philip Sidney,* in his *Apologie for Poetry.*

POETS.

As some do vse an Amethist in compotation agaynst drunkennes: so certain precepts are to be vsed in hearing and reading of poets, least they infect the mind. *Plut. & Plin.* lib. 37. cap. 9.

As in those places where many holsome hearbes doe growe there also growes many poysonfull weedes: so in Poets there are many excellent things and many pestilent matters. *Plut.*

As *Simonides* sayde that the *Thessalians* were more blockish then that they could be deceiued of him: so the riper and pregnanter the wit is the sooner it is corrupted of Poets. *idem.*

As *Cato* when he was a scholler woulde not beleeue his maister, except hee rendered a reason of what he taught him: so wee are not to beleeue Poets in all that they write or say, except they yeelde a reason. *idem.*

As in the same pasture the Bee seaseth on the flower, the Goate grazeth on the shrub, the swine on the root, & Oxen, Kine, & Horses on the grasse: so in Poets one seeketh for historie, an other for ornament of speech, another for proofe, & an other for precepts of good life. *idem.*

As they that come verie suddainlie out of a very darke place are greatly troubled, except by little & little they be accustomed to the light: so, in reading of Poets, the opinions of Phylosophers are to bee sowne in the mindes of young schollers, least many diuersities of doctrines doe afterwardes distract their mindes. *idem.*

As in the portraiture of murder or incest we praise the Art of him that drewe it, but we detest the thing it selfe: so in lasciuious Poets let vs imitate their elocution but execrate their wantonnes. *idem.*

Some thinges that are not excellent of themselues are good for some, bicause they are mcet for them: so some things are commended in Poets which are fit and correspondent for the persons they speak of, although in themselues they bee filthy and not to be spoken; As lame *Demonides* wished that the shoes that were stolne from him might fit his feet that had stoln them. *idem.*

As that ship is endaungered where all leane to one side, but is in safetie one leaning one way and another another way: so the dissensions of Poets among themselues doth make them that they lesse infect their readers. And for this purpose our Satyrists Hall, the Author of *Pigmalion's Image* and *Certaine Satyres,* Rankins, and such others are very profitable.

As a Bee doth gather the iuice of honie from flowres, whereas others are onely delighted with the colour and smel: so a Philosopher findeth that among Poets which is profitable for good life, when as others are tickled only with pleasure. *Plut.*

As wee are delighted in the picture of a viper or a spider artificially enclosed within a precious iewell: so Poets do delight vs in the learned & cunning depainting of vices.

As some are delighted in counterfet wines confected of fruites, not that they refresh the hart but that they make drunke; so some are delighted in Poets only for their obscenity, neuer respecting their eloquence, good grace, or learning.

As Emperors, Kings, & princes haue in their handes authority to dignifie or disgrace their no-bles, attendants, subiects, & vassals: so Poets haue the whole power in their handes to make men either immortally famous for their valiant exploites and vertuous exercises, or perpetually infamous for their vicious liues.

As God giueth life vnto man: so a Poet giueth ornament vnto it.

As the Greeke and Latine Poets haue wonne immortall credit to their natiue speech, beeing encouraged and graced by liberall patrones and bountifull Benefactors: so our famous and learned Lawreat masters of England would entitle our English to far greater admired excellency if either the Emperor Augustus, or Octauia his sister, or noble Mecænus were aliue to rewarde and countenaunce them; or if our witty Comedians and stately Tragedians (the glorious and goodlie representers of all fine witte, glorified phrase, and queint action) bee still supported and vphelde, by which meanes for lacke of Patrones (O ingratefull and damned age) our Poets are soly or chiefly maintained, countenaunced, and patronized.

In the infancy of Greece they that handled in the audience of the people graue and necessary matters wcrc callcd wise men or eloquent men, which they ment by Vates: so thc rest, which sang of loue matters, or other lighter deuises alluring vnto pleasure and delight, were called Poets or makcrs.

As the holy Prophets and sanctified apostles could neuer haue foretold nor spoken of such supcrnaturall matters vnlesse they had bin inspired of God: so *Cicero* in his Tusculane questions is of that minde, that a Poet cannot expresse verses aboundantly, sufficiently, and fully, neither his eloquence can flow pleasantly, or his wordes sound well and plenteously, without celestiall instruction; which Poets themselues do very often and gladly witnes of themselues, as namely Ouid in 6 Fast.

Est Deus in nobis; agitante calescimus illo. &c.

And our famous English Poet Spenser, who in his *Sheepeheards Calender,* lamenting the decay of Poetry at these dayes, saith most sweetly to the same,

'Then make the wings of thine aspiring wit,
And whence thou camest fly backe to heauen apace.' &c.

As a long gowne maketh not an Aduocate, although a gowne be a fit ornament for him: so riming nor versing maketh a Poet, albeit the Senate of

Poets hath chosen verse as their fittest rayment; but it is the faining notable images of vertues, vices, or what else, with that delightfull teaching, which must bee the right describing note to knowe a Poet by. *Sir Philip Sidney* in his *Apology for Poetry.*

A COMPARATIUE DISCOURSE OF OUR ENGLISH POETS WITH THE GREEKE, LATINE, AND ITALIAN POETS.

As Greece had three poets of great antiquity, Orpheus, Linus, and Musæus, and Italy other three auncient poets, Liuius Andronicus, Ennius, and Plautus: so hath England three auncient poets, Chaucer, Gower, and Lydgate.

As Homer is reputed the Prince of Greek poets, and Petrarch of Italian poets: so Chaucer is accounted the God of English poets.

As Homer was the first that adorned the Greek tongue with true quantity: so *Piers Plowman* was the first that obserued the true quantitie of our verse without the curiositie of rime.

Ouid writ a Chronicle from the beginning of the world to his own time, that is, to the raign of Augustus the Emperor: so hath Harding the Chronicler (after his maner of old harsh riming) from Adam to his time, that is, to the raigne of King Edward the fourth.

As Sotades Maronites, the Iambicke Poet, gaue himself wholy to write impure and lasciuious things: so Skelton (I know not for what great worthines surnamed the Poet Laureat) applied his wit to scurrilities and ridiculous matters; such among the Greeks were called *Pantomimi,* with vs, buffons.

As Consaluo Periz, that excellent learned man, and Secretary to King Philip of Spayne, in translating the 'Ulysses' of Homer out of Greeke into Spanish, hath by good iudgement auoided the faulte of ryming, although not fully hit perfect and true versifying: so hath Henrie Howarde, that true and noble Earle of Surrey, in translating the fourth book of Virgil's *Æneas;* whom Michael Drayton in his *England's heroycall Epistles* hath eternized for an *Epistle to his fair Geraldine.*

As these Neoterickes, Iouianus Pontanus, Politianus, Marullus Tarchaniota, the two Strozæ, the father and the son, Palingenius, Mantuanus, Philelphus, Quintianus Stoa, and Germanus Brixius have obtained renown and good place among the ancient Latine poets: so also these Englishmen, being Latine poets, Gualter Haddon, Nicholas Car, Gabriel Haruey, Christopher Ocland, Thomas Newton with his *Leyland,* Thomas Watson, Thomas Campion, Brunswerd, and Willey haue attained good report and honourable aduancement in the Latin empyre.

As the Greeke tongue is made famous and eloquent by Homer, Hesiod, Euripedes, Æschylus, Sophocles, Pindarus, Phocylides, and Aristophanes; and the Latine tongue by Virgill, Ouid, Horace, Silius Italicus, Lucanus, Lucretius, Ausonius, and Claudianus: so the English tongue is mightily enriched and gorgeously inuested in rare ornaments and resplendent abiliments by Sir Philip Sydney, Spencer, Daniel, Drayton, Warner, Shakespeare, Marlow, and Chapman.

As Xenophon, who did imitate so excellently as to giue vs *effigiem iusti imperii,* "the portraiture of a iust empyre," vnder the name of *Cyrus* (as Cicero saieth of him), made therein an absolute heroicall poem; and as Heliodorus writ in prose his sugred inuention of that picture of Loue in *Theagines and Cariclea;* and yet both excellent admired poets: so Sir Philip Sidney writ his immortal poem, *The Countess of Pembrooke's Arcadia* in Prose; and yet our rarest Poet.

As Sextus Propertius said, *Nescio quid magis nascitur Iliade:* so I say of Spencer's *Fairy Queene,* I knowe not what more excellent or exquisite Poem may be written.

As Achilles had the aduantage of Hector, because it was his fortune to bee extolled and renowned by the heauenly verse of Homer: so Spenser's *Eliza, the Fairy Queen,* hath the aduantage of all the Queenes in the worlde, to be eternized by so diuine a Poet.

As Theocritus is famoused for his *Idyllia* in Greeke, and Virgill for his *Eclogs* in Latine: so Spencer their imitator in his *Shepheardes Calender* is renowned for the like argument, and honoured for fine Poeticall inuention and most exquisit wit.

As Parthenius Nicæus excellently sung the praises of his *Arete:* so Daniel hath diuinely sonetted the matchlesse beauty of his *Delia.*

As euery one mourneth when hee heareth of the lamentable plangors of Thracian Orpheus for his dearest *Euridice:* so euery one passionateth when he readeth the afflicted death of Daniel's distressed *Rosamond.*

As Lucan hath mournefully depainted the ciuil wars of Pompey and Cæsar: so hath Daniel the civill wars of Yorke and Lancaster, and Drayton the civill wars of Edward the second and the Barons.

As Virgil doth imitate Catullus in the like matter of *Ariadne* for his story of Queene *Dido:* so Michael Drayton doth imitate Ouid in his *England's He-roical Epistles.*

As Sophocles was called a Bee for the sweetnes of his tongue: so in Charles Fitz-Iefferies *Drake* Drayton is termed "golden-mouth'd" for the purity and pretiousnesse of his stile and phrase.

As Accius, M. Atilius, and Milithus were called *Tragaediographi,* because they writ tragedies: so may wee truly terme Michael Drayton *Tragaediographus* for his passionate penning the downfals of valiant Robert of Normandy, chast Matilda, and great Gaueston.

As Joan. Honterus, in Latine verse, writ three bookes of Cosmography, with geographicall tables: so Michael Drayton is now in penning, in English verse, a Poem called *Poly-oblion,* Geographicall and Hydrographicall of all the forests, woods, mountaines, fountaines, riuers, lakes, flouds, bathes, and springs that be in England.

As Aulus Persius Flaccus is reported among al writers to be of an honest life and vpright conuersation: so Michael Drayton, *quem toties honoris et amoris causa nomino,* among schollers, souldiours, Poets, and all sorts of people is helde for a man of vertuous disposition, honest conuersation, and well gouerned cariage; which is almost miraculous among good wits in these declining and corrupt times, when there is nothing but rogery in villanous man, and when cheating and craftines is counted the cleanest wit, and soundest wisedome.

As Decius Ausonius Gallus, *in libris Fastorum,* penned the occurrences of the world from the first creation of it to his time, that is, to the raigne of the Emperor Gratian: so Warner, in his absolute *Albion's Englande,* hath most admirably penned the historie of his own country from Noah to his time, that is to the raigne of Queen Elizabeth. I haue heard him termd of the best wits of both our Vniuersities our English Homer.

As Euripedes is the most sententious among the Greek Poets: so is Warner among our English Poets.

As the soule of Euphorbus was thought to liue in Pythagoras: so the sweete wittie soule of Ouid liues in mellifluous and hony-tongued Shakespeare, witnes his *Venus and Adonis,* his *Lucrece,* his sugred *Sonnets* among his priuate friends, &c.

As Plautus and Seneca are accounted the best for Comedy and Tragedy among the Latines: so Shakespeare among the English is the most excellent in both kinds for the stage. For Comedy, witnes his *Gentlemen of Verona,* his *Errors,* his *Loue Labors Lost,* his *Loue Labours Wonne,* his *Midsummers Night Dreame,* and his *Merchant of Venice;* For Tragedy, his

Richard the 2, Richard the 3, Henry the 4, King Iohn, Titus Andronicus, and his *Romeo and Iuliet.*

As Epius Stolo said that the Muses would speake with Plautus tongue if they would speake Latin: so I say that the Muses would speake with Shakespeares fine filed phrase if they would speake English.

As Musæus, who wrote the loue of Hero and Leander, had two excellent schollers, Thamaras and Hercules: so hath he in England two excellent poets, imitators of him in the same argument and subiect, Christopher Marlow and George Chapman.

As Ouid saith of his work,

Iamque opus exegi, quod nec Iouis ira, nec ignis,
Nec poterit ferrum, nec edax abolere vetustas;

and as Horace saith of his,

Exegi monumentum aere perennius
Regalique situ pyramidum altius,
Quod non imber edax, non Aquilo impotens
Possit diruere, aut innumerabilis
Annorum series, et fuga temporum:

so I say seuerally of Sir Philip Sidney's, Spenser's, Daniel's, Drayton's, Shakespeare's, and Warner's workes,

Non Iouis ira, imbres, Mars, ferrum, flamma, senectus,
Hoc opus vnda, lues, turbo, venena ruent.
Et quanquam ad pulcherrimum hoc opus euertendum,
    tres illi Dii conspirabunt, Chronus, Vulcanus, et Pater
    ipse gentis.
Non tamen annorum series, non flamma, nec ensis;
Aeternum potuit hoc abolere Decus.

As Italy had Dante, Boccace, Petrarch, Tasso, Celiano, and Ariosto: so England had Matthew Roydon, Thomas Atchelow, Thomas Watson, Thomas Kid, Robert Greene, and George Peele.

As there are eight famous and chiefe languages, Hebrew, Greek, Latine, Syriack, Arabicke, Italian, Spanish, and French: so there are eight notable seuerall kindes of Poets, Heroicke, Lyricke, Tragicke, Comicke, Satiricke, Iambicke, Elegiacke, and Pastoral.

As Homer and Virgil among the Greeks and Latines are the chiefe Heroick Poets: so Spencer and Warner be our chiefe heroicall Makers.

As Pindarus, Anacreon, and Callimachus among the Greekes, and Horace and Catullus among the Latines are the best Lyrick poets: so in this faculty the best among our poets are Spencer (who excelleth in all kinds), Daniel, Drayton, Shakespeare, Bretton.

As these Tragicke Poets flourished in Greece, Æschylus, Euripedes, Sophocles, Alexander Ætolus, Achæus Erithriœus, Astydamas Atheniensis, Apollodorus Tarsensis, Nicomachus Phrygius, Thespis Atticus, and Timon Apolloniates; and these among the Latines, Accius, M. Atilius, Pomponius Secundus, and Seneca: so these are our best for Tragedie, The Lorde Buckhurst, Doctor Leg of Cambridge, Doctor Edes of Oxford, Master Edward Ferris, the author of the *Mirror for Magistrates,* Marlow, Peele, Watson, Kid, Shakespeare, Drayton, Chapman, Decker, and Beniamin Iohnson.

As M. Anneus Lucanus writ two excellent tragedies, one called *Medea,* the other *De incendio Troiae cum Priami calamitate:* so Doctor Leg hath penned two famous tragedies, the one of *Richard the 3,* the other of *The Destruction of Ierusalem.*

The best Poets for Comedy among the Greeks are these, Menander, Aristophanes, Eupolis Atheniensis, Alexis Terius, Nicostratus, Amipsias Atheniensis, Anaxandrides Rhodius, Aristonymus, Archippus Atheniensis, and Callias Atheniensis; and among the Latines, Plautus, Terence, Næuius, Sextus Turpilius, Licinius Imbrex, and Virgilius Romanus: so the best for Comedy amongst vs bee Edward, Earle of Oxforde, Doctor Gager of Oxforde, Master Rowley, once a rare scholler of learned Pembrooke Hall in Cambridge, Maister Edwardes, one of Her Maiesties Chappell, eloquent and wittie Iohn Lilly, Lodge, Gascoyne, Greene, Shakespeare, Thomas Nash, Thomas Heywood, Anthony Mundye, our best plotter, Chapman, Porter, Wilson, Hathway, and Henry Chettle.

As Horace, Lucilius, Iuuenall, Persius, and Lucullus are the best for Satyre among the Latines: so with vs, in the same faculty, these are chiefe, *Piers Plowman,* Lodge, Hall of Imanuel Colledge in Cambridge, the Author of *Pigmalion's Image* and *certain Satyrs,* the Author of *Skialetheia.*

Among the Greekes I will name but two for Iambicks, Archilochus Parius and Hipponax Ephesius: so amongst vs I name but two Iambical Poets, Gabriel Haruey and Richard Stanyhurst, bicause I haue seene no mo in this kind.

As these are famous among the Greeks for Elegie, Melanthus, Mymnerus Colophonius, Olympius Mysius, Parthenius Nicæus, Philetas Cous, Theogenes Megarensis, and Pigres Halicarnassæus; and these among the Latines, Mæcenas, Ouid, Tibullus, Propertius, C. Valgius, Cassius Seuerus, and Clodius Sabinus: so these are the most passionate among vs to bewaile and bemoane the perplexities of loue, Henrie Howard, Earle of Surrey, Sir Thomas Wyat the elder, Sir Francis Brian, Sir Philip Sidney, Sir Walter Rawley, Sir Edward Dyer, Spencer, Daniel, Drayton, Shakespeare, Whetstone, Gascoyne, Samuell Page, sometimes Fellowe of Corpus Christi Colledge in Oxford, Churchyard, Bretton.

As Theocritus in Greek, Virgil and Mantuan in Latine, Sanazar in Italian, and the Authour of *Amintæ Gaudia* and *Walsingham's Melibœus* are the best for Pastorall: so amongst vs the best in this kind are Sir Philip Sidney, Master Challener, Spencer, Stephen Gosson, Abraham Fraunce, and Barnefield.

These and many other Epigrammatists the Latin tongue hath, Q. Catulus, Porcius Licinius, Quintus Cornificius, Martial, Cnœus Getulicus, and wittie Sir Thomas Moore: so in English we have these, Heywood, Drante, Kendal, Bastard, Dauies.

As noble Mæcenas, that sprang from the Hetruscan Kinges, not onely graced Poets by his bounty but also by beeing a Poet himself; and as Iames the 6, nowe King of Scotland, is not only a fauorer of Poets but a Poet, as my friend Master Richard Barnefielde hath in this disticke passing well recorded,

> The King of Scots now liuing is a Poet,
> As his *Lepanto* and his *Furies* show it:

so Elizabeth, our dread Souereign and gracious Queene, is not only a liberal Patrone vnto Poets, but an excellent Poet herselfe, whose learned, delicate, and noble Muse surmounteth, be it in Ode, Elegy, Epigram, or in any other kind of poem, Heroicke or Lyricke.

Octauia, sister vnto Augustus the Emperour, was exceeding bountifull vnto Virgil, who gaue him for making 26 verses, 1,137 pounds, to wit, tenne *sestertiæ* for euerie verse (which amounted to aboue 43 pounds for euery verse): so learned Mary, the honourable Countesse of Pembrook, the noble sister of immortall Sir Philip Sidney, is very liberall vnto Poets; besides, shee is a most delicate Poet, of whome I may say, as Antipater Sidonius writeth of Sappho,

> *Dulcia Mnemosyne demirans carmina Sapphus,*
> *Quaesiuit decima Pieris vnde foret.*

Among others, in times past, Poets had these fauourers, Augustus, Mæcenas, Sophocles, Germanicus, an Emperor, a Nobleman, a Senatour, and a Captaine: so of later times Poets haue these patrones, Robert, King of Sicil, the great King Francis of France, King Iames of Scotland, and Queene Elizabeth of England.

As in former times two great Cardinals, Bembus and Bibbiena, did countenance Poets: so of late yeares two great preachers haue giuen them their right hands in fellowship, Beza and Melancthon.

As the learned philosophers Fracastorius and Scaliger haue highly prized them: so haue the eloquent Orators Pontanus and Muretus very gloriously estimated them.

As Georgius Buchananus' *Ieptha* amongst all moderne Tragedies is able to abide the touch of Aristotle's precepts and Euripedes's examples: so is Bishop Watson's *Absalon*.

As Terence for his translations out of Apollodorus and Menander, and Aquilius for his translation out of Mcnander, and C. Germanicus Augustus for his out of Aratus, and Ausonius for his translated *Epigrams* out of Greeke, and Doctor Iohnson for his *Frogge-fight* out of Homer, and Watson for his *Antigone* out of Sophocles, have got good commendations: so these versifiers for their learned translations are of good note among vs, Phaer for Virgil's *Æneads*, Golding for Ouid's *Metamorphosis*, Harington for his *Orlando Furioso*, the Translators of Seneca's *Tragedies*, Barnabe Googe for Palingenius, Turberuile for Ouid's *Epistles* and Mantuan, and Chapman for his inchoate Homer.

As the Latines haue these Emblematists, Andreas Alciatus, Reusnerus, and Sambucus: so we haue these, Geffrey Whitney, Andrcw Willet, and Thomas Combe.

As Nonnus Panapolyta writ the *Gospell* of Saint Iohn in Greeke hexameters: so Iervis Markham hath written Salomon's *Canticles* in English verse.

As C. Plinius writ the life of Pomponius Secundus: so young Charles Fitz-Ieffrey, that high touring Falcon, hath most gloriously penned *The honourable Life and Death of worthy Sir Francis Drake*.

As Hesiod writ learnedly of husbandry in Greeke: so hath Tusser very wittily and experimentally written of it in English.

As Antipater Sidonius was famous for extemporall verse in Greeke, and Ouid for his *Quicquid conabar dicere versus erat:* so was our Tarleton, of whome Doctor Case, that learned physitian, thus speaketh in the Seuenth Booke and seuenteenth chapter of his *Politikes: Aristoteles suum Theodoretum laudauit quendam peritum Tragaediarum actorem, Cicero suum Roscium: nos Angli Tarletonum, in cuius voce et vultu*

omnes iocosi affectus, in cuius cerebroso capite lepidae facetiae habitant. And so is now our wittie Wilson, who for learning and extemporall witte in this facultie is without compare or compeere, as, to his great and eternall commendations, he manifested in his challenge at the *Swanne* on the Banke Side.

As Achilles tortured the deade bodie of Hector, and as Antonius and his wife Fuluia tormented the liuelesse corps of Cicero: so Gabriell Haruey hath shewed the same inhumanitie to Greene, that lies full low in his graue.

As Eupolis of Athens vsed great libertie in taxing the vices of men: so doth Thomas Nash, witnesse the broode of the Harueys!

As Actæon was wooried of his owne hounds: so is Tom Nash of his *Isle of Dogs*. Dogges were the death of Euripedes; but bee not disconsolate, gallant young Iuuenall, Linus, the sonne of Apollo, died the same death. Yet God forbid that so braue a witte should so basely perish! Thine are but paper dogges, neither is thy banishment like Ouid's, eternally to conuerse with the barbarous *Getæ*. Therefore comfort thyselfe, sweete Tom, with Cicero's glorious return to Rome, and with the counsel Æneas giues to his seabeaten soldiers, *Lib*. I, *Æneid*.

> Pluck vp thine heart, and driue from thence both feare and care away!
> To thinke on this may pleasure be perhaps another day.
> *Durate et temet rebus seruate secundis.*

As Anacreon died by the pot: so George Peele by the pox.

As Archesilaus Prytanœus perished by wine at a drunken feast, as Hermippus testifieth in *Diogenes:* so Robert Greene died of a surfet taken at pickeld herrings and Rhenish wine, as witnesseth Thomas Nash, who was at the fatall banquet.

As Iodelle, a French tragical poet, beeing an epicure and an atheist, made a pitifull end: so our tragicall poet Marlow for his Epicurisme and Atheisme had a tragical death. You may read of this Marlow more at large in the *Theatre of God's judgments,* in the 25th chapter entreating of *Epicures and Atheists*.

As the poet Lycophron was shot to death by a certain riual of his: so Christopher Marlow was stabd to death by a bawdy Servingman, a riual of his in his lewde loue.

Checklist of Further Readings

Bibliographies and other reference materials:

Arber, Edward, ed. *A Transcript of the Registers of the Company of Stationers of London, 1554–1640 [Stationers' Register]*, 5 volumes. London, 1875–1894.

Bietenholz, Peter G., and Thomas B. Deutscher, eds. *Contemporaries of Erasmus: A Biographical Register of the Renaissance and Reformation*, 3 volumes. Toronto & Buffalo, N.Y.: University of Toronto Press, 1984–1987.

Eccles, Mark. "Brief Lives: Tudor and Stuart Authors," *Studies in Philology*. Texts and Studies 79 (Fall 1982): 1–135.

"English Literature/1500–1599," in *MLA Bibliography of Books and Articles on the Modern Languages and Literatures*. New York: Modern Language Association, annually.

Fédération international des sociétés et instituts pour l'étude de la Renaissance. *Bibliographie internationale de l'humanisme et de la Renaissance*. Geneva: Droz, annually.

Hamilton, A. C., gen. ed. *The Spenser Encyclopedia*. Toronto: University of Toronto Press, 1990.

Hardin, Richard F. "Recent Studies in Neo-Latin Literature," *English Literary Renaissance,* 24 (Autumn 1994): 660–698.

Harner, James L. *English Renaissance Prose Fiction, 1500–1660: An Annotated Bibliography of Criticism*. Boston: G. K. Hall, 1978.

Harner. *English Renaissance Prose Fiction, 1500–1660: An Annotated Bibliography of Criticism, 1976–1983*. New York: G. K. Hall, 1985.

Harner. *English Renaissance Prose Fiction, 1500–1660: An Annotated Bibliography of Criticism, 1984–1990*. New York: G. K. Hall, 1992.

Hogrefe, Pearl. *Women of Action in Tudor England: Nine Biographical Sketches*. Ames: Iowa State University Press, 1977.

Ijsewijn, Jozef. *Companion to Neo-Latin Studies*. Amsterdam: North-Holland, 1977.

Lanham, Richard A. *A Handlist of Rhetorical Terms,* second edition. Berkeley: University of California Press, 1991.

Lievsay, John L., ed. *The Sixteenth Century: Skelton through Hooker,* Goldentree Bibliographies. New York: Appleton-Century-Crofts, 1968.

Marcuse, Michael J. "Literature of the Renaissance and Earlier Seventeenth Century," section O in *A Reference Guide for English Studies*. Berkeley: University of California Press, 1990, pp. 323–338.

O'Dell, Sterg, ed. *A Chronological List of Prose Fiction in English Printed in England and Other Countries, 1475–1640*. Cambridge, Mass.: MIT Press, 1954.

Ousby, Ian, ed. *The Cambridge Guide to English Literature*. Cambridge: Cambridge University Press, 1988.

Pollard, A. W., and G. R. Redgrave, eds. *A Short-Title of Catalogue of Books Printed in England, Scotland, and Ireland, and of English Books Printed Abroad, 1475–1640 [STC]*, 3 volumes. London: Bibliographical Society, 1926; revised and enlarged by W. A. Jackson, F. S. Ferguson, and Katharine F. Pantzer. London: Bibliographical Society, 1976–1991.

Preminger, Alex, and T. V. F. Brogan, eds. *The New Princeton Encyclopedia of Poetry and Poetics*. Princeton: Princeton University Press, 1993.

"Recent Studies in the English Renaissance," *Studies in English Literature, 1500–1900*. Annually, Winter.

Ruoff, James E. *Crowell's Handbook of Elizabethan and Stuart Literature*. New York: Crowell, 1975.

Schweitzer, Frederick M., and Harry E. Wedeck, eds. *Dictionary of the Renaissance*. New York: Philosophical Library, 1967.

The State of Renaissance Studies: A Special Twenty-fifth Anniversary Symposium in Honor of Dan S. Collins. English Literary Renaissance, 25 (Autumn 1995).

Stephen, Leslie, and Sidney Lee, eds. *The Dictionary of National Biography from the Earliest Times to 1900 [DNB]*. London: Oxford University Press, 1885–1900; reprinted with supplements, 1967–1968.

Watson, George, ed. *The New Cambridge Bibliography of English Literature [NCBEL]*, volume 1: *600–1600*. Cambridge: Cambridge University Press, 1974.

Ziegler, Georgianna M. "Recent Studies in Women Writers of Tudor England, 1485–1603 (1990 to mid-1993)," *English Literary Renaissance*, 24 (Winter 1994): 229–242.

Anthologies, collections:

Alexander, Nigel, ed. *Elizabethan Narrative Verse*. Cambridge, Mass.: Harvard University Press, 1968.

Byrne, Muriel St. Clare, ed. *The Lisle Letters*, 6 volumes. Chicago: University of Chicago Press, 1981.

Dodd, A. H., ed. *Life in Elizabethan England*. New York: Putnam, 1961.

Donno, Elizabeth Story, ed. *Elizabethan Minor Epics*. New York: Columbia University Press, 1963.

Ferguson, Moira, ed. *First Feminists: British Women Writers, 1578–1799*. Bloomington: Indiana University Press / Old Westbury, N.Y.: Feminist Press, 1985.

Henderson, Katherine Usher, and Barbara F. McManus, eds. *Half Humankind: Contexts and Texts of the Controversy about Women in England, 1540–1640*. Urbana: University of Illinois Press, 1985.

Hurstfield, Joel, and Alan G. R. Smith, eds. *Elizabethan People: State and Society*. New York: St. Martin's Press, 1972.

Mahl, Mary R., and Helene Koon, eds. *The Female Spectator: English Women Writers before 1800*. Bloomington: Indiana University Press / Old Westbury, N.Y.: Feminist Press, 1977.

Manley, Lawrence, ed. *London in the Age of Shakespeare: An Anthology*. London: Croom Helm, 1986.

May, Steven W., ed. *The Elizabethan Courtier Poets: The Poems and Their Contexts*. Columbia: University of Missouri Press, 1991.

Millward, J. W., ed. *Portraits and Documents: Sixteenth Century*. London: Hutchinson, 1961.

Myers, James P., Jr., ed. *Elizabethan Ireland: A Selection of Writings by Elizabethan Writers on Ireland*. Hamden, Conn.: Archon, 1983.

Otten, Charlotte F., ed. *English Women's Voices, 1540–1700*. Miami: Florida International University Press, 1992.

Rollins, Hyder E., and Herschell Baker, eds. *The Renaissance in England: Non-dramatic Prose and Verse of the Sixteenth Century*. Lexington, Mass.: Heath, 1954; reprinted, Prospect Heights, Ill.: Waveland, 1992.

Shepherd, Simon, ed. *The Women's Sharp Revenge: Five Women Pamphleteers from the Renaissance*. New York: St. Martin's Press, 1985; republished as *The Women's Sharp Revenge: Five Women's Pamphlets from the Renaissance*. London: Fourth Estate, 1985.

Smith, G. Gregory, ed. *Elizabethan Critical Essays*, 2 volumes. Oxford: Oxford University Press, 1904.

Travitsky, Betty, ed. *The Paradise of Women: Writings by Englishwomen of the Renaissance*. Westport, Conn.: Greenwood Press, 1981; revised edition, New York: Columbia University Press, 1989.

Williams, Penry, ed. *Life in Tudor England*. New York: Putnam, 1964.

Wilson, Katharina M., ed. *Women Writers of the Renaissance and Reformation*. Athens: University of Georgia Press, 1987.

Woudhuysen, H. R., ed. *The Penguin Book of Renaissance Verse, 1509–1659,* selected by David Norbrook. London: Penguin, 1992.

Recommended works:

Allen, Don Cameron. *Mysterious Meant: The Rediscovery of Pagan Symbolism and Allegorical Interpretation in the Renaissance*. Baltimore: Johns Hopkins University Press, 1970.

Alpers, Paul J., ed. *Elizabethan Poetry: Modern Essays in Criticism*. New York: Oxford University Press, 1967.

Anderson, Judith H. *Biographical Truth: The Representation of Historical Persons in Tudor-Stuart Writing*. New Haven: Yale University Press, 1984.

Bainton, Roland H. *The Reformation of the Sixteenth Century*. Boston: Beacon, 1952.

Bakhtin, Mikhail M. *Rabelais and His World,* translated by Hélène Iswolsky. Cambridge, Mass.: MIT Press, 1984.

Beilin, Elaine V. *Redeeming Eve: Women Writers of the English Renaissance*. Princeton: Princeton University Press, 1987.

Benson, Pamela Joseph. *The Invention of the Renaissance Woman: The Challenge of Female Independence in the Literature and Thought of Italy and England*. University Park: Pennsylvania State University Press, 1992.

Binns, J. W. *Intellectual Culture in Elizabethan and Jacobean England: The Latin Writings of the Age*. Leeds: Cairns, 1990.

Black, J. B. *The Reign of Elizabeth, 1558–1603,* second edition, volume 8 of *The Oxford History of England,* edited by George Clark. Oxford: Clarendon Press, 1959.

Booty, John E., and others, eds. *The Godly Kingdom of Tudor England: Great Books of the English Reformation.* Wilton, Conn.: Morehouse-Barlow, 1981.

Bradner, Leicester. *Musae Anglicanae: A History of Anglo-Latin Poetry, 1500–1925.* New York: Modern Language Association, 1940; republished with supplement in *Library,* fifth series 22 (1967): 93–103.

Briggs, Julia. *This State-Play World: English Literature and Its Background, 1580–1625.* Oxford: Oxford University Press, 1983.

Brooke, Tucker, and Matthias A. Shaaber. *The Renaissance (1500–1600),* book 2 of *A Literary History of England,* second edition, edited by Albert C. Baugh. New York: Appleton-Century-Crofts, 1967.

Burckhardt, Jacob. *The Civilization of the Renaissance in Italy,* translated by S. G. C. Middlemore. Oxford: Oxford University Press, 1944.

Bush, Douglas. *Mythology and the Renaissance Tradition in English Poetry,* revised edition. New York: Norton, 1963.

Bush. *Prefaces to Renaissance Literature.* Cambridge, Mass.: Harvard University Press, 1965.

Bush. *The Renaissance and English Humanism.* Toronto: University of Toronto Press, 1939.

The Cambridge History of Renaissance Philosophy. See Schmitt and others.

Camden, Charles Carroll. *The Elizabethan Woman.* Houston: Elsevier Press, 1952.

Campbell, Lily B. *Divine Poetry and Drama in Sixteenth-Century England.* Berkeley: University of California Press, 1959.

Carlson, David R. *English Humanist Books: Writers and Patrons, Manuscripts and Print, 1475–1525.* Toronto: University of Toronto Press, 1993.

Colie, Rosalie L. *The Resources of Kind: Genre-Theory in the Renaissance,* edited by Barbara K. Lewalski. Berkeley: University of California Press, 1973.

Craig, Hardin. *The Enchanted Glass: The Elizabethan Mind in Literature.* Oxford: Blackwell, 1966.

Dobson, Eric John. *English Pronunciation: 1500–1700,* second edition, 2 volumes. Oxford: Clarendon Press, 1968.

Dowling, Maria. *Humanism in the Age of Henry VIII.* London & Dover, N.H.: Croom Helm, 1986.

Dubrow, Heather, and Richard Strier, eds. *Historical Renaissance: New Essays on Tudor and Stuart Culture.* Chicago: University of Chicago Press, 1988.

Eccles, Mark. "A Biographical Dictionary of Elizabethan Authors," *Huntington Library Quarterly,* 5 (April 1942): 281–302.

Ferguson, Margaret, and others, eds. *Rewriting the Renaissance: The Discourse of Sexual Difference in Early Modern Europe.* Chicago: University of Chicago Press, 1986.

Ferry, Anne. *The "Inward" Language: Sonnets of Wyatt, Sidney, Shakespeare, Donne.* Chicago: University of Chicago Press, 1983.

Ford, Boris, ed. *Renaissance and Reformation,* volume 3 of *The Cambridge Guide to the Arts in Britain.* Cambridge: Cambridge University Press, 1989; republished as *Sixteenth-century Britain,* volume 3 of *The Cambridge Cultural History of Britain.* Cambridge: Cambridge University Press, 1992.

Foucault, Michel. "What Is an Author?," translated by Josué V. Harari, in *The Foucault Reader,* edited by Paul Rabinow. New York: Pantheon, 1984, pp. 101–120.

Fox, Alistair. *Politics and Literature in the Reigns of Henry VII and Henry VIII.* Oxford: Blackwell, 1989.

Fox and John Guy. *Reassessing the Henrician Age: Humanism, Politics and Reform, 1500–1550.* Oxford: Blackwell, 1986.

Fraser, Russell. *The Dark Ages and the Age of Gold.* Princeton: Princeton University Press, 1973.

Fraser. *The War against Poetry.* Princeton: Princeton University Press, 1970.

Grant, Leonard. *Neo-Latin Literature and the Pastoral.* Chapel Hill: University of North Carolina Press, 1965.

Greenblatt, Stephen Jay. *Renaissance Self-Fashioning from More to Shakespeare.* Chicago: University of Chicago Press, 1980.

Greene, Thomas M. *Light in Troy: Imitation and Discovery in Renaissance Poetry.* New Haven: Yale University Press, 1982.

Guy, John. *Tudor England.* New York: Oxford University Press, 1988.

Hannay, Margaret P., ed. *Silent but for the Word: Tudor Women as Patrons, Translators, and Writers of Religious Works.* Kent, Ohio: Kent State University Press, 1985.

Haselkorn, Anne M., and Betty S. Travitsky, eds. *The Renaissance English Woman in Print: Counterbalancing the Canon.* Amherst: University of Massachusetts Press, 1990.

Haugaard, William P. "The Preface," in *The Folger Library Edition of the Works of Richard Hooker,* volume 6, part 1. Binghamton, N.Y.: Medieval and Renaissance Texts and Studies, 1993, pp. 1–80.

Helgerson, Richard. *Self-Crowned Laureates: Spenser, Jonson, Milton, and the Literary System.* Berkeley: University of California Press, 1983.

Heninger, S. K., Jr. *Touches of Sweet Harmony: Pythagorean Cosmology and Renaissance Poetics.* San Marino, Cal.: Huntington Library, 1974.

Hoffmann, Ann. *Lives of the Tudor Age, 1485–1603.* London: Osprey, 1977; New York: Barnes & Noble, 1977.

Hogrefe, Pearl. *Tudor Women: Commoners and Queens.* Ames: Iowa State University Press, 1975.

Howell, Wilbur Samuel. *Logic and Rhetoric in England, 1500–1700.* Princeton: Princeton University Press, 1956.

Hull, Suzanne W. *Chaste, Silent, and Obedient: English Books for Women, 1475–1640.* San Marino, Cal.: Huntington Library, 1982.

Javitch, Daniel. *Poetry and Courtliness in Renaissance England.* Princeton: Princeton University Press, 1978.

Kay, Dennis. *Melodious Tears: The English Funeral Elegy from Spenser to Milton.* Oxford: Clarendon Press, 1990.

Keach, William. *Elizabethan Erotic Narrative: Irony and Pathos in the Ovidian Poetry of Shakespeare, Marlowe, and Their Contemporaries*. New Brunswick, N.J.: Rutgers University Press, 1977.

Kelley, Donald R. "The Theory of History," in *The Cambridge History of Renaissance Philosophy,* edited by Charles B. Schmitt and others. Cambridge: Cambridge University Press, 1988, pp. 746–761.

Kernan, Alvin. *The Cankered Muse: Satire of the English Renaissance*. Yale Studies in English 142. New Haven: Yale University Press, 1959.

Kerrigan, William, and Gordon Braden. *The Idea of the Renaissance*. Baltimore & London: Johns Hopkins University Press, 1989.

King, John N. *English Reformation Literature: The Tudor Origins of the Protestant Tradition*. Princeton: Princeton University Press, 1982.

Kökeritz, Helge. *Shakespeare's Pronunciation*. New Haven: Yale University Press, 1953.

Kristeller, Paul Otto. "Humanism," in *The Cambridge History of Renaissance Philosophy,* pp. 113–137.

Lathrop, Henry Burrowes. *Translations from the Classics into English from Caxton to Chapman, 1477–1620*. University of Wisconsin Studies in Language and Literature, no. 35. Madison: University of Wisconsin Press, 1933; New York: Octagon, 1967.

Levao, Ronald. *Renaissance Minds and Their Fictions: Cusanus, Sidney, Shakespeare*. Berkeley: University of California Press, 1985.

Levin, Carole, and Patricia A. Sullivan, eds. *Political Rhetoric, Power, and Renaissance Women*. Albany: State University of New York Press, 1995.

Levin, Harry T. *The Myth of the Golden Age in the Renaissance*. Bloomington: Indiana University Press, 1969.

Lewis, C. S. *The Discarded Image: An Introduction to Medieval and Renaissance Literature*. Cambridge: Cambridge University Press, 1964.

Lewis. *English Literature in the Sixteenth Century, Excluding Drama,* volume 3 of *The Oxford History of English Literature,* edited by F. P. Wilson and Bonamy Dobrée. Oxford: Clarendon Press, 1954.

Lovejoy, Arthur O. *The Great Chain of Being: A Study of the History of an Idea*. Cambridge, Mass.: Harvard University Press, 1936.

Mackie, J. D. *The Earlier Tudors, 1485–1558,* volume 7 of *The Oxford History of England,* edited by George Clark. Oxford: Clarendon Press, 1978.

Marcus, Leah S. "Renaissance / Early Modern Studies," in *Redrawing the Boundaries: The Transformation of English and American Literary Studies,* edited by Greenblatt and Giles Gunn. New York: Modern Language Association of America, 1992, pp. 41–63.

Mason, H. A. *Humanism and Poetry in the Early Tudor Period: An Essay*. London: Routledge & Kegan Paul, 1959.

Matthiessen, F. O. *Translation: An Elizabethan Art*. Cambridge, Mass.: Harvard University Press, 1931.

May, Steven W. *The Elizabethan Courtier Poets: The Poems and Their Contexts*. Columbia: University of Missouri Press, 1991.

Mayer, Thomas F., and D. R. Woolf, eds. *The Rhetorics of Life-Writing in Early Modern Europe: Forms of Biography from Cassandra Fedele to Louis XIV*. Ann Arbor: University of Michigan Press, 1995.

Maynard, Winifred. *Elizabethan Lyric Poetry and Its Music*. Oxford: Clarendon Press, 1986.

Mazzaro, Jerome. *Transformations in the Renaissance English Lyric*. Ithaca: Cornell University Press, 1970.

McLean, Antonia. *Humanism and the Rise of Science in Tudor England*. London: Heinemann Educational, 1972; New York: Watson Academic, 1972.

Miller, Edwin Haviland. *The Professional Writer in Elizabethan England: A Study of Nondramatic Literature*. Cambridge, Mass.: Harvard University Press, 1959.

Mueller, Janel M. *The Native Tongue and the Word: Developments in English Prose Style, 1380–1580*. Chicago: University of Chicago Press, 1984.

Norbrook, David. Introduction to *The Penguin Book of Renaissance Verse, 1509–1659*, selected by Norbrook, edited by H. R. Woudhuysen. London: Penguin, 1992, pp. 1–67.

Norbrook. *Poetry and Politics of the English Renaissance*. London: Routledge & Kegan Paul, 1984.

Parker, Patricia A. *Literary Fat Ladies: Rhetoric, Gender, Property*. Berkeley: University of California Press, 1987.

Parker and David Quint, eds. *Literary Theory / Renaissance Texts*. Baltimore: Johns Hopkins University Press, 1986.

Patrides, C. A., and Joseph Wittreich, eds. *The Apocalypse in English Renaissance Thought and Literature: Patterns, Antecedents and Repercussions*. Ithaca: Cornell University Press, 1984.

Patterson, Annabel. *Censorship and Interpretation: The Conditions of Writing and Reading in Early Modern England*. Madison: University of Wisconsin Press, 1984.

Pearcey, Lee T. *The Mediated Muse: English Translations of Ovid, 1560–1700*. Hamden, Conn.: Archon, 1984.

Peterson, Douglas L. *The English Lyric from Wyatt to Donne: A History of the Plain and Eloquent Styles*, second edition. Princeton: Princeton University Press, 1990.

Pitcher, John. "Tudor Literature (1485–1603)," in *The Oxford Illustrated History of English Literature*, edited by Pat Rogers. Oxford: Oxford University Press, 1987, pp. 59–111.

Relihan, Constance C. *Fashioning Authority: The Development of Elizabethan Novelistic Discourse*. Kent, Ohio: Kent State University Press, 1994.

Ricks, Christopher, ed. *English Poetry and Prose, 1540–1674*, revised edition, volume 2 of *[Sphere] History of Literature in the English Language*. London: Barrie & Jenkins, 1986.

Ridley, Jasper. *The Tudor Age*. Woodstock, N.Y.: Overlook Press, 1990.

Rivers, Isabel. *Classical and Christian Ideas in English Renaissance Poetry: A Students' Guide*. London: Allen & Unwin, 1979.

Rose, Mary Beth, ed. *Women in the Middle Ages and the Renaissance: Literary and Historical Perspectives*. Syracuse, N.Y.: Syracuse University Press, 1986.

Rubel, Veré L. *Poetic Diction in the English Renaissance from Skelton through Spenser*. New York: Modern Language Association, 1941.

Salzman, Paul. *English Prose Fiction, 1558–1700: A Critical History*. Oxford: Clarendon Press, 1985.

Schmitt, Charles B., and others, eds. *The Cambridge History of Renaissance Philosophy*. Cambridge: Cambridge University Press, 1988.

Sheavyn, Phoebe. *The Literary Profession in the Elizabethan Age,* second edition, revised by J. W. Saunders. New York: Barnes & Noble, 1967.

Sloan, Thomas O., and Raymond B. Waddington, eds. *Rhetoric of Renaissance Poetry from Wyatt to Milton*. Berkeley: University of California Press, 1974.

Smith, Hallett. *Elizabethan Poetry: A Study in Conventions, Meaning, and Expression*. Cambridge, Mass.: Harvard University Press, 1952.

Southall, Raymond. *The Courtly Maker: An Essay on the Poetry of Wyatt and His Contemporaries*. Oxford: Blackwell, 1964.

Stauffer, Donald A. *English Biography before 1700*. Cambridge, Mass.: Harvard University Press, 1930.

Stevens, John. *Music and Poetry in the Early Tudor Court*. London: Methuen, 1961.

Stone, Lawrence. *The Crisis of the Aristocracy, 1558–1641*. Oxford: Clarendon Press, 1965.

Stone. *The Family, Sex and Marriage in England, 1500–1800*. New York: Harper & Row, 1977.

Tayler, Edward Williams. *Nature and Art in Renaissance Literature*. New York: Columbia University Press, 1964.

Thomas, Keith. *Religion and the Decline of Magic*. New York: Scribners, 1971.

Tillyard, E. M. W. *The Elizabethan World Picture*. New York: Macmillan, 1944.

Travitsky, Betty S., and Adele F. Seeff, eds. *Attending to Women in Early Modern England*. Newark: University of Delaware Press, 1994.

Trinkaus, Charles. *The Scope of Renaissance Humanism*. Ann Arbor: University of Michigan Press, 1983.

Tuve, Rosemund. *Allegorical Imagery: Some Medieval Books and Their Posterity*. Princeton: Princeton University Press, 1966.

Tuve. *Elizabethan and Metaphysical Imagery: Renaissance Poetics and Twentieth-Century Critics*. Chicago: University of Chicago Press, 1947.

Vickers, Brian. *In Defence of Rhetoric*. Oxford: Clarendon Press, 1988.

Vickers. "Rhetoric and Poetics," in *The Cambridge History of Renaissance Philosophy,* pp. 715–745.

Waller, Gary. *English Poetry of the Sixteenth Century*. London: Longman, 1986.

Warnicke, Retha M. *Women of the English Renaissance and Reformation,* Contributions in Women's Studies, no. 38. Westport, Conn.: Greenwood Press, 1983.

Whigham, Frank. *Ambition and Privilege: The Social Tropes of Elizabethan Courtesy Literature*. Berkeley: University of California Press, 1984.

Wilson, K. J. *Incomplete Fictions: The Formation of English Renaissance Dialogue*. Washington, D.C.: Catholic University of America Press, 1985.

Wilson, Katharina A., ed. *Women Writers of the Renaissance and Reformation*. Athens: University of Georgia Press, 1987.

Winters, Yvor. "The 16th Century Lyric in England: A Critical and Historical Reinterpretation," in his *Forms of Discovery: Critical and Historical Essays on the Forms of the Short Poem in English*. Chicago: Swallow, 1967, pp. 1–120; reprinted in *Elizabethan Poetry: Modern Essays in Criticism,* edited by Alpers, pp. 93–125.

Woodbridge, Linda. *Women and the English Renaissance: Literature and the Nature of Womankind, 1540–1640*. Urbana: University of Illinois Press, 1984.

Wright, Louis B. *Middle-Class Culture in Elizabethan England*. Chapel Hill: University of North Carolina Press, 1935.

Zocca, Louis R. *Elizabethan Narrative Poetry*. New Brunswick, N.J.: Rutgers University Press, 1950.

Authors and Works in *Sixteenth-Century British Nondramatic Writers, First Series* through *Fourth Series*

Contributors

Ursula F. Appelt .... *State University of New York at Stony Brook*
James P. Bednarz .... *Long Island University*
Elaine V. Beilin .... *Framingham State College*
Kenneth Borris .... *McGill University*
Richard H. Branyan .... *Grace–St. Luke's Episcopal School, Memphis*
Donald Cheney .... *University of Massachusetts, Amherst*
Edward Doughtie .... *Rice University*
Konrad Eisenbichler .... *University of Toronto*
Raymond-Jean Frontain .... *University of Central Arkansas*
John Gouws .... *Rhodes University, South Africa*
Wyman H. Herendeen .... *University of Windsor*
Elise Bickford Jorgens .... *Western Michigan University*
Dennis Kay .... *University of North Carolina at Charlotte*
Arthur F. Kinney .... *University of Massachusetts – Amherst*
Michael McClintock .... *University of Toronto*
Jerry Leath Mills .... *University of North Carolina at Chapel Hill*
Debora K. Shuger .... *University of California, Los Angeles*
L. M. Storozynsky .... *University College of the Fraser Valley*
Carolyn R. Swift .... *Rhode Island College*
Frederick O. Waage .... *East Tennessee State University*
Charles Whitworth .... *University of Montpellier*
Robert Wiltenburg .... *Washington University*
D. R. Woolf .... *Dalhousie University*
Jenny Wormald .... *St. Hilda's College, Oxford*

Cumulative Index

Dictionary of Literary Biography, Volumes 1-172
Dictionary of Literary Biography Yearbook, 1980-1995
Dictionary of Literary Biography Documentary Series, Volumes 1-14

Cumulative Index

DLB before number: *Dictionary of Literary Biography,* Volumes 1-172
Y before number: *Dictionary of Literary Biography Yearbook,* 1980-1995
DS before number: *Dictionary of Literary Biography Documentary Series,* Volumes 1-14

B

Edwards, James
[publishing house] DLB-154

Effinger, George Alec 1947- DLB-8

Egerton, George 1859-1945 .... DLB-135

Eggleston, Edward 1837-1902 ...... DLB-12

Eggleston, Wilfred 1901-1986 ...... DLB-92

Ehrenstein, Albert 1886-1950 .... DLB-81

Ehrhart, W. D. 1948- DS-9

Eich, Günter 1907-1972 .... DLB-69, 124

Eichendorff, Joseph Freiherr von
1788-1857 .... DLB-90

1873 Publishers' Catalogues DLB-49

Eighteenth-Century Aesthetic
Theories DLB-31

Eighteenth-Century Philosophical
Background DLB-31

Eigner, Larry 1927- DLB-5

Eikon Basilike 1649 .... DLB-151

Eilhart von Oberge
circa 1140-circa 1195 .... DLB-148

Einhard circa 770-840 .... DLB-148

Eisenreich, Herbert 1925-1986 ...... DLB-85

Eisner, Kurt 1867-1919 .... DLB-66

Eklund, Gordon 1945- Y-83

Ekwensi, Cyprian 1921- DLB-117

Eld, George
[publishing house] DLB-170

Elder, Lonne III 1931- DLB-7, 38, 44

Elder, Paul, and Company DLB-49

Elements of Rhetoric (1828; revised, 1846),
by Richard Whately [excerpt] ... DLB-57

Elie, Robert 1915-1973 .... DLB-88

Elin Pelin 1877-1949 .... DLB-147

Eliot, George 1819-1880 ..... DLB-21, 35, 55

Eliot, John 1604-1690 .... DLB-24

Eliot, T. S. 1888-1965 .....DLB-7, 10, 45, 63

Eliot's Court Press DLB-170

Elizabeth I 1533-1603 .... DLB-136

Elizondo, Salvador 1932- DLB-145

Elizondo, Sergio 1930- DLB-82

Elkin, Stanley 1930- DLB-2, 28; Y-80

Elles, Dora Amy (see Wentworth, Patricia)

Ellet, Elizabeth F. 1818?-1877 ...... DLB-30

Elliot, Ebenezer 1781-1849 .... DLB-96

Elliot, Frances Minto (Dickinson)
1820-1898 .... DLB-166

Elliott, George 1923- DLB-68

Elliott, Janice 1931- DLB-14

Elliott, William 1788-1863 .... DLB-3

Elliott, Thomes and Talbot DLB-49

Ellis, Edward S. 1840-1916 .... DLB-42

Ellis, Frederick Staridge
[publishing house] DLB-106

The George H. Ellis Company DLB-49

Ellison, Harlan 1934- DLB-8

Ellison, Ralph Waldo
1914-1994 ....DLB-2, 76; Y-94

Ellmann, Richard
1918-1987 ....DLB-103; Y-87

The Elmer Holmes Bobst Awards in Arts
and Letters Y-87

Elyot, Thomas 1490?-1546 ....DLB-136

Emanuel, James Andrew 1921- DLB-41

Emecheta, Buchi 1944- DLB-117

The Emergence of Black Women
Writers DS-8

Emerson, Ralph Waldo
1803-1882 ....DLB-1, 59, 73

Emerson, William 1769-1811 ...... DLB-37

Emin, Fedor Aleksandrovich
circa 1735-1770 .... DLB-150

Empson, William 1906-1984 .... DLB-20

The End of English Stage Censorship,
1945-1968 .... DLB-13

Ende, Michael 1929- DLB-75

Engel, Marian 1933-1985 .... DLB-53

Engels, Friedrich 1820-1895 .... DLB-129

Engle, Paul 1908- DLB-48

English Composition and Rhetoric (1866),
by Alexander Bain [excerpt] DLB-57

The English Language:
410 to 1500 .... DLB-146

The English Renaissance of Art (1908),
by Oscar Wilde DLB-35

Enright, D. J. 1920- DLB-27

Enright, Elizabeth 1909-1968 .... DLB-22

L'Envoi (1882), by Oscar Wilde DLB-35

Epps, Bernard 1936- DLB-53

Epstein, Julius 1909- and
Epstein, Philip 1909-1952 .... DLB-26

Equiano, Olaudah
circa 1745-1797 ....DLB-37, 50

Eragny Press DLB-112

Erasmus, Desiderius 1467-1536 .... DLB-136

Erba, Luciano 1922- DLB-128

Erdrich, Louise 1954- DLB-152

Erichsen-Brown, Gwethalyn Graham
(see Graham, Gwethalyn)

Eriugena, John Scottus
circa 810-877 ....DLB-115

Ernest Hemingway's Toronto Journalism
Revisited: With Three Previously
Unrecorded Stories Y-92

Ernst, Paul 1866-1933 .... DLB-66, 118

Erskine, Albert 1911-1993 .... Y-93

Erskine, John 1879-1951 .... DLB-9, 102

Ervine, St. John Greer 1883-1971 ....DLB-10

Eschenburg, Johann Joachim
1743-1820 ....DLB-97

Escoto, Julio 1944- DLB-145

Eshleman, Clayton 1935- DLB-5

Espriu, Salvador 1913-1985 ....DLB-134

Ess Ess Publishing Company DLB-49

Essay on Chatterton (1842), by
Robert Browning DLB-32

Essex House Press DLB-112

Estes, Eleanor 1906-1988 ....DLB-22

Estes and Lauriat DLB-49

Etherege, George 1636-circa 1692 ....DLB-80

Ethridge, Mark, Sr. 1896-1981 ......DLB-127

Ets, Marie Hall 1893- DLB-22

Etter, David 1928- DLB-105

Ettner, Johann Christoph
1654-1724 ....DLB-168

Eudora Welty: Eye of the Storyteller ... Y-87

Eugene O'Neill Memorial Theater
Center DLB-7

Eugene O'Neill's Letters: A Review Y-88

Eupolemius
flourished circa 1095 ....DLB-148

Evans, Caradoc 1878-1945 ....DLB-162

Evans, Donald 1884-1921 ....DLB-54

Evans, George Henry 1805-1856 .....DLB-43

Evans, Hubert 1892-1986 ....DLB-92

Evans, Mari 1923- DLB-41

Evans, Mary Ann (see Eliot, George)

Evans, Nathaniel 1742-1767 ....DLB-31

Evans, Sebastian 1830-1909 ....DLB-35

Evans, M., and Company DLB-46

Everett, Alexander Hill
790-1847 ....DLB-59

Everett, Edward 1794-1865 ...... DLB-1, 59

Everson, R. G. 1903- DLB-88

Everson, William 1912-1994 ..... DLB-5, 16

G

M

Malamud, Bernard
1914-1986 .....DLB-2, 28, 152; Y-80, 86

Malet, Lucas 1852-1931 .... DLB-153

Malleson, Lucy Beatrice (see Gilbert, Anthony)

Mallet-Joris, Françoise 1930- DLB-83

Mallock, W. H. 1849-1923 ...... DLB-18, 57

Malone, Dumas 1892-1986 .... DLB-17

Malone, Edmond 1741-1812 .... DLB-142

Malory, Sir Thomas
circa 1400-1410 - 1471 .... DLB-146

Malraux, André 1901-1976 .... DLB-72

Malthus, Thomas Robert
1766-1834 .... DLB-107, 158

Maltz, Albert 1908-1985 .... DLB-102

Malzberg, Barry N. 1939- DLB-8

Mamet, David 1947- DLB-7

Manaka, Matsemela 1956- DLB-157

Manchester University Press DLB-112

Mandel, Eli 1922- DLB-53

Mandeville, Bernard 1670-1733 .... DLB-101

Mandeville, Sir John
mid fourteenth century DLB-146

Mandiargues, André Pieyre de
1909- DLB-83

Manfred, Frederick 1912-1994 ....DLB-6

Mangan, Sherry 1904-1961 ....DLB-4

Mankiewicz, Herman 1897-1953 .... DLB-26

Mankiewicz, Joseph L. 1909-1993 ... DLB-44

Mankowitz, Wolf 1924- DLB-15

Manley, Delarivière
1672?-1724 .... DLB-39, 80

Mann, Abby 1927- DLB-44

Mann, Heinrich 1871-1950 ..... DLB-66, 118

Mann, Horace 1796-1859 ....DLB-1

Mann, Klaus 1906-1949 .... DLB-56

Mann, Thomas 1875-1955 .... DLB-66

Mann, William D'Alton
1839-1920 .... DLB-137

Manning, Marie 1873?-1945 .... DLB-29

Manning and Loring DLB-49

Mannyng, Robert
flourished 1303-1338 .... DLB-146

Mano, D. Keith 1942- DLB-6

Manor Books DLB-46

Mansfield, Katherine 1888-1923 ... DLB-162

Mapanje, Jack 1944- DLB-157

March, William 1893-1954 ...... DLB-9, 86

Marchand, Leslie A. 1900- DLB-103

Marchant, Bessie 1862-1941 ...... DLB-160

Marchessault, Jovette 1938- DLB-60

Marcus, Frank 1928- DLB-13

Marden, Orison Swett
1850-1924 .... DLB-137

Marechera, Dambudzo
1952-1987 .... DLB-157

Marek, Richard, Books DLB-46

Mares, E. A. 1938- DLB-122

Mariani, Paul 1940- DLB-111

Marie-Victorin, Frère 1885-1944 ..... DLB-92

Marin, Biagio 1891-1985 .... DLB-128

Marincović, Ranko 1913- DLB-147

Marinetti, Filippo Tommaso
1876-1944 .... DLB-114

Marion, Frances 1886-1973 .... DLB-44

Marius, Richard C. 1933- Y-85

The Mark Taper Forum DLB-7

Mark Twain on Perpetual Copyright Y-92

Markfield, Wallace 1926- DLB-2, 28

Markham, Edwin 1852-1940 .... DLB-54

Markle, Fletcher 1921-1991 ....DLB-68; Y-91

Marlatt, Daphne 1942- DLB-60

Marlitt, E. 1825-1887 .... DLB-129

Marlowe, Christopher 1564-1593 .... DLB-62

Marlyn, John 1912- DLB-88

Marmion, Shakerley 1603-1639 ..... DLB-58

Der Marner
before 1230-circa 1287 .... DLB-138

The *Marprelate Tracts* 1588-1589 ....DLB-132

Marquand, John P. 1893-1960 ...DLB-9, 102

Marqués, René 1919-1979 .... DLB-113

Marquis, Don 1878-1937 ....DLB-11, 25

Marriott, Anne 1913- DLB-68

Marryat, Frederick 1792-1848 ...DLB-21, 163

Marsh, George Perkins
1801-1882 ....DLB-1, 64

Marsh, James 1794-1842 ....DLB-1, 59

Marsh, Capen, Lyon and Webb DLB-49

Marsh, Ngaio 1899-1982 .... DLB-77

Marshall, Edison 1894-1967 .... DLB-102

Marshall, Edward 1932- DLB-16

Marshall, Emma 1828-1899 .... DLB-163

Marshall, James 1942-1992 .... DLB-61

Marshall, Joyce 1913- DLB-88

Marshall, Paule 1929- DLB-33, 157

Marshall, Tom 1938- DLB-60

Marsilius of Padua
circa 1275-circa 1342 ....DLB-115

Marson, Una 1905-1965 ....DLB-157

Marston, John 1576-1634 ...... DLB-58, 172

Marston, Philip Bourke 1850-1887 ...DLB-35

Martens, Kurt 1870-1945 ....DLB-66

Martien, William S.
[publishing house] DLB-49

Martin, Abe (see Hubbard, Kin)

Martin, Charles 1942- DLB-120

Martin, Claire 1914- DLB-60

Martin, Jay 1935- DLB-111

Martin, Johann (see Laurentius von Schnüffis)

Martin, Violet Florence (see Ross, Martin)

Martin du Gard, Roger 1881-1958 ...DLB-65

Martineau, Harriet
1802-1876 .....DLB-21, 55, 159, 163, 166

Martínez, Eliud 1935- DLB-122

Martínez, Max 1943- DLB-82

Martyn, Edward 1859-1923 ....DLB-10

Marvell, Andrew 1621-1678 ....DLB-131

Marvin X 1944- DLB-38

Marx, Karl 1818-1883 ....DLB-129

Marzials, Theo 1850-1920 ....DLB-35

Masefield, John
1878-1967 ....DLB-10, 19, 153, 160

Mason, A. E. W. 1865-1948 ....DLB-70

Mason, Bobbie Ann 1940- Y-87

Mason, William 1725-1797 ....DLB-142

Mason Brothers DLB-49

Massey, Gerald 1828-1907 ....DLB-32

Massinger, Philip 1583-1640 ....DLB-58

Masson, David 1822-1907 ....DLB-144

Masters, Edgar Lee 1868-1950 ....DLB-54

Mather, Cotton
1663-1728 .... DLB-24, 30, 140

Mather, Increase 1639-1723 ....DLB-24

Mather, Richard 1596-1669 ....DLB-24

Matheson, Richard 1926- DLB-8, 44

Matheus, John F. 1887- DLB-51

Mathews, Cornelius
1817?-1889 .... DLB-3, 64

Mathews, Elkin
[publishing house] DLB-112

Mathias, Roland 1915- DLB-27

Cumulative Index

Viramontes, Helena María
1954- DLB-122

Vischer, Friedrich Theodor
1807-1887 ....DLB-133

Vivanco, Luis Felipe 1907-1975 ....DLB-108

Viviani, Cesare 1947- DLB-128

Vizetelly and Company DLB-106

Voaden, Herman 1903- DLB-88

Voigt, Ellen Bryant 1943- DLB-120

Vojnović, Ivo 1857-1929 ....DLB-147

Volkoff, Vladimir 1932- DLB-83

Volland, P. F., Company DLB-46

von der Grün, Max 1926- DLB-75

Vonnegut, Kurt
1922- DLB-2, 8, 152; Y-80; DS-3

Voranc, Prežihov 1893-1950 ....DLB-147

Voß, Johann Heinrich 1751-1826 ....DLB-90

Vroman, Mary Elizabeth
circa 1924-1967 ....DLB-33

W

Wace, Robert ("Maistre")
circa 1100-circa 1175 ....DLB-146

Wackenroder, Wilhelm Heinrich
1773-1798 ....DLB-90

Wackernagel, Wilhelm
1806-1869 ....DLB-133

Waddington, Miriam 1917- DLB-68

Wade, Henry 1887-1969 ....DLB-77

Wagenknecht, Edward 1900- DLB-103

Wagner, Heinrich Leopold
1747-1779 ....DLB-94

Wagner, Henry R. 1862-1957 ......DLB-140

Wagner, Richard 1813-1883 ....DLB-129

Wagoner, David 1926- DLB-5

Wah, Fred 1939- DLB-60

Waiblinger, Wilhelm 1804-1830 .....DLB-90

Wain, John
1925-1994 ....DLB-15, 27, 139, 155

Wainwright, Jeffrey 1944- DLB-40

Waite, Peirce and Company DLB-49

Wakoski, Diane 1937- DLB-5

Walahfrid Strabo circa 808-849 .....DLB-148

Walck, Henry Z. DLB-46

Walcott, Derek
1930- DLB-117; Y-81, 92

Waldegrave, Robert
[publishing house] DLB-170

Waldman, Anne 1945- DLB-16

Waldrop, Rosmarie 1935- DLB-169

Walker, Alice 1944- DLB-6, 33, 143

Walker, George F. 1947- DLB-60

Walker, Joseph A. 1935- DLB-38

Walker, Margaret 1915- DLB-76, 152

Walker, Ted 1934- DLB-40

Walker and Company DLB-49

Walker, Evans and Cogswell
Company DLB-49

Walker, John Brisben 1847-1931 ....DLB-79

Wallace, Dewitt 1889-1981 and
Lila Acheson Wallace
1889-1984 ....DLB-137

Wallace, Edgar 1875-1932 ....DLB-70

Wallace, Lila Acheson (see Wallace, Dewitt,
and Lila Acheson Wallace)

Wallant, Edward Lewis
1926-1962 ....DLB-2, 28, 143

Waller, Edmund 1606-1687 ....DLB-126

Walpole, Horace 1717-1797 ....DLB-39, 104

Walpole, Hugh 1884-1941 ....DLB-34

Walrond, Eric 1898-1966 ....DLB-51

Walser, Martin 1927- DLB-75, 124

Walser, Robert 1878-1956 ....DLB-66

Walsh, Ernest 1895-1926 ....DLB-4, 45

Walsh, Robert 1784-1859 ....DLB-59

Waltharius circa 825 ....DLB-148

Walters, Henry 1848-1931 ....DLB-140

Walther von der Vogelweide
circa 1170-circa 1230 ....DLB-138

Walton, Izaak 1593-1683 ....DLB-151

Wambaugh, Joseph 1937- DLB-6; Y-83

Waniek, Marilyn Nelson 1946- ...DLB-120

Warburton, William 1698-1779 ....DLB-104

Ward, Aileen 1919- DLB-111

Ward, Artemus (see Browne, Charles Farrar)

Ward, Arthur Henry Sarsfield
(see Rohmer, Sax)

Ward, Douglas Turner 1930- ...DLB-7, 38

Ward, Lynd 1905-1985 ....DLB-22

Ward, Lock and Company DLB-106

Ward, Mrs. Humphry 1851-1920 ...DLB-18

Ward, Nathaniel circa 1578-1652 ....DLB-24

Ward, Theodore 1902-1983 ....DLB-76

Wardle, Ralph 1909-1988 ....DLB-103

Ware, William 1797-1852 ....DLB-1

Warne, Frederick, and
Company [U.S.] DLB-49

Warne, Frederick, and
Company [U.K.] DLB-106

Warner, Charles Dudley
1829-1900 ....DLB-64

Warner, Rex 1905- DLB-15

Warner, Susan Bogert
1819-1885 ....DLB-3, 42

Warner, Sylvia Townsend
1893-1978 ....DLB-34, 139

Warner, William 1558-1609 ....DLB-172

Warner Books DLB-46

Warr, Bertram 1917-1943 ....DLB-88

Warren, John Byrne Leicester (see De Tabley,
Lord)

Warren, Lella 1899-1982 ....Y-83

Warren, Mercy Otis 1728-1814 ......DLB-31

Warren, Robert Penn
1905-1989 ..... DLB-2, 48, 152; Y-80, 89

Die Wartburgkrieg
circa 1230-circa 1280 ....DLB-138

Warton, Joseph 1722-1800 .....DLB-104, 109

Warton, Thomas 1728-1790 ...DLB-104, 109

Washington, George 1732-1799 .....DLB-31

Wassermann, Jakob 1873-1934 ......DLB-66

Wasson, David Atwood 1823-1887 ...DLB-1

Waterhouse, Keith 1929- DLB-13, 15

Waterman, Andrew 1940- DLB-40

Waters, Frank 1902- Y-86

Waters, Michael 1949- DLB-120

Watkins, Tobias 1780-1855 ....DLB-73

Watkins, Vernon 1906-1967 ....DLB-20

Watmough, David 1926- DLB-53

Watson, James Wreford (see Wreford, James)

Watson, John 1850-1907 ....DLB-156

Watson, Sheila 1909- DLB-60

Watson, Thomas 1545?-1592 ......DLB-132

Watson, Wilfred 1911- DLB-60

Watt, W. J., and Company DLB-46

Watterson, Henry 1840-1921 ....DLB-25

Watts, Alan 1915-1973 ....DLB-16

Watts, Franklin [publishing house] ...DLB-46

Watts, Isaac 1674-1748 ....DLB-95

Waugh, Auberon 1939- DLB-14

Waugh, Evelyn 1903-1966 ......DLB-15, 162

Way and Williams DLB-49

Y